Blind Man's Bluff!

By

Geri Taeckens

Music Rights

FIVE HUNDRED MILES, By Hedy West
1964 (renewed) Unichappell Music Inc. (BMI) and Atzal Music Inc. (BMI)
All rights administered by Unichappell Music Inc.
All Rights Reserved.   Used by permission.

SCARLET RIBBONS, By Jack Segal and Evelyn Danzig
1978 EMI Mills Music Inc.
All Rights Reserved.   Used By permission.

FOR WHAT IT'S WORTH, Words and music by: Stephen Stills
1966 (renewed) COTILLION MUSIC INC., TEN EAST MUSIC,
SPRING ALO TOONES and RICHIE FURAY MUSIC
All rights administered by WARNER-TAMERLANE PUBLISHING CORP.
All Rights Reserved. Used by permission.

SATISFIED MIND the composition by Joe "Red" Hayes and Jack Rhodes
Copyright 1955 By Fort Knox Music Inc. and the Trio Music Company
in the United States

ISBN: 978-0-9774546-1-7

Blind Man's Bluff! Copyright 2007 by Accessibilities,
Sault Ste Marie, Mi
accessibilities@isahealthfund.org
All Rights Reserved

Acknowledgments

Before I began this endeavor, I used to pass over the acknowledgement page when reading books because I figured, "Ah, no big deal." Now I know, first hand, what a big deal this page really is. People who help writers reach the point where they can place the last punctuation mark on their manuscripts should be honored and cherished forever! The problem comes in deciding how many people one should list in this section and in what order they should be identified. To sort out this problem, I will thank everyone who had anything to do with this book. You all deserve first billing.

—All the members of the Yahoo Critical Writing group in 2004; Moira Wilson, a fellow author who wrote "Revolutionary Fires"; Ardeth Marchetti; and my Belgian cousin, Jaak Taeckens, who provided most helpful feedback in the development of the book.

—Deborah Carney, illustrator, and her husband Mark, who helped me lots!

—Dinah Savoie, Cris Roll, and James Wilson, who helped edit the manuscript.

—One of my best friends, Linda Hunt, for her continual feedback, which kept me honest. Without Linda and my classmate, Marsha Yager, I might never have survived my early school years.

—Cody Sanford, who cared more about befriending me in junior high than giving in to peer pressure. Her belief in my validity will be forever cherished.

—My best friend Jody Burton Slowins, who shares an innate understanding of the concepts I portray, for giving me feedback on the many drafts I sent her.

—All the people who inspired the characters in my book after enriching my life with theirs. I have only changed your names to protect your innocence. (Smile!)

—My wonderful brother and sisters, who were great siblings to their baby sister.

—My loving husband, Billy Park, my wonderful son Nolan Glore, and my super guide dog Kojak. I thank them so much for their patience and belief in this eight year effort.

—Rex Schechter, chief editor, who has believed in my story from the very beginning and who gave me endless hours of his time and support despite the fact I almost drove him crazy.

—My Mother and Father, whose love and support I will always cherish. Without them I would never have become who I am.

Part I

Chapter I

Childhood

Pencils on a Corner 1957

"Goody!" I squealed. I was excited to go with my dad for our Saturday morning ride downtown and rushed up the stairs to get dressed. "Ouch! Darn it!" I said, rubbing my head. In my hurry, I'd failed to duck, conking my head on the sloping cork ceiling of the attic. At age five, I was proud to be standing tall enough for such a mishap. I breathed in the hot stuffy air of the loft and wiped sweaty hair from my neck. I couldn't wait to get out of the heat and go with my father. My brother and sisters were five, seven, and nine years ahead of me, so I was the only one interested in such outings.

I threw off my pink flowered baby doll pajamas and grabbed my favorite red dress with blue and yellow flowers from the floor. I threw it over my head and quickly searched for what to put on next.

"Mom? Where are my red socks?" I yelled, pulling open drawers. As rolled pairs tumbled to the floor, the red ones emerged.

"Never mind," I hollered, "I got 'em!" I pulled the socks over my toes and rummaged through my closet. I tore through heaps of tangled clothes and finally found my favorite black and white saddle shoes. I hastily stuck my feet inside and tied two bows.

"Don't forget to brush your hair," my mother called from below.

"I won't," I said, and hurried to the vanity for the hairbrush with the dancing ballerina on the back. I dragged it through my board-straight hair and looked at my reflection in the mirror. A pair of grey-blue eyes peered back at me through a flurry of yellow strands.

"Mom, I need my bangs cut."

"You need all of that stringy mop chopped off!" she said from below.

"Uh-uh, no, Mom! I like my hair long. Just cut the front part, okay?"

"We'll see. You'd better hurry, your father's ready."

I tossed the brush back onto the dresser and headed down, two stairs at a time, happy to leave the oven that doubled as a bedroom for my sisters and me.

Dad was waiting in the kitchen dressed in his yellow t-shirt. "You ready to get some needles and thread for your mother?" he asked, reaching for the car keys on the pegboard by the back door.

"Yup," I answered, pushing past him so I could beat him to the car.

"Hey, take it easy. Let's not shove one of us into the cellar now, okay?"

The damp, musty smell of our Michigan basement filled the air near the landing. The dirt floor and walls gave it a strong odor that was oddly inviting.

I was delighted at the prospect of getting ahead of my father, so I opened the screen door and ran to our rusty '52 Chevy.

"I beat ya!" I called, gripping the hot metal handle.

"Ouch!" But Dad didn't hear me cry out, so he simply commented on my announcement of success.

"I can see you did!" He walked over to the driver's side.

"Beat ya again!" Giving him a big smile, I slid across the wide bench seat.

"You sure did!" Shutting his door, he moved in next to me, flashing me one of his famous tight-lipped grins. Instantly the air felt suffocating.

"How about rolling those windows down, Geri, it's pretty hot in here."

With both hands, I did as he asked. I sucked in the fresh air and leaned back against my father's shoulder, curling my feet up under my bottom so I could see over the dash. I liked the smell of his Aqua Velva shaving lotion. I wished I could taste it.

"Do I get to start it?" I asked.

"Sure enough." He handed me the keys. I slid them into their spot on the dash and pushed the starter button with my pointer finger. The motor revved, making the car lurch and me jump.

I giggled at my startled reaction, but Dad just gave me another grin.

After a few more sputters from the engine, he put the gear in reverse and backed out of the driveway onto the busy street.

I watched our dirty yellow clapboard house fade away as we headed down the road. Leaning forward, I asked, "Okay, Daddy?"

"Okay, take over."

I reached for the stick shift attached to the steering wheel. As the car speeded up, the sound got louder and higher. Dad pushed in the clutch and I knew it was time to move the shifter to second gear. The motor slowed again, so I pulled with both hands to put the lever into third. The engine hummed. I knew this meant the car had reached the speed Dad wanted. Everything is fine, I thought.

"Okay, that's good. We're off," Dad said. I felt a little rush of excitement as he and I joined in with the other automobiles. I loved being one of the crowd.

"We going to Kresge's to get Mom's stuff?"

"Yes sir!" Dad announced as I watched the many houses whiz by. As we neared the railroad tracks, the street trolley came up behind us. Its bell clanged loudly as it pulled all its passengers along. We crossed the track and neared the corner of Franklin and Robert T. Longway Boulevard. I heard the motor sound go lower this time, so I put the shifter into the slot my dad called neutral.

"Good job. Now what direction are we going?" Dad asked as we waited for the red light to change.

"South."

"And what street are we going to turn on?"

"Robert T. Longway," I said, looking up into his face. His twinkling hazel eyes smiled at me.

As the car idled, I watched a lady in a blue checkered dress push a baby buggy past the hood of our Chevy. She smiled as she glanced in the window and saw me leaning on my father. I waved at her. I was proud to be my dad's driving partner.

The light changed, but we didn't move. "Just a minute, Geri. Looks like the trolley lost its connection."

He pulled his white handkerchief from his pocket and wiped the sweat from his forehead.

"It's really hot, ain't it, Dad?" I said.

"It sure is!" he said, "Especially without the wind." Together we watched the driver get out. He started fiddling with something.

"What's he doing, Dad?"

"He's trying to reconnect that rod with the electrical wire above. It needs to be in the right place so the electricity can turn the trolley's motor."

"How does the wire make the motor go?"

"Well, Geri, it's kind of like an electric cord."

"What d'ya mean?"

He scratched his head. I could tell he was thinking of what to say. "You know how our radio has a cord that plugs into the wall?"

"Uh huh."

"That rod does the same thing. When it connects with the wire and the motor, it sends electricity through it to make the wheels go."

"So where is the motor that makes the radio play?" I asked, trying to picture how Fibber McGee and Molly, one of my favorite Friday night radio shows, could be driven into our big cloth covered speaker.

"Uh huh! Well, never mind there, Geri," he laughed.

"Why ya laughing, Dad?" I giggled, but he didn't answer. It didn't matter though. I just liked his smiles.

Soon the driver returned to his seat. He rang the bell to signal he was about to move.

"Okay, we're on our way again. Can you tell me what direction we're going to turn now?"

"West!"

"That's right." Heading down Robert T, I moved the shifter through the gears until we were finally back in third.

A few blocks later, the skyline of downtown's tall buildings came into view. The weather ball that sat atop Citizens Bank glowed bright red.

"Let's sing our song, Dad."

"Okay! You ready?" We sang together.

"When the weather ball is blue, cooler temperatures are due.

When the weather ball is red, warmer temperatures ahead."

We finished the silly rhyme as Dad turned south onto Saginaw Street. I resumed my job as shifter.

After we rounded the corner onto Harrison, Dad slid the car neatly against the curb. He pulled the keys from the slot on the dash, stepped out of the car, and opened my door. I took hold of his hand and leapt out onto the sidewalk.

"There ya go," he announced as he handed me three pennies from his pocket. I proudly walked to the parking meter. One at a time, I dropped them into the slot and turned the four-pronged knob.

"Erk-clank, erk-clank, erk-clank," the meter clanged.

"The needle went to three six, Dad."

"Okay, let's head on to the corner, then."

I skipped along behind my dad and watched my black and white saddle shoes flash in front of me. My dress flounced as I twirled. I liked the way it made the yellow and blue flowers swirl all together.

"Step on a crack, break your mother's back," I sang softly to myself.

"Are you coming?" my dad called. He was already several steps ahead. He'd soon be turning west to cross Harrison.

"Yeah, wait up. Don't cross without me, Dad!" I hollered, jumping over a crack in the sidewalk.

"Come on, we only have a little more than half an hour. You don't want me to get a ticket now, do you?"

I had to run to catch up. I wondered how he could move so quickly. "Okay, I'm coming."

I was just about to reach him at the corner when Dad's large warm hand gripped mine. I took one last leap and plopped next to him.

"Well, that was quite a landing, Geri."

"I know!" I said, looking up into his gentle eyes, giggling at his lop-sided grin. Without a word, we both broke into big wide smiles, feeling our special connection.

When the light changed and we arrived at the other side, Dad let go of my hand. I decided to hop over the cracks, one footed this time.

As we neared Kresge's, I saw an old man in raggedy overalls, dirty fishing cap, and dark sunglasses sitting at the bus stop. A shoebox and a tin can sat next to him. I wondered what the man was doing.

Without warning, my dad walked over to the strange man. He dropped a couple of coins in the tin can and picked something from his box.

"There you go, honey," he said proudly, handing me two pencils.

Puzzled by his actions, I took them. "What ya giving me these for? We already have some at home."

Without warning, Dad grabbed my free hand and whisked me indoors. "Shh!" he whispered.

Though somewhat shaken, I couldn't help but notice the smell of freshly made fry-cakes coming from the doughnut maker just inside the entranceway. I longingly eyed them as they slid down the chute of the machine. The inviting aroma couldn't compete with the feeling of something being wrong, however.

"What's the matter, Daddy?" I asked nervously. The sound of many feet clunking against the wooden floor pounded in my ears.

My father looked behind him. He was eyeing the door suspiciously. When it finally closed, he squatted down and said, "Now Geri, that man, he's blind, so I thought we should buy his pencils."

"Why?" I asked, still not understanding.

"Well," he said, scratching his ear thoughtfully. "This man—you know, honey—he can't see.

"So, we still don't need his pencils."

Dad looked around at all the people moving in and out of the store. "Come with me," he said, wearing his very serious face. He took my hand and guided me through the crowd.

When we neared the jewelry counter, he stopped once again and spoke to me. I heard his knees crack as he lowered himself to my level.

"I know we don't really need his pencils, Geri, but—it's just that—I mean, blind people, they can't work, you know? They aren't able to really take care of themselves, so it's up to people like you and me to help them out when we can. Understand?"

I looked down at the two yellow wooden sticks I was rolling back and forth with my thumb. Shamefully, I shook my head, no.

Once more my father rose and moved us forward. We passed the candy aisle. My eyes bugged at the glass bins filled with colorful sweets. The sight of pink marshmallow ice cream cones, toffee nut chews, and orange and yellow candy corn made my mouth water. I felt a sudden attack of hunger pangs. I remembered Dad's policy about asking for unnecessary junk. But when we came across the case containing red, yellow, green, brown and purple M and M's, I couldn't hold back.

"Can I have some candy, Dad?"

"Not now, honey, we've got to find the thread and needles for your mom."

"I wish I could get candy instead of those pencils you got."

Suddenly Dad turned toward me. He squatted down yet again. Though I knew he was upset with me, I noticed how perfectly his shirt matched the yellow candy disks.

"Now Geri, you mustn't be selfish. God would not be pleased with your putting candy over helping someone. Buying pencils from that man gives him money so he can buy food and things."

My tummy tightened as I dared to question why he was making such a fuss. "So how come you didn't just give him the money, Daddy? We've got lots of pencils already!" I still thought the sweets would have been a much better buy. Instead of scolding me, however, Dad looked upward as he considered my question.

"Oh, uh, I didn't want to insult him."

"What does 'installed' mean?"

"The word is 'insult'," he corrected. "Let's go over here and I'll explain it better." Together we squeezed through the crowd to the back of the store. When we reached the notions section, there was no one around.

"Okay, let's see," he began. "Insult means to hurt someone's feelings. I didn't want to make this poor man feel any worse than he already does."

"Why does he feel bad?" I asked sadly, looking over the rows and columns of colored thread. I liked how they lay on a shelf which was tilted at an angle. They reminded me again of the mix of colored treats. I considered asking Dad one more time if he would buy candy for me, but I was afraid he'd be angry. I didn't like him to be mad at me.

Before I could decide what to do, he said, "I guess the man feels pretty awful about being blind, ya think? The poor guy isn't able to see anything. I mean, just imagine all the pretty things he misses, like flowers and pretty smiles like yours."

I felt the corners of my lips turn upward, mimicking the movement of my father's. I wondered if the man would want to see all those colorful candies and threads.

"Just think," my father went on, "He can't drive a car and he isn't able to work a real job, either. I'll bet he feels happy when he can give a person a pencil for the money they give him. He'd feel sad if he only took the money."

"Why?" I asked, rolling the spools of thread around with the writing tools now in question.

"Well, you know how much you like to help Mom and me in the kitchen. Right?"

"Yeah! I like making cookies."

"I know you do. Now, think if you couldn't help Mom stir the batter, or lick the beaters! You wouldn't like it much, would you?"

"Nope!"

"Well, that's like the blind man outside. If he could never do something nice, like give people something to write with, then he would feel very sad, too."

"Oh, yeah," I agreed, not quite sure what I was agreeing to.

"Yup, I guess if that man only had people giving him money and he could never give anything back, he would not be able to live with himself."

"Who would he live with then?"

My dad let out a big chuckle. "What I mean is, the man would feel so bad about not working for his money that he maybe wouldn't want to live at all."

"Oh," I said, more confused than before Dad started talking. I decided this must be one of those times he was figuring out the same thing he was trying to teach me.

"Well, you'll understand someday, Geri. Just remember that it is always nice to help other people, even if it means you don't get candy."

Picking up a spool of blue thread, Dad strolled down the aisle. He soon found the sewing needles and took a pack from the shelf. At last he announced it was time to check out.

After standing in line for a long time, we left the store and headed to the car. I did my best not to stare as we passed the odd-looking man on the corner. Though I knew God and my father would be disappointed, I still wished I had candy in my hands instead of the dumb pencils. *Why did God have to make that man blind, anyway?* I thought, feeling bad for being so selfish. But as we turned the corner, the man disappeared from my sight.

Chapter 2

Stark and Cold

November 1959

Days 1 and 2

"A—a dog," I groaned between clenched teeth. A lady with a bright smile and sparkling eyes had just asked if I had a pet.

"What's your dog's name?" Her voice was so kind, I wanted to be polite and answer her. But I also wished I could be still. With great effort I moaned and said, "Ti-ippy."

"Oh, Tippy, that's a nice name for a dog. What kind of dog is Tippy?"

I closed my eyes tightly and tried to muster the strength to answer. Like a toothache, the pain surged up my back and down my legs. My body jerked forward.

"Now, you want to stay as still as you can, Geraldine," the man's voice behind me warned. "Just a little bit longer."

I tried not to move. The pain started to disappear. I relaxed a bit and opened my eyes. The lights were so bright. It was not easy sitting on a hard table doubled over a pillow. I looked down. All I could see were the lady's white shoes and the silk stockings covering her legs. I imagined shooting the pain out the end of my pointer finger as I traced the black squares checkering the linoleum.

The nurse repeated her question. "What kind of dog did you say Tippy was?"

I scrunched my eyes tightly together and croaked, "A boxer."

"Oh, a boxer. They are so cute. I had a boxer when I was a kid, too. Does Tippy like to play fetch?"

Another burst of pain ripped through me. I let out a whimper. I wanted to cry, but I was afraid it would make the pain worse.

I grimaced, hugging the pillow tightly as the nurse patted my arm.

"The doctor's almost done now. You're doing a great job! Do you have any brothers and sisters?"

"Two sisters and a brother."

"What are their names?"

I searched my tangled thoughts but couldn't find the words.

"Ginnie, Grace, and Joe," I grunted. "Ow! Oh!" Another dose of electric pangs forced my eyes shut. Frantically, I jabbed my finger repeatedly at the floor I couldn't reach.

"I know, it really can smart, can't it?" the nurse said, wiping sweaty hair from my face. "How old are your sisters and brother?"

Her words spun around in my head. When the gush of pain was over, the answer came.

"Joe is sixteen, Grace is fourteen, and Ginnie is twelve."

"Oh, so you're the youngest, are you? I'll bet you get a lot of attention."

Her words faded as I tightened my fists in distress. I wanted to keep track of what was happening to me, but the nurse kept asking me about my home and family.

"Tell me about the house you live in, Geraldine."

I couldn't think. Didn't she know shock waves were ripping up my spine and through my brain? I worked my finger faster now, blasting the pain at the floor. Another momentary calm washed over me, clearing my head.

"Better now?" she asked kindly, once again wiping my forehead. I nodded.

"Good! So, tell me about your house. What color is it?"

"Yel—I mean, green," I corrected. We'd moved to a new house on the north side of town the previous winter. How could I have forgotten?

"Green's a good color. What's it like?

"It's got four bedrooms and a big kitchen," I said, forcing the words out.

"It does? Do you have a room of your own, or do you share with one of your sisters?"

"I have my own room," I said, wishing I didn't. *Everybody has a room upstairs except me,* I thought, still upset by my parent's decision.

"Wow, that must be nice."

I did not agree. After sharing a room with my sisters for six years, I felt left out. In an attempt to reassure both of us that I was still a part of their evening affairs, I said, "Sometimes I sleep with them, though. My sister Ginnie reads me fairy tales and Grace sings songs."

"That's really nice. So you like to sing, do you?"

Before I could answer, another torturous jolt interrupted our conversation.

"I'm sorry, Geraldine," the doctor apologized, "It won't be too much longer."

"Ow! Can we be done now?" I begged.

"Almost finished. This will be the very last one. I'm going to pull the needle out of your back—"

"Ow!" I yelled.

"—and we're through!"

After a series of small pinches, the pain was gone. Sweat gushed from my forehead, then all over my body. The nurse dabbed my face gently with a cool, wet washrag. The soft cloth felt so soothing. The nurse pulled the pillow from under my tummy. In a gentle voice she said, "Okay now, Geraldine, why don't you lie back on the gurney here. I'm sorry, but I can't give you a pillow. You'll have to lie very flat for twelve hours. This means for the rest of the day and through the night. Do you think you can do that?"

"Okay," I answered weakly. "Why do I have to be flat?"

"The doctor has taken out some fluid from your back. It's like a liquid that we all have in our spines. So, until your body has a chance to make more of it, you could get a very bad headache if you sit up or move around too much. Even though you may want to get up and play later, you must be quiet. Okay?"

"Okay," I said, terrified my body wouldn't know how to make more of the liquid.

Filled with fear, I slowly wiggled my way into as comfortable a position as possible. A couple of men came into the room. The tall one looked like Kingfish on the Amos and Andy show. The other guy reminded me of Jerry Lewis except he didn't have his funny voice.

"Is this the pretty litta lady we get ta escort back ta the ward?" the colored one asked with a smile.

"Yes, sir," the nurse said. "She's been a real trouper, this one. Never dropped one tear through the whole ordeal."

"Ya never even cried?" the Jerry one said with surprise.

"Well, you is a brave one then, you is, young lady," said the colored man. "Heck, if that Dr. Sharp was ta give me a spinal tap, I'd be bawlin' like a baby. Man, Isa don't even likes ta come inta the room until it's all over. Ida fainted clean away if Ida hads ta watch that doc puts that needle in youse back. Youse a tough cookie, you are, little mama."

I felt a smile cross my lips. The nurse opened up what looked like an oven door and then turned back toward me. I snuggled in tightly as she wrapped a warm blanket around my shivering shoulders. I felt safer now, despite having been tortured by all these strangers.

"Well, ya ready for a nice ride, young mama?" the colored guy asked. "I'd sure be honored ta push a courageous youngun like y'all back to da room."

"Okay," I answered shyly. I was happy to go anywhere that took me far away from this chamber of horrors.

In no time, the two nice men slid me into my bed as gently as they could. It had become mine only the day before. I stared at the wallpaper of clowns and circus animals surrounding me and felt safe. I wondered if I should be so comfortable there after going through such a horrible experience.

I lay there, trying to understand how and why my folks had left me all alone as I thought about the previous day's events.

My parents and I had driven an hour in the cold autumn rain to sit endlessly in the outpatient waiting room of the university medical center. We made this trip because Mrs. Nicer, my second grade teacher, told my folks about her concerns. Since I'd started second grade she had worried about my trouble doing schoolwork. Despite my protests, she believed I couldn't see the blackboard or the letters in the reading books. After Dr. Gruch, the eye doctor in Flint, couldn't figure out what was wrong, they decided I had to go to this big university to see a specialist.

As I sat in my blue plaid dress, waiting to see the doctor, my dad kept me entertained with several games of Nim and I Spy. Mom sat next to us reading magazines and knitting. My mother wasn't good at playing with me or my brother and sisters. She was best at making flannel pajamas, knitting colorful mittens, growing great tomatoes in her garden, and cooking and cleaning the house.

At last I heard someone call for Geraldine. I cringed at the sound of my formal name. A nurse in a starchy white uniform ushered us into a tiny room. We sat for another long time until, finally, a parade of men in white coats squeezed through the door.

"Hello, I'm Dr. Biggs," the first guy said. He shook both my folks' hands, ignoring me altogether.

"These are medical students here at the university," he explained. "They will be examining your daughter along with me so they can become good ophthalmologists."

"That's fine," my dad replied, never considering whether I might be interested. The doctor continued to ignore me as he asked them a lot of questions.

Upon hearing about my difficulties at school, the doctor began his grueling examination.

"Geraldine, would you sit up in this chair?"

I hate that name! I thought. But seven years of training to be a polite young lady told me I'd better do what he asked.

The torture series began with each doctor shining a bright light in my eyes, insisting I stare without blinking. Next, Dr. Biggs put stinging drops in them, which made the sockets feel like they were filled with marbles. More time passed while the drops took effect, then the doctor announced his plan.

"We're going to play a letter game."

My tummy tightened. I dreaded this so-called game. Dr. Grutch had played it with me back home in Flint and it wasn't fun at all. I gripped the arms of my seat tightly, remembering how he'd accused me of not knowing my alphabet.

I wish I could get out of here! I thought. He'd better not tell me I'm faking to get attention! I warned him in my mind, recalling how Dr Grutch had made this ridiculous statement after my dad told him how smart I was. It was only when both my parents insisted I was not pretending that Dr. Grutch suggested I see a specialist. I could tell these doctors were not much better. I had to fight the urge to keep from leaping out of my chair.

"Can you read the top line?" Dr. Biggs asked.

With sweaty palms and stretched-out neck, I struggled to sound confident, "E."

"Good. Now the next."

"W, M."

"Okay, the next line," he commanded.

"M, uh, no N, E, W, uh no, M, S?"

A sense of failure swept over me as he picked up a clipboard and wrote something on it.

"Okay, now I'm going to look into her eyes," he told my parents.

He moved in closer and placed the little lollipop light between his eye and mine.

"Stay still now," he said, blasting coffee and cigarette smells up my nose. Reeling my head backwards, I almost gagged. Somehow I managed to stop myself, knowing it would not be polite.

"Open—keep your eyes wide open," he commanded, making me want to retch. Between my stomach churning from the putrid odor and my eyes burning from the blinding light, I couldn't help myself from shrinking farther down in the chair.

"You need to sit up straight, Geraldine!" Dr. Biggs snapped. "It's just going to take longer if you don't cooperate."

This guy was making me mad. I didn't like him accusing me of doing something bad. I decided to prove him wrong. I pursed my lips and shot upright, daring him to make me blink. When I didn't, he never even noticed.

When he finished, I had to do it all again. One by one, the rest of the men in white coats took their turns. I never complained, even though none of them smelled any sweeter.

When at last the ordeal was over, I couldn't wait to get out of there, but I didn't get far. Dr. Biggs announced that a few days in the hospital would give him a chance to examine me further.

Despite my protests, the grownups all stuck together, telling me how great it would be to spend the night. "It's for your own good," my dad insisted, handing me the white hanky he'd been storing in his pocket. Reluctantly, I took it.

I pouted, walking behind my folks, who followed another stiff-suited lady for a very long way. She took us to the children's ward and showed me my room.

Though the pink bedspreads and colorful wallpaper looked inviting, they didn't help. The room felt cold and foreboding. Three of the four beds were empty. The small chairs and tiny dressers made the place look even more barren.

"This is your bed, and I'm Nurse Ellen," the lady announced, giving me a warm smile.

"What pretty red hair you have," my dad said to the nurse.

"Why, thank you. Geraldine? Do you like to be called Geraldine?"

I was grateful when Mother answered for me. "I think she prefers Geri."

"Geri it is, then. This is Edna. She'll be your roommate. You girls have the whole place to yourselves for a while."

"Hi," a tiny voice said from under the pink mound in the bed across from mine.

I attempted a kind hello despite my unwillingness to agree to all this.

"This is your dresser. Oh, and here, you've got this really neat rolling table you can raise and lower to your liking." Nurse Ellen demonstrated the moving counter.

"Over here we have some games and some very unloved stuffed animals," the nurse said as she moved in front of a row of shelves lined with toys and dolls and various objects. She pulled a big black and yellow tiger off the top shelf.

"This guy hasn't been hugged in ages. Think you might have room in your bed for him tonight?"

I hesitated, not yet willing to admit I'd be sleeping in this place.

"Well, at least give him a quick squeeze for now. You can decide later if you've got room for him."

Reluctantly I took the animal. I didn't want to be rude or hurt either of their feelings. His soft fluffy body did feel pretty cuddly. Hoping no one was looking, I managed to give him a quick hug, just to be sure he didn't feel rejected. He did come in handy after my folks left. Though Mom assured me she'd make me some of my favorite molasses cookies, their promises to return every other day did not take away my worry.

Now, lying here alone, with no pillow or tiger, I scolded my parents for deserting me. They never said anything about the horrible things those doctors were going to do to me or that I would have to lie flat and be still.

"Did they know they'd put needles in my back?" I wondered aloud. Suddenly I became quiet, listening to hear if my words woke Edna. Though the sound of her steady breathing was reassuring, I figured I'd better keep my mouth shut. Edna seemed nice enough, but she slept a lot.

My thoughts turned back to my parents. *They told me they wouldn't leave me in bad hands!* The muscles in my back tightened as I realized they had lied to me. The sharp pain I had experienced earlier returned. With nowhere else to go, the tears that I had so cleverly held back began oozing from the corners of my eyes. Like a river overflowing after a hard winter's thaw, the stream of salt water gradually increased until a steady flow washed over my cheeks, soaking the sleeve of my hospital gown.

I guess I'm not brave after all, I thought, my heart aching as I pictured my mom standing over the oven door pulling out trays of molasses cookies. I longed to grab hold of my dad's arm and play 'I Spy' with him.

How could they leave me all alone in this awful place? No, I can't feel safe here. I decided. Not even with smiling elephants and laughing clowns on the walls. With no one to talk to, only sleep brought relief.

Chapter 3

Shades of Red

November 1959

Days 3 through 6

The third day of my hospital stay proved to be much better than the second. I woke feeling no pain and was elated when Nurse Ellen said I could get up. When I saw Mom and Dad walk through the door, I leaped into their arms.

"Wow, hold on a minute there, Geri!" my dad exclaimed with a chuckle. "You're going to make me drop all your things."

Dad juggled the old brown overnight bag and my brother Joe's gray duffle, set them on the bed, and gave me a big hug. My mother, too, had to recover from the impact of my charge.

"You don't want to make me spill all these cookies, do you?" Mom added as she gave me the container she was holding.

"I get to keep all of these?" I asked, clutching the large red cookie tin typically used for the entire family.

"They're all yours. You can share them with your roommate though."

"Oh, I will!"

"Where is she, by the way?"

"They took her down for tests this morning," I said, hoping they weren't doing to Edna what they did to me.

We all shared big hugs, then Mom opened the gray duffle and pulled out something blue.

"I got you some new pajamas," she said proudly.

"Oh, they are so silky. Are these dragons on the top?"

"Yes. That's what they call a kimono style."

I was glad to ditch the open-back hospital gown the nurses made me wear the day before. I slid my legs into the pants and threw the top over my head.

"Oh, you look very pretty in those snazzy PJs," Dad said with a whistle.

"Thanks," I said, feeling the shiny material swish around my legs as I modeled my new lounging attire.

Dad sat down at the little round table in the center of the room and asked me how I was doing. I told them all about the terrible things the doctors had done to me the day before, but Dad insisted it was all for my benefit. I knew it would do no good to argue, so I decided not to say anything more.

Dad and I played Nim while Mom knitted mittens for the Christmas bazaar. Eventually Edna returned and my father invited her to join us for I Spy. Though it was hard to hear her soft voice, she was good at the game. While we played, we discovered we were both seven. We chatted about all kinds of things. With a new-found friend, it was not so hard to say goodbye when Mom and Dad left.

"You got nice parents," Edna said.

"Yeah, I know."

"Mine will be here soon. They got a hotel near the hospital."

"That's nice. How long you been here?"

"Oh, I think five days so far, this time."

"This time? How many times you been in the hospital?"

"Lots!"

"This is my first time and I'm never coming back!" I said firmly.

"So why are you here?" she asked.

I thought for a minute. "Everybody is worried 'cause I don't see all the letters."

"You can't see very good?"

"I can see fine. I keep trying to tell them that I only need to sit closer to the blackboard. My teacher said I could, but my parents want me to get all these tests."

As we talked, I rummaged through the duffle bag. I pulled out my new pack of paper dolls and laid them on my bed. A box of my favorite pencils lay underneath.

"Oh, look! My mom got me Cinderella and Prince Charming! I've wanted these guys for so long! Hey, Edna, you wanna play with my cutouts?"

"Sure! I have some, too. In the last drawer. Can you get 'em?"

I opened the drawer and pulled them out, then placed them on her rolling tray and slid it next to her.

"Here ya go."

"Thanks."

"Who you got?" I asked.

"Pat Boone and Millie! I got another girl and guy I named Roy and Shelly."

"I got Millie, too, but I don't think Mom brought her," I said as I pulled my bedside table over by Edna and placed my cutouts on it. I noticed Edna struggling to sit up. She was grabbing her bed rail for help. I wondered if I should do something, but she managed on her own.

"Does it hurt to sit up?" I asked. I returned to pull the rest of the items from the gray bag and stuffed them in the drawers of the little dresser.

"No," she said, catching her breath. Then she added in a whisper, "I'm just weak."

"Why?"

Edna took a few more slow deep breaths.

"I've been having problems with my kidneys. They had to take one of them out and the other one isn't working too well."

"What's a kidney?"

"It's this thing in your body, between your belly and back, that makes you go to the bathroom."

"Oh!" I stopped looking through my stuff and felt my sides and spine.

"You can't feel it from the outside, silly," she giggled. "It's inside."

I tried to picture what it must look like. I imagined a brown blob floating around in my belly.

"So can't you go pee?"

"Yeah, I can, but it's not the right kind."

"What's the right kinda pee?"

I put the last pair of socks in a drawer and shoved the duffle bag under the bed.

"First of all, it's supposed to be light yellow. Mine is real dark, more orange. The other thing is that I don't go very often."

"Yeah, so what's wrong with that?" I asked, as I opened the tin of molasses cookies sitting atop the dresser. "Wanna cookie?"

"No, thanks."

I bit into one. The snappy taste of ginger and molasses made my tongue tingle. With great pleasure, I sank my teeth into the chewy texture. My mouth still full, I asked, "So what is the matter with not going pee as much?"

"Whenever somebody goes potty, they are getting rid of yucky stuff that's in their body. My kidney isn't working right, so it isn't making enough pee for me to go the way I should."

I took another bite, savoring the rich combination of flavors.

"Why don't you just drink more and that would make you pee more. I know it does me," I suggested.

"Well, actually I'm not supposed to drink a lot. It makes my sick kidney work too hard. That's why I can't eat cookies and lots of other stuff. Because it won't get rid of the poison in me."

Really? I placed what was left of my half-eaten cookie back in the tin. I looked at Edna, trying to picture poison inside of her. Edna's brown eyes looked soft and kind. Chestnut hair fell in soft waves around her face. It seemed like she always had a warm smile. I leaned closer to look at her. Her face was very pale and there were creases that spread out from the corners of her eyes. They reminded me of the ones around my mom's.

"They're going to fix your kidney, aren't they?" I asked.

"Mom and Dad say they can't really fix it. They gave me some medicine to try and help clean out the poisons, but I don't think I will get strong like I want to."

I picked up the brown overnight, set it on the bed, and unzipped the lid. "Hey, look at this!" I said, holding up a brand new book. Mickey Mouse smiled out from the cover.

"101 Connect-the-Dots Coloring Book," I read aloud.

"Wow! That's the biggest one I've ever seen."

"Yeah! Me too. Wanna do one?"

"Sure!"

I took the book over to her bed. Her small, thin hands slid out from under the blanket and gripped it weakly. I helped her pile up the cutouts she had spread across her table top. Edna flipped through the pages slowly, reviewing each array of dots.

"Can I do this one? I think it's going to be Mickey Mouse doing something with Donald, but I can't tell what."

"Sure!" I said, peering closely at the page. I couldn't imagine how anyone could see anything by staring at all those dots. "Here, I'll get you one of my best pencils Dad sent."

"Thanks. Wanna see Teddy?" she offered, handing over a small brown bear with a red bowtie and movable limbs.

"Oh, he's cute. He sure is huggable!" I said, squeezing the bear tight to my chest.

"Mom gave him to me the last time I had to come to the hospital. I love him. I never, ever go to sleep unless he is under the covers with me."

I gave a last hug to Edna's teddy and then laid him back beside her, tracing the outline of his smiling red lips with my finger. I noticed how perfectly they matched the satin ribbon around his neck. His shining shoe button eyes seemed to wink at me as Edna pulled him close.

"So, is it hard to go to school with a bad kidney?"

"I haven't really gone to school for a couple of months. The last time I went it wasn't much fun anyway." Edna moved Teddy to the other side, and then repositioned the dot-to-dot book so she could begin drawing.

"Why not?"

"Lots of the kids tease me."

"About what?"

"About being sick all the time and missing so much school."

"That's not your fault," I said, pulling a chair over beside Edna's bed. I sat down to sort my cutouts.

"I know that, but all the kids say I'm a sicky-face, and it makes me really mad."

"I'd be mad, too. What do you do when they make fun of you?"

"Not much. If I could, I'd slug them all. But I am too weak, so I just end up crying."

We were quiet for a while. Edna worked on another dot-to-dot, while I searched for a dress to cut out for my new Cinderella. I found a pale pink gown with puffy sleeves and ruffles around the neck and hem. I looked through the brown bag, opened up some small boxes of crayons and clay, then finally found one with a pair of scissors. I was happy my mom remembered to pack them. I sat down to cut out the paper gown.

After a while, Edna spoke. "You know, of all the kids that tease me, I think Martha Madden is the worst."

"How come?"

"She says really mean things. The thing I hated her saying the most was that I wasn't really sick. She said I was faking it 'cause I was a 'Mama's girl'."

I looked up from my project. "That's awful! I had a doctor that said that about me, too. That Martha sounds as mean as Karen Worster."

"Who's that?"

"She's this mean ol' bratty girl that lives next door to me. She is always making fun of me for something."

"What does she make fun of you for?" Edna asked.

"Sometimes, because I have some trouble reading, she calls me stupid," I said.

"That's mean!"

"I know. I hate it when she does that. She says it in front of everyone when we're out on the playground, too."

"Oh, that's terrible," Edna declared. "I think we should make Martha and Karen have to go to a hospital and take yucky tasting medicine and get needle pokes and stuff."

"Darn it!" I yelled.

"What's the matter?"

I hesitated for a second, not wanting to tell Edna what I had done.

"Did you cut your finger?"

"No, I—well, I cut Cinderella's dress. I hate it when I do that."

"I'm sorry," Edna said. "Let me see."

I didn't really want to show her.

"It's okay, I won't laugh."

I stood up and held out the dress, pointing to the cut sleeve.

"Oh, that don't look too bad. I think we can tape it."

"I just hate it when I do that. I always do stuff like that," I said, disgusted with myself.

"I make mistakes like that, too. Let's see, where can we get some tape?"

Just then, one of the nurses came through the door pushing a big cart.

"Okay, young ladies, time to share a bit of yourselves with Nurse Ellen."

"Oh, do we have to?" Edna moaned.

"Of course you do. You too, Miss Geri. Get those sleeves rolled up, missies. The vampire nurse has come to take your blood!" she said, trying to mimic a scary Dracula accent.

Edna and I laughed.

"Okay," Edna said reluctantly.

"So, are you going to be first, Edna, dear?"

Edna held out her arm, which looked more like a toothpick with skin on it. Nurse Ellen picked out four glass tubes from the box on her cart. From her pocket she pulled a roll of medical tape, a pen, and scissors.

"Hey, Nurse Ellen?"

"Yes, my dear?"

"Can me and Geri have some of your tape? Geri has a tear in her paper doll's dress."

"Oh heavens, we can't have one of your lovely ladies dressed in shambles now, can we?" she exaggerated. "Let me see it, Geri. Not only am I a nurse and the daughter of Dracula, I'm a seamstress as well."

Edna laughed. I managed a smile as I shamefully handed the ruin I had made to nurse Ellen.

"Oh, what a breathtakingly beautiful gown. Did it come from Paris?" Again she talked in an accent. This time she pretended to be someone from high society. "Where's the tear?" She proceeded to turn the paper dress over in her hand. "Oh, here it is. That's nothing, Geri. This shall only take a moment, my dear. Would you like some champagne while you wait for the designers to mend your lovely creation?"

I smiled bigger, and Edna gave what was for her a hearty-sounding laugh.

Nurse Ellen placed the dress on her cart and snipped tape from the roll. In a second she turned back to me and said, "Voila! There you go, my dear. Good as new. No one at the ball will ever notice, not even Queen Elizabeth."

"Or her court," she added as an afterthought.

Nurse Ellen returned to her original task of labeling the bottles. When she finished, she removed a needle from a plastic package.

"You gonna look this time?" she asked Edna.

"Of course."

Gaining strength from Edna's bravery, I added, "Me, too!"

"You too, huh? Okay, you warrior women. You two are my only customers that dare to watch. What'sa matter with you girls, anyway? You like seeing all that blood or something?"

"I just want to be sure you know what you're doing!" Edna said.

Falling back into her dramatic role, Nurse Ellen said, "What's that? Edna, you don't trust ol' Nurse Ellen? Oh, I'm hurt." She pretended to cry.

"I learned a long time ago not to trust any of you medical people when you've got needles in your hands," Edna teased.

I giggled, but watched carefully as Nurse Ellen proceeded.

"Okay now, hold still for me."

With quick fingers, Nurse Ellen stuck Edna's arm, snapping on one of the bottles. The tube filled with bright red blood. She repeated this process three more times, then pulled the needle out as fast as she had put it in. From another pocket came a purple band-aid which she stretched across the tiny puncture she'd made.

"Okay, guess whose turn it is now?" she taunted.

I wanted to look as calm as Edna but tension pulled my muscles tight. I winced as the needle pierced my vein. No sound left my lips, however, as I kept my eyes fixed on the bottles filled with blood.

Nurse Ellen slapped a bright yellow band-aid on my arm and added four more tubes of blood to her collection. In a flash, she was out the door.

Edna and I chatted, but once more we were interrupted. An orderly came to take Edna for an x-ray. She complained cheerfully as the nice man moved her rolling table and helped her into a small wheelchair.

"See ya later," she said, as he whisked her out the door.

The smile I wore when we said good-bye left as quickly as she did. I noticed Tiger back on the shelf. I took him down, plopped him on my bed and stared up at all the cute little animals on the wall. I liked the green elephants best. They were so big and easy to see against the light yellow background. They looked cute wearing different colored saddles. I counted them as I thought about Edna and how nasty it was for that Martha girl to tease her.

Karen Worster came to mind. I wondered which of them was meaner. Then I remembered something that happened at school just before I went to see Dr. Grutch.

It was a chilly day in September. I sat in my second grade classroom, listening to the sound of the old iron radiators, clunk, clunk, clunking to keep us warm. This sound, coupled with the autumn decorations on the bulletin boards, made me feel all cozy inside. My daydream ended when Mrs. Nicer, our teacher, announced it was time for reading. Everyone would take a turn reciting a page from our Dick and Jane book.

Though I wanted to read like everyone else, I knew I didn't do it as well as the others. I'd always read a few lines ahead so I would be prepared when Mrs. Nicer called on me. It didn't help a lot, but rehearsing my lines was a daily habit. This day there were three sentences on my page. I felt my heart pound as Mrs. Nicer called my name.

"Sal-ly, loo, loo-ked, looked, ou, out the, wi, wind, windo, the window," I managed. But in the background, I could hear Karen Worster sitting behind me, snickering under her breath. I kept reading. "Sal-ly, Sally, sai, said, loo, look, Ja, Jane, see Sp, ot, Spot."

Before I could finish, Karen giggled louder, Sherry joined her.

"What a stupe," Karen said.

My hands shook. The letters wiggled in front of me. My eyes filled up with tears. I did not want to cry, but I felt so bad.

"Look!" I heard Karen say. "I think she's gonna cry. What a stupid idiot."

"Yeah, I know," Sherry agreed.

I couldn't hold my tears back any longer. I put the book down and ran from the room. When Mrs. Nicer found me sobbing in the bathroom, she promised the girls would be punished. It didn't comfort me. I figured Karen would just be meaner to me if she got in trouble.

Now, tracing in the air the outline of one of the elephants with my finger, I couldn't help wondering why I wasn't seeing the letters together. *Why did Edna have to be so weak?*

The muscles in my face grew heavy. "Why does everything have to be so unfair, God?" I asked. When I didn't get an answer, I turned away from the happy figures and pulled Tiger close. Things just didn't seem right. A chill ran through me. I curled my body around him and covered my head with the pillow. Just as I had the night before, I cried until sleep rescued me from all my unhappy feelings.

When I woke, Edna was back in her bed and chatting with her parents. They did not include me in their conversation, so I played quietly until they left. Unfortunately, Edna was so tired she fell asleep.

The next day we played together again. More interruptions stole some of our time away. Edna went for more x-rays, while I endured an electroencephalogram, or EEG. Unlike the spinal tap, it was not painful, but very nerve wracking. For two hours, I sat with wires glued to my head while another gray-haired lady in a starchy white uniform scolded me for not sitting perfectly still. By the time I returned, my hopes for playing with Edna after dinner quickly faded as she again drifted off to sleep.

On the fifth morning, I gave Edna my usual greeting.

"Mornin,' Edna!" I called across the room, but she didn't answer.

"You okay?" I asked. Again, she did not make a sound.

I moved over to her and placed my hand on her shoulder. She was breathing, but her skin felt sweaty and cold.

I ran to the nurses' desk and found Nurse Ellen. She thanked me and followed me back to the room. I huddled with Tiger under my covers, feeling very scared as I watched many medical people rush to Edna's bed. Though I didn't understand most of the words, I could tell they were giving her an oxygen tent and an IV. I wanted to ask questions about what was happening, but I was afraid.

After the equipment was set up and the treatments were done, everyone but Nurse Ellen left the room. She told me not to worry and asked if I wanted to play with my paper dolls. I got the dot-to-dots, as cut-outs weren't much fun without a friend. I wished I had someone to talk to as I drew Edna a picture.

After a while, Edna's parents came. Her mom thanked me for getting the nurse when I did. She told me I was a good friend. After that, she only spoke softly to her daughter. She and her husband took turns staying beside Edna while the other went and got lunch or took a walk. I played quietly by myself, except when the man who looked like Kingfish came to take me for another x-ray. He was the only one I laughed with that day, and I wished I could hang around with him instead of going back to my room.

Edna's parents left after suppertime, and only after the nurses assured them they would take good care of their daughter.

When Edna and I were alone, I crept over to her. Nervously, I looked through the plastic curtain of the oxygen tent. I couldn't see if she was awake.

"Hi, Edna," I whispered. She moved her head toward me.

"Hey, you okay?"

I heard a faint voice say, "Yeah." I was glad to hear her speak.

"You scared me, Edna. Do you hurt?"

She moved slightly and I thought she was trying to answer "no."

I didn't want to make her talk any more, so I continued to tell her about my day.

"I sure missed playing paper dolls with you. There isn't anyone else around who likes to play them. You tired?"

"A little," she whispered with her eyes closed.

"Want me to sing you one of the songs my sister sings me?"

She reached her hand over in my direction. I took it in mine. When she squeezed it, I knew she was saying yes.

"Okay." I thought about the many songs my sister Grace had sung to me. I decided to pick my favorite, Scarlet Ribbons.

I peeked in to say good night, and then I heard my child in prayer.

And for me, some scarlet ribbons, scarlet ribbons for my hair.

All the stores were closed and shuttered. All the streets were dark and bare.

In our town, no scarlet ribbons, not one ribbon for her hair.

I went on singing the song that told the story about a mother who overhears her daughter's wish to receive red ribbons for Christmas. The song ends with the mom peeking back into her daughter's room, singing

I peeked in and on her bed, in gay profusion, lying there,

Lovely ribbons, scarlet ribbons, scarlet ribbons for her hair.

Edna seemed to be asleep. I squeezed her hand still folded inside mine and took a minute to say my own prayer, then went to bed.

The next morning my friend was no better. Though she was able to whisper to me a little, she was still very weak.

"Can I do something to help, Edna?" She mouthed something, but I couldn't hear. I leaned closer.

"Teddy for me?" she softly asked.

"Sure." I felt around for Teddy. He had been shoved down under the covers, almost to her feet.

"Here ya go. I think the nurses forgot to put him back when they fixed your oxygen tent this morning."

"Yeah."

"Anything else you need, Edna?"

"No."

"Okay. Wanna hear another song?"

She gave another nod. This time I sang Bingo and then Old McDonald.

When I finished, Edna whispered that she wanted to hear Scarlet Ribbons again. I gladly sang, and each time I finished the song Edna's hand squeezed mine. I knew she wanted to hear it again. Finally she drifted off to sleep.

Worried and tired, I flopped back in my bed, hugging Tiger as hard as I could. Sleep, I was learning, was a great thing. This time, however, I did not wake up feeling better.

I heard people rush in and out of the room. Staying safely under my covers, I held onto Tiger. People spoke in low voices next to Edna's bed. I recognized two of them as belonging to her parents. Nurse Ellen was another. Despite the frantic sounds of shuffling feet and moving carts, there was a continual melody of loving words flowing from Edna's mother's lips.

Soon the noise from the others stopped. One by one, I heard all the people file out of the room.

"I think she's sleeping," Edna's mom said to her husband.

"Yes," he answered.

Edna's mom sniffled and began to sob. I peeked out from under my covers to see her husband put his arm around her. The oxygen tent was gone. Nurse Ellen returned.

"We're just going to take her to another room now, okay?" she said gently. My favorite orderly arrived. As I watched them wheel Edna past me, I caught a glimpse of Teddy's red bowtie on the bed next to her. Her mom gently picked him up, cradling him tightly for a long time. I shivered uncontrollably, pulling the covers back over me and Tiger.

Though I wasn't sure why, I had the feeling Teddy would not be sleeping with Edna anymore.

Chapter 4

The Diagnosis

November 1959

Day 7

The next morning turned out to be bittersweet. The mood of the ward was heavy. The staff spoke in whispers, and I wondered how my new friend had disappeared so quickly.

When Nurse Ellen brought my breakfast tray, she announced, "Hey there, missy, I hear you're leaving us today."

"Really?" I jumped with excitement, almost knocking the tray from her hands.

"Yuppers! We gave your folks a call this morning. They're on their way."

"I gotta get dressed." I plowed past her to my little dresser.

"Hey, wait a minute there, girl. You'd better eat some breakfast. They won't be here for an hour, and you don't want to go on that long ride without any food in your tummy, now do you?"

"I'm not hungry. Besides, my dad will stop and get a lemon-filled doughnut at the bakery on the highway!"

Nurse Ellen shook her head. "A doughnut is hardly breakfast, Geri girl. You sure you don't want some of this good bacon and scrambled eggs?"

"No, thanks. I'll just get dressed so I'm all ready to go."

"Okay, but in case you change your mind, I'll keep your tray at the nurses' station. We're gonna miss you around here. You and Eh—you were one of my best customers when it came to those blood draws, you know."

I knew she was going to say Edna, but I guessed she didn't want to spoil my excitement by talking about something so sad.

"I'm gonna miss you, too, Nurse Ellen. You're really nice. You're the nicest nurse here."

She set the tray on my bed table and gave me a hug.

"You take good care of yourself, Geri, and give that dog of yours a pat for me. Okay?"

"Okay."

"You know, you've taken such good care of Tiger here, maybe you'd like to take him with you?"

I looked at the comforting animal and thought about what to do. I was torn between not wanting to desert him and my desire to forget about this place forever.

Finally I said, "I think Tiger should stay to help other kids who have to spend the night here."

"You know, I think you're absolutely right!" Nurse Ellen said, bending down to give me a kiss on the top of my head.

I couldn't get dressed fast enough. I threw on the blue plaid dress I wore to the eye clinic so long ago. I rushed with anticipation, slipping on my saddle shoes. I packed all my things and tried to wait patiently for my folks to arrive. I wanted to go home so badly. Despite some of the nice folks I met, I wanted to be where people didn't poke or prod or disappear.

Eventually, I heard them coming down the hall. I ran to the doorway and almost knocked Dad over as I jumped into his arms.

"I thought you'd never get here!" I scolded affectionately.

"You did?" he chuckled, squeezing me tight. He lifted me into the air and gave me a big kiss on my cheek. When he put me down I hugged my mom around the waist. She patted my shoulder lovingly. I whisked my bag off the dresser.

"I'm all packed. Let's go," I said, moving toward the door.

"Hold on," my dad said. "We've got to talk to the doctor before we head home."

"I don't want to see any more doctors, Dad. I just want to go."

"It shouldn't be too long," my mom reassured.

But it was. Again Dad and I played Nim and Mom read from her *Reader's Digest*. After what seemed like an eternity, Nurse Ellen came to tell us the doctor was coming. She directed us into the office behind the nurses' counter. It felt like a privilege, as we kids were not allowed back there. My sense of being special quickly faded as the next chapter of my life unfolded.

I scanned the forbidden room carefully. My first impression was how stupid it was that such a place, containing only a desk and three chairs, had been off limits. It was stark and colorless, with nothing of any value or interest.

Mom sat down, and Dad took the seat near the door. The only chair left was behind the desk, so Dad invited me to sit next to him on the corner of his seat. I was more than glad to do what he asked. I felt a definite change in the air and snuggled in next to him. It seemed like we waited forever for Dr. Biggs.

He finally came, and behind him there were two other medical men. Dr. Biggs took the empty seat, while the others stood against the wall. He cleared his throat several times and opened a large folder and shuffled through it. As he reviewed the papers, I noticed a strand of thread hanging from my dad's jacket. I wound it about my finger, enjoying its tight grip. At last the doctor spoke.

"Mr. and Mrs. Taeckens, after reviewing all of the tests, we have concluded that your daughter has a disease that is affecting her eyes."

My mom shifted in her seat. Dad cleared his throat. "So what does that mean?"

The doctor turned another page and continued, "The disease is called *retinitis pigmentosa*."

I felt my father stiffen. I released the string from my finger and wound it up again, tighter this time.

"Can you explain what that means?" Dad asked.

"Yes. It is a disease of the retina, which is the disk in the back of the eye." His words made no sense to me. My mother's face looked confused as well. She was wringing her hands like she always did when she was upset.

Another string found its way around my finger. I started winding the two up together just to make things more interesting.

Dad asked, "So what does that mean if this disk has a disease in it?"

The doctor went back to turning pages. I noticed he was not looking at my parents or me, only the folder in front of him.

"The thing is, the disk is the part of the eye that turns the light into the image you see. It's like the film of a camera. The light hits the film, then the retina turns it into a picture."

Dad's muscles tensed up again. I was afraid he might yell, so I leaned hard into him. He took a deep breath. I felt him relax a bit. I could tell he was trying to control his voice as he asked, "So, Doctor, what exactly will this disease do to Geri?"

I jerked at the sound of my name. Suddenly I felt sick. I thought of Edna. *Do I have a disease inside of me, too?*

The doctor dropped his folder. I jumped at the sound. He looked at us for the first time. There was a long silence. I glanced at the door, only inches away. I wanted to run from this dreary place. As I was about to ask Dad if we could go and play Nim, my mother spoke.

"How much vision will she lose?"

"She will lose it all," he said frankly.

I turned my attention to Dr. Biggs. The two doctors were still standing behind him like mannequins. No one moved. *Is anyone breathing?* I wanted to ask. The end of my finger felt numb. *What is everyone talking about, anyway?*

Dad took in another deep breath. Finally he spoke. This time he used a word I understood all too well.

"You mean Geri is going to go blind?"

Instantly an image flashed into my mind of the tattered old man in dark sunglasses who had sold us pencils so long ago. I remembered what my dad had said about him.

"Blind people, they can't work, you know? They aren't able to really take care of themselves, so it's up to people like you and me to help them out."

I felt the same jolt of fear I did when Dad scolded me in Kresge's.

Will I have to sell pencils when I grow older? I wondered.

I remembered how Dad had shushed me. *Will Mom and Dad end up feeling sorry for me?* Suddenly I felt terribly ashamed. I pulled my hand roughly from my father's jacket. The sound of ripping strings broke the silence. I prayed nobody noticed as I hid my thread-covered fingers in the folds of my skirt.

Still no one spoke. I knew I shouldn't ask my next question, but I just couldn't sit there any longer.

"Come on, Dad, let's go home, can we?"

Chapter 5

That School

January 1960

    Not long after I sat as the invisible patient listening to the verdict of my future, my life changed. No longer did I get to walk the block and a half to the neighborhood school with my friends. Instead, I was forced to ride in a big yellow taxi to a new institution of learning.

    I'll never forget the day I first visited "That School." It was a cold and bleak January morning when I rode there with Mom and Dad. I felt as worried as my mother looked. The closer we got, the more the knot behind my belly tightened. Though I wore my favorite black and white checked skirt with ruffles along the hem, white blouse with baby doll sleeves, and my faithful saddle shoes, my mood did not improve. My new glasses with sparkling blue frames and Coke-bottle lenses didn't help either. I thought they made my eyes look like giant bugs. At least that's what Karen Worster said. If my father hadn't insisted I wear them, I would have gladly thrown them in the garbage.

    The first thing I noticed when we entered the building was the handrails running along the hallway. Everything looked drab. I followed my folks into the main office, wrapping my red wool coat tightly around me.

    A tall skinny lady with a beak nose and long stringy hair came out from behind a counter. I heard her high heels click purposefully as she shot toward us. She looked as if she had just arrived from the Land of Oz. In her long-sleeved black dress, she resembled the Wicked Witch of the West. Her high pitched voice only increased my suspicions.

    "I'm Mrs. Hecklebottom, the Principal," she said, reaching out to shake my father's hand. When she completed this ritual with my mother, she turned to me. "And you must be Geraldine. I trust you will have a good stay with us, my dear."

    I nodded my head, too scared to speak.

    "Very well. As long as you follow the rules I shouldn't need to see you in my office. Come with me and I'll take you to your new classroom."

    I kept a generous step behind the grownups and thought of Mr. Starr, the principal at my real school. I wished it was him I was walking with at that moment.

    "Your room is on the second floor, Geraldine," Mrs. Hecklebottom said. Her use of my full name added more discomfort to my belly. She didn't lead us to a staircase. Instead we ascended a series of ramps which zigzagged back and forth.

When we reached the top, we walked down a long hallway where we met a group of students. I watched as they filed out of a classroom, and we stopped so they could pass. I tried not to stare, but my eyes wandered to each boy and girl. Never had I seen children with so many differences. There were kids in wheelchairs, kids with hearing aids, and kids who were much smaller than their classmates. One child was not able to contain the saliva in his mouth, which caused him to drool. My parents had explained to me before we arrived that I would be in a class with children who had vision problems, but I had no idea about these others.

When we finally reached the entrance to my new room, I crept up tight behind my mom. Mrs. Hecklebottom stepped inside for a moment and then returned.

"You may go in. I apologize for my brief time with you, but I have a very important meeting in my office." And then—whoosh—she was gone, her high heels echoing down the hall.

I peeked through the doorway. Nine very odd-looking children sat at strange desks shaped like the letter L. Metal contraptions looking like they came from outer space sat atop each one. The voice of Rod Serling came to mind. *Maybe I'll be entering The Twilight Zone too*, I thought, feeling a chill run up my spine.

Just then I heard heavy steps. I turned and saw a large lady in a navy knit dress coming to greet us, a big smile on her face. She reminded me of my friend Katie's grandmother with her puffy hair tipped blue at the ends. A pair of glasses hung from a chain around her neck.

"Well, hello there!" she said, holding out her hand to my father. "I'm Margaret Cartacker, the Special Education teacher. Glad you could accompany Geraldine on a visit to our school." Another smile spread across her entire face, showing off her big white teeth.

I winced at the sound of my full name, while Dad shook her hand.

"Glad to meet you, Mr. Taeckens. And you must be Mrs. Taeckens?"

"Yes," said my mother, hesitating before taking the teacher's hand.

"Welcome to our classroom, Miss—what do you like to be called, Geraldine or Geri?"

"Geri," I answered.

"Welcome, Geri."

"Hi," I replied, feeling relieved she'd bothered to ask.

"Let me show you and your parents where to hang your wraps."

After we placed our coats on hooks near the door, I scanned the room once more. It was larger than I had realized. The teacher's desk was just inside the doorway. To the side of the student desks sat two square tables. The wall next to them held shelves of games and toys. A huge world globe stood on a pedestal in the opposite corner from the door, standing about as tall as me. The other far corner held a large easel, but I couldn't tell what was on it. Cardboard cards with felt dots arranged in different patterns hung across the top of the blackboard at the other end. One entire wall was filled with big thick books in green covers.

"Would you like to meet your classmates?" Mrs. Cartacker asked, jolting me back to the discussion at hand.

I didn't know how to answer this, as I surveyed the questionable-looking children. The kids sitting behind the strange desks were doing even stranger things. Some had their fingers in their eyes and another was rocking back and forth. The students in my real school never did stuff like this. I shot a questioning look at my folks as I secretly noted how sighted I really was.

"Of course!" Dad interjected. "Geri surely would like to meet her new schoolmates, wouldn't you, Geri?"

"Uh, yes," I answered, knowing I'd better be polite. *Is this what blind kids are all about?* I wondered.

"Boys and girls, I'd like you to meet the new member of our class. I want you to say hello to Geri Taeckens."

In unison, all the hands dropped from the eyes, and with a sound like a chorus out of tune, I heard, "Hello."

"I'd like each of you to tell Geri your name and how old you are. Janice, would you like to go first?"

A tiny girl with dark eyes and frizzy hair took the lead. "Hi, I'm Janice Pearl and I'm 8 years old." It was freaky watching her quick movements as she rocked back and forth to the rhythm of her words.

"Anthony, you're next," the teacher prompted.

In a drawn out flat tone, the young boy with an army haircut responded, "Hi. My. Name. Is. Anthony Smart. I. Live. At. 3. 2. 1. South. Lyon. Road. My. Phone. Number. Is--"

"That's okay, Anthony," Mrs. Cartacker chimed in. "Your name is good enough."

Relieved by the teacher's suggestion, I let out the breath I'd been holding after mentally helping Anthony complete his speech.

"Who's next?" Mrs. Cartacker continued.

"Me, I think," said a cheery voice. "Hi, Geri, I'm Linda Dowit. Glad you're in our class. If you want, I'll show you around after you get your desk and everything."

"Uh, okay," I said, surprised at her normalcy.

"Donna?" called Mrs. Cartacker.

Pulling fingers from her eyes, Donna lifted her head, exposing a drooping left eye and crooked smile. Once more I felt the muscles in my jaw tighten as I strained to understand what she was saying.

"H-i Ga-re, wool-come to the cl-aa-ss. My dame ziz Don-na. I yam eight-a years ol'. I hop-a yul li-ke go-wind to stool whit uz."

I resisted the urge to ask, "What?" Instead I just said, "Thanks."

Mike was next. In speech that closely resembled that of a gangster in an Eliot Ness show, he said, "Yeah, ah, hi. The name's Mike. I'd prefer to get ta know ya before I tell ya much more bout myself. Not ta be rude or anything, but we get lots a folks commin' in here askin' about us kids, see, so it gets a little tirin' after a while."

"That's fine, Mike," the teacher interjected. "Let's not scare Geri away on her first day now, shall we? You'll find, Geri, that Mike is the rebel of our group. He likes to get on his soapbox from time to time. Not that I mind, I like a young person who thinks for himself. Just try to save it for the right times like we talked about, okay, Mike?"

But I didn't feel at all afraid. My family watched Eliot Ness, and I thought Mike was kind of neat.

I listened anxiously as the rest of the students took turns saying their names. Travis, Jade, Maria, Sally, and Annie were all older than me.

After the introductions, Mrs. Cartacker and my folks huddled at her desk. While they discussed me, Linda gave me a tour of the place. I was surprised to see how easily she sprang from her chair and walked over to me. She didn't even bump into the desks she passed. Amazingly, she located my hand, grabbed it, and pulled me to her unusual work station. Her sandy brown hair was tied back into a ponytail with a blue ribbon. It matched the dotted Swiss dress she wore.

"What school did you used to go to?"

It took me a second to answer. Her blue eyes distracted me. The left drooped, while the right one stared straight ahead, never moving.

"I go to the parochial school in my neighborhood," I answered, as I watched her bring another chair from an empty table. I continued to stare in awe at Linda's ability to walk through several obstacles without even touching them.

"If I went to my local school, it would be Lincoln. Got any brothers or sisters?" she asked.

"Two sisters and a brother," I said, sitting down across from her.

"I only have a younger brother and a dog, Buster. You got any pets?"

"Uh, yeah, I have a dog named Tippy."

"What kinda dog?"

"A boxer-collie mix. He's brown and white, with a white tip on his tail. That's how he got his name."

"Oh, that's neat. So, how old are you?"

I watched as Linda arranged things on her desk without moving her eyes to look.

"I'll be eight next week."

"Oh, you're going to have a birthday? Mrs. C always brings cupcakes for birthdays. What day?"

"January twenty-eighth. How old are you?"

"I just turned seven," she called as she walked to the bookshelf and took one of the green books, again maneuvering through tables and chairs.

Linda's confidence confused me. How can she be so normal and be blind, too? I wondered, as a picture of the man selling pencils flashed in my mind.

"This is what we write on." She took my hand and placed it on the contraption I'd noticed earlier. I felt its cold metal surface. "It's called a Braille writer. Our desks are shaped like the print letter L so it can hold these big Braille books while we write," she said, tapping the book she'd laid on the desk. Linda took my finger and ran it across the back end of the machine. "See, the paper slides under this roller, but you got to pull these clips back or it won't go in." As she talked, she whipped a piece of paper out from underneath her desk. She slipped it efficiently into a slot and rolled it in so it almost disappeared.

Crunch, crunch, crunch, ding. Linda went from pushing some weird-looking keys at the front to pulling back on another thing-a-ma-bobble which had no describable shape. Before I could ask what she was doing, Linda placed my fingers on the strip of paper. "Here, can you feel them?"

I rubbed my pointer finger across some clumps of dots.

"Yeah! That's Braille?" I asked in surprise. I hadn't imagined anything like this. "You can read it? It doesn't look like any letters to me!"

"Oh, it will eventually. See those big cards hanging over the board at the back of the room?"

"Yeah?" I said, looking in their direction.

"Well, those felt dots are the Braille alphabet. That's how you're gonna read. Don't worry, you'll catch on."

"I will?" I asked, feeling doubtful.

"When I first started learning," Linda continued, "the dots felt like nothing to me at all, but it doesn't take long to figure out the patterns. You totally blind or are you a partial?"

"What do you mean?"

"Are you totally blind or partially blind?"

"I'm not blind!" I said feeling annoyed.

"Then you're a partial."

"What's a partial?" I asked, my irritation rising.

Linda gave a knowing smile. "Somebody who can't see very well."

"I can see okay!" I lied.

"Then why are you coming to this school?" I didn't like her questions. I also didn't like how her smile was getting wider.

"I just have a little trouble seeing letters on a chalk board."

"Must be more than that if you're coming here!" she insisted.

I thought about my friends sitting in the classroom back home. I glanced at my folks and saw they were still talking to the teacher. I wanted to rush over and demand to leave, but I knew I couldn't. Instead I searched for a clock. Spotting one over the Braille cards, I could see it was 10 o'clock. I realized my friends at my other school were doing math, my least favorite subject, and I felt a little better.

"Well, are you gonna tell me why you're in this class or not?"

"Huh? Uh," I said, trying to come up with an answer. I remembered the words the doctor used when telling my folks I needed to go to a special school. "I'm just learning to read with my hands so I don't strain my eyes."

The smile left Linda's face. She thought for a minute. "That don't matter," she proclaimed. "In this class, you're either a total or a partial."

I glared at her. My cheeks grew hotter, keeping pace with the anger welling up inside me. I glanced nervously at my folks, who had no clue what was happening. With great effort, I held my arms tight to my sides, clenched my teeth and said, "I am not a partial. I just have a little trouble reading sometimes."

Linda continued, "So, you gonna lose more sight some day?"

I balled my right hand into a fist and considered hitting her as I silently screamed "Shut up!"

"Well, are you?" she said again.

I answered slowly and with deliberation. "I told you, I don't have trouble seeing. I just need to read with my fingers so I don't strain my eyes."

"Okay!" But I knew she didn't believe me. The slight grin crossing her lips told me so. Linda started pounding on her machine. It made me jump. My fear disappeared, however, as I watched her fingers move swiftly over the funny-looking keys. In no time, she unrolled the paper and handed it to me.

"Here ya go," she said, thrusting it my way.

For a second the fear returned, and I thought she was going to hit me. I took the paper from her hand although I really didn't want to.

"What is it?"

"It's the Braille alphabet. Take it to show your parents and friends."

I felt like throwing it back in her face, but I thanked her instead. *I'm not showing it to nobody!* I thought.

"Wanna see the Braille map of the United States?" she asked.

"Okay," I answered, silently slipping the unwanted offering onto her desk. I checked my folks to see if they were done talking, but they were still very much in conversation. It turned out okay, though. I liked the map a lot. It was a big puzzle on the easel stand I'd noticed earlier. Each state was a different color and could be removed. The mountains, lakes, and rivers were all raised or indented, so they could be felt. I forgot being mad at Linda as she named them all. When she was done showing me the map, she took me over to the big globe. It, too, had raised mountains and borders.

When we were done, she asked, "Wanna play a game?"

"Sure. But what can you play?"

"Oh, we got lots of games. How about tic-tac-toe?"

"Okay." We went over to the shelves near the tables. As I watched her pull a box from a shelf, I was still curious to know how she knew what she was doing.

"You wanna be Xs or Os?"

"I don't care," I answered, sitting down at the table.

Linda set down the board.

"Feel this."

I did as she asked. Four raised lines made up the nine squares of the game.

"That's neat!" I said.

"It's so the Xs and Os don't slide out of their spot. Here's the markers." Linda handed me five metal Xs. "You go first."

So I did. We ended up playing seven rounds before I heard my dad call. "Ready to go?"

Quite willing to leave, I answered. "Oh, yeah."

"That makes four and three," Linda announced, "I'm ahead." She gave me a triumphant smile. "I'll keep the scores until next time."

My heart sank as I realized I would be coming back. I jumped up and headed for the coat rack.

"Goodbye," I managed to say as I moved as fast as I could through the exit.

During the ride home, I considered whether to ask the question I'd been holding in all day. Though I already knew the answer, I dared to say, "Dad, do I have to go back there?"

"Of course, honey. Didn't you like your new school?"

"I just want to stay with my friends."

"I thought you liked the little girl, what's her name?"

"Linda," I answered sulkily.

"Yeah, Linda. It looked like you and Linda were getting along just fine."

"She's okay, but I want to go to school with Sherry and Katie and the other kids."

"Mrs. Cartacker seems real nice," my mom offered.

"Oh, she is. I just like Mrs. Nicer really a lot and I want to go back to my own school."

"Well," my dad said, "for now, I think you're going to have to go to this one. Mrs. Cartacker says she's going to teach you how to read with your hands. They have a really nice pool. Oh, and guess what?"

"What?"

"You get to ride in one of those yellow taxis we see driving around town."

Despite my dad's effort to comfort me, I finally lost control.

"I don't wanna ride in a taxi!" I yelled. "I just wanna walk like everybody else! Dad, please don't make me go to school with all those weird kids. Please!"

There was silence for a few minutes. I prayed he was changing his mind.

Eventually he said, "Geri, I don't like you calling any child weird. You have a vision problem. Your school can't teach you to read with your hands. Besides, you'll learn things you need to know so you don't have to use your eyes all the time."

I thought about the secret I'd been keeping since I sat scrunched on the chair with my dad at the hospital. I had decided that day the doctor was wrong. Just because I didn't see all those letters on their charts didn't mean I would go blind. I knew that if I just worked at it, I could make my eyes be okay. Though I had wanted to tell this to my parents, I feared it would only make them repeat the doctor's words. Maybe I should tell them now.

"Dad?"

"Yes."

"I can see just fine, honest."

"I know you can, honey, but you won't always be able to. That's why you need to learn new ways to do things."

"No, that's not what I mean! I know I can't read letters too well, but I can work harder at it. I can do lots of homework, Dad. Besides, my new glasses are helping lots. I think they're gonna keep it so I can do fine. Just let me stay at school with my friends, Dad, please?"

"Now, Geri, you know you need to learn Braille. You'll get used to your new school and love it in no time."

"But, Dad! Those kids…"

"What about those kids?" my dad asked.

"They're not normal, Dad!"

"Young lady, I don't know what you think normal is, but God made each and every one of those kids, and they all seemed to be very nice. I'd suggest you treat them like you would any of your friends."

Even with his scolding, I did not feel any guilt. *Grownups are supposed to say that stuff anyway*, I told myself, slumping back in my seat. My words were not very reassuring, however. Instead I felt defeated. I was already behind one match of tic-tac-toe, and I was losing at the game of tug of war. I threw the bottom of my coat over my head and pictured the students sticking their fingers in their eyes. *Will I be sticking mine there too?* I asked no one, wishing I could scream.

No! I insisted, I am not going to go blind!! I am going to be normal!

Chapter 6

Dividing the Squares

January 1960 to January 1963

When my mother became overwhelmed with the demands of the household, I would hear her say, "Sometimes I feel like I live on more than one planet." I knew what she meant. I'd been straddling two worlds for three years now. This was not an easy task, particularly when one of them turned out to be the Twilight Zone after all. The gap between home and school was growing wider. This made doing the splits more challenging. My survival depended on keeping the zones separate.

It was bad enough to deal with Karen Worster's normal bullying. If she ever heard the horrid details of my days at That School, I'd never live it down. She'd already caught on to how jealous I felt about being away from Katie and the other kids. If I was to avoid further rejection, I could never reveal how awful it felt to spend every day just waiting for time with the teacher.

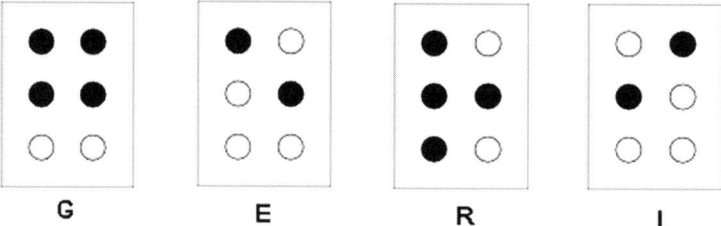

The first few months were tolerable, except for adjusting to some of the oddities of the place. Mrs. Cartacker spent a fair amount of time teaching me Braille. I felt privileged learning to read words with my fingers, even though it wasn't as difficult as most thought. Mrs. C. explained how this new system worked using a number six domino as an example of a Braille cell.

"Each dot has a pretend number name," she said, sitting beside me at the table where Linda and I had played tic-tac-toe. "The top left dot is number one." She took my right pointer finger and touched it to the indented circle on the domino. "Below it is dot number two, and the bottom left is number three." She moved my finger down the left side of the domino as she spoke. "Now we have to go back to the top and start on the other side." There was affection in her voice. I liked the clean smell of her perfume. The gentle touch of her warm hand on mine felt so nice. "Feel the top right dot?"

"Uh-huh."

"That is number four, below it five, and finally—can you guess what the bottom right dot's number is?"

"Six!" I said proudly, even though I knew anyone would have figured it out. "So how can that make letters?" I asked.

"Here, touch this," she said, placing a piece of paper with a real Braille cell on it in front of me. I rubbed my index finger over the rectangle of bumps. "Hey, I can feel them!"

"That's good."

"But I still don't get how this makes letters."

"It's quite simple really," she assured me. "By using specific dots or mixtures of dots, it will make a particular letter."

"Oh, I get it. I'm not supposed to use all six of them all the time."

"That's right."

"So how do I make the dots?" I asked.

"You are always one step ahead of me, Geri," Mrs. C chuckled. Once again a warm, satisfying feeling came over me. The way she spoke to me reminded me of my dad when he'd praise me for moving the gears in the right place.

"This is what you use your embosser for," she continued.

"Oh, yeah!" I giggled, looking up into her wide smile.

Mrs. C pushed the Brailled paper to the side and replaced it with the odd looking machine. After rolling a piece of paper in, she placed my hands on six of the nine keys.

"Okay now, when you push one of these keys, it will punch out a specific dot on your paper."

"But there's nine of them," I protested, confused.

"You're correct about that. The funny looking one in the middle is the space bar. This round one on the left rolls the paper out and the round one on the right is the back space. Understand?"

"Got it," I said, giving her another smile.

"So this leaves the rest for making Braille. Each key has a number assigned to it, just like the dots in the Braille cell.

"You mean one, two, three, four, five, and six?"

"Yes, Miss Smarty, that's exactly right."

"So which one is one?"

"I'm getting to that," she laughed. Mrs. C proceeded to answer my question. I quickly understood the concept. The key for dot one was under my left index finger, two and three under my middle and ring finger. On the other side of the spacebar, numbers four through six were in the same position.

"So which ones do I push to make letter G?" I asked, curious to know how to write my name.

"Slow down!" she said jovially. "Let's do this systematically, shall we? If you learn them out of order, you're more likely to forget. Let's start with 'A' first, okay?"

"Okay." I agreed, giggling at our playful interaction.

For the next two weeks, Mrs. C taught me the number combinations of each letter. With my lessons only lasting fifteen minutes twice each school day, I felt frustrated that I couldn't learn faster. I ached to be able to read so I could get on with other subjects.

Learning to recognize letters by touch was another matter. When my teacher told me I had to develop my tactile sense first, I complained. I insisted I could do it without wasting time with training, but she still made me follow the long and boring process. This included feeling felt shapes which were glued in rows across the pages of a little book. The goal was to identify, through touch, the various shapes as I moved my fingers left to right. Though these figures were eventually reduced to the size of a Braille cell, and placed closer together, it didn't happen fast enough for me. Once Mrs. C decided my fingers were fine-tuned enough, she allowed me to graduate to a book filled with Braille letters.

Though I enjoyed her attention, I felt discouraged with the slow pace of the lessons. When I became bored, I'd distract myself by admiring the colorful cluster of pearls she wore on her ears and neck. The jingling of her jewelry was a welcome sound, as it always signaled the teaching of something new.

"Today we're going to learn about numbers," she announced one morning, rattling the double string of silver beads hanging between her generous breasts.

"Braille has numbers?" I asked, realizing I hadn't thought about this possibility before.

"Absolutely! There are numbers in Braille, too, you know. They are the same as the letters, except you have to put a number sign in front of them."

"What's the number sign?"

"Dots three, four, five, and six."

"A backwards V?" I already knew the answer, as V was dots 1, 2, 3, and 6.

"That's right! Very good! If you put a number sign in front of the letter A, you have the number one. If you put it in front of the J, you have the number zero."

Instantly I understood. "So C-J means the number thirty, right?"

"You are very quick!"

Even though Mrs. C knew I caught onto things rapidly, she didn't tell me about Grade Two Braille until the beginning of my second year.

"Because Braille takes up so much space on a page, we have to find a way to shorten things up," she informed me. "So far you've only been using Grade One, which is simply the letters of the alphabet. I am now going to show you contractions, which are kind of like short hand."

It took the rest of the school year and most of the next to learn the shortcuts making up this alternative language. This included the numerous dot combinations for "ing," "and," "er," "ed," "the," and many others. I learned that each letter of the alphabet, except for "O," stands for a word when used alone in a sentence. "B" stands for the word "but," "K" means "knowledge," "P" means "people," and "Z" equals "as." If this wasn't enough to remember, additional multiple letter combinations would create a new word, like "PD" for "paid," and "PCV" for the word "perceive." If I added "D" to the end of "PCV" it became the word "perceived." Mrs. Cartacker also taught me how adding one or two dots in front of a letter would give it another meaning. If dot six were placed before an "N," it would stand for "ATIO." Therefore, the word "nation" would be written, "n," dot 6, "n." If dots four, five and six were placed in front of the letter "M", it would make the word "many."

Having to learn all the signs and symbols was overwhelming.

Matching all the rules and regulations with what my fingers were feeling took time. I did eventually become pretty good at reading. Not as fast as Linda, though. She could read better than Mrs. Cartacker and made sure I knew it.

The slate and stylus was the next challenge I faced. Mrs. C didn't introduce it to me until the beginning of my third year. "This handy little device will allow you to write Braille wherever you go," she explained, handing me a two by eight inch metal rectangle, hinged on one end. She showed me how the paper slid in between the two sides. The paper would then be secured by clamping the mechanism shut.

The top plate of the device contained a line of four rows of twenty-eight windows. Each was slotted with six grooves. They corresponded to the bottom plate which held the same number of cells, all of them with six holes in the shape of a number six domino.

Mrs. C handed me a metal stylus with a wooden knob on the end. She showed me how to use it for punching out Braille. Because the dots came out on the bottom, the numbering of each cell had to be reversed. Instead of dots 1, 2, and 3 being on the left side, I had to reverse the numbering so they were on the right, with four, five, and six on the left. This made it so the letters would be punched out correctly. I also learned the necessity of writing right to left so when the page was flipped over, the words would read properly.

At first it was slow going. When I finally caught on, Linda and I would challenge each other. We'd see who could write an assignment the quickest. Unlike tic-tac-toe, I usually won.

Once the private lessons with my teacher stopped, the boredom I had experienced in between my Braille lessons increased. Mrs. C had lots to do with so many students with different abilities. Anthony and Janice were still learning the first part of the alphabet, and it took a lot of effort to get Maria to even talk, let alone learn much of anything.

Shortly after my arrival at That School, I learned that Maria was the product of serious child abuse. Linda and I overheard Mrs. Cartacker talking to another teacher in the hallway. Maria had been adopted after her real mother tried to burn the devil out of her with an iron. This explained the scars on her face and arms.

Jade was another story. Periodically, in the middle of a lesson, she'd start throwing chairs and books or whatever she could get her hands on. Mrs. C would wrestle her down. If she got really bad, one of us had to tell the teacher who taught the blind pre-schoolers in the next room. Though Mrs. Cartacker attempted to give math and spelling lessons, she was mainly busy keeping everything under control.

The greatest challenge of the day was finding something to do. As long as I was quiet and didn't disturb Mrs. C while she was busy, I could pretty much do what I wanted.

My old classmates would have found this a dream come true, but I thought it torturous. My desperate attempts to avoid going stir crazy included a new version of Beat the Clock. This had to do with trying to see the exact moment the large minute hand moved from one of the black dots to the next. Although I was quite able to see the contrast between the white face and the black figures, it appeared as if the hands somehow magically jumped from one spot to the next. Eventually this activity also turned monotonous, so I searched for things to occupy my mind.

I initially avoided spending time with the other kids. Their strange behaviors were way too weird. Fingers in the eyes, rocking, jiggling legs, the clicking sounds made by Annie's tongue, and Travis's intense body odor were more than annoying. Linda was the one who eventually shed light on these various traits.

"It's like ya got to fill in the blank spot," she told me after I asked her why she always stuck her fingers in the socket of her left eye. "Even though I can't see, I know there's supposed to be something happening there, so if I push up against my eye with my knuckles, it feels better."

"But it looks weird!" I told her.

"I think it's weird that you don't," she said sarcastically.

"So how come you never put your fingers in your right eye then?"

"Cause it's artificial and I don't have any feeling there." Although I found the idea of a fake eye repulsive, I decided not to say anything more.

Linda also informed me that rocking was her way of running.

"It's not always safe for us blind kids to move fast or go dashing from one end of the house to another like my brother does. If I can sit in a rocking chair, I can get rid of all kinds of energy."

"Well, a rocking chair's okay," I admitted, "But moving back and forth in a regular chair looks stupid."

"So bring me a rocking chair and I'll be glad to sit in it instead," she snapped.

"Mrs. C wouldn't let us have one of those at school!" I argued. "You just need to sit still and look normal."

"Normal shwormal," Linda said with a laugh. "Why can't you see normal if you think it's so easy? Personally, I read abnormally fast, so I wouldn't want to be normal anyway!"

Clicking tongues were another area Linda and I argued about. She told me that making a continuous sound helped to know if an object was in the way.

"If I snap my fingers or make a noise with my voice, the sound bounces back off a wall or a shelf or something, and I can tell how close I am. Annie does this too, when she makes her clicking sound. Some kids use singing like Janice does."

"I think singing is more normal than clicking tongues," I proclaimed, but Linda simply informed me once more she didn't give a darn about normal.

I also learned the reason for Travis's body odor. It was not the result of poor hygiene as I had thought. Linda said there was something wrong with his kidney which made his body smell. I accused her of lying. Edna had never smelled badly. I secretly forgave Travis anyway.

Although we squabbled, Linda's company turned out to be the best solution to the long empty days at That School. When we weren't engaged in an activity with Mrs. C, she and I would play games of checkers or Scrabble, and take turns reading part of the one hundred and four volumes of the Braille World Book Encyclopedia. These were the green books which lined the entire wall of the room. I hated that she read ten times faster than I did, but I loved sharing the information I drank from this wondrous book.

During my third year at That School, I had to endure yet another degradation. Although the majority of the school was for special education, the top floor housed general education students. When Mrs. C announced that Linda would be spending half her day attending classes with the regular kids, I grew green with envy.

This is when I realized how much I cherished our times together. Every day I'd watch her leave the place I called prison, forcing me to stay with the others. I desperately wanted to ask Mrs. Cartacker if I could go with her, but I was afraid she'd tell me I was too stupid.

I hated staying behind, but it did force me to get to know the rest of my classmates. Linda's explanations turned out to be helpful. With no one else to talk to, I discovered they weren't so bad. I wasn't particularly interested in wrestling and baseball like Mike and Travis, but we did share a fondness for the game of checkers and a love for rock and roll. Sally liked to play kids' records, so we'd sing together if Mrs. Cartacker said it was okay. Donna turned out to be great at Scrabble, while Annie kept us laughing with her good sense of humor as she regularly mistook the closet for the hallway door. I ended up reading the Braille version of Susan Barton, Student Nurse to Sally, Jade, and Maria, which made me feel really important, but still I wanted to be with Linda.

Surviving through each day proved to be more and more difficult. I looked for anything that would help brighten my time at That School. This included the small heated swimming pool and Girl Scouts. Both were held on Wednesdays. This helped to have something to look forward to at the beginning of the week, but left me with little afterwards.

The greatest degradation I endured at That School still makes me cringe. After lunch, we were forced to take naps on cots. This rule came from our principal, Mrs. Hecklebottom, who believed blind kids were not safe on the playground. I'd lie there angry, fuming about the unfairness of having no freedom while my friends at home were out playing. I hated the humiliation I felt each day. I couldn't even count on sleep to help me escape from my shame. Instead, I spent the endless thirty minutes lying there, tracing in the air the outline of the cardboard squares with felt dots, wondering how long I could keep my two lives separate.

Chapter 7

To Tell the Truth

May, 1963

With each passing year, my awareness of my differences grew. It became harder and harder to push back the shame I felt about my secret life at That School. Each time the big yellow taxi pulled into my driveway to pick me up or drop me off, I'd pray that no one would be around to see. When they did, I'd hear about it, particularly if Karen Worster saw it.

"Takin' a ride in your funny yellow bus there, Geri?" Or "Don't forget to tip the driver. Tell him he should get a better looking bus."

But the worst thing was seeing the kids walking home from school together carrying book bags filled with homework. Sometimes I'd hang out at my best friend Katie's house while she studied. When she'd read from her book and write down answers in nice neat letters, I ached to be able to do the same. Going to the library with my dad had the same effect. The rich smell of all those books filled with knowledge taunted me. I'd run my fingers along the colorful bindings, like I did with the spools of thread, yearning to find out what was inside. Sometimes I'd pull out one of the books and pretend to read. I felt so important thumbing through them, but all the information was out of reach. I don't believe a day went by that I didn't feel angry or jealous about my situation.

I couldn't find anyone to be mad at, though. Sometimes at home I would get really upset if I couldn't get the line of my socks to lay straight across my foot. If the toothpaste didn't come out of the tube just right, or if I had too many tangles in my hair, I'd throw myself on the floor and kick and scream that nothing was right. Every day I'd tell myself I was going to be a good girl, but something always bothered me and I'd throw a tantrum.

Although I couldn't admit it, my vision had slipped since my initial hospital visit. This made it harder for me to join in some of the neighborhood activities in the cul-de-sac near our house. I had to ask whoever was turning the jump rope to stop it until I stood beside it. When I played kickball, I had to ask for a special favor, as Karen so unkindly put it. I was unable to see a moving ball, so I needed to have it placed right in front of my foot. My ability to stay within the lines for hop scotch turned into a nightmare, so I usually found an excuse to bow out. The game of tag quickly joined my "no way" list, as running fast in uncertain territory went beyond even my safety index.

Ironically, the only game I could play well turned out to be Blind Man's Bluff. Though putting the scarf over my eyes brought back the image of the blind man, I did appreciate the leveled playing field. Already I had learned to use my ears more than most kids. It never took me long to find the others simply by listening for their breathing or the rustle of a bush. My victories made Karen Worster mad, however, so eventually this game became obsolete. Karen's position as the neighborhood queen meant she got to pick what we played. Unless she happened to be away, Blind Man's Bluff stayed out of sight.

There were so many secrets I had to keep, at times I thought I'd burst apart with anger. The strange events at That School, feelings of jealousy, inferiority, and all the other bad thoughts inside me were overwhelming. I needed to find a way to feel better somehow. I did find the means to accomplish this, but I often did so in a less than honorable fashion.

One Wednesday afternoon I climbed out of the big yellow taxi. I looked up and down my street, hoping it was empty. To my dismay, I saw Sherry Grumble crossing the road toward my house. Sherry could be a friend, but if Karen Worster happened to be nearby, Sherry always found a way to win brownie points with her by cutting me down. As she approached, I acted as if coming home in a taxi were a normal everyday thing. I swung my gym bag nonchalantly in my hand, then whipped it up over my shoulder. I ignored the cold wet spot forming on the collar of my pink striped seersucker dress, scolding myself for never wringing out my bathing suit.

"So, what'd you do at school today, Geri?" Sherry asked in a snide tone.

I shifted the dripping bag under my arm.

"Went swimming," I answered.

"Oh, yeah? How many times did you almost drown there, Ger?" she asked, releasing a malicious chuckle.

"Real funny!" I answered as we walked together toward my front porch. "Hey, I'm too good a swimmer to drown. In fact, we practiced the breast stroke for our meet next week."

"Is that the only stroke you know?" she asked.

"Nah, I know the back and butterfly, too, but it's the breast stroke we need to work on most."

We stopped at my front stoop as Sherry and I continued talking. I hoped she wouldn't notice the water now dripping down my side.

"So where's this meet gonna be held at?" I could tell by the way she looked around she wasn't really interested. I decided to see if I could get her attention.

"It's gonna be in Florida."

"Florida! I'm sure," she mocked.

"Really! Heck, Florida's no big deal. Last month we went to California. I won the gold at that one." I gave her a smile, daring her to challenge me.

Counting on Sherry's bad grades, I felt safe she knew little about geography. Luckily, I had the big puzzle map of the states at That School to help me out.

Besides, Sherry and the others bought my story last month when I told them my class had flown to New York to visit the Statue of Liberty.

I tried to assure myself the story was only a slight exaggeration, but the commandment "Thou Shalt Not Lie" did cause a bit of internal conflict. It didn't stop me from adopting Mrs. Cartacker's story of her Easter trip to visit the statue, however. I decided the risk I took was worth everyone listening intently as I shared how we all walked up 354 steps to the crown.

Now standing by the stoop, I wondered if Sherry was buying my fish story. She looked straight at me through her tortoiseshell glasses. I couldn't look back. Her busy red and blue paisley print blouse made my eyes bug. Nonetheless, I kept a straight face.

"Oh, yeah? Then how da ya get ta all them places?" she asked, maintaining her stare.

"We take planes, of course. We have to be back in time for the end of the school day, you know."

Sherry finally looked away. "I'm sure," she said in disbelief.

"It's true!" I insisted, encourage by her submissive response. "Once a month, on a Wednesday, all of us kids get to go to other cities and compete. They have gold, silver, and bronze medals for the top three winners. I win a lot 'cause Mr. Benchly says I'm one of the best."

"That ain't true. You're lying."

"I am not," I said indignantly. "You can ask my mom. She even had to sign a permission slip so I could ride on the airplane. All the kids' moms did. Once in a while we don't go 'cause they have the meets here. But mostly I go every month."

I could tell Sherry was struggling to think of something to say. Of course, I knew she'd never ask my mother. I also knew that Sherry would give anything to be able to go anywhere. She had a lot of brothers and sisters, and I never knew her family to take a vacation. In fact, I kind of figured Sherry didn't get a whole lot of attention from anyone except for me and Karen.

"I'll show you the gold medal I got last time if you wanna see it," I said, remembering a little twenty-five cent medal I really did win. "Want me to get it?"

"Nah," she said, "I'll see it some other time." Sherry stuffed her hands in the pockets of her jeans and bowed her head. She scuffed her canvas tennies back and forth on the edge of the bottom step. Feeling slightly ashamed of myself for causing her to feel bad, I smiled, triumphant that I made her jealous.

As I was about to leave Sherry said, "We got to go to a play today. Karen and I got to sit together, too."

"That's nice," I lied, a pang of envy tearing through my gut.

"Yeah, it was about a bunch of nursery rhymes. One of them was Three Blind Mice. Karen said that you should have been one of the mice. Ha-a-a. Good one, huh?"

"Uh, yeah," I laughed, hoping to cover up my hurt. "Is she home from school yet?" I prayed the answer was no.

"Yeah, she's in changing her clothes."

"What latest fashion is she wearing this time?" I asked. I hated how Karen always had something new to wear. Her mom bought her every new style that came out. Karen got the twist blouse, square-toed shoes, the latest Nehru jacket, and any other popular item advertised on TV or in the magazines.

"I dunno, but she'll be out in a minute."

Big deal, I thought but didn't say. "You wanna come in?" I asked instead.

"Nah, I think we're gonna play kickball when she comes out. Wanna play?"

My heart sank with this announcement. I thought about making up an excuse, but I hated being left out of things.

"Uh, well, I guess so. When you playing?"

"As soon as we round up some others."

"Okay," I said, with all the enthusiasm of someone agreeing to be escorted to the electric chair. "I gotta change first."

"Okay, but hurry, I need you to help find some players."

I raced to my room, threw off my soggy dress and slid into a pair of jeans and a t-shirt. I removed my heavy glasses and rubbed my tired eyes before switching my pink plastic headband for a white one. After making sure my bangs were tucked neatly under this modern day hair piece, I returned the thick lenses to their spot on my nose. Before I ran out the front door, I made sure my folks knew I'd be hanging out at the corner with my friends. It took about fifteen minutes for Sherry and me to round up four other girls to play the dreaded game. Katie, thank goodness, was one of them. In the four years we'd palled around with each other, she never teased me or anyone else. Katie, always in pigtails, was the picture of sweet innocence. I never knew her to do anything unkind despite the fact her father was always yelling at her.

Mary, Margaret, and Elaine were the other girls who joined us. This was good. They were all neutral members of the group. They didn't particularly get off on teasing or sucking up to Karen. As far as I was concerned, I could trust them.

We all gathered at the edge of the dead end road. Our little corner was a great place to play, as the only cars that came around were related to one of us kids. Sherry leisurely bounced her ball as we waited for Karen.

Finally, the queen arrived. A picture of loveliness, she was dressed in matching navy shirt and stretch pants, auburn sausage curls bouncing as she walked. She moved into the group like she owned us.

"Okay, let's call teams," Karen directed. "Sherry, you're with me, right?" Before Sherry could even answer, Karen continued. "Mary, you going to be the captain of the other team?"

Of course she was. Karen said so, didn't she? I mused.

"Okay," Mary answered,

Karen continued. "Elaine, you wanna be with me?"

"Sure," Elaine answered.

Karen held up her hands, signaling Sherry to throw the ball. She yelled, "Good. Katie, you're with us, too. You get Margaret and Geri, Mary," she announced, catching the ball. Karen glanced in my direction, sneered briefly, and then dribbled the ball as she walked.

I thought I saw Mary scrunch up her face. Though I wasn't completely sure, it seemed like Mary was annoyed. She cleared her throat, about to say something, then shook her head slightly as if changing her mind.

Karen walked slowly around, surveying the group. No one spoke as the tension grew. Katie, who stood on the opposite side of the road, stared directly at me. I gave her a look of concern. I felt pretty sure Karen was purposefully creating a problem for my benefit by picking teams the way she did. Katie must have read my thoughts.

"Karen?" she ventured.

"Yeah, what?"

"Well, uh, I wouldn't mind being on Mary's team," Katie said.

"Yes!" I murmured to myself. "Thanks, my best friend."

"I called you first! Right, guys?" Karen insisted. She again flashed an even bigger smile at me. I felt a chill run up my spine.

"I don't mind, I want to be on Mary's team," Katie insisted.

I held my breath.

Karen stopped dribbling. She placed the ball firmly under her arm, staring hard at Katie.

"I said, I called you first. First one to call team members gets the pick. You know the rules."

Katie shrank back. It made me angry. "Rules, my foot," I grumbled under my breath.

Karen resumed pounding the pavement with the ball as she marched around the group.

Mary carefully spoke, "But, Karen?"

"Yeah, what?" Karen answered.

"Well," Mary continued. "I don't think it's fair that you have four on your team and we have three."

My stomach tightened, the muscles in my arms and legs followed.

"Well, if you have Katie, I'll only have three on my team. Since I called first, I think I should be the captain who has four!" Karen insisted, stopping and standing right in front of Mary.

"Well…" Mary said, hesitating.

"Yeah, well, what?" Karen said, egging her on, putting her face right up to the girl who dared to question her authority.

Mary stepped back. I could hardly believe my ears when Mary found the guts to challenge this self-proclaimed ruler once again. "Well, it would be fairer if the team that has Geri has the extra person on it."

There was dead silence. Finally Mary spoke. "I mean, well, no offense, Geri, but…"

Karen jumped in, taking advantage of Mary's tongue tie. "Just say it, Mary. Just say how you don't want her on your team cause she can't play, right?" With a look of satisfaction, Karen turned toward me, flashed a triumphant grin, and started bouncing the ball, harder this time. Again no one spoke. It was Karen who broke the silence. "Why don't you just say it, Mary?"

Mary looked down at her feet, then at Karen. Her face was filled with resignation. In contrast, Karen's had a smile as big as the Cheshire Cat's.

"Go on, tell Geri why you don't want her on your team. Tell her it's because she's a bumbling idiot and she don't know how to play!" The knot behind my belly tightened as Karen walked toward me, continuing to badger me.

I winced.

"You know, Geri," she said, emphasizing my name as she pounded the ball. "If you didn't always have to play, we'd have an equal number on each team. Then Mary, here, wouldn't feel like she got gypped."

Until this moment, I had managed to keep myself steady, only occasionally exposing my fear to Katie. Now my lips were quivering. Despite my effort, tears began filling my eyes. My cheek muscles sagged with the weight of sadness. Terrified I'd fall apart, I tightened my arms and fists, pushing them hard against my body.

My effort to hold myself together failed. I could not combat the force now pulling my body down into a slump, nor could I resist the desire to hide in the warmth and security of my bed. I yearned to feel my soft comforter and fluffy pillow. I longed to curl up in my favorite position, the one I was in before my life began. Saving face didn't seem so important any more.

Far away, I heard the voice that I trusted. "It's okay, Geri. I'll be on your team," Katie said.

Through watery eyes, I saw Karen hold the ball in check as she stared in Katie's direction. "No you won't!" she yelled, flashing an angry look at Katie.

How can she be so cruel? I thought, certain I would crumble into a million pieces. Karen suddenly noticed me and said, "Oh my God, you're not going to cry, are you? Oh, you are."

I put my hands over my face and rushed toward the corner. Streams of tears ran down my cheeks while snot dripped from my nose. My stomach heaved. Unable to see through the blinding tears, I tripped over a crack in the sidewalk and fell to my knees.

Dribbling the ball harder now, Karen yelled from behind, "Way to go, stupid!" The pounding of the ball on the pavement controlled my heart. I wanted to cover my ears and drown it out. Instead, I got up and raced for home.

As I gripped the handle of my front door, I heard her squealing back at the corner, "And she thinks she can play kickball? Boy, is she stupid. Aren't you stupid, little cry baby? Ha ha ha! Look at her, trying to run away. Stupid, stupid, stupid."

At last I managed to get the screen door open. I dashed to my bedroom as fast as I could, passing my father, who sat watching baseball in the living room. My seventy-five pound dog was right behind. Tippy always knew when one of us was upset. He jumped on the mattress next to me as I buried my face in my pillow. My dad had noticed my distress as well and arrived soon afterwards. He found me curled up on my bed next to Tippy, a blanket over my head, sobbing uncontrollably.

"What's the problem, did you get hurt?"

Choking and gagging, I couldn't get control over my breathing.

"You're not cut or anything, are you?"

"Nuh-no, no," I managed to squeak out between convulsive breaths. Telling him about my knees would only make him want to dump alcohol on them.

"Well then, tell me what's the matter. That's an awful lot of crying for not being hurt," he said affectionately, pulling the blanket from my head. He reached into his pocket for a handkerchief. Gratefully, I took it and wiped my eyes and blew my nose.

Again I worked to speak between sobs. "The uh, the uh, the kids, Karen."

"What about the kids? Did one of them hit you?"

"No," I squeaked, wadding up the hanky as I continued crying. A consoling Tippy ran his tongue up my arm.

"Well then, did a dog bite you? I know it couldn't have been Tippy!"

"No," I said, an annoying smile threatening to destroy my moment of grief.

"Did a car hit you?"

"No!" I pretended to be irritated.

"Something must have happened to make you cry so much. Tell me all about it."

It took me a minute to be able to talk. After a few more sobs and another wipe of the nose with the balled-up cloth, I snuffled out, "Well, Karen—we were gonna play kickball and…" The tears welled up again. My dad leaned down and cradled me in his arms. Tippy lay back down, satisfied I was being cared for. Dad held me for a few minutes, though I wished it had been forever. His big, strong arms were so comforting. His voice always soothed me. He loved me and I knew it.

After a bit, he sat up, still keeping his hand on my shoulder and said, "So, try to stop crying now and tell me what happened. You were going to play kickball with the girls and something about Karen, right?"

"Yes. Well, Karen, she was calling the teams, like she always does."

"I can imagine that. Go on."

"Well, she had three girls on her team and Mary had me and Elaine…" Once more I began to weep.

"Now, hang on a minute, you haven't told me the whole story yet."

"Okay," I unrolled the hanky looking for a dry spot. I dabbed at my eyes, took a deep breath and went on. "When Mary only had three girls on her team, and one of them was me, she had to say that I wasn't a good player." But my confession only unleashed more tears. They made their way down my already wet cheeks as I leaned back into my dad.

"Hang on, now," he insisted. "Why did Mary have to say you weren't a good player? What does that have to do with three players?" Reluctantly I pulled back from my father's comforting body.

"Because, there were four girls on Karen's team," I answered, annoyed.

"Oh, you didn't tell me that the teams were uneven."

"Oh. Yeah."

"So why, just because Karen had four and Mary had three, what does that have to do with saying you aren't a good player? I mean, somebody has to have one girl less, if there is an uneven number. Do I have this right?"

"Dad!" I was getting really irritated now. "She had to say that because if you are three against four, and I'm one of the three, it makes it real unfair to the team that's got me." I felt my cheeks burn with anger. Having to spell it all out to my father was exhausting. I tightened my fingers around the soggy handkerchief, squeezing it hard with my fist. "I hate being the kid nobody wants on their team!" I yelled.

"Ah, yes, I get it now," my dad said with a nod of his head. "I understand why that might make ya feel a bit crummy."

"A bit crummy!" I sat up on the bed, slapping my hand on the pillow beside me. Tippy jumped up again, leaning his big wet nose closer to my face. I gave him a quick pat and took a deep breath.

"I hate it, Dad! I hate that Karen, too. She purposely made the teams that way, so Mary would have to say something."

"Oh, did she now?" he asked, as if there was some doubt.

"Of course she did," I insisted, standing up and stomping my foot on the floor.

"Hmm," my dad pondered.

"Well, she did!" I demanded.

Tippy looked nervously at my father then back at me. Dad reached his hand out to comfort the dog and said, "It's okay, boy. She's just having a bad moment." He scratched Tip's head as he thought about what I had said.

"You're probably right about that one. Karen can be a bit of a stickler now, can't she?"

"A stickler? She's downright mean."

"But tell me, why did you leave the game and come crying home?'

Astonished, I stared straight into my dad's eyes. "What do you mean, why did I come home?"

"I just wonder why Mary saying that you weren't the best player made you run home."

Enraged, I yelled, "Because I don't wanna be the baddest player! Nobody wants me and I hate it!" Startled, Tippy jumped off the bed and ran out of the room. This made me feel even worse. I burst into tears again, rolling my body up as I fell back onto the bed. Once more I buried my nose and mouth into the handkerchief.

My dad turned to me and patted my back. In a gentle but firm voice he said, "Geri, there is nothing wrong with being the worst player. Everybody has something they are the worst at. It doesn't mean that you're not wanted or that you have to feel embarrassed about it. Besides, it makes sense that you aren't the best. You have a vision problem, which gives good reason as to why you have trouble kicking and catching the ball. Heck, what excuse do I have?"

My father's words caught my attention. Despite the cringe I felt at hearing the term, "vision problem," I managed to ask between soft continuous sobs, "What do you mean? You can play kickball, can't you?"

"Well, maybe I could do okay with kickball, though I can honestly say I really don't know, as I'm almost fifty-four years old and I haven't played that game since I was a kid. It's football that I'm talking about. Years ago, when I was going to college at Notre Dame in South Bend, Indiana, I wanted to be on that football team so badly I could taste it. Do you know that the most famous football coach who ever lived was the coach at that university when I was going there?"

"No," I answered, not sure what he was getting at, but listening intently for his answer.

"Yes sir, Knute Rockne. Man, what an amazing guy." His eyes turned upwards as he remembered his days as a youth. "His teams were unbeatable. Heck, the only reason I went to that school was because I wanted to play football under him. Uh, and because my father insisted I go there."

"So did you get on his team?" I asked hopefully.

"I tried. I tried hard. I had to get up every morning and run 18 miles, lift weights, and work out with the rest of the rookies. But, no matter how hard I tried, I didn't make it. You see, I'm small by comparison to the other guys, and—"

"I think you're the biggest, strongest man in the world, Dad!"

He chuckled as he lovingly patted my shoulder. His soft hazel eyes twinkled as we exchanged smiles. "Well, when you're up against some of those guys, five foot ten ain't real big. But I did get to play on the scrimmage team."

"What's a scrimmage team?"

"Well, it's kind of like…"

I held my breath, waiting for my dad to continue.

"You're not the greatest. It's the guys the real team practices against so they can get good. The scrimmage team doesn't get to play the other college teams in front of the fans. They never win trophies or play in college bowls."

I suddenly felt very sympathetic toward my father. It never occurred to me that he had disappointments in his life.

"That must have been awful!"

"I felt pretty let down," he admitted. "But what do you think would have happened if, when the coach chose his teams, I went crying home because I didn't get picked for the big one?"

I hung my head with understanding.

"I think you've got it, Geri. If I had gotten all upset in front of everyone, I wouldn't have been able to play for the scrimmage team and work with the best coach in the world."

"But didn't you feel sad, Dad?"

"Oh, I sure did. I still do, a little, but if I had shown my upset in front of the coach, I would have been laughed off the campus. I thank my lucky stars that I got to be a part of that era of football. I mean, I got to work under the same coach that trained the Gipper."

"What's a gipper?" I asked.

"What's a Gipper!" my dad replied with astonishment. "He was only the best player in the history of football."

I was enjoying Dad's reveling in the past and urged him on. "Why was he so great?"

"He was a record breaker. Heck, he never even played football before he got to college. One year he and the Fighting Irish won 27 games. He made 21 touchdowns, and not one pass got by him when he was on the defensive end. His real name was George Gipp, but they called him the Gipper."

"Did you ever get to play against him when you were on the scrim— team?"

"Scrimmage team," he corrected. "Nah." A sad look came over his face. "No, the Gipper died before I ever thought about going to college. He died in 1920. I guess I must have been about 11 when he passed away from strep throat."

"Strep throat? Hey, I had that in January."

"I know! Back then they didn't have the good medicines they do today. Anyway, the story goes that the coach, Knute Rockne, went to see him in the hospital. The Gipper knew he was dying, so he told the coach to tell the team to win one for the Gipper. He did, and the team won. Even today, before the Fighting Irish head out to the field to play, they all yell, "Win one for the Gipper!" Not every young man who dreams about becoming a famous football player gets to play for the team the Gipper played for."

I watched as Dad's eyes returned to the present. They were now looking directly at me, filled with concern and affection.

"So, you have to someday come to accept that you aren't the best at everything, Geri. You also have to realize that, because you have trouble seeing, you aren't going to be as good as others at things that require vision."

"I know!"

"Well, I think Karen might be a good teacher for you, just like Coach Rockne. She told you the truth, and the truth is the best thing a person can have."

"What do you mean, Dad? She called me stupid!"

"Well, she shouldn't have called you that, but you do have to admit, it was pretty stupid to get upset because she said you didn't play well. If you had just agreed with her, she wouldn't have had much else to say, now, would she?"

I lowered my head again, thinking about this new revelation. "No, I guess not," I finally said. I thought about my dad's story. I pictured that football player dying in his hospital bed. Memories of Edna came to mind. Then I thought about mean ol' Martha Madden and Karen Worster. It was all so unfair.

"I just don't understand why God made everything so hard," I said, clenching his hanky and looking up at him.

"I don't know all the answers, Geri, but don't go blaming God. You're the one who has to decide how you act when you get teased. If you don't toughen up a bit, you're going to be spending a lot of time in your room crying. You've missed a fun game with the girls today. It's a lot more enjoyable playing outside instead of being in your bedroom with a tear-stained face."

I slumped back in my bed, frustrated with no real answer to my questions. Dad bent down and gave me a kiss on the forehead.

"Speaking of games, I have to get back and see how the Tigers are doing. Come on out and I'll make a party plate for us if you want."

I pictured my father's special platter of cubed sharp cheeses, crackers, and my mother's homemade bread and butter pickles all neatly arranged by his hand. I wanted to follow him, but I felt exhausted from this confusing ordeal.

"I'll be out in a minute," I said instead.

"Okey dokey."

My dad left me alone, and Tippy peeked in the doorway.

"Come on in, Tippy," I said. "I'm sorry I upset you, boy." I patted the bed. Tippy leaped across the room, plopping down next to me. After a few kisses, he laid his head on my pillow, and I stroked his ears.

The discussion with my father ran through my mind. "That dumb ol' Karen told the truth," I told my dog. Feelings of shame came over me. Sherry's sad face appeared in my mind. Wincing, I continued with my confession. "I shouldn't have told her those lies, boy. I'm worse than that ol' Karen Worster." Tippy lifted his head and licked my hand. Sherry's face suddenly changed into the image of the man selling pencils so long ago. Startled by this vision, I couldn't help wonder if the old man had also been teased. I hugged Tip more closely and struggled to keep the face of the man in dark glasses at bay. I didn't want mine to take his place. Again I looked to sleep in hopes it would rescue me from the awful thoughts in my head.

Chapter 8

The Do-Gooders

September through December 1965

The black hands of the clock moved slower than molasses. Time at That School seemed to stand still. After two years of enduring oddities and tedium, I dreaded having to face yet another year. Outside the school zone, life was not much brighter than twilight. Good ol' Karen Worster kept her job as neighborhood regional director, badgering me any chance she got. Although I'd learned not to react with tears, her words still cut deep.

I kept insisting I could see just fine even though my vision was slipping. This required more creative explanations to convince myself and others why I did some of the things I did. In June of this year, I personally introduced myself to the trunk of a big red car. I must admit, imbedding one's face in such an unyielding surface can prove to be rather painful. The girls from my neighborhood and I were heading to Forest Park on our bikes for a picnic lunch, when it jumped in front of me. Of course Karen Worster made a big deal about me running into a parked car, complaining I'd spoiled everyone's fun. Katie assured me it was not my fault, however. The mixture of bruises to my body and ego made it impossible for me not to cry.

A different set of allegations greeted me upon my arrival home. Instead of blaming me for messing up lunch, my folks focused more on the reasons behind my close encounter.

"It has nothing to do with not seeing the car!" I said to my parents as Dad led me into the bathroom to tend my wounds. "I was looking behind me when I crashed!" I insisted, but they didn't buy my excuse.

"I don't think so, Geri," Dad said, shaking his head as he dabbed alcohol on my injuries. I was covered with cuts and scratches on my face, arms and legs.

"Ouch! That stings!"

"Try not to jump. I almost spilled the whole bottle," Dad said, wetting another corner of his hanky. "I think it's time to put up the bike for good," he announced as a matter of fact, making it sound like it was no big deal.

"No!" I cried out, panicked. "It's got nothing to do with me not seeing, Dad! I had my head turned, that's all!"

"But Geri, you could have really hurt yourself," Mom countered. "What if that car had been moving?"

"But it wasn't, Mom. If it was moving, I would have seen it, honest! I didn't hear any cars so I went ahead and turned around to see where Katie was!

Please don't make me put my bike away! Please! I need it, you guys!" I begged. "I won't be able to hang out with the kids if I don't have a bike!"

Both my parents were silent as Dad closed up the bottle of alcohol. I thought hard to field off my father's game plan. He was about to tackle the issue of my bike in the same aggressive manner he used when taking care of my injuries. He would approach the problem with his football mentality, just like his heroes, the Fighting Irish. It was now up to me to intercept him—and quickly.

The many reasons I gave for keeping my vehicle to freedom were rapidly being shot down by both my folks, so I did what any respectable child would do when faced with such a catastrophe. With each successive no, I escalated to begging and finally to a full-blown tantrum. After I threatened to never leave my room, eat, or talk to them again, they eventually gave in. This agreement did not come until I promised to move my head back and forth a lot when riding. I also promised to travel in familiar territory.

Although I refused to admit it, I was beginning to experience the tunnel vision Dr. Biggs had predicted. I knew my peripheral vision was slowly disappearing. I saw objects fairly clearly in my central view, but things out to the side simply did not exist.

To my dismay, the vision check up I had in August exposed the truth to my parents. Not only did the doctors not buy my story about seeing okay, they insisted it was worse. I had to go through all their grueling tests again. There was the long and boring field of vision exam, numerous fingers counted, letters read, and breath held to avoid smelling theirs while they stuck their lighted eyes in mine. The test results led to a prescription for new glasses. Although I was not happy with thicker lenses, I appreciated the opportunity to advance to a more mature color. Even though I didn't want to look like Sherry, tortoiseshell frames were the "in" fashion.

Dr. Biggs also informed my parents they were considering a new drug called cortisone to treat my disease. He convinced my folks it was worth a try. Of course nobody ever asked me what I thought. They also didn't bother to mention some of the interesting things it might do to me.

After four weeks into the medication regime, I entered school looking like a beach ball on legs. The pills caused me to retain water, forcing me into clothing two sizes larger. Though I was at an advantage going to school with blind kids, it didn't help how I felt about myself. Worst of all, good ol' Karen Worster had a heyday. She happily added my appearance to her list of torments.

I was almost glad to return to school after the trials of the summer. I knew my classmates would not tease me about my shape and size. Though I wouldn't admit it, they had become a part of my life. I felt ashamed of myself for keeping secret how much I cared about them.

One morning, we were all hanging out in the back of the room, biding our time while Mrs. C worked to calm Jade down after one of her chair-tossing tantrums.

This usually meant we'd have to occupy ourselves for a good thirty to forty minutes. Linda sat rocking in the chair Mrs. Cartacker so wisely purchased the previous year, while I joined Annie, Donna, Anthony, and Marie at the square table.

"I hate that Karen Worster!" I said, telling them how she'd tried to keep me from playing hide and seek the night before.

"Well, at least you got some friends to hang out with," Mike said from his favorite perch atop the wooden cabinet. "There aren't any kids in my neighborhood that will even speak to me. They must think I got cooties or something."

"Heck, I must be lucky," Linda said, her body moving back and forth in rapid motion. "I don't have any neighbors to tease me. I just have my brother and me. We go over to the church graveyard next door and read the headstones. Did you know they have raised letters on them? I learned the whole print alphabet feeling those stones!"

"You're lucky all right, Linda. At least, I think you are. You never know, though. One of them dead people might find a different way ta tease ya," Travis said in a spooky tone. "Do-do-do-do. Do-do-do-do," he sang, mimicking the theme song to "The Twilight Zone." We all laughed. Travis was sitting on the windowsill at the side of the room. He thoughtfully kept his distance from the rest of us. He knew he smelled bad even though he wore cologne to cover it up.

"I think you're pretty safe there, Linda," Mike said. "You got the best neighbors around. Them dead people ain't gonna bug ya."

"I wish I had neighbors like that," I said.

"No, you don't, Geri!" Linda said, rocking more furiously now. "You don't know how good you got it! I was joking when I said I was lucky. I sure wish I had some friends around to play with all the time. Dead people don't do a thing for loneliness."

I did not appreciate her scolding, so I ignored Linda and turned my attentions to Maria.

"Do you have any friends you play with at home, Maria?" I asked. But she didn't answer. She just sat across from me, fingers in her eyes. In the silence we could hear Mrs. C trying to reason with Jade, who she held cradled in her arms on the floor.

"Let me up!" Jade screamed. We just kept ignoring her as we were quite accustomed to this scene.

"So, Maria, do you have any friends at home?" I asked again, knowing repeating my question sometimes prompted a reply.

In her very quiet voice, she finally said, "No."

"That's too bad. How 'bout you, Donna?"

"We al-ways got a lot of fam-uh-lee at my house. I got lots ta do."

"That's good!" I said.

"Geri, think you can get the loom and loops?" Annie asked.

Turning toward the front of the room, I judged the distance between the supply shelves and Mrs. C and Jade and decided it would be safe. We'd all been warned to keep our distance when Jade went through one of her episodes.

"I think so," I replied.

"Can you get da tic-tac-toe game, too?" Donna asked.

"I want the Lincoln Logs," Anthony commanded.

"Okay." I tiptoed to the cupboard, careful not to make any noise. I located the three items and stacked them neatly to avoid dropping them. After I returned to the table, I handed each of the objects to their prospective users.

"Thanks, Geri. Do you want to play?" asked Donna.

"Okay," I said, taking the Os.

"Well I sure don't have no friends," Annie offered. "I never go outside. I'd get lost sure enough. You know me, I can't find my way out of a paper bag, let alone a place with no walls."

We all laughed.

"Don't you ever get bored, though?" Linda asked her.

"Nah! I just play my records and dream about Little Stevie Wonder." I watched as her fingers wove the colorful pink, blue and green cotton loops into a hot pad.

"I dream about the Beatles!" I confessed, sliding my elbows forward on the table in a gesture of hopeless longing. The poster hanging on my bedroom wall of the Fab Four flashed into my mind.

"You like the Beatles?" Linda asked.

"Oh, yes! They are so cool!"

"They're okay, but I like folk singers like Joan Baez better."

"Got any Beatle records?" Annie asked. "I got 'Meet the Beatles' and 'Introducing the Beatles'."

"Hey, can you bring them in?" Travis asked.

"Sure! You like them too, Travis?"

"Yeah, they're okay."

"I like the Beach Boys, too," Linda added, sticking her fingers in her eye. I wanted to tell her to put them down. It continued to scare me I might do the same some day.

"I like dem Beach Boys, too!" Donna chimed in, working to place an X on the center square of the board. The combination of her talking and manipulating her fingers must have caused one of her palsy spasms. In a flash, the metal X shot across the room and onto the floor.

"Way ta go, Donna!" I said. "You almost got a point with that one."

"She did get a point," Travis declared. "It hit me right in the foot."

We all cracked up laughing. Flying objects propelled by Donna's muscle spasms were rather common, and always a comic relief, particularly on a Jade day.

The intensity in Jade's voice was lessening. We figured by the tone it would be another ten minutes or so. Travis picked up the X and returned it to Donna while Annie continued the discussion of favorite rock groups. "The Beach Boys are okay, but Ray Charles and Little Stevie Wonder are the greatest."

"I'd love to go on a date with Ringo," I said in a dreamy tone.

"Yeah, that'll be the day," Mike laughed. "They'd never give any of us the time of day."

"And why not?" Linda asked.

"Cause they sure wouldn't be wantin' ta spend time with a buncha blind kids. They only go for them good-lookin' girls," Mike said.

"Hey, Geri, am I good looking?" asked Linda, removing her hands from her eyes.

"I think you are," I answered.

"My mom says I am, but she's my mom."

"How about me? Do I look pretty, Geri?" Annie asked.

"Annie, you've got the best bunch of braids I've ever seen."

"You got braids, Annie?" Linda asked.

"Yeah. My mum puts them in every Saturday morning. Didn't you know that?"

"No! Let me see 'em." Linda stood and moved over to Annie. She started feeling the cornrows piled all over her head, while the other students took turns asking me to describe them.

I felt strangely powerful telling them about their appearance. I managed to compliment everyone, even though some didn't fit the picture of loveliness. Most of my friends' eyes were distorted, with a lot of the white showing. Some did not take good care of their hair or clothes. Linda was probably the best dressed and groomed of us all, but even she looked odd with one eye always closed.

Though I didn't understand the phenomenon of being patronizing at the time, judging my classmates' appearance made me uncomfortable. This was not the first time I experienced a sense of superiority. Whenever I helped a student find or do something requiring vision, I felt self-important. I didn't like believing I was better than them, yet I did. The resulting conflict kept me separate, which I also liked and disliked.

At last Mrs. C called us all back to our seats, and our day went on the same as always.

The only variation in our experience at That School came when The Do-Gooders, as we called them, came to visit. Mrs. Cartacker tried to convince us these visitors were very important people. She told us they were ladies and gentlemen who donated money to help run the school. Five or six of them would file through the door, walk around the edge of the room, and then stare at us. Comments like "Isn't it amazing?" or "Aren't they so special?" would be whispered between them. Once in a while a Do-Gooder would get brave and ask us a question.

"What's that you're doing, honey?"

"Sweetie, can you tell me who helps you get dressed in the morning?"

"You have such a lovely ribbon in your hair, darling. Can you tie it yourself?"

"Oh, you are so handsome, young man. Does your mom comb your hair for you?"

Sometimes the questions were more reasonable, but mainly they were insulting to us kids.

After one group had come and gone, Mike got bold and started mocking the visitors. "Hey Travis, I hear you wear diapers."

"Yeah, and I drink my beer from a baba," Travis snickered.

"Now, boys," Mrs. Cartacker scolded. "That isn't very nice."

"Yeah," Annie said. "It isn't very nice of them to talk to us that way either."

"I know," Mrs. Cartacker said, "but it's our job to help them understand."

"I don't like them comin' a-lookin' at us like we're animals in a zoo," Mike insisted.

"Yeah!" Travis agreed.

"It's weird having a bunch of people just walk around and stare at us and whisper like we can't hear them," I protested.

"Now class, most of these people have never met a blind person before. They have no idea how you all get along. We have to be patient and show them how Braille and other tools can make you able to do the things that other students can do."

"Da-n't they weel-lize," Donna asked, "Dat eve-ven dey do things widt out look kin? I mean det's not dat dif-frant dis it? I mean lots ov pe-po turn off de light on de wall ba-fore dey go to deir bed. And not eve-rry-one watches eve-ver-ry ding dey do, like type-pen."

"Secretaries don't look at the keys, yet lots of people ask us how we can type," Sally chimed in. "I just don't get it."

"Right, man!" Mike said, talking in his typical jive manner. "What about when the power goes out and stuff like that? My mom made a whole meal without lights or gas for the stove. We had ham sandwiches. She even poured the milk without any light. She said she learned how to do that from me. I never spill the milk if I have my finger over the edge of the glass like you taught us, Mrs. C."

"My dad has to feel for junk under the cars he fixes," said Travis. "He says light don't get in to some of the parts underneath. He even said he'd show me how to fix cars next summer. He thinks I'd be good at it because I don't have to use my eyes to find stuff."

"That's right, Travis," Mrs. Cartacker acknowledged. "Fixing cars, cooking, and many other jobs are very reasonable occupations for people who do not see. I met a gentleman at a convention this summer who owns a construction business. He himself is the carpenter. He is totally blind and does beautiful work."

"Really?" we all said at the same time.

"Oh yes," she continued. "He uses regular power tools, but he adjusts his work area with tactile guides so he doesn't put his fingers in the wrong place. He makes intricate carvings and trim for walls and doorways, but he is very conscious about keeping his workshop safe."

"Wow!" exclaimed Travis. "Really?"

"Oh yes, and he also makes book shelves and wood cabinets," Mrs. C. added.

"I wish you would have told those people who just came through here about that man. I bet if they heard that, they'd stop asking us about how we get dressed in the morning," Linda said.

"I hate people thinking I can't do nothing, too," I announced. "I can do most anything my friends in my neighborhood can do 'cause I can still see."

"Don't matter whether you can see or not," Linda said, scolding me. "Nobody wants to be treated like they can't do anything."

"But it's even worse when they think you can't see, when you can," I insisted, suggesting I had it worse than the rest.

"Oh, Geri!" Linda said, exasperated. "Because you can still see don't mean you get people thinking you're like a baby any more than the rest of us."

Mike ignored our spat. "Well, I don't get it. Why do we got to put up with them peoples' ignorance? It ain't our job ta have ta answer all them questions that have nothin' ta do with our comin' ta school."

"I understand, class, but if you don't help others understand what you can do, they will never change how they think about blind people. It is up to each and every one of you to help change people's thinking. You must remember you are the representatives of the blind. If you are nice and kind, others will think all blind people are nice and kind. If you are rude, well, then—"

"That's the dumbest thing," Mike said with disgust.

"You may not like it, Mike, but it's true. It's up to you to decide how you represent your fellow blind folks."

Mike gave no more argument to Mrs. Cartacker's words. However, when Christmas came a few months later, he and the rest of us all struggled to follow her advice.

Each year a local community group took Mrs C's class to lunch. The younger class of blind kids came, too. We'd eat at the Durant Hotel, one of Flint's most luxurious establishments. It contained a fancy restaurant the average family would never even hope to see. In our younger days, we students loved to go.

Everybody would get all dressed up. We were thrilled that we'd have a chance to see Santa, who always had a present and a bag filled with candy for each of us.

It was a big deal for the grownups as well. The businessmen dressed in suits and brought their wives in fancy dresses. The local newspaper and television reporters were always there. They'd do a heartwarming story on what a wonderful thing this group was doing for the blind children of the area.

Mike led the way as we tried to explain how we didn't want to attend a party for little kids. When Mrs. C tried to encourage us, we flat-out told her how much we hated going. But all our begging and pleading to stay at school did not change her mind.

"Remember, class, these people help buy some of your supplies. They're the ones who bought us the encyclopedia. They make sure we get all the latest volumes as the book is updated. Besides, this is likely your last year, so make a good go of it."

The collective mood of the group suddenly changed upon hearing Mrs. C's last words. There were no more protests. The heavy silence fell hard as the atmosphere moved from enthusiastic griping to oppressive defeat. There was no question we were all contemplating our inevitable fate. As much as we disliked our school, most of us didn't want to think about where we would soon be going. Our next stop would be the state residential school for the blind. Except for a couple of my classmates, we had no interest in living away from our families for weeks at a time.

When the day of the Christmas party finally came, we all piled into the bus to go downtown. We were met at the door by our prearranged hosts. Mrs. Cartacker introduced me to Mr. and Mrs. Snobe.

"Well, hello there, young lady!" Mr. Snobe said, helping me off with my coat. "My, don't we look pretty today? Don't you think Miss... uh, Miss..."

"Geri," I offered.

"Yes, don't you think Miss Geri is dressed so lovely this afternoon, Marge?" he said to his wife.

"Ah, yes," she answered, gazing out over the crowd.

I glanced down at my oldest sister's blue jumper gathered around my very huge waist. My mother had hemmed it so it didn't hang to my ankles, but my sister's clothes were about all I could wear with my new cortisone look. To make matters worse, my father had taken it upon himself to cut my hair only weeks earlier. He got a little carried away, and I now wore a hairdo which was similar to the style worn by military men. Looking quite the sight, I didn't feel the least bit lovely.

Mr. Snobe nervously continued. "Well then, why don't we go and find our seat now, uh, Geri? That's right, isn't it? Yes, Geri."

"That's right," I said, wishing I were somewhere else.

"Uh, how about if I… How 'bout if I take your hand there, Geri? Would that work?" Mr. Snobe asked, reaching for my hand. Instinctively I pulled it back.

"I can follow you okay," I said.

"Oh. Oh, you can? You can follow me okay?"

"Uh-huh," I answered.

"Well, that's nice. Okay then, follow me," he said reeking of uncertainty as his jerky movements propelled him forward. "You too, Marge, you'll come right along with Miss Geri and I, won't you, Marge?"

Mrs. Snobe did not answer. She simply gave a sigh as she followed us into the Grand Ballroom.

I couldn't keep myself from admiring this truly magnificent place. The sparkling crystal chandeliers hanging high above our heads would lift anyone's mood. Decorations of holly-covered wreaths, angels, and bells were everywhere. Ceramic winter scenes sat atop long tables covered in white linen, with red and green ribbons intertwined across the middle. These adorable little centerpieces triggered my imagination as I fantasized what it would be like to live in a picture-perfect land. Suddenly I remembered this was kid stuff and scolded myself for being drawn into such silliness.

I followed Mr. Snobe's effort to locate our seats. We were constantly interrupted by introductions and greetings. The waiters and waitresses moved in between us as they placed cut glass dishes filled with holiday candy on the table.

While I waited for my Do-Gooder to run through another welcome, my eyes wandered to the front of the room. Once again I was mesmerized by the sight. A noble tree stood as tall as the ceiling would allow. I couldn't help smiling. It looked so dressed up in dazzling ornaments, candy canes, and zillions of lights, with a shimmering silver star on the top.

Finally we were seated. My pubescent nature reemerged. I refused to allow myself to appreciate the festive atmosphere filled with songs about Frosty and Santa coming to town. This was so much harder than answering a few questions from the visitors who came to our room. I dreaded having to interact with these folks for two hours, and wondered how the rest of the kids were doing.

"We have a wonderful party planned for you children today," Mr. Snobe announced from the seat on my left. His wife sat to my right.

"That's nice," I lied.

Funny sounds emerged from Mr. Snobe as he struggled to think of something to say.

"And how old are you, young lady?" he asked.

"I'll be fourteen next month,"

"So, you're thirteen years old. My, and what a pretty young thirteen year old you are at that."

I swallowed hard. Oh, brother, I mused, knowing I looked like a bloated bug with my round tortoise-shell glasses outlining my moon face.

"Thanks," I answered, instead of responding with the, Yeah, right! which I snidely said inside my head. I let out a sigh of relief as I saw Mike and his caretaker coming down the opposite side of my table. I was even more grateful when he sat directly across from me.

"Hi, Mike."

"Hey!"

"You know where Linda's at?"

"Nah. I heard her meeting her Do— uh, people, in the lobby there, but don't know where she went."

"Oh, is this your friend?" Mr. Snobe asked.

"Uh, yeah. This is Mike," I said, introducing them.

Mr. Snobe stood up and stretched his arm across the table. He reached out his hand for Mike to take, then quickly pulled it back, realizing Mike couldn't see it.

"Uh, hello there, Mike. I'm Mr. Snobe."

"Yeah, hi there," Mike said.

"So, Tom, you got yourself a fine young lad there."

The man now sitting on Mike's right answered, "Yes sir. Mike here tells me he likes baseball."

"Baseball? Well, that's great. Who's your favorite player, Mike?" Mr. Snobe asked.

"Mickey Mantle, of course," Mike answered.

"Hey, kids! I'm Mr. Slater's wife," a lady in a sparkly blue dress announced. "Aren't you guys so excited about the party?"

"Yeah," I said at last when I realized no one else was willing to respond.

Next to me, I could hear occasional moans coming from Mrs. Snobe. I did hear her say a few words to the lady on her right, but for the most part, she sat stiff and quiet. I kept looking for Linda. My heart sank as the seats across from me filled up with the littler kids. Mr. Slater's wife sat down on Mike's left.

As the grown-ups continued to talk to us like babies, I ached to sink beneath the table. From the look on Mike's face, I figured he wished he could do likewise.

"So, have you all been good this year?" Mrs. Slater asked, her big white teeth shining so brightly I could almost count them.

I decided to help things out. "Oh, yes, we've all been ever so good."

Mike chuckled. I was glad Mrs. Cartacker wasn't around.

"That's wonderful!" Mrs. Slater said. "And I hear that this year Santa has something extra special for you children. Oh, can you hardly wait?"

"Oh, I can hardly wait," Mike exaggerated. I wished he could see me smile, so I kicked him gently under the table instead.

"You should see all of the extravagant gifts piled around our beautiful Christmas tree. They are wrapped in red, green, and gold paper and tied with lovely ribbons," she went on.

Even Mrs. Snobe became increasingly annoyed, and more sighs escaped her lips while she shifted uncomfortably in her seat.

"Do you think he brought me a truck?" Travis asked. I knew I had smelled him, but didn't see him sit down on the other side of Mr. Snobe. I wondered how his Do-Gooders were handling his body odor.

"Could be!" Mrs. Slater said. Her smile looked so phony and her voice was so sickly sweet I half expected frosting to ooze from her lips. "What else do you think Santa brought you?"

I almost gave in to the urge to ask about a baby doll, but I thought better of it. I mainly wished I could find a way out of the inevitable activity following lunch. We all dreaded having to line up in the procession to the tree where a dressed-up Santa would hug us and ask us if we had been good all year. The nature of the presents was childish and disrespectful of those of us who were mainly excited about members of the opposite sex.

By the time lunch came, I still had no way to avoid the journey to Santa's lap.

Despite my desire not to be there, the food smelled very inviting. It was delivered in fine serving bowls, gravy boats, and rectangular butter trays. Wicker baskets full of hot rolls were passed around. The china plates in front of us were loaded with fried chicken, mashed potatoes, and steamed vegetables. Long-stemmed crystal goblets were filled with water and milk.

"Can I butter you a roll?" asked Mr. Snobe after filling my plate.

Oh, brother! I thought. *Looks like it's time to ward off the Do-Gooders' need to help.*

"No, thanks. I can do it myself," I said, trying to hide my irritation.

"Are you sure?" Mr. Snobe asked.

"I'm sure."

"Well, just let me tell you that your mashed potatoes are at two o clock, your chicken is at—"

"I know!" I said, hating the clock method used to help blind people know where their food was situated. "I can see my food, thank you," I added, hoping to smooth over my initial response.

As I asserted my independence with my caregiver, I noticed Mike and his custodians were having a private conversation. The man kept whispering to him. I couldn't quite make out what he was saying, but I could tell Mike was bothered by it.

"Why don't you just let me scoop your potatoes in a little ball on your plate," my guardian said, reaching over with his spoon, performing the task before I could refuse.

He's not gonna get it, I told myself, resisting the impulse to slap his arm. "Okay. Thanks," I managed to say.

"How about some gravy?" Mr. Snobe asked, once more moving his hand over my dish and dumping some on my potatoes without even knowing if I liked the stuff.

"I can manage my own food!" I snapped, feeling a mixture of shame and anger. Though I never worried about containing my frustrations at home, I worked hard to be polite in public.

"Oh, yes, uh, that's right," he said, returning to his own plate.

Once more the conversation across the table drew my attention. I could hear Mike whispering.

"I know," he said, "I will. Yeah, I know how."

I tried to imagine what they were talking about.

Suddenly, Mike slid back in his chair with a big sigh. Mr. Slater reached behind Mike and pushed him forward.

"It's just while you eat," he said.

"That's right, Mike," Mrs. Slater agreed, "It's only for a little while."

"But I don't want to," Mike insisted, his voice louder.

"Come on, Mike, let me just put this on you," said Mr. Slater, standing behind him.

"What are you doing?" Mike asked.

"Just placing this on your shirt so you don't get it dirty," said the man.

"No, thank you," Mike insisted.

Mr. Slater continued to fiddle with the item in his hands. "Like I said, it's just for while you eat."

"No, thank you," Mike said emphatically, reaching up to his neck.

Everyone stopped eating, giving their full attention to the disagreement across the table. I could tell Mike was trying really hard to keep his cool.

"Now, Michael, you have such a nice shirt on and you don't want to get it dirty if you spill something, do you?" Mrs. Slater explained.

"I'm not going to spill anything," he said between clenched teeth.

We were all holding our breath, waiting to see what would come of this skirmish. Still gripping something in his hands, Mike started to rise.

"Sit down now, Michael," Mr. Slater commanded.

I was surprised to see Mike do as he was told. His willingness to sit did not stop his protests however.

"It's just for while you eat," Mr. Slater insisted, as he pulled the object out from Mike's fist and spread it across his chest. I could now see it was a baby's bib, complete with a teddy bear on the front. I couldn't believe my eyes. I was glad Mike could not see the full effect of the childish item.

"I do not want to wear a bib."

"It's okay," Mr. Slater insisted. But it wasn't. In a flash, Mike lost it. Actually he found it.

In one big whoosh, Mike ripped the bib off his neck and threw it across the table. The back of his hand collided with one of the crystal glasses. CRASH! The goblet toppled, tipping another in its path. The second one hit the gravy boat just right. The domino effect created a river of water, milk, and gravy which traveled down the path of the red and green ribbon, over the linen tablecloth, and into the laps of several sharply dressed Do-Gooders. Everybody jumped up, backwards, forwards, and sideways. Kids who couldn't see and had no clue what was going on screeched and yelled. The Do-Gooders, already anxious about taking care of a bunch of poor blind kids and keeping them safe and happy, were in a total panic. The comical nature of this vision of pandemonium made it hard for me not to laugh.

Although the teachers and Do-Gooders tried to smooth everything over and go on with the festivities, the atmosphere could not be resurrected. It seemed like the rest of the party was all in fast motion. We finished eating, saw Santa, and headed out the door and back to school.

Mike served his punishment honorably. Mrs. Hecklebottom pronounced him insubordinate and sentenced him to sit in her office for a week during lunch.

"I tink it's so unfair dat Mike can't dalk wid us!" Donna said the second day of his punishment.

"Me, too!" Annie agreed.

"Man, that principal. She's got a lot a nerve, punishing Mike when it's those stupid Do-Gooders who should be disciplined," Travis said.

"Yeah, what do you think they should have to do for trying to make Mike wear a bib?" I asked.

"I think they should have to wear one when they're at one of their big important business lunches," Travis answered.

Laughter erupted from the group.

"Yeah!" Annie said. "And while they're eating, we get to sit around and ask them who dressed them and how old they are."

Linda chuckled, "I'll just bet them old ladies would love to tell us their age."

"I think it's funny," I interjected, "that some of them, especially the ones who thought they were Mike's babysitters, had to sit through the rest of the party with gravy in their laps." Again giggles, hoots, and other expressions of amusement filled the room.

"I sure hope we don't have to go to those dumb parties any more," Travis said.

"Sure would be nice," said Annie. "We're always being told how much good they do for us children."

"Yeah, right!" Linda said. "But what they don't see is, those Do-Gooders don't do so good!"

"You're not kidding!" Travis said. "There are none so blind—"

Annie finished the statement.

"As those who cannot see!"

Chapter 9

The Times They are a Changin'

February 1966

An invisible charge filled the air. I didn't need to see it to know things were different when I returned to school after the holidays. The others felt it, too. By the end of our first week, most of us had become vocal about our dissatisfaction with our learning establishment.

The Do-Gooders' party certainly played a role in our oppositional mood. Christmas break could not wipe away the outrage we felt about such a fiasco. The grownups wanted to blame it all on puberty, but we kids knew it was more. The signs of the times likely played a role, too. The protest movement of the Sixties was well underway. The spirit of resistance touched even those of us who felt cut off from the mainstream of life as we listened to the music of Bob Dylan, Joan Baez, Barry McGuire, and others. Whatever the cause being expressed in the music or on TV, the collective message of our group boiled down to one simple concept: "We're not gonna take it any more!"

Thank heaven for Mrs. C, who despite pressure from the powers that be, gave up her lunch break so we could hang out together instead of taking naps. She also developed an orientation and mobility program to teach independent traveling skills. This addition to our daily routine gave most of the kids a greater sense of freedom.

I was not among them. It did not make me at all happy to learn to use a white cane. I resisted the endeavor the best I could, insisting I could see just fine. The grown-ups did not agree. They constantly reminded me how this would not always be the case. Their insistence only made me more resentful. Initially I threatened not to go to school. My tantrums didn't work, however. Despite my objections, my parents and Mrs. C made sure I learned how to get around without seeing. Each time I was forced to put on a blindfold, I seethed with anger. As we walked along together tapping the hideous white sticks, I swore I would never be like the others. It annoyed me how the rest of the students appreciated the independence they gained. Everyone made a big deal about their new-found confidence. Even Annie, who was terrified the first time she walked down the sidewalk on her own, learned to love being able to find her way around the school all by herself.

My life outside the classroom also changed. I began to bridge the gap between my two lives. My relationship with Linda was growing stronger. I had reached the point of accepting Linda as an intelligent and somewhat normal human being. During Christmas break, we spent time at each other's houses. In order to avoid comments from Karen, I only introduced her to Katie. Sometimes she would come over and read teen magazines to us, but usually Linda and I would hang out in my bedroom alone.

One Saturday afternoon in late February, we were sprawled across my bed listening to music up in the room I had taken over after my sisters moved away. A Simon and Garfunkel LP played on the turntable. The words to "He was a Most Peculiar Man" were consuming our attention. The sweet tenor voice of Paul Simon sang the story of a man who didn't fit in. The lyrics struck a chord in me.

"That's how I feel sometimes," I said.

"Not me. I got a lot a good stuff going on in my life. Besides, you're not like that guy, Geri," Linda mumbled into my pillow. I couldn't see her face with her long brown hair draped around her head. I noted our typically opposing viewpoints as I examined her straight thin body. Thanks to her mother's eye for fashion, Linda was outfitted in stylish attire. I was green with envy as I admired the matching denim jacket and pants with flowers embroidered on the pockets. I was glad she couldn't see how frumpy I looked in my sister's old rust-colored sweater that clashed with my yellow pedal pushers. I reached out and gave Tippy a pat, hoping to gain some sense of comfort from him. He lay between us without a worry in the world.

"I know, but I still feel like I don't belong. I really do feel like hiding away, especially when I hear about junk my friends do at school." I reached over and turned up the volume.

Paul continued singing about the friendless existence of the lonely odd man while I lay back down, supporting my head on my arm. As I stared at Linda, the image of the blind man on the street corner popped into my head. *Did he live in a tiny room all by himself like the peculiar man?* I wondered.

I braced myself for the climax as I heard Linda sigh. We'd heard the song before, but it seemed we both hoped for a different ending. But Paul could not change the inevitable. He sang on. Once again, the lonely odd man could not face his isolated existence any more. Instead, he returned to his tiny room and gassed himself to death.

"It scares me," I said as I heard the melodious intro to "April," the next song on the "Sounds of Silence" album, begin to play. "Though I certainly would never kill myself, I do worry about whether I might end up like that peculiar man."

"Oh Geri," Linda said, "you'll never be like that guy." I did not share Linda's confidence. When I thought about my future I'd feel this nagging fear in the pit of my stomach. My thoughts about the odd man continued, despite Paul singing about a mysterious girl who elusively moves in and out of her lover's life.

My trusty dog was not the least bit worried, however. His interests were primarily focused on food and affection. When Linda leisurely rolled to her back, stretching her arms out wide, he let her have it.

"Oh, yuck!" she exclaimed.

Without warning, Tippy had plastered a big wet sloppy kiss on her face. I let out a hearty laugh as my belly sprang free from fear's grip. "I think Tip thought you invited that," I said through chortles. My buddy slapped his tail in agreement.

"Oh, Tippy!" she said, wiping his saliva from her cheeks. "You've got some wonderful breath there, dog."

"I know," I said, still sniggering. "I tried to brush his teeth once, but he just thought the toothbrush was something to chew on."

"Well, Buster's breath ain't much better," she giggled, placing her arm crosswise over her face to ward off any future affection.

Tippy settled back down, and Linda and I got quiet again. The harmonious story of April brought feelings of melancholy to my heart. As the song ended, Linda lowered her arm and rolled in my direction.

"Sounds like Paul's having no luck with love."

"I think he's trying to say that nothing ever lasts."

"Well, at least April got to experience love. My mom thinks I never will. She's convinced I'll live my life without a husband.

"That's crazy! Heck Linda, you're smart and nice, and—"

"And blind," She added.

"That don't mean you won't get married though."

"Ah, don't worry 'bout it, I'm not," she said, springing up into a sitting position. "I got lots of interests, and my folks are really good about supporting my goals for college, but I do feel like a Martian for the most part. Except for you and the kids at school, I don't really fit in with the rest of my age group."

"Well, I hate not fitting in," I said, slapping my hand on the bed. Tippy lifted his head and stared at me. I rubbed his ears.

"Honestly, I really, really hate it!" I gripped my thighs tightly and felt my baggy yellow pants. They reminded me of how uncool I really was.

"Even though I'm not as bothered about it as you are, Geri, I can see how it might upset you. I'm used to being an outsider, where you had to leave a group of friends and stop doing the things you used to do because of going blind." Her words stung me hard.

I almost protested, but she kept on talking. "I've been able to find other interests like reading and learning, which are just as important to me as being cool is to you. Plus I'm very involved in the church choir and we're always doing something fun with my big family. But you're right about being an outcast. I mean, magazines, radio, TV, you never find anyone like us being portrayed among the teenagers."

"No kidding! I know there's nobody looks like me on them magazine covers. They're all thin and, except for Twiggy, they've all got flowing long hair and straight teeth." I stood up and walked over to my dresser mirror. I fixed my eyes on the gawky drab figure before me. The girl who looked back disgusted me. My hair had grown enough to be styled in a Sassoon haircut like Twiggy's, but it was hardly complimentary. This popular hairdo cut around the ears exaggerated my chubby cheeks. My features were accentuated by the tortoise-shell spectacles and super thick lenses I was forced to wear. Even the weight I'd lost after the failed cortisone treatments could hardly put me in the category of slim. To top it off, my back and shoulders were developing a permanent slump. I couldn't decide if this was because I was always jutting my head forward to see better, or because I felt weighed down with all my worries. Whatever the reason, my hunched profile did not look cool.

"I hate watching American Bandstand," I sighed, trying to stand straighter. Linda slid back down on the bed.

Tippy licked her arm affectionately. "Not my face, boy," she reminded, patting his head until he returned it to the mattress.

"I know they'd sure never let me on that show!" Linda said with a chuckle.

"Me neither." Feelings of jealousy resurfaced. Linda seemed so unbothered by it all. I was no longer able to look at my ridiculous self so I returned to my spot on the bed. Once more, I rested my head upon my arm and looked intently into the face of my friend. "It really makes me mad!" I announced, studying her droopy left eye and knowing it would never be on camera. "Heck, I'd just be happy to be in the audience of Shindig or Hullabaloo, but they only let the pretty girls in."

"Yup!" Linda said. "We've been kicked out of the Pepsi Generation, and we don't have the look you want to know better."

Both of us gave a resigned chuckle. Without warning, Linda sat up and began rocking back and forth on the bed.

"Part of the problem is," she said, moving rapidly now, her need to release energy making it hard for me to watch her, "we don't have a lot of people to look up to. I mean there's Judge Shaker, but not too many others.

"I'm talking about cool people, Linda, not judges! Besides, blind people ain't the only ones who aren't seen on TV or the movies. Ugly people aren't considered cool either!" I was hoping to put the focus on something other than blindness.

I sat upright examining Linda further. I was curious about her perceptions of things.

She seemed calmer now, using her forearm as a pillar to rest her head on her hand. She looked like that painting of The Thinker, except her left index finger was in her eye, not on her chin. After a thoughtful moment, she added. "I guess there's Little Stevie Wonder and Ray Charles. They made it big, at least as musicians."

"Wow, two out of how many?" I asked. The face of Little Stevie Wonder flashed in my mind. As a teenage idol, he did not match my image of cool. I pictured how he moved his head stiffly from side to side when he sang. Did Linda realize that she, too, did not move her face normally when she spoke to me?

"We can't forget Helen Keller," Linda reminded, still plugging her left eye and keeping her face down instead of turning it toward me like a sighted person would.

"Oh, come on, Linda," I said, annoyed. "What, she's about 80 something? Just what I'm looking to model myself after. I told you, I want to be admitted into the pop music audiences, not vaudeville."

Finally she pulled her head from her finger, turned her face up toward the ceiling and said, "Heck, I'd settle for any kind of person who had something in common with us. Even a newscaster or spokesperson for commercials. The other day I was cleaning the bathroom sink. I hollered at my mom, telling her how nice and smooth the new bathroom cleaner made the sink feel, and she said I sounded like a commercial. What better person to do an advertisement for cleanliness than a blind person. I mean, don't we have the best feel?"

"Or feel the best," I said with a giggle. "Problem is, no boy wants to have anything to do with a girl like me, let alone fee—"

"Oh, Geri," Linda blurted warningly. "You don't want to go thinking those kinds of thoughts."

"Oh, yeah?" I said mischievously. "I think them more than you want to know, Linda."

"I'm not the only one then, huh?" she asked, the bouncing bed revealing her increased nervousness.

"No way!" I assured her. "The problem is that people don't think blind or ugly girls have any feelings about that stuff at all, but when I see a cute guy—"

"Oh, Geri!" she said jumping up. "It gives me the willies talking about this stuff. Like you said, folks just don't expect such feelings from kids like us. Besides, if my mother knew—well, I—you know what I mean!" she said in her shrill voice.

Amused by Linda's conflicting thoughts, I egged her on. "No, I don't know. What do you mean?"

"Well she…she'd think I was sinnin'."

I continued my affectionate taunt as I casually lay back on the bed. "Heck, if my mother knew the feelings I get down—"

"Geri!" she squealed. We both let out a hoot.

"Well, even if you can't say or hear it, Linda, your face sure shows you're interested!"

"What do you mean?"

"It's as red as a beet!"

"Geri!" she again scolded me through snickers. "Stop that!"

I was amused and concerned by Linda's struggle with the prim and proper mindset toward sex. My frustration thrust me forward. I moved around her and scooted my butt on the edge of my dresser while she rocked heel to toe to the beat of her anxious heart. I let out a heavy sigh. "I just don't get why it's so sinful if everybody seems to be feelin' it, even us blind and ugly girls," I said, demanding an answer from somewhere.

"Let's talk about something else," Linda said, still smiling.

I hesitated, considering whether I dared raise the subject which haunted me daily. "Linda…"

"What?"

"Well…uh, do you ever wonder about God and stuff?"

"What do ya mean?" she asked, sitting back down.

"I don't know. I just wondered if you ever thought about why things are so unfair and all?"

"Heck, yes."

"Really? I mean, I'm terrified of being blasphemous, but sometimes I don't understand God. I even have a hard time not feeling mad at him for all the suffering in the world."

"I know!" she agreed. Bringing her finger to her eye, she went on. "I learned quickly in Sunday school not to ask any real questions about what they teach."

"You telling me you talked about this stuff in Sunday school?"

"Only once," she said, resuming her jiggling of the bed. "I got my mouth washed out with soap once for suggesting that God maybe wasn't so nice to be threatening us with hell every time we made a mistake."

"No kidding? You got your mouth washed out? That's awful."

"I know. Took me days before anything tasted normal again."

"I'll bet," I said, cringing at the idea. "I never dare say anything about what I think, but I sure do say a lot of Acts of Contrition though. I just can't stop myself from always questioning what they teach me in church." Linda's restlessness had taken my box springs to new levels, turning them into a trampoline.

"I know! It drives me crazy, too!" Linda agreed.

"Heck, when I look at the cover of my catechism book, I can hardly believe anyone would call it the teaching of God. It's horrible."

"How so?" Linda asked.

"Well, first of all, it's got this terrible picture on the front cover showing a bunch of anguished faces all burning in a fire. I mean, come on, I can't figure if God is love, how am I supposed to trust this guy?"

"You want my answer or my Sunday School teacher's answer?" Linda asked with no intentions of waiting for a reply. Instead, the bed fell motionless as Linda stood, turned toward me, and in the tone of a properly speaking adult she said, "God gave us free will. It is up to us to decide how we live our lives. You have the choice to follow his laws or to disobey him and be damned forever and burn in the eternal fire of hell. If you choose to follow, it must be done with blind faith, for questioning is the pursuit of evil and knowledge is the cause of original sin. So choose your path and accept the consequences of your actions."

"You got it," I said, impressed with her mockery of the teacher. I felt fear rising in my gut. I was not sure being mutually mystified by the paradox of religious teachings would help us at the pearly gates. My fear did not stop me from speaking what I'd been holding in for a long time, however.

"God gives us the gift of thought, and tells us not to use it. Even the preacher talks about how he blessed humans with the gift of curiosity. He tells us how we were purposely separated from lower animals, giving us the desire to learn and know, and yet we're supposed to not be curious and ask questions. He blesses us with free will and yet we'll burn if we use that, too." The freedom I felt as I released my demonic thoughts was quickly replaced with a sense of impending doom.

"Problem is, free will don't answer being left out of things because you're blind," Linda said defiantly. "If God's so darn good, why would he make blindness, deafness, and all the sickness in the world, not to mention poverty, war, and other junk?"

"So do you think we're gonna burn for saying all this?" I asked, beginning a mental Act of Contrition just in case.

Sitting back down, she replied, "I don't know. Either God ain't so loving or these Bible teachers don't got it exactly right."

Linda's sensible words soothed my soul. The anxiety over being a Doubting Thomas returned shortly after our visit ended.

Later in the evening I was sitting in my pajamas alone in the dark. I leaned on the windowsill and looked out. The soft glow from the windows below brought a warm, comfortable feeling to my heart. Tippy's rhythmic snores added to my sense of well being as I stared at the street lamp at the end of our cul-de-sac. It stood like a beacon in the night, warding off intruders while guiding the late night workers home.

I could see in the distance, beyond the schoolyard, a stop light change from green to yellow to red. While only an occasional set of car lights traveled underneath, the signal lights continued on, marking the passage of time. They looked like three little eyeballs, each taking their turn, winking reassurance and security to whoever bothered to notice.

A light in one of the living room windows disappeared. As I watched my sleepy neighborhood turn in for the night, an infectious thought disturbed the precious scene. Reaching behind me, I scratched the soft warm fur of Tip's ears. He let out a worriless sigh.

"It sure must be nice to be a dog, ol' Tippers. You just lie there and soak it all in, never worrying about what it's all about."

Tippy remained silent. He simply wriggled closer so I could scratch him better.

His soft warm body urged me to leave my perch and move in closer to him. I dug my nails deeply into his fur and proceeded to tell him my worries.

"I don't get it, Tippy. How can it seem so peaceful and safe, while people somewhere out there are suffering?"

But again Tippy said nothing. He simply rolled to his back, exposing his belly. I obliged him, massaging his fur and making sure I rubbed under his armpits. He moaned in ecstasy, tilting his head backwards, lifting his paw so I could rub him more deeply.

"You don't even care, do you, boy? I wish I didn't." I considered my earlier conversation with Linda. I worried I might go to hell if I died in the night, but I couldn't hold the thoughts back. Unfortunately, my dog was oblivious to my need for answers, so I redirected my conversation.

"I can't hold back my questions, God! I don't understand it! Why would you let me think this way, but threaten to make me burn forever?"

Like Tippy, God did not reply.

"I'm a Doubting Thomas," I said to both of them. "I have to see it to believe it."

A momentary thought skittered through my head. *Maybe that's why God is making me go blind.* I shook my head to rid my mind of this idea.

Tippy rolled back onto his side, indicating he'd been petted enough.

I returned to my window. The gleaming spectacle was mesmerizing. Suddenly I noticed the stoplight now shone yellow. A rush of excitement hit me. "I can see that light!" I said out loud. "It's at least three blocks away and I can see it just fine."

A sense of joy came over me. The scene reminded me of Christmas when we lit our tree for the first time.

The momentary sense of relief I felt was quickly replaced with anxiety. It occurred to me God might be sending some kind of warning through the colorful blinking lights. Maybe if I stop questioning his existence and pray harder, I might be able to keep seeing. I flung myself over top of my companion and held on for dear life.

"I don't understand it, boy. I can't help these ideas running around in my head. Nothing makes any sense any more."

A chill ran through me. I was afraid to let go of my friend in order to reach the covers scrunched at the bottom of the bed. Instead, I gripped the edge of the blanket with my toes, inching it up as close to my upper body as I could. Still unable to reach it, I let go of my hairy life raft and grasped the edge. Tucking the comforter around me tightly, I snuggled safely between the warmth of the blanket and my dog's toasty body. It did not take long for Tippy and me to join our slumbering neighbors.

Chapter 10

In the Eye of the Beholder

Fall 1966

Joe Kewl was his name. He was a fine looking guy with black curly hair that hung casually around his face. Windswept strands draped carelessly down the back of his neck just below his collar. The long, thick lashes surrounding his dark brown eyes gave a mysterious quality to his appearance. If that wasn't enough to turn a girl's head, the shadow of a beard added to his masculinity, stimulating my desire to kiss him.

I watched this member of the opposite sex strut into the room in his skin-tight hip-hugger jeans. He triggered a longing inside me that hurt oh-so-good! The carefree manner in which he tucked the blue shirt with green polka-dots into his wide leather belt inspired devotion from his many female admirers. I couldn't help the growing ache of longing filling my unworthy heart, even though I knew he was out of my league.

I sat at my desk staring at him and realized how much my life had changed. I surely hadn't expected to find myself here. On the contrary, Linda, Mike, Travis, Annie, and I thought we were going to the residential school for the blind. Luckily for us, the signs of the times turned out to be on our side. With the civil rights movement of the Sixties and the call for desegregation, the special education system fell under inspection as well. Fortunately many of our parents joined Mrs. Cartacker in making Flint one of the leaders in mainstreaming disabled students into the general education system.

When Mrs. C explained the plan to transfer us to one of the junior high schools, we were ecstatic. I was especially thrilled as the chosen school was one point two miles from my home. Though my parents were concerned this was too far, I insisted I could do it. No more rides in the stigmatizing taxi. At last I could be like my neighborhood friends, even if I couldn't go to the same school.

Mrs. C told us she'd be going with us as the resource teacher to transcribe our assignments into Braille and read tests. Some were comforted by this arrangement. I was annoyed. Although we were thankful to Mrs. C for having given us so much kindness and support, Linda and I agreed we were ready to break free of anything reminding us of That School.

With my new found hope for having a normal future, I could hardly wait to walk into a regular school with normal kids. At last I would be like everybody else.

The first day of school arrived. I had hardly slept. Before my mother could give me the first wakeup call, I was already out of bed. I was too excited to eat, so I grabbed my glasses and dressed in the clothes I had laid out the previous evening. I proudly put on my white blouse with the Peter Pan collar and my sister Grace's gathered skirt with red flowers on it. I thought of a fashion article Katie had read to me. It described how this year's style would include matching knee socks, cardigan sweaters, and skirts, so I slipped my feet into long red socks and then put on my Mary Jane black leather shoes. I walked to the mirror and ran my childhood brush through my collar length hair. The glasses still did not help my appearance, but my face definitely looked better now that it was thinner.

I kinda look like Margaret on the Dennis the Menace show, I mused to myself. Can't look all that bad if I resemble a TV star, I decided, forcing myself to stand straighter.

My confidence was firmly in place by the time I reached the stairs.

"I'm leaving!" I hollered to my parents eating breakfast in the kitchen.

"You be careful crossing those streets, Geri!" my mother warned.

"You sure you don't want me to give you a ride?" Dad asked.

"Nah," I said, part of me wishing I could say yes.

I picked up my new red book bag from the table near the door. It contained my Braille math, English, and science books, given to me by Mrs. C at the orientation two days earlier. I swung it over my shoulder and stepped out the door. I mentally ran through the directions my father had shown me several times throughout the summer. Though I was nervous, I quickly squelched the urge to go back and ask for his help just one more time.

You're not gonna miss that jog by the school, I firmly told myself, wishing I didn't have to worry. I'll bet the other kids don't get all bugged about this stuff, I thought, feeling angry at losing my confidence again.

But as I began walking down the road, I felt a sense of pride welling up inside me. Each time I crossed another street and took the proper turn, my self-assurance grew. My dream to be more independent had finally come true.

"Step on a crack, never ever have to go back!" I sang aloud, hoping the memories of That School would disappear with each step.

I maneuvered through the zigzagged streets and triumphantly located my new school. It looked glorious with its wide glass entranceways beckoning me to join the students now sauntering in.

The closer I got, however, the tighter my stomach became. I saw other students walking in pairs or groups. None of them carried book bags, especially red ones. As they filed past, their chatter and laughter made me uneasy. Just as I reached the door, two students in front of me opened it. They walked through, totally ignoring me, letting the door shut in my face. When I stepped in, the overwhelming scene told me I didn't belong.

I felt like Pygmalion as I surveyed the students nearby. Their stylish attire immediately told me these girls dressed far differently than the females at That School. The makeup they wore was so thick even I could see it. They all seemed to have beauty parlor hairdos. I wished I had a hat to cover my drab dishwater strands. Their matching skirts, tops, and knee-highs suggested they'd all conferred on what to wear.

Whether this was true did not change the fact that I looked nothing like them. Their outfits were more subdued in colors of plum, rust, and olive green, as opposed to my girlish floral. Though I knew it was important to dress with fashion in mind, I had no idea of the extent. The only time my former classmates and I considered our clothing was when we went to the Do-Gooder's party. Besides, knowing about fashion and possessing the vogue attire were two different things. Ginnie and I simply accepted our fate of wearing Grace's hand-me-downs without question.

My reverie was cut short when one of the girls in a brownish colored coordinate said, "What you lookin' at, girl?"

Flinching, I quickly looked away and said, "Nothing."

"Who is that?" she asked, turning back to her friends, "And what planet did she get dressed on?"

I glanced down at my attire. My hemline fell far below theirs. I ran my fingers down the buttons of my blouse, wishing I hadn't. My action had only drawn more attention to its unstylish look.

"I don't know," I heard the voice of a different female say. "But she sure grabs that schoolgirl look, don't she?" Snickers and laughter followed. My face flushed with embarrassment. My effort to console myself with the fact I had ditched my saddle shoes two years earlier was short-lived. As my eyes fell to the floor, I suddenly realized the Mary Janes were likely as bad, if not worse, than the black and whites. There was not one girl who wore strapped shoes. Tied brown leather oxfords speckled the lobby floor, emphasizing how ridiculous mine looked.

The bell rang, startling me. I mustered up my nerve and searched for my homeroom through the mayhem of students. In the chaos, the landmarks I had identified when the place was empty were now completely skewed. I tried my best not to look visually impaired as I struggled down unfamiliar hallways. Eventually I found my way, locating my locker. I opened the combination lock labeled in Braille, removed my math and English books, and quickly stuffed my bag inside.

By the time I entered Mrs. Greenly's room, I was filled with anxiety. I wished my books weren't so bulky as I tried to hide them under my left arm so the rows of students on my right couldn't see them. I hoped my tense muscles didn't over-ride my effort to look casual. I decided if I held out my free hand and discreetly touched the edges of the desks as I walked by, no one would notice. It seemed like an eternity before I spotted an empty place at the far side of the room. I let out my breath and eased into the desk. Certain I looked like a complete weirdo, I mentally ran through my closet trying to pick out something more stylish to wear the next day.

Suddenly he walked in. The chatter momentarily stopped. Then, like a row of dominoes falling, all the girls said one after the other, "Hi, Joe! Hi, Joe! Hi, Joe!" When the greetings ended, I joined the other females as they fixed their gaze on this creature now sitting three rows away.

I could never have a chance with this one! I thought, as I studied his every movement. I found his fluttering lashes mesmerizing as he responded to girls who dared to speak to him. He reeked of confidence, tilting his head in a most endearing manner whenever he nodded his approval. I tingled with excitement as my hand fell to the excess material draping around my legs.

He's definitely out of my league! I assured myself, surveying my Orphan Annie attire. Nope, he'd never accept someone like me, that's for sure!

The fifteen minutes in homeroom quickly ended. The bell rang. Everyone shot from their seats and rushed to the door. I decided to wait. As the others filed out, I moved tentatively toward the exit. Instinctively I kept my left hand subtly out in front of me while holding the cumbersome texts in my right. This was not an easy task. I figured if I could keep my elbow tipped outward, it would hit an object before my body did. With all my concentration focused on my hands, I suddenly realized I was jutting my head forward, bugging my eyes wider than ever. I snapped my head upright, hoping no one noticed the obvious movement.

The door seemed miles away. My tummy began to spasm with each step. I felt little beads of sweat spilling out at my hairline, threatening to make my glasses slip down my nose. I was fearful my cheeks might flush, so I forced myself to smile and act like nothing was wrong. Fortunately, no one paid much attention to me as I gingerly walked behind the crowd.

What is so different about this school? I asked myself. I never had trouble crossing a room or going through a door before.

The knuckles of my left hand clunked against an empty table. I looked down, realizing I could not tell the difference between the tabletop and the same colored floor. My attempt to compensate by moving to my right caused me to bump into the teacher's desk.

Much to my dismay, Mrs. Greenly noticed. Assuming she needed to help, she rushed over and grabbed my arm. I pretended I was simply repositioning my books, but she guided me to the door anyway.

"Do you know how to find your next class?" she asked more kindly than I wanted. As I struggled to remember the layout of the sprawling school, I realized I didn't even remember the correct room number for my first-hour class. I slid my hand into the front cover of my math book and scanned the Braille schedule I'd placed there earlier.

"First hour, Room 112," I read aloud.

"That's the hallway to your left, Geraldine," Mrs. Greenly directed.

"Oh, yeah!" I said, attempting to sound nonchalant. I shot out of the room and turned left, feeling grateful no one else, especially Joe, saw this little episode. *Maybe there's not the same amount of light in this school,* I wondered, looking up to the ceiling to check.

The true cause of my disorientation had nothing to do with light, however. In a familiar environment, in which distances and objects never changed, I could instinctively maneuver through them with little problem. During six years at That School I didn't notice my vision gradually slipping away. Unless I bumped into something, I did not see what I did not see anymore. Though I wasn't able to realize all this at the time, I knew in my heart it had nothing to do with the lighting.

I carefully moved closer to where I expected my room to be. The bell rang before I got there. Fear gripped my stomach harder as I tried to focus on the numbers posted to the left of each doorway. To my dismay, all I could see were black blurs against the gray cinderblock walls. I frantically tried to make sense of the numbers. Slowly their outline came into focus. I thought I could make out a one, one, and a three, or maybe a two? I couldn't be sure. As the clock in my head ticked faster, I decided to enter what I prayed was the correct room.

With heart pounding and cheeks hot with embarrassment, I could not see an empty seat. All I could make out was a sea of blurry blobs. As I stood there, not sure what to do, the teacher spotted me.

"Oh, you must be Geraldine," he said in what seemed to be an overly sweet voice. "Come on in."

I was certain his niceness was because he recognized me as one of those "special" students. I felt ashamed as I stepped further into the room.

"Here, let me show you a seat, my dear," he said, grasping my elbow and pulling me forward. I could feel all eyes on me as I allowed myself to be dragged to a seat on the opposite side.

"Miss… ah, what's your name?" he asked the girl in the front row.

"Alice."

"Yes, Alice, would you mind moving to that desk in the back? Geraldine should be up here in front so I can help her when she needs it."

I wanted to die. More than ever I wished I could shrink into nothingness. As the teacher discussed the plans for the term, I vaguely heard him mention words like "homework" and "points for being on time with assignments." Instead I spent the majority of the class period trying to decide what the others were thinking of me. I scolded myself for not having remembered the layout of my classes and vowed I'd do better.

The rest of the day did not improve, however. I was late for most of my classes. Lunchtime turned out to be a nightmare as well. Navigating the food line in the cafeteria took every ounce of cleverness I had. I hoped no one was watching, as I moved my face as close as I could to the steaming glass bins, struggling to see what foods lay behind them. When I finally got my tray filled with items I didn't necessarily care for, another challenge lay ahead.

Carefully, I carried my tray to a table partially filled with students. I sat down midway, making sure to leave a couple of chairs between me and the next person.

"You can't sit here!" the voice of a girl commanded.

"Oh, I'm sorry! I didn't know this seat was saved," I apologized, starting to get up again.

"It's not!"

Confused, I hesitated, wondering if I misunderstood.

"We just don't want gawky girls like you sitting this close to us!" the female across from the first one said.

"Oh. Okay," I said, accepting their rejection. My cheeks flushed with embarrassment as I realized my plan to be a regular student was now foiled. Feeling totally defeated, I found an empty table at the far end of the cafeteria and sat down, alone. *At least Joe is not here to witness this,* I thought. But I didn't feel terribly consoled by this fact.

Over the next month, I continued my study of the social norms and values of the adolescent race. I was careful not to reveal my examination of the females, as I noted their every gesture, intonation, pattern of speech, and article of clothing. I practiced some of the "in" phrases on Tippy when we were alone in my room. Grace and Ginnie also lent a hand by helping me improve my wardrobe. They each donated a few fairly fashionable tops and sweaters. After a bit of begging and pleading, my father took me shopping for two new skirts. He recommended navy blue and tan, suggesting the neutral colors would go with anything. He also let me get matching knee-highs and a pair of shoes. I felt pretty spiffy in my new pair of Hush Puppies and stylish attire.

But thick glasses and stringy hair still made me stick out like a ragamuffin. No matter what I did, my board-straight hair would do nothing but part in the middle. Each time I looked in the mirror I saw a yellow-haired Raggedy Ann. Makeup was another barrier, as Mom, due to her straight-laced upbringing, did not think girls younger than eighteen should be wearing the stuff.

Overall, I still had the aura of Cinderella before her encounter with the magic wand. Unfortunately, having the right clothes didn't stop my classmates from referring to me as "one of those kids." With this stigmatizing label, no one talked to me. They'd whisper, thinking I couldn't hear them. They'd make cruel jokes about my big books or my glasses. Once the girl next to me made fun of how I stuck my face close to the desk when I printed my answers on dark lined paper. I almost discontinued this independent effort, but it was one less reason I had to go to Mrs. C's resource room.

I hated being taunted, but it was even worse coming from Joe. Once I overheard him make a wisecrack to one of his buddies, but I decided peer pressure was the culprit. I knew a guy as cute as Joe could never purposely hurt my feelings. Just in case, I had to disassociate myself as much as possible from my former classmates. I didn't want to be "one of those kids." I figured if I was ever going to be accepted by the "cool kids," I had to stay as far away as possible even though they were the only ones who really cared anything about me. I hated myself for disregarding my friends, especially Linda, but I was obsessed with becoming accepted. I wanted more than anything to be normal, to share in the homeroom gossip, and to show them that I could be funny and cool, even though I didn't believe it myself.

But I can learn, I told myself. If I keep watching and listening, I can be cool, and maybe even Joe will notice me.

When the end of the first term drew near, my wish finally came true; at least the part about Joe noticing me. After walking the long distance to school in the bitter cold with nothing covering my legs except a skirt, I was ready to sit down in my home room and warm up. I dumped my coat and other junk in my locker and headed into the room.

"Ooo, ouw, oh!" Crash, clunk! "Ouw ouw!" I moaned, finding myself sprawled on an overturned desk.

"Hey, what's a matter—didn't you see that, blind girl?" Joe asked, using Karen's favorite reference to me.

I felt a surge of pain. The sound of his words cut me deeply. I quickly forgave him, however, as I heard him say, "Got her."

But his gallant gesture did not come. At first I was confused. I didn't want to believe Joe's intentions were less than honorable, so I continued to expect him to whisk me to my feet. Surely he'd realize I was hurt and apologize for finding my unfortunate mishap funny.

But he did not come, and he did not apologize. The voice of another boy revealed why. "Good one, Joe! You finally got her good!"

I was devastated. I realized it was Joe who purposely slid the desk into my path. *Had he tried other times?* I wondered.

I was hardly able to believe this could be happening to me as I attempted to untangle myself from the rungs of the desk. Pushing myself up with my hands, I pulled one leg from between the cross bar and the floor, as Joe let out a hoot. "Woo, would you look at them panties! Pink ones—wow!" More laughter burst from the students, followed by whistles and a catcall.

I was totally humiliated. I reached behind me to pull down my skirt. The movement made me lose my balance. I fell back on the overturned desk.

"Smooth move," a girl called.

The blow of the metal frame did not compare to her comment. I wanted to run away and cry. For the first time, I wished I were back at That School.

I don't belong here, I thought. I stood up. Horrified, I realized I did not have my glasses. My things were scattered everywhere. Tears threatened to rob me of the little dignity I had left. I was terrified to move. All eyes were on me. I felt their stares burn into my back.

My teacher was talking outside the door. The pressure to hurry urged me on. I did not want her to find me in this state. I wanted nothing else said about the catastrophic affair. I quickly turned the desk upright and squatted down, sweeping my hands across the floor. I was desperate to find my glasses. I suddenly felt their plastic rim, snatched them up, and shoved them on my face.

I could still hear my teacher talking. She was at a safe distance, so I continued with my frantic search.

"Hurry, girl, hurry!" Joe whispered, now aware of my reaction to the voice in the hall.

My fingers groped the floor. The harder I tried, the clumsier they became. For a moment, I thought my stomach might erupt.

I swallowed hard, keeping the bile from exploding. It was a race against time.

"Okay then, I'll catch you at lunch," Mrs. Greenly said.

I had already gathered up several papers with my sweaty hands. I scanned the area one last time. Do I have them all? I asked myself.

One final sheet grazed the tip of my finger. As if this paper were my last hold on life, I snatched it up and slid it atop the pile. With not a second to spare, I located my desk and sat down.

"What were you all laughing about?" Mrs. Greenly asked, totally oblivious to the nature of her pupils' actions. "Sounds like you were having a good time."

"Oh, we sure were, Mrs. Greenly," Joe said in his most innocent voice. I could not look at him or anyone else. After I replaced my papers in my books, I propped my bowed head up with folded fists.

"Well, it's always good to hear laughter from you young'uns," Mrs. Greenly added, as she walked to her desk to take roll.

I locked my knees tightly against my seat trying to steady myself, as thoughts and emotions pitched and swelled inside me. I didn't want anyone to see the waves of shivers threatening to shake me into a collapse.

Why me? I asked God. It's not fair. I didn't do anything to deserve this. Why did Joe do this to me?

The anguish was unbearable. Memories of Karen Worster brought the taste of bile into my mouth. I swallowed hard. Another ishy feeling threatened to send it right back, but I willed it down again.

As Joe continued to lead the others, snickering and jeering at me, an answer came. Good old Joe Kewl was the reason. He loved to be in the spotlight. He'd used me just to get a laugh and be the center of attention. *I didn't think boys were like that!* I thought, as I considered the motive behind his actions. *He's no better than Karen Worster! Martha Madden, too!* I remembered, as Edna's sweet innocent face popped into my mind. I felt rage inside. *How dare these kids be so mean?* I asked Edna as I stared at Joe. His eyes did not seem mysterious any more. The casual wisps of hair that hung on his neck no longer looked inviting. Instead, it made him appear sloppy and unkempt. I wondered how I could have ever found him so attractive.

I'll show you! I told him in my mind. I'll show all of you. I'll find a way to be as cool as you. I don't know how, but I will be normal. I will.

Chapter 11

The Metamorphosis

January through May 1967

The term rat fink was the expression Linda and the others used when referring to me. In all honesty, it was far too good a name for describing how rotten I acted.

Even Mrs. C expressed her disappointment in me. However, all their chastising was nothing compared to the mental punishment I gave myself on a regular basis. Every time I walked past Linda or another former classmate and pretended I didn't know them, I cringed. *How can I be so cruel?* I asked myself daily. *How can I act like those snobs I hate? I'm no better than they are.* I thought about how they ignored or teased me, making me feel like an outcast. There was no doubt about it. I deserved every bit of the loneliness I felt.

If having no friends and being a jerk wasn't enough to make me feel awful, my father's disappointment in my poor academic performance did the trick. The educational void at That School left me feeling like an idiot. Though this was not my fault, I still felt like I was to blame. For five years I longed for a real education, and now it was too late. After years of getting information through osmosis, I had not learned how to learn. My poor semester grades were the result.

A new semester started shortly after Christmas break. This required me to find two new classrooms. I dreaded this task. I nervously searched for numbers and prayed I wouldn't enter the wrong room. With bulging eyes and stretched out neck, I eventually found my history class. Luckily the seat closest to the door was empty. I slid between the desk and chair and breathed a sigh of relief.

"I hear Mr. Gleason's pretty tough," said a soft voice behind me.

I turned, recognizing Cody Jentell from the previous semester's geography class. Being in the presence of one of the most admired girls in school definitely made me nervous.

"Uh, yeah," I stammered.

"Well, I hope he's not too hard. History isn't my favorite subject."

I tried to think of something cool to say as I stared at her. Her luxurious chocolate locks were dripping down her shoulders like swirls of ice cream.

"Ah, nice hair," I said, my face flushing with embarrassment for making such an obvious remark.

But Cody just thanked me and continued, "Sally had him last semester. She says he's nice enough, but his tests are long and he makes you remember a whole bunch of dates. I hate memorizing dates, don't you?"

"Yeah, I don't like dates, either," I said, chastising myself once more for sounding so stupid.

"Well, maybe we're lucky. I hear Mr. Dander, who teaches the other section, gives lots of homework. I'd rather remember dates than have lots of that stuff, wouldn't you?"

"Oh yeah, me too," I said.

"Actually, I'd rather have a date than remember them!" she added with a girlish laugh.

I was dumbfounded by her attention. I didn't know how to respond.

"Get it? I'd rather have a date with a guy than memorize them?" she repeated, showing me her beautiful white teeth.

"Oh, uh, I get it!" I said, as sweat collected in my armpits. Cody gave me a big smile and continued.

"Mr. Gleason's better looking, too," she said. I glanced in his direction.

"Are you able to see him?"

"Oh, sure!" I said, wondering if I sounded too certain for a girl who was supposed to have a vision problem.

"That's cool. Well, check out his big blue eyes and those silver sideburns. He's very handsome!" She gave me a wink, sliding her tongue around her lips in a sensual motion. Her deep brown eyes grew wider.

I couldn't help stare at her pretty face. *Why is she paying so much attention to me?* I wondered.

"I hear he's only twenty-five. Played football for a big university. Get a load of those muscles, would ya?"

I was feeling totally inadequate carrying on this conversation. Somehow I managed to muster a "Wow!"

"I love football players, don't you?"

"My dad played football, too," I said, containing my excitement for finally saying something reasonable.

"Really? That's neat. He must be a big guy too."

Before I had to come up with something else to say, Mr. Gleason called out the first name on the attendance roster. "Jake Adams?"

My contact with Cody ended for that day, but she resumed her friendliness on the next. Although I felt anxious in her presence, it was nice to be talking to someone as if I were a regular teenager. By the end of the week, I started questioning her motives, though. *Why is she telling me so many things about herself?* I wondered. When she revealed a crush she had on Andy Swavemore and asked me if I thought he was cute, I figured my suspicions had to be correct.

After all, I was the girl that everyone taunted or rejected, the girl no guy would give the time of day to. There was no way Cody, or anyone else for that matter, would discuss their interest in boys with someone like me unless they had a less than honorable reason. When Cody invited me to walk home with her after school, I decided this was when the dastardly plan would be revealed. Talking with me in school was one thing; being seen hanging out with me on the outside was another.

I recalled a story Katie once read me from the teen magazine about a girl viewed by her peers as looking hideous. This made me grow even more certain the character's fate would become mine.

The story told how a group of the in crowd got together to play a cruel joke. They made a plan to have the most popular guy invite this frumpy poor girl to the prom. Surprised and elated, she accepted the offer, only to be made the brunt of their joke. When they walked into the dance arm in arm, he suddenly let go of her and jumped to the side. The onlookers hurled mud at her, ruining her pretty new dress and crushing her spirit. I made sure I would never be placed in such a position, so I continued to refuse Cody's invitations. I made up all kinds of excuses for why I couldn't join her, while growing more and more fearful she and her friends would find some other way to ambush me.

After a couple weeks of Cody practically begging me to meet her after school, I decided to be brave.

"Why do you keep asking me to walk with you?" I dared, trying not to let her inviting smile keep me from finding out the truth.

"I just thought it'd be fun," she said, giving me a wink.

I resisted her endearing trait and stood my ground. "For who?"

My question seemed to catch her off guard. Her bright smile evaporated.

"For us!" For a second I almost believed her.

"Which 'us'?"

"Huh?"

"Don't play dumb with me, Cody. I know why you keep bugging me."

"What do you mean?"

"Come on! I know what you're up to."

"What are you talking about?" she asked, glancing in the teacher's direction. For a second, I wondered if he could be in on it, too.

"You know there's another reason you want me to go with you," I said sarcastically.

I watched as Cody searched to come up with an excuse. Her hand nervously grappled with her hair, pulling it back behind her ear. I knew she was stalling now.

"Well... I see you walking down Holmes Road, which runs alongside the field I cut through, and thought you might want to take the short cut and hang out with me on your way home."

"And if I did, what would that do for you?"

Her confused look made me doubt my theory. "What do you mean, Geri?"

"Look, Cody," I said firmly. "I don't know what you've got up your sleeve with your friends and all, but I am not falling for it." Cody sat speechless, staring wide-eyed at my discovery.

I got her, I thought, figuring her expression was due to the disappointment of being found out.

But she just kept looking at me for the longest time. I turned away.

Eventually she spoke, "Geri. Do you really think I'd do something mean to you like that?"

Looking back at her, I snidely said, "Why not? Everybody else does."

She reached out her hand and placed it warmly on my upper arm.

"I'm so sorry!" she said.

I instinctively jerked back, daring her to touch me again.

Her lips turned into a frown. She scrunched up her cheeks, distorting her pretty features. When she closed her eyes I wondered if she might cry.

"Look, its okay. I don't really care. Just forget about me and we'll both be fine," I said, my doubts now turning into shame.

Cody sniffled quietly. I clenched my fist in anger. After praying so hard for a friend, I had messed up my only chance. I wanted to console her, but instead I looked away.

"Geri," she said gently, "I've heard some of the mean things those snobby kids say about you, but I didn't think you knew about it."

"What? Do you think I'm deaf, too?" I snapped, turning back toward her.

"No, no! I mean, I'm just so sorry you have to hear that stuff. Some kids are so mean."

"No kidding," I agreed, my heart softening. "Look, if you weren't plannin' to do nothin' to me, sorry I said anything," I said, reverting to the slang I used when jive talking with friends or feeling inadequate. This time it was the latter. "But it don't make no sense somebody like you would want to hang with me. You're gonna lose friends if you get seen with me anyway, so why don't you forget it, okay?"

"No, Geri, I like you. You're one of the few friends I have that doesn't seem to be spendin' time with me because...well, 'cause some of the boys think I'm pretty. Lots of the girls kinda use me. They think I'm going to magically get them a boyfriend by walking home or down the halls with them. Lots of times I don't know if a girl is really my friend or trying to get a date or something."

"Really?" I asked, astonished.

"Really!" Cody took her purse from under her desk and pulled out a tissue. She delicately blew her nose. I took note of her feminine gesture and decided I'd try to blow mine that way next time. I typically sounded like a foghorn when performing this task.

"I'm sorry," I said, feeling rotten now. "I didn't mean to hurt you. I was sure you and your friends were trying to get your jollies off me. If you still want to, I'll walk home with you after school today."

"Sure!" Cody said, as Mr. Gleason called the class to order.

I was happy to have a true pal, but Cody's friendship took some getting used to. Over the remainder of the school year, Cody had to remind me many times how she liked me because of who I was. We mainly had fun talking about boys and hanging out at each other's houses.

I took advantage of her natural inclination for fashion and asked her advice on changing my dowdy image. We agreed that, although looks aren't everything, they could be of great help in the game of boy meets girl. Cody became my fashion consultant and personal cosmetologist, eventually transforming me into a rather sharp-looking chick.

It was hard work, though. Experimental hairstyles that required sleeping all night on hard plastic rollers definitely took some getting used to. But it paid off. We ended up settling on a hairstyle that gave me height on the crown and a gentle curl that turned under at the ends. This made for a rather sweet, innocent look, except for my thick ugly tortoiseshell glasses.

Makeup turned out to be a bit trickier. First I had to convince my mother to modernize her old fashioned notions about painted faces. I'm not sure whether my arguments swayed her or if she gave in to my constant hounding to maintain her sanity. Whatever it was, my next challenge was to avoid stabbing my eyeball with a mascara brush. I eventually caught on, but not until I ditched the mirror and learned to sense the brush as it neared my lashes.

The toughest alteration had to do with a little extra baby fat I carried. This is when I learned how to capitalize on my stubborn streak. It took three long months of starving to bring myself from a size sixteen to a twelve. At last I met my goal in April.

There were pros and cons to losing weight. I liked that it accentuated my long-awaited bosoms. But I didn't like the way my clothes hung on me. I knew very well how difficult it would be to acquire a new wardrobe knowing my parents' frugal nature.

One day I mustered up the courage to approach my dad. The hand-me-down policy stood pretty firm in our house unless nothing fit or everything had too many holes. The fact I had received two new skirts the previous fall made getting another outfit unlikely. Dad must have heard the desperation in my voice, however, when I asked if I could go shopping with Cody for a few essential items. I was totally amazed when he handed me forty dollars and told me to have fun.

I felt like one of the girls in the magazines as Cody and I traversed the stores and explored the racks of Flint's downtown department stores. By the end of our spree, Cody had fixed me up with some very mod outfits. The beige wrap-around skirt with pale green top tucked in at the waist accentuated my curves in all the right places. The orange ribbed top and diagonal orange and brown plaid skirt would definitely get me noticed. Although both skirts were fairly short, it was the blue plaid mini skirt and navy scoop-necked top which really sent me! The problem was, it would also send my mom right into hysteria. The top had a choker strip that buttoned on the left side under my neck, exposing a circle of skin above the breast line. This definitely went against the values of my mother's era. Cody agreed that I shouldn't wear it around my mother and took it home so I could change at her house on Monday morning.

"Wow! Would you look at her!" said Debby Simpleton in her Southern-accented voice. She was in my girls' glee club and English class. We ran into each other most mornings before the first bell. Checking makeup one last time before joining the masses was an absolute must for those considered cool.

"Geri, is that you?" Chris Gabner asked, walking in behind her. Chris, too, sang in the club. She and Deb sat next to each other in the alto section, not far from Cody and me. Though they never went out of their way to talk to me, they seemed nice and sometimes sent a bit of gossip my way.

"Geri, where'd you get that outfit?" Chris asked.

"Smith Bridgman's."

"You are lookin' really terrific!" Deb announced.

"Thanks," I said, acting like it was an everyday thing.

"Where's your glasses, honey chile?" she suddenly asked.

"Oh, uh, they broke," I lied.

"How y'all gonna do your English assignments?"

I waved her concern away, but I felt a twinge in my stomach. I thought I might be sick. When I decided to leave the thick-lensed glasses hidden in my dresser the previous evening, I didn't realize it might make me nauseous. I had convinced myself I could do without them. I now questioned my judgment.

When I switched my outfits at Cody's earlier that morning, her approving comments overrode any doubts I harbored.

"Wow, you really look cool in that outfit, Ger," she said, pulling me to her full-length mirror.

I stared at the blond with the hourglass figure. She warmed my heart. "How could this be me?" I asked, as I watched the girl pivoting from side to side, posing like a model inside the looking glass.

"It's you, girly girl!" Cody said with a whistle, as she moved in beside me, giving me a big hug.

"Not without your help, Code," I said, returning the affection. Cody touched my shoulders and stepped back, surveying me thoroughly.

Suddenly she gave a hard squeeze and said, "Girl, where's your glasses?"

"It's a long story," I said, pulling away and throwing on my coat. Cody did likewise, and we left the house. We walked in silence to the field. The April wind whipped at our faces and bare legs. Being experienced winter travelers, we both knew the pointlessness of talking between chattering teeth. Wearing hats and leggings under our skirts would have kept us warmer, but we would have rather died first. By the time we stepped onto the path that ran across the open field, our bodies had acclimated enough to converse.

"At least it's not a blizzard," Cody finally said.

"I don't know. I hate this damp wind. Sometimes being frozen doesn't get to me as much."

"Know what ya mean."

"This short skirt don't help me neither. Will it ever warm up?" I complained.

"Oh, it will. Just wish it were now," Cody said, turning to walk backward against the wind. I saw her look up at me. Instinctively, I knew what she was about to say.

"So, where's your glasses?"

Giving her a sheepish smile, I said. "I decided I look better without them."

"Well, yeah, but—"

Before she could finish, I interrupted, "I hate those damned glasses, so I ain't gonna wear them."

"But Geri, you can't see without them," Cody insisted, turning to walk forward beside me again.

"I'm okay," I lied.

"But you need them to see!"

"I can make it without them."

Cody was silent for a bit. I knew she was trying to come up with something to convince me otherwise. "How 'bout getting some cool wire rims then?" she suggested.

"I've been thinkin' about that. Problem is, my dad would never pay for them, particularly after handing me forty bucks for clothes."

"But, Geri, you gotta wear your glasses. Heck, girl, you got enough trouble keepin' from falling and bumping into things. And what about schoolwork? You know you won't be able to write on the lines and see what you're printing without them."

"I know," I said, thinking about how happy I was when I first discovered teachers could read my printing. Looking like the other kids while doing schoolwork was the most important thing to me, but if I could get by without the darn Coke bottle lenses, I had to try.

"I figured I'd put a ruler at the edge of the lines to keep my place," I explained. "I don't want to use the slate and stylus, that's for sure! That thing definitely makes me stand out. Besides if I wrote stuff in Braille, I'd have to go to the Sped Room so Mrs. Cartacker could transcribe it for the teachers."

"How come you always go there from Miss Ankle's class?" Cody asked.

"Cause she insists I use 'the proper tools for the blind.' She says my printing is not acceptable. You know how she is about everybody using cursive. 'Mrs. Cartacker is there to help you'," I said, mimicking the English teacher's nasal voice. "It's like she wants to shove blindness down my throat. Let's just hope I can still print without the glasses."

"I guess so. But, Ger, you just gotta stop worrying 'bout what them other kids think. They ain't worth it, girl!" she said affectionately.

"Darn!" I yelled, feeling my ankle twist as I stepped off the edge of the sidewalk.

"That's what I'm talking about," Cody scolded, taking my arm until I regained my balance. "Geri, you're gonna hurt yourself."

"I'll be okay," I said, hoping not to expose my doubts. A wave of nausea passed through me. Since removing my specs, my perception of objects made them appear to be set off to the right. This created momentary bouts of confusion. Earlier in the morning I had misjudged the location of my dresser corner, hitting it with my hip. When I left my house, I found myself reaching for the doorframe instead of the handle.

"I really can't even think about putting those glasses back on!" I insisted, pleading with Cody to understand. "Besides…"

"Besides, what?" Cody asked.

"Well, I kind of told a bit of a lie."

"What lie did you kind of tell?"

"Well, I told my parents I lost them."

"You didn't."

"I did. Last night I took a walk over to Katie's. We hung out at the park, and then, on my way home, I slipped them into my jacket and told my folks I'd lost them."

"Whoa, not a bad idea you got there, Ger."

"Yeah, right!" I said, lowering my head. "Not bad until they wanted to go out in the dark and try to find them. Can you imagine how many Acts of Contrition I'm gonna have to say for breaking the fifth and ninth commandments?"

"Oops!" Cody said, raising a hand to her mouth. "What'd you do then?"

I quickly returned my glance from Cody to the sidewalk. Concentrating hard on every step, I replied, "What could I do? I tried to tell them there was no way they could be found. I made up a story about how we were climbing the sand hill when I slipped and fell. I explained how when I rolled down the hill, they flew off somewhere along the way. They insisted on looking for them. So at nine o'clock last night, my Dad and I went traipsing through the sand with flashlights to look for something I knew wasn't there. My dad wanted to call Katie to see if she could help, but I told him she was feeling sick and was probably in bed."

"Oh, good move."

"No kidding! Katie saw me wearing them walking home. She doesn't know what I did. I only thought of it as I was heading up my driveway."

"So, now what?"

"Well, my dad still wants to go back there after he gets home from work. He's probably going to call the recreation department or something to get those darn things back."

Guilt resurfaced in my gut. Considering what I had done, I expounded on my ideas of retribution. "I have half a mind to run home and sneak over to the sand hill with them, so he can find them. I figured if they were all scratched up, he'd buy me new ones, but they'd probably only replace the lenses, not the frames. God, I hate lying to him. He looked so upset!" I pictured his drawn face in my mind. *But he's so tight with money*, I reminded myself, arguing justification for my actions. "Man, if he ever finds out…I can't even think about how hurt he'd be."

"Yeah, you've got a nice dad, that's for sure. Heck, my father would have killed me even if I truly did accidentally lose something like that. He gets upset if we use too much toilet paper."

The guilt of my lie slipped away as compliments similar to Chris and Deb's continued throughout the day. I felt like a new kid on the block. This time I wasn't the ugly duckling, but a cool chick. One of the boys whistled as he walked past me in the hallway. Without a doubt, I felt like Cinderella on her way to the ball after being enchanted by her Godmother's magic wand.

The additional skewing of my vision with no corrective lenses made it more difficult to navigate through the hallways, however. I quickly learned to touch the back of my seat before actually sitting. I almost landed on the floor in first hour, as the chair appeared closer to me than it was. Printing on the lines turned out to be easier than I thought, though I did need to keep the finger of my left hand under my pencil. At least it was less conspicuous than a ruler, I decided.

The day wore on, and I felt unusually weary. I realized I'd been rubbing my eyes a lot. They were weak and longed for their magnification. I felt almost cruel depriving them of the crutch they'd used for so many years. But the reception I was getting from my fellow classmates was helping to ease the discomfort.

The next morning I met Cody at our usual corner. This time I wore the beige and green outfit.

"Well, did your father give up on trying to find them?" Cody asked first off.

"Yeah. He never asked me to take him back to the hill. Didn't have time."

"So, what's gonna happen?"

I smiled sadly. "I guess I'm getting new rims. He's driving me down to the eye doctor after school today. You probably shouldn't wait for me. He's picking me up."

"All right!" Cody said.

"Yeah. I just wish I didn't have to be so sneaky about the whole thing. If my Dad ever finds out, he'll really be disappointed in me."

"Ah, don't worry about that. Just get rid of the other frames, and you'll be safe. Did you tell Katie what you did so she don't say nothin'?"

"No, but I will. I hate to bring her into this. She's way too nice to be a part of something so awful."

Later in the evening, I confessed my terrible crime to Katie. She didn't say so, but the look on her face told me she did not approve. A couple of weeks later, when my new glasses arrived, I forgot about my deception. The wire rims were a definite improvement over the tortoiseshell spectacles I'd worn. It was necessary for my eyes to make a reverse adjustment after being without them. Now when I put my new glasses on, everything moved in the opposite direction. Again, I misjudged where things were. On top of this, a couple of students made fun of my new mod look. Others told me I looked much better without them. I decided to keep them in my purse unless I needed to write something.

With each passing day, I grew more confident. I discovered I could now say hello to Linda and the others without fear of being lumped in with 'those kids' by passersby. I kept these contacts brief, though.

Girls like Deb and Chris were inviting me into their conversations. Candace Seeker, the most popular girl in the eighth grade, even talked to me. Joe Kewl said hi once, and I scolded myself for saying hi back. I could hardly believe it was all happening.

The end of my first year in regular school was drawing near. I was diagramming a sentence in English class when the girl who sat across from me spoke.

"Hey, uh, Geri?"

I turned toward her. She had never talked to me before.

"Yeah?" I asked, annoyed with her disruption.

"Got an extra piece of paper you can give me?"

I stared at her as I flipped the pages of my notebook to find a blank sheet. Her stringy dishwater hair hung partly in her face. A drab brown dress hung loosely over rolls of skin. As my eyes traveled from her head to her feet, I couldn't believe what I saw. This girl had committed the greatest of fashion taboos, wearing white anklets over hairy legs. I had never really noticed her sitting near me before.

Without a word, I thrust the paper her way.

"Thanks," she said.

I turned back to the assignment I'd been working on, but my thoughts stayed with the girl.

Boy, what a grunge, I mused. I can't believe how weird she looks. I'll have to tell the others about this gawky girl. They won't believe she doesn't even shave her legs! Suddenly, shame flooded my heart.

You are disgraceful! I told myself, using the words my mother would if she knew what I was thinking. *Who do you think you are, acting like such a snob?*

I couldn't answer myself. Instead, I continued fantasizing about how we'd all feel so cool talking about how ridiculous she was. I loved the feeling of belonging I got when bringing good gossip to the group. Sometimes I'd worry about what Cody thought, as she just listened and never said anything mean. I was jealous of her kind heart. Though I wanted to be like her, when I was in the presence of my new friends, I couldn't resist the pleasure I got from cutting others down.

But when evening came and I lay alone in my bed, the terrible things I had said about the girl could not be justified.

"How can I be so mean when I know how much it hurts, Tippy boy?" I asked my dog, lovingly petting his soft ears. "I'm as bad as Karen Worster and even dumb old Joe Kewl!" I admitted, "But I do it anyway."

I pictured myself huddled in the corner of the music room chatting so normally with Chris and Deb. It reminded me of the reason for my cruelty. *At least I wouldn't be a part of a plot like those kids in that story,* I thought. *Or would I?* My question scared me. "Nah, I wouldn't do that! It's just that it feels so good to be a part of it all!" I told my furry pal. "I wish I were a dog sometimes, Tippers. You dogs would never do such awful things, would ya?"

My discussion with my canine friend did nothing to ease my internal struggle. Being a member of the cool clique was the most important thing in the world. After years of waiting for the fairy Godmother to set Cinderella free, I had no intention of turning back into the poor ragged girl I'd evolved from. Before I allowed remorse to threaten my successes of the day, I quickly shoved these thoughts out of my mind.

"Nope, this fairy tale is not going to end at midnight if I can help it," I told my trusted friend, hoping sleep would soon rescue me from my awful self.

Chapter 12

Fallin' For Love

January 1969

"Hey, guess who I just saw walking this way?" Cody asked, running up behind me in the hallway.

"Really?" I said, my body already knowing the answer. The funny twinge I'd been feeling lately shot through my thighs and into my hips. "Wonder what he's doing in the music wing?" I pondered aloud, as Cody and I continued on to the choral room. The high school I'd been attending since September was rather large. It took a full five minutes to go from one end to the other. The building was laid out in five sections, each identified by the subject taught. The music wing, where a certain someone never ventured, was far from the academic areas.

"Don't know," Cody replied. "Maybe he's joining band or chorus."

"Nah!" I said, wishing she were right. "It's too late to add classes in October. So, what's he wearing?"

"Green v-neck sweater with a black turtleneck dickey."

"Oh, I love him in green. It really suits his eyes, don't it?"

We were discussing my new love, Donny Wansome. I first laid eyes on Donny at the Wildcat's pep rally two weeks earlier, where he helped sell confetti for the cheerleading club. As he handed me my bag filled with shredded green and white paper, I felt an electric surge the instant our fingers touched. His emerald eyes twinkled as he flashed a lopsided grin. Later in the evening, I noticed him at the football game sitting three rows ahead. Instead of putting my attention on the game, I spent the entire time whispering to Cody, trying to decide whether to talk to him or not. Although my confidence had grown in the previous year, I still didn't have the courage to initiate a conversation.

I was irritated with myself for blowing a perfect opportunity, so I challenged myself to find another way to catch Prince Charming's eye. Never before had I longed to be with someone every waking minute of my life. I eventually coerced Cody and a few other friends to help me discover Donny's daily routine so I could keep track of his every move. Once I figured out his schedule, my perfect attendance slipped away. In one week I collected seven tardies. I rationalized my deviant behavior as part of my adolescent development. After all, running into Donny in between breaks could certainly be counted as part of my social education. His school activities weren't the only thing I learned about. I was elated to find he lived five blocks from my house. Unfortunately, his home was in the opposite direction from where I walked, so I simply went out of my way to stalk him. Donny did not appear to notice me despite all my efforts. In my shyness, I never made sure he did.

"He's pretty cute, Ger," Cody said, giving me her devilish smile. We entered the chorus room and found our seats in the soprano section.

"I just love the way that sandy hair hangs over his collar and eyes."

"Yeah, I know," Cody said, a dreamy look crossing her face. "Andy's hair's like that, too."

"So, does he let you touch it?" I asked hopefully, having no clue what guys did and didn't like.

Cody pulled her compact from her purse and removed the powder puff from its tray. "Last week he let me braid it, but he made me promise not to tell anyone."

"Well, your secret's safe with me. I'll never tell," I promised, peering into the tiny mirror. A smile crossed my face as I spotted my reflection. I flicked my chest-length hair over my shoulder admiring the feminine gesture. "God, what I'd give to run my fingers through that thick mane of his," I said, wondering if he'd find mine attractive. "I so love lots of hair on guys."

"Me, too! Turns me on every time," Cody agreed, dabbing her cheeks with peach blush.

"Okay, guys and gals, I'm going to start with section rehearsals," Mr. Randal J. Emerson announced. He waddled to the front of the concave risers and stared at the eighty-eight chorus members perched in their theater chairs. "If you are quiet, you can talk softly—and I do mean softly—if I'm not working with your group." He pointed at the basses sitting to our left, using his silver baton. "You guys have a lot of work ahead of you if you're going to sing up to my standards by Christmas. So far these ladies are singing you out of a job. So get out your sheet music for Sleigh Ride."

"Good!" I said, glad to continue talking with my friend.

"If only I could get Donny to notice me," I moaned, wondering whether flipping my hair in front of him might do the trick.

"Have you managed to talk to him yet?" she asked.

"Uh, well… not yet, but I will."

"Geri, you've got to say 'hi' if he's ever gonna notice you."

"I know, but he's always with a bunch of his buddies. I can't very well say hello to just him."

"Then talk to all of them. At least you'll let him know you're alive. It's an important start, Geri," Cody said, pinching my cheek

"Well, I've got an idea," I said, giving her a devious look via her mirror.

"What's that?" Cody asked, grinning in anticipation.

"Well, I heard that Donny is in the ski club."

"Yeah?"

"Yeah!"

"Geri, you're not thinking what I think you're thinking, are you?"

I smiled.

"You are," she said, snapping her compact shut and returning it to her purse.

"Do you like to ski?" I asked.

"Yeah, I've done it a couple of times, but…"

"But what?" I dared, knowing exactly what she was thinking.

"Well, how are you gonna ski?" she asked.

"With my feet, silly."

"Yeah, I know that, but what about seeing trees and people and other things that are out there for you to run into?"

"Well, I'll have you to help me, won't I?"

"How am I gonna help you? I can't very well be tapping you on the elbow out there on skis, can I? And I don't think you're gonna be able to hear me whistle or click my tongue, either."

She was referring to the system we'd developed to help me keep my greatest secret from the world. Since I'd given up the glasses, I'd run into a few little problems, literally. Objects to my left had a nasty way of jumping out at me. Although I managed pretty well in familiar territory, foreign environments tended to challenge my ability to stay upright. Bumps and bruises were no big deal, but when stairs disappeared, then reappeared without warning, my adrenal system tended to become over-taxed. For some unnerving reason, the sensation of falling produced pure, unadulterated terror in me, which I definitely didn't care for.

I think it had a similar effect on Cody. In her concern for my safety, she offered to hold hands with me when we walked in unfamiliar territory. I refused. There was no way I would let guys—or anyone else—see me holding onto my girlfriend in public. I assured Cody I could live with the few scrapes and bruises I incurred, which actually tended to be daily. But when my lack of depth perception caused me to fall down a flight of stairs at Kresge's, Cody came up with a plan. We agreed the key element was me being able to follow her as we walked. Since contrasts were easier for me to see, she'd always wear a color that stood out in the environment we planned to be in. Dark surroundings warranted light colored tops, and vice versa.

Next we developed signals for potential danger. If we walked side by side, I'd keep a half step back so I might see the movement of her shoulder. She'd tap my leg once if there were stairs going up and twice for down. When we were out of reach of each other, she'd click her tongue or whistle the same numbers. If we were side by side and an object entered my pathway, she'd gently bump her hip into mine, pushing me away, or touch my elbow and pull me toward her. Other unexpected hazards resulted in my name being spoken in a loud firm tone. Amazingly, it worked. After a couple of practice sessions, we were in sync. Slowly but surely, the cuts and bruises disappeared.

Now, as I sat there thinking about my new idea, I explained my brilliant plan. I first reminded her of how strong and agile we'd become from the exercises we'd both been doing. Then I mentioned how most ski hills were pretty wide open. I would be able to see her dark blue jacket clearly against the white snow.

"I'll stay behind you," I said, "and if I look like I might hit something, you could yell stop."

She thought about this for a minute, then reminded me about the moving chair lifts.

"You know how hard it's gotten for you to ride a bike. You told me yourself how much trouble you have seeing things that are moving, like when you're in a car."

I considered her words carefully. "Well then…"

"Well then, what?" she asked.

"I'll just ask the lift operator to stop the lift for me."

"Yeah, right!"

"I will. Heck, if it means I get to go skiing and maybe run into Donny, I'll do it."

"What about the ski advisers? Mr. Chansler might go for it, but Mr. Stickles, well, I know someone who has him for history, and they say he's pretty rigid."

"I'm not planning to tell either of them," I told Cody. "Heck, that's the beauty of this place. There are so many kids that most teachers don't know I'm one of the Special Ed students."

"You're not gonna tell them?"

"Nope! Don't see no reason to. I've got a right to join the ski club just like anybody else."

Cody shook her head, looking doubtful.

"Will you do it?"

After a brief pause, she smiled. "Aw, heck, why not? I'm game if you are."

"All right."

The next barrier I faced was my parents. I pulled out my creative ability to slant the truth and explained to my mom and dad how the ski club was starting a program for the Special Ed kids. I assured them that a trained instructor would guide each blind student on the bunny hills. Convincing them was not as easy as maintaining my bike privilege, however. It definitely didn't look good, as my folks insisted on contacting the club advisers.

My conniving mind quickly came up with a twisted plot. I innocently suggested one of the advisers could contact them. When a friend of mine, Dale Cohort (alias Mr. Stickles) gave them a call explaining the exciting opportunity now being offered blind children, they couldn't resist.

I felt a tad guilty as I excitedly prepared for my first skiing adventure. I arranged to spend the night at Cody's to avoid my father meeting the advisor when he dropped me off at school. A great plan, except for one minor hitch. I forgot the trip was supposed to be only for blind kids. I was caught off guard when my dad asked why Cody was going.

"She always—" I began, then suddenly checked myself. "I mean, she's such a good skier, they've asked her to come along to assist us." I felt my cheeks flush. I hoped they didn't give me away.

When the day arrived, Cody and I awoke at five thirty. We threw on our clothes and trudged through the crunching snow to the school. Thankfully it was five blocks closer. We boarded the bus, but Donny was nowhere to be found. I was sick with disappointment when the driver left the parking lot. Any hopes I had for connecting with my new love had vanished.

As time went on I felt nothing but relief as my foolish notions were realized. Skiing had looked so easy. I figured all I had to do was stand at the top of the hill and slide down. I had no clue about what I was supposed to do. Experience ended up becoming my teacher.

The first challenge was renting and putting on my skis. Even with Cody's help, it took a good forty minutes to arrange myself so I could make my way to the chair lift. Challenge two had to do with mustering up the courage to talk to the lift operator.

"What should I say?" I asked Cody.

"All you have to do is tell him you can't see real well and ask him if he'll stop the lift."

"He's gonna think I'm crazy!"

"You are!" Cody said with a laugh.

"Oh, God, Cody, what'd I get us into?"

"A whole lot of fun. Go ahead, Ger. This guy don't give a darn about what you do. Just ask him to stop it for a sec."

"You're a real pal, Code." I approached the lift operator. "Uh, excuse me, sir?" I ventured.

"Yeah?"

"Uh, I don't see very well, so I'm wondering if you could stop the lift for me?"

"What ya doin' skiing if you can't see?" he asked, chuckling and shaking his head.

"Well, I can see, but I have trouble with getting on moving things."

"Skis move, honey. Don't you know that?"

"I know, but it's not the same."

"How's it different?" the man asked, his tone suggesting he was enjoying heckling me.

Exasperated, I asked, "Can you stop the lift or not?"

"Okay, if you say so, but I ain't responsible if you break your neck."

"Ah, she ain't gonna break her neck," Cody chimed in. "You're gonna do fine, Ger."

"Thanks, Code." An empty chair soon stopped in front of us.

"Do you know to lift your skis when it starts up?" the guy asked.

"Uh, I think so."

"You have to be sure you tip your skis up so they don't get caught in the hill and pull you out."

"Oh, yeah." I was catching on to the potential danger, and it made me a little nervous. Cody and I climbed aboard, enjoying the view as we ascended.

Challenge three came at the top of the hill. I lined up my skis side by side and maneuvered to the edge to wait for Cody.

"You ready?" she asked.

"I'm ready!" I gave her a nervous smile. *Should I really be doing this?* I wondered.

"Okay, I'm heading out!" Cody said.

Off she went. I watched the movement of her dark jacket as she glided down the white expanse of slope.

This is it! I told myself, hesitating. You'd better go or you're gonna lose sight of her!

I leaned forward and felt myself begin to slide.

"I'm doing it!" I said aloud, as I floated gently over the snow. My smile widened. Wind filtered through the spaces between my teeth. *I feel so free!* I thought, my hair flying out from the furry ear muffs I wore.

But the sensation of freedom quickly changed to fear. The steady balance I'd been able to maintain at cruising speed was fast becoming compromised. My inner thigh muscles began to quiver as I struggled with all my might to keep my skis from splitting apart. Faster and faster I saw the white earth rush beneath me, making my body tip back and forth like a clown on stilts. Suddenly, I zipped past what I assumed to be Cody.

"Oh, my God!" I hollered out, praying there was nothing in my way. "Where's the end? Damn it, where's the end?" I yelled, struggling as hard as I could to slow myself with my poles. The gesture jammed my forearms up into my shoulders. The impact threatened to throw me off kilter. I was certain I'd shake apart from the momentum and frantically tried to think of what to do. Just then I heard from far away a voice like Tarzan's bellow out "STOP!"

Instantly I dropped my butt and fell to the ground. My exhausted muscles spasmed as I collapsed. I was never so grateful to hug the solid, still earth with both arms.

"Hey, girl! What ya tryin' to do, join the Olympics?" Cody asked, gliding up beside me and lowering herself to my level.

"Sorry 'bout that, Code. God, I feel so stupid! Did anybody see me?"

"Jeez, Ger. A better question might be, are you hurt?"

"Nah. Only my pride," I said, half laughing. "I had no idea skis would make me go that fast!"

"I think you need to know how to snow plow," she giggled, reaching over and pulling off my ear muffs. "God, girl, you scared the shit out of me!"

"Aw heck, it's not a big deal, really. I mean the worst thing that happened is I fell into a pile of snow."

"Uh, I don't think so!" Cody said.

"What do you mean?" I asked, not sure what she was getting at.

Cody took my hand and helped me into a sitting position. She continued to pull me forward.

"Check this out!" she commanded, placing my hand on a familiar object. There, only a few inches from where I had plopped my rear, stood a birch tree. I patted it gently.

"Sorry there, tree," I said, my stomach turning over with the prospects of what might have happened. I worked to regain my composure, repositioning myself so I could get up. As I did so, I learned about challenge four. This feat of human endurance turned out to be the greatest exploit one had to face in the sport of skiing. It did not take long to comprehend the importance of not falling. Although one might expect such a danger would be obvious, it had nothing to do with getting hurt. Even with Cody's suggestion to use the tip of my pole by hooking it over the end of my boot, I still could not find the strength in my arms to get up. Finally, out of exasperation, I inched my way over to my new-found friend, and borrowed its strength to stand. "Thanks there, pal," I said, patting its trunk.

I retrieved my ear muffs from Cody and followed her to the lift. We had decided it was best to get back on the horse right away, before we both lost our nerve. But before we did, Cody showed me a few pointers. Among these were zigzagging when traversing a hill, and the technique of snow plowing, which Cody assured me would make my life longer. She was right. Not only did I finish out my day without falling, I tested my skills on unsuspecting souls in dark coats, to see if I could become more independent. Happily, I ended my first ski trip without any casualties.

Several more ski trips came and went. Unfortunately Donny attended the two I missed. I was disappointed with only catching glimpses of him between classes, but my love for this sport was incentive enough to go. Together Cody and I worked on our techniques by attending free instruction offered by various lodges. My motivation to learn overrode my embarrassment for exposing myself as a visually impaired person. I was surprised at how free I felt asking for extra demonstrations. My aversion to sympathy was balanced out by the skill I gained. I had to admit I enjoyed the extra hands-on attention given to me by good looking instructors. There was something about their manly touch that overrode their feeling sorry for me. By January, I could ski with the best of my classmates. In fact, I was able to join them along with the unknowing advisors on five mile trails through rugged terrain.

The end of the season trip, scheduled in late February, required a three-hour bus ride to Boyne Mountain in Petoskey. I had heard through the grapevine Donny would be going to Michigan's most renowned ski resort. I sat next to Cody, excited and waiting for him to board the bus. But when Mr. Stickles started the engine, once more my heart sank.

"Everybody ready for a great time?" Mr. Chansler called.

We all answered in unison, "Yeah!"

"To the North Country then, Mr. Stickles," Mr. Chansler directed. Instead of heading straight to highway 23, Mr. Stickles made a turn down a familiar side road. When the bus stopped in the middle of the street and opened its doors, Cody explained.

"Geri! It's Donny! They're picking Donny up at his house!"

"Oh, my God!" I squeaked. "Pinch me, I can't believe it!"

Donny climbed onto the bus and found a seat two rows in front of us. When he slipped back the hood of his black nylon jacket and his hair tumbled out, I thought I'd faint.

For two hundred miles I held my breath for fear of saying or doing something stupid. Cody gabbed away, but I could hardly concentrate on anything she said.

At last we arrived. Everyone clambered off the bus and scattered in various directions, including Donny. As I struggled to see which way he went, the snow-covered slopes caught my eye. By the time I looked back, I had lost sight of him. Giving up the idea of finding him, I stared at the beauty before me. I watched specks of colored dots scattering themselves like ants across the slopes. I had to remind myself they were really skiers making their way to the bottom. Chair lifts moved continuously like snakes along the edges. The sight reminded me of a giant ice cream cone covered in candy sprinkles, and I wanted to take a bite. It was a winter happening and I was ecstatic to be a part of it, even though I'd lost track of my love.

Cody and I trekked our way to a small hill to warm up. Eventually we got separated and just did our own thing. In my enjoyment, I forgot about Donny. It just felt good to move so freely with the wind in my face. More than confident in my newfound athletic skill, I decided to face the challenge of Mount Olympus. It was the biggest hill in Michigan, and only the best of the best dared to take it on. I maneuvered my way to the line for the three-person chairlift. I tried to ignore the twinge of doubt now nagging at me.

I wonder if I'm ready for this? I asked myself.

Before I could chicken out, someone behind me spoke. "So you're gonna try the big one, are you?"

I turned to see who belonged to this strong masculine voice.

"I hear it's a killer!" he warned.

My difficulty with recognizing faces made me unsure if this was anyone I knew.

"I know," I answered shyly.

"I've done it a few times myself. Gotta be careful about them moguls."

Before I could ask how big they were, the voice asked, "You're Geri, right?"

Suddenly I realized the guy standing right in front of me was none other than Donny Wansome. Oh, my God! I almost said aloud.

"Oh, uh, yeah," I managed to answer. With knees knocking and palms sweating, I willed myself not to quiver. Thrilled and terrified all in one swoop, I worked to steady myself. I managed to squeak out, "You're Donny, aren't you?"

"Yup, that's me," he said, ever so confidently. His deep green eyes gave me a wink, and my knees threatened to crumple.

"How long you been skiing?"

"A few times," I said, wishing I had thought up something less honest.

"You really think you're up for this mountain?"

"Uh, yeah."

"Well, be careful. Like I said, it's full of moguls and the slope gets pretty steep in places."

"Oh, uh, okay," I said, showing my verbal versatility.

Donny continued to make conversation and I continued to give my three-word responses. My heart was racing, my armpits were dripping, and an increasing tremor threatened my collapse. The line moved forward, and I suddenly remembered the need to reveal my secret to the chair lift operator. If Donny thought I shouldn't try this mountain as an amateur skier, what would he think if he knew I had a vision problem?

As he talked, the wheels in my brain turned. I periodically rotated my face away from him to focus on the area of the lift. I felt a boost of confidence when I saw one of the swinging benches pass my visual field at the two o'clock position. It disappeared for a count of five but reappeared at the bottom. I calculated these movements and was amazed at my ability to hold up my end of the conversation. As we talked I noticed the chair which would eventually carry me and two others was in the two o'clock spot.

I counted to myself. *One, two, three…*

The guy in front headed for the chair.

Four, five. I followed.

Like clockwork I sat my butt down on the moving lift just in time. In the heat of this most exciting moment, I felt Donny's warm body snuggle tight next to mine. Unfortunately, my joy lasted for only a moment. My cleverness had not extended very far. After successfully maneuvering onto a moving target, I failed to remember other important aspects of riding the lift.

"Ow!" I screamed.

"I got you!" Donny yelled as he grasped me around the waist. The hands of the other passenger clutched my shoulders hard.

"Ow! Oh, my God! Ow!"

"Hang on!" Donny yelled. "Hold on to the chair with your hands."

But I was in the center, and there was no place to grip.

"My leg, my leg!" I cried out. "Oh please, my leg!"

"Here, let me see if I can get my ski under yours to hold it up," Donny gallantly offered, as we continued to ascend.

In a moment the intensity of the pain lessened as Donny picked up my dangling ski with his own. In an effort to be cool, I hadn't followed the advice of the heckling lift operator. Just as he had promised, my ski caught the side of the mountain and pivoted around. My foot was now pointing backwards and excruciating pain was shooting up my leg.

For what seemed an eternity, Donny held me tightly as we continued to climb the hill. The other guy also did his best to assist, but Donny's arms mattered most. When we at long last reached the top, it was Donny who spoke comforting words to me as paramedics lifted me into the emergency bobsled.

As I lay in Boyne Mountain's medical center, Donny held my hand in his. I couldn't believe my luck. A dream come true for any girl, I figured. Unfortunately, a familiar voice interrupted my private drama.

"Why didn't you tell me you can't see?" asked Mr. Stickles.

Suddenly, the beauty of this magnificent moment faded. I wanted to die. The boundaries of the fairy tale I'd created were starting to cave in around me. My lies were now exposed. Without a doubt, I knew more would follow. Picking my words carefully, I continued my effort to get out of my predicament as best as I could.

"I can see. I just forgot to lift my ski, Mr. Stickles," I said, praying he'd leave it alone.

"Your friend Cody says you're one of those Special Ed students."

Darn her! I thought, then reminded myself she was not someone who could lie.

"I'm sorry, Mr. Stickles. I guess I should have told you, but I really can see well enough to ski."

"I can see that," he said sarcastically.

I turned toward Donny. I wondered what he thought.

"I don't think your parents are too happy, either."

"They know?" I asked, trying to imagine the impact of being found out.

"I just got off the phone with your father. I gather he was under the impression this was a ski club for blind students?"

I wished I could shrink below the blanket, so I did the only reasonable thing a girl could do. I cried. It started as a trickle, then moved on to convulsive sobs. Mr. Stickles didn't seem to be particularly moved by my dramatic response, but Donny was, and that's all that mattered. Leaning forward, Donny gently patted my shoulder.

"Ah, he's just an old coot," he said. "It'll be okay."

I was in heaven. Though I knew I'd have to face my father when I got home, I decided for now I'd let Donny sooth me all he wanted. In all my fantasies I had never dreamed up something this good. My leg hurt, but it didn't seem to matter much. The shot the nurse gave me was now spreading like warm butter all through me. With Donny's hand firmly around mine, I absolutely knew this was heaven. To top things off, my friend arrived just at the right time. When she saw our entwined hands, she smiled her approval. With Cody as my witness, no one could doubt my story.

At last the time arrived to leave the magic of the winter wonderland infirmary. I was dressed in hospital pajama bottoms with my leg firmly secured in a straight-leg cast. I hobbled my way to the bus on crutches with Donny right beside me. We rode home together in the back of the bus, Donny cradling me in his arms. Like all good things, the tender sympathy I received came to an end. As we pulled into the school parking lot, I braced myself for what I knew I deserved.

My heart filled with shame when I saw my dad at the bus door. He didn't say a word. The only thing I could do was hand him a bag of torn pants. He silently took them, and then he and Mr. Chansler helped me down the stairs and into the car. I wiggled my way into the back seat. My dad climbed in the driver's side and we headed for home.

I waited, but he said nothing. *Maybe he wants to get on the main road before he starts yelling*, I thought. But he still said nothing. *Is he gonna let me have it at home so Mom can get in on it?* But after we got into the house, I realized Mom was in bed.

"You can sleep on the couch," Dad said, "No point in trying to climb the stairs."

I sat on the edge of my mother's stuffed rocker waiting patiently for him to direct me further. His matter of fact demeanor scared me. He took a sheet and blanket from the hallway linen closet and spread them over our red sofa. He then took my ski jacket from behind me and hung it in the closet. I felt guilt rise inside me with every effort he made. I moved to the couch and watched as he took my torn pants into the kitchen, where I heard them drop into the wastebasket.

"Need anything else?" he asked.

"No."

Why isn't he saying anything? I asked myself. I wished he'd yell or something. But he just turned and headed to the bedroom.

"Dad?"

"Yeah?"

"Aren't you going to yell at me or ground me?"

"No," he said simply.

"Why not?"

"You already know what you did," he answered. "Night now. Holler if you need anything."

I don't think I could have received a worse punishment. I refused to let myself cry, however. I knew it would bring my father back to my side, if for nothing else than to give me his hanky. I did not deserve such a kindness. I thought about saying a prayer asking for forgiveness, but I calculated God was running out of absolutions for me. It took a long time before sleep relieved me from my unworthy self.

I'm not sure why I could never keep my promises to do better, but when Monday rolled around, any feelings of remorse I had dissipated as my celebrity status became clear. The story of the ski trip traveled far and wide. Walking on crutches brought me even more attention. For the first time ever, most everyone in the school knew who I was. Like magic, they wanted to be near me.

Donny's affection never went beyond the ski trip, however. I was disappointed, but realized my jealous nature would have gotten in the way of any relationship with him. I learned quickly that Donny needed lots of attention from many girls. In time, he faded from my mind.

"Hey, I got a scoop on Donny Wansome!" Cody announced. The end of the school year was near and my leg was almost healed. We were sitting in our usual place in the music room.

"Yeah, what'd you hear?" I asked, leaning closer.

"Well, I heard that Donny's in the hospital."

"Really? What for?"

Cody took out her nail file and began to saw them down. I grabbed another emery board from her makeup kit and joined her.

"Well, apparently he took a dare to jump off the Flint River Bridge."

"You're kidding, right?"

"Nope."

"Somebody dared him to dive into that stream of human waste? How gross."

"No kidding."

"So, did he?"

"Yes, he did."

"That's disgusting!" I said, imagining his pretty face covered with the brown slimy water of the river, which doubled as the city's toilet.

"Yeah, Ger," Cody continued, "I think, in a way, you're pretty lucky."

"How do you figure?"

"Well, knowing what I know now about Donny, I think it would have been a shitty relationship after all."

Chapter 13

A Brave New World

Summer 1970

Paranoia strikes deep

Into your life it will creep

It starts when you're always afraid

You step out of line, the man come and take you away

You've got to stop, children, what's that sound?

Everybody look what's going down

As the words from the song *For What It's Worth* rang out, my gut wrenched.
How could they know how I'm feeling? I wondered, sitting on the grassy hill at the outdoor music festival.

Only seconds before, a pair of legs connected to no one had passed in front of me. Again the feeling of disorientation made me want to vomit. But as always, I said nothing to anyone. I simply continued listening to the words written by Stephen Stills that so well expressed my secret fear. I breathed in the familiar smell of marijuana, half wishing I had accepted the offer to take a hit from the long-haired hippie sitting behind me. At least I would have a more tolerable excuse for my distorted reality.

Applause erupted from the crowd of flower children surrounding the bandstand. It was obvious they all agreed a concert held at Flint's natural amphitheater was where it was at.

"They're great, aren't they," Candice timidly said.

"Yeah, they're far out!" I replied, hoping excitement would override my nervousness.

Candice Seeker read the lineup on the billboard near the bandstand while the first group left the stage.

"It looks like Bob Seger's next. I hope he does *Heavy Music*."

"Me too," I said, wondering if she could see the anxiety I was certain must be written all over my face.

I pretended to wipe out debris by digging the knuckle of my index finger hard into my right eye. Of the two, this one was the most reliable, though it was getting harder to call it that. My effort was in vain. As hard as I tried, I could not wipe away the chaos in front of me. I could not find the bodies that belonged to the sea of legs now milling around.

They have to be there, I told myself. But the flashing light flickering in and out of headless appendages created a strobe effect, forcing me to close my eyes in defeat. The warm and wonderful sun which provided a life giving force to the Earth and its inhabitants was quickly becoming my enemy. I had tried wearing sunglasses, but they worked a little too well. They not only took care of the glare, but they blocked out anything else I could see. I had to abandon them, which left only scattered images for me to see. It reminded me of how the bright lights of an oncoming car blinded the driver with a dirty windshield. Unfortunately, I was unable to blame this craziness on a car ride.

Candice continued talking. I could hardly concentrate. I wanted to tell her how crazy everything looked to me but, like the song said, I was afraid. I wasn't exactly sure why I couldn't speak, particularly after what had transpired between us earlier in the day.

In the past year Candice and I had become close friends. When Andy Swavemore dumped Cody for several other girls, she fell madly in love with an older guy she'd met at a fraternity party. He turned out to be the possessive type, so she apologetically spent less and less time with me.

I missed Cody a lot, but Candice filled the void very well. I could hardly believe I could find another beautiful, intelligent, and popular friend to give me the time of day. Our connection came during choir class when Candice expressed an interest in reading to me. She overheard me talking about having trouble finding required books in Braille. Since she, too, was a soprano, and Randal J. Emerson generously provided us with lots of free time, there was plenty of opportunity for chatting. Fortunately, it didn't stop there. Her interest in school rubbed off. She ended up helping with other homework after school. My grades improved greatly during our junior year.

With the anti-establishment movement of the late 60s and our increasing book list expanding into consciousness-raising literature, we discovered we had a lot in common. We both grew passionate about exploring controversial topics and searching for the truth.

After the assassination of Martin Luther King, Jr. in 1968, many students, black and white, came together to protest some of the segregated and oppressive teachings of the educational system. Candice and I found ourselves at many of these rallies. When a student protest broke out in our school in the spring of 1969, Candice and I left the tear gas-laden building and carried protest signs on the sidewalk outside. We also spent more and more time at Wilson Park, Flint's downtown hippie hangout. There we defaced some of the surrounding dilapidated buildings by writing heartfelt graffiti on them.

"HELP I'M DROWNING IN LIFE AND I CAN'T SWIM!" was my contribution to the walls of prose. I and many authors of such words of wisdom wrote with the hope that some passerby might give a darn.

But books were what brought Candice and me together. We drank in the knowledge of cherished words that soothed our souls. By summer we'd completed many new books, including *Brave New World, 1984, Stranger in a Strange Land, Letters from the Earth*, and *Tropic of Cancer*. As we digested the writings of great authors like Aldous Huxley, George Orwell, Robert Heinlein, Mark Twain, and Henry Miller, our questions about the many facets of life intensified.

"I wonder why living has to be so painful?" Candice asked, setting the book down on the table next to my bed. We'd just finished Salinger's novel, *Catcher in the Rye*. His character Holden, who goes a little crazy, also questioned his painful existence as a social misfit.

"I don't know," I said, moving from the bed to my new bean bag chair in the corner. "God is supposed to care about us. He's supposed to be just and fair, but look at all the horrible stuff people have to go through," I said, remembering similar conversations.

"I know. My preacher says we have free will and that we have choices. He keeps saying we can make our life better. But what about all those kids in foreign countries who have nothing to eat? Where's their choice?" Candice stood up and walked over to my dresser. She picked up my childhood brush and ran it through her silky white hair. We were almost carbon copies of each other in terms of personal style. Since we'd joined the hippie cult, blue jeans cut-off or long, t-shirts, and love beads were the extent of our wardrobe. We didn't feel we should be spending money on material things when so many had so little. My blond hair tended to be more on the golden side, but we both wore our hair to our waist and parted severely in the middle. Her eyes were deep green, and her complexion milky white. I liked my new appearance, but she was strikingly beautiful.

Watching Candice sensuously move the brush through her hair, I wondered if she'd ever felt like an outcast.

"Life is so different than what they told me it would be," I remarked.

"What do ya mean?"

"Well, I mean like *Leave It to Beaver* or *Father Knows Best*. Those shows were supposed to be like the All-American family. Me, I never understood why mine wasn't."

"Me neither," Candice said, turning to look at me. "Heck, you'd never find my father sitting down and discussing school with me or sorting out an argument between me and my sisters. In fact, you'd never find him at my house at all."

"Really?"

"Nah. He's always working in Ohio or someplace. He sends my mother guilt money and comes home maybe once a month for a visit."

"Don't your Mom get lonely?"

"I guess, though I expect she's used to it."

I couldn't imagine life without my father. "Once, I thought my folks might get a divorce," I told her, repositioning myself in the cushion. "They didn't talk to each other for weeks. I tried to figure out who I'd live with and it about killed me. I couldn't stand to have either of them away."

Candice put down my brush. She moved over and lay on my bed, propping her head up with her elbow. "It's no big deal, I guess," she said unconvincingly. Though I couldn't see her expression across the eight foot distance between us, I pictured her full pink lips frowning. "I only wish my mom weren't so stupid."

"What do ya mean?"

"I mean she's stupid. All she does is cook and clean and baby my little sister. She hardly ever goes anywhere. Going shopping is her big outing for the week and she gets all dressed up to walk through Kroger's."

"Well, my mom don't go too many places either. Come to think of it, neither does June Cleaver or Margaret Anderson." We both gave half-hearted chuckles. "I guess we have something in common with those dumb TV shows after all," she said.

We continued to discuss how confusing it all seemed. "Why haven't we heard about people like Holden before?" I asked, directing my question to the heavens. "I figured I was the only one who feels crazy sometimes."

"Me, too," Candice said.

We were both silent for a while. Suddenly Candice sat up. With a force in her voice I'd never heard before, she said, "Why don't they show how awful it feels when a kid comes home from school to find their mom crying, and there's a present in the mail that their long-lost dad sent them?"

My mind saw the tears I knew were running down her soft pale cheeks. My heart went out to her. I thought of my own father. Without a doubt, I could not even begin to know how hard life would be without him. Candice fell back on the bed, hiding her head in her arms. I heard her breathless sobs and walked over to her, gingerly sitting beside her. I reached my arm around her shoulders. She responded by crying harder. Instinctively, I knew this was a good thing, so I leaned in closer. She turned up slightly on her side then buried her head in my chest. I began to cry too.

"I don't understand why it all has to be so difficult," I said, wishing some invisible force of wisdom could hear us. We lay together until our spasms of grief subsided. Then Candice lifted her head and said, "And they have the nerve to tell us we have a loving God who watches out for us."

She dropped her head again and wept. Although Candice and I had hinted at our doubts about religion, particularly after reading *Letters From the Earth*, we never came right out and admitted the depth of our skepticism. "Don't you believe in God?" I asked gently, hoping she did, yet wishing she didn't.

"No! I don't!" she cried, shaking her head back and forth in the crook of my shoulder.

"Me neither!" I choked. I lay my face on hers. Our tears mixed together, flowing down our chins, soaking the necks of our t-shirts. A sweet sadness poured from my soul as I stroked Candice's satiny hair. The sense of oneness overpowered me. Our mutual catharsis intensified my affection for her.

"Oh Candice!" I quietly whispered, deciding to confess my secrets. "I have never said it, but it's true. I can't find anything to make sense out of all the garbage I've been listening to at church all these years. I want there to be a God, but I can't find any evidence. None of it makes any sense!"

"I know, I know!" she said, pulling her head out from under mine. I reluctantly lifted my arm, regretting the severing of our bond. She sat up and pulled a tissue from its pink holder on the dresser. I did likewise, dabbing my face and eyes.

Like a swan delicately dipping its beak into a pond, Candice gracefully tipped her nose into the tissue and blew it with nary a sound. I found her action impressive. I decided Candice could likely perform the most disgusting act, and still look sensuously feminine. I felt both jealous and privileged she would spend time with me at all. Candice dropped the dirty tissue into the wastebasket.

"It's the hypocrisy that drives me crazy! 'Judge not lest ye be judged.' What the hell is that all about?" She demanded, slapping her thigh. I jumped at the unexpected sound. I'd never known Candice to be so animated. "I hate going to church!" she continued. "If the other churchgoers aren't staring at me because I don't have on a pretty dress, they're whispering to their friends and making nasty comments about hippies and druggies."

I nodded my head in agreement as I located a string hanging from my cutoffs. I began wrapping it around my finger. "No shit!" I said, adopting Candice's infectious fury. "If you want to find a rigid critical person, look for a Bible thumper or a politician. Anyone who supports the Vietnam War and says they're Christian is talking out of both sides of their mouth."

"I know," Candice agreed, gathering up one of my pillows and cradling it in her arms like a baby. Except for the sound of ripping threads, we sat silent for several minutes.

At last Candice spoke. "Actually, I think Jesus was pretty cool."

"Yeah?" I asked, curious to hear what she had to say.

"He was a pacifist. He understood that people make mistakes and that there are times for everything. Just like in the book of Ecclesiastes where it says, "To everything there is a season."

"Yeah, right!" I agreed, thinking about the song *Turn Turn Turn* by The Byrds. I fetched the other pillow and held it tight, hoping to prevent my shorts from being torn apart.

"I really don't get the whole idea that God is love and can do anything, but he'll send you to hell if you don't get baptized and have original sin wiped from your soul," I said. I waited a second to see if Candice had a comment, but she simply nodded affirmatively. I went on. "I mean, it don't make a darn bit of sense. We're taught to forgive and forget, turn the other cheek, be understanding, yet God will sentence us with eternal damnation for a sin that got committed by somebody else a million years ago."

"I know!" she said, nodding her head multiple times, her gesture reassuring me of our bond. With Candice as my comrade, I found I had more courage to reopen this taboo subject. Exposing the years of hidden resentment brought an incredible sense of relief. I'd been keeping these doubts to myself since the days of my discussions with Linda. Now I didn't have to manage them on my own. Tossing my pillow hard against the wall, I continued.

"How unreasonable can people be, for God's sake? If God is so smart and all knowing, why couldn't he figure out a better way to manage his flock?" I asked, throwing up my hands in the air. "Damn it all anyway?" I yelled, slapping my bare thighs hard.

This time it was Candice's turn to jump. Instinctively she pulled her pillow up tighter against her chest, waiting for me to go on.

"Heck, our own court system is more fair than this crazy plan they say God has. If he created all of us in his own image, then why would he go and torture us with the threat of eternal fire, not to mention all the tragedies he torments us with on Earth."

Candice gave a half-hearted chuckle.

"Remember what Mark Twain said in *Letters from the Earth*, when he was talking how heaven ain't necessarily set up for the average Joe?"

"Oh yeah," she said with another half laugh.

"Well, just think, Candice, after we get through all this pain and suffering on Earth, we get to go to heaven and listen to a bunch of angels play horns."

Her giggle made me smile. "I can hardly wait!" I noticed her stuffy nose. She pushed the pillow away and started to get up. "I agree with you, though," she said. "It's the original sin idea that gets me. I sure don't figure why I and all the others, including innocent babies, have to pay for some dumb chick eating an apple."

"God is going to send his wrath on us for talking this way Candice."

"I know, but I can't pretend I believe something I don't believe any more."

I liked watching Candice's feminine movements. I took note that I would adopt her gestures for my own.

Candice reviewed her reflection in my mirror. "Well, just in case it's all they say it is, I pray to God every night to forgive me for being such a Doubting Thomas," she said.

"You're doing better than me then, Candice. I gave up praying a long time ago. If there is a God, I figured he's so sick of hearing the same apologies with no mending of my awful ways, that I'd give him a break."

Candice reached over to my dresser. She retrieved her keys to the Olds her father had given her and started for the door. "Wanna head to the concert?" she asked.

"Sounds groovy!"

We were still waiting for Seger to get set up when I saw two legs approach.

"Hey, girls." His words were slow and drawn out. I lifted my arm and held up my index and middle finger in the shape of a V. Without seeing it, I knew the hand of the voice did the same. Flashing the peace sign was standard greeting procedure for hippies.

"Hi Fred!" Candice replied. "Wanna sit down?"

"Right on!" he said, lowering himself to my visual level. I could now see his shaggy blond hair straggling down around his face.

"Hi, ladies," another quieter voice said. It belonged to Fred's best friend, Wally. I offered the symbol of peace to him as well.

We'd been hangin' out with Fred and Wally all summer. They were both classmates. We'd be seniors in September. They wore the trademark clothes of hippie-freaks too.

"I got some really good stuff, ladies?"

I was able to see Fred's endearing smile. It was the one he always gave us when he tried to get Candice and me high.

"Gonna try it this time?"

"Nah," Candice said with hesitation. From discussions we'd had, I knew she was as curious as I was about pot. The fact it seemed to make whoever smoked it feel mellow enticed us both. Mellow sounded very inviting to me at this moment. I leaned over to Candice's ear.

"Wanna try it this time?" I whispered, not wanting to experiment alone.

"Ah, I dunno."

"Ah, come on, Candice, you know you're curious," Fred urged. "I tell ya, you won't regret it. Just try a couple of hits to start. If you don't like it, it won't last very long and you'll be none the worse off. Honest."

"Let's do it, Candice. I mean, whatta we got to lose, right?"

"Uh…"

"Here, come on, take a little drag. Geri, show her how it's done." I heard the strike of a match, then the aromatic smell of the hemp leaf drifted into my nostrils. A combination of burning leaves, religious incense, and a pungent earthy smell called to me. Fred seemed to read my mind as he held the burning offering to my lips. Unable to see it coming, I jerked back.

"Whoa girl, it won't bite you."

"Oh, the smoke went up my nose," I lied, not wanting him to know I hadn't seen it. This time we connected.

"Now just suck in a little. I'll hold it for you."

I hesitated. It felt like I was about to plunge off a high dive. I worried I'd hit the bottom and never come up.

"Go ahead."

I knew Candice was watching. *Do it!* I commanded myself. Without another thought, I breathed in deeper than planned and choked.

"Easy. Easy there, Ger," Fred said, drawing out his words. "Gotta breathe in a little slower, more shallow, but you'll get the hang of it," he said chuckling. "Okay, Candice, your turn."

I heard the crowd moan as the announcer informed everyone about a few technical difficulties that would delay Bob Seger another five minutes.

"Okay," Candice said. I tried to watch while Fred held the joint up to her mouth. She apparently learned from my mistake, as I did not hear her choke. *Would Candice ever make such awful noises?* I wondered. *Would she sound as gross as me?*

"Far out!" Fred complimented. "Ready for another toke, Ger?"

"I guess so." He repeated his gallant gesture several more times. I felt no difference.

"What's it supposed to do to ya?" I dared to ask.

"Oh, just make you feel a little mellow."

"Well, I don't feel any different."

"Me neither," Candice agreed.

"You will. Here, have a couple more tokes to be sure."

But after a few more puffs, mixed with a bit more choking on my part, nothing noticeable occurred.

Finally a cheer from the crowd welcomed the introduction of Bob Seger. He was a native of the area and was well loved by his Flint audience. His famous animalistic, guttural growl rang out as the drummer hit the downbeat to the song I longed to hear. The crowd gave another roar as Bob sang the words to *Heavy Music*. The connection was strong as we all grooved to the music of his most popular song.

While tapping out the rhythm with my hands and feet, I had a strange sensation. The music seemed to slide from the area of the speakers on the stage, down a silver thread, into my mind. As I heard Bob sing about going deeper, I was amazed at the Fantasia being performed inside my head. It was just like Disney's movie. The colorful string began to change hue. Like neon, the iridescent silver strand now dissolved into metallic blue, coiling into a circle around itself. Various shades began sprouting from the center point, sliding through the spiraling image. I watched as luminescent yellows merged from chartreuse into tangerine. As the intensity of Bob's gravelly voice shouted out, turquoise sparkles exploded into a dazzling fireworks display.

As this magical kaleidoscope unfolded before me, childlike amusement tantalized me. I was no longer focused on the strobe lights from the sun. With my eyes gently closed, I lay on the cool grass totally absorbed in what heaven should be like. Without realizing it, I started to laugh.

"Oh, my God, I think I'm high!" I shouted, louder than I'd planned.

Candice was laughing as well.

"Told ya," Fred said mischievously.

"Pretty far out!" Wally added.

More giggles and cackles erupted from my gut. The muscles of my stomach contracted. The convulsive movements seemed to match the beat of the music, making me roar even harder. I couldn't tell whether Candice was laughing at me or something in her own head, but I was too fascinated with the light show in mine to ask.

When the music stopped, I sat up and opened my eyes. Like a fireball shot from a cannon, the harsh sunlight blasted my eyes, sending blinding stabs of pain deep inside. The joy and lightheartedness I'd experienced left as quickly as it came. When my pupils adjusted the little they could, everything appeared far more blurred. I could hardly manage the chaos before me. With my stomach churning, I curled my body forward, attempting to steady myself. I rolled onto my side and tried to focus on my connection to the earth.

Then I heard Fred ask, "What'sa matter, Ger?"

Does he know? I thought, panicked.

"Nothing," I said, with a voice that was not my own.

"You sure?"

He knows! I told myself. How can he know?

Candice stopped laughing. Her voice sounded concerned. She asked the same question. "You okay, Geri?"

"I'm fine," I lied, knowing my face didn't match my words.

"Here, have another hit." Fred's fingers touched my lips. I jolted upright as if he'd put a knife to me.

"No!" I said sharply. But again, my voice sounded foreign.

Bob started up with another song. The tempo was much slower this time. The mellowness helped. I turned over and burrowed my head in crossed arms, gripping the grass to anchor myself to the earth. The contrast between the quiet darkness behind my eyes and the nightmare I saw when I opened them terrified me. As I struggled to calm myself, I hoped the guys would just think I was grooving to the music and forget about me.

Candice leaned over. "Just let the music take you, Geri. It'll be okay."

Her kind words help me relax. I managed to conjure up the colored strings again, but it was more subdued now. A lingering nervousness kept their beauty at bay.

"Pretty far out, don't ya think?" Candice asked, scooting closer. Her gesture comforted me.

"It's far out, all right. Thanks for being my friend," I said, hoping I wouldn't cry.

"You, too."

The colors drew near. They flowed gently to the music.

All you have to do is keep your eyes closed, I told myself. Just don't look and you'll be all right.

Chapter 14

An Unexpected Distraction

September 1970

Day 1

The leather tie holding back my hair gave way. Instinctively, I brushed the strands from my face.

"Weird hair ribbon," a deep voice said.

Turning in its direction, I held out my hand.

"Hey, give it back! What'd you do that for, anyway?" I asked. But instead of my band, all I got was a slap on my palm. The light coming from the hallway helped me see the face in front of me. A cute guy stood there with a big smile on his face. His medium brown hair hung over his ears just the way I liked it. With deep blue eyes and pearly teeth, he looked like a model advertising toothpaste in a magazine.

"You look better without it!" he said, grabbing a fistful of my hair and wrapping it around my face and mouth.

"There, you've got a mask," he announced, chuckling. "You could tuck these golden locks in your pants if you wanted!" he said, running his hand down the strands. When he tried to stuff them in the belt of my hip-hugger jeans, I slapped his arm away.

"Ah, come on, that looked pretty cool!"

"I don't think so."

"Wanna dance?"

Throwing my hair back over my shoulder, I answered. "Sure! As long as you give back my tie and don't touch my hair."

"Hmm!" he said, turning toward the dance floor. "Come on then."

"Hey, you gotta give it back first!"

"After we dance."

I gingerly followed his light blue shirt through the couples as they swayed to the romantic melody from above. With great effort, I swished through the crowd trying not to entangle myself in the extra yards of denim making up the bells of my pants. I hoped he didn't notice me ricocheting off entwined elbows.

Finally, he stopped and turned to me. I felt his arm slip around my waist and reciprocated the gesture. My body quivered. I hoped he didn't notice.

"So what's your name?" he asked,

"Geri."

"Geri what?"

"Geri Taeckens."

"Hmmm, yes, I will."

"Will what?"

"Take you!" he chuckled, pulling me to him, almost making me fall.

"Hey, watch it!" I warned, regaining my balance. "So now tell me, what's yours?"

"Ken."

"Ken what?" I asked, mimicking his request, finding myself melding back into him.

"Herald."

"Herald! Now that's an interesting name. Ken Herald. So how come you got two first names?"

"Cause I'm important!" he said, pulling me nearer, this time without throwing me off. A nervous silence interrupted our conversation. My mind raced. *What do I say next?* I wondered as I struggled to keep track of where my feet were. I was intoxicated by the smell of his cologne and the spellbinding words of Chicago's *Color My World*. My legs threatened to collapse under me. Ken's next question sobered me.

"You one of them hippie chicks?" he asked.

I surprised myself with my wit. "Is it the love beads that told you?" I asked, pretending that hanging out on a dance floor with a guy was an everyday thing.

"I figured as much," he said with a snide tone, now hooking his thumb over my wide leather belt. "The army jacket is a dead giveaway."

"So you like my threads, do you?" I asked, pulling away and looking down at the jacket my father loaned to me.

"Didn't say I liked it now, did I?" Ken said, digging his fingers into my back.

"Don't tell me you're one of those straight guys?" I countered, noticing how easily we moved together.

"That depends on what you mean by straight."

As I was deciding how much I should disclose, Ken maneuvered us in and out of the other couples. This guy had a real style to his step. Unlike most, he was not satisfied to simply shuffle back and forth in one spot.

"Ever done pot?"

"Nope."

"Then you're straight," I said, pulling back a little.

"Have you?" he inquired, pushing against my resistance. The sensation of his open palm against the small of my back sent chills up my spine. The tender words to Chicago's love ballad circulated around the room.

"Would it make a difference?" I asked, as the lyrics suggested love should be promised between those who are near.

"Probably not," he said abruptly. But his firm grip said the opposite.

We continued edging around the other couples, sashaying in and out, advancing and retreating in a gentle gliding motion. The poetic words, now supported by a melodious flute, spoke of being together forever. As the music cast its spell, Ken leaned his head in to mine. I was nervous, but it felt so natural being in the arms of someone I'd never met before. As the flutist brought the enchantment to an end, I felt the mournful notes. But instead of Prince Charming disappearing in a puff of smoke, Ken kept hold of me as we returned to the side of the gym.

"Hey, there you are," Candice said, walking up beside us. She looked down, noticing our coupled hands. "Oh, just checking on you. Gotta go find Chris."

I gave her a smile as she headed off.

"She's a looker!" Ken noticed. "She your friend?"

For a minute, I thought my new find would put his sights on something prettier than me. Much to my delight, his grip grew firmer, as he pulled me toward the door. When we got outside his questions continued.

"So, you smoke pot, do you?"

"Why are you so interested in that?" I asked, annoyed.

"Just curious. Your friend a hippie, too?"

"Didn't you see her love beads and jacket?" Candice's father hadn't served in the armed forces, but she made sure to wear a buckskin coat with fringes.

"Boy, you're a feisty one, aren't you?"

"You're a nosey one, aren't—"

But before I could finish, he bent over and kissed me hard on the lips. Something inside me exploded. Tingling sensations spread all through me. I felt my hips compress. More bursts of pleasure found their way to places I didn't even know I had. I pressed hard against his warm moist lips, savoring the moment. Together we let go, but it left me wanting more.

"Not a bad kisser," he said as if he were some kind of authority.

I responded, trying to pretend a kiss like this was no big deal. "You're all right for a straight guy," I said, surprising myself with such a clever comeback. Without hesitation, I leaned over and kissed him back. This time our tongues met. I had never been kissed before in any form or fashion, but I instinctively knew what to do. It wasn't at all disgusting like I had once thought. Instead, it fed a hunger I didn't know I had. Little tingles trickled up my neck and down my spine as Ken fondled my hair with his delicate touch. Once more my thighs squeezed together in reply.

When we finally came up for air, I pushed him away.

"So, where's my hair tie?" I scolded, hoping the gesture would keep me from blushing.

He laughed, "Wouldn't you like to know?"

"I would," I said firmly, as I checked both of his hands with mine.

He opened them wide. "Not there."

"So, where is it?" I demanded.

"I've got it in a very safe place."

"I need it," I said, shaking my long hair as Candice would. He grabbed a fistful. "See, that's why I need my leather band. Besides, I hate my hair in my face," I lied.

"I like you better with it down. It makes you look like an angel. Though I doubt angels smoke pot."

We laughed.

"Come on, give it to me."

I reached in his pocket, feeling the soft leather. But before I could snatch it up, Ken pulled away.

"Now, now, I told you, I'll keep it safe." Once more he grasped both my wrists firmly, kissing me again.

I wanted to surrender to him. I'd never been pursued like this before. I loved it. I was Cinderella all over again.

Slowly, the old worry seeped in, distracting me from the glorious moment.

What's he gonna think when he finds out? I wondered.

"Hey, what's the matter?" he asked, giving my shoulders a squeeze.

"Nothing," I lied, noting I must be careful about expressing fear on my face.

He kissed me again.

We were now sitting on a cement planter near the entranceway playfully bantering and teasing each other about our interests and beliefs. As we cradled each other around the waist, we argued about the Vietnam War, legalization of marijuana, and free love. I purposely avoided my revelations about religion as he disclosed that he went to a church similar to mine. Despite the fact that we took opposite positions on almost everything we discussed, it was so easy to be with him. By the end of the evening we'd swapped phone numbers with plans to go to a movie the next weekend. When Candice hollered her last call for a ride home, we kissed goodbye several more times.

As I climbed into Candice's car, she commented on my new glow. "Don't need any lights in here with your lit-up face," she said laughing. "Who is he, anyway?"

"His name's Ken. He goes to our rival school."

"He's cute!"

"He thought the same about you," I admitted.

"Yeah? Well, he's definitely interested in you, Geri. It was written all over his face when I saw you guys in the hallway."

"Seems that way, don't it?" I said, grinning widely.

"So, tell me more?"

"He's a pretty cool kisser."

"Ooh, Geri. You do move quickly."

My smile grew wider. I liked having to stretch my cheeks so far. Sweet sixteen had come and gone without my lips being touched by a kiss. I welcomed the residual soreness that came from rubbing his five-o-clock shadow.

"So, we go to The House tomorrow night?" Candice asked.

Suddenly I felt a pang of regret. The happiness I'd been feeling started to slip. The mention of The House brought conflict to my mind, dampening my spirits.

"Uh, well…" I finally answered.

"Ah, come on," Candice urged. "You can still have fun with your little Ken doll. He'll still be there when you get back."

"I know. It's just that…"

"What? You afraid he'll find out and not like you?"

"No. He wouldn't find out. Don't worry, I'm going. It just feels kinda funny now."

As I left Candice and headed into my house, I wondered how Ken would feel if he knew what I did on most weekends. I had two secrets to keep now. *Oh well,* I said to myself, *he'll ditch me anyway, as soon as he figures me out.*

The sweet taste of his kisses lingered. They left me craving more. I had to figure a way through this quandary. *I've straddled two worlds before*, I reminded myself. *I've been living two lives a lot lately anyway. I can keep them separate*, I promised. Despite my convictions, doubt twisted the knot in my stomach as I wondered how long I could keep it up.

Chapter 15

The Den of Iniquity

September 1970

Day 2

"Did you tell your mom you were staying at my house tonight?" Candice asked, as I climbed into her boat-sized Olds.

"Yeah. You, too?" I replied, noticing how green her eyes looked with the kelly sweater she wore. We had both decorated our necks with leather chokers. The silver peace sign which dangled in the center accented our scoop-necked collars. With bell-bottom jeans and brown leather boots, the only difference in our attire was the rosy pink t-shirt peeking out from behind my army jacket.

"Ditto," came Candice's answer. "I sure hope she never bothers to try and get ahold of me one of these times."

"No kidding!" I agreed, the thought of it making my knees go weak.

"I've got my Doors album this time," Candice announced.

"Cool," I said. "I so love that song, '*Break on Through*'."

"I know," she said with a groan. "You've only listened to it a million times. I'm surprised the grooves are still there for the needle to find." We laughed.

As Candice drove east out of the city toward our destination, I couldn't help admiring the view. An expanse of thick forest unfolded before us. As Davison Road wound its way through the red, yellow and green treetops, it looked like a Scottish plaid ribbon was stretched across the skyline. Despite the crisp air, I rolled down my window and breathed in the sweet smell of dying leaves.

"Isn't it so pretty?" I asked, already knowing the answer.

"I know," Candice said. "Check out that watermelon colored one on the right."

I turned to look. "Oh, yeah!" I said, feigning I had found it, wondering why I did. Though I could see the mass of trees in their brilliance, picking one out of the bunch was impossible. "They look so fake, don't they? It's almost like they're made from crepe paper decorated for Halloween or something."

"Yeah, they do!" Candice agreed.

A worried thought hit me. *What if I won't be able to see them someday?* I pushed the thought away. *Nah! They look too real to disappear.*

Candice gave a deep sigh, unaware of my internal debate. "Ain't it weird that the trees are at their best when they're about to die?" There was sadness in her voice. "It seems like nothing pretty or good ever lasts."

"I know!" I said, sharing her feeling.

We drove in silence for a while. I wondered what Ken might be doing. I wished I could ask Candice to turn around, but I knew how much she wanted to go to The House.

At last we arrived. Candice pulled into the driveway and we headed to the door. As we approached the white aluminum-sided dwelling, I inhaled the crispy fall air one last time. When the door opened, an overpowering mixture of patchouli oil and burning incense momentarily suffocated me. I reminded myself I would adjust to the lack of oxygen and took shallow breaths as I entered.

A familiar gravelly voice greeted us. "Hi girls," it said. The voice belonged to the lady of the house. She was in her early forties, but her cropped brown hair and wrinkled face made her look as if she were sixty.

"Hi, Caribou!" Candice and I said in unison.

Caribou wore her usual apparel. A brightly colored floral house duster hung so loosely around her it was hard to tell her true size, which I had learned was bone skinny. Her white-socked feet seemed to always dwell in fluffy blue slippers. We made our greetings from the little vestibule which stood at the top of the basement stairs, dividing the kitchen from the living room.

"Hang up your coats, gals. How was your week?"

"Okay," I said, throwing my dad's jacket over one of the hooks on the wall near the entrance.

Caribou pulled her pack of cigarettes from the front pocket of her housedress. She stuck one in her mouth and retrieved her gold Zippo lighter. The click of the metal top told me one of her favorite vices was lit. I dreaded having to breathe the smoke, but I resisted the urge to go outside. The wrongness of the place made me homesick, a feeling I'd been able to keep at bay on previous visits there.

"Danny's downstairs," Caribou said, blowing her smoke directly our way. "Got a new crossword book if you wanna join me later."

"Sure Caribou," I said, more aware of her deceptive kindness this time. Although she was always welcoming, Candice and I quickly learned that she had expectations for her son's friends. This included keeping her company and doing crosswords. There were others that unfolded as we continued our visits, a mutual agreement to keep quiet about what went on at The House being the most important expectation of all.

Other facets of this unlikely mother would have been hard to believe had I not experienced them for myself. I was not sure if it was the death of Danny's father ten years earlier or if there existed flaws in her character, but Caribou provided for her seventeen-year-old son in ways they never mentioned on *Leave It to Beaver* or any other TV show for that matter. Caribou's support of her version of the game of football was the one that was most obvious.

As Candice and I started down the basement steps, Caribou called, "There's some bean soup on the stove if you're hungry, girls."

"Maybe later," Candice said.

But Caribou persisted. "It's a good idea to eat something before you play football, you know."

"Yeah, we'll be sure to grab some beforehand," I said. "Thanks."

"Well, at least have something to drink. You know you'll need that." She walked over to the fridge and grabbed two Cokes. I turned and headed back up the few stairs I had already descended. Spurt-clink, spurt-clink, came a most familiar sound. My homesickness grew as she slipped the bottle tops of the eight-ounce glass Cokes into the combination bottle opener and top catcher. A similar contraption mounted on the side of the cupboard could be found in my kitchen too.

She placed the two bottles in my outstretched hands. "Thanks," I said, handing one to Candice, hurrying down the steps before she could think of something else to hold us up.

When we reached the bottom, we found Danny and his band setting up their instruments. They always practiced on the weekends when they didn't have a gig. Danny played lead guitar, Rob the bass, Mike keyboards, and Jim played the drums.

We'd met them the last Sunday in August at one of the Wilson Park Battle of the Bands concerts. This phenomenon was a monthly event put on by WTAC Radio. Candice and I never missed going. Bands competed for money and a chance at a recording session. The winner was picked by votes, which could only be given by concertgoers who bought slices of pizza from Palace Pizza House.

We were sitting on the grass not far from the stage when Danny's ghost-like figure approached. With the sun behind me, even I could see he looked like death warmed over. He was tall, pale and skinny, his long stringy white hair hanging down as far as mine and Candice's did. He wore a tie-dyed t-shirt and frayed jeans that I assumed were bell bottoms. Several gold chains sparkled in the sunlight around his neck.

"I had to come and touch you." He bent down and placed his hand on Candice's shoulder. "You are such a radiant beauty!" he said to her in a slow spacey voice. "You looked so far out from the stage. And you are just as beautiful close up."

With a nervous laugh, Candice said, "Really?" I could tell she was both embarrassed and flattered by this guy.

"Yeah, man. Your hair…it made an illuminating aura around you. It looked like the sun behind you was emanating from your spirit. You are so filled with radiance."

Candice's girlish giggle gave her away. She was definitely getting off on the poetic charm this guy was bestowing on her. In no time, the two of them were walking through the park, hand in hand, while I hung with other freaks I knew.

During our ride home that evening, Candice told me about her new love.

"He wants to be a rock star."

"That's cool," I said. "How old is he?"

She brushed her hair back over her shoulder as she drove.

"Seventeen."

"Where does he go to school?" I asked, mimicking her gesture.

"He doesn't. He dropped out last year."

"Really? Does he live alone?"

"No. He lives with his mom, who sounds really cool. She thinks Danny is so smart that school was boring him, so she let him quit. He loves to read books like we do and has lots of the same ideas as us."

"Far out," I said, despite feeling a bit skeptical.

"He wants us to come visit him. He lives in Davison."

"Davison? That's about half an hour away, ain't it?" I said, scolding myself for sounding like a questioning adult.

"I can drive it. Wanna go with me next Saturday?"

"Right on!" I said.

"He says we can spend the night since it is a bit far. I figured we could just tell our folks we are at a sleepover at a friend's house or something. His mom'll be there and everything."

"Well, sure, why not?" I said.

Despite the nag of doubt in my gut, it felt delightfully naughty venturing off to hang at a musician's pad. When we got there, the difference in the home atmosphere was instantly noticeable. The aroma alone was the first giveaway. Calling his mother 'Caribou' was another clue their relationship was not typical.

Maybe because of the oddities, or despite them, Candice and I both thought the place was pretty groovy. Long strings of wooden beads hung over the entranceway to the basement, making a rich hollow sound when they parted. Visitors to Danny's lair were enveloped by a blue and purple parachute hanging from the ceiling. Candles and black lights cast elusive shadows around the room, creating a mystical effect.

Though this den of ghostly silhouettes made my visual acuity diminish to almost nothing, it didn't matter. Here I felt accepted. The straightforward approach by Danny and his friends regarding my visual impairment was so inviting. At times I purposely did not try to find things. I was growing fond of the special treatment I received by the freaks. Instead of being obnoxiously independent, I allowed my hand to be taken to guide me. I figured there was no harm done, as the guys seemed to gain pleasure from their gestures.

But now, despite some of the comforts and after visiting every weekend for six weeks, the coolness of the place was fading. In fact, it felt foreign and foreboding. It took a certain amount of mental energy to grapple with the conflict between right and wrong. Though I was rebellious, my parents and the religious teachings instilled in me continued to have a hold on my conscience. I liked the idea of hanging with a counterculture of people who believed that weirder was better, but I also knew what I was doing was deceitful. I couldn't pass up the chance to be accepted with no worry about being fully sighted. Besides, I'd lived weird most of my life. I simply couldn't decide whether it was better to be a good girl and try to fit in with the normal world or to do bad things to belong and fight my sense of right and wrong. Having met Ken, a genuine good guy, battling my conscience seemed harder.

"Where the fuck you been, Candice?" Danny scolded as we pushed our way through the beaded doorway.

"I told you I couldn't get here 'til five, Danny," Candice said obediently.

"Then sit the fuck down here and send me that energy of yours that makes me play so good!"

I winced at the sound of the forbidden "F" word, scolding myself for still being so prissy. Until I joined the hippie cult, I'd never dared to even hear that word, let alone speak it. But for most of my freaky friends, the "F" word seemed to give some sort of catharsis.

Candice did as he said. I sat on an overstuffed pillow covered in tapestry material, one of many that made a circle around Danny's stool.

The other musicians were setting up behind him.

"Hey there, foxy ladies!" Rob said, fiddling with something.

"Hi Rob," I answered, giving him the peace sign. Candice gave her greetings as well.

"Far out shirt there, Geri," Danny said complimenting me in a voice much kinder than the one he used with Candice.

"Thanks," I said, using my forefinger to trace the scooped neckline of my new pink shirt. I took hold of the medallion to secure the momentary experience of feeling pretty. Compared to Candice's extravagant beauty, I tended not to feel terribly attractive.

"Gonna play football with me tonight?" Danny asked. Though he directed the question to me, Candice answered, "Sure!"

"How 'bout you, Geri?"

"Well, I think we should eat something first, don't you, Candice?"

"Spoils the jag!" Robby warned. "It cuts into the intensity."

"I can handle it," Candice said. "Besides, I like that it makes me so I'm not hungry. Saves that many more calories."

Both Candice and I got off on the fact that a month of playing football helped us lose weight. We now understood why Caribou was so thin. After all, she was the one who so kindly organized the supplies. I preferred to take her advice to eat beforehand, however, as I didn't particularly like the ache I got from playing with an empty stomach.

"So, ya ready to drop then?" Danny asked. I heard the snap of his little plastic box. The sound of his movements told me he was holding out his hand.

"Let's play ball," he said, as if announcing the beginning of a baseball game.

"Thanks, Danny," Candice said.

"Here ya go, Geri," he offered, placing his fingers on mine. "May you score a touchdown!" I knew he was not referring to the kind that came from carrying a pigskin a hundred yards through an H-shaped goal. I thought of my father and worked to ward off the never-ending guilt. I responded to the kindness in Danny's voice by opening my hand and accepting two of his little oval-shaped pills. Had I been able to see them in the black light, fluorescent red lines would have revealed a familiar outline. There was no doubt they were intended to imitate the object of the sport my dad so proudly played in his college days. *What would he think?* I asked myself, as shameful thoughts slipped into my mind.

"Groovy," I lied, sounding cool despite my hesitation. I popped them into my mouth and swallowed them down with a swig of Coke. I felt my stomach tighten in an all-too-familiar way. It twisted up with a mixture of emotions that I didn't want to know about. *How could I feel so good about Danny's thoughtful gesture when he was giving me such a questionable gift? How could I like his compliments when he was being so rude to Candice?* Thoughts of Ken found their way to my mind, complicating matters.

Don't worry, it'll all be gone in a few minutes, I told myself. But it's not real! I argued in my head.

Danny strummed his guitar.

"Play something," Candice said affectionately.

"Whatta ya wanna hear?"

"How 'bout *Blowin' in the Wind?* I love the way you do that one," she said.

"All right by me. We'll hit it without the juice," Danny said to the other musicians. I was glad they would play the song acoustically. I leaned back, wiggling my body into the overstuffed pillow. Typically the amplified music was unbearably loud, making me feel truly blind. My decision to relinquish my usual need to act sighted came in handy. Spending time in Danny's basement had forced me to realize how much I used sounds to figure out my surroundings. Sometimes the intensity of the music made me feel trapped. So far I'd managed to keep this to myself.

"Ah, man!" Robby complained, "I been wantin' to try out the new amp."

"Take a chill," Danny barked, "This song's acoustic. Can't groove to folk music if it's electrified."

"Ah, shit!" Robby muttered as I heard him flip open his case. I assumed he was replacing his electric bass.

Jim rolled his drums and Mike adjusted the volume on his mini keyboard.

"And a one, and a two, and a three," Danny counted softly, and then strummed the six strings for the first chord. The others joined in, each doing their part for the introduction of the song.

As we sang Bob Dylan's questioning lyrics about hypocrisy and what is really important in life, I thought about my own doubts and felt glad that someone with credibility had put them to music. I heard Candice go flat on a couple of notes as the words to the chorus rolled off our tongues. I hoped Danny noticed how much better my singing was, and then chastised myself for thinking such thoughts. We finished the song with my voice dominating everyone else's.

"That was really cool, Danny," Candice said, apparently unaware of my obnoxious attempt to take over.

"Yeah, Danny, play *Where Have All the Flowers Gone*, will ya?" I urged, knowing I did this one exceptionally well. He started the chord sequence to the melody. The band members filled in the empty spaces. Again, Candice and I provided the poetry.

As we sang, I became aware the thump in my heart was getting stronger. I felt the familiar rush of blood running through my veins. The troublesome thoughts plaguing my mind were disappearing. Danny strummed the last round of chords. My voice gained power. I held the final note long and beautifully. I could hardly contain my excitement as my vocal cords vibrated with a rich trill.

"Far out!" Jim said. "You're pretty darn good at them vocals."

Holding back my joy at the compliment, I privately gloated over my performance. Singing meant a lot to me. I loved showing off and secretly wished Danny would ask me to sing in his band.

"You sound like Joni Mitchell," Danny said.

My heart burst with joy. I couldn't have asked for a better tribute. I'd been practicing with Joni every chance I got. I'd put her records on my turntable and followed along with her in the privacy of my bedroom. I'd worked and worked to figure out how she breathed and flipped her larynx from one end of her voice box to the other. She had a range and control as good as, if not better than, Barbra Streisand, another vocalist I admired.

"Really?" I said, my guilt and worries no longer present.

"Yeah, you're pretty far out. Try singing her version of *Woodstock*."

"Uh, not sure I know all the words, but I can try."

Mike tapped out the first four notes on his ivory. There was no place for the other instruments in this intro. I listened as he repeated them. When he hit the fifth note, it would be time for me to start.

I began to sing.

Jim hit the downbeat on his drum and Danny and Robby strummed their notes. With the power of benzedrine behind me, I let myself go.

As I sang, I thanked Joni for her Ladies of the Canyon album. Though Crosby, Stills, Nash, and Young had made the song popular after the famous Woodstock outdoor concert in 1969, it was Joni who actually wrote it. I loved her use of minor and major chords together in the same song. The variant sound matched my soul, squeezing out emotions I would not have reached otherwise.

Like butter, my vocal cords slipped up and down and across the octaves Joni so loved to play with. The melody ended with the do-oo-oos unique to Joni's version of the ballad.

"Right on!" Rob said. Once more I had ended with perfect pitch.

"That was pretty far out, Geri," Candice said. I knew she meant it. Again thoughts of deceit and betrayal slid across my mind. If she had sung so beautifully, I would be green with envy. Candice was far too nice for such jealous thoughts and I knew it, but the thrill of the moment helped me push the nasty feelings aside. I felt so powerful and capable.

"You got yourself a mighty voice there, lady!" Danny added.

The affection he sent my way both excited and scared me. I flashed to Ken, then thought about how stuck on Danny Candice was. I felt thrilled that someone who hit on Candice was sending me affectionate vibes, but I dared not act on them. To cover up my devious impulse to take over the evening—including Danny—I said, "Let's all sing something together. What do you wanna sing, Candice?"

"I don't care."

There was irritation in her voice. Fearing she may be on to me, I persisted. "Come on, you pick this time Candice."

"I really don't care what we sing, Geri!" she insisted. The power of the speed began to cloud my perceptions. *Is she mad at me?* I wondered. *Can she tell what I'm thinking?* Wanting to counteract my hidden desires, I said, "But Candice, you should have a turn. I don't want you to feel left out."

The guys were fiddling around on their instruments. The discord of sound aggravated me further. Candice turned abruptly in my direction.

"I didn't know I was being left out," she said, annoyance, now without a doubt, present in her voice.

I grasped a hunk of hair and pulled it across my face like Ken had. Hiding behind a mask seemed like the safest thing I could do at the moment.

"You're not," I said, my voice sounding phony. I tugged hard on my hair until it hurt. Letting it drop, I tried to rectify the situation. "I mean, I only want you to have some say in what we do."

Candice stood.

"Where ya goin'?"

"Upstairs."

"Ah, come on, Candice, stay down here. We'll sing your favorite song, then. You like *Five Hundred Miles*. Let's sing that one."

"Yeah, sit down!" Danny ordered. "Nothin' upstairs for ya. We're singin' now."

She stopped moving, but didn't sit. I could tell she was angry. I didn't like the way Danny bossed her, but I was glad he'd told her to stay.

"Sit the fuck down, I said!"

"I wanna go see Caribou," she said, obviously upset.

"You don't need ta see Caribou. I thought ya came ta see me."

"I told her I'd do a crossword with her."

"So do it later. We're singin' right now."

Candice didn't move. I knew she wanted to leave and probably go cry in the bathroom or something.

"Sit the fuck down!" Danny yelled. I winced. Candice did what she was told. I felt ashamed and sorry for her.

"You like *Five Hundred miles*, do ya?" Danny said, a little nicer this time. Candice didn't say anything.

"'Five Hundred Miles' it is. Hit it, Guys. One, two three…"

All together, the band began the sequence of chords that led to the beginning of the melody. Despite my guilt, I sang. *"If you miss the train I'm on, you will know that I am gone, you can hear the whistle blow a hundred miles."*

But my friend wasn't singing. I nudged her with my shoulder.

"A hundred miles, a hundred miles—" I squeezed her elbow this time.

"Come on." I whispered to her. "Join me."

In a soft tone, Candice did as I asked.

"You can hear the whistle blow a hundred miles. Not a shirt on my back—"

Moving closer, I lowered my voice so hers could be heard. She sang a little louder. I gripped her wrist and squeezed it affectionately. The gesture felt condescending. The students from That School came to mind. Despite my internal reprimands, a sense of power surged through my speeding body.

As the song continued, my kind gesture of staying even with Candice's voice disappeared. I sang more beautifully than ever, again hoping it would be noticed. *God, it feels good to have all this energy and control over my voice,* I thought. *It can't be all bad feeling like this, can it?* Ignoring the little voice in my head telling me otherwise, my euphoria overrode any desire to be considerate to my friend.

Five hundred miles, five hundred miles,

Five hundred miles, five hundred miles,

Lord I'm five hundred miles away from home.

Chapter 16

A Head-On Collision

December 1970

From the far recesses of my mind, I heard a faint call. "Geri." I lifted my head out of the pillow and listened. Deciding I'd been dreaming, I dropped my befuddled head back into its nest.

"Geri!" This time the voice was loud and clear. There was no doubt. It belonged to my mother.

Too tired to lift my head, I answered into the pillow, "What?"

Unable to hear me, she yelled louder. "Geri, do you want to answer the phone or not?"

With her mention of the phone, I managed to croak, "Wait a minute!"

"Hurry up, he's already been waiting on the telephone for ten minutes. I'll be surprised if he's still on the line."

"It must be Ken," I decided. I realized it was Sunday afternoon and my irritability rose. "Why didn't you make sure I got up sooner, then?" I scolded, using my nastiest tone. Tippy ran from his place next to me. Anger pushed me from my bed. I stomped across the floor and whipped my terrycloth robe from its hook. I felt a twinge of shame as I threw it over my shoulders, thinking about how she'd made it for me last Christmas.

"Then why aren't you up before four in the afternoon if you don't want to miss calls?" my mother barked back.

"It's the weekend!" I screamed, pulling the sash of the robe around my waist and heading down the stairs. Prickly electric sensations shot up and down my legs as I forced the tendons to stretch and flex.

"It's still way too late to be sleeping in," she argued.

My mother's voice grated on my ears like fingernails running down a chalkboard. "I can sleep in as late as I want!" I shrieked.

"If that's how you're gonna treat me, then I'll just let you sleep the next time."

"Better not," I mumbled under my breath as I stepped off the last stair.

"What smart-aleck remark was that?" she dared me to answer.

"Nothin'," I snapped, rushing past her to the kitchen to get the phone.

"Hello?" I said, wincing at the unbelievable switch I'd made to a pleasant voice.

"Oh, brother," I heard my mother say as she opened the fridge.

I flashed her a warning look. She knew how I felt about her hanging around when I talked on the phone.

"Hi." It was Ken for sure. He typically called Sunday afternoons. I'd been seeing him every Friday night since our first meeting four months earlier. We held opposite views on many subjects, but we'd really hit it off. We spent the majority of our time going to the movies, holding hands, driving around town in his father's car, and stopping to neck in out-of-the-way places. Singing to the radio was the best. Sometimes Ken would croon to me. His deep bass voice and exaggerated movements always made me laugh. Of course, *Color My World* by Chicago turned out to be our song. No matter where we were, car or grocery store, if it came on the radio, he'd wrap his arms around me and sing it in my ear. Ken would have been glad to take me out Saturdays as well, but I reserved that time for Candice and our trips to The House which he, of course, knew nothing about.

"Did ya get lots of studying done at Candice's last night?" Ken asked.

"Ah, yeah," I lied. "How 'bout you, did you have fun with Kurt and John?"

"Yeah, we went and shot some pool, then bowled a few games. I lost."

He's so wholesome, I decided, picturing Ken and his buddies throwing a ball down an alley to knock down a bunch of pins. *What would he think if he knew I'd dropped six hits of speed since seven yesterday evening?* He had no idea that I'd stayed awake until nine this morning. How would he feel about me if he heard me using the F- word intermingled with 'far outs' and 'right ons?' Brushing the tangles from my face, I willed these dangerous thoughts away.

"Bummer!" I said, keeping my secrets well hidden.

"Wanna go cruise the A with me? I got my dad's wheels. I can be over in a few if you're free?"

"Sure," I said, recalling how much he loved driving through the A&W, waving to his buddies who did likewise with their girls. Typically this little root beer and hot dog stand only stayed open in the summer. This year they'd decided to brave the winter weather. Except for the poor car hops who delivered orders to the customers in the freezing cold, most of us young cruisers were pretty happy about the idea.

"I can be ready in about fifteen. Just give me a chance to comb my hair and put on something besides my bathrobe."

"I'll be glad to brush your hair for you," he said suggestively, "and there's no need to change out of your bathrobe on my account."

He is so straight, I mused to myself. His choice of words and charming comments were almost too much to take. The hippie guys I hung out with would simply ask a girl if she wanted to ball. There'd be no subtle suggestions or flirtations leading to romantic interludes.

"It's a terrycloth robe," I informed him. "It don't make me look all that attractive if you wanna know the truth."

"I'll bet you'd look good in a gunny sack," he complimented. "I'll be over in a few."

"Okay. See ya."

I hung up the phone. Hoping to avoid my mother, I hurried past her to the stairs. "I don't suppose you'd think of asking permission to go out," my mother scoffed, scrutinizing me from her chair.

"I'm almost nineteen. I shouldn't have to ask permission to go out on a Sunday afternoon!"

"You still live in my house. I'd think it'd only be a sign of respect. Neither of your sisters would have gotten away with such behavior."

I stopped at the stairwell entrance and turned to look at her. As I considered my retort, I absorbed the view. The living room where I'd spent much of my life looked so foreign. I could hardly believe it was the same place that once held a bunch of rambunctious kids. Even then my mother's scolding didn't curtail our roughhousing on the furniture. Looking at her now, I decided her small demeanor must have fostered my disregard for her feelings. But as she sat there in her burnt orange overstuffed rocker, I knew I had no right to blame her for my ugliness. I quickly revived my critical notions of her though. I hated how hideous she looked in the worn, faded red cardigan sweater she always wore. Not only did it clash with the burnt orange chair, but neither went well with the ancient red couch. As I admonished her in my mind for having poor fashion taste, I failed to include how much she always sacrificed to be sure her children could have better. For years she'd dreamed of new carpet, furniture, and real curtains instead of Venetian blinds. One year she got as far as ordering a gold rug, but a need arose for one of us kids, so once again she did without. Now, only a few days shy of sixty-one, she remained mismatched with totally gray hair. The glasses framing her small face made her look old and frail.

"Well, I ain't my sisters," I informed her, disregarding the goodness in her heart.

Nothing was said for a few moments. She just sat there in her usual position staring at me. Her right elbow rested on the arm of the chair with her hand in the air. She held a cigarette between her first two fingers. All I saw was an enemy.

"I don't know what's gotten into you, Geri," my mother said, softening her tone. "For the last two months you spend every weekend at that Candice's house, come home Sunday morning, sleep all day, and talk to me like I'm a piece of dirt. Your father won't let me say boo to you. He thinks you have to figure it all out for yourself, but I'm getting really tired of your nasty tone and mean, disrespectful comments."

"Well, maybe if you'd leave me alone like Dad says I wouldn't be so nasty." But my words didn't ward off the truth that haunted me every time I found myself in my mother's presence. I knew she knew something was up. I don't know if I figured being nasty would keep her from finding out or if it was to let her know she was right about something being wrong.

As I turned to get away from her, I saw her reach down to her lap and pull something up toward her face. In a second, I realized what it was. She was now dabbing at her eyes with one of my dad's white hankies. With a hint of affection in her tone, my mother revealed a confidence that shook me deeply.

"You might be able to convince your dad that you're old enough to be independent and do what you want, but I know that something is not right." She paused briefly, swallowing hard. "You've lost weight, you always have bags under your eyes, and you fly off the handle at the drop of a hat. I don't know what you and that Candice girl are doing every weekend, but I know it isn't homework. Your father knows it, too. He's just too worried about you to say so," she warned, her sadness turning back to anger.

"Why is he worried about me?" I asked defensively, not sure I really wanted to know. "I'm fine. I'm losing weight because I want to."

She blew her nose and continued. "You don't need to lose any more weight, Geri. Whether you believe me or not, your dad worries about you every single day." The image of my Father's troubled face made my heart ache.

"There is nothing to worry about," I pleaded, hoping I would be believed.

"Easy for you to say, but you can't fool me. I try to tell your father you need more discipline, but he won't hear of it, so I have to sit here and do nothing!"

"Well I don't get why he has to worry so much," I said, ignoring my mother's concerns altogether.

"Because..." she began.

"Because why?" I demanded. Turning her head away from me, my mother took a long drag off her cigarette. Impatiently, I repeated my command.

"Because why?"

"Because...He thinks if you're going blind, you need to have friends."

Astonished at these words, I challenged my mother's interpretations. "He wouldn't think that! I've always had friends. Why would he think such a thing?"

"Because you're not getting any more sighted, Geri. You're losing vision, and it's getting harder for you to blend in with the others. And those are your dad's words, by the way. He says that even if you're not always doing exactly the best things, at least you have someone to spend time with."

I struggled between feelings of rage and fear, but refused to accept what I was hearing. "That's ridiculous!" I yelled. "You're lying!"

"I'm not!" she countered.

"But at my last checkup the doctor said my eyes haven't gotten worse for two years now!"

"You only hear what you want to hear, Geri. They said the remaining red pigments in your retinas haven't died out for two years, but that your peripheral vision had narrowed."

"Bullshit! How can my vision narrow if my pigment hasn't blackened anymore? Those doctors don't know what they're talking about anyway. Hell, they'd have it so I didn't ride my bike or do anything according to their stupid tests. I can do exactly the same things I've always done, and I don't even wear my glasses most of the time!"

"Have it your way. No one can tell you anything, anyway, Geri. But you can't stop the rest of us from worrying about you."

"You've got no business worrying about me!" I screamed louder. "Especially Dad!"

"Think what you want. He's no dummy, Geri. He knows you're up to something that's not good, just like I do."

Did he know I was into drugs? I wondered. Did he think doing drugs was the only way I could get friends? Was doing drugs okay if a kid was losing vision? Realizing I could not sort this all out, I switched my tactic.

"You're jealous 'cause Dad likes me, and you don't!" I said through clenched teeth.

I heard my mother sigh. Once more she raised her cigarette to her lips and took a puff. When she exhaled, she spoke. "There is nothing further from the truth. You don't have to believe me if you don't want to, but this has nothing to do with jealousy. It has to do with you and how you act. Geri, your dad loves you. He's afraid for you. But if you're spending time with boys or having sex or getting drunk on the weekends, then you're headed for trouble."

Despite the slight tinge of relief I felt when I realized my mother had not included using drugs in her list of possible wrongdoings, my indignation prevailed.

"So that's what this is all about," I said. "You're just afraid I'm having sex. You are jealous of me! You've never wanted me to be pretty or hang out with boys. That's why you're being so mean to me."

But she didn't say anything. She simply stubbed out her cigarette in the ashtray, got up, and headed into the kitchen. I heard her descend the basement stairs. I knew she would be crying down there. My momentary sense of triumph in manipulating the conversation quickly faded. I knew there was no justification for my unsuitable behaviors or fabricating my mother's wrongdoings. Instead, my illusion of victory was replaced with sorrow. "You're rotten!" I told my evil self. Climbing the steps, Tippy following behind, I wondered how things between my mother and I had gone from bad to worse. When I reached my room, Tippy found his spot on the bed. Another rush of guilt tore at my heart, as I pulled off the robe she'd taken such care to make. "How could I accuse her of such terrible things?" I asked my dog, remembering how she'd always gone to such trouble to make us kids snuggly flannel pajamas. "How could I be so mean to her, Tippy?" I said, wishing I could run back, find her, and tell her I was sorry.

In my hesitation, I decided it would be too risky. Ken would be here any minute. Besides, I was afraid I'd confess to all the terrible things I'd been doing. The strain of living two lives was wearing on me. "It's getting harder to keep them apart," I told the two of us as I slid my flower-covered stovepipe jeans over my butt. Threading the end of my wide braided belt into the ornate brass buckle, I couldn't prevent my mother's comments from filtering through. The last hole in the belt no longer pulled the pants snug enough around my hips. In the past, I would have had to lie back on the bed in order to zip them up. Now a size six would likely fit perfectly if I could round up the money to buy a pair.

I ran the brush through my snarls when my eleven-year-old dog leaped off the bed, ran down the stairs and started barking at the front door. I quickly slipped on my clogs and clunked my way down to open the door.

"Hey!" Ken said, stepping in. Tippy wagged his tail, jumping up to greet him. "Hi, Tippy," Ken said, patting him and holding him back at the same time.

"Come on, Tippy. Don't get your hair all over Ken, you silly boy," I told him, signaling him to lie down.

"Okay, it's your turn," Ken said, giving me a big hug. The familiar smell of his cologne made the tension in my neck relax. His big, wide smile melted my harsh mood. He certainly was cute. A blue turtleneck peeked out of a light blue wool V-neck sweater that showed between the open flaps of his brown corduroy jacket. With his five-eleven frame, my sixty-four inch body with shoes made me stretch to reach his lips. I wanted so badly to collapse into his arms, confess the sins of the last twenty-four hours and all the weekends before, but he would be too shocked. He'd never believe how awful I had acted toward my mother.

Ken would never have bad-mouthed his parents. He was on a fairly short leash compared to lots of guys his age. He had an eleven o'clock curfew, had to earn the use of his dad's car, and he never called his mother Mom. Whenever I suggested that he should be treated more as an adult, he explained that he had no problem with the rules his folks laid out. Unlike me, he believed that his parents were the providers, the adults, and he was lucky to have the privileges he did.

"You look really pretty in that green sweater," he said. "Is it new?"

"It's, uh, Candice's," I admitted, almost telling him it was mine. I let out a sigh of relief, glad I hadn't told another lie.

"Ready to go?" he asked.

"Sure. Let me grab my coat." I walked over to the hall closet and reached for my camel suede jacket complete with fringed sleeves and double-breasted gold buttons. My hair cascaded over my shoulders, as I pulled it out from under my collar.

Before we headed out the door Ken asked, "Aren't you gonna say goodbye to your parents?"

"Ah, well, Dad's playing bridge and my mom's in the basement. She knows I'm going."

"Okay," he said uncertainly.

As we headed out, I thought about the words my mother had spoken to me. *What would Ken think of my dad's worries about me having friends?* I wondered.

Ken had always been up front about my vision. On our first date to the movies, he'd simply asked about it straight out. It had been a mild fall evening with no need for a jacket. I wore a long sleeved cotton blouse with dark green pin-stripes that warded off any chill. It also warded off any comments Ken might make about my weird attire. I had reluctantly shunned the jeans and put on matching green cords. Walking my typical half step behind him, I smiled at how well I'd matched his preppy look. He wore a pin-striped shirt with color-coordinated pants. The only difference was the color. He wore blue.

As we walked from the car to the theater, I strained to be sure I didn't bump into anything or fall down stairs. He must have noticed something because, while standing in line, he turned and said, "So, what's wrong with your eyes?"

I was astonished, uncertain of how to answer him. I decided to play dumb and ask. "Uh, what do you mean?"

"You don't see right, do you?"

I looked behind me, half expecting to find someone holding up a sign tipping him off.

"I can see okay!" I lied.

"No, you can't," he said emphatically. "You've got something wrong with your vision. What is it?"

I struggled to cover my distress when I asked, "Who told you about it?"

"Nobody. I can just tell. Your right eye is always turned to the side and you walk with your head stuck out in front of you. I know you're straining to see."

My jaw dropped. I was horrified. Ken reached out and tenderly gripped my shoulders.

"It's okay, you know," he said gently, his kindness threatening to make me cry.

Afraid of exposing my feelings, I pulled back and firmly said, "It's really no big deal."

He stared at me, lips parted, shaking his head from side to side. I knew he didn't believe a word I was saying.

"Really. I mean, I do have some trouble with depth perception, but other than that, it's okay."

"Are you sure?" he asked. "How come you can't read, then?"

"Why do you think I can't read?" I asked, terrified to hear his answer.

"Because, when we went to Coney Island for dinner, you had the menu upside down!"

Suddenly, all the blood in my entire body raced to my face. I was mortified. *How could I have been so careless? I should've made sure the big letters were upright!* Ken wrapped an arm around my shoulders and let out an affectionate chuckle. "It's okay, Geri. I don't care. I thought it was cute, you sitting there trying to act like you were reading the menu."

I buried my face in his chest and wished I could melt into nothingness.

"Really Geri, it's okay. I knew you didn't see well the first night I met you, but I guess I didn't realize how bad it was. You must be one of those blind kids."

I pulled away hard, stomped the ground with my foot, and said, "I ain't one of them blind kids! And if you think you're doing me some big favor by taking me out cause you feel sorry for me, forget it. I can grab a bus and take myself home if that's what you think you're doing."

I left the line and walked away. Ken came after me, taking hold of my shirt sleeve. I wished I had the protection of my army coat and jeans. I felt vulnerable behind the thin layer of the blouse.

"Geri wait!" he said firmly. I stopped and turned back to him. "You've got it all wrong. Believe me, I'm not taking you out because I feel sorry for you." Ken gripped a handful of my hair as he had done on our first meeting. He slid his palm down the strands, pulling me closer. "I only mentioned it because I know there's other blind kids at your school. I don't care whether you can see or not. I was only curious, that's all."

"Well I care," I said pushing his wrist away. "I don't like being lumped together with 'those blind kids'. Just because I can't read a menu, don't mean I'm blind."

"So, you gonna be someday?" he asked, the innocent curiosity returning to his voice.

Instead of getting mad or denying the suggestion, I heard myself say, "Some of the doctors think I will." I couldn't believe my own voice. As I wondered why the heck I admitted to this possibility, another genuine question left his lips.

"Really? Are you scared about that?"

Again I heard myself give an outrageous answer, "Yes."

He studied me a second. "Yeah, I can imagine. I know I would be!"

But my moment of truth was over. Terrified the dam I had built would break and release a flood of endless tears, I straightened up, looked him square in the face and said, "But there's only a rare chance it'll happen. I'll be fine." He continued to look inquisitive. I thought he would ask another question, but he took my hand and said, "Well, come on. Let's go see the movie. I'm looking forward to holding your hand in the dark."

As Ken and I headed down my snow-dusted steps, I wondered what he might think about my mother's revealing story. I was disheartened and troubled that my father shared my fear that I might lose friends. We cut across the yard to his father's Impala as snowflakes fell against our cheeks. The usual thrill I'd get from this wondrous occurrence didn't show itself. Instead, I became acutely aware of the painful absence of joy.

An invisible barbed wire fence seemed to separate me from winter's beauty. I felt disconnected from it. *Am I losing my sanity?* I wondered, resisting the urge to push my make-believe barrier away. Ken was saying something to me, but this ghostly image made it impossible to hear him. I wanted to experience the peaceful winter scene, to feel the enchantment of the Christmas lights surrounding neighborhood houses. But all I felt was a cold emptiness.

"Don't ya think?" I finally heard Ken say.

"Uh, yeah," I said, hoping I was supposed to agree.

"If this keeps up, we're gonna get a white Christmas after all."

I climbed in the car and slid over next to him. *Should I tell him what my mother said?* I wondered, uncertain if I could avoid confessing everything in such an attempt. *Sure, go ahead, see if you can swindle some sympathy from the guy!* I scolded, despising my self-serving nature. *You can blame her all you want, but you're the Goddamn liar, not to mention the two-faced crap you're pulling on Candice.*

I moved my arm so it firmly held my gut, as thoughts of my devious behavior flooded my mind. Recently, I'd been accepting some of Danny's affection behind Candice's back. It started out rather innocently when Danny offered to teach me how to play the guitar. But the proximity of our bodies evoked certain thoughts, changing the focus of our contact. Although the motivation to explore other realms was primarily Danny's, I couldn't resist accommodating the affection given by someone Candice liked. Even though I knew she wouldn't see it this way, I told myself my response to Danny's kisses was really a tribute to her in a weird sort of way. If I weren't so desperate to be like her, I would never have risked my relationship with Ken and agreed to overtures from a guy I didn't find attractive. At least that's what I told myself. Sheer jealousy also played a role in my dishonorable conduct, though I tried to convince myself otherwise. In truth, I was a traitor with no scruples. I relentlessly battled my conscience but continued to act in ways that could eventually hurt everyone.

After we were situated in the car, Ken backed out of the driveway, took my hand in his, and headed toward our destination. "So, did you and Candice get a chance to do anything fun after you worked on your report?" he asked, giving my hand a loving squeeze. Resisting the urge to pull it away, I pressed my lips together. I hoped this gesture would help me keep my secret.

Oh, God, how can you be so naïve? I wanted to shout out. Don't you get it, Ken? I didn't study with Candice last night. I'm a bitch, a jezebel. I did drugs all night, fooled around with Candice's boyfriend, and then came home and slept it off until I woke up and treated my mother like shit!

"Uh, well, we watched a movie on TV," I lied instead, pinching myself hard on the thigh. *Why do I always have to make something up?* I begged my subconscious to let me know.

"You feelin' okay?" he asked.

His words took me by surprise. Fearful he could read my mind, I acted like I didn't know what he was talking about.

"Yeah, sure."

"Why are you so uptight, then?" He lifted my hand in the air as if to indicate that it had told him to be concerned.

"I'm okay," I said sheepishly.

"Well, you don't look too hot and you're as tense as they come."

"Thanks," I laughed, attempting to make light of his worry.

"You been crying or something?"

"No. Why do you keep asking me this stuff?"

"Because you seem upset, and your eyes are all red."

He let go of my hand as he made the turn into the A&W. I was glad to see there were only a few cars, and I hoped none of them were owned by anyone we knew. Ken pulled into a parking spot and left the motor running so we'd have heat.

"Ah, now I can do what I've been wanting to do for two days," he said with a hunger in his voice. After he turned in my direction, Ken wrapped his arm around me and pulled me tight. The gesture was so loving. I couldn't hold back any longer. I started to cry. Burying my head in his shoulder, I could no longer prevent my dammed-up quagmire from bursting forth.

"Geri," he said tenderly, "What's the matter?"

I couldn't speak. I just continued to weep. All the pain, fear, guilt, and sadness of my whole life poured out. My body contorted with each eruption of emotion. Like a geyser, tears gushed out in rhythmic intervals. Instinctively, Ken held me tighter, using his arms and torso to keep me from falling apart. Suddenly there was a knock on the window. I jumped. Ken shifted, letting go of me.

"Hang on, I gotta order. Want something to eat?" I shook my head, declining the offer. Ken rolled down the window. "Two beers, please."

"Sure," the carhop said. While the waitress went to fetch our drinks, Ken apologetically removed his other arm from my shoulder.

"I gotta get my wallet. It'll only be a second."

Fearful I would fall apart as Ken managed the real world, I curled up in a ball and fell onto his lap. With my nose dripping, I reached my hand into my coat pocket. There it was, one of my dad's trusty hankies. Thoughts of my father and how he always soothed me made me cry even harder. Likewise, Ken simply patted my head and let me sob.

In a couple of minutes, the girl returned with two mugs of root beer. It seemed like an eternity before Ken finally situated the purchases on the dash, returned his wallet to his pants pocket, rolled up the window, and resumed his hold on me.

"So tell me," he asked softly, "What is the matter?"

With my face firmly planted in the soggy wad of hankie, more tears came. I thought I might never stop, but the waterworks eventually subsided enough to let me speak.

"Ken," I said, but the tears flowed once more.

"What is it, Geri?" he asked with urgency.

"Ken, I've been so awful!"

"You've been so awful?" he chuckled. "You're not awful."

"Yes, I am. You have no idea."

"What?" he asked, pulling his head back, sounding a bit fearful for what I might say.

"Well, uh, I haven't exactly been totally honest with you."

"What do you mean, you haven't exactly been honest?" There was caution in his voice. Though I wanted to surrender to the tears again, I decided it wasn't fair to keep him waiting any longer. I wiped my eyes with Dad's hankie and replied.

"I mean, on Saturdays, when I've told you I've been doing homework and stuff with Candice—"

"Have you been dating someone else?" he asked, panic evident in his voice.

"No, no, not that."

He gave a sigh of relief and hugged me harder.

"But I have been doing some bad things," I admitted.

"What bad things are you talking about, Geri? Can you just tell me, please?"

"I'm sorry," I said. "It's, well, it's hard to admit." I quickly organized my thoughts so I could be honest without getting into Danny kissing me. I figured it would be pointless to confess to such actions when I really had no feelings for the guy. I especially didn't want to hurt Ken unnecessarily. Most of all, I didn't want to lose him.

"I've been experimenting with drugs."

He pulled back again, this time so he could look me straight in the face. "Why are you doing something dumb like that? What kind of drugs, anyway? Is it pot?"

"No," I said, wishing it were. I assumed Ken would understand the idea of me smoking marijuana, since he'd thought this when he first met me. Though I'd never admitted to it, I was pretty sure he knew.

"What, then?"

I hesitated. "Uh, well, amphetamines," I finally said, bracing myself for his response. There was no going back. I'd confessed, and now I'd have to pay the consequences.

"Geri, speed? You've been doing speed?" He pulled me to him once more. Squeezing me hard, he said. "Geri, that stuff is so dangerous. I knew you haven't looked good. Oh, why are you doing stupid stuff like that?"

I began to cry again.

"Ken, I just can't take it! I just can't take the pressure of always trying to be something I'm not."

"What are you talking about?"

"I don't know."

"You are yourself," he insisted.

"No, no I'm not. I feel so phony. I've always felt that way." Covering my face I tried to think back over my life. *Did I really think that?* I asked myself. I was so tired, so strung out from speeding all night. It always left me feeling weak and wiry. It made my nerves raw. Lights, sounds, everything intensified.

I continued to weep. "I don't know what I mean, Ken. I don't know anything anymore. All I know is I just can't handle it." Cradling me in his arms, he rocked me back and forth as if I were a baby. "I love you, Geri. I don't want you to do that stuff anymore. Promise?"

I struggled to imagine what it'd be like not to go to The House ever again. *What would Candice do if I didn't go?* I was worried about her, too. She had also lost lots of weight. Her face looked hollow, like she was empty inside. If she knew what I'd done with Danny it would really hurt her, hurt our relationship. Our friendship was already strained with the secrets I'd been keeping. Sorting out what I could and couldn't say, worrying if she would or wouldn't find Danny and me sneaking around, filled me with anxiety and guilt. This made it impossible to relax in her presence and created a wedge in our friendship. In spite of my deceitful behavior, I really cared about her. Ironically, it worried me how she fell for a guy who treated her so badly, even though I was part of that treatment.

"Promise me, Geri. Promise me you'll never do that stuff again!" Ken begged.

"I won't," I heard myself saying from some place far away, in a voice that seemed to belong to someone else. *You can't believe her!* I secretly warned, loathing the girl who could not be trusted.

Unable to tolerate the affection Ken was bestowing on me, I suddenly pulled away. He took a root beer off the dash and offered me a drink. "Have a sip of your beer," he said, holding it up to my lips. With shaking hands, I took the handle of the heavy glass mug. I was barely able to keep it steady as I drank. I quickly admonished myself for enjoying its refreshing effect.

"Thanks," I said.

We sat in silence while Ken drank from the other mug.

"Do you mean it?" he finally asked hopefully. Though I wanted to assure him, I didn't really know if I could give up the drugs.

"I think so," I said honestly. "I'll try. I guess that's all I can say. I understand if you don't want to hang around me, though."

"Don't be silly!" he said, kissing me on the top of my head, "I'm with you Ger, all the way."

Ken returned the mugs to the dash. He gathered me up in his arms once again, though this time his body felt tense. Despite his effort to hang on to me, it felt like I was slipping away. I was so tired I couldn't think straight. I wanted to go home and sleep, but I had one more question to ask.

"Ken?"

"Yeah, Ger?"

"If I ever went blind, would you still love me?"

But he didn't answer. Instead, he removed his right arm from around my shoulder and flashed his headlights, signaling to the carhop he was ready to leave. By the time he'd rolled down the window, the waitress was there, retrieving the empty mugs. Terrified by his silence, I waited, but Ken simply rolled up his window and shifted gears. Taking the wheel with both hands, he eased out of the parking space and turned toward the main road. When it was clear of traffic, he moved onto the street and headed for my house. I wondered if he was telling me he'd had enough of me. Finally, he spoke.

"Geri?"

"Yes?" I dared to ask.

"Do you think you'd still love yourself if you went blind?" Totally surprised at his question, I was not at all shocked at my instantaneous reply.

"No!"

Chapter 17

On the Road Again

May 1971

"Are you ready, Geri?"
"Almost. Be down in a minute."
"Can't wait to see you!" my dad said.

I nervously dabbed the corners of my eyes. Never sure if there might be traces of mascara left behind, I used this backup method as an insurance policy. Wiping my sweaty palms with a tissue, I opened the tiny bottle of White Shoulders perfume my sister Grace had given me for the occasion. Little flutters of excitement rippled through my stomach as I placed a tiny drop of the delicate fragrance behind each ear. When I leaned forward to be closer to the mirror, I couldn't help smiling at the girl who was happily smiling back.

"Not bad!" I remarked to Tippy, who watched inquisitively from the bed. "Not bad at all." Tip wagged in agreement. I turned toward the mirror once more.

What I saw boggled my mind. The angelic figure now standing in front of me was such a contrast to the dragged-out hag who stood there two months earlier.

"Whoops!" I said, noticing a potential fashion taboo. I reached up and centered the yellow bow decorating the crown of my head. Hours of hard work and the help of Aqua Net hairspray had turned my straight hair into Shirley Temple locks. It only took half the can to coax the curls to stay piled high above the ribbon. The sausage tresses cascading over my bosoms looked so pretty. To prove to myself they were really mine, I fingered them gently. *I really do look like Cinderella after all,* I thought. My focus moved to the string of pearls so kindly loaned to me by my mother. They were one of the few items of value she possessed. I felt privileged to wear them as I fondled the beads that reflected the scooped neckline of the pale yellow dress. Their femininity added the perfect touch to the innocence of the baby doll sleeves tied with polka-dotted ribbon. The sophisticated childlike style I'd created made me chuckle as I realized it went well with my resurrected spirit. I moved my hands over the gown, my fingers absorbing the delicate texture of chiffon.

"Don't I look pretty, Tippy?" I asked him as I twirled in my spot. As the many taffeta layers of the full-length skirt followed, the whooshing sound made Tippy's ears pop up.

"Pretty cool, ain't it, Tippy boy?" I said giving him another pat. "It's really me! Tippy, can you believe it?" I asked my loyal pal.

Leaning back into my reflection, I noticed how rosy and healthy my cheeks looked. I wondered how I had ever managed to return to such an image of innocence after all I'd done. With one last affectionate pat, I slipped on my white two-inch pumps and rounded up the essentials to put in my sequined handbag. Deciding to take one last look in the mirror, I held my breath, fearful I might be dreaming. To reassure myself of the reality of my metamorphosis, my mind forced itself to reminisce one last time.

Even though I'd confessed to Ken that Sunday evening in the parking lot of the A&W, I returned to The House the very next weekend. I don't know if I thought feeling guiltier justified my actions, but I ended up doing more footballs than usual. If that wasn't bad enough, I made a point to hang out in one of the bedrooms upstairs so Danny could find me alone and available. Over the next several weeks, the intensity of Danny's attention grew, and so did the level of my rage toward myself and my mother. By the end of January, I looked like death warmed over and could hardly say a kind word to anyone.

School was also growing more and more difficult to manage. I found myself popping half a football in the mornings just so I could get out of bed. I discovered the other half worked well to help me focus on my assignments in the classroom. Despite my belief in the power of the drug, my report card at the end of that term showed my fruitless effort. I had dropped my grade point from a 3.75 to a 1.5, flunking most of my classes except chemistry. Amazingly, I maintained an A in that subject, which is the only reason I had a grade point at all.

The last week in January, the day after I'd brought my report card home, I took my last trip to The House. My dad had just finished his lecture about how important school was and how I was so much smarter than I allowed myself to be, when I heard Candice honking in the driveway. I climbed into her car and hoped she'd be in a better mood. The last few times we'd been together, she hardly spoke to me. When she did, it was short and irritable. Candice also had lost lots of weight, looking more pale and worn-out than ever.

"Hey Candice," I said, hoping I might hear the old affection she used to send me.

"Hi," she said flatly, barely parting her lips to speak, her voice directed at the windshield.

"Did you get your report card?" I asked, pulling my heavy jacket up around my chin, preparing for the cold ride ahead. The old car's heater could barely kick out enough juice for the windshield to stay clear, let alone warm the two of us.

"Yeah. I'm droppin' out," she answered in a sullen tone. Unable to see her in the early darkness of the winter day, I pictured her drawn, expressionless face.

"Really?"

"Yup."

"You do bad, too?" I asked, knowing the answer.

"Three E's."

"What were the others?" I asked, wiggling my toes to keep them from turning into icicles.

"Two C's and a D."

"At least you did better than me. Heck, I got all E's, a D, and an A."

She said nothing. We drove for a while. I pondered Candice quitting school.

"Jesus, it's cold in here," she finally said, rubbing her right hand up and down her thigh.

"No kidding!" I agreed, glad to hear we concurred about something.

"You really gonna quit?" I asked.

"Yup."

"But Candice, you're too smart for that. I mean, I know we've been screwin' off lately, but we can pull the grades up if we try. Heck, graduation's only a few months away. I'd hate to see you not finish."

"Don't give a shit," she simply stated.

"But Candice, you are so damned smart!" I said touching her shoulder affectionately. As if stung by a bee, she instinctively pulled away.

"I said I don't give a shit!" she snapped. Resisting the urge to react, I kept silent. Candice had never spoken to me so harshly before.

After along pause, I dared to speak. "But Candice, I'm worried about you."

"Yeah, right," she said.

"I am!"

"Yeah, then why the fuck you been messin' with my boyfriend?"

My heart sank. Realizing how unprepared for this I was, I wondered how much Candice could know about Danny's attraction to me. I thought I'd played it cool, at least when she was around the two of us. Had she figured out that Danny's trips upstairs to the bathroom were really trips to see me? Could she know I was really secretly meeting Danny in his mother's den to kiss and neck instead of doing crosswords? Danny and I had never connected for more than fifteen minutes. *There's no way she could know*, I told myself. Deciding to dare her assumptions, I managed to look directly at her and say, "I ain't fucking with your boyfriend, Candice. I wouldn't do that."

"Don't lie," she said, still looking straight ahead. "It makes it even harder when you lie."

"But I'm not lying!" I protested, speaking truthfully on the technicality of the word fucking. Somehow I doubted Candice would appreciate my version of playing horseshoes, however. I was curious to know what prompted her to confront me at this moment.

"Why are you accusing me of screwin' with your boyfriend?"

"I'm not stupid, Geri," she said, her voice frighteningly calm, eyes still on the road. "I've been watching Danny fall all over you and you sucking it up for weeks now. I'm sick of it! Really fuckin' sick of it!"

My muscles tensed. Despite my fear, I felt a smile threaten to show itself across my lips. A diabolical sense of pleasure came over me knowing Candice had acknowledged her boyfriend's interest in me. I quickly admonished myself for having such thoughts, as my self-hatred grew. *How could I be so cruel?* I asked myself, hastening to pull the muscles of my cheeks in a downward motion. Why do I need to boost my ego at Candice's expense?

Falling back on my compulsion to lie, I said, "But Candice, I'm not doing nothin' with Danny. He's nice to me sometimes, that's all."

The car powered forward. Unaware of the cold, I huddled tighter into my jacket, shivering at the impending danger.

"You are the worst excuse for a friend anyone could ever have!" she spewed. The Olds accelerated faster now. "I am so sick of your sweet, innocent phony bullshit. I used to think you were a real honest-to-goodness love child. You cared about things, about me, about what is right. But all you care about is yourself. You don't care how you do it, but you always manage to get exactly what you want."

I gripped the handle of the door, certain the wheels were about to leave the road. Candice continued maneuvering through the winding artery. My temperature rose with the feverish pace of the Olds flying past an endless row of tree trunks. It was all so surrealistic, like being in a car chase scene of a movie. But terror quickly brought me back to reality. With all the bravery I could muster, I squelched the urge to tell her to slow down, certain this would only make her drive faster. The gas pedal seemed floored now, and I wondered if hitting a tree would be any worse than the crashing of her words on my most deserving heart.

"I am so sick of tryin' to help you pretend you can see," she went on, her cold steely voice cutting right through me. "I have to tell you when there's steps or whisper where things are. I have to be careful not to talk too loud when I let you know who walks through a door. If we're at a party, I can't freely do my own thing, I have to keep track of when you need me so you don't have to give yourself away. I'm sick of being your eyes, Geri. I'm sick of helping you pretend. But I do it anyway, and then you cop out on me. I told you how much I like Danny, and the minute you could, you tried to steal him from me. How could you?" she asked, swerving around a hairpin curve. The car shook so hard I thought it would break apart. As she forced it beyond its limits, Candice screamed, "How could you?"

The impact of the truth collided with my brain, hurling its way deep into my soul. For a split second, I was sure we had crashed. As the car slowed down I was sorry we hadn't.

Shaken by the impact of her words, I thought I'd crumble with the weight of both our pain. Although I was devastated by the knowledge of having become Candice's charge, I hated how deeply I had hurt her. I desperately wanted to tell her I was sorry, but I was certain it would only make things worse. Instinctively I knew she needed to hate me. I thought about all the times we'd spent together and questioned how I could have been so blind to her feelings. I turned my head toward the passenger window and began to cry.

"Don't cry," she said, calmer now. But her words only added to my grief. I tried harder to be silent, but the need to take a breath after holding in the tears naturally gave me away.

"I'm sorry," I managed to squeak out. "I know it doesn't mean much to you now, but I am sorry."

"Okay, okay!" she said. I knew she wanted me to shut up. Despite my desire to oblige her, I only cried harder.

"Please stop crying," she begged. "We're almost there. You can drop a few footballs in a minute and forget about it."

But instead of consoling me, the idea made me want to retch. It sounded so sick, so crazy, so wrong. I'd dared to consider it myself many times, but never admitted it. Initially I'd taken drugs out of curiosity. I'd never allowed myself to think I used them to escape reality. That was something addicts did. People with real drug problems. Not a cool hippie freak experimenting and exploring alternative states of consciousness. I had to deny the possibility that I was using drugs to cover up emotional pain, to hide from truth about myself.

Candice's words sobered me briefly. I sat up and looked directly at her. "But I don't want to do footballs so I don't feel bad."

"Why not?" she asked, surprised. "That's what I do. Works every time."

I stared at her, stunned by her admission.

"So they make you feel better about being around me?" I asked, afraid to hear her say yes.

"That's not the hurt I'm talking about," she said in a tone suggesting I was an idiot.

"What do they cover up for you, then?" I asked, fearful for what she would say.

With a sarcastic laugh, Candice roared, "Oh my God, Geri, don't you get it? You don't get it, do you? I just fuckin' told you for God's sake. Now let's see, what pain do they cover up for me? You're so busy worrying about being sighted, you couldn't recognize somebody else's struggle if it bit you in the ass."

Reeling back from her harsh words, I pressed hard against the door. I wished I could run from this stranger sitting beside me. What was she talking about? She'd never told me about any emotional pain, other than her father being gone all the time.

"What?" I asked. "What don't I get because I'm so selfish?"

"Don't you get it? Can't you see? I told you. I told you how much I loved Danny. I'm crazy about him. But just like my dad, he never has any time for me. If he's not sneaking up to see you, he's busy playing his guitar, or practicing with the band. So many times I've wanted to cuddle with him, kiss him, lay with him and have him hold me, but he doesn't notice. If I'm lucky, he'll give me a kiss hello, or when I leave, but mainly he just treats me like shit. Then you sit there and take all the compliments. You sing, and he adores you. He likes what you wear, he follows you upstairs. He even tells me to stay down with the others, and I know it's so he can go find you. Then you go home and you've got Ken calling you. You tell me how he treats you so nice and holds you and kisses you. But no, that's not enough for you, Geri. You've got to tag along with me every Saturday night and steal the only guy I've ever cared about."

Though I realized on some level my common sense could explain why Candice would be upset, I sat astonished at what she was telling me. All this time I had felt inferior. I'd tried to raise myself up to her level by accepting the attention of someone I didn't even like, simply because the girl I admired liked him. I couldn't believe that all this time Candice was feeling lonely like me. Once more a spark of glee flashed in the recesses of my mind. Once more I loathed myself for being so shallow. *Do others have such evil thoughts?* I wondered. *Are other people as deviant as I am? Why in the hell do I have to be so damn aware of everything I think anyway?* I asked no one.

The car slowed to turn down Danny's street. More than ever I wished I'd stayed home. I wasn't ready to deal with The House, but I could hardly wait to get out of the Olds. Candice pulled in the driveway, turned off the motor, and pulled the emergency brake. The grinding sound made me jump. As she opened her door, Candice turned and asked, "Can ya just keep your hands off him tonight?" Her face moved close to mine. I pictured her deep green eyes glaring at me. "Can ya just not sing any of your stupid songs?"

I nodded my head slightly in agreement, wishing I weren't hearing the end of our friendship.

"Good! Just leave me alone then, and everything will be just fine."

I sheepishly walked silently behind her to the door. I dropped only one hit of speed while I helped Caribou with a crossword puzzle. But the effects of the tiny oval pill did little for my mood. Holding to my bargain, I refused Danny's invitations to sing or sneak to the bedroom.

On the ride home, I told Candice again that I was sorry, but she said nothing. I suggested that it might be best if I didn't come back to The House anymore, hoping she'd disagree, But she didn't. She simply said, "Okay."

When we finally reached my house that Sunday morning, I opened the door to leave. I could see her now in the bright winter sunshine. Despite Candice's ghostly features, her silky white hair glistened in the light. I tried to imagine the power Danny's original comments had over her. What kind of spell had he cast? Why didn't she reject him like she had rejected me? I wanted to ask, but decided against it.

Waiting for me to take my leave, Candice gave an exasperated sigh. Unable to stall any longer, I got out of her life and headed for my house. On Monday, Candice did not show up for school. Each day I looked for her, but she didn't come. I awkwardly warded off questions about her from mutual friends. On Friday one of the school counselors called me into her office.

Candice had not only failed to return to school, she hadn't gone home, either. Sick with worry, her mother hoped I'd let the counselor know where she was. Torn between further betraying her and concern for her well-being, I finally relented and gave the counselor Danny's number.

Two weeks later Candice returned. Hearing the news by way of the grapevine only fed my sense of rejection. Everyone knew Candice and I shared everything. When classmates caught on I had not known where she'd been, gossip about our crumbling friendship spread like wildfire.

In the weeks following, every time I overheard bits and pieces about what Candice was doing, I cringed. Tormented with hope, I initially positioned myself in the hallways I knew she'd be passing through. As I was unable to see her in a moving crowd, it would be up to her to make the first overture. When it didn't come, I gave up, crushed and defeated.

One day in the spring, while I was walking through a rather empty hallway, I thought I heard her voice. I moved closer to the sound and noticed the distinctive color of her hair. Though I wanted to rush up and hug her, I held back, anxiously waiting for her to finish talking to some girls. When she was done, I hurried up behind her.

"Hi Candice!" I said with hopeful expectations.

"Oh, hi,"

"Glad you're back," I said, now only a step behind her.

"Thanks." She kept walking.

"You doing okay?" I asked, moving up beside her, the familiar essence of her presence making it hard not to embrace her.

"Yeah, I'm fine."

"That's good. I was worried about you," I said, praying she'd appreciate my concern and slow down. But instead of responding to my affectionate gesture, she stopped, turned toward me, and said, "One thing you need to do, Geri."

"What's that?" I asked, my spirits rising.

"You need to forget about me," she said firmly. "Okay?"

Devastated, I couldn't answer. I'd been holding out hope she'd eventually forgive me and want to spend time together like we did in the past. With the failure of my last-ditch effort, there was no way I could go to class. Instead, I darted into the nearest girls' bathroom and wept. It was really over. My friendship with my best friend, who I loved, was really over and I had no one to blame but myself.

While I sat sobbing on one of the stools, the picture of the footballs that I hadn't touched in almost a month popped into my head. I'd dumped the last few in the toilet only two weeks earlier. Now I felt regret at my hasty action. The pain in my heart was way too hard to take.

Unaware of the passage of time, I contemplated my options for managing this moment of truth. The ideas I considered were frightfully dark, coming from a place deep inside my soul. Suddenly my reverie was disturbed. The sound of giggling females entered my den of anguish. I looked at my watch. It was lunchtime. I'd been crying for almost an hour. My father would be picking me up in a few minutes. I had to pull myself together.

The last term of my senior year included a course in work-study. Every day my dad would drive me to the vocational rehab center on the other side of town. This was where mentally impaired adults worked on a mini assembly line, sorting car parts for General Motors. My job was to assist the two supervisors, John and Tim, in overseeing their work and to help encourage their productivity. Although I loved my job, I dreaded going. Instead, I wanted to run and hide.

Maybe I'll tell Dad I'm sick. I hastily dampened paper towels and tried to wipe the red from my eyes. *I look like shit!* I told myself. "Dad's going to know you've been crying, stupid," I said under my breath.

I was right. As soon as I climbed into the car he expressed his concern. "How come you been crying?" he asked.

But instead of answering, I started with the waterworks all over again. In his usual manner, Dad pulled a handkerchief from his pants pocket and handed it to me. I took it gratefully, burying my face in its softness. As he drove out of the parking lot, he asked, "So, what's the matter?" His kindness made me cry harder.

I resorted to the fetal position again, difficult to maintain in the front seat of a moving automobile. After driving for a while, I was able to tell him.

"Dad, I've hurt Candice's feelings. I haven't been very nice to her and now she won't talk to me any more."

"Oh, I doubt this will last forever," he said in an attempt to console me.

"No, Dad, I know it's over. It has been for a while, but now I know it's true."

"That's too bad," he said simply. "You and Candice have been friends for a long time."

"I know. She's always been so nice to me, Dad! She's been the best friend I ever had. She reads to me all the time, and now I can't even talk to her." More tears fell. I thought my heart would break in two.

My dad waited patiently, letting me cry. After a while, he spoke. "Do you deserve to lose her friendship?"

I hesitated. Finally I admitted I did. He thought for a minute.

"Well, I gather some of the things you've been doing with Candice aren't the best?"

Totally unprepared for such a question, I hoped he didn't know exactly what those things were. "What do ya mean?"

"Well, I did get a call from one of your friends a while ago."

"Who?" I asked, astonished at his words.

"Never mind who. I just want to know if their suggestion that you and Candice were doing drugs is true, that's all"

Horrified at his knowledge, I became hysterical.

"Dad, I'm sorry," I wailed. But he said nothing. "Oh, Daddy, Oh, Daddy! I've been so awful!" I screeched at the top of my lungs, hitting myself in the head with my fists. "I hate myself, Dad. I hate myself."

"Geri, Geri! You've got to stop that!" he urged, pulling into a parking lot and turning off the car. He took my wrists firmly into his big warm hands.

"Now Geri, you've got to stop this!" I could feel him shaking. It frightened me. I relaxed my arms.

"I'm sorry, Dad," I said. He released my hands and placed a comforting arm around me, patting my back gently.

"It's okay, Geri. It's okay," he said softly.

But I couldn't stop crying. I wept so forcefully I could hardly breathe. When I managed to exhale, I choked out, "No, it's not! I'm awful, Dad. I've done awful things. I've hurt you and Mom, and I've lost my best friend. I don't blame her for ditching me, but I want her back."

"Geri, Geri," he said anxiously.

"Oh, Dad. What am I going to do? I don't know what to do." I wept, collapsing my head on his lap.

Dad let me cry for a while. He patted my hair gently, worry still evident in his gesture. "I wish I had an answer for you, Geri, but I don't. Sometimes we do stupid things, and then we have to pay the price."

"I know," I wept.

"You are already doing better," he said. "I know you're not doing those drugs any more.

"But I don't feel better," I cried.

"Maybe not this moment, but I can see you are looking lots healthier."

"I don't feel it, though," I protested.

"I know you don't right now, but your mother and I have noticed that you've been improving at school. You're not so angry any more. Geri, I don't know if you realize how worried about you we've been, but lately we've been very proud of you!"

As usual, his wise words helped soothe my aching heart. I was still crying, but the fear of bursting my lungs was subsiding.

"How long have you known?" I asked, curious about who told him and when.

"Oh, I guess I suspected last fall. But when that friend of yours called me in December and told me where you were going every weekend, I knew for sure."

My original suspicion that it was Ken who told him had to be wrong. Though Ken knew about the drugs, he had no clue about The House. With diminished tears, I straightened myself up and asked, "Can you please tell me who it was?"

"Oh, I'm not going to say who called. That doesn't matter anyway."

"But why didn't you say something, yell at me, or keep me from going?"

"Would it have stopped you?" he asked.

I thought for a minute. "Well, if you told me I couldn't go, I probably wouldn't have been able to sneak out as often."

"Maybe not," he sighed. "But where there's a will there's a way. Believe me, it hasn't been easy watching you leave the house on those weekends. I wanted to make you stay home, but I learned from your brother and sisters that, at this age, there's little we can do to stop you from doing what you want to do."

I considered my dad's words. I wondered if he or my mother could have done anything to prevent me from going to The House. The answer was clearly no.

"Heck, when I was a kid," my father continued, "I used to hop the train from Detroit to Chicago with my buddies. We'd hang out at the jazz clubs and smoke marijuana behind the buildings. If my dad had ever caught me, even when I was twenty-five, he'd have tanned my hide. But it's just something I had to do."

Stunned at his words, I tried to imagine my dad smoking weed. Part of me wanted to ask him about getting high, but a bigger part of me cringed at the idea.

"I guess I figured this was a phase you needed to go through," I heard him saying. "I'm just glad you figured it out."

It felt peculiar listening to my father talk so frankly about his own delinquency, let alone his parental decisions. Somehow it didn't sound like something a parent should be saying. Oddly enough, I felt much better despite this unconventional discussion.

"I wish you could have stopped me anyway," I said. "I ended up losing a good friend by being so stupid."

"Consequences are everywhere, Geri. I didn't say you shouldn't pay a price. I suspect you learned the hard way how damaging drugs can be."

"What about you, Dad? Did you pay a consequence for smoking dope?"

"Well, I guess I lucked out there. I did almost jump out of my skin one time, though."

"What do ya mean?" I asked.

"What I mean is, I never ran so fast and far in my life as I did the night the cops chased me and my buddies down the back alleys of Chicago. I'm afraid I'd have paid a big consequence had I gotten caught and thrown in a Chicago jail with illegal drugs. I tell ya, it sure kept me from doing things like that again!"

Picturing my father being chased by the police was almost comical. A smile crossed my lips, despite the muscles of my cheeks pulling them back to a deep frown.

"Does Mom know about what I've done?" I ventured to ask.

"Well, she suspects. I didn't tell her about the phone call, but she's no dummy, Geri. She sat up many Saturday nights, worried sick about where you were and what you might be doing."

Guilt ripped through me again like a freight train heading from Detroit to Chicago. Feeling drained and exhausted, I ventured a question.

"Think I could call in sick, Dad?"

He thought for a moment. "That's up to you," he finally said. "But you've got some people counting on you at the rehab center. Letting somebody down because you've been let down is not necessarily an even swap. But if you can't go, you can't go."

I thought about the people I'd grown so fond of in such a short time, and then John and Tim came to mind. I was not at all impressed with their treatment of the workers. In fact, I had to work hard at times to hold my tongue. Their condescending comments and incorrect assumptions about the capability of the workers reminded me of my experiences at That School. I found myself constantly countering John and Tim's disrespectful remarks. I used my sarcastic humor to engage them while putting them in their place, making sure they had no knowledge of my intent. I had no doubt that my presence helped the line staff and knew they would be disappointed if I didn't show up.

After wiping my eyes with his hanky, I instructed my dad to take me to work.

Walking through the door of the center with bulging red eyes and a dark cloud hanging over my head was not easy. I was fearful I'd be asked what was wrong, so I forced myself to smile. I wondered if I was truly up to the expectations of the workers, but the welcoming greeting of the employees quickly washed away my fears

"Hi Geri," said several happy voices.

"Hi guys," I replied, my own voice sounding as if it belonged to someone else.

After stuffing my purse into my locker, I walked toward the row of assembly tables. I still anticipated inquiries about my tear-stained face, but most of the eight assembly line employees were only interested in my attention.

"Did you have to stay longer at school today, Geri?" Sheila asked from behind the assemblers' table.

"Uh, yeah, just a bit," I said, not wanting to explain anything.

"We were worried about you, Geri," Martha said. "I was afraid you were in a car accident."

"Sorry, Martha," I said, remembering how she worried about every little thing. "I'm fine. I would have called, but there wasn't a phone." I hoped this would explain why I hadn't notified John, who was presently reviewing some of the work.

"Just glad you made it," John acknowledged.

"It won't happen again," I said, wondering if he noticed I'd been crying.

"Hey, Geri, I like your earrings. Did you get them from a bird?"

I reached up and touched the soft blue feather hanging from one of my ears. "No, Donald, I'm not sure where these feathers are from. I bought them in a store."

"They goes real good with your dress, Geri. You look real purty in blue."

"Thanks, Emily," I said. "I like your blue blouse, too."

"It's got lots of flowers on it."

"Yes, I can see that. It looks very nice on you."

"Gonna challenge us again today, Geri?" asked Raymond.

"Sure!" I said, my spirits lifting a bit. Despite what John and Tim thought, sorting nuts and bolts or stringing mesh nets for holding car parts was a boring task for anyone. Just because these workers didn't possess a so-called normal intelligence didn't mean they weren't frustrated with these mundane tasks.

To help improve working conditions and reduce complaints, I would challenge the workers a bit. Every Friday I'd buy a pop for the person who met whatever goal I set up. Sometimes it would be for the one who best improved their productivity for the week. Other times it was for those who beat their previous week's achievements. Once John kept track of who complained the least. On this day, I came up with a different plan.

"Okay, think about how much you did or didn't want to come to work this morning."

"I likes coming to work," Donald said. "I likes seeing you, Geri."

"Thanks, Donald. You're my best fan." My smile was growing wider now. "So if you really wanted to come to work today, pick the number one. If you wanted to come, but not a whole lot, pick a number two. If you would have rather stayed in bed or stayed home to watch TV, pick a number three. If you really, really didn't want to come to work at all, pick a number four."

The workers chatted among themselves, truly intrigued by my proposal.

"Okay guys, now you have to match the number to how you feel."

Without a doubt I knew who would pick a number four. Up until today, I had been unable to figure out a way to make sure George would win. Always a bit surly, George held the worst attendance record of the group. Even though he lived in a foster care home with other residents, he isolated himself, staying in his room a lot. At work he made sure he kept clear of the others as well. He responded to my efforts to get him to talk, but I could tell he'd rather not.

Making sure I called on him last, I said, "George, what number did you pick?"

"A four," he said in his gruff voice.

"George wins!"

"George?" said the others in amazement.

"Yessir!"

"Why does he win if he hates to come to work?" Sheila asked.

"Because, even though you hate to come to work, George, you're here anyway. That takes some real doing in my book," I said, thinking about my own self. "For that, you deserve a pop. What kind do you want, George?" I asked, forgetting all about my aching heart.

Stunned by his win, George replied, "I don't know."

Retrieving some coins from my purse, I invited him to accompany me to the machines. "Well come on then. Come pick it out with me."

George dropped what he was doing and bustled out from around his work station. He studied the choices thoroughly. As we stood there, I realized I had never seen him drink a soda before. Finally after he had surveyed the options for a very long time, George picked a 7-Up.

By the time I left the rehab center that day, life seemed better. I couldn't help wondering how far my loyalties to this group would go, however. I could recognize them each for their own significance and appreciate the important lessons they taught me, but I also knew I would likely betray them as I had my classmates from That School. Although I could feel comfortable in this setting as an assistant supervisor, I surely would have little to do with any of them in a public social setting.

It's that darn "us and them" syndrome, I decided, as I stood before the mirror enjoying what I saw. I wondered if I could ever be truly accepting of others. My father's voice broke through my trance.

"Ken's here, Geri!" he called.

My critical thoughts evaporated as the excitement of the moment brought happier thoughts to mind.

"I'll be right there!" I said, daintily lifting my skirt for the trek down the stairs. As I clicked my way down in my big girl shoes, I was glad to leave behind the harsher realities of life. Tonight I was going to the prom with Ken. Tonight I would be Cinderella after all.

Part II

Chapter 18

The Age of Enlightenment

Fall 1971

Time is such an elusive thing. At any given moment an experience can feel so real, while at the same time so distant. If something is painful it seems like it will never end. If it's joyful it slips away so quickly, yet the memories can be powerful and permanent. As I reflect back on the star struck evening I spent with Ken at the prom, I can't decide which was more tangible: the actual moments or the memories. Either way, the thoughts propelling me along through the rest of that summer were filled with hope. Just like the days when I'd skip along behind my father in my red dress and saddle shoes, protecting my mother's back by jumping over cracks, I felt footloose and fancy-free. Finally I'd been able to figure out what made me happy and what did not. Leaving Ken did not make me happy. Being accepted into the college next door to the university medical center where I had spent too much of my childhood did. So, when September came along, I, with my newfound sense of wisdom, packed my most precious belongings, said goodbye to Ken, my parents, and Tippy and headed off into another chapter of my life.

Unfortunately, good things often come to an end all too quickly. In late October, after being away from those I loved most for several weeks, the sense of well-being I'd attained began to fade. It hit me suddenly one Saturday afternoon as I stared out of the tenth story window of my dormitory room. Although I'd tried to suppress it, I became acutely aware of how my new environment had affected what I could or could not see. All the familiar cues I'd used to function as a normally sighted female were being compromised right along with my confidence.

As I stood in front of the full-length glass, attempting to comprehend the ominous view, I feared that the gray clouds now hovering over the campus might swoop down and suck me up. Imagining what it might be like to be lifted from my burdens, I struggled to anchor myself by remembering what my earlier excitement had felt like. A profound notion came to me: *Nothing ever lasts!* The resulting shock wave moved me out of my melancholic state and gave me the urge to push through the protective pane that separated me from the courtyard below. An invisible set of fingers grabbed hold of my body, counteracting the self-destructive impulse. A rush of panic followed. I stepped back and wondered if the invisible hands would have kept me safe had the window been open. Though my heart pumped anxiety-producing adrenaline through my system, anger quickly took over. *Can't count on anything, Geri. It doesn't matter what you figure out, good things always disappear.*

I slammed my hand down hard on my desk as one tiny tear escaped from the corner of my eye. I watched the little dots I knew to be students make their way among each other below. My mind humanized them, placing them in pairs or groups, as they moved with purpose along the thin grey strips I knew to be sidewalks. I told myself they couldn't all be with friends, but I was certain the single ones had a destination better than mine. With nowhere to go and no one to talk to, I thought of how much I missed Ken. The urge to grab the phone almost overpowered my practical reasoning. Luckily, my fear of my father's disappointment held my hand back. *You can't call,* I told myself firmly, crying harder now. The memory of telling a lie to my father didn't help. I moved over to the bed and curled into a ball. Hugging my pillow, I thought about the incident which prompted my dishonesty.

Two days earlier my scarcely-seen roommate stopped by to get more clothes to take to her boyfriend's place. She'd only spent a few nights in the dorm since school started. She picked up the mail on her way up to the room and handed me an envelope. I was grateful for the gesture. I hated trying to search through the endless rows of same-colored mailboxes, hoping no one would notice my spectacled face smashed tightly up against them looking for the right number.

I was anxious to find out what was in the letter, but I waited until she left. It was the phone bill. Filled with worry, I took it to my desk so I could try to read it under the light of the fluorescent tube hanging from the shelf above. In my family, long distance phone calls were made only on holidays, birthdays, and to report someone's death. I hoped my frequent usage for unsanctioned reasons would not be too excessive.

It's going to be my demise, I thought, as I held the multi-page bill nervously in my hand.

I located my magnifying glass, put on my faithful wire rims and prepared myself for the dreaded chore of finding the actual charge. Squinting, I slid the magnifier slowly over the page. The words and numbers were so small, melting into each other, even with the use of both tools. If this task wasn't hard enough, the shiny paper caused the light to scatter, making the inky forms wiggle. I got up and closed the shades to create a more direct light. At last, after scanning all the columns and rows on three separate pages, I found the word I was looking for-- Total.

Now to find the number that corresponded with the word. My eyes were burning with exhaustion as I struggled to track a straight line with my finger across the page. No image came to my aching eyes. With growing frustration came nausea. Keeping my finger on the word I had found, I stood up, rubbing my sockets under the rims of my specs. Light headedness forced me to steady myself as I sat back down. I realized I could not follow an imaginary line so I pulled a ruler from my drawer and lined it up between the word total and the opposite side of the page. At last, I got it. There, clearly marked, was the answer. I zeroed in on the figures and tried to steady my focus.

"No way!" I said out loud. I pulled off my glasses and dug my knuckles into my watery orbs. My eyeballs throbbed from the combination of tears and strain. I repositioned the paper under the light and shoved my specs back hard against my face, certain I had read it wrong. Once more, with great effort, I worked to find the spot where I'd seen the number. There it was again.

"Oh shit!" I said, stamping my foot. "Dad's gonna kill me! I couldn't have talked for a hundred and twenty-six dollars worth of time, could I?" But I had. A hundred and twenty-six dollars for long distance phone calls in 1971 was a lot of talking. It would be similar to talking for several days on end, at least in terms of how my father would view it. Both my folks lived through the depression. They were very frugal. Writing too many letters requiring three-cent stamps was considered frivolous. Talking on a telephone for a hundred and twenty-six dollars was outrageous! With a heavy heart, I flopped on my bed and wondered how I'd figure my way out of this one. Not only would I have to obtain the money to pay for the bill, I also knew my phone calls to Ken would have to stop. Though he might be able to call me on occasion, the little he made as a gas jockey had to be spent on his education at Flint Community College. Eventually I considered a lie, one that I figured my dad wouldn't question.

I guiltily forced myself off the bed and moved back to my desk. I pulled my Smith Corona from its spot on the shelf, carefully positioned my university stationary into the feeder, rolled it into place, and then began a letter to my dad. Making certain to bow my head in shame, I concocted an elaborate story about needing money to pay for two more books not listed in my syllabus. I made sure to blame the university for this error. In order to make my story more realistic, I ventured one step further in my deception. The State of Michigan provided funds through an agency called Aid for the Blind. Not only did this program pay for my college tuition, room and board, but they also allotted a limited amount of money to pay for readers. Most books were taped by volunteers ahead of time, but such assistance was needed for doing library research or other miscellaneous reading. I exploited my need for this service by explaining to my father how I would now need to secure additional money for such help as these new books had not been taped. After completing the page filled with nothing but lies, I wrote another to Ken, telling him I could not call any more.

When I was done addressing and stamping them both, I laid them on my desk and returned the typewriter to the shelf. I hoped I'd change my mind before my roommate came back for more clothing. When she showed up again the next evening, I placed the letters in her hand, feeling totally numb as I did so.

Now, as I lay curled on my bed, still recovering from the whirlwind notion of plunging ten stories to my death, I admonished myself for both of these sinful actions.

"Grow up, you stupid girl!" I said out loud, now sitting up. "Stop pitying yourself for being a jerk. Your'e gonna play, you're gonna pay." I only wished I could have paid with money instead of the hatred I now felt for myself.

Standing upright to take action, I wondered what I should do. "You've got to get it together somehow, you stupid idiot." I said, louder this time, but no ideas came to me.

With no immediate solutions for how to make myself become a better person, I finally decided to study. Unfortunately, the growing hunger pains counteracted my plan. I would have endured them if my brain would agree, but I typically could not concentrate under such conditions.

If I could just walk to that restaurant on the other side of campus, I could probably afford one of those twenty-two cent hamburgers, I thought. But the guilt about spending money gave me a good excuse not to leave the confines of my safe familiar room, with nice square walls and no one to hide my secret from. Even without the issue of money, mustering up the necessary energy to traverse the campus at this point was out of the question. My increased familiarity with the place helped improve my maneuverability through the many barriers of benches, raised gardens, and curbs, but I still found myself wanting to stick my head forward to see. I had already done a flip over a bike rack near the library, not to mention the fall I took down three unexpected steps when I exited the wrong door of the science building. Though I told myself such accidents were in the past, my present delicate state told me to stay put.

Since I'd been at the university, I hadn't been eating much. I'd lost almost ten pounds after finally returning to a reasonable weight in May. Losing weight was not my goal; avoiding the cafeteria was. I hated going there. Negotiating the commons area during mealtimes created too much distress, so I managed to stay alive by resorting to less conventional methods. I made do by heating soup and baked beans in a popcorn popper, which doubled as a hot plate and sauce pan. Once in a while, out of desperation to avoid malnutrition, I managed to muster up the guts to go through the cafeteria line. This was very difficult. As the food lines were at angles to the entrance and the bordering walls, I found it hard to locate their beginning. Sounds of clinking silver, banging trays, sliding chairs, and hordes of chattering students also interfered with my mission, totally drowning out any auditory cues that might help me orient myself. Asking someone to explain the layout was, of course, out of the question for me. As a result I avoided the cafeteria like the plague.

With my final decision to avoid any and all social situations, I walked over to my closet and started planning dinner. I located the cord to my popcorn popper, pulled it down and placed it on the bathroom counter. Next I searched for a can of soup, but couldn't find one. I reached farther, but only touched boxes of crackers. Desperate to find something to eat, I frantically shuffled my stash until my fingers wrapped around a can. It felt like a can of beans, but to my dismay, when I shook it, I could hear too much liquid sloshing around inside.

"Darn, it must be fruit." I said aloud. Continuing my search, I hoped I might find a container of tuna. But the only other foods I located were the salt and pepper, a packet of instant hot chocolate, and a box of Sugar Pops.

"Damn it!" I yelled, "I need more than just fruit." But I settled on the box of cereal and whatever I had in my hand. I returned the popper, opened the drawer in the bathroom, and pulled out my can opener. The aroma released by the first turn told me that peaches were my main course for the evening. I sat down on the closed lid of the toilet and sucked back the slippery slices. Bowl or utensils were not necessary at this dining establishment. I especially liked the "no dress code" aspect.

After finishing the last morsel, I tossed the empty tin in the garbage, rinsed and dried the opener, returned it to its place in the drawer, and took my box of cereal to my bed. As I pulled out a handful of Sugar Pops, I noticed how much they looked like the "footballs" I used to hold in my palm. I quickly pushed the thought aside and stuffed the wad of crunchy oval treats into my mouth.

Before long, I felt a bit of relief from the sullen mood I'd been in. My hunger pangs were gone and there was a slight rush from all the sugar I'd consumed. I was still a bit worried about how long my food supply would last, but my newfound energy would allow me to study.

I returned to my desk and reached underneath to find the handle of a square metal case. I pulled the heavy tape player out and felt for the wall socket. Making sure I kept my fingers clear of the connection, I plugged in the cord. My next task was to flip through a stack of tapes and read the Braille labels. When I finally located the one that said "Chemistry Tape #3," I removed the reel from inside.

"Now for the hard part," I said to no one, letting out a sigh. I hated the tedious task ahead. The requirements for threading the magnetic tape through a series of pegs and cylinders took steady hands, nimble fingers, and patience. Just get it done! I told myself, placing the reel filled with hours of text on the left peg of the machine. It took seven tries before I managed to weave it in and out to the empty spool perched on the right. I slipped my index finger into the narrow space. Finally, after several more attempts, I was able to lace it through and wind it securely.

Before I turned on the player, I pulled my heavy Braille writer off the top shelf and set it on the desk. Feeding a piece of thick paper into the familiar contraption, I sat down and prepared to listen. I heard the familiar crunching as I labeled it "Chemistry, chapter #13."

"And now for the even harder part!" I said out loud, taking a deep breath to help manage the frustration I was about to experience. I turned the lever to fast forward and began counting.

"One thousand one, one thousand two, one thousand three…"

After a few seconds, I stopped the tape and put it in play mode.

Not yet! I told myself, hearing I was still in Chapter Ten. I repeated this process once more, only to find I was now in Chapter Eleven. Again and again I fast-forwarded the tape, counted, stopped the tape, played the tape, and listened, discovering I needed to keep going. After the fifth try, I listened once more.

"Study questions for Chapter Thirteen." I heard the female voice of the reader say.

"Shit!" I yelled, knowing the study questions were always at the end of a chapter. "I've passed the damn spot!" I told my walls. "I spend half my study time looking for the right place. I wish I had a tape player for every chapter I need to read!"

Eventually, I located the beginning of Chapter Thirteen. As the monotone voice read from the text, I pounded significant information on my trusty but cumbersome Braille writer. When an hour or so of listening passed, my wrists began to ache. Switching the lever back and forth and taking notes typically caused a tingling sensation in my fingers. I stood up and shook my hands. I paced the room and felt envy toward students who could lie back on their beds, read, and jot down notes with a pencil and pad. I wanted to get out of my little cell and take a walk in the crisp fall air, but I'd have to endure so much stress.

Maybe if I just go down and sit on one of the benches in the courtyard, I thought. *Yeah, but then you'd have to find a bench that was empty,* I argued. *There are lots of people down there today. What if you try to sit on a bench thinking there's a space left on it, and you sit on nothing, or worse, someone's lap?* But despite my argument forbidding me to go, the need to feel the fresh air on my face won out. Before I could change my mind, I grabbed my University emblem sweatshirt off my bed pole, threw it over my head and bolted through my door. A terrifying thought hit me as I patted my jeans pockets. Fear was quickly replaced with a wonderful sense of relief when I felt the familiar outline of my peace sign key chain. Thank heaven I don't have to find someone to help me get back in. The momentary scare proved helpful, as the released adrenalin energized me to continue my venture outside.

After looking around to be sure I was alone, I kept going. I turned down the three hallways leading to the elevator, practicing walking with my head erect. Keeping my eyelids at normal width felt awkward. When I reached the elevator, the nice round black button against the white wall looked so nice. With great ease, I reached out my finger and pushed it. As I waited for the elevator to take me to the lobby, I considered how often I had the impulse to feel things. Each time I did so, I pictured the behaviors of old classmates from That School. *You gotta stop bugging your eyes out!* I scolded. I had recently become aware of how I looked when scanning unfamiliar environments. One day I was trying to locate the end of the food line, when a student asked me if I was stoned. When I told him I wasn't, he suggested I must be crazy. I was devastated by his comments, but I figured my pupils must be dilated in order to let more light in.

The elevator doors opened. I stepped into it as more self-deprecating thoughts circled through my consciousness. Without warning, I let out a painful squeal as an argument with my father came to mind. Why did he have to insist? I asked myself. "I should have told him," I said as an afterthought, admonishing myself for another unkindness I had committed against him. "Why couldn't you just tell him you took the darn thing? It would have eased his mind you big brat!" I said aloud, thinking of the folding white cane I had hidden in my underwear drawer. As long as I'm in familiar territory, I'm fine, I told myself, justifying my resistance toward my father's concerns.

Sure Geri, I thought. *Just as long as the sun's not too bright, you're not nervous, aren't tired or have a cold, have clear contrasts, and you're not moving too fast, then you can fake it pretty good.*

The panels before me squeaked open, reminding me of the sound-effects used in scary movies. A sudden chill ran up my spine as I recalled a scene from The Twilight Zone. A woman had been sleepwalking when she entered an elevator. After she stepped out, she found herself in a morgue. An attendant announced, "Room for one more?" *I should be so lucky!* I thought, certain such an invitation would be in order for someone as awful as me.

The blur of moving objects and loud voices suggested the lobby was filled with students. A football game played on the television, and chatter mixed with laughter told me that everyone was doing just fine. Carefully, I walked across the reception area and exited the glass doors.

The courtyard lay ahead. Separate raised gardens, supported by cement walls, were positioned in front of each of the three ten-story dormitories. They were arranged in a triangular formation with walkways weaving in between. Only one path continued on through an open field to the main campus. I nervously scanned the surrounding area. The benches that I knew were next to the gardens all looked filled. Apparently others felt the same desire to be outside in the fall air. Though cloudy with the threat of rain, the atmosphere was mild. It held that sweet smell of dying leaves I so loved and wondered about. I still wanted to know why decay brought such brilliant colors and sweet aromas.

I gingerly walked around the garden directly in front of me. I really didn't want to sit with anyone, even if there was an empty spot. As the one near my entrance bore no empty seats, I sauntered to the next. When I got to the far side, there were two benches clearly vacant. Grateful for my find, I sat down, forcing myself to look nonchalant. Considering the position of my body, I crossed my legs, folding my hands on my exposed knee. Then I remembered how my psychology professor said crossed limbs equaled a guarded personality. Quickly I dropped my foot to the ground and opened my arms, resting my hands on either side of me. *This has to look too proper,* I thought. So I again placed my leg over top the other and draped my right arm over my lap.

This could also mean I'm closing myself off from the world. Unfolding my arm I lay my hand halfway down my thigh. It was a slight improvement, but I imagined self-consciousness written all over my worried face. Attempting to change my pensive mood, I turned up my lips in a smile. I abandoned this idea however, certain I must look more like a clown with a plastered smile than a happy college chick.

I wished I'd brought a book with me. I should look like I'm doing something. With that idea, I reached in my pocket and pulled out my keys. I jingled them as if I were waiting for someone. *That's good!* I thought. *If someone sees me, they'll think I'm meeting someone to go somewhere. I wonder why keys make people feel so important?* I thought, remembering how envious I was of Candice and others jingling their car keys. *I guess it's a sign of control or maybe power,* reflecting on how people always seemed to be leaving whenever they made the sound.

I continued to process more obsessive thoughts about how I appeared to the world or whether I had a right to be sitting in the courtyard. It suddenly dawned on me the whole reason for coming to this place was now lost. I hadn't even noticed the fresh air, let alone eased my stress.

Just as I was about to get up and head back in, I heard a voice ask, "Anyone sitting here?"

I looked up. A rather tall fellow with dark brown hair hanging disheveled to his shoulders drew near. As he spoke, a broad smile parted his bearded face.

"Uh, no," I said.

"Care if I sit down?"

"Uh, no," I said again, scolding myself inside for retreating to my shy mode of interacting.

"You live here?" he asked.

"Uh, yeah," I answered, slapping myself in my mind. *Think think*, I told myself, searching for more than two word comments.

"I live up on central campus. Thought I'd check out this end for a change. Name's Mike."

"Hi, Mike. I'm Geri. Which dorm you live in?" I asked, glad to think of something more to say.

"South Hall," he said. "Not for long, though. I'm finally gonna get an apartment next term. Can't wait. I'm not into the jock thing like most of the guys from that dorm. Not sure why I haven't found my way out of there before now. Been there for three years already!"

"Oh," I managed.

"Nope. Not into the sports thing, you know. Don't make much sense a bunch of guys going out on a field, fighting over a pigskin and killing each other."

"Yeah, I know what you mean," I said, knowing my father would not approve of this conversation.

"This your first year?"

"Yeah."

"Ya like it?"

"Uh, yeah," I said, lying. It must have shown on my face.

"It's hard to get used to it, ain't it?" His tone was sympathetic.

Afraid I'd cry at his insightful recognition, I didn't answer.

"Met any friends yet?"

Before I could stop myself, I answered truthfully. "No." I said, dropping my head in shame.

"Hey, that's understandable. Man, I had a hard time myself when I first got here a few years ago. Still don't really fit in, ya know. I mean everybody's into this rah-rah-rah stuff as far as the football thing goes. And I sure don't much agree with the educational system to begin with. Makes me mad I have to pay money so I can get a piece of paper saying I'm smart enough to get a job. Heck, university doesn't make you smart. Life makes you smart."

I stared at him, drinking in every word. He was like an angel of mercy. Terrified I'd scare him away with how needy I felt, I simply nodded my head.

"You think that too?" he asked, a smile crossing his lips.

"Yeah," I answered, my tongue tying up once again. Though I could easily see the clear contrast his facial hair made, the motion of his moustache helped to animate his face. Moving my gaze upward, I focused on his dancing eyes, fully enjoying his expression.

"I mean, I know school's important, but most of what I've learned has been through experience."

"What are you studying?" I managed to ask.

"Philosophy," he said with a laugh. "I know, I know, it's a nowhere degree." He threw up his arms, palms spread wide. "At least that's what my father says to me every time I go home."

I chuckled with him as he continued, "I love reading all those guys and considering their wisdom. They don't make people like Socrates anymore. How about you, what're you studying?"

"I haven't decided yet. I'm taking a couple of classes for a psychology degree, but I'd also like to teach…special ed, I think."

"Really? That's cool. I like psychology, too. Have you taken abnormal yet?"

"Got it now."

"So, what pathological disorder do you have this week?" We both laughed. It was true. With each new disorder discussed in class, I would run down the list of symptoms to see if maybe that was what was wrong with me. The professor warned us about this, but it didn't help. Everyone did it, and now Mike confirmed it as well.

With each passing question and answer, I grew more relaxed. I also became more animated, nodding my head enthusiastically when in agreement, tossing back my hair signaling my attentiveness when Mike expounded on one of his philosophical theories.

"Were you going somewhere?" Mike asked.

"No!"

"Do you always hold your keys in your hand?"

I had forgotten that I still had them. I let out a chuckle.

"Don't tell me you were trying to look like you were going somewhere?"

I squelched my instinct to make an excuse and simply smiled more broadly.

"You were!" he said, throwing his head back and giving a hearty laugh. "So you were looking for someone to join you, were you?"

"No, not that." I protested. "Needed to get out of the room, but didn't have anywhere to go. I guess I felt a little stupid just sitting here with nothing to do."

"Good plan, good plan," he said, nodding in an exaggerated manner.

Just like with Ken, the normal discomforts when getting to know someone did not seem to exist between this passerby and me. This time, however, I was acutely aware of my vulnerability. The intense loneliness I'd felt only seconds before his arrival made me want to lean into his arms and grab hold for dear life. His natural style of empathy told me to check my body space as we continued our conversation. Thoughts of Ken and what he would think helped keep me in check as well.

It began to rain. Thinking this would be a natural ending point, I suggested it was time to go inside. But Mike misunderstood my meaning and thanked me for inviting him into the dorm. Suddenly, the boundaries of our relationship changed. The feeling of equality and camaraderie which had developed between us felt threatened. Anxiously I flicked my eyes in the direction of where I believed the entrance to the building to be. *Can I make it without hesitating?* I asked myself. *No jutting your head forward!* I warned. I decided I could probably slip a half step behind him if he wasn't the chauvinistic type.

It worked, but once we were inside a new worry surfaced. Where to sit? There was no way I could locate two empty places in the chaos before me. Cleverly, I turned to Mike. "Where would you like to hang?"

"How 'bout over here?" he asked, angling off to the left. Gratitude filled my heart as I followed him to an empty plastic couch. Sitting in the student lounge with a friend made me feel so normal. Envy of the residents disappeared. Instead I felt cool, sitting with all the others having company of my own.

During our conversation, Mike told me about a group he belonged to. "It's called the Help Line. It's an organization of students who want to help anyone whose havin' a hassle in their life. We rap with callers about anything and everything, especially if they are having a problem with drugs. They might be depressed or have relationship problems, but a lot of the calls are stoned-out hippies having a bad trip."

Mike went on to clarify the parameters of the program. The Hotline, as he called it, wasn't to criticize anyone, bust anyone for having drugs, or even talk them out of using them.

"Heck a lot of us who volunteer turn on, if ya know what I mean. Anyway, we mainly just help turn bad trips into good ones and if someone is thinking about killing themselves, well, we either talk them out of it or call the police. The other thing we do is provide information and referrals."

"What's that about?" I asked.

"Well, Amy compiles most of the list, but it's a Rolodex filled with numbers of people and places that can help for whatever reasons. I mean, we only deal with the immediate crisis. Sometimes people need to get more long term counseling or detox or even medical help. So we keep a list of those agencies."

"Right on!" I said, not knowing what else to say. It felt good to be using hippie slang for a change.

"You think you'd like to join us?" Mike asked.

The same thought had crossed my mind, but I resisted asking, afraid of appearing overzealous, maybe pushing him away. My recent revelation—nothing ever lasts—still lay in the forefront of my mind. Would this guy have asked me this same question if he knew hours earlier I'd had the urge to jump out of my tenth story window? Would he ask me if he knew I couldn't read the information and referral materials?

Mike sensed my hesitation. "Don't feel like ya have too. You sure as heck don't have to give me an answer right away. I can imagine you must be overloaded with classes."

"No, it's not that at all!" I quickly replied. "It's just, well, I'm not sure how I would manage the information stuff. You see, well, I don't know if you noticed, but I don't see very good."

"Yeah."

Startled, I shot a look at him. Did he mean yeah-go-on-tell-me-more or yeah-I-realized-that?

"Geri, just talking to you, you seem to be a very kind and understanding person. That's what we need on the phones."

"What about reading the information?"

"Oh, yeah, that. Well, we always work in pairs. If you need to get a number just ask your partner."

I smiled at his common sense.

"So, you knew I didn't see too well?" I asked, my burning curiosity overriding my embarrassment.

"Yeah, I kind of figured as much," he said.

"Can I ask what gave it away?"

"Well, you don't really look at a person directly. And when we walked in here, I looked back and could tell you were really straining to see."

Damn! I thought I'd fixed that.

"Why don't you want people to know?"

"Ah, well. I guess I'm always a little nervous about whether I'd be, well…"

"Accepted?" he offered.

"Yeah," I answered, amazed at how quickly he caught on.

"Have you been rejected in the past because of it?"

"I don't know if rejected is the word, but a lot of kids weren't really into hanging with a chick who didn't see too well. I mean, nobody wants to bother with giving extra directions, or always having to look out for me. But mostly I don't like people feeling sorry for me."

"Uh, yeah, I can see that," he said, rubbing his beard thoughtfully. "Well, do you think maybe you expect too much from people?"

Astonished at his boldness, I didn't have time to feel offended.

"It's possible, but I'm not sure exactly what you mean by that."

"Well, maybe you expect too much from people. Maybe since you seem to be one who doesn't want to show your vision problem to the world, you rely too much on others to keep your secret."

This guy was blowing my mind. How could he figure this out after spending less than an hour with me?

"How'd you know that?" I decided to ask.

He laughed. "Forgive me for being so blunt. I get myself in trouble speaking what I see as the truth sometimes. You just seem a little nervous about how you come off. Even now, you are sitting rigid, trying to act relaxed, but you're not."

I wanted to ask him to tell me more, to speak my inner thoughts for me, to tell my pain. He was so insightful. Ken was kind, but he would simply tell me not to feel bad. This guy was really catching on to me. Though it scared me, I was intrigued. I shifted in my seat as I grew uncomfortably self-aware.

"I didn't mean to make you so self-conscious," Mike apologized. "It's okay to be guarded. Heck, we just met. It wouldn't be right to expose everything about yourself in such a short time. I fear I've let my tendency to be psychoanalytic slip out again. Please forgive me. You are a cool chick, and there's no need for you to explain yourself to me."

"No!" I blurted. "I mean, it's okay that you're so honest. It's refreshing, actually. I don't know, Mike, sometimes I get so tired of pretending to be what I'm not. You're right about me expecting too much from people. I want their help, but I don't want their help. I don't want their pity, but I act pitiful. Since I've come to school, I've mainly avoided everyone so I don't have to deal with any of it."

He looked at me with sad eyes. Reaching over, he placed his hand over mine, which lay on my leg in a balled up fist.

"It has been hard for you, hasn't it?"

With all my might, I struggled to hold back the tears now threatening to spill. I turned my head away, biting my lip hard. His warm hand squeezed mine. He very kindly waited until I recovered. I was so glad he didn't say anything, as I truly did not want to cry in front of the others.

At last I was able to regain my composure. I surprised myself when I looked back at him. "I'm all right," I assured him. "It's going to take time to get used to a new place. I'm glad I'm here, just a little lonely, that's all."

"Well, then, you've got to join the Help Line. We've got training coming up in two weeks. You'll have to go through that first, but you can come to the next staff gathering to get a head start on meeting everyone and learn about the organization. Heck, I'll give you a personal tour of the place next Saturday if you want."

"Okay," I said, hoping I didn't sound too eager.

"Can I get your number? I'll call you Friday night and set up a time to meet you."

"Sure."

He let go of my hand and pulled a pen and pad from the leather pouch on his belt. I gave him my number and memorized his.

"Well, I guess we'll be in touch," he said.

As I climbed on the elevator to head back to my room, I could hardly believe all that had transpired. In less than an hour, I'd poured out my deepest secrets to a perfect stranger. Thoughts of Ken threatened to ruin the joy I felt, but I quickly dismissed them, telling myself it was normal to have friends. *Besides,* I decided, *how can I keep myself from spending time with someone who can see right through me?*

Chapter 19

Looking through the Window Pane

December 1971

"Hey, that sounds cool, man. Can you tell me what else you're seeing?"
"Far out!"
"Hey, hey, its okay, that's normal, man. It's just the way it goes when you're taking a ride like this. So can you tell me more about the Christmas lights on your tree?"
"Oh cool! That's got to be beautiful."

I had been listening intently for over an hour as Mike talked down the tripper on the other end of the line. I figured he'd be tied up long past our Friday graveyard shift. It was already 3:50 a.m. and we were scheduled to leave at four. *Never leave a tripper alone* was rule number one at the Help Line. An acid head under the influence of LSD, particularly one who shows signs of freaking, can easily plunge into a bad trip if left abruptly. A help line worker who needs to transition a tripper to another phone worker has to do it very carefully. I knew Mike would opt to stay on the phone to the end.

I'd observed interactions like this several times since joining Help Line. Though I'd only handled two acid calls myself, Mike said I was a natural. The experience definitely raised my curiosity. The more I listened, the more tantalized I became with this phenomenon called tripping.

Mike was impressive to watch as he skillfully moved his caller from negativity to happiness. I must admit, however, it made me ponder the resulting paradox. I couldn't decide which was true. On the one hand, Mike possessed a quality about him resembling that of a spiritual teacher as he guided his pupil through the world of psychedelica. On the other hand, he was affirming the use of a powerful mind-altering substance which, by most people's standards, was terrible, awful, even evil. Despite my doubts, I felt drawn to him. After all, he'd spotted my greatest secret on first meeting, and had offered me total acceptance. So often I found myself wanting to surrender to him. Give up any thoughts of my own and let him decide for me what I needed, while at the same time resisting the attraction with all my might. *How can I give myself over to a man I've only known for two months when I'm still in love with Ken?* I regularly asked myself. Sitting transfixed in my chair observing Mike's every move, I heard the door of the center bang open. My contemplative spell was broken.

"Hey, Geri, what's happenin'?" It was Carl, one of the phone workers for the next shift.

I placed my finger over my lips to indicate Mike was on a call. "Hey, Carl," I whispered.

Motioning him to follow me, I went into the lounge. When we were out of Mike's earshot, I proceeded to bring him up to speed.

"He's on the phone with a tripper. Did four hits at once from what I can gather," I said, taking a seat in the overstuffed chair where I could easily see Carl on the couch across from me.

"Far out! Four hits at once? Bet he's buzzed."

"Yeah, Mike's been able to keep him up, but there were some freaky moments when I thought he'd lost the guy."

When I saw Carl's rust-streaked beard move upwards, I assumed he was making a responsive gesture. His words confirmed my hypothesis.

"Whoo! Bet he's way past the ozone layer by now!"

"No kidding," I agreed, as I noted how frequently I'd been using overt cues to help me fill in the blanks of what I didn't see.

"So, anything else?"

"Not much. Had a female caller worried about end of semester grades. I think she'd been drinking a bit. Got her roommate on the line, and she's gonna keep an eye on her tonight. Pretty depressed. Got a rich daddy she needs to please real bad."

"Bummer."

"Also got a mom looking for her fifteen-year-old daughter. Thinks she ran away. I gave her the number for the runaway hotline. Sure felt sorry for her. She was pretty upset. I told her she could call back if she needs to."

"Good, good!" Carl said, nodding. As he did this, I admired his long curly locks which matched the red in his chin. Both hair and beard were so long they almost touched his waistline. I wondered if his hair was as long as mine, given he was much taller than me by about a foot. The compulsion to reach out and grab it was difficult to resist. It looked so soft and inviting. I wasn't attracted to him by any stretch of the imagination, but I loved his wiry animated movements which matched his comical style. He had a practical sense about him, especially when it came to working the phones.

"Anything else?" he asked.

"Mike had another call before this one, but not sure what it was about. I was on the other line."

"Okay. Well, not too heavy for a Friday night. Sounds like you guys got it all under control." He flashed me a big smile.

I felt a warm sensation of belonging as I finished my evening report.

Just then Crystal came in. Instantly my stomach reacted with its usual twist. Ignoring me completely, she walked between the two of us and turned to Carl.

She gave him a big kiss on his head. When she bent over to hug him, her petite butt almost landed in my face.

"Hey, Carl! Good to see you. Couldn't wait to give ya that kiss, honey buns. Great party last Saturday. That was some good shit ya had. Took me a couple a days to get my head screwed back on. Man, was I strung out. Almost didn't make it to my Monday morning class."

Carl laughed. "Yeah, you were really suckin' back on that bong like it was a baby bottle. Gotta slow down a bit there, Crystal, so you don't fuck yourself up so bad."

"Ah, I can handle it. That was nothin' compared to some of the stuff I've done. Takes a real woman ta keep up with you boys, ya know!"

Even though she was disregarding my presence, I had the notion she was trying to impress me. When she stood, I couldn't help take pleasure in how ugly and stringy her mousy brown hair looked. It hung way past her bottom and was uncombed and frizzy at the ends. She threw it over her shoulder in a flirtatious manner as she turned away.

"Oh, hi, Geri!" she said, as if noticing me for the first time. "How ya doing, honey?"

I worked hard to resist the urge to react to her condescending tone and simply replied, "Hi, Crystal."

"Well, did you get to answer a call tonight?"

"Yeah."

"Far out! How'd ya do, honey girl?"

"Fine," I said, wishing I could puke.

She pulled up a folding chair from the corner of the room and sat it right in front of me. When she plopped herself down, we were uncomfortably close. I had the feeling she'd purposely blocked Carl from my view. He may have taken her gesture as a signal to leave; he got up and went into the phone room.

"So tell me about your calls. Was Mike able to help you out?"

Despite my growing anger, I bit my tongue and pretended she wasn't bothering me. I was new to the group of flower children making up the Help Line crew. My natural tendency to take on a less than equal status made it hard for me to assert myself and tell Crystal where to get off. I had already learned that this commune of hippy freaks was really just a fraternity-sorority in disguise. There was a hierarchy of love children that was totally opposite to the preaching of the "God, Love, and Rock-and-Roll" philosophy. I knew this counterculture offered me far more sanctuary than some of the other cliques and groups at the university, but I was smart enough to see through the illusion being projected. Crystal was not the only person who hid behind the uniform of bell bottoms and love beads advertising, "Love is all you need," when really she was saying, "I am all you need." There were several others at the Help Line who, despite their peace signs, were filled with competition, jealousy, and the desire for power.

"No big deal. Carl can fill you in," I said, getting up from the chair. My knees brushed hers as I wiggled out from the human barrier she had strategically placed in my way. As I did so, I tripped over her booted foot and fell back. She grabbed my arm and let out a gasp.

"You okay, Geri?" she asked, as if I'd just fallen dangerously far.

"I'm fine," I said, freeing myself from her grip. But as I attempted to stand, she continued to hold on, insisting I was unsafe without her help. When I finally wrestled myself away from her, her short little body strengthened my character. The urge to shove her down almost escaped me. Just then, Crystal pushed upward, causing me to lose my balance once more. Like a cow being rounded up by a nippy little collie, I leaned back into her, resisting her attempt. Our awkward connection tangled us up so badly we both ended up falling into the chair.

"Are you okay, Geri?"

I almost laughed at her patronizing tone, particularly when I was the one crushing her.

"I'm fine!" I reiterated, pushing myself up, breaking free of her. As I quickly moved out of her reach, she said, "Geri, you should be more careful."

More careful? You little— But my insecurity kept me from speaking my thoughts. *Why can't I stand up to this idiot?* I brooded, as the moment for a comeback slipped away. Instead I rationalized my failure to tell her off by reminding myself how truly ridiculous she was.

Crystal prided herself on breaking the social norms any chance she got. I'd overheard her more than once talking about how Americans were too formal about their greetings.

"In other countries," Crystal would say, "there's a lot more hugging and kissing, and people stand a lot closer to one another. I think it's groovy to be close. It's all about love, you know." Then she'd proceed to push her toes up to the person she was talking to and hug and kiss them no matter how uncomfortable she made them feel.

She never notices what another needs unless she's performing on the phone, I told myself.

I left the lounge without a word and headed to the crash room. This is where transient hippies would sleep if they were hitchhiking through the area and needed a place to spend the night.

As I drifted off, I thought I heard Crystal talking about me. Not wanting to let her upset me further, I thought about Mike. I consoled myself with the likelihood that we'd probably walk to Big Bob's when he was through. This all-night hangout, situated on the main drag next to the university, served the best, greasiest hamburgers any time of the day or night. It was one high calorie meal I could count on at least once a week.

"Ready to go?" For a second I couldn't remember where I was. I wiped the sleep from my eyes, noticing a figure pulling a coat off a hook. "Hey sleepyhead, you gonna stay here all day? It's almost six, and I'm starved." It took a second for slumber's fog to lift before I recognized Mike's voice.

"Uh, yeah, sure. Let me hit the john and I'll be ready."

I headed off, taking care of my business and splashing cold water on my face. When I completed my personal duties, I bundled up in my coat and headed out the door with my friend. Fresh snow had fallen through the night. The city, now blanketed with silence, created a sweet stillness in me. It didn't last long, however. A similar scene from only a year ago disturbed my quiet. Peace of mind was non-existent then. Remembering how Ken had helped pull me through such an awful time, I wondered how he'd feel about the secret desires I now harbored.

"Well, that was sure a long phone call," I commented, hoping this question would shake the haunting image from my mind.

"Yeah," Mike chuckled. "The guy was pretty buzzed."

"What's it like?" I asked.

"Whaddya mean? Talking to a tripping hippie or doing acid?"

"Dropping acid."

"It's far out, that's for sure."

The squeaking sound of our boots crunching through near zero snows made me think of early childhood scenes. The contrast between such memories of innocence nearly halted my plan of pursuit. Just as I was about to ask my burning question, the sound of a buzzing street lamp triggered images of playing games of hide and seek. The melancholy feelings now filling my heart threatened to keep me from my impending folly. But my passionate desire to search for something more was battling hard against my virtuous nature. In an effort to hang on to my innocence, I said, "Don't you love the sounds of winter?"

"Yeah, doesn't it make ya feel warm inside, even though it's freezing cold?""

"I want to do it," I blurted, scolding myself as I spoke.

"Do what?" Mike asked with surprise.

"I want to drop acid."

"Oh, I don't know about that one, Geri. You got enough to deal with."

"What do you mean I've got too much to deal with?"

"First of all, you got exams coming up. This is a heavy time for any student. You don't want shit like that hanging over you when you drop acid."

"So, what about after exams?"

"Man, I don't know. Acid's a funny thing. Whatever is on your mind at the time you drop gets exaggerated big time. There's a ton of stuff you're dealing with, Geri. We've talked about it lots."

The many nights of conversations with Mike rolled through my mind. I'd shared more with him in two months than I ever shared with Ken. He was truly a thinker. He understood the many questions I had about life, people, and how it all got started. But Mike had somehow come to terms with it all. Me, I still couldn't accept that things were so unfair.

"That's because you haven't accepted your own self," Mike said to me one night, sitting at the center waiting for calls. He had dared to challenge my protests by telling me I could never truly be okay with myself until I got honest about my impending blindness. Despite my arguments, Mike held firm, eventually replying with broad smiles instead of words.

As we walked, I continued bugging him to agree. "You said yourself if you have a good guide, acid can be very enlightening. It might help me."

He gave a combination laugh and moan. "Oh-a-a-ah, Geri. What am I going to do with you? You are too curious for your own good. Using acid to uncover your neurosis is not necessarily the way to go."

"Timothy Leary thinks so. And what about Janoff? He says it's only through primal scream that one can truly release their pain."

"Somehow," Mike said, wrapping his arm affectionately around mine, "you don't strike me as a Timothy Leary type. And as far as Janoff, he's a pretty far-out character. I don't think you want to be unleashing demons on acid. It could be pretty destructive if you ask me. Besides, if you need to scream, I'll help you make it primal." He pulled me close, putting his arm around me as we walked.

I knew what he was alluding to. Mike was definitely interested in me in more ways than friendship. Though I admired him and possessed a hidden desire to totally surrender to him, my loyalty to Ken was strong.

"So, whaddya think? How 'bout being my guide after exams? That gives me two weeks to think about it and be sure it's what I want."

"Geri, Geri, Geri. I don't think you know what you're getting into."

"Come on, Mike. It can't be that bad. You've done it, lots of people have done it, and they're all right."

"There's one thing I can tell you about dropping acid, Geri."

"What's that?"

"Once you've done it, there's no going back."

"Twelve hours, right?"

"I don't mean it like that. I mean that your life will change forever. It opens a door that can never be shut. Not that it's necessarily bad, mind you, but you will never be the same."

His words only fostered my obsession to know. It was snowing again and we were almost to the restaurant. I couldn't imagine what this world of psychedelics was all about. Some said it was kind of like marijuana, but not. Even though I'd seen some mental images of color, those who'd tripped said my experience was not a true hallucination.

I'd experienced some enjoyable times on pot, but I eventually grew to not like it. Whenever I was high, my self-consciousness always increased, yet my confusion from the drug made it harder for me to tell how I was coming across.

The end result was a kind of paranoia. With my decision to stop smoking and to give up speed in March, I had not touched a drug in nine months. Even though my newfound friends at Help Line, especially Mike, helped to reduce my depression, I felt a growing urge to do something to alter my state of consciousness.

The next two weeks were a blur of classes, studying, and exams. I only saw Mike once more when we manned the phones together at the center. As we chatted between phone calls, I brought up my desire to trip with him again.

"You sure you want to do this, Geri?" he asked, hopeful I had changed my mind.

"I really do. You've said yourself, what's life without adventure?"

"I did say that, didn't I? But Geri, this is not a typical adventure."

"Have you ever had a bad trip?"

He thought for a minute. "Well, no, but I've known people who have."

"And how are they now?"

"Well, they're okay I guess, but it was pretty hard on them. I don't want to get you in a bad frame of mind about this, as I can tell you're hell bent on doing it, but there are some who haven't really recovered, you know."

"Who?"

"Well, I'm not really sure."

"Lots of people say it's all propaganda. That parents are saying this stuff because they don't want to let their kids grow up and explore ideas and realities that they don't understand."

"Who knows?" said Mike. "I just think you should really reconsider this."

"Look, I'm done with exams on Thursday. How 'bout you?"

"Wednesday at five for me," he said happily.

"Then let's say we do it Thursday or Saturday night. I am leaving for home on Sunday."

"Yeah, me too.

"So which day then?"

"Actually, Friday would be better. If I can get someone to take our shift for us, that is. It'll give us some space between exams and going home."

"Sure, that'd be even better."

"Okay. I'd ask you to reconsider but I can tell I ain't gonna change your mind on this. You're one stubborn chick, Geri. Smart, likable, and I love that you are so curious, but man…"

"Oh, stop," I said. "I don't know why you're babying me about this. Most of the chicks at the Help Line have done the stuff. I don't know why you think I'm so fragile."

The next day Mike called to say we were on for Friday night. He let me know he'd scored the drug, careful not to say the actual word. I'd learned this was the code of making such deals as no one wanted to get busted. There was an atmosphere of paranoia when participating in such activities, as most believed the FBI were tapping phones, especially campus lines.

The evening finally arrived. The dorm hallways were alive with the hustle and bustle of students. They were hauling suitcases up from the storage closets to pack for Christmas vacation. Since my roommate permanently moved her things out in November, all of my belongings were already in my room, packed and ready to go. I wanted nothing to worry about during my upcoming adventure.

Mike knocked on the door around six.

"You got it?" I asked.

"Right here," he said, holding out his hand. A small medicine bottle lay in his palm. He opened the lid and dropped a tiny fleck of something in my hand. It was about the size of a pinhead. I was unable to see it and could barely feel its plastic texture.

"This is it?"

"That's it. I tried to get microdot, but the guy said it got exposed. You have to keep that stuff in the freezer or it evaporates."

"So what's this stuff if it ain't microdot, purple haze?"

"Nope, this is Windowpane. It's dropped onto film to keep it more stable."

"Really?" I said, admiring the minuscule object in my hand. "I can't believe that this little…uh, whatever it is, is such a big deal."

"Well, you will!" Mike assured me. "This is some pretty pure stuff. Windowpane is of course the best, as it doesn't have any additives in it. Purple haze is often laced with speed, or PCP, which can really fuck you up."

I stared down at the invisible window in my palm. I thought of the words Grace Slick sang about pills making you larger and smaller.

"So this is like Alice through the looking glass?" I remarked.

"I guess you could say that," Mike chuckled. "Well, you ready to drop?"

"Don't we need some water to wash it down with?"

"Sure, that'll work."

I nervously put the tiny piece of film back into his bottle, being careful not to drop it on the floor. While Mike slid off his jacket, I went to the bathroom and filled two glasses. By the time I returned, my body had broken into a noticeable sweat. With a jittery hand, I gave him his drink.

"Hey, no need to be nervous. You're in for the time of your life. Here you go," he said.

I sat down across from him and accepted the minuscule particle. *This is your last chance to turn back!* I told myself. But I knew I had made up my mind.

"Ready to partake in this communion?" Mike asked, raising his glass and clinking it against mine.

"I am," I said, licking the plastic wafer off my hand.

"Bottoms up!" Mike said, sucking back his drink.

I quickly followed his lead, washing down the thin host that held the molecules to a world unknown. *How can something this small do all that I've heard?* I wondered, feeling my adrenal glands send me another zap. *You'll never be the same!* I thought. Fear filled my veins. Sweat dripped from my arm-pits. *What did you do?* Mike must have seen the look on my face.

"Uh-uh. No worried thoughts from here on out. From this moment on we're going to have fun, fun, fun."

I smiled. "Okay. Just a little nervous, that's all."

"Nah, nothing to be nervous about. I had to try and talk you out of it before, but it's really okay. Heck, that's the job of any good guide. It's important to me that you were sure you really wanted to do this. But you've made your decision and now you're in for the time of your life."

"So what do we do 'til it hits?"

"Let's play a game."

"Scrabble?"

"Yeah, I gotta beat you after losing the last two, don't I?"

"Never!" I growled, giving him a wide-eyed sneer. "You will never beat me as long as I am alive!" As I turned my scornful face back into a smile, Mike and I both started laughing. He pinched my cheek. I retorted by ruffling his hair.

This game had become a favorite pastime for us. I was terrible at spelling, but I was darn good at making words from odd combinations of letters. I placed the board on the desk, and Mike and I situated ourselves on the only two chairs in the room.

I was surprised at how easily I kept my focus. I expect my love of competition helped. Beating Mike was definitely a good motivator. It didn't keep me from frequently glancing at the clock, however. After about twenty minutes I wondered if I'd swallowed a placebo. Maybe Mike had chickened out of taking me on this trip.

"You didn't give me elephant shit, did you?" I asked, half smiling, knowing some dealers passed such excrement off as hashish.

"Nah, I wouldn't give you something like that. Don't worry, you'll know it when it hits you, and it won't be long now."

Another little jolt of fear ran through me. But this time my heart seemed to stay pumping faster even though the rush was gone. When I returned my attention to the game, the letter tiles were quivering. I started to laugh.

"What ya laughing at?" Mike asked, chuckling.

"The letters. Mike, can you see them moving?"

He looked down at the board. "Sure can. Pretty cool, eh?"

"It is!" I picked one up. Instantly it stopped. "Hey, it looks normal now!"

"Ah hah! It's trying to trick you!"

"Oh stop!" I said, giving him a slap. "Really, Mike, how come it ain't wiggling in my hand?"

"Who knows?"

I looked down at the letters once again. This time the entire board came alive, twisting and turning and adding color to itself.

"Hey! Look, they're spinning!"

"That they are!"

"Come on, do you really see that?"

"Sure I do!"

"Really? You're not just humoring me?"

"No, ma'am, wouldn't do that to a fellow traveler. Bad policy. Only the truth when taking a trip like this."

Gazing once again at the menagerie before me, I watched it expand into a three dimensional whirlwind.

"They're growing!" I squealed. "The tiles, they look like alphabet chimneys!"

"Woo hoo!" he hooted, taking his finger and swirling them around in a circle.

"It looks like psychedelic ice cream! The pink, blue, and red squares are melting into each other and making rainbow sherbet!"

"Far out!" Mike said, as we hooted and snorted, flicking them back and forth at each other.

"Check it out! Can you see those misty waves of light following the tiles?"

"Those are tripping trails!"

"What are tripping trails?"

"Well, some folks think it's a form of hallucination."

"Really? It looks so cool!"

"Yeah, it's a weird phenomenon, that's for sure. But I don't think it's a hallucination, I think it's real!" Mike informed me.

"How so?" I asked, doubting such misty traces of light could truly exist.

"I think it's simply the particles of light which are normally invisible to us when we're not high."

"What do you mean?"

"Acid, it's a strange thing. It does weird stuff to the brain. It acts on the neurotransmitters, making the nerves that carry thoughts go a little crazy."

Although I'd heard this term in psychology class, I couldn't recall the details of what it was. "What are neurotransmitters?" I asked, finding it odd to be asking such a normal sounding question.

"It's this stuff in our brains that makes nerves transmit. Get it, neurotransmitters?" he said, drawing out the syllables of the word.

"I… get… it," I said, giving him a smile.

Mike waved his hand in the air. Once again I saw the luminescent line follow his movements. I glanced upward and saw the overhead light. Its usual dull bulb now showed as bright as the sun, causing me to squint.

"So anyway," Mike went on, "This fluid, if there's too much or too little of it, will affect how nerves fire. LSD affects the neurotransmitter called serotonin. This fires the nerves that are related to our thinking. Hence, LSD makes you think weird!"

"I love it when you talk smart like this, Mike." I smiled, trying to decide if this conversation was reasonable in the state of mind I was in.

"You silly girl!" he said, reaching over and pinching my cheek. "Don't you want me to tell you this stuff?"

"No, no! I love it, really! It's just you sound so serious when I'm feeling so crazy!"

"Ain't it the truth!" he said, throwing his head back like he always did when he was laughing at himself.

"So go on. Tell me more. Why does having too much of this sera…"

"Serotonin."

"Yeah, serotonin, make us think weird?"

"Have you ever noticed how when you dream, people can change form, and the sequence of events don't make sense?"

"Yeah!" I said, beginning to catch on as other objects in the room started to sway.

"You know, our bodies produce dimethyltryptamine, the chemical we've just consumed, but not in such a concentrated dose. However, at night, or under high stress, like days without sleep, people can get a 'natural high' so to speak."

"So why does everything seem so warm and beautiful? My dreams aren't necessarily like this," I asked, finding it hard to concentrate with my attention wandering to the weirdness in the room.

"As your nerves go all haywire, so do your senses. It's like everything is experienced to the nth degree 'cause all the cells in your entire system are wide open. Heck, little kids feel stuff like this all the time, at least until the stress of life teaches them to close themselves off."

"Too bad! I'm sure feeling pretty groovy right now," I said, as I looked around. Everything had a rich glow about it. Even the chalky white walls looked creamy and soft, as if they were painted with vanilla pudding.

"You are, are you?" Mike replied, reaching over and kissing me on my cheek. As he did so, another trail of light followed the movement of his head.

"There it is again!"

"What's that?"

"The tripping trail."

"Ain't it cool? Even you can see a part of the light spectrum with the help of LSD that straight folks can't."

"Hmmm! Maybe I'll just keep taking the stuff so I can see better." We both laughed.

"I have a hunch you might get a little exhausted from sorting out light waves from all the other stuff you have to look at. By the end of our trip, you're gonna feel pretty strung out from all the stimulation coming your way."

"Bring it on! I's a ready!"

"Right on! How's 'bout we check out the brave new world!" Mike said, getting up and slipping on his jacket.

"Okey dokey!" The floor beneath my feet seemed to tilt as I walked over to get my coat.

We found our way outside, but not before I fondled every Christmas decoration lining the doors on the way to the elevator. I couldn't believe I hadn't noticed their beauty before.

"Mike, touch this! It's like velvet, but I know it's not supposed to feel this soft."

"Ain't it grand!" he agreed, fingering the plastic wreath.

"It's so green!" I exclaimed. "It looks like it's made of emeralds."

"Oh, you are going to be a gas! Can't wait to show you the universe."

Despite Mike's joy at watching me trip, there were a few important rules I had to learn. One of them had to do with keeping our journey a secret. After I commented to a girl in a pretty dress how nice she would be to hug, Mike had to remind me that this was not a good idea. He also told me to keep my opinions about basketball fans between the two of us. I gathered that I had offended a few of them as we passed the athletic building.

Mainly my oo's and ah's about what I felt, smelled, heard, and saw, took up most of the time we shared. I felt like a kid on my first trip to Disneyland, certain we must be in a fairy tale.

As we walked along the path from the dorm to campus, the snow on the branches glittered like diamonds. The lampposts lit the way, shining like halos as they stretched on into infinity. As I gazed across the shadowy field, I half expected the faun from Lewis's *The Lion, The Witch, and the Wardrobe* to appear.

"This is like Narnia!"

"Yeah, you're right." Mike agreed, taking my hand in his.

"I just hope the White Witch never lets the snow melt!"

With the greatest joy I'd ever known I started skipping down the walkway.

"Come on, let's skip our way to Oz!" Mike followed my lead as we laughed and giggled along the way. But reality soon found its way into our fantasy. When I slipped and fell on a patch of ice, my illusion that I could float was squelched.

There were other elements of harsh reality that showed themselves as well. We were walking past rows of houses decorated with Christmas lights. I could hear church bells ringing. It sounded like the rims of millions of crystal goblets were being circled by wet fingers, creating overtones which resonated in perfect pitch. Above me ethereal notes were carried on the wings of angels as they whisked by.

Suddenly Mike screamed. I felt his arms grab me. Instantly my joyous mood plunged headlong into terror.

"Geri, you've got to be careful!" I heard his frightened voice say.

I doubled over in fear. Bright lights whizzed by me from out of nowhere.

"It's okay now," I heard Mike say, but I couldn't pull myself from the nightmare in my mind. "Geri! You're okay now. Take in a deep breath."

Even though I could feel his arms around me, he sounded far away.

"You're okay now. You just forgot to watch for the cars. Breathe in now. Come on, take a deep breath," he coaxed. Gradually I noticed we were both huddled on the ground. Car lights were zooming past us.

"Come on, breathe in deep." Mike demonstrated. The contagious action caused me to mimic his gesture.

"That's good. Now again." Listening to our breathing made me forget about my fear. In fact, I got so into it, Mike had to tell me to stop.

"I think you're ready to go scuba diving!" he laughed. I started laughing, too. I stood and we waited for traffic to clear. I gripped his hand tightly as a stream of headlights seemed to barrel straight at us.

"Pretty freaky, aren't they?" he suggested.

"No kidding!"

As he led me across, I felt like a child. My heart started swelling with love as the image of my father came into view.

"I wish my dad could know what this is like," I told Mike.

"Well, I don't think I'd tell him if I were you."

"Oh, I won't, but Mike, this is just like being in heaven. Everything is so so beautiful and rich. Well, almost everything. Man, I thought I was gonna die back there."

"Yeah, that's the risky part about tripping. It's hard to keep track of safety stuff and all. But we're back on track now."

Mike suggested we stop in at Bob's.

"Not good to trip on an empty stomach."

As we sat at the white counter waiting for our food, little flecks of color began to magically appear.

"Mike! Can you see this?"

"What's that?"

"Look, there's little, like, snowflakes in the counter!"

"Uh huh! I know! Plain white surfaces are the best! This is where you can really have some fun."

"What d'ya mean?"

"Pick a spot on the tabletop."

"Okay."

"Now stare at it for as long as you can. Tell yourself you can see whatever you want, and then watch."

I thought for a minute. "I want to see cotton candy."

"Okay, concentrate on what it looks like and see what happens! Go for it!"

Before I knew it, little puffs of pink cotton candy came into Technicolor view. At first there was one, then two, then three, until finally, the entire counter was covered. They looked so real. I was amazed I could see every detail, right down to their texture.

I want blue ones, I thought. Slowly but surely icy blue fibers began swirling around.

"Hey, I'm watching spun sugar!" I announced, laughing at my humorous remark.

"Sh-sh!" Mike said, putting his finger to my lips. "Remember, we don't want others to know."

"Okay!" I whispered back, giving him a wink. "But, Mike, this is amazing!"

"Sure is!" he chuckled.

Now I want mint green!" I commanded. "Voila!" I said as a cluster of cool green cotton balls magically appeared.

"Oh, my God, Mike, it's like the horse of a different color, like in the Wizard of Oz!" I squealed. But this time Mike did not shush me. Instead, he threw his head back and started cracking up.

"Abracadabra!" I said, waving my hand in the air, "I want all the colors!" My wish was granted. "Ta dah! I did it! Gosh Mike they are so pretty! They look so inviting, I want to reach out and pick them up and eat them!"

"Ain't it glorious?"

"So Mikey, what are you seeing?"

"I'm seeing ruby red hearts and they all belong to you," he said, reaching over and giving me a kiss on my cheek.

I looked up at him. His sparkling eyes were filled with warmth.

"You sure have big pupils!" I remarked.

"The better to see you with, my dear!" As we hugged and kissed, a voice from across the way said, "Wonder what they're on?"

I was just about to tell them, when Mike squeezed my neck and shushed me.

"Oh yeah, right." I smiled, then burst out laughing.

The act of eating took quite some time as each morsel of food took on a life of its own. I could not find a word to describe the magnificence of each mouthful. Eventually we did manage to complete our meal and left the restaurant to continue our adventure.

Mike and I glided down various side streets. We laughed and giggled at everything we saw. My joy was interrupted however, when I suddenly became aware of where we were.

"Where we going?" I asked suspiciously.

"Thought we'd drop in at Normal House."

Instantly, the brilliance of the white snow darkened. Once more I dropped to my knees, holding my stomach so it didn't heave.

"Geri, what's the matter?" Mike asked, his voice filled with urgency.

"I can't!"

"What can't you do?"

But I was not able to answer. My brain was so flooded with emotion I could no longer express my needs. Instead, bits and pieces of ideas flew by, all of them filled with fear and negativity. I was trapped in a conflict between both our desires, and I did not know what to do.

"Geri, can you tell me what is upsetting you?"

"Normal House," I finally managed.

"You don't want to go there?"

I nodded my head vigorously.

"I can't go to Normal House."

"Is that all?" he chuckled.

"No, no, Mike, it's not funny. I just can't!"

"Hey, it's okay. Do you know why?"

"Crystal lives there."

I watched Mike lean back on his heels and slap his forehead. "Oh Geri, I didn't even think about her. See your point. No need to worry. It's about face for you and me!" With that, he stood up, pulled me by my hand, and started heading the other way.

Though it took a while to settle down, the walking helped. Powdery snowflakes commenced to dust our faces, rekindling the beauty I'd temporarily lost.

"It's snowing Mike!"

"I know! Ain't it pretty?"

"Yeah, it's just like in the Wizard of Oz. It's making me feel all better again!"

"Makes you wonder if somebody ain't watching out for us after all!" Mike suggested.

"Maybe," I conceded. "It's pretty strange though."

"What's that?"

"Well, I mean, already I've moved from happiness to fear a couple of times tonight, and it's pretty freaky," I said, squeezing Mike's hand hard. "Maybe Paradise and Hades are right there in our own minds."

"I think you're right about that one, Geri. The trouble with acid is, it can get pretty intense."

"No kidding! Man, I didn't really like getting all screwed up like that."

"I know, it can make you pretty vulnerable," Mike agreed, wrapping his arm around me and pulling me closer. "I mean, you're kinda like a leaf in the wind. That's why it's a good idea to trip with someone you're really comfortable with. Never been one to drop with just anyone myself. It's also the reason why you don't want nothing heavy on your mind. The stuff will exaggerate everything big time, good or bad."

I now understood what Mike was telling me earlier, when he'd tried to talk me out of taking the drug.

"I'm sure glad I'm with you, Mike!"

He stopped abruptly and turned to me.

"Me, too!" he said, hugging me hard. We stood there in the cold, warmth emanating from both of us. Once more the desire to surrender to him almost won out. Again, I saw Ken's smiling blue eyes waiting for me back home.

I released my hold on him. Mike let go and we walked on.

"Well, since you're not interested in visiting Normal House, how's 'bout we go over to the Dean's Den?"

"Okay."

Dean's Den was much less austere than Crystal's place. You didn't have to be a super hippie to hang out at Dean's. There was no pretense or condescension there. When we arrived, he was sitting in his favorite chair with headphones on listening to music. He didn't notice us at first. Not only couldn't he see us in the dim light, his temporary deafness kept him from hearing us as well.

"Hey there, buddy!" Mike said loudly, waving his hand in Dean's face.

"Oh, hi guys!" he answered, pulling off the head phones. "Glad you stopped by. Wanna beer?"

"Ah, no thanks," Mike said. "Geri and I are doin' a little tripping."

"Far out!" he said enthusiastically. I pictured a big smile forming across his face. "Geri! Didn't think you were one to be dropping acid. How's it going?"

I was a bit nervous with the new environment, so I simply smiled and said okay.

"Hey, come on over here," he said, struggling to get up from his overstuffed perch, his big bear-like body lumbering a bit as he stood.

"Ya got to check this out!" Dean wrapped his beefy arm gently around my shoulder, pulling me forward. I didn't know him well, but Dean had a cuddly quality about him. He was a three time college dropout, not much interested in his future, but he loved to party. He'd tried to hit on me a few times for a date, but when I didn't respond, he seemed satisfied just to be friendly. He was sexually unappealing with his scruffy look and unwashed clothes, but I never heard an unkind word come from his lips.

He pulled me off balance, sending a rush of anxiety through me. I wished I could get back to Mike, but Dean kept moving me to the chair.

"Here, let me take your coat."

I reluctantly gave it to him.

"Now, sit down here, Geri, and listen to this."

I did as he asked, letting him place the headset on my head. The ear pieces felt greasy as they rested against my lobes. My polite upbringing prevented me from tearing them off. Instead, I endured their gooey texture, imagining gobs of goop dripping into my ears. But my discomfort lasted only for an instant. As if a warm velvety mist were being washed over my body, I felt myself falling into a deep state of bliss.

Like floating ice crystals on the wings of angels, the delicate sound from Pink Floyd's *Ummagumma* drifted through my ears and into my brain. As the music continued, each note came alive, performing a wondrous dance in my mind's eye.

Fantasia's back! I said to myself, remembering my first experience with marijuana. *Only much better!* I mused, as I merged into oneness with the colorful images flowing inside me.

I'm not sure how long I stayed in the magical land of melody, but when the music ended, I felt deeply saddened. Dean and Mike insisted that I share my joyous experience, so the headphones were unplugged, and the turntable speakers took over.

Since I no longer needed to hear the music from Dean's chair, I returned it to him, crossing the room to the couch where Mike sat. He patted the spot next to him. I appreciated this auditory gesture. I was unable to organize my inner and outer visions to orient myself in the poorly lit room. I snuggled in close as Dean placed another record on the stereo.

His choice of music couldn't have been better. Moody Blues' *Days of Future Past* followed by Iron Butterfly's *In-A-Gadda-Da-Vida* engulfed my spirit, molding it and shaping it into wondrous motions that matched the movement of the notes. To top it off, Mike's body formed warmly around mine, fusing us together in the musical universe.

"Mike, I can't believe how beautiful I feel!" I whispered in his ear.

"We're peaking," he whispered back, sounding like he was right inside me.

"So this is peaking?" I asked, having heard this term before.

"You have arrived at the height of heights, my love!" With that, Mike kissed me hard on the mouth. My desire to respond to him fully was suddenly disrupted by fear. My panic at no longer knowing where I ended and he started, kept me from plunging into his being. Before I could slide back down into a darkened abyss, the rich sound of Carlos Santana's *Black Magic Woman* resurrected my senses. The sweet high-pitched trill of his solo guitar penetrated into my soul, lifting me higher than before.

The door opened. The sound of voices interrupted our ecstasy. Reality once more plunged me downward, confusion and paranoia churning inside me. I couldn't handle the normal occurrence of friends dropping in for a visit.

"How dare they intrude on our world?" I whispered to Mike, digging my fingers into his neck.

"Relax, Geri. It's okay," he murmured in my ear, gently prying my fingers free.

"But, Mike!" I quietly snarled between clenched teeth.

"I know, I know. Just gotta go with the flow. It's the only way to handle the stuff."

As I listened to the conversations, I couldn't believe how nonchalant everyone was. They were chatting like nothing unusual was happening, while I tried to process whether they knew how I felt. When one of them asked me how I was doing, I thought my heart would pump right out of my chest.

"Okay," I heard my voice say, hardly able to believe it was mine. *I've gotta get out of here!* I didn't say.

"Hang on, Geri, we're gonna leave soon," Mike said, making me wonder if he read my mind.

"Sorry to head out so quick guys, but you know how it is," he said, letting out a phony sounding laugh. "Me and Geri are on the road again, aren't we, girl?"

"Uh, yeah," I managed. *Isn't this rude?* I thought. *Shouldn't there be more time between them coming and us going?* In my contemplation, Mike had to nudge me with his knee. He was already up with his jacket on.

"Hey there, Geri, you coming with me?" Mike said, ruffling my hair affectionately.

"Oh, yeah!" After Mike helped me on with my coat, we said our goodbyes and left.

"I'm glad we were on the same wavelength." I said, grasping his hand tightly. "I just hope we weren't too rude."

"Nah! Anybody who's done LSD knows when you get the urge to do something, you gotta do it. That's how to keep a good trip going."

"Sure wish they hadn't come over though."

"Ah, no big deal. We're back on track again." I smiled, glad Mike knew the way.

"Wasn't that so incredible, though?" I asked, as we walked back to the university.

"Sure was!" he agreed, holding me close. Again it seemed we were sharing the same body.

When we passed the athletic building, I felt so far above the world of reality, I couldn't remember what it was like to be straight.

"They have no clue," I told Mike as we ambled by the spectators leaving the basketball game.

"I know," he said

"How can they stand it? How can anyone be satisfied with life when there is so much more?" I asked, now knowing the strain of keeping such a secret. "This is unbelievable, Mike. Everyone should live here."

For the next couple of hours, Mike and I walked and walked. We traveled through all the neighborhood streets admiring the holiday decorations. Sometimes we'd stop and just stare at the lights for a long time. I befriended one little green bulb perched on an evergreen branch. Its emerald glow reached deep into my soul, making me one with its beauty.

In time, however, pink fingers of light pushed back the edges of night's comforter. With the threat of dawn, I realized my mystical journey was about to end. The rapture I'd felt for so long was fading as the rotation of the Earth continued. No longer under the sanctity of the peaceful night, Mike and I decided to go back to my dorm.

When we arrived, he sprawled himself over my roommate's bed. I did likewise on mine.

"So, did you like your trip?" he asked.

"It's amazing!" I said, still in awe. Despite the familiar feelings of being strung out, I could still see little polka dots of light spinning around my vision.

"How 'bout you, did you have fun, too?" I asked, realizing I had barely thought about how Mike felt.

"It was fun watching you. You are still such a little girl, Geri. Don't ever grow up."

"I wish I didn't have to." I agreed, worry already seeping into my thoughts. One of them would be waiting for me when I got home. Even if I didn't tell Ken about Mike, it would be different with him.

"So what kind of stuff went on in your head, Mike?" I asked, fearful I already knew the answer.

"Well, to be honest, I had to struggle with my feelings for you, Geri."

"What do you mean?"

"I mean I really had fun and I enjoyed you so much, but I wanted to be with you. I mean really with you."

With a mixture of guilt and sadness, I admitted to Mike that I already knew.

"It's okay. I understand you're not ready to be with me. You may never be ready, but I wanted you just the same."

I got up off my bed and moved in beside him. He welcomed me into his arms.

"Mike, I'm really sorry. It's not because I don't care about you. If I let myself, I'd feel the same way you do. But Ken…"

"I know. It's okay, really. I'm glad to be with you any way I can. It's just that the acid, it makes everything so much more intense. My feelings for you are so…" He started to cry. I pulled him close and hugged him hard. Though I couldn't tell him, love flowed freely through me as I embraced his warm, wonderful body. He buried his face in my chest and wept. We held each other for a long time. With all my heart I wished I could give myself to him, just as I had wanted to back at Dean's. Memories of Ken's loving affection would not allow it, however.

In time, we both drifted off into a kind of sleep. My dreams were far from normal, however. Psychedelic colors and exaggerated images caused me to flitter in and out of consciousness.

At one point I awoke. I was lying in a cold sweat. Suddenly, I became acutely aware of life's stark reality. It was then that Mike's warning came to me. "Once you've opened that door you can never go back."

I now understood what he meant. I'd taken a trip to heaven. Instinctively I realized that my visit was premature. After all, once you've been to heaven, how do you live in hell?

Chapter 20

Can't Have One without the Other

January 1972

"Frequent callers are those individuals who are using the agency compulsively," Jack was saying. He was the faculty adviser to the Help Line volunteers. "We need to be careful about encouraging some of these folks, as they are likely becoming dependent on the crisis line, substituting all of you for friends."

"So why is that so bad?" Crystal demanded from her spot in the center of the group, most of whom were sitting cross legged on the floor. As the Help Line office was too small to hold the Sunday evening meetings, we gathered in the basement of the campus church.

"Because, if we are always there to listen to their every concern, they may never learn to develop more socially appropriate relationships."

"What if they don't know how to do that?" Liz asked.

I thought about David, the twenty-nine-year-old man who always managed to call on my Friday night shift. Others had mentioned him calling as well. He was a brilliant man who came close to receiving his Ph.D. in algebraic topology before he had a schizophrenic breakdown, as he called it. He had taken too many acid trips, which resulted in several psychiatric hospitalizations. Although he was lonely and without friends, he didn't fit the picture being painted here.

"Is it can't or won't?" Jack challenged.

The atmosphere grew pensive. I could hear several of the twenty-one bodies shifting uncomfortably in their places.

"Another problem with the frequent callers that we need to think about," said Tom, the assistant adviser, "is that they tie up the phone lines when someone in a real crisis could be trying to get through."

"We've got two phone lines, for God's sake," Crystal said. "If we make sure one is free when one of our FC's is doing their best to connect their spirit to one of ours in this inhumane world we live in, then I don't see what harm it does. I mean, what the fuck are we all about if we can't be there for someone who needs a listening ear?"

"Whoa!" Jack said, holding up his hands as if to defend against the words that were coming at him. "I'm not saying you can't talk to these folks. All I'm saying is we need to be thoughtful about how we talk to them."

"Sounds awful damned judgmental in my book," Crystal snapped, whipping her long hair behind her.

"Come on, Crystal," Jack said, in his characteristically mellow voice. "You know me better than that. I don't appreciate the attitude you're copping. These meetings are our opportunity to discuss concerns and situations. If you're gonna be laying a trip on me for expressing a concern I and some of the others have, it's only going to make everyone uptight."

"Sorry, Jack. Just freaks me out when we have to discuss our fellow human beings in terms of categories like this."

"I know, I know," Jack said, "but sometimes it's a necessary burden if we are going to be sure we provide the best service to everyone out there."

I couldn't see his face from where I sat at the back of the room; I pictured his soft brown eyes looking downward with regret. Jack was a really cool guy who worked in the student counseling center at the university. It seemed as if every girl in the Help Line group had a crush on him, including me. I so admired his even tempered ability to lead discussions and address Help Line situations.

"Well, what if we set a kind of time limit with them?" Jan suggested from her place on the far side of the basement.

"That'd be weird! 'Woops! Times up. Hold that thought 'til next time you call'," Jeff said in a mocking tone.

"No! I don't mean it like that!" Jan said. "I just mean, explain to the FC's that we do have to keep the lines open so we can really only give them a few minutes a call, or something like that."

"Well, I think we should start talking to them about who else they might rap to besides us," Carl said.

"And if they don't have anyone else?" Crystal challenged.

"Well, I guess I figure it's part of our job to at least help them explore other possibilities," Carl explained. "Though I don't think we should cop out on anyone, we gotta keep them movin' on!"

"Shit!" Crystal exploded. "For fuck sake, what the hell ways can we give to a screwed up, burned out freak who ain't got no friends! I mean if they ain't caught on to how to make friends by the time they get to us, we for damn sure ain't gonna be able to fix 'em with a few flimsy how-to-get-friends slogans at this stage of their trip. We're the best most of these guys got. All we gotta do is just give them a little rapping time, man!"

"Right on!" Kevin agreed. But Kevin always agreed with whatever Crystal said.

What a hypocrite! I thought, wishing I could say it out loud. I felt my muscles tense with disgust as I digested Crystal's pompous attitudes. She was always talking out of both sides of her mouth.

"That's what I mean, Carl!" Jack said, obviously ignoring Crystal and her side kick. "We need to at least talk to them about why they don't have anyone else, and how they might go about finding friends."

Mike murmured behind me. "We need to get off this unsolvable subject," he growled. Until this moment, I had not known where he was in the room. Being the first Sunday back after Christmas break, I had not spoken to him since taking our psychedelic journey together. Even though I arrived early Saturday, I couldn't bring myself to call him. Now, hearing his voice made my stomach do flip flops. *I wish I had skipped this stupid meeting,* I told myself, wondering how I could slip out early to avoid him.

"Other ideas?" I heard Jack asking, Mike's comment apparently unnoticed.

With half my focus still on Mike, I yearned to say something. Unfortunately, my usual feelings of inferiority and intimidation kept me mute.

"I like the time line idea," Sherry said.

What if we used several approaches, different ones at the best times? I thought, vaguely hearing someone from the other side of the room reply to Sherry's comment.

It wouldn't sound too stupid, I told myself, *silently trying to ward off any doubts. If we were busy, we could kindly ask the person to call back, or we could call them when we were free,* I considered as distant voices continued bantering back and forth. *We could just ask callers who are misusing the listener to call back when they are willing to be polite. Yeah, that would work,* I thought, hoping I might encourage myself to chime in. After I rehearsed this scenario in my mind a few times, I readied myself to speak. But when I tuned back in to find a way into the conversation, my heart sank. Nancy, one of the most long winded phone line workers, was in the middle of conveying her opinions.

"Could we make a kind of evaluation check list that we, I mean, whoever you think should make it, Jack, make this check list of signs, I mean, symptoms of what we look for if a frequent caller is showing signs of the bad things, I mean, saying the kind of things that would suggest the reason they are calling ain't so good? You know, like whether the person was calling just to pass the time of day or if they really had a problem, and if it was just so these guys were just calling us to shoot the shit, we'd nicely tell them we had to go, maybe? And—"

Doesn't she ever take a breath? I wondered, feeling irritated.

"What if—" Nancy was saying, when Crystal pounced on her with her know-it-all reasoning.

"Sometimes shootin' the shit is a cover up for the problem! Don't you know that by now, Nancy?"

"Damn her!" I mumbled under my breath. She beat me to the punch. She is so fucking belittling. *That broad's got some nerve!* I decided, slumping sideways onto the floor, totally frustrated. *If Nancy can stumble over her words, why can't I give it a try?* I asked myself. But I knew the answer to my own question and wondered how I might avoid Crystal's opinionated responses and relay my ideas anyway. Dean's hearty voice cut through my thoughts. "I'm thinking if we keep it simple and just tell 'em to only call once or week or something, that'll help folks use us for the right reasons. Freaks sometimes do better when they just know what to expect!"

I couldn't help smile at Dean's simplistic view of things. Despite his own difficulty with following rules, he was willing to give them to others. For a moment, I wished I could be sitting next to Mike so we could exchange knowing smiles.

"Nah, you can't do that with people's feelings," Jeff was saying. "Man, what if they were wantin' to commit suicide, but they'd already called that week. I sure as hell wouldn't want that on my head. Joe, I mean, one of the FC's who calls, I like the guy. He's had some heavy shit to deal with in his life and I don't blame him for needin' to rap with us several times a week. We're all he's got to hold on to, for fuck sake!"

The room was silent for a minute. In the quiet I urged myself to speak. As I mustered up the guts to open my mouth, Jack began.

"I know what you're saying, Jeff. I personally don't have a problem with that. I'm only saying we need to think about each person, their situation, and what they are trying to gain from their phone calls. If they're somebody who is misusing our service by tying up our phone lines, trying to hit on the listener, or refusing to take any steps to help improve themselves, then we need to discuss that and find better ways to help move them to a healthier state of mind. The bottom line is we need to be sure we keep at least one of the lines open, no matter who is calling. If your partner is on the phone and you get a call, make sure one of you gets off as soon as you can to free up one of those lines."

As I listened, I realized Jack had summarized my idea. *I don't know if I've gotten better or worse,* I thought, no longer paying mind to the goings-on in the room. *God, how I wish I didn't have to analyze every damn thought I have. By the time I decide what I want to say, it's either been said or lost.* I am so sick of feeling inferior.

The meeting ended with a plan to have Jack and Tom explore possible resource information for the volunteers. They would specifically look for training that addressed the problems of phone line management and frequent callers. Hotlines like the Help Line were popping up on several university campuses. It was a sign of peers helping peers handle the "turn on, tune in, drop out" motto of the drug culture. Jack thought it might even be good to have paraprofessional counseling training for those of us who possessed those skills. Secretly, I ached to have such an opportunity. I quickly dismissed this possibility, however, as I figured I was not well regarded by the hierarchy of members who pretty much ran the show. I was well aware of my reputation for being meek and insecure.

Nervously, I scooted toward the exit, hoping to avoid Mike. As we filed up the stairwell heading into the main part of the university chapel, I was careful to watch the person in front of me. I knew it was Liz by the unique color of her hair. I kept my eye on how it contrasted with her blue jean shirt. I wanted to reach out and touch her so I knew how high to climb, but I resisted the urge. It turned out she was very easy to follow, though, so I was able to relax by the time we got to the top. She remained in front of me as we walked through the vestibule near the outside door. I grabbed my jacket off the rack and confidently headed to the exit. No longer feeling the need to be cautious, I did not watch Liz as she moved to the door.

Kersplat! Having forgotten the three exit steps, down I flew, barreling headlong into the back of Liz's knees and landing on my bad one. Out of the corner of my vision I saw Liz hit the door, which opened slightly as she did so.

"Uh uh!" I grunted, hoping to keep the sound as much to myself as I could.

"Oh, Geri!" someone screeched.

Oh, shit! I said to myself, hearing the high pitched dramatized voice of Crystal as she rushed frantically through the crowd.

Suddenly, she flung herself down beside me. "Geri, are you all right?" she asked, totally panicked.

"Yeah, I'm fine," I lied, struggling to sound nonchalant, like falling down steps was an everyday thing for me.

"Oh, my God, girl! You've got to be more careful."

Fuck! I screamed inside my head. *Why did she have to see this?*

"Oh, it's no big deal, Crystal," I said, reassuring her and everyone who was now stopping to stare. But as I worked to get up, my knee was telling me otherwise.

Just like before, Crystal grabbed my upper arm and started pulling on me, throwing my balance off and causing me to fall to the side. I wanted so badly to yank her hand off me and tell her to leave me the hell alone, but I didn't.

"If you'll please let go, I can get up myself," I said.

But Crystal just kept holding on and pulling me.

"I think she's okay, Crystal," Liz said.

"No! She's hurt!" Crystal urgently replied.

"She's okay, Crystal. If you give her a little room to breathe, I'm sure she'll be fine." I looked up and for an instant, thought I saw my old friend looking down on me. Her beige-blonde hair gave her an uncanny resemblance to the girl I still deeply missed. Bittersweet emotions momentarily overwhelmed me. I now knew why I had been avoiding Liz despite her gentle unassuming demeanor.

"You okay?" I asked her, remembering she, too, had been hurtled down the stairs.

"Yeah, I'm fine. Let me know if you need a hand," Liz replied. Her sensibility calmed me. I followed her practical lead as I considered what to do next.

But Crystal still held her grip.

"Crystal, I need you to let go so I can use both hands to get up," I said, mimicking Liz's style. It took a few seconds, but finally Crystal did as I asked. I rolled over so both palms were on the floor, my good knee holding most of the weight. Though it was painful, I pushed myself up quickly and stood.

Crystal put her arm around my waist and warned, "Geri, you have got to be more careful! Maybe you should get one of those special white sticks to help support you when you move around. You really shouldn't be taking such risks with your poor eyesight."

Blood rushed to my face. I was overcome with humiliation and rage. The urge to strangle her for making such an audacious remark almost overpowered me. My thoughts moved to my secret hiding place. *Could she know?* I wondered, panicked she might have found out. I quickly pushed my paranoid perceptions away, scolding myself for even considering such notions. Not even Mike knew about the object I had hidden in my underwear drawer. Despite my shame, I forcefully shoved her hand off my waist.

"I don't need a cane!" I said, sounding like a rebellious child refusing to eat the peas and carrots that everyone knows make a person big and strong.

"But Geri, you can't see fine. You just fell down three stairs and hurt yourself. You need to stop being in denial. Everyone says they're worried about you and how you take so many risks."

Once more Crystal's condescending words caused my spirit to sink. *Everyone's saying it?* I repeated her message in my mind. *Oh my God, everyone!* Knowing I could not stand against 'everyone', I wished I could die, right then and there. *Don't let yourself have a total emotional meltdown!* I begged, as I looked for a wall to steady myself. My knee was surging with pain. I wished someone would hold me up as I grew more and more unstable in body and mind.

"Crystal, you need to mind your own business," I heard Liz say as she moved between us. The strength in her voice was contagious.

I don't have to take this! I told myself.

"Well, she's gonna get hurt!" Crystal warned.

"It's none of your concern." I said, drawing on Liz's confidence. Liz reached out and opened the door. I thanked her and gingerly walked through it. The crisp evening air cleared my head. I wished I could have expressed my gratitude better for the dignity Liz gave me.

"Hey, Geri, you walking home?" Mike said, running up beside me.

I turned and looked up at him. The late hour of the winter's evening made it impossible for me to see his expression.

"Yeah."

"Good, I'll come with you then, if you don't mind."
"If you want."
"So, how was your break?" Mike asked.
"Oh, it was okay."
"Really?"
"Yeah, how about yours?"
"It was shit. When did you get back?"
I hesitated and then decided to tell the truth. "Yesterday morning."
"Yesterday, huh?" We walked in silence for a bit. Finally, Mike put his arm around my shoulder.
"You're limping."
"Uh, yeah, a little," I admitted.
"So, you really did hurt yourself falling down those stairs, didn't you?" I could hear he was smiling. I pushed his arm off of me.
"Glad it makes you so happy!" I said.

Mike also had periodically bugged me about being so stubborn, telling me I should be more careful. Only once had he dared to suggest I use a white cane. Only once had I given him my wrath.

"Ah, come on, can't help it when you know I told you so."
I remained silent.
"Okay. What's the matter?"
"Nothing," I lied.
"Come on! I know you, Geri. I know you're upset. Hell, you didn't even call me when you got back. And it's the first time you didn't sit with me either. Did you fall back in love with your Ken doll?"

I was surprised at how flippant he was acting.
"Mike!" I said. "That's not very nice. I've been honest about Ken with you. I thought you understood!"
"That's before I spent Christmas vacation thinking about you back home in his arms. Can't blame me, Geri. Then I see you for the first time since you're back, and you ignore me. What the fuck am I suppose to think?"

Again, I fell silent.
"Well, I'll tell you what I'm thinking. I'm thinking you went home, realized how much in love with the guy you are, and now you want to dump our friendship completely."

The pain I'd been feeling since I went home and spent time with Ken surfaced. Unlike other sad situations which brought tears and an aching feeling in the heart, this state of conflicting affairs left me feeling empty and hollow inside.

As I searched for the right words, all I could come up with was. "You're wrong."

"I'm wrong? Well, that's great!" Mike said, stopping to hug me with both arms now. But I didn't respond.

"Why are you so uptight then, Geri? If it's not that you are giving up on me, then what is the matter?"

"I didn't say I don't love him any more, Mike. I didn't say I don't love you. I just said I didn't go home and realize I only loved Ken."

We started walking again. Mike was quiet. Finally he said, "Yeah, I see what you mean."

"Mike? What am I going to do? I love both of you! But I can't love both of you. I feel so awful!"

We didn't say anything for a long time. Finally Mike asked, "So, did you tell him about me?"

"A little," I said.

"Does he have any idea how you feel?"

"Probably," I admitted. "He could tell I wasn't as connected to him. He kept asking me what was wrong, but I couldn't tell him. God, Mike, it was awful. The whole time I was with him I was thinking of you. Everything seemed so stupid. I mean not just Ken, but everything and everybody."

"I'll bet," Mike said knowingly.

"It's true what you said. I'm in a different world now. I kept looking at everyone, listening to them talk about everyday stuff, knowing they had no clue where I'd been. I felt so separate from them."

"You can't say I didn't warn you."

"Come on, Mike. Don't give me that 'I told you so' shit. I don't need no guilt trippin'! I'm not saying I regret taking acid, I'm just not sure how to handle things now that I've been to heaven. I feel like I've got this incredible secret that I can't share with anyone, yet I want to share it with everyone."

"That'll pass, Geri. You'll get used to having that secret, and it won't bother you as much that you have to keep it to yourself or at least between fellow trippers."

"Maybe," I said doubtfully, "But I do know that it'll be hard to be close with someone who doesn't know where I've been."

Mike took my hand as we turned down the path to my dorm. "There's a price to pay for everything, Geri. You can't have good without bad. It's the old yin-yang."

"What's yin-yang?" I asked.

"It's the Buddhist philosophy. They teach that everything comes in opposites. Dark and light, happy and sad, good and bad. It's the way of the world. For every action there's a reaction. Oops, no, that's Isaac Newton," he said with a chuckle.

"Can I come up?" Mike asked as we reached the dorm.

"I don't know. I just feel so shitty. I won't be very good company."

"I don't mind. You don't have to be in a good mood for me, you know. I'm so glad to see you."

As I thought about the compromising position we could get ourselves into upstairs in my dorm, I decided to bow out.

"Think you can wait? I really feel like going to bed as soon as I'm done studying. I got an eight o'clock class, and I need to get a head start on the first chapters so I don't get behind." Mike reluctantly accepted my request. With little left to say, I opened the dormitory door and said, "I'll see you Friday, okay?"

"Okay!" he said, bending down to kiss me on the top of my head.

I stepped into the elevator. With each level of ascent, I felt more down. When I entered my room, the emptiness magnified the sense of isolation growing inside me. Any ability I may have thought I had for studying disappeared. I decided to set up the stereo my mom graciously loaned me. Despite the loneliness I felt, there were advantages to having the entire room to myself. Dormitory space was at a premium, and I had double of everything. I set up the stereo on my roommate's desk and then squatted down in front of a box of records in my closet. One at a time, I began to read the Braille labels I'd placed on them the previous summer. It would be another tedious but necessary task if I was going to locate the one I knew I had to hear. *When did I stop being able to read the labels on these things?* I asked myself, straining to remember. I could still read them if they didn't have to put all that fancy writing on them! But the nasty word spoken by Crystal earlier hit me.

"Denial!" I said aloud. "Like she fuckin' knows it all!" I continued ranting, shaking my head back and forth. "She needs to learn to mind her own business!" I shouted, yanking LP's out faster now. "Where is that stupid album anyway?" I said in as nasty a tone as I could, bolting upright with pain I could no longer contain. "Fuck it!" I said, giving the box a kick with my already hurt leg. "Damn, I want to hear Joan!" I whined, glad I hadn't invited Mike up. Sitting down on the floor this time with my bad leg outstretched, I continued rummaging through the records. At last, I located what I was looking for.

Farewell, Angelina read the dots beneath my fingers. I took my prized album over to the stereo and felt for the tiny dot of glue I had cleverly put on Side 1 of all my LP's. After finding it, I carefully manipulated the cumbersome disk so its hole sat balanced on my index finger. I guided the edge of the record with my other hand so as not to let it get scratched in the process, located the top of the spindle and slid the hole onto its tip. I made sure to manually move the record down past the eject switch so it didn't have to drop while the turntable was moving. I had learned this is how most of the scratches in the vinyl occurred. I hated the sound of crackles and pops made by such mars in the record. As a result, most of my collection sounded very rich and unscathed.

Once more I felt grateful Mike was not around. Even as accepting as he was, I had not yet performed such delicate tasks in front of him, or Ken, for that matter.

I would have given the job to either of them before I'd allow them to watch me use tactile alternatives for performing visual duties.

As I flopped on my bed, the deep rich voice of Joan Baez, one of my favorite folk singers, began with the title words to *Farewell Angelina*. The bravado of her strong female voice was so rich and soothing as she sang Bob Dylan's words about the pain of life and moving on. Curling up once more in my favorite position, I melted into the music, releasing the pain of my existence.

But as the needle floated gently through the grooves of the vinyl, memories of the awkward moments with Ken pushed their way to the surface. At first he didn't notice how distant I felt. He was so glad to see me when he picked me up at the bus station on Sunday night, he didn't notice my guarded mood. As he hugged and kissed me in the front seat of his dad's car, he had no clue I'd been to another world. But, after our third meeting, he could no longer overlook how I'd changed. He finally forced me to explain.

"You feelin' okay, Ger?" he asked, sitting across from me at the restaurant where I had so foolishly given my secret away.

"Yeah, sure," I lied.

"Well, you sure don't act it."

"Whaddya mean?" I said, wishing I hadn't.

"I don't know. You haven't been as talkative as usual. And you, well, you don't seem as affectionate."

I felt my cheeks flush. Though I tried to dispel his concerns, I heard my voice crack and then I flinched.

"You met somebody else," he blurted out.

I was caught completely off guard. Before I could stop myself, I shifted uncomfortably, letting out a nervous cough.

"You have, haven't you?" His look was serious now. In the bright light, I saw a wrinkle of pain run across his face. For one brief moment, I considered taking advantage of this question to tell him the truth.

"No!" I insisted instead.

"But Geri, I can tell! "

"No, really, Ken," I said with more confidence, remembering from my childhood how believing what I said was the way to tell a lie. "I mean, I have met some other people, guys too, but not a boyfriend." My voice was stronger now. I decided I couldn't hurt him with the full truth.

"Positive about that?" he asked, his face and voice more relaxed.

"Of course. I told you about the Help Line. I've met lots of really cool people who work there."

"But nobody special?"

"Well, there's a couple special folks, but you're my boyfriend," I said, reaching across the table and taking his hand in mine. The gesture felt condescending and I hated myself for it. He didn't notice, however, and I figured it was because he didn't want to. Internally, I questioned myself about why I was leading him on, while sharing in his sense of relief. After spending time together over the Christmas break, I realized his sweet innocence was a quality which no longer satisfied me. I wanted to talk about life, its meaning, what acid was and what it did to the consciousness. I wanted to understand where I'd been when I ventured through the windowpane. Why does swallowing a few molecules make everything become so rich and intense? I wanted to go back there, and I couldn't even tell Ken that I'd already been there.

As I remembered how he'd hugged me tighter than ever before, the second song of Joan's album, *Colors*, began to play. Distracted by the new melody, I forced the parting scene with Ken from my mind. I did not stay focused on the song for very long, however. A new rush of emotions, generated by a replay of the evening's earlier scene, once more pumped rage into my blood.
"Damn her!" I blurted out to no one, wishing they could hear. *Who am I telling this to, anyway?* I asked myself, doubling over in anguish. The pain in my gut burned the loneliness deep into my bowels, branding me an outcast forever.
I searched for my rag of comfort, but it was not under my pillow. I remembered I had not unpacked it yet. *You got no reason to cry anyway,* I scolded. Like the record on the turntable, round and round my thoughts went. Feelings of guilt turned to passions of wanting to know more about the acid experience. My emotions rose and fell, until I thought I'd puke from the confusion. The last song of the album started to play. The words caught my attention.

> *How many times have you heard someone say?*
>
> *If I had his money, I could do things my way?*
>
> *Little they know that it's so hard to find*
>
> *One rich man in a hundred with a satisfied mind.*

What the hell is that? I thought, mocking the last phrase. Who really can have a satisfied mind in this world?

> *How many times, have I heard someone say*
>
> *If I had his money, I'd do things my way.*
>
> *Then suddenly it happened, I lost every dime.*
>
> *I'm richer by far, with a satisfied mind.*

"I'll never have a satisfied mind!" I yelled out, as the needle lifted from the LP and the player automatically shut off.

That's what I'm looking for! I suddenly realized.

"So where is it?" I yelled once more. "I feel less satisfied than I did before!" I whined to my walls. "Hey, you're the one who chose to go through the door," I answered myself back. "What did you expect, to find a satisfied mind on the other side, you stupid idiot?"

In the context of this new revelation, I reflected back on all the manipulations and cons I'd performed over the majority of my life. Did I think lying would get me such a state of mind? Anger raged through my veins. The constant figuring, pretending, lying, drug taking, and now dividing my love between very special men made me feel crazy. "When will it all end?" I yelled out loud. "When you confess your sins, you asshole!"

"I'm guilty, I'm guilty!" I hollered. "So charge me, punish me. Put me in jail and throw away the key!" As I listened to my insane conversation, a stream of words coupled by a melody began pouring out of me.

I'm guilty as charged for all that you say.

But whether it's true, don't matter any way.

I throw myself down on the court's great mercy,

Oh please don't go on…

I rushed over to my desk, quickly pulled the Braille writer off the shelf and rolled a piece of paper into it. Fearful that I might lose the honesty of the words now waiting to be released from my fingers, I punched the first three lines out into their appropriate dot formations.

Oh please don't go on…,

"Come on! Come on!" I begged myself to think of the words which would complete the first verse of the poem. Using the alphabet I went through all the letters to try and find the best word to rhyme with mercy.

"I plead no (barky?), no (fercy?), (dispercy?)," Finally I found one which when sung out in syllables, would do the trick.

Oh please don't go on…, I plead nolo contendere.

The next verse came freely.

Oh Joan,

No Joany.

Oh Joany you've sung of so many a kind.

I'm in there for sure, I'm not hard to find.

You've sung of the rich ones, you've sung of the poor,

You've sung of those great ones who have something more.

"But the melody!" I asked, as I considered the possibility of forgetting it by morning. Suddenly it hit me. As if racing against time, I whisked the tape recorder out from my desk, ignoring the surge of pain it brought to my still-aching knee.

I wish I could play guitar like Danny! I thought, remembering the chords he'd shown me. Linda, too, had demonstrated the A, F, and G-minor cords on her new guitar when we visited over Christmas break. Despite her boasting in knowing one more thing I didn't, I gladly endured her willingness to teach me the thing I'd been longing to do for some time now. But I didn't have a guitar, and I had to find a way to remember this music now floating around in my head.

I desperately fumbled through the boxes of reels, searching for a blank tape. "Come on, come on!" I said, feeling as if I were in a life and death situation. Finally I found one. But hurrying and threading a reel to reel tape could only create a greater delay. I forced myself to take a deep breath and slowly wrapped the tape through all the spindles. I retrieved the microphone from my top drawer, plugged it into the machine, and flipped the lever to "record."

"Testing, testing!" I said. Quickly I rewound the tape and played it back. I heard myself loud and clear. Reading from the page in the Braille machine, I paired the written words with the melody still circling in my mind. Relieved to know the first two verses were now safely recorded, I wrote down the rest of the poetry now ready to be let loose. In a matter of a half-hour, I finished the song.

I've listened so carefully and I still don't know why,

I'm not one of those, with a satisfied mind.

What a terrible crime, what a terrible sin,

To be both rich and poor from without and within.

The punishment will last for eternity,

If you've never been blessed with a mind that is free.

For it's the free that are cleansed of all troubles and horror,

How great it would be to have something more.

How great it would be to have something more.

Chapter 21

None Who Are So Blind!

April 1972

"Hey, Geri!" I heard a female voice call from the pathway to my left. Not sure who it was, I turned and spoke as if I knew her well.

"Hi!"

"Congratulations!"

"Uh, thanks," I said, still uncertain who the voice belonged to. I slowed, allowing her to catch up to me as I headed toward the science building.

"Karl told me last night when I was doing my shift."

"Oh, yeah, thanks!" I said, now realizing it was Liz congratulating me on being one of the five Help Line workers hired to do paraprofessional counseling. The interviews were held the previous week and were conducted by the Listening Ear, a crisis hotline from a nearby city. When I received the word three days earlier, I could hardly believe it. I was certain, had the interviews been performed by the board members from the Help Line, I would have been last on the list.

As it was, Mike told me there were rumors going around that I should be reconsidered. "After all, how could someone in denial be a good candidate for such a position?" he said, mimicking the words spoken by a certain someone, as he relayed what he had overheard. With denial being the operative word, it didn't take a genius to figure out who was trying to undermine my success. The other major clue was that Crystal had not been chosen. Mike said it wasn't a pretty picture when she got the word. He happened to be at the center when she received her review by the Listening Ear interviewers.

"You could hear her from the back room all the way to the front door," Mike explained. "When she ran past me she was flinging her hair like a wild woman. She only stopped to ask if I knew who else had been picked. When I said no, she ranted about how pissed off she was that they wouldn't tell her who made it. You should have seen her stomping around in her big boots. I thought the door would come off the hinges after she slammed it." When Crystal found out later that I had been chosen, she used me to make her wine from sour grapes.

While Mike reported the news of Crystal's histrionic snit, I felt a delightful sense of vengeful triumph, as I wallowed in the knowledge that I had been one of the chosen ones. I decided it would not be good to share my exuberance with Liz, so I quickly changed the subject.

"You headed to class?" I asked her.

"Yeah, got a botany lab this morning. How 'bout you?"

"I got a biology lab. You're in your third year, right?"

"Yup, only one more, but first I've gotta get through next week's exams. They sure can be a drag."

"I know. If I can just pass biology with a B, I'll be so happy," I said, nervousness rising as I felt Liz move in beside me. Slowing my pace a bit, I situated myself a half step behind her, feeling a tad more comfortable with this new juxtaposition.

"Hey, Geri?'"

"Yeah?"

"You takin' classes this summer?"

"Uh huh," I said, watching the edge of the grass carefully.

"Where you staying?"

"Oh, I guess the dorm."

"Well, Jan and I were thinking of getting a year lease, but the apartments we're looking at are a bit much for two of us."

"Bummer," I said, half listening. I was concentrating on keeping a steady pace without veering off the sidewalk.

"So, you think you might be interested in rooming with us for a year?"

Totally shocked at this very unexpected proposal, I couldn't think to speak. Could Jan and Liz be reacting to my new status with the Help Line? I wondered suspiciously as I felt the spongy texture of the grass slide under my foot. I quickly shifted my weight toward the left until my feet touched the hard surface again.

"Actually, I tried calling you last weekend, but you weren't home, so I'm glad I bumped into you," she continued.

Delighted that she hadn't noticed my bumbling, I listened with growing anticipation.

"Jan and I talked about who we might want to have room with us, and we thought about you."

Thought about me, I said to myself, realizing this well-planned offer was not a reaction to my recent success. Astonished, I tried to think of what to say.

"You don't have to give an answer right away, Geri. And if you aren't interested, that's okay. We just thought you might want to get out of the dorms."

"Oh, yeah! Well, uh, sure. How much would it cost?" I stammered, still amazed at her unexpected proposal.

"We figured about $66.66 a month, with an additional penny every three months for each of us." Chuckling, Liz added, "But if you can't handle that extra penny, I'll foot ya for it."

"Oh gee, thanks," I said awkwardly, wishing I could join more fully in her humor.

"Can I think about it for a few days? I gotta figure out my finances so I'm sure I can afford it," I said, wondering why I didn't simply say yes, knowing I could manage the money.

The previous Saturday I had been interviewed by the vice president of the university and his wife to baby sit their kids. Apparently they were impressed with my description of how I believed children should be managed, and they accepted my explanation of how I accommodated my visual impairment and hired me. I had plans to save up for a guitar, and working four days a week through the summer with two weekends a month during the regular school year would get me the rent money.

"Oh sure! Can you call me, say, by Friday at four? That'll give us 'til five to let the complex office know."

"What apartments are they, by the way?" I asked.

"Oh, shit. Yeah, I guess that'd help." Liz said, as I heard her slapping her head with her hand. The sound made me want to look her way, but I knew I'd better keep my eyes peeled on both shoulders in front of me, Liz's to my left and the sidewalk's to my right. "It's the ones with the pool, behind the university, on the other side of the railroad tracks from your dorm. It wouldn't be but an extra five minute walk to classes."

"Oh, yeah, those are nice apartments," I said, trying not to let the thrill of this new possibility make me mess up and fall into her.

"And we'll have to pay electric, which I think is around $15 a month," Liz added. "That'll be $5 per each of us."

"Ah, yeah, thanks," I said, calculating the total in my head.

Liz went on to explain how we could share groceries to make it cheaper.

The idea of having roommates was too good to be true. No more eating out of popcorn poppers! No more hassle with cafeteria lines! I wanted to jump for joy. I resisted the urge to accept her offer right then and there. Instead, I told her I'd call her on Friday.

Before we went our separate ways, Liz tore some paper out of her notebook and jotted down her phone number. "Did I make it big enough? I can redo it if you need," she said matter of factly.

I looked at the ragged slip with large darkened numbers in my hand.

"Yeah, I can read this just fine. Thanks," I half lied, knowing I'd need to be out of the sunlight to see it clearly.

I could hardly concentrate as the lab assistant helped me dissect a fetal pig. Not only was I excited about Liz's offer, I had plans to meet with the dean of the special education department to declare my major directly following my lab.

At last the time had come. As I carefully walked to the appropriate building, I thought about my motives for my recent decision. After enrolling in a course my second semester called Educating the Exceptional Child, I found myself outraged at the messages of condescension still being fostered about children with disabilities. The very title of the class carried with it undertones of segregation, attaching the word 'exceptional' to certain children, instead of viewing kids as kids.

"Why are children with disabilities exceptional?" I asked Mike one Friday night after hanging up with Dave, the guy who still regularly called me at the Help Line.

"Well, I think they're just trying to find a nice way to identify the group of kids they're talking about," Mike said.

"Then why can't they just say 'Educating Children with Disabilities'?"

"Too long."

"Too bad!" I barked. "It's the old 'us and them' syndrome. The 'us' or 'we' being those who always know what's best for 'them'."

"Well you gotta admit, Geri, if you're gonna be a teacher, you'd better know what's best for the children you're teaching."

"No no no!" I said, pounding my fist on the desk. "I'm not talking about teachers and students."

"Well, what the hell are you talking about then?" Mike asked, letting out a nervous laugh.

"I'm talking about the general way these instructors refer to people with disabilities. I mean, I don't have a problem when they are explaining how you use this tool or that strategy for teaching a student who is deaf, or blind, or who uses a wheelchair. That's just dandy. It's when they stand up there and talk about how 'those kids' are this way and 'these kids' are that way that drives me crazy! The worst is when they show slides of these cute little cripple kids; going on and on about how sweet and adorable and amazing they are."

"So you don't think they're cute or amazing?"

"Mike!" I half yelled. "You're not hearing what I'm saying." Again he chuckled. "I mean all kids are cute and sweet and amazing. But they are sensationalizing these kids. They are saying that because they have an illness or disability, they are extra amazing, extra cute. Heck, some of the kids they show are downright ugly!"

"Now you're discriminating against kids who are ugly."

I threw up my hands in disgust. "Oh, you are too stupid," I said.

"Now you're discriminating against me! It's not my fault I'm not as smart as you," he said, laughing harder now.

I struggled to regain my composure so I didn't act on my urge to punch him. I took a deep breath and lowered my voice.

"Mike, don't you get it? Don't you see how they are grouping these children into a box of specialness? I mean, it's the same thing that they did to the colored people, only instead of looking at these kids as bad, they make them special. Either way, they are separate, segregated."

"But don't you think it's different? I mean it's not like they have to drink out of a different fountain, or go to the back of the bus!"

"Oh, no!" I mockingly laughed. "They fuckin' can't even get on a bus, unless it's a special one for going to school. And when's the last time you saw a kid in a wheelchair getting a drink in a public fountain? Hell, they can't even reach one, it's too high up."

Mike thought for a moment. "You got a point there."

"I know I do! All I'm saying is that any time you make somebody special or bad, you've done the same thing to them."

"Well, I'll give you one thing," Mike said. "You sure are passionate about this."

"Damned straight I am. Spent too many years at the Do-gooders Christmas parties to put up with this shit."

"Do-gooder's what?" Mike asked, genuinely confused.

I proceeded to explain to Mike about some of my experiences at That School. I was amazed at the sense of relief I felt as I poured out some of the events of my youth.

"Holy shit!" Mike said, as I told him about nap time and how we kids couldn't go out at recess. He finally began to catch on to what I was saying by the time I finished the story about my old classmate being asked to wear a bib.

As I entered the education building, I reminisced about this conversation. More than ever, I wanted to become a special education teacher so I could teach students they were as okay as anyone else.

"May I help you?" the lady behind the desk asked.

"Yes," I said, sounding grown up as I stood there in a blue shirtwaist dress with my hair tied back in a metal clasp. "I have an appointment with Professor Powers."

"Your name?"

"Geri Taeckens."

"Have a seat, Miss Taeckens. Dr. Powers is presently with a student. He'll be with you as soon as he is finished."

"Thank you," I said.

As I sat in the two-chair waiting area, my excitement grew at the prospect of finding and following my newfound path. I hoped none of the remnants from my earlier activities had seeped through the lab coat as I smoothed the skirt of my dress, trying to make it longer than it was. Reaching up, I followed my hairline back to the barrette to be sure no strands were out of place. I had purposely dressed more conservatively for the interview.

Rumor had it this professor was rather old fashioned. As head of the department for the visually impaired division of the special education program, he carried a reputation for being very strict. I'd overheard one student in the Exceptional Children class tell how he didn't feel he was a good instructor unless he flunked fifty percent of his students. I felt confident, however, as I figured he'd view my visual impairment as an asset.

A half an hour passed. Worried I might miss my next class, I double checked with the secretary to be sure he knew I was waiting.

"He's with a student, Miss Taeckens. You'll have to wait or make another appointment."

"I'll wait," I said, figuring I could miss English Lit, if I needed to. I was way too excited to pass up this opportunity. Finally, after fifty-five minutes, the door to my left opened and a female student emerged. A couple minutes later, I heard my name.

"Miss Taeckens," the stern voice of Professor Powers boomed.

I started at the sound.

"Yes, I'm Miss Taeckens," I said, attempting to look as sighted as possible. I reached out my hand, but he did not shake it.

Instead he turned his back and walked into his office. I assumed I was to follow him in.

"You may sit down," he said flatly.

The room was rather dark, only the dim glow of a lamp lit a small section of his desk positioned between us. I inched myself in further, struggling to feel a chair with my leg. I felt a cold metal object through my nylon. Assuming it belonged to the item I was looking for, I bent to sit. But instead of a seat hitting my bottom, the sharp corner of a projector stand jabbed me in the butt. Instinctively, I bolted forward to avoid the pain, tripping over a cord that was running across the floor.

"The seat is farther to your right," Dr. Powers said.

"Oh, yes, thank you," I said, totally freaked. Nervously, I turned and looked, but all I could see was mounds of clutter. Being as inconspicuous as I could, I nonchalantly moved my hand over several items strewn across more items. Still I could not find a platform to rest my now aching derriere. Noticing my predicament, Professor Powers stood up, walked over beside me, and patted the cushion of an office arm chair.

"Thank you," I said, grateful to have a place to anchor myself. Blood rushed to my cheeks, signifying my usual state of embarrassment. But his next response dispelled my fear of having blown the interview.

"How can I help you, Miss Taeckens?" he asked, behaving as if nothing unusual had taken place.

"Well," I said, clearing my throat. "I've been taking the Exceptional Child course, and I'm very interested in teaching."

"Yes…"

"Well, uh, well, I am particularly interested in becoming a teacher of the visually impaired."

"Oh, really?" he said, a slight inflection in his voice this time. Accepting this as a sign of his interest, I forged on.

"Yes! I am very interested in education and the fact that I have a similar experience to the children I'd be teaching, I have decided to declare my major in this area. That is," I said as an afterthought, "with your permission, sir."

"The blind can't teach the blind," he said matter of factly, returning to his original unimpressed tone. "Anything else, Miss Taeckens?" he added, shuffling some papers in his hands.

Flabbergasted, I couldn't believe what I was hearing. *Anything else?* I repeated in my mind. *What the—*

But before I could respond out loud, Dr. Powers stood and said, "I'm sorry, Miss Taeckens. I realize that you are likely under the impression that you would make a good teacher. I commend you, of course, on your desire to be a role model or whatever it is you think you would be adding to the profession of teaching, but trust me, it does not work that way. I've been in the business of teaching teachers for many years. I've had the unfortunate task of overseeing two such university students who possessed the characteristic of blindness during that time. I found it to be disastrous and I feel it my responsibility to you and the students who might potentially be under your charge, to avoid wasting your time and theirs. It has not, and cannot, work. I would strongly recommend that you use your desire to help others of your kind by concentrating in the field of social work or psychology, or one of the other helping professions."

I was stunned, sitting motionless, glued to my chair.

"Is there anything else, Miss Taeckens? I do have to get to class." He stepped closer to me, urging me to get up and leave.

"But, Dr. Powers!" I finally managed. "What you're saying is totally wrong!" The abruptness with which Professor Powers stopped and turned toward me was scary.

"Young lady. I hope you realize that I am not the least bit interested in your opinion of the rightness or wrongness of my decisions. I didn't make head of the department on the advice of students like you who have no life experience, particularly in the area of teaching. You are naive and I must insist you get on with your education, but not in my department! Now if you will excuse me!"

Contrary to Professor Powers' attempt to intimidate me by speaking to me in such an authoritative manner, I did not cower. Instead, his audacity only exploded the rage I had told Mike about. Standing now, I stamped my foot on the ground and looked directly in his face.

"But Dr. Powers, you don't even know me, or what I can do. You have decided my fate without giving me any opportunity to prove myself. It's not fair that you won't even give me the chance to follow my dream to help kids like me. I'd think you'd realize that because I have a vision problem, I would better understand how students with vision impairments learn best."

"It doesn't take a vision loss to know how to teach a blind student, Miss Taeckens," he snapped, brushing past me. "And in terms of fairness, I would hope that by now you would realize that the concept of fairness does not exist on this planet. As I said, it's my job not to waste your time or your money by authorizing you to major in this area. Now I apologize, but I must be off to class. Good day, Miss Taeckens."

With that, he held the handle of the door, waiting for me to pass so he could shut it. With all my strength, I moved forward, pushing through the wall of my own resistance which threatened to hold me steadfast. My fists tightened as I took the last step past the professor, still standing like a bouncer, ready to grab me and toss me out the door. I couldn't believe what had just transpired. Never in my wildest dreams would I have expected the reaction I got from this bullheaded, narrow-minded idiot.

Fuming, I left the education building and hurried back to my dorm. I tried calling Mike, but he wasn't home. Three times I dialed Ken's number and three times I hung up before his phone could ring. *It'd be cruel to call him*, I told myself. Spring break had not gone well for us. Since I was unable to make a commitment, Ken had suggested we not communicate for a while. As badly as I wanted to hear his sympathetic comments, and as certain as I was he'd give them to me, I knew it would not be fair to pull on his heartstrings. Instead, I changed back into my jeans and t-shirt to try to gain some level of comfort. But it didn't help. I felt like I couldn't contain my rage another minute so I grabbed my keys, charged back out the door and headed to the counseling center. I didn't know who would be doing emergency drop-ins, I just knew I had to talk to someone.

When I arrived at the student center building, where a variety of support programs were offered, I found my way to the counseling office. The lady behind the desk took my name and told me the counselor on call would soon be available. When Jack called my name, my heart sank. I hadn't thought about him as a possibility. I wondered how I could get out of this.

"Hi, Geri, come on in." His voice was so calming I decided to take a chance. I followed him into his office and sat down on the clearly displayed chair in his uncluttered room. Grateful that I didn't have to fumble to sit myself down, I sighed.

"You look a little frazzled. How can I help?"

The offer was overwhelming. Before I could catch myself, I began to cry. Jack patiently waited. As I wept, I tried to think of where to begin. I was upset about so many things. Finally, I regained some semblance of control.

"I don't know how much you are aware of my situation, but you know I don't see too well."

"Yeah, I know about you having problems seeing. Go on."

"Well…well, sometimes it is just so overwhelming. Other people, I mean. I mean how other people perceive me." I paused, choking back the tears.

"Today...well, I mean, today I decided I'd go over and declare my major. I want to be a special education teacher for blind kids," I said, looking up at him through watery eyes.

He looked at me intently. "Go on."

"I went over to get the department head to officially accept me into the program, and he refused." More tears fell from my eyes. I was doubled over, head in hands, hiding my face from Jack and myself.

"Oh, God! I just hate people and how they judge. I just hate always having to ward off their ideas about me. If they don't think I need to use a cane, they think I can't teach blind kids. They don't even know me, yet they think they know everything about me."

I cried some more. Jack reached over and handed me a box of tissues. I took several and blew my nose, sopping up the moisture on my face.

"I see what you mean," he finally said. "I can tell you've been struggling with this for a long time, Geri."

I nodded my head.

"Well, I must say, you certainly don't show it."

"What do you mean?" I asked.

"I mean, I see you every Sunday, and you go about your business, doing your thing on the hotline and hanging with the crowd."

"Oh, you have no idea..." I said, beginning to cry again. I continued to tell him about my self-consciousness. About how I analyzed everything I said or did. How afraid I was to move in front of others for fear of bumping into things or tripping. He listened quietly.

"Wow! Geri, I don't know how you do it. I can't imagine how much energy you use just trying to do what, for others, are ordinary things."

Jack's words hit me. I had never considered such a notion before. Suddenly I realized I only noticed what I couldn't do, never what I could.

"I guess that's what makes you so good," Jack continued.

"What do you mean, 'so good'?"

"What I mean is, I've overheard you on the phone on several occasions. I imagine having first hand experience with managing such tough issues would impact your ability to be a good listener. The reports from the folks at the Listening Ear confirm this. They rave about your ability to assess other people's needs and be empathetic. You also scored very highly in the problem solving arena. Matt, the big guy with the beard who interviewed you?"

I nodded.

"He's the director of the agency, you know, and he said you were the best of the bunch."

Dumbfounded, I stared at Jack, wanting to be sure his face matched his words.

"Me?" I finally asked. "You're sure they're talking about me?"

"Geri?" Jack said, a serious tone in his voice, "You don't have a clue that you have value, do you?"

Again, the tears welled up and rolled down my face. "No. No, I don't feel like I have much of anything good in me," I admitted, dropping my head into my hands. Suddenly, I felt years of secret pent up pain erupting from my heart. I wanted to wail, cry out, for all the terribleness I felt about myself, but I stayed quiet. Terrified I would lose total control, I only allowed the slight sound of my breathing to escape my lips. When I eventually managed to calm myself, Jack spoke.

"Geri?" he asked gently. "Have you ever considered getting some counseling to help you work through all you are dealing with?"

I shook my head no.

"Maybe you should consider this then. You've got quite a burden, and you don't have to do it alone, you know."

In view of his words, I lifted my eyes out from their hiding place.

"Other people don't have to get help. Do you think I'm so bad I can't take care of things by myself?"

Jack let out an affectionate chuckle. "Oh, Geri, you and so many others think emotional pain is meant to be managed alone. Of course I don't think you are so far gone. I'm just suggesting handling your situation doesn't have to be so hard! Heck, we all need other people. If we didn't, you wouldn't need to be working the phones at the Help Line."

"So, I'm like the people who call?" I asked, fearful of his answer.

"What's this judgment call I hear coming from you? You know better than this, Geri. If you didn't, you wouldn't be as good as you are on the phones. It's not us versus them. It's people helping people."

The many critical opinions I held about Crystal surfaced. *I'm just like her!* I thought, scolding myself further for looking down on the organization's clients.

"I'll bet you'd be surprised," Jack continued. "There are many Help Line phone workers who are in counseling."

"Really?"

He gave another heartier laugh. "Oh, Geri, you get fooled by the pretense many of your coworkers project about being cool, or hip, or havin' it together."

I nodded my head. "You're right," I admitted. "But I wouldn't know who to go to anyway, even if I did think it would be a good idea."

"What about me, then?"

I looked up at him again. "You?" I asked, once more surprised someone as together as Jack would even think about meeting with someone like me.

"So you think I'm not good enough, huh?"

"No, no! I mean…"

"I know what you mean, Geri. Even more reason why you should plan to meet with me once a week. It sounds to me like you could use some support as you figure out how to think nicer about yourself."

I nodded. "I'd like that."

"The other thing you need to do is to file a complaint against Dr. Powers. What he is doing is blatant discrimination. We have an office of student rights at this university. I believe you need to make them aware of this situation."

A glimmer of hope unwound a portion of my aching heart, allowing it to beat more freely. "I didn't know about that," I said.

"Yeah, I'll give a call to Joan over there. It's just around the corner from the counseling office. If she's in, you can walk over there right now if you're up to it."

I wanted to address the Dr. Powers issue as soon as possible, so I agreed. Jack made a quick call and told me Joan would be waiting.

"Be sure to make an appointment with Teri, my secretary, before you leave, Geri. Have her set up a standing weekly appointment. I'm working through the summer if you're planning on being here."

"I am," I told him.

It felt like a thousand pounds had lifted from my shoulders as I left Jack's office. I filled out a grievance form in the student rights department, then headed back home. As it had so many times before, sleep transported me to a place where troubles were out of view.

Chapter 22

Relativity Theory

June 1972

"'*I think, therefore I am!*' Who can tell me what Descarte meant when he made this statement about reality? Yes, Mr. Sanders?"

"I think he was saying that reality has to do with thoughts, not emotions."

"Okay…anyone else have an idea? Yes, Miss Wilson, how about you, what do you think he meant?"

"I think he was suggesting that you have to be conscious in order to experience reality."

"Yes, yes, I do think he is referring to consciousness. Mr. Zimmerman, you had your hand up?"

The student sitting next to me in the back of the classroom spoke. "I think he is saying that reality is what you make it."

"Good point, Mr. Zimmerman," Professor Masters said. "I agree. I believe our friend Descarte is suggesting that reality is what you think it to be. What do you think about that, Miss Stevens, is it?"

"Yes," said the quiet voice of the girl in the row in front of me. "Well…"

"Go ahead then."

"Well, I don't believe that makes sense."

"And why not?" Professor Masters asked.

"Well, I mean, if this is a chair that I'm sitting on, and I don't see it is a chair, it still really is a chair, isn't it?"

"Good point. I can tell you're thinking carefully about this concept. So you're saying that because a group of people have decided that the thing you are sitting on is a chair, and if you don't think that, then who is right, the group of people or you? Am I right in interpreting your statement in this way?"

"Yes," she agreed.

"What if," Professor Masters went on, "you were sitting in that chair, but you were unconscious, so you didn't think about that chair, you're not experiencing that chair. Then, is that chair a part of your reality?"

"Well it's still a chair," she said.

"According to whom?" he challenged.

"To us," a voice near the door said.

"Ah, yes, but is that not the reality of each of the people who make up the us, not the person who is unconscious?"

As I sat listening to the discussion taking place in my summer semester philosophy class, the obscure notions being bantered around made my head spin. I decided I'd better take a few notes, so I took the stylus, which I'd been using to poke the palm of my hand, and rotated it outward between my thumb and fingers. I began punching out the appropriate dots on my slate.

Descarte, "I think, therefore I am," I wrote, wishing my writing didn't make such a loud thud. Objects real according to whom?

I hope I've written enough, I thought, knowing the less I wrote the less noise I made.

As I pondered the concepts of the discussion, I thought about the notion of what reality might be. The question of what is truth and reality were ideas I struggled with frequently. I figured there must be something I was missing as the actuality of my own life was growing more difficult. Now, with my upcoming plans for this evening, I added one more question to my deliberations. What is tripping? I wished I could raise my hand and ask what happens to reality when you swallow lysergic acid diethylamide, but I dared not.

While the professor continued debating with the students, my thoughts wandered into troubled arenas.

I'd been living with Liz and Jan for a little over a month now. Though it was great having a real apartment to move around in, I did not feel totally comfortable with them. They had been friends for a couple of years. Though I was happy to have one of the two bedrooms to myself, their time together in the evening added to my sense of separation. There were many idiosyncrasies the two of them shared as well. I never felt like Jan or Liz purposely excluded me, but they had many inside jokes and experiences which increased my feelings of being left out. Every time I heard "Remember when…" or "I'll never forget that time when you…" I was reminded of the strength of their bond.

The other disturbing change in my life had to do with Mike. We were working the graveyard shift together the last Friday in May when he laid it on me.

"I'm leaving Sunday."

"Really. Where you going?" I asked.

"California."

"That's nice, how long you going for?"

"Not sure. Got accepted into Berkley."

It took me a minute to register what he was saying.

"What do you mean?" I asked, suddenly alarmed.

"I got accepted into their anthropology program. Though the semester don't start 'til August, they've offered me a grad assistantship which starts there week after next. Heading out Sunday so I have time to get set up."

"Mike!" I yelled. "Why…When…I had no idea you even applied out there."

"Yup. Never thought I'd make it, but they want me, so I's a-goin'."

"Well, that's real fuckin' nice!"

"Aren't you glad for me?"

I stared at him, stunned that he was acting so offhanded about the whole thing.

"Why the hell…" I couldn't think what to say, and started to cry.

"Geri! Why the tears? I thought you'd be happy for me."

"Happy for you?" I said, sniffling. Getting up, I reached out my hand and searched the cluttered desk for the tissues. Figuring I was in for a good one, I snatched several out of the box.

Mike got up too, walking over to me. He started to put his arms around me but I just pushed him back hard with my hand.

"How could you?" I yelled.

Just then the phone rang.

"I guess I better get this one. Help Line, can I help you?" I heard him say.

I went into the other room and threw myself on the couch, struggling to process the gravity of what I'd just heard. *I can't believe it!* I thought, opening and clenching my fists. *How could he lay this on me like this? And in this setting, for God's sake! What am I gonna do without him?*

My mind ran through all the times we'd spent together. Mike had accepted me like no one else had. His endless words of wisdom, his honesty, his ability to call me on my stubbornness were qualities I'd never found in anyone else. He was such a support in my life. He'd also been a pressure. Although my relationship with Ken was pretty much over, I still had not let go of him fully. Mike wanted more from me and I could never bring myself to completely commit to him. I wondered if this was his way of paying me back. Whatever his intentions, I was about to lose him.

I heard him hang up. He came into the group room and cautiously sat beside me.

"I guess I didn't think you'd be so upset," he finally said.

I lifted my head out of my tissue filled hands. "How could you not think that? How did you assume I would react? 'Oh Mike, I'm so glad you're leaving me so I can't see you or talk to you or hug you any more?'"

He put his arm around me. Reluctantly, I let him.

"You've always known I wouldn't stay in this area forever, Geri. I didn't tell you about the applications 'cause I honestly didn't think I'd get chosen. I'm always sending them out to universities. Most of the grad programs at the really good schools only allow a few students in each year, let alone give assistantships. Gotta have that to pay the way, you know. Even with my 4.0 the competition is great, and I'm a white male, which makes it even harder. The fact that I'm not a resident of California also made me think I wouldn't make it."

Some of his rationale was plausible, but I couldn't buy it.

"You could have at least kept me informed. When did you find out, anyway?"

I felt his arm stiffen. He didn't answer. I pulled back, turning to look him square in the face.

"Well, when did you get the word?"

"Uh, two weeks ago."

I stood up, rage pumping through my veins.

"Two weeks ago!" I yelled. "Mike, how could you not have told me for two whole weeks?"

"I didn't want to spoil the last of our time together," he said, raising his voice defensively.

"But, Mike, that's not fair. You have no right to decide that."

"Look, Geri," he said more firmly. "It's not easy for me to leave. I don't do so good with goodbyes, okay? I just didn't want everyone knowing and having to deal with everyone getting all gaga about the fact that I'm moving on. If it's any consolation, you're the first person I've told. Nobody else knows and actually, I'd just a soon they not find out until I am in California."

"But, Mike, that isn't fair! You have no right to take away everyone's need to get used to your leaving. Come on, we talk about that stuff in training all the time, how we're supposed to help people deal with loss and saying goodbye and all that. Just because it's uncomfortable don't mean it shouldn't happen. Besides—" I started crying again. "I don't want you to go."

Once more the phone rang. Giving a frustrated sigh, Mike went into the other room and answered. "Help Line, can I help you?"

I was thankful it was only a quick information call. When he returned, he put both arms around my shoulders.

"I don't know why you chose to tell me here, either. How did you figure we'd be able to answer phones while dealing with this shit?" I yelled, punching him hard in the shoulder with my fist. "I hate you for this, Mike. I hate you for leaving me."

I buried my head in his chest, wrapped my arms tightly around him, and held on to him for dear life. "What am I going to do without you?"

He ran his fingers through my hair and down my neck. The familiar erotic sensation I often felt when we cuddled together made me want to give in to him right then and there. "Geri, it wasn't working with us. How much longer do you think I could handle being with you and you not fully responding. I've wanted you for so long now, and you haven't been able to completely accept me. I don't blame you but, I mean, a guy just can't keep a longing like that going forever, you know," he said with a chuckle.

For a brief moment, I considered acting out my secret yearning, but something held me back.

"I'm sorry," I said, tears gushing from the corners of my eyes. "I know it's been tough on you. I've wanted to surrender to you, Mike. So many times I have wanted to, but I couldn't."

"I know, I know," he whispered. "It's just the way it is. I'd hoped it would change, but I realized a while ago that you aren't ready yet. And that's okay," he said as an afterthought. "The one thing that keeps me going is accepting what is, not what I want something to be. We gave it a good try, but the time is not right."

"Oh, God! I wish it were, I wish it were," I cried. It took all my strength to keep from promising him I'd change. I squeezed his middle, hugging him with all my might, wishing I could hold on to him forever.

"Oh, Mike…I don't want you to go away."

He placed his hands on my shoulders and pushed me back. "You know, I'm not leaving the planet. Just because I'm going for now, don't mean I won't be back. My roots are in Detroit and I'll have to come around someday to get all my philosophy books, you know." He gave a half-hearted laugh. "Who knows, maybe you'll follow me out to California after you get missing me too much."

"I might," I said, leaning back into him.

But I doubted I ever would. Whatever the future held, I responded as if our time together was through. I saw Mike one more time before he left. He came by my dorm room the next morning and handed me a small paper bag. In it was the tiny bottle he'd put our windowpane in, that fate-filled night.

"Just a little memorabilia for you to remember me by," he said. "You sure are a trip, Geri Taeckens. It was a pleasure being your guide that night," he said, taking my hand and giving it a shake.

"You take care, okay?" he said more tenderly.

"You too," I said, tears welling in my eyes.

"Now, now, no more of that. We've said our goodbyes already. I'm not going to tell you I'll write, because I won't. Let's just treasure the times we had together and look forward to what else life brings us."

Despite his words, silent tears streamed down my cheeks. I didn't know whether to admire his ability to be so accepting of life's situations or to be angry about it. After he left, I lay on my bed, wondering if I should have begged him to stay, promising him I'd be his partner. But the same words came to me. *No! It wouldn't have worked.* I didn't understand why my instincts told me Mike wasn't the right man for me. Maybe the very fact that he up and left the way he did was a clue, but I wasn't sure about that.

"Read Chapters Seven through Ten by Monday." Professor Master's voice said, pulling me back from my painful memories.

"I know it's a lot," my instructor went on, "but the unfortunate thing about these summer classes is that we have to double up on assignments. Have a great weekend."

At once the students stood and started filing out the door. I undid my slate from my tablet and slid both into my bag, dropping the stylus into the pocket of my jeans. Throwing my large canvas bag over my shoulder, I headed out the door. I carefully found my way to the stairwell, pretending to be locating something in my bag. This was a great way to cover up the fact I was really being very cautious. I sashayed along until my foot slithered over the edge of the first step. I felt the familiar rush of triumph which came whenever I made it to the stairs without someone trying to help me. I loved to fool passers-by, as it gave me a sense of superiority.

With my surroundings clearly understood, I rapidly descended the stairs, proud of myself for not touching either railing. Traversing the campus through barriers and moving students was not as easy. It required several other tricks to make myself look normal. Stopping to adjust my bag, using it to block the sun, bending down to tie a shoe, or scratch my knee were all devices I used to orient myself. Eventually I reached the field leading to my apartment. Only then could I relax and contemplate the evening's plans.

I wish Mike were here to join us, I thought, longing for his presence. "I hope I can keep it together with out him," I said aloud, worry now setting in. *Should I change my mind? They'd think I'm weak*, I told myself. *I'd have to come up with a reason. How can they all seem so cool? I sure wish I could be as hip and easygoing as Liz!* I recalled her questions about my refusal to take hits off joints. Though she never criticized me, her face always looked puzzled when I declined such offers.

"Feel like mellowing out there, Ger?" she'd ask, after she'd spent a long day at school. "Sure helps me unwind. Have trouble getting those numbers out of my head after calculating data all day."

Liz was a biology and psychology major. I admired her aptitude for numbers. I also admired her ability to get stoned without getting paranoid. My level of self-consciousness increased so badly when I smoked pot that I ended up with full blown anxiety attacks.

But tripping's different, I told myself, as I stood waiting for the traffic to clear. *Pay attention now!* I warned myself. There was no light or stop sign at this rather busy crossing, so I needed to really concentrate. Eventually the street was silent, so I continued on my journey. *You don't want to bow out of the group trip, do you?* I scolded, thinking of the plans we'd all made two weeks ago. *You'd really alienate yourself for sure if you did! Besides, you could use a good high after all you've been through lately. It'll be nice to step back into heaven again,* I reminded myself.

When I walked into the apartment, Liz and Jan were sitting at the dining room table.

"Hey, Geri!" Liz said. She looked so cute in her pink halter top dotted with what I knew to be butterflies. Except for her blond hair, she might have passed for Pocahontas with her two braids hanging past her bosom. "Ready to go traveling?" she laughed. Jan joined in with a hearty chuckle.

"Right on!" I said, hoping to conceal my worry.

"Dean and Karl should be over soon," Jan said. "Wanna glass of wine while we wait?" Jan's warm smile was easy to see. Her voluptuous lips, the color of dark cherries, framed her sparkling white teeth.

"It's really good!" she said, sensuously sliding her tongue around the outline of her mouth. Contrary to Liz's light complexion, Jan's skin always looked tan. Her long thin face contained huge dark brown eyes, accented by chestnut hair. Complying with the look of any respectable hippie chick, she also wore it long and straight, parted in the middle. The bright yellow halter top she wore not only accentuated her dark skin, but emphasized her feminine features quite well. At five foot eleven, she could have easily been a model. Instead Jan's plans were to be an English teacher.

"Uh, nah. Don't want to cloud the trip," I said, relieved to have a good answer for not wanting to mix drugs.

"I think I'm gonna take a shower before they get here," I said. "Man, it's hot out there. I got all sweaty walking home."

Shortly after I showered and changed, Dean and Karl arrived. We were all sitting at the table. Despite my rather fashionable attire of red flowered halter top and cut off jeans, I still didn't feel cool or hip. No matter how hard I tried, I continued to view everyone as superior to me. Karl was taking some things out of a big bag and Dean was thumbing through a stack of LPs he'd brought.

"Got some groove tunes for you ladies!" Dean announced, walking to the stereo that I'd transferred to the living room for the occasion.

"Cute little setup ya got here. Whose music box is it?"

"Mine," I said. It made me nervous to be so excited about my contribution to the evening's affair.

You're gonna have to find more than this to make you feel like you belong, I warned myself, wondering how I was going to make it through a twelve hour trip.

"Well, we're ready, ladies," said Karl.

As I listened to the music of The Doors begin to play, I tried to prepare myself for another acid ride. *Man, I wish Mike could be with us!*

Karl took an envelope from his pocket and opened it up. He pulled out a piece of paper. "Meet Mr. Natural," he said, slicing the page with a knife he had hooked on his key chain.

"Why do they call it Mr. Natural?" Jan asked.

"Because...See, I'll show you." He held out one of the pieces for everyone to see. I could make nothing of it.

"Geri, it's got a drawing of a little stick man on it," Liz explained. "What is that? Litmus paper?" she asked.

"Yuppers. Keeps Mr. Natural from disappearing on us. Here ya go!" he said, handing it to Liz. "Got one for you, too, Jan." He repeated the process. "Geri, hold out your hand."

Reluctantly, I did as he asked. I stared at the square of paper in my palm, knowing this was not a good idea.

"Want something to wash that down with, Geri?" Liz asked, handing me her glass of wine.

"Thanks, I'll just get some water." I stepped into the kitchen and grabbed a cup out of the cupboard. As the sound of the filling container heightened in pitch, so did my anxiety. *You should drop this in the basket!* my inner voice warned, but instead of following my own advice, I popped Mr. Natural in my mouth and washed him down. *You'd better get with the program!* I told myself as more bad feelings ran through me. *God, I wish Mike were here!* But my yearnings did not help the isolation I felt.

I heard the group at the table laughing about something. I laughed, too, even though I didn't have a clue what had been said. "Fake it 'til you make it," I heard Mike tell me.

"Okay, I have brought with me in our travel bag some necessary items for a good trip," Carl announced. "We have here—" he lifted something up in the air. "A box of dominoes!"

"Woo!" Liz said, clapping her hands.

"And—pickup sticks!"

"Yeah!" It was Jan this time. "I love those! I wonder if I'll be as good at them stoned as I was as a kid."

"Same difference, I hear," Dean said. "Acid's just a way to get ya back there, to being a kid, I mean. Their brains don't screen out all the neat stuff reality has to offer like our adult minds do, you know?"

As I heard Dean speak Mike's familiar words, my tension eased. *These guys know what they're doing*, I reassured myself, as Carl chimed in.

"Right on!" He reached into his bag again. I watched his red locks jiggle as he did so.

"And here we have a kaleidoscope."

"Far out!" Liz said, bending over to take the toy.

Another lift of Karl's hand. "A deck of cards. That's for strip poker when we're so fucked up we forget our body parts."

More laughter.

"And, Ta Dah! A jar of bubbles!"

"Groovy!" Jan said, drawing out the word as if it were three syllables long. "Ever done bubbles when you're trippin', Geri?"

"Uh, no!" I said, my voice sounding more nervous than I wanted. My moment of encouragement had not lasted long as I definitely did not feel a part of this group.

"Oh, yeah, and I got some Fizzies!" Liz exclaimed, walking into the kitchen. I stared at her with envy as she bounced back to her chair, totally free of worry. In her hand she carried a package. "They are the best!"

"What are they?" Dean asked.

"They're the little tablets you drop in water and it makes a fruity drink that's all bubbly."

"Oh!"

"They are really freaky when you are peaking and you put one in your mouth without water."

"Ho ho!" Karl said. "Sounds pretty far out for sure."

As they all continued playing in their upbeat, fun-loving way, I became more and more apprehensive. I was sure my laughter sounded contrived as I forced my lips to turn upwards to make a smile.

I've got to get out of this state of mind! I told myself, panic setting in. Karl started dealing cards to everyone.

"Blackjack it is. Loser drinks a glass of wine in two gulps!"

In order to participate in this event, I needed to use my glasses. I headed off to the bedroom and hoped no one would make a big deal about it. In the process of pulling out my dresser drawer to get them, I caught sight of myself in the mirror. Leaning forward, I looked into my dark and foreboding eyes. The sight of them scared me.

I wish I could change into a t-shirt, I thought, feeling totally exposed. *But they'll know I'm worried if I do that!* I said in my head.

Calm down, Geri! I told myself. *Think about the wonderful world of color you saw before.* Memories of the brilliant Christmas lights came back to me. I sighed and focused on the laughter from the next room. *They're all having a good time! Just relax*! But as I headed back to the table, my doubts increased.

I slipped on my glasses and picked up the two cards Karl dealt me.

"Hey, Geri, I didn't know glasses helped you," Karl said.

"Yeah, they do," I said, hoping we wouldn't get into a deep discussion about what I could and couldn't see. This question was one everyone asked, but one I couldn't give an answer to. It was often followed by someone holding up their hand and asking, "How many fingers?" After Karen Worster had relentlessly teased me in this manner, I did not appreciate this method for evaluating my level of vision. Besides, what I could see in one situation, I couldn't see in another. In this case, I was definitely having trouble recognizing the various numbers and figures on the cards. With more light being let in from the dilation of my eyes, the usual glare from the shiny surface increased. This, coupled with unsteady hands, threatened to keep me from playing. I still wanted to be a part of the group, so I strained as hard as I could to see, counting the characters rather than looking for the numbers.

The reject switch on the stereo clicked. The ear-shattering sound of the second record slapping down on top of the first made me jump. *Why would he stack the records like that?* I asked myself, surprised Dean would take such poor care of the vinyl.

Jefferson Airplane began to play.

"Want a hit?" Karl asked me.

"Uh, just a minute," I said, attempting to focus. *One two three four five six seven... one two three four five six seven eight?* I counted, but the characters were now taking on a three dimensional form. *This is just like the scrabble tiles, remember?* I said trying to calm myself. *Don't take too much time!* I warned, as the figures became unrecognizable. "Yeah, hit me," I finally said, terrified I may have taken too long to decide.

"You got a three. Want another hit?"

As he said this, Jan started cracking up.

"Yeah, I'll have another hit!" she said. "You'll have to anchor me down so I don't leave the Earth, though," she snickered. "Get it, another hit?" Everyone roared.

I suddenly caught on to Jan's reference to a hit of pot. *Is she trying to trick me?* I asked myself. I let out a phony laugh. *Can they tell I'm faking?* I wondered, covering my mouth with my hands.

"Okay, okay!" Karl chuckled. "So, Geri, you want another hit?" Before I could wade through the confusion enough to answer, Jan reached over and gave me a slap. The sensation was electrifying.

I leaped up, startled by this unexpected gesture.

Jan started hooting louder than ever. "You're gonna need unanchoring there, Ger!" she said. "Get it, unanchoring? That means you are disanchored, flying high in the sky."

I'm not flying, I thought. *No, she's teasing, I think.*

"There you go!" Karl said, sliding another card in my direction, totally ignoring what was happening inside me. "You just look like you need another hit, so I'm giving you one!" he announced.

I look like I need another one? I asked myself. Do I look bad? It must show that I'm having a bad time if he thinks I look like I need another hit. A wave of terror raced through my stomach. I wanted to double over from the pain.

He's just talking about the game of cards, the voice in my head said, but it didn't help. I have to get out of here! Stay calm, stay calm.

By this time cards were being flipped back and forth between everyone at the table. They spun and darted, creating elusive trails behind them, telling me I was well on my way to tripping.

"Caught it!" Jan laughed. "Catch this one!"

Grace Slick's voice was now in full focus. I listened carefully as she sang about Alice and pills making you larger and smaller. Suddenly I saw Alice slip through the looking glass on the wall behind Karl.

"You okay, Geri?" Dean asked. His question hurled my stomach into a spin.

"Why, don't I look alright?" I asked, hearing panic in my voice.

"I don't know. You've got a strange look on your face."

Jan burst out laughing. "You do! You look so serious, Geri."

"Nah, she's just a little spaced out, that's all," Carl said.

But it was too late for any more excuses. I pushed back my chair and doubled over. Dean's hand reached out and touched my arm.

"You okay?" he asked, his voice very concerned.

"Am I having a bad trip?" I heard my own voice ask matter-of-factly.

"It's okay, Geri," Liz said. "Here, have a sip of wine, it'll help you chill."

She held her glass up to my lips. But the taste of the bitter substance made me spit it back.

"No, I don't want that. I've got to go to my room," I said, getting up from the table.

"I'll come with you," Dean said, starting to follow me. But Liz warned him to stay put.

"We've gotta get somebody over here," she said, panic in her voice.

"I'm having a bad trip, aren't I?" I asked. But my practical words were not matching the terror I was now feeling.

"She's right," Karl agreed. "We can't deal with this ourselves. No point in messing everyone's trip up. Maybe Crystal can come over and sit with her."

"No!" I yelled. "No, not Crystal. I'll be okay. I'll just stay in my room. Don't bring Crystal over here."

"Okay, Geri, we won't," Liz said.

I darted to my room, shutting the door behind me. The orange flowered pattern of my bedspread spun mercilessly before me. Though I was afraid I would be twisted up inside it, I dove in. I curled up into a ball and wrapped my arms tightly around both knees. As I rocked back and fourth, waves of horror undulated through my veins. Tides of fear rose and fell with each beat of my heart. I could hardly breathe as the force of an undertow pulled me deep into an ocean of terror. Certain I would drown in the emptiness, I pushed past the suffocating panic and took in a deep breath. *It's the acid,* I told myself.

This momentary awareness of my drug induced state allowed me to breathe more freely. The trip-tide soon returned, however, dragging me back into the abyss.

As I lay on the bed, convulsing wildly, I repeated out loud, "What is tripping? What is truth? What is reality?" With each thought, I saw in my mind's eye the letters that spelled out these words. They were made up of emissions from a sky writing rocket flying past. Instead of the brilliant iridescent colors of my first acid experience, the letters were smoky gray, melting into ghostly blobs, disappearing into the chasm of my mind.

On and on through endless time, I became lost in eternity. The sound of my voice was the only thing keeping me in touch with reality. "I'm not going to make it!" I'd say over and over and over again. "Oh God, I'm not going to live through this."

Eternity had passed when I heard my door open. A voice was explaining something to me.

"Open your eyes," I thought I heard it say. But when I did, I could only see blackness. The emptiness brought more fear as I wondered if I had gone blind.

I'm doomed! I thought, plunging back into the void.

"Geri, it's Jeff," I thought I heard from far away.

"No! No! I don't want them to know," I said, maintaining some deluded notion I would be destroyed if I didn't remain isolated.

"Let's go for a walk, Geri. Come on, I'll take your hand."

"No! No!" I yelled, writhing up and down on the bed. "Go away!" I begged. "I want to be alone." Despite my protest, I felt a flicker of hope just knowing there was a link to the outside world.

Eventually the dreaded voice vanished. Once again I was left alone in the den of iniquity I had so resolutely designed. The momentary sense of relief quickly turned to horror as the craziness returned. "Hold on!" I kept repeating out loud as I moved in and out of worlds unknown, oscillating between a fear or wish to die.

I must have become unconscious at some point, aware of nothing until I heard another knock on my door. Liz's voice echoed from far away.

"You okay now, Geri?"

Am I in a tunnel? I wondered calmly. My serenity was quickly shaken however, as I opened my eyes and saw nothing but darkness.

I am blind! I decided, a deep ache penetrating into the center of my heart.

"Is it okay if I come in?" Liz asked, opening the door a crack. A slice of light stimulated my optic nerve, rescuing me from my worst fear.

"Not really up for company much," I heard myself say.

"Yeah, sure, I understand. But I really am glad you're back!" Liz exclaimed.

I suddenly became aware I was lying in a puddle of sweat; my top half off, all screwed up around my chest. I reached for my blanket and pulled it up over me.

"Thanks, me too," I said tentatively.

"Well sure is good to hear you sounding better, Geri."

"What time is it?" I asked, glad to be interested in such an everyday thing.

"It's about two in the morning. You've been in here about seven hours now. You had a pretty rough ride."

As I struggled to orient myself, I suddenly realized the darkness was the result of the night. The events of the evening began trickling back.

"Where is everyone?" I asked, holding back the joy now filling my heart. *I didn't die or go permanently crazy!* I thought with amazement, as Liz went on.

"Oh, we're all here. I mean, we did go out for a bit. Had too. You were really wailing for a while there. Jeff came by to stay with you while we went to the Botanical Gardens, though."

"Oh, I'm sorry!" I said, still feeling a bit confused..

"Hey, no problem. We had a great time! Just sorry you weren't able to come with us. We made sure you were covered, though. Wouldn't have left you alone. Good rules of trippin', you know. Don't try to help if you're high, but don't leave nobody in a bad trip without support."

As I remembered the code of ethics Liz now recited, a sense of shame came over me for having to be the one who needed to use them.

"Thanks," I said. "I appreciate that."

"No problem. You're welcome to join us."

I had no desire to be in their company. Unlike me, they'd been able to keep it together. I wondered if I would ever live this down. Like Hester Prynne in Hawthorne's Scarlet Letter, I'd soon be branded as one of those weak minded hippie chicks who didn't know how to 'tune in and turn on'. Besides, I assumed the others were still buzzing, and I was only a step away from Pluto's door step.

"I think I'll just ride out the rest of the night alone," I replied, wishing she'd leave.

"Okay, well it'll be cool if you change your mind."

"Thanks, Liz."

"No problem!" and then she left the room.

The urge to pee welcomed me back to reality. Having been out of touch with my body for such a long time, I was glad to feel again, even if it meant discomfort. I quickly did my business, rushing to and from the bathroom, praying no one would see me pass through the hallway. I gathered up my pillow and stuffed it into the crook of my arms as if it were my best friend. *Sleep will take me away*, I thought, hoping it would prevent the pending reprimands now lurking at the door of my consciousness. But sleep did not come easily. As I watched dull trails of light swirling around in my agitated mind, angry voices sent debasing messages of humiliation to my soul. *You are so God damn stupid, you fuckin' idiot!* an inner voice raged. *How many times you gonna try to be what you're not?*

Other voices joined in, roasting every part of me at various levels of Dante's Inferno.

You ought to be dead, you worthless piece of shit! You're never gonna make it in this complicated world.

But I'm trying! I insisted, begging them to understand, but none of the voices listened.

In the restless slumber that followed, my thoughts continued to plague me. "What is reality?" I said out loud. *Is my questioning at this very moment really happening?* I asked myself. *Are my dreams real too? What would Descarte think?* I mused. *So if I think myself to be in heaven, then why don't I feel like I am?*

I wish I could ask him this question directly, I thought. There's never a philosopher around when you need one, I chuckled to myself. *Descarte must not be thinking himself alive at the moment.* As I dipped back into dream land, a sudden revelation hit me. I guess reality is what you make it. I just wish I knew how to make mine good.

Chapter 23

Psychotic Reactions

August 1972

Some might say I'm a slow learner. They'd be absolutely right. In my efforts to discover reality, I spent several hours of my life visiting hell not once, but several times. It took three additional bad trips before I figured it wasn't quite worth it. Any hopes of returning to heaven were squelched.

I did learn, however, that these exploratory journeys took their toll. By the end of August, an anxiety developed within me that I couldn't shake. I adopted a nervous tick, wiggling my right leg up and down rapidly whenever I felt uncomfortable or bored. Since this covered most of my waking hours, I packed in a lot of exercise simply by sitting down. These biological gyrations unfortunately transferred over into the classroom. I tried to control them to the best of my ability, but the desks at school turned out to be excellent conductors of sound and motion. With the additional thud-thud-thud of my slate and stylus, my ever present sense of self-consciousness grew, blowing my efforts to remain inconspicuous.

The other unique attribute I acquired as a result of my pursuit of happiness included the flickering of light radiating around the periphery of my vision. Unless the illumination in my environment was very subdued, this stimulus remained constant, creating a strobe-like effect.

Initially I told myself this phenomenon was just a normal aftermath from tripping. I knew most acidheads got flashbacks from time to time. A sudden return of psychedelic perceptions was quite common. But after weeks of looking at objects surrounded by flashing light, I grew more and more scared. In fact, I became so frightened I made an appointment with the ophthalmologist I had vowed to avoid for the rest of my life.

"What your daughter is experiencing is *nistagmous*," Dr. Biggs said, continuing to direct his explanation to my parents, ignoring my presence just as he had done each time since I was seven. Despite my strong irritation toward the man, I listened as he went on to say how this is a disorder which eventually accompanies retinitis pigmentosa. Part of me felt relief at this disheartening news, but I wondered if I might have brought it on a bit sooner by my reality studies. I certainly never noticed it before my journey to the underworld.

To combat the strain of my existence, isolation became my favorite choice of refuge. I used the need to study as my regular excuse to spend most of my free time in my room. Though I did do some reading, I focused a lot on writing heartfelt poetry. With my steady babysitting job, I was finally able to purchase the instrument I had longed for. At last I could work up melodies on my very own guitar.

In addition to my distress, another loss ensued. My relationship with Ken came to an absolute end. I was so uptight when meeting him two weeks after a bad trip I took in July that he became suspicious. He responded to my nervousness and avoidance of intimacy by accusing me of being involved with someone else. In order to convince him this was not true, I broke down, confessing I had become re-involved with drugs. Initially this evoked a desire in him to help me get straight, but it didn't last. By the time the third disastrous voyage to psychedelica land took place at the end of July, he realized I was not the girl he was looking for. Even though I had known for a long time we were not meant to be, his rejection gave me one more reason to feel unworthy to be alive.

Fortunately, there were a few things which kept me going. Like crazy glue, weekly visits with Jack helped keep the little sanity I had left intact. Liz and Jan's friendship also pulled me from sliding too deeply into the caverns of depression. Although my roommates were not as enticing as the memory of the footballs still signaling me to play, nevertheless, I was grateful that they regularly invited me to join them. Their interest in my music really meant a lot to me. Their requests for me to entertain them gave me an opportunity to sing my songs. I resisted their plea to take my music to local coffeehouses. Performing in front of strangers took a confidence I did not possess.

I did agree to go with them on Saturday night outings to the bar. I longed to accept offers to dance, but I refused invitations every time. Maintaining visual contact with a moving partner was out of the question, particularly under strobe lights without any physical contact.

Though not a substitute for heaven, beer had a way of toning down the glowing embers radiating around my eyeballs. Tapping one's feet to the beat of the music turned out to be an excellent cover for my frenzied extremities as well. I remained quite content to stay firmly planted on my bar stool. That is, until one night, after drinking a few beers, Liz decided to do a little orchestrating. I was sitting at the table with my roommates, dressed in an orange and pink tie-dyed backless top with matching stovepipe pants, when a guy walked past our table.

"Wanna dance, big boy?" Liz asked. I listened to her bold gesture as I gyrated to Steppenwolf's *Born to be Wild*.

"Sure!" I heard the deep voice boom back. His close proximity made me glad I had a reason for my moving foot.

"Great!" Liz said. From out of the blue, I felt her hand grasp mine. "This is my roommate," she said, placing it in his. "She can't see too well, but she's a great dancer. Take her hand and keep track of her on the floor, would ya?"

I was totally freaked as a warm set of fingers wrapped around mine.

"Sure! Far out. Come on, uh, what's your name?"

"Geri," I yelled over the booming speakers, hoping he wouldn't notice my panic. "But you don't have to. It's okay, that's just my crazy roommate," I said, trying to get out of this unexpected dilemma.

"Nah nah! Come on, let's see you dance," the guy said, pulling me from my chair.

Unable to resist, I decided to let John Kay's electrifying guitar arouse the dormant erotic creature within. My inhibitions evaporated as I found myself following him onto the dance floor. They resurfaced when my partner let go of my hand and visual nonsense disoriented me once again. Flickering lights bombarded my eyes as the disco ball twirled above us. Which one is mine? I asked myself, straining to see. A new fear entered my thoughts. *How am I gonna get back to my table?* I wondered, sure I had been abandoned by now. As John Kay bellowed out he was born to be wild, a hand gently touched my wrist. The gesture rekindled the thrill of the moment, and I let go of the wild child within me. I boogied like crazy, grinding my hips and gyrating my shoulders, reclaiming my primordial soul. When the music ended, my anonymous partner proposed we stay on. *I hope he's not doing this out of pity*, I thought, still doubtful anyone would really want to dance with me. The notion was replaced with the desire to move freely as the thundering beat of Argent's song, *Hold Your Head Up*, grabbed my spirit.

But all good things must come to an end. When the music changed pace, John Doe thanked me for our time together and escorted me back to my chair. My devious cohort was apparently out on the floor when I returned to find Jan sipping her beer. Before I finished a few swallows of my own, I heard Sly & the Family Stone begin singing *Thank You (Falettinme Be Mice Elf Agin)*. As I joined them in song, I was once more interrupted.

"Wanna dance?" the voice of an invisible person asked.

"Sure, but I don't see very well. You'll have to keep track of me, okay?"

I don't know which surprised me more, my bravery or the guy's reply.

"Uh yeah, sure." I found his hand and allowed him to lead me away.

When I left the bar that night, I took with me a happiness I hadn't felt for a while. The magical formula conveyed to me by my insightful roommate stayed with me as well. The words, "I don't see very well, can you…?" instantly erased questions about why I didn't look directly at a person, or why I might be feeling objects with my hands. These simple seven words, originally spoken by Liz, allowed me to expand my independence. Instead of relying on my roommates or my mother to shop, I started venturing into stores on my own. Though I still tried to appear as sighted as possible, I now had something to fall back on.

My babysitting job also added a semblance of sanity to my crazy world. Kids' automatic acceptance of me certainly turned out to be good for my soul. The vice president and his wife, Tim and Joan, were so happy with my care of their two children that they referred me to other professors.

I wished Professor Powers could get wind of my great work with kids. The fact that I had to keep pursuing my grievance reinforced my steadfast belief—there is no one to answer such fanciful prayers.

By the time August rolled around, I was straddling life again. The yin and yang existence Mike told me about certainly described my reality. As I worked to balance between my images as a dancing queen, a Nervous Nelly, and a Mary Poppins, I added one more persona to my identity. I became a Suzy Social Worker after completing the paraprofessional counseling training in May

Dave, the frequent caller who faithfully talked to me every Friday evening, became one of my customers. Though I didn't mind talking with him on the phone, I found myself anxious about a face-to-face connection. Dave had a quality about him which both attracted and repelled me. I was initially intrigued by his discussions on alternative realities and visual distortions. However, my growing anxiety about my own perceptual changes made me want to avoid this topic altogether.

Having only talked by phone, Dave did not know about my visual limitations. Though he encouraged me to discuss aspects of my life, Help Line counselors were encouraged to limit self-disclosure.

"What's wrong with your eyes?" was the first question he asked as he strode mechanically across the room, and sat down in the seat adjacent to mine. Filled with a sense of importance and knowledge, I closed the door to the converted crash room. I carefully seated myself, resisting the urge to shake my leg. I felt a little awkward in my professional attire, a white nylon blouse and navy pants. I decided I'd go for a more casual style next time, if only to feel more like myself. I placed my arms on the rests of the chair, figuring an opened body posture would convey the message of acceptance.

"So what's wrong with your eyes?" Dave asked again.

"I have retinitis pigmentosa," I said, feeling a bit taken aback.

"How much can you see?" Dave asked, delivering his words as he did on the phone, slowly and deliberately.

"Well, that's a hard question to answer. It all depends on if I'm tired or have a cold or something," I replied.

"Can you see me?"

"Of course," I answered, uncomfortable with the role reversal; Dave directing questions to me.

"What do I look like?"

"Don't you know what you look like?" I said, giving him a reproachful smile.

"You've got a beautiful smile," he said.

I was concerned he might be trying to hit on me, which made me shift uncomfortably in my seat.

"You don't need to be nervous," he offered. "I just think you have an exceptionally beautiful smile."

"Thank you," I replied, clearing my throat and crossing my leg, the stiff material of my pants resisting my effort.

"So what do I look like?"

Deciding to play it safe, I simply commented on his size. "You're well built and very tall."

"How tall do you think I am?" he asked.

"I'd guess about six foot two or three."

"Hey, you're right, six-two. What else?"

Surveying his face against the contrast of the plain blue wall behind him, I was able to see him fairly clearly. The direct light of the lamp beside him also illuminated his features. He had a Nordic face with wrinkled forehead, revealing that this man of twenty-nine had been through a lot. If his disheveled hair were combed and trimmed, I suspected he could look rather handsome. Hoping we could cut the game of twenty questions short, I said, "You've got brown hair just past your ears, blue eyes, a long, distinguished nose, and you also have a nice smile."

"What color shirt?"

"Blue, but you should know that," I suggested, hoping he'd get the hint.

"Right!" After a short pause, he asked, "Mind if I smoke?"

I wasn't sure if I was happy to have passed his eye exam or sad the room would soon be depleted of oxygen. I lied and said no.

With slow jerky movements, Dave reached into his shirt pocket and touched what I assumed was his pack of cigarettes. With another pause, it looked like he was trying to register if the item he saw was the item he wanted. Finally, his actions looking like that of a robot, he pulled out the pack and methodically tapped the open end upside down three times on the palm of his right hand. He grabbed what I presumed was a cigarette with his fingers, thoughtfully switched it to his other hand and returned the pack to his pocket. With what seemed to be great effort, Dave leaned onto his right side and in the same slow manner, reached back with his left hand and pulled a lighter from his jeans. He put the cigarette in his mouth and lit the tobacco. Returning the lighter to his pants took as long if not longer than the original process, as Dave appeared to consider every move prior to executing its action.

After holding the smoke in his lungs for an inordinately long time, I heard him exhale in a purposeful manner. I thought about the old TV show Sea Hunt, as Dave's breathing mimicked the sound of the regulators they used on that program. I found myself worrying about whether he would get enough air before he passed out. I also wondered how he ever managed to get the simplest of procedures accomplished, let alone make it to the level of post graduate work he'd achieved at one of the top universities in the nation. My next thought scared me, as I considered whether all the acid trips he took could be part of why he behaved so oddly.

When I wrinkled my nose in response to the odor, Dave said, "You don't like smoke, do you?"

"It's okay," I lied.

"I'll only have this one, okay?"

"Okay." Hoping to redirect the conversation, I recalled some of the techniques we'd learned in our training.

"So, what brings you here today?"

"You sound so pro-fes-sional," he said, drawing out the syllables of the last word. He always seemed to end each phrase with a pause. "I suppose, now that you've got this nice new position, you're gonna turn into one of those cool co-lec-ted counselors, aren't you?" His question, spoken more as a statement, caught me off guard.

"I guess I'm not sure what you mean."

"You're trying to act so like a 'Susie Social Worker'," he explained, still drawing out every word. "Here you are, sitting there, dressed so nice, with all that open body language, but you're very uptight," he informed me. "The muscles in your face and arms are all tense." He glanced down at his left hand resting on his leg and looked at the cigarette. He mechanically raised it to his mouth and took a deep drag. The embers sputtered as Dave drew hard on the tobacco. His idiosyncrasies were really difficult for me to deal with. I countered my discomfort by crossing my arms and resting them on my lap. "Well, I'm not trying to be a Susie Social Worker. I'm just here to listen if you feel you have a problem," I said, hearing the words from the training manual.

After a long pause, Dave released the smoke in his lungs and spoke. "Why don't you talk to me like you do on the phone then?"

"I guess I don't know what you mean," I said, giving him a half hearted smile.

"Are you always so nervous?" Dave asked. "You don't sound nervous on the phone. Usually you sound nice and kind and understanding. I hope you don't let the machine of psy-cho-logy let you turn people like me into lab rats."

Instinctively I understood what he meant. I didn't like how this was going. In my desire to protect my position of being the counselor, I reflected back to the role plays conducted in the training. My other two clients were much more cooperative keeping their place in the client-therapist relationship.

"Talk to me," I heard Dave say. "Ask me how my day went or how things are going with the schiz-o-phren-ia." I had come to realize that this word held mixed emotions for him. He explained to me on previous occasions how this diagnosis both relieved and scared him.

After struggling with periods of hallucinations and delusions that began when he was at Berkeley two years earlier, Dave hadn't a clue what was happening to him. Since his psychiatric hospitalization and diagnosis, he understood that schizophrenia was likely a biochemical disorder, probably triggered by a combination of genetics and too much LSD. He explained this new causation theory was still not well accepted by professionals in the field of psychiatry, but he believed it to be true. Not only did he have other relatives who suffered from similar symptoms, he told me how he'd been helped by psychotropic medications.

Although unable to tolerate the stress of a full time job, the anguish of living in an altered state of mind had disappeared. Dave told me how he could hardly communicate with others prior to taking medication. He constantly saw things that were not there and heard people talking about him and conspiring against him. The struggle with visual distortions and anxiety was still present, but he described living with his parents as fairly comfortable.

Hearing his story over the phone had brought much more sympathy and understanding. Now, sitting across from him, watching his reptilian movements and enduring his intrusive questions, I found myself feeling an aversion toward him. This guy was messing up my "accept everyone" philosophy, causing great internal conflict. Keeping my professional stance, I followed his directive.

"So, Dave, how's your day?"

"It's a fairly nice day," he said, pausing to clear his throat. "I really wanted to meet you…but the visual distortions are both-er-ing me somewhat."

"That's too bad," I said, thinking about my own. The strobe-like phenomenon situated around my circle of vision had become more prominent. With the back of my right hand, I reached up and swiped it across my eye in an attempt to wipe it away, an idiosyncratic gesture now very much a part of me.

"Eyes bothering you, huh? Do they do that a lot?"

The pressure of being under this man's microscope was disconcerting. Exasperated, I heard myself say, "Look, Dave, I'm not sure what this is all about, but I'm not here to answer a bunch of questions about myself. If you want to talk to me, you can, but I really don't like you commenting on my every movement."

"Yeah…I forgot. The patient is sup-posed to act like a patient," he said, sounding irritated as he spoke. Moving in a much more fluid manner, Dave raised his arm to take another drag. "Fred used to tell me that," he said, his measured speech disappearing and becoming more rapid with inflection. "He was my psychiatrist after I got back from Berkley. He was pretty neurotic, Fred was. He hated that I called him Fred and kept reminding me that I was the one who needed to answer the questions. I kept asking them anyway. He taught me a lot, though," Dave said, a devious closed lip smile crossing his face. "He taught me how crazy sane people can truly be, and how truly sane crazy people really are!"

"Look, I don't know what you're trying to say, but I think maybe this is not a good situation for either of us."

Dave's lips began twisting nervously, first one side turning upwards then the other. With another clearing of his throat, he continued, reverting back to his deliberate pattern of speech. "Ah, gee, Ger, I'm sorry. I didn't mean to upset you, really. I am curious about you. I find you a very interesting person," he said, sounding sincerely worried now as he shifted uncomfortably in his seat. "You are acting so differently than you did on the phones. You are such a natural, you know?" I felt a bit of shame as he continued to twist up his mouth. "You are the best Help Line listener they've got. I talk to lots of them, you know, and well, you're the only one that seems to really care about what I say." He inhaled, but he barely had time to enjoy his vice as he exhaled almost immediately. "You don't cut me off, tell me I'm crazy, or tell me I need to stick with more pro-fes-sional help." As Dave drew out the syllables again, he stubbed out his cigarette in the ashtray.

I simply stared at him. With a mixture of sympathy and repulsion, I had no clue as to what to say or do. He finally broke the silence.

"If I promise not to analyze you and not smoke any more cigarettes, can I still come and see you?"

As I had difficulty rejecting anyone for any reason, I considered his plea. Finally I said, "Okay, but I think we need to stop for now. I've got to be at another appointment soon," I lied.

"Can I come next week at the same time then?" Dave asked, sounding more like a hopeful child.

"Yeah, sure," I said, not liking how important he seemed to be making me. Training concepts popped in my mind. Don't feel responsible for your client. Burn out comes from taking on your client's pain. As I thought about how to avoid a next visit, I told myself it wouldn't be my fault if he had a nervous breakdown.

"Thanks," Dave said, clearing his throat once more. "Cut me a little slack, Geri. I have to admit, I was taken by surprise when I first saw you. I wasn't expecting a blind girl, after all."

With his emphasis on the word blind, his words cut through me like a knife. Being identified with such a harsh and dirty label turned my sympathy into anger. The vision of the man with the dark glasses I had kept at bay for some time now momentarily returned.

"I did it again, didn't I?" Dave said, twisting his lips several more times. "I know I'm blunt. Never been good at that social a-pro-priat-ness that every-body seems to catch on to. I think something, I say it. Guess that's why I haven't many friends. Maybe you could teach me about that stuff, Ger?"

I gave him a disapproving look at the sound of my nickname.

"I guess I shouldn't have said that?" He sounded genuinely puzzled.

"No, you didn't say anything wrong," I said, acting more reassuring than I felt. "But I do have to go" I said, standing up and opening the door.

"I've really messed things up, haven't I?" he said, walking sheepishly to the door, his hands interlocked behind him, totally exposing his outer surface to the world.

Relying once more on my old lying tactic, I said, "No, you didn't. Don't worry, everything's okay."

"Well, I hope you will forgive me. Maybe I will eventually see you again some day?"

"Okay," I said, guiltily realizing we both understood the ending of this meeting.

I felt exhausted as I flopped back into my chair, attempting to process what had transpired. The mixture of sympathy and repulsion pulled at my conscience. I hated criticizing someone who obviously suffered so much.

"He scares the hell out of me," came my answer. I glanced downward and noticed my jerking leg. I gripped it tightly with both hands, bending over in fear. "Stop it, stop it!" I heard myself say out loud. I prayed no one else heard as I felt the struggle between my restless leg and my desire to be still. I dropped my head and spoke quietly into my lap. *Oh, Geri!* I pleaded. *You've just got to stop taking those chemicals. You've just got to! Oh God, please don't let me end up like that! Please!"*

Chapter 24

Special Delivery

June 1973

"Hey, Ger, you got a package!" I heard Liz call from the living room.

"Oh, yeah?" I said, surprised at this unexpected announcement. I was still dressed in my dad's white t-shirt, which doubled as a night dress. The apartment door slammed as I watched Liz struggle with a large box. She also wore her night clothes. In contrast to mine, hers was the color of buttercups, flared with a slightly more feminine touch. "Hope George wasn't too disappointed," Liz said with a giggle. "Got no pockets for change in my nightie."

"Ah, don't worry, he got his tip!" I said, chuckling back at her. "Sometimes I think he'd be willing to hire someone to send us packages, just so he can get a chance to catch a peek, especially at you!"

"Don't know about that," Liz said. "You're probably right though. He does seem to be the only one in the front office who brings us our stuff. But I'm not the only one hanging out in peejays around here."

"Maybe not, but it's you he likes all right!" I kidded. "Face it, Liz, you'd look good in a gunny sack."

Liz laughed and snorted away my flattery as she carried the huge box to the kitchen table.

"Wow, what the heck is it?" I asked.

"Not sure. Let's see." She shoved the package wrapped in brown paper onto the table. "Woops!" she said, as it collided with the pile of dirty dishes and school books scattered about, causing a notebook to land on the floor. I resisted the urge to use this instance to illustrate the value of putting things away, so I simply went over and tossed the notebook back in its spot.

"I got it," I said. "So who's it from?"

"No name. The return address is Belleville, Michigan. Know any one from there?"

"Uh, no. Can't think of anyone," I said. "I'll get a knife and open it up."

"Good idea," Liz said, sitting down to watch.

With my dad's favorite knife he had unwittingly loaned me the last time I visited, I began tearing through the wrapping of the mysterious parcel. Liz picked something from the middle of the mess. I saw her manipulating it around her hair while I cut open the cardboard box. I tore off the brown paper and walked it to the wastebasket hidden under the kitchen sink. Again I bit back the desire to comment on how little effort it took to throw things away. I hated having to decipher the hodgepodge my roommates created, but I didn't want to come off sounding like their mother.

I carefully severed the heavily taped flaps. Liz's hands were still fluttering about her neck. *It's a hair tie*, I told myself, glad to finally give the invisible object a name. My compulsive need for order overrode my desire to open the mysterious box. Instead, I walked back to the kitchen cupboards and placed my knife in the drawer. Satisfied with my diligent action, I resumed my task.

"It's a book!" I announced, lifting out a text bound in a black cover. "There's two more exactly the same," I told Liz.

"I thought your books usually come in those big black boxes with the straps."

"You're right. They come from the Library of Congress. Not Belleville, Michigan. I sure didn't order these," I said, examining the volume more closely. "There's no string attached for marking the page," I explained, running my fingers around the edges once more to be sure. "I can't imagine who sent me these!"

"So what's the title say?" Liz asked, leaning closer.

I picked up one of the volumes and sat down adjacent to her. With no room on the table, I placed it across my lap. Sliding my finger over the Braille, I read aloud the title, *An Epilogue for the Birth, Death, and Rebirth of the Sun,* by David… Oh, shit!" I said, recoiling from the page. "It's from that FC who used to call me at the Help Line all the time! I should have guessed by the address."

"Yeah, I remember him."

"I thought for sure he'd finally gotten the message that I didn't want to deal with him. Why's he sending me his book now?"

"What'd he do, write a novel or something?" Liz asked, picking up a brush out of the clutter and smoothing her bound hair.

Skimming the table of contents, I read several titles. I noticed they were only one or two pages in length.

 "No, at least I don't think so. I think it must be a collection of his poetry. I remember him telling me he wrote sonnets and stuff, but I didn't think he'd put it into a book, let alone have it Brailled and sent to me!"

"Cool!" she said, reaching out and running her hand over the dotted page. "When's the last time you talked to him?"

"Oh, gosh, not since last year sometime. I saw him once for a counseling session, but after that I only allowed him to talk to me on the phone, and then just a couple a times," I replied, wincing at my condescending words.

"How come?"

"Oh, I don't know," I half-lied. "He made me nervous, I guess. Didn't feel comfortable around him"

"He try to hit on you?"

"Well, not really, but he kept wanting to know everything about me and I didn't like that."

"Hmmm!" she said, pursing her lips. "Well, sometimes, despite that silly rule about no disclosure, I tell callers about myself. If he freaked you out, then I guess that makes sense."

"It's not like I wanted to be mean or anything," I said defensively. "It's just, I don't know…he was so weird!" But as I listened to my excuses, they didn't seem like a reasonable justification for rejecting someone.

Liz stared at me with kind eyes. I looked down at the book in my lap.

"Well I guess we're all a little weird," she finally said.

"I know," I admitted. "But it sure seems odd that he went to all the trouble to send me his stuff in Braille!"

I opened the cover and began reading the title page. A single Brailled sheet of paper unexpectedly flew out. Liz picked it up and handed it back to me.

"What's this?" she asked.

Placing the dotted page on the opened book, I fearfully read the top line. Dear Geri.

"I think he wrote me a letter," I said, quickly tossing it back in the box. "I'll check it out in a minute." I did not want to read it aloud. Instead, I ran my fingers over the title page.

"What's it say?" Liz asked.

"The Church of Truth," I read.

"The Church of Truth! This guy's religious?" Liz asked.

"No, that's who did the transcribing."

"Really? Cool church to do that."

"Oh, lots of those religious organizations do this stuff. They train volunteers to transcribe all kinds of junk in Braille."

"Is that who does your textbooks?"

"Some of them, but not this particular church. The ladies I work with will do anything you send them really, except maybe devil worship literature," I chuckled.

"Far out!" she said, once more reaching over and thumbing through the multitude of pages. "So, do you think his poetry is any good?"

"No clue. Not even sure I want to read it."

Propping her chin up with her hand, Liz challenged me, "Why not?"

Do I dare tell her the truth? I asked, sweat forming on my fingers. Do I tell her how scary this guy makes me feel when he asks me blatant questions about my vision? What if she knew I have some of his same symptoms of insanity? Even though I had not done any drugs for over a year, I was still plagued with many odd thoughts and visual distortions. I looked at Liz's clear blue eyes. Her genuine interest in me and her compassion for everyone increased my sense of unworthiness. No, I can't tell her, I decided.

"Oh…I don't know really," I said, trying to stall while I figured out what to say. "It's hard to put my finger on it, but I want nothing to do with him. Guess I feel a bit guilty for cutting him off, but at the same time the guy gives me a strange feeling, like I can't trust him."

"Well, I guess you know him better than me, but simply reading his stuff don't seem like it'd hurt anything."

"I suppose," I said, continuing to avoid her eyes, which were looking very disapproving.

"Don't ya think he must have some good about him? I mean the guy's gotta have some passion to take the trouble to send you his writings, and in Braille, don't ya think?"

"You're right," I said, lowering my head in shame. "I'll check out the book and maybe drop him a thank you note or something."

"That'd be a nice gesture, Geri," Liz said approvingly. She stood and moved toward the kitchen.

I was glad for the opportunity to end this conversation. I quickly gathered up the volumes and headed to my room. Sitting down on my bed, I stared at the pile of books stacked neatly in their cardboard case. Remembering the letter, I picked up the top volume and took the Brailled sheet from underneath. I began running my fingers over the dotted words.

Dear Geri,

I know you would rather I didn't contact you, but I can't help myself. Since our conversations have ended, the loneliness has returned. Alone in my world of perceptual distortions, the only morsel of hope I feel is the memory of your kind words.

Please accept this collection of humble prose as my gift to you for all those richly filled nights you listened to me on the phone. Even if we never speak again, I will always remember your kindness and how you pulled me back into a world I thought I could never touch again.

Living in the hell of schizophrenia, where everything is sharp and cold, as if my mind were fenced in with barbed wire, the soft sounds of your voice were like ointment to my wounds. I won't lie and pretend that my gift of poetry to you is not an effort to bequeath your acceptance of me, because it is. I would do almost anything to be able to share my thoughts with you again. But that remains to be seen.

I hope you can at least enjoy the imagery I have painted with words. The short story, The Magic Mushrooms, is about you.

If you should have a change of heart, you can contact me at the number below. My parents go to bed early, so it's best if you call before 8 p.m. Take care of yourself, and I hope your eyes are doing okay.

Dave

Refusing to touch the phone number at the bottom, I angrily crumpled the thick paper into a wad and tossed it across the room. *How dare he intrude into my life again?* I thought, warding off his comment about the barbed wire. "What is with this guy?" I said to my walls. I retrieved the paper ball and stuffed it into the box with the books. *Is that another symptom of schizophrenia?* I asked myself, remembering the feeling I'd experienced the winter evening with Ken so long ago. *It's got to be the drugs!* I told myself, recalling the last time I felt the razor sharp image of the fence separating me from reality. *Yeah, Christmas, six months ago!* I counted in my head. "I was stone drunk!" I said out loud. I folded the four flaps over the box and shoved it into my closet.

I picked up the alarm clock off my nightstand and held it close to my face. It was almost eleven. I was scheduled to be at a para-pro staff meeting at noon. I grabbed my brush off the dresser and ran it through my hair. Thinking about how hot and sweaty the two-mile walk to the center would be, I made braids on each side of my head and pinned them up in a ball over each ear. Staring into the mirror, I waited for my eyes to adjust so I could see my reflection. It took about a while before a sweet innocent face came into view. I watched her as she grimaced at the ridiculous contrast between image and reality.

"You look like Gidget," I said out loud, admonishing myself for looking so misleading. *I wonder if she was as deceptive as I am,* I asked, picturing Sally Field from the old Sixties TV show. *Too bad I am so mean!*

Careful not to undo my braided ear balls, I gingerly worked the large neckline of my makeshift night gown over my head and threw it on my bed. I put on my favorite peace sign t-shirt and cut off shorts. I stuck my feet into my wedgie sandals, grabbed my bag off the bed, and clunked to the front door.

"You headed out?" Liz asked.

"Yeah, gotta meeting at the Help Line."

"I got to try doing my hair like that," Liz commented. "It's really cute! I love it when you wear it like that."

As always, her compliment made me nervously happy. I hoped it meant there were no hard feelings left over from our earlier discussion.

"Not sure my hair will hold. It's so damn fine," she added.

"Oh, it's easy!" I assured her. "It's got more to do with the length than how fine the hair is. Once it's in the braid, with a few bobby pins, nothing moves it."

"You think so?"

"No doubt!"

"Got any pins I can borrow?"

"Got lots. They're in a heart-shaped box on my dresser," I said, overjoyed to be of help.

"Thanks."

"No problem!"

"Hey, don't forget, I've got classes today until five and Jan's on some field trip with her sociology class," Liz reminded.

"Yeah, she mentioned it. If you guys want, I'll make some dinner and we can eat at six," I offered, hoping this might help get the pile of dishes done.

"Sounds good to me," she said, raising her hand in the air. "Peace!"

"Peace!" I replied, returning the gesture.

I worried about being late as I swiftly clicked to the center, my backless shoes snapping at my heels as I went. Three times I slipped off them, and three times I blamed the shoes for making me veer off into the grass. By the time I got to the center I was drenched with sweat.

The meeting with the para-professional counseling team was a mixed bag for me. As Jack always led the meetings, my dual role with him brought confusion. I knew he would never tell anyone I was in therapy with him, but still I felt exposed, knowing he knew my deepest, darkest secrets. Though I found the discussions about each counselor's clients interesting, my internal efforts to constantly ward off feelings of inferiority were exhausting. The level of anxiety I endured invariably gave me the urge to shake my leg. I only hoped no one noticed how my hand was always clutching my knee.

Jack opened the meeting. He gave his usual reminder about the importance of confidentiality. Star, one of the para-pros, was the first to discuss a client. "I learned last week that my eighteen-year-old college girl has been partaking in probably the worst drug imaginable."

"What drug is that?" Jack asked.

"It's the one that robs a person of their spirit. The girl is truly strung out on amphetamines."

An unexpected rush of energy jolted me. My heart began to pound. The image of Danny dropping a football in my hand both startled and pleased me. A burst of sweat followed as a wave of anxiety overwhelmed me. I found it necessary to grab my leg with two hands as it accelerated past the speed limit. *Why are you getting so freaked about this?* I asked myself. *You haven't touched the stuff in over two years!*

In the background, the words crystal, meth, and paranoia were all being passed around. As the group continued their analysis of the girl, I engaged in a self-assessment.

Your life is good now, you like your roommates, and your grades are great! I told myself, listing the pros for staying clean. Jack says it looks good for beating that old coot and your vision's been the same for a year! Why would you want to mess it up? Let getting drunk on the weekends be enough!

My preoccupation gave me little opportunity to share in the group discussion. Amazingly, I was able to respond appropriately when one of the members asked me if I agreed.

"Yup, speed kills!" Jack commented after I apparently reinforced the girl would likely not get better until she addressed her substance problem. Other cases were discussed, but I was barely able to comprehend what was said.

"I'd like to ask a few of you if you'd be willing to help with that training," I heard Jack say.

What training? I asked myself, my inattentiveness interfering with my need to know.

"We're going to adapt the encounter model for incoming volunteers before they work at the center. I know you are all busy with school in the fall, but I'm thinking if some of you would be willing, maybe you could do the training some weekend in October."

I wanted to jump at this opportunity. Unfortunately, I didn't know yet what my fall schedule would be like. In hopes my grievance would soon be resolved, I made sure I signed up for as many education related courses as I could. If it did go through by September, I would have to catch up by enrolling in the methods classes Professor Powers presently banned me from taking. As it turned out, I was not the only one at the meeting who could not commit to Jack's request. He closed the session with the hope we would know more about our schedules later in the summer.

I was glad the meeting was over, so I headed to the phone area to see who might be working.

"Hi, Geri!"

"Hey, Dean!" I said, always glad to see him.

"What's up?"

"Ah, not much. Trying to stay cool in this heat," I said, my uptight mood melting away with Dean's jovial manner.

"Yeah, we've sure had a warm one so far."

"Who you workin' with this afternoon?" I asked.

"On my own. Star usually works with me, but she had to go to your meetin' there and then study. I told her there's enough folks toolin' around here that I could grab help if I needed it."

"That's mighty nice of you, Dean."

"You takin' classes this summer, pretty lady?"

"Yeah, I got a tough one, too."

"What, you got a math class or somethin'?"

"About as bad. I have to learn all the parts of the eye and understand how they work with the brain," I said, describing the requirements of my Anatomy of the Eye course.

"Phew. Over my head. Only use 'em, don't much care about knowing what they're made up of."

We both laughed.

"It wouldn't be so bad, but I can hardly seem to concentrate these days."

"Nah?"

"Nope. I'm too young to be gettin' senile I think, but I used to be really good at memorizing stuff. Heck, I was pretty good at chemistry and biology, but for some reason I can't grasp this info. I mean, the eye is only one part of the body. You wouldn't think it'd be so hard. But I keep going over and over this stuff and it ain't sinkin' in," I said, wondering why I was bothering to explain this all to Dean.

"You amaze me, Geri," Dean said. "Don't know how you do any of it havin' to listen to tapes and junk."

"Oh, Dean, don't you go being one of those people who thinks I'm amazing 'cause I go to school with a vision problem."

"No really! Heck, if I were you, I'd just sit back and let the government pay my way through life. I mean, you got a good excuse not to have to go to school and all that. Might as well take advantage."

If anyone else had said these things to me I would have been offended. But coming from Dean, it was okay. Not only did he have a special affection for me which would never allow him to purposely offend me, he had an interesting attitude on life. "Never do more than you have to and enjoy what you do" were his words whenever he noticed someone getting bent out of shape. Of course, Dean was usually high on something, so his mellow nature was to be expected. He worked as a taxi driver only when he had to, dealt drugs for extra money, got high, and listened to music the rest of the time. "Well, Dean, if I flunk this class, I just might consider your idea. I'll get that government money, and you and I will live happily ever after."

"Well, if you really wanna pass that class, I got something that'll help ya study!" he said, a slight smile coming across his face.

"What?" I asked, suddenly aware of my uncharacteristic comments to Dean. I rarely complained to anyone about my struggles with studying.

"Crystals," he whispered. I felt my mouth twist against the deviant smile threatening to form on my lips. "What's with the face, Geri? The stuff will help you out." His enticing words made the familiar knot behind my navel tighten.

"Oh, yeah?" I heard my voice say, as my inner voice simultaneously screamed "NO!"

"Yuppers! Good stuff. Not too strong, but enough to pull an all nighter. Gave some to another Help Liner and they agreed it got 'em through a tough exam."

"NO!" the voice said again. *But what about that endless list?* another voice argued as I considered all the eye parts I still had to learn.

"It's amazing how clear headed this stuff makes ya," Dean went on. "And this batch don't seem to give you that strung-out feelin' when it's over."

No no no, the first voice begged. *It'd just be this once* came the other's reply.

"Well…I don't know" I heard my real voice say.

"It's up to you," Dean said, "But if you wanna pass that class and avoid welfare, might not be a bad idear."

"Got 'em here?" I said, hardly believing I could ask.

"Nah. You know the rules about drugs at the center. Wouldn't do somethin' stupid like that. But I can get 'em to you later."

"How much?" I asked as the battle between my selves raged on.

You've done well. You deserve a break once in a while. You've gotta get a good grade. It's just this once, my irrational voice implored.

But it's not a good thing. It's gotten you in trouble. Don't do it to yourself again, the other part of me begged.

"Ah, for you Geri, say, a buck a pop?" Dean answered.

"Gee, I don't know…"

"Come on, it's not that much. Just tell me how many you want?"

"Okay, you gotta deal. I'll take five," I heard myself say, the wise part of me disappearing with regret.

"I'll swing by your house about four then?" Dean said, all smiles.

"Okay. See ya then."

As I was about to exit the center, someone on the other side opened the door.

"Hey Ger! How ya doin'?"

"Hi Clifford!" I said, happy to have a good excuse to forget about what I had just done.

Cliff came on board as a Help Line listener in February, and he turned out to be one of the most fun-loving characters of the bunch. He really got into partying and spending time with us at the bar on Saturdays. A ladies man, he loved to flirt. He could make any female feel special. We all learned quickly however, never to try and pin him down. For me, this was a perfect arrangement, as I enjoyed his attention without feeling the need to develop a commitment.

"So, how ya doin'?" he asked, grabbing my cheeks with both hands and smiling at me. I looked into his blue tinted glasses.

"Groovy!" I said, forcing any negative energy out of my mind. Tossing my bag on the floor, I wrapped my arms round his tall slim body and gave him a big hug. He returned the affection, and then kissed me on the forehead. I copied the gesture, barely able to reach his chin; tasting a mouthful of his wooly beard.

"So what's up, kiddo?"

"Just got done with a meeting. How's about you?"

"Stoppin' by to grab some Help Line pamphlets. Gotta give a speech tomorrow and decided to do it on the Help Line."

"Good idea! Not only will you get a good grade, you'll be doing some good PR for the place."

"That's what I figured."

We decided we should get out of the doorway, so I followed him back into the phone room.

"Hey there, Dean!" Cliff said.

"Hiya, Cliff. Come by to share the shift with me?"

"Sorry buddy, I got the graveyard tonight, otherwise I would."

"Ah, that's okay. Isa just kiddin' anyway."

"So Geri, where you off to now?" Cliff asked.

"Oh, I was headin' back to the apartment to take a swim. Wanna join me?"

"Sure! Can I swim in my cutoffs?"

"Not supposed to, but our lease is up in August, so I don't much care if they threaten to kick us out."

"All right! Wanna ride?"

"You got your car?"

"Na, got the cycle!"

"Well I got the hairdo for it," I laughed, cupping a braided bun with each hand.

"You certainly do!" Cliff said smiling. Once more he gripped my cheeks and pinched them affectionately.

"You guys are making me jealous," Dean said.

"Well, bring your suit when you come over later, Dean, and you can join us."

"Right on!"

When we reached the apartment, Cliff headed to the pool while I ran up to my room to change. Before I did so, I checked the kitchen to find the pile of dishes still stacked in the sink, their crusty surfaces taking advantage of the additional hours to harden. The pungent aroma of fermentation confirmed the good use of the passing time as well.

"Damn!" I said to no one, resigning myself to the necessary chore ahead. *I suppose it all washes out in the end*, I told myself, thinking about the rides and other favors Jan and Liz did for me. Hurriedly, I dressed in my wildly colored two piece suit. Pulling two towels from the linen closet, I headed to the pool to meet Cliff.

"Who's that far out lookin' chick over there?" Cliff hollered, as I fumbled with the lock on the gate.

I looked in the direction of his voice, but I could hardly see his body for the bright sun. I finally caught a glimpse of something blue and figured it was him. At two in the afternoon in the middle of the week, we had the pool to ourselves. I walked to where Cliff lay stretched out on a lawn chair and tossed him a dry towel. He'd already disrobed, and his shirt and shoes were piled next to him on the cement.

"Think I'll get hot first," I said.

"Oh, baby, you are hot!" Cliff said seductively.

"Oh yeah?" I said, walking to the pool.

"Hey, I thought you said you were gonna sunbathe first," Cliff said, lifting his head off the chair.

"I am." Holding my hands steady, I walked slowly back toward him.

"What are—oh, you! That's cold!" he yelled, jumping up and running after me.

Expecting his reaction after tossing water on him, I darted to the other end of the deck.

"You're gonna get it!" he taunted, closing in on me fast. Struggling to keep my eye on the contrast between the blue water and the white deck, I rounded the opposite end of the pool. I didn't have to keep track for long, however. I soon felt Cliff's firm hands around my waist, lifting me in the air.

"Clifford, no—"

Kersplash! Under the water I went. I soon found the bottom of the five foot deep pool. I struggled to my feet, my left hair ball now dangling in its original braid. But before I could climb out and retaliate, Cliff plunged in after me, dunking me again. We wrestled around for a bit, splashing and playing and laughing. Without a worry in the world, I moved free and easy in the cool water. Nothing to bump into, no thoughts to consider.

After a bit we climbed out and returned to our respective perches. I pulled out the bobby pins remaining in the rolled up braid and slid them on the edge of the towel. I decided that soggy pigtails looked better if they matched. As we dripped dry, Cliff asked me an unexpected question.

"Wanna room with me?"

"Huh?" I said, taken by surprise.

"Do you wanna share a place with me next year?"

"What do you mean?" I asked, not sure what he was getting at.

"Well, I gotta find a place by the end of August. My lease is up and my roommate's heading to Georgia. I found this house for two hundred and fifty a month, but I gotta find roommates. It's got five bedrooms, so if five of us shared, it'd only cost fifty bucks a month."

With Liz heading East for grad school and Jan deciding to move back with her mom, I knew I had to secure something soon if I didn't want to go back to the dorm.

"Who else would we get to room with us?"

"Well, Jeff and Ted seem kind of interested, and I thought about asking Carl or George."

"Well, I'll think about it," I said, flashing to the sink full of dishes and wondering if guys could be as messy as girls. "What about electric and heat?"

"All included."

"Wouldn't mind having an extra twenty dollars a month," I said. "Where is this place?"

"That's the best part. It's right across from the main campus. 'Bout two blocks away on University Street."

"Far out! Wouldn't mind givin' up those walks across that windy field in the winter."

"No kiddin'. It'll save me gas for driving that big boat of mine fifteen miles every day, let alone not havin' to find parking."

"When ya need to know?"

"Pretty soon. The guy's got a few interested people, so the sooner we round up enough folks, the better chance we've got of getting it."

"You opposed to askin' another lady?"

"Heck no! Always room for more beautiful women in my life, or my home, or my bed. If I had it my way, I'd have five females rent the place and I'd provide gigolo services. Of course I'd be willing to rotate sharing a different room every night. The lucky ones would get me a second time on a weekend," he laughed.

"You dirty minded chauvinist!" I said, slapping him with my wet towel.

"You're gonna get it now!" he warned as he got up and lifted me off the lounge chair and carried me over to the water. I kicked and wiggled, protesting his manly grip on me, but his hands held firm.

"Don't you—" I said as he hurled me once more into the heavenly sanctuary, floating me into freedom. As we tumbled and played like children, a voice called out, threatening the lost innocence I'd found .

"Hey guys! I got relieved from my shift early."

I looked up from the spot in the middle of my oasis. It took great effort to focus, as the fiery rays of the sun played havoc with my eyes. For an instant, I thought I saw the devil standing where Dean should be. In an alluring voice I heard him say, "Hey, Geri, your delivery man has arrived!"

Chapter 25

Slipping on Appeal

November 1973

"Hey there, Ger, got the sauce going for tonight?"

"Yup, just gotta throw in a few more things and it's ready to simmer. Jeff bringing Star?"

"Think so."

"What about Ted? Is Faith coming with him or did they break up for good this time?" I asked as I chopped a clove of garlic.

"Oh, who knows? I can't keep track of when they're off or on. Here, let me cut up these fun-guys for ya."

Cliff picked up the carton of fresh mushrooms and moved to the end of the kitchen counter. He took another knife from the drawer.

"Got another cutting board?"

"Nah, but you don't need one for mushrooms. They're soft, and you can cut them in the air for heaven's sake."

"Not if you wanna save your skin!" Cliff whined.

"Oh, here, you big scaredy cat. Use mine. I can cut anything without one. All ya gotta do is feel when the knife's about to hit your skin and stop." I scraped the tiny morsels of garlic into a bowl and slid the slab of wood down to Cliff's end of the counter. Like the knife in my hand, the homemade butcher block handcrafted by my father had surreptitiously left its spot in my parents' kitchen. It had become another one of those permanent possessions unknowingly provided to me by my folks. The chopping sound of Cliff's efforts forced me to wonder just how upset Dad would be if he witnessed this family heirloom being used by my male roommate. My next thought brought reflections of the day I announced to my folks I'd be moving in with four guys.

"It's wrong!" my dad said angrily.

"But Dad, I'm only going to share a house and rent with four other people, nothing more."

"Well I don't like the idea of you sleeping in a house with four grown men. What do you think the neighbors would think if they found out?"

"It's not right," my mother agreed. "Even if those boys say they're not going to do anything, you can't believe that. Once they get you into that house they'll be taking advantage of you before you know it."

"Oh mom," I said, exasperated at her primitive viewpoint regarding members of the opposite sex. "I promise, that is not going to happen. We're each going to have our own room. Think of it as living in an apartment, but we share the kitchen. I saw the house and I've got a really big room with the bathroom right next door, so I don't even have to come out unless I want to eat something."

But my comment was less than reassuring.

"That's another thing," she continued. "How are you going to be able to share one bathroom with all those boys and not have something awful happen?"

"Oh Mom. I'm not going to shower with them, if that's what you mean. There is a lock on the door. I promise to lock it every time I have to go. Honest."

"Well," my dad said in the harshest, firmest tone he could muster. "I promise you this. If you move into that house with those boys, I will never step foot inside." My father rarely spent much time in my place of residence when he drove to pick me up or bring me back to school, but I didn't want him to boycott my home. It puzzled me to experience my father treating me so sternly in contrast to his leniency during my teenage years.

Is the potential of having sex with a male roommate at age twenty-one so much worse than doing drugs every weekend in twelfth grade? I wondered. As I sat in my parents' living room listening to protests about my activities as an emancipated adult, I couldn't figure it out. My father, especially, was behaving more differently than he ever had before. One thing stayed the same however. Once my dad made up his mind about something, I knew he would never change it, even if the earth threatened to freeze over. So with all my effort, I begged.

"Aw, Dad, please don't say that, please! Right now I just don't have any other place to live and really, these guys are all very nice. They all work at the Help Line, and I absolutely know it's not going to be like you and Mom think. I won't let anything like that happen, Dad, please!"

"If you don't have any place else to live, then you can move back to the dorm."

"Dad, I hated that. I had such a hard time finding friends, and I hated the cafeteria."

"You heard me. You move into that house, and that's it. I'll still drive you back and forth, but don't even think about asking me to step even one foot inside that place."

"How small you want these, Ger?" I vaguely heard Cliff ask. My father's words still echoed in my mind. It took a second to register Cliff's question.

"Jare-ree!" I heard Cliff calling.

"Uh, oh, I don't know, maybe in quarters."

"Okey dokey. Where were you anyway?" he asked. "Little lost in thought there don't you think?"

"Oh, I was thinking about my father. I sure wish he'd accept my decision to move in here with you guys. If he'd just come in and meet everybody, I know he'd feel better."

"What about your mom, will she come in?"

"Heck, no! My mom hates to drive long distances. But even if she rode down here, there's no way she'd step foot in this house of ill repute. She's got some notion that all we do is lay around and have orgies or something."

"Not a bad idea!" Cliff joked.

I gave him a slap. "If only my dad could see how normal this place is, I know he'd feel better about it all. If Dad accepted it, my mom would feel better, too."

"Let's be honest Geri, how normal is a place called Banana House?"

Carl was responsible for giving us the name of our new pad. One Sunday night at the Help Line meeting, Jeff mentioned that he, Cliff, Ted, George, and I would be moving in together. When Carl learned I was the only lady, he said, "They're gonna drive you bananas, Geri." Jeff's girlfriend Star found this comment rather humorous and asked me why I'd want to live with such a group of monkeys. Hence, Banana House became our home's official title.

Chuckling at Cliff's comment, I said, "I know. But honestly, this is the best arrangement I've been in yet. I mean I liked living with Liz and Jan, but they made such a big deal about cleaning schedules and all, yet they were both terrible at keeping up with their bargain. I like our arrangement much better. If somebody sees that something needs doing, they do it, no big deal. Don't have to keep track of whose week it is to carry out this or that."

"Right on. Chicks get into that stuff, don't they?" Cliff said, cleaning off his knife under the tap. "Want these dumped in the pot?"

"Nope, leave those 'til last. Wanna do an onion?"

"Aw, Ger, they make me cry!" he moaned.

"I'll make you cry, you big baby! Now chop! It's all nice and peeled for you."

I dumped my bowl of two chopped garlics into the pot. I opened the fridge and reclaimed the two green peppers I'd purchased that morning. I commenced cleaning them in the sink while I resumed the conversation.

"Anyway, I feel just awful that my folks are so upset with me."

"Well, for what it's worth, you're not alone in the parent department."

"No? Your folks won't visit you 'cause you're living with a female?" I said smiling.

"Silly girl!" Cliff said affectionately, pinching my cheek with an oniony hand. "Always a funny!" Returning to his task, he went on. "Nah, but I never quite measure up, either. I don't know, my dad's such a great success and everything, but when I don't pull all the A's and I wear my hair long and all, I don't come off lookin' too good to the guy."

"I'm sorry, Cliff," I said, looking at him with sympathy for the first time. "That's gotta hurt."

"Oh, well. Some day he'll get over it, I'm sure."

"What about your mom?"

"She's okay. My folks are divorced and she's remarried, so I don't get a chance to see her too often."

"Where she live?"

"Chicago," Cliff said, emphasizing the end of the word. "Good old Chicago."

"Then where do you get your little Southern accent."

"You noticed that, did you?"

"Oh yeah. I can hear a hint of something there for sure!"

"I grew up in Oklahoma as a kid, so I guess I must still be hangin' on to it a little bit."

"Well, I like it," I said, reaching up and giving him a kiss on his hairy chin.

"Thank ya, ma'am!" he said, reciprocating the gesture.

Cliff finished cutting his onion. With a dribbling nose he excused himself from the kitchen, explaining he'd better get to his room to do bills before I roped him into another smelly task.

George walked through shortly after he left. I heard him sniff the air.

"M-m-m! Something surely does smell goo-ood!" he said.

"It better," I said.

"You do make the best sketti sauce I ever did eat."

"Thanks, Georgie boy."

"Can hardly wait! Six, right?"

"Yup. Is Amy coming?" I asked.

"Think so. Haven't talked to her since yesterday, but she usually manages to get here."

"I figured as much. Wanna be sure I made enough. I think Jeff is bringing a couple of folks from his work along with Star."

"Oh, reminds me, here's my share," George said, reaching into his pocket. He jingled some coins and handed me fifty cents. Each week Banana House residents chipped in so we could hold a dinner for our friends. It took a total of two and a half dollars to buy enough ingredients for at least fifteen people plus a gallon jug of Gallo wine. Most of the guests would bring a bottle or dish to pass, and we'd eat and drink 'til we were ready to burst.

Our Friday night feasts were always followed up by a trip to Mackinaw Jack's, a dance bar in the next city over. My new lifestyle made it necessary for me to forfeit my Friday night graveyard post after almost two years. I had to switch to the Sunday afternoon shift with Carl. The new arrangement turned out to be a welcome change. I learned a lot from Carl and I was glad to have a more expanded social life. I felt like these guys were really my friends. I didn't find I compared myself to them like I did with Liz and Jan. My sense of inferiority seemed to magically disappear in their presence.

"Hey, Ger!" I heard Ted calling from the front of the house.

"Back here, Teddy," I called.

"Got some mail for you, Ger." In a second Ted bounced into the room with a letter in his hand.

"M-m-m! Smells good as always," Ted said. "Love that aroma of simmering sauce!"

"Faith coming?" I asked.

"Who knows?" Ted said.

"She mad at you again?" George asked, chuckling.

"Always!" he said with a smile. "Guy's gotta have a gal to give him a hard time, ya know. Keeps me in my place!"

"Yeah, and we all know you need that!" I said. "You're such a mean guy and all."

"What can I say?" he said, tapping me on the shoulder with the letter.

"Well, you don't deserve it," I said, rinsing my hands.

"Ah, she don't mean nothin' by it. She's just got lots on her plate with her physical therapy internship," Ted replied.

"You're too nice," I scolded, walking back to him and shaking the water off my hands so it splashed in his face.

"Thanks, Ger. Just for that, I ain't givin' you your mail." Ted let out one of his high pitched giggles as he wiggled backwards, playing "keep away." Cute was the best word to describe him. Standing three inches shorter than me, with a head full of thick brown curls, he could have been an advertisement for Toni perms. He had an elfish face with a Sonny Bono moustache and small brown eyes that were always smiling. He would have made a great clown with his comical movements. Faith picked the right guy to be going or ungoing with, as the case might be at any given moment. It didn't matter how unreasonable she could be, he put up with anything, never getting upset. Even in the middle of Help Line meetings, Faith would give him the "what for" over absolutely nothing. Ted would apologize profusely, sneaking a wink at his friends, never accepting the guilt she tried to lay on him. He'd tenderly reach out and touch her shoulders, only to have her slap him and yell at him more. Though he was truly an understanding guy, he wouldn't fit the definition of wimp or whipped. He was simply patient and kind, using humor to ease tense situations.

"Okay, I apologize!" I said, holding out my hand for the letter.

"Now now…" he teased. "What ya gonna give me if I give it to you?"

"I'll send you to bed without your supper," I warned.

"Okay, okay, you got me there. Can't pass up one of your good spaghetti dinners. Here you go."

"Can you read who it's from?" I asked, not expecting mail in the middle of the month.

He took it back to read. "Oh, it's from the university, grievance department?"

My knees went weak.

"This what you've been waitin' for?" Ted asked gently.

"I think so," I said, glad the guys were aware of what this could mean. "Not sure I really want to know. If it's bad news, I hate to ruin a good party."

"Gotta find out some time," Ted urged.

"Don't worry Geri," George said. "Whatever it says, we'll make sure we're with you tonight."

"Thanks, George."

"What are friends if they can't share bad news?"

"Ah, it ain't gonna be bad," Ted said in his usual optimistic style. "Let's open it and get it over with."

"Okay, but let me sit down first."

I went over to the stove and made sure the burner was at simmer. Then I headed into the dining room and sat down at the big table. Sigmund jumped up and crawled onto my shoulder. Sigmund was our pet white rat who had been saved by George from the psych lab incinerator in August. I started to pet him and gave Ted the signal to go ahead.

"Okay, read away," I commanded.

With each tear of the envelope, my anticipation grew. I no longer cared about my shaking leg and let it jiggle up and down without resistance. Ted tugged at the contents inside. I heard the sound of ripping paper. I wanted to yell at him for taking so long. Suddenly Sigmund dug his claws into my skin. He leaped from his perch to snatch up a tiny scrap that had fallen on the table. In a flash he ran off to hide his prize. As Ted continued to meticulously work to release the embodiment of my future, the urge to reach out and rip it from his hands almost overpowered me. Finally, the object of my torment was free. Contrary to Ted's usual jerky manner, he methodically unfolded the one page letter.

"Come on! You're not handling a historical document that's gonna disintegrate for God's sake! What's it say?" I commanded, no longer able to keep my cool.

"Hold on, hold on," Ted said, now looking at the fully opened page. "Let's see… okay, here we go. I'll skip over all the letter headings and junk, okay?"

"Yeah, good!"

"Dear Ms Taeckens:

After reviewing your grievance against Dr. Albert Powers, and the Special Education Department, VI—"

"What's VI mean?" Ted asked.

"Visually impaired," I said, annoyed at his question. "Go on."

"We have determined that your pursuit to declare a major in the area of Special Education for the visually impaired--"

"They just said that!"

"Ted! Just read, okay?" I said impatiently.

"Sorry. Uh, let's see, where was I?"

"Ted!"

"Okay, okay!"

"We have determined that your pursuit to declare a major in the area of Special Education for the visually impaired is your right as a student at our institution of higher learning, an equal opportunity university—"

"All right!" I screamed at the top of my lungs. "Far out!"

"…And we apologize for any inconvenience…" Ted read louder now. But I didn't hear too much more of what he relayed.

"Oh my God, I can't believe it."

"Hey, what's up? Sounds like somebody's killin' a pig!" Cliff said, walking down the hallway toward us.

"I beat him! I really did it, I beat that pious bastard Powers. Oh my God, I just can't believe it passed. It took them a fuckin' year, but they finally figured out what a discriminatory nearsighted chauvinist that guy is."

"All right, Geri girl!" Cliff said, lifting me into the air. Ted and George hooted and hollered as well. It was hugs all around as I jumped and twirled, too ecstatic to know what to do with myself. I felt tears form in my eyes as I released the fear I'd held for so long. I fell back in my chair, uttering expressions of disbelief. Sigmund returned, joining in my excitement as he wiggled and squirmed in and out of my hands. I picked him up and brought his little pink eyed face up to mine.

"Can you believe it, Sigmund? We made it, you and me. Neither one of us is going to the gas chamber." We all laughed as Sigmund wiggled his whiskers, squiggled out of my grip and ran to my neck, wrapping himself in my hair.

"And they call you a rat, Sigmund," I said.

"He may be the rat," Ted said, "But he's not the fink you've had to deal with!"

"No kidding," Cliff agreed as everyone hooted at the joke.

"Problem is, I'm gonna have to deal with him eventually. He teaches half the required VI courses, so I'm gonna have to take him as an instructor."

"Yeah, but he can't mess with you if you pass the tests. It'll be a little more objective, harder for him to hassle with you."

"I don't know about that," I said as Sigmund now ran down my arm and off to somewhere unknown. "I wouldn't trust that guy as far as I could see him, and according to him that's not enough." Everyone chuckled.

"Well, you got your foot in the door anyway," Ted reassured.

For the next few hours, Banana House filled and emptied of occupants. Likewise, my emotions rose and fell with the revelation of my news. Hardly knowing what to do, I found myself thinking of people to call, while intermittently tending to the sauce. Linda was one of my contacts. She, too, had been experiencing similar problems in her efforts to get into law school. She had been very understanding, and I wanted to be sure to give her my news. My folks were also very happy to hear I'd won this battle, though they both maintained their disapproving tones as we talked. I almost wished I hadn't called them as, each time we spoke, I hung up feeling both guilty and angry.

After running out of people to call and things to do in the kitchen, an unwanted image seeped into my mind. Though I tried to suppress it, it kept nagging at me. I found myself wandering into my bedroom. I walked to my dresser and opened the lid to my jewelry box. Along with my peace sign choker, earrings, and love beads, there sat two little pills. I managed to save them from the stash Dean had sold me a few months earlier.

These will be markers of my personal progress with self control, I remembered telling myself after using two to study for the anatomy of the eye class. Though I had taken one more the very next day to celebrate the B I earned, I promised myself it was my last.

But now the longing grew stronger as the minutes ticked by. Three times I managed to pull myself away from the stash, and three times I went back to the box. *Why do you want one now?* I asked myself. *You're already happy. You don't need a pill for that.*

It's a way to celebrate! I told myself. Nothin' wrong with that. Everybody uses something to have fun or rejoice with.

But you know it's not good for you, my practical voice said.

What about weddings and cultural events? I argued, thinking about a lecture in history class. Even my professor had acknowledged the traditions of ancient man using mood-altering herbs and mushrooms.

"You know this isn't good!" my out-loud voice retorted. "I'm already happy. What's the point in getting happier?"

I went back to the kitchen and focused my attention on my creation. The familiar call of the drug kept nagging at me as I stirred the rich red brew. Friends soon filtered in for dinner. As it was about to be served, I filled a glass of water and snuck away to my room. Opening the wooden box, I stared once more at the contents. There they were again, sitting like pearls among the colorful array of jewelry,

"What is it inside those that make a person feel so darn good?" I asked, receiving no answer.

Once more my conscience tried to squelch my growing urge. *Think of how crazy it makes you feel later.* But my argument could not stop me from reaching in and picking up both pills and putting them in my mouth. I slugged them back, placing the half empty glass on my dresser.

"This is a two pill celebration," I said. "Besides, with them both gone, I won't have to be tempted any more."

I lowered the lid and then lifted the cover once more. I retrieved my choker, deciding it would go well with my navy v-neck sweater. I centered myself in front of the mirror, and put it on. The ghost like figure reflecting back told me I must not have dusted the glass for a while.

"I guess I haven't really looked at myself much lately," I said out loud, forcing my tone to sound matter of fact. I stepped into the hallway, opened the linen closet, and pulled out a rag. I snatched up the bottle of Windex and went on with my task. I dampened the cloth with the solution and wiped the shiny surface clean. But the smoky figure was still there. A nagging fear tugged on my gut. I retrieved the lamp off my night stand and moved it to the dresser.

"How long since I've looked?" I wondered out loud, pulling out the dresser to plug in the light. But flipping the switch did not erase the fog. The same misty figure remained.

Suddenly an idea hit me. I quickly ran to the bathroom and turned on the light. When I looked in the mirror, tears exploded from my eyes. "Thank God!" I whispered so no one could hear, "Thank God it was only the poor lighting!"

My sense of relief lasted only for a moment however. As I dabbed my eyes, trying to ready myself to join the others, the truth of my situation hit me. *How long can I keep on pretending?* I asked myself. *How many light bulb changes and pills will it take to keep me from seeing that my vision is slipping away?*

Chapter 26

There's More than Meets the Eye

January 1974

"Geri, you and Tom are in 109. Star and Kevin, your group's in 107 next door. Faith and Jeff, you guys are farther down the hall in 102, and Carol and I will be in 105."

The second training for Help Line volunteers was about to begin. After hearing Jack's instructions, we all filtered to our prospective rooms in the counseling center. Conducting this training the first weekend of the semester, had paid off. Twenty-five potential volunteers enrolled, a record for the center.

The ten by twelve foot room was void of furniture. Jack had arranged for all the desks and chairs to be removed, as sitting on the floor was supposed to be a grounding experience and a key component to the encounter training model. "Everyone on the same level," we'd all been told. Tom closed off what remained of Friday evening's sunlight by shutting the drapes and then joined me on the floor in the opposite corner. This provided a balance between the facilitators and the trainees. Though I could see his figure, he was too far away for me to notice facial expressions or subtle gestures.

"So, who's assigned to us?" I asked, wishing I could be closer to him.

He flipped through the pages and found the group lists.

"Let's see. We've got a Mary, a Jasmine, Nathaniel, or Nate, written in parentheses, then Peggy, and a Dave."

I repeated the names in hopes I'd get a head start on remembering them. First names only was the rule. This was to avoid any preconceived notions about heritage, or any possibility of former knowledge of a trainee. Tom and I reviewed some of the ground rules and chatted a bit about strategies. We'd worked together in the previous training and I felt very comfortable with him. Eventually people started straggling in. I could hear Carol in the hallway directing folks to their assigned rooms. By six p.m. everyone had arrived.

"Welcome all," I said in a quiet voice. "You are about to participate in a rather unique and intensive weekend. We ask that you try to avoid taking bathroom breaks or leaving the room except during specified times, as it can disrupt the encounter process. You need to be aware that you will be expected to share your personal thoughts, feelings, and experiences as much as you can, and respect the expressions of other members of this group."

I paused for effect, brushing my hair back over my shoulder. Everyone sat perfectly still. I wished I could read their facial expressions. I was filled with the glow of self-importance as I continued with the rules of the training.

"It will be absolutely essential that everything that is said in this room stays here. I'm not trying to cop an authoritative attitude here, but you need to know that you will be instantly dismissed if you are discovered disclosing anything to anyone else. This holds true for when you become a Help Line listener as well."

Once more I allowed for a moment of silence, believing the quiet would give my words more impact. Eventually Tom asked, "Any questions?"

No one spoke. Fingering the double string of colorful love beads which hung almost to my hip hugger bells, I went on. "Okay, now that we've established the most important ground rule for the group, why don't we go around and introduce ourselves and say why you decided to become a phone worker at the center." I looked around the room. When no one spoke, I said, "I guess I'll start. My name is Geri. I've been working at the Help Line for over two years. I love helping others and learning to understand what makes people feel or do some of the things they do."

I nodded to my partner, indicating I was through.

"I'm Tom, the other facilitator of this group," he said, pausing. I heard him shift his body. I figured he'd moved into his favorite lotus position. "I've been round the Help Line for 'bout four years. I too think it's far out to hang with folks when they're up tight or just needing to chat. Learned lots from the folks that call. Get lots of good feelings from it all. Okay, now it's your turn."

More nervous silence filled the room.

"How 'bout you?" Tom asked, his long dark beard dipping down the front of his pink t-shirt. I assumed he must be nodding to one of the participants. A tiny voice from his right spoke.

"I'm Jasmine. I'm studying to be a psychologist. I want to learn how to talk to people and get some experience for my degree."

"Far out! Thanks, Jasmine," Tom said. "And you."

The person to Jasmine's right now offered his name. "Hello, I'm Nate. Not really sure why I'm here. Saw the announcement and thought it might be cool to do a little volunteer work for somebody. Had the weekend free, so thought I'd check it out."

"Great!" Tom said. "Some of our best listeners didn't really have a clue why they signed up. Right on, man!"

I was next in line, so I turned to the person to my right and asked her name.

"I'm Mary. This is my second semester at school. I wanna major in social work and I've already taken Psychology 101. I've done a lot of volunteer work like this before. We had to go through something like this when I worked at a nursing home back in high school. I'm from Grand Rapids, and we have wonderful volunteer programs for the elderly. I like older folks. They're so sweet, and they just love to tell their stories to anyone who'd listen. I found it fascinating to hear how they used to have to live. No water, no phone, cooking and cleaning without any electricity. I just can't imagine, can you? Anyway, I must have spent most my junior and senior year down at the home. Summers, too. Heck, sometimes I even do my school work there. They just love having somebody sitting near them, you know. Don't matter if you're talking with them, just so you're in the room with them. I figured that out and figured heck, might as well study there as home and make them happy."

"That's really commendable, Mary," I managed to slip in. "Sounds like you're really enthusiastic about helping others."

"Oh, I am, I am. It's one of the funnest things, you know."

"Okay, well, shall we hear from the person next to you now?" I suggested, deciding Mary would be our toughest customer in terms of time management.

"I'm Peggy. I'm a nursing student. I'm in my third year. I need to accumulate thirty hours of non-medical interpersonal volunteer experience by September of next year. I thought this might be interesting."

"Well, it sounds like this might meet your needs then, Peggy. Welcome," I said, sensing she was a little uptight.

"And you?" I asked nodding to the large fellow in the blue striped shirt sitting near the door.

"Well, I'm Dave," he said, clearing his throat. "Actually, I've used the Help—"

My heart sank. I couldn't believe it. At the clearing of his throat I instantly knew who it was. Gripping my beads tightly, I considered running out of the room to find out how this had happened. When it dawned on me he was blocking the door, my anxiety increased. My panic went unnoticed as Dave continued.

"—Line many times. The staff have been very helpful to me, and I thought I might be able to give something back to others," he said in his distinctive hesitating style.

"Well, that's really cool!" Tom said. I wanted to jump up and run over and whisper to him. *No, no, Tom, it's not cool! This guy should not be a Help Line listener. He's crazy, he's weird!* I told him in my head. Liz's earlier comments whispered back, however: "Well, I guess we're all a little weird."

But I can't handle being in this type of setting with him! I protested to her image, now clearly visible in my mind.

Gratefully Tom was carrying the ball. He was explaining the next rule of using "I" statements, when responding to someone who is sharing a problem. "It's bad news to tell someone not to feel something. Advice is cheap. Being open and accepting may take you a bit of effort, but it beats doing a turn off. Right, Geri?"

"Uh, yeah!" I agreed, twisting my necklace so tightly it was choking me. Tom continued. I could see he was fully animated, moving his hands in all directions.

"As one of the phone listeners, you're not here to judge or try to tell someone how to live. If you do have an idea for someone, you need to own it as your own. Do you know what I mean by this?"

No one replied.

"Well then, let me give you an example of how you might phrase an idea as your own. "When I am in a similar situation, I do this, or that. Get it? Instead of just telling them what they should do, I simply share my experience. Less threatening, you know."

As Tom droned on, trying to teach the benefits of "I" statements, I continued to obsess about Dave's presence. As I did so, Liz's words took center stage, impairing my ability to focus. "Geri, this does not sound like you. You are always so tolerant of everyone," I heard her say.

Why am I being so critical? I asked myself. I'm doing the 'us and them' thing that I hate so much! You'd better get it together. You wouldn't want visually impaired people banned from the training.

"Right, Geri?" Tom asked. Not having heard a word, my face flushed with embarrassment.

"I don't think she heard you," Dave said. "I think she's a bit surprised to see me."

I wanted to kill him for alluding to our previous connection. *How far is he going to go with exposing me?* I wondered. *Will he pay me back for rejecting him and share my cruelty with this group?* Terrified, I quickly decided to change tactics.

"Yes, Dave, I was a bit surprised to see you. But I'm very glad you have taken an interest in the center this way. I think it'll be a good experience for you."

"Thanks, Ger," he said.

Wincing at his casual use of my name, I felt the noose I'd made squeeze tightly against my Adam's apple. Totally unaware of what I was dealing with, Tom continued.

"Well I was saying, Geri, that it's hard sometimes not to wanna fix folks when they call with a big list of woes and stuff."

"Oh, yes," I said, sounding more professional than I wanted to. "One of the things we're going to do soon is role play a situation," I announced, swinging my love beads loosely back and forth across my chest, hoping to appear more relaxed than I truly felt. "First we want you to think of a problem, not too stressful, that you might share with another," I explained. "The person who's helping needs to figure out a way to listen, support, and explore ideas without giving advice."

"Oh, and you gotta remember that if a person does get upset or something, don't rush to rescue them by hugging 'em or layin' a bunch of I'm sorries on 'em," Tom added. "Sympathy ain't really all that helpful. Empathy is saying you understand and accept why they are upset. Sympathy is doing that rescue thing."

"Thanks Tom," I said, admonishing myself for forgetting to mention this. "Anyone interested in trying this out?"

"I'll do it," Nate offered.

"I'll be the listener," Mary volunteered.

Tom instructed them to move to the center of the room. He asked the others to be quiet.

"Okay Nate, go ahead," I said.

"Gotta chick I really like," Nate began. "She's really purty and I've been trying to get a date with her for three months now."

"Oh, yeah?" Mary replied. "I knew a guy once who I really really liked. Oh, he was so dreamy looking. Big brown eyes and soft curly brown hair. I thought he really liked me, too, but after the first date he didn't ever call me again. I'd leave messages with his mom but he'd never return them. I saw him—"

"Mary, you might wanna stay a bit more focused on Nate," Tom suggested.

"Oh, yeah, right," she giggled nervously. "Uh, so, what's she look like?"

"Well, she's got long brown hair and blue eyes," Nate explained. "She's tall and thin and has this cute little walk. I try really hard to be nice to her. She lives in my dorm, you know and, though she's kind of nice to me, she always says she's busy. If she just told me she doesn't want anything to do with me, I'd let go of the whole thing, but she kind of leads me on a bit, you know?"

"Well, if you ask me," Mary said, "if she's been givin' you the brush-off for three whole months, you probably ought to give it up, you think?"

Listening to Mary dominate the conversation, throwing out comments directly opposed to the ideas which were recently discussed, told me I needed to do something. Sensing Dave's eyes staring at me blocked my usual ability to intervene, however. I glanced over at him. As I suspected, his face was turned directly at me. Without a doubt, I knew he was watching and waiting for me to mess up. As Mary continued expounding on how Nate should handle his situation, I frantically tried to think of something clever to say.

"Well, you should just drop her. I mean, I finally was able to convince the guy I liked to ask me out, but I ended up not really liking him too much. You could keep trying to force yourself on her, I guess. Just don't let it get to you. I learned I shouldn't have let it get to me, so you shouldn't. If someone don't like you, they don't like you, and you can't do much about that anyway, can you now?"

Desperate to interject something, I finally asked, "Nate, how do you feel when Mary says something like this to you?"

"Well, I gotta admit I don't exactly feel supported."

Still concerned about Dave's surveillance, I ventured further.

"Mary, do you understand how telling him your opinion could maybe hurt his feelings?"

"Well, gee, he asked me if I understood. It's pretty obvious, don't ya think, if a girl keeps giving excuses, that she isn't really interested, then it's best to forget about her?"

As I processed with Mary the pros and cons of her intervention, my belief about Dave's desire to see me falter impaired my ability to speak. Despite my experience, my tongue became tied, and concepts evaporated from my brain. Instead of helping her identify the result of her statements, I found myself scolding her for doing it all wrong. Before I knew it, we were arguing.

"You can't tell a client what they should do," I insisted.

"But he asked me for my opinion. Besides, it's pretty obvious the girl ain't interested in him. He's gotta realize that!"

"Well the thing you gotta think about Mary," Tom said, "is that sometimes it's better to help the caller figure out why they might be havin' trouble letting go, instead of just telling them what you think the problem is. The important thing is you gave it a try and you were able to identify the problem right off, which is good!"

The contrast between my critical approach and Tom's gentle encouragement made me want to run and hide. I suddenly realized I had been displacing my anger about Dave's presence onto Mary. Certain my secret admirer must be gloating over my ridiculous behavior, I hoped it might discourage him from any further admiration.

"Well, gee, I didn't mean to hurt your feelings, Nate," Mary said, looking in my direction.

"Ah, it's okay," Nate said. "It's really not a big deal. You said not to bring up anything too serious, and I've kinda given up on the chick for a while now."

"It's all about learning, Mary," I tried to assure her. "We don't expect you to know how to do empathic listening right off the bat," I said, switching my angry tone to one of condescension. You're blowing the trust thing! I warned myself, thinking of how I must be coming off to the others. Chill out! But I couldn't stop obsessing about Dave looking at me under a microscope.

I was more than happy to let Tom offer to model the listener in the next vignette. Jasmine agreed to be the caller. When they finished, we discussed the pros and cons of the interaction.

Dave and Peggy were the last to engage in a mock scene. They each took a seat in the center of the room. Dave played the role of the helper. I grasped my beads, pressing them hard with my fingers as the muscles in my body grew equally tense. My mood became pensive as I listened to the interaction unfold.

"Hello Peggy," he said.

"Hi," she replied.

"What brings you here?"

"Well, I'm a nursing student. I'm doing well with my grades and I only have one and a half years to go before I graduate."

"That must make you feel good," Dave said.

"That's the problem," Peggy explained.

"You aren't happy about your good grades or graduating?"

"Both! I've spent all this money and worked very hard and I want to quit the nursing program."

"Boy, that must be very frustrating. Why do you think you don't like nursing?"

"Because I never liked it."

"Did you pick it as your major because your parents wanted you to?"

"Yes!" Peggy said. "My mother was a nurse and my grandmother was a nurse, and therefore, I have to become a nurse."

"What would happen if you changed your mind?"

"My parents would hate me."

"Are you sure about that?"

"Well, pretty much."

"It's hard to be a disappointment to your parents, isn't it?"

"Yes!" Peggy said, her voice sounding amazed at Dave's suggestion. I shared her sentiment, even though I found myself upset by Dave's competence.

"I know my parents think I'm a disappointment."

"Really?" she asked, her previously rigid body now leaning forward toward Dave.

My feeling changed to jealousy as I watched him engage this uptight lady with ease.

"I was a student studying at Berkley in the area of math. I liked math and all, but I ended up having a nervous breakdown right before I completed my Ph.D."

This will put a stop to her comfort level! I told myself, cringing at his taboo disclosure. But as Dave shared his experience with schizophrenia, her response was not adverse. Instead, she became more animated, her voice rich with emotion.

"Sometimes I feel like I'm going to have a nervous breakdown, too," she said.

"It can feel scary, can't it?"

"Yes, it can," she bowed her head. Inching forward, I tried to see her face. The poor lighting made it impossible.

"Pleasing our parents is probably at the core of our being," Dave said. His astute observations were pissing me off.

"It is, it is. I can't think of anything worse than having my mom or dad being disappointed in me!"

"Freud always said that everything we do is to protect the bond of our existence, which is of course our parents, our givers of life. I can understand why it feels so scary to you."

"I just don't know what to do," Peggy said.

"You seem like a very self-aware young woman, Peggy. The fact that you understand this before having a nervous breakdown means you have a good chance of working through it okay. It probably wouldn't be a bad idea to start seeing a professional counselor to help you with this problem, though."

A sinister smile came across my face, as I delighted in Dave's misguided suggestion. *He's insulted her for sure!* I mused.

"Do you really think that would help?" Peggy asked hopefully, as my smile plunged into a frown.

"I do. It's never good to try and hold emotional pain in."

"Gee, maybe I should consider that."

While Dave provided her with information on counseling agencies, I scolded myself for having such an overgrown ego.

"The other thing that helped me," Dave went on, "Is I sat down with my mom one time and asked her if she would love me any less if I could never work or finish my Ph.D."

"What'd she say?" Peggy asked.

"She was very kind and assured me that she would always love me, no matter what. I think most parents would feel this way."

With Dave's heartfelt testimonial, Peggy began to cry. She dropped her head in her hands, sobbing profusely. I reached for the box of tissues I had sitting beside me and slid them in her direction. She pulled a few from the box as she went on with her cathartic release.

"Shouldn't somebody hug her or something?" Mary asked. Remembering the no touching rule, I shook my head no.

"Crying is a good thing," Dave calmly said. "It's good you can cry, Peggy. I wish I could cry more, but I'm blocked. You have a lot of potential if you can weep so freely like this."

"Thanks," Peggy managed to say between sobs. She blew her nose a couple of times and wiped her eyes. "I didn't know I would get so upset," she explained. "I never told anyone how I felt about school before. Maybe I should say something to my folks, you think?"

But Dave did not give her a yes or a no. He simply told her she would do what she needed to when she was ready.

The wisdom that flowed from his lips blew my mind. By the end of Friday's session, I was so full of shame I couldn't stand myself. He had spoken so honestly. His capacity for cutting to the chase while displaying empathy and personal insights was truly exemplary.

But despite my acknowledgement of Dave's capabilities, I still felt an aversion toward him. Throughout Saturday and Sunday's sessions, I continually avoided him as he attempted to make conversation with me during breaks. Like two magnets that repel each other when placed close together, I felt a powerful force driving me back.

At last the final hour of the training arrived. At four p.m. on Sunday afternoon, each pair of facilitators brought their apprentices to the counseling waiting lounge.

Jack did his closing exercise, having everyone share how they felt about their experience. He went over the rules for volunteering at the Help Line one more time and explained the three month probationary period. Everyone signed confidentiality agreements and the new members were dismissed. The rest of us hung back for a short debriefing, then Jack sent us on our way.

"Wanna go have a beer at Bob's?" Tom asked the group. Everyone except me agreed. Exhausted and emotionally drained, I couldn't wait to get home and be alone. I stopped at the bathroom, and then located the last jacket off the rack in the break room nearby.

"Hi, Ger," I almost jumped out of my skin. I thought I was the only one left in the place. I hadn't expected to hear anyone's voice, let alone Dave's. In my surprise, I dropped my buckskin coat on the floor. I quickly picked it up and put it on, repressing my desire to snap at him for cornering me.

"Hi," I said instead.

"You did a nice job facilitating, Ger," he said kindly.

"Thanks. You, too."

"You're having more trouble seeing, aren't you?"

His words hit me hard. I couldn't hold back my anger any longer.

"Dave, why do you say things like that? I don't like it."

"Why does that make you mad?"

But I didn't answer. I simply turned away. He was blocking the hallway to the front door, so I headed toward the back entrance. He continued calling after me. "It must be hard. I can tell you keep struggling to see people's faces, but you're not able to, are you?"

I turned on my heels and yelled, "Yes, I can!"

"Not like you could the last time I saw you."

I decided to ignore him. Instead, I rushed off, turning down another hallway, flying out the back door.

The setting sun brought with it the confusing shadows of black and gray. Dusk always made travel harder than ever, especially when the landscape was spotted with dirty snow. If distinguishing the sidewalk from the ground were not challenging enough, I now added the blur of my falling tears to the treacherous mix. Frantically wavering back and forth, I wondered why the hell I was crying.

My wandering became aimless as some unknown force drove me forward. Suddenly the sidewalk split. Uncertain of which way to go, I panicked. I took the left path. Anxiety grew with each step. As I picked up my pace, I was certain of being followed. Thoughts of boogie men triggered more childish fears. *You must escape!* I told myself, urging my feet to go faster. *Hurry, hurry!* I demanded, recalling the exodus I took so often as a child as I ran from basement ghosts. *It's gonna get you!* the child within me warned.

Suddenly there was something in front of me. I stopped dead, scanning the area. A monstrous object stood before me. Though I told myself it must be a building, it seemed to undulate as I stared. I listened. An eerie sound like a space ship grew louder. I was paralyzed with fear. "Where am I?" I said to no one, my voice shaky with doubt. Everything looks so strange! I'm so dizzy, so confused! I said as the earth beneath my feet began to spin. Desperate for comfort, I reached my hand into my pocket. Grateful to find my security blanket so helpful in such times, I buried my face in the crumpled handkerchief and longed for my father's arms. Having lost all sense of myself, I crouched down in the middle of nowhere retching into the wadded cloth.

"I'm sorry you're so sad," a voice said as a hand gently touched my shoulder. "It must be very hard to be so alone and scared."

With no ability to control my reactions any longer, I stood and buried my face in a large, tall man. He wrapped his sturdy arms around my back and held me firmly, comforting me as I cried.

"It's okay to cry, Geri. It really is." As Dave's tender voice expressed genuine concern, I felt myself surrender as I had with only one other person. Just as my father had comforted me as a child, assuring me it would all be okay, Dave responded with the same loving caress. Though my submission lasted for only a moment, I now knew the depth of my despair. The experience of getting lost in my own back yard now forced me to see a clear glimpse of my fate.

Chapter 27

In The Dead of Night

February 1974

Wiping my eyes, I picked up the bottle of Coke beside me and took a sip. My effort to swallow turned into a fit of choking as an unexpected sound caught me off guard.

"Whoa! You all right?" Ted's voice asked. I nodded my head, holding up one finger to indicate he should wait. When I regained my composure, I said, "Went down the wrong pipe."

"Hate that. See you're up late again. You ever gonna go to sleep tonight there, Ger?"

"Yeah, but I have to turn in this report by noon and got classes all morning," I said, sitting at the desk situated just inside my bedroom.

"You always got classes and reports, girl. When you gonna rest?" Ted's small hand reached out and tousled my hair. Working as an ambulance driver, he never got home before one a.m. No matter when he came in, Ted always checked on me before heading upstairs to bed. "It's already 1:45. Even if you went to bed now, you'd only get six hours of sleep," he warned.

"I know." I looked up from my typewriter. "You worry too much about me, Teddy boy," I said, extending my hand and pulling him toward me, giving him an affectionate smile. Responding to my tug, Ted stepped forward and wrapped both arms around me, rubbing my shoulders through the plaid flannel shirt. I slid my arm around his waist. He felt so cuddly in his thick Scandinavian sweater. Even with me sitting and him standing, he still barely stood a few inches beyond the top of my head. We gave each other a squeeze and then released our grasp.

"Seriously, Geri, you've been up most nights 'til three or four. How long you think you can burn the candle like this? You got bags under your eyes, girl!" He gently took his finger and traced a line under each of my eyes. "You look awful!" I felt his warm hand on my shoulder.

"Ah, I'm okay," I said, shoving him backwards in a playful manner to lighten the moment. "Heck, all students do it from time to time. I just got a lot going on this semester, what with the center training wrapping up, and adjusting to the nanny job."

"Well, maybe it would've been wiser not to take twenty credits in one term, if you get my drift. What's that all about, anyway?"

"It's only a few credits more than normal, and I've got to catch up with the Special Ed course work, thanks to that turkey, Powers. If you wanna get on someone's case about my workload, give him a call right now and tell him off for me, would you?" Smiling up at him again, I brushed my hair from my face.

"I don't know," Ted said, shaking his head at me. "Whatever the excuse, it's not cool for somebody to take this many credits, plus do trainings, plus take care of two little rascals most every evening and all weekend to boot."

Ted was referring to my recent undertaking. I'd been hired by the Dean of Admissions to care for his two children, Oliver and Kamiah, ages four and six respectively. His wife had gone on a sabbatical back to her homeland in Nigeria, so he needed someone to watch his kids three evenings during the week and every other weekend. Sometimes this required overnight stays at either his home or mine. Though I had to forfeit the after dinner outings on opposite Friday evenings, I typically kept Oliver and Kamiah at Banana House on spaghetti night so as not to disappoint my roommates and friends. The kids loved helping me cut vegetables for the sauce, and Oliver loved playing with Sigmund. It was fun to watch the guys' paternal instincts emerge as they gave piggyback rides or read books to the kids. Ted took particular interest in this boy and girl, teaching them karate moves, building houses out of popsicle sticks, or making explosions with baking soda and vinegar. Cliff also took a liking to them. Not a Friday went by since landing this job in January that Cliff didn't bring them some kind of surprise. He even became temporary nanny the weekend I trained the new Help Line listeners.

Of course Cliff had a particular investment in these little balls of energy. Right before Christmas break, he bounded into the kitchen where I was making a big pot of chili for the Help Line holiday party.

"Hey Geri!" he said in his usual animated fashion. Standing at the stove with my back to him, he wrapped both arms around me and kissed me first on one cheek, then the other.

"What's up, Cliffy dear?" I asked, keeping my focus on my rotating wooden spoon.

"Oo! Your famous chili, huh? Smells like a killer batch."

"Only the best!" I gloated.

"Well, I got this great idea."

"What's that?"

"How'd you like to take a trip to Europe next summer?"

"Far out! How you gonna arrange that for me? Is this all expenses paid?"

"Yeah, right," he laughed. "No, seriously, I got flipping through this magazine on backpacking through Europe, and I figured we could do it on five bucks a day."

"No kiddin? Problem is, where do I get five bucks a day?"

"Well, if we could get someone to sublet our rooms from us this summer, we could use the rent money, plus whatever we could earn from now 'til May or

June. I looked up air fares and you can get a flight from Toronto to London for three hundred bucks."

"Three hundred bucks is a lot of money, Cliff, and I don't have a job, remember?"

"So get one."

"Doing what?"

He thought for a minute. I wondered if Cliff had forgotten that grabbing a minimum wage job as a clerk or a waitress was out of the question for a person with a vision problem.

"Uh, well you're creative, come up with something, Ger."

Beating him to the idea, the wheels in my brain began to turn. This venture sounded very enticing, and I wasn't about to pass it up.

"How long would we be there?" I asked.

"I guess that depends on how much money we pull together, but I was thinking six weeks or two months at the very least."

"Wow! Far out! Wouldn't that be so cool? Oh gosh, Cliff, I'd love to do it."

"What about babysitting?" he suggested. "You've done some of that since you've been at school. Maybe if you put your shingle up, you could get some jobs."

"I wonder if Joan and Tim know of someone at the university whose child needs care," I said, thinking of the vice president and his wife. They rarely needed my services these days, as Joan had quit her job to have another baby. "Well, all I can do is give it a try," I said.

The next day I gave them a call. I was amazed when Joan told me of the dean's search for a part-time nanny. She contacted him for me and within three days and a home interview, I had the job. For $250 a month, I figured I'd be able to swing the cost of the trip with no problem.

The kids were lots of fun, but they required a great deal of attention. Unfortunately, my plans to study while they played did not turn out the way I figured. With the combination of their missing their mom and my difficulty saying no to them, I spent most of my time doing whatever they wanted. As a result, my only study time came after ten p.m. Ted was right. I could only run on a few hours of sleep for so long, at least without a little help.

Now, as I sat listening to Ted's warning, I held within my brain my secret worry about the risky energy boosters I'd been using. No one except Dean knew of my questionable activity, not even Jack. Though I wanted to tell him, I feared he would think less of me, as I would expect he should.

The only other person who was instinctively aware of my concealment was Dave. Despite my moment of catharsis that desolate winter day, the need to guard myself against his beautiful wisdom grew stronger. However, his probing inquiries continued. Cleverly, he'd arranged his Help Line shift to be directly before mine, which was now Sundays at eight p.m. He'd hang around for a bit conjuring up ways to converse with me. Making an effort to be friendlier, I nervously allowed for some interaction. Two weeks earlier he had caught me off guard.

"So, Ger?" he said. "You doing drugs?"

Having dropped some speed the night before, I felt my face react. My astonishment at his insight must have shown.

"You are, aren't you?"

"No, I'm not," I insisted. But his perceptiveness could not be swayed.

"Ger," he said in his most endearing tone, "you could really hurt yourself. Don't hurt yourself, Geri. You've got a lot to give."

"I'm not!" I protested, but we both knew I was lying.

As I listened to Ted's concerns, I knew I had to dispel his fears, and keep my secret safe. "Oh, shoot, that reminds me," I said, hoping to change the focus, "I forgot to find somebody to swap my shift with me this Sunday so I can take care of the kids. I sure wish I could find someone to do a permanent change. I'm needed more frequently than the dean thought and scrambling every week like this is a drag."

"Like I said, you've bitten off more than you can chew, silly girl."

"What you talkin' about, Teddy boy, I still got three days to find someone," I laughed, noticing my leg start to shake.

"Give me one of your great back rubs, and I'll do it for you," Teddy offered.

"Really, you would?" I said, dropping to my knees in an effort to steady them. I grabbed his hand and feigned desperation, acting like a damsel in distress.

"I would, me lady! In fact, for a weekly back rub I might even consider switching shifts permanently with you."

"Really?" I said, allowing him to help me back into my chair. "You got Wednesday mornings four to eight, right?"

"Yuppers!"

"Hmmm, yeah, I think that'd work."

"Well, gotta hit the sack. I ain't no masochist like you, pretty lady. I need my beauty shut eye. At least eight hours for this handsome devil."

"Well, since I'm already beautiful, I shouldn't have to sleep at all!" Despite my seemingly fun loving appearance, inwardly I felt completely drained. I couldn't remember the last time I slept eight hours. I doubted if I'd got much more than three hours each night this week, and even these were fitful at best.

As I heard Ted climb the stairs, I rubbed my eyes and reflected on how my crazy schedule came to be. Two days before classes resumed, I received notification in the mail to report to the Special Education office. Terrified that Professor Powers found a way to once more thwart me from my career goal, I almost went crazy until I could make the necessary contact. When the moment of truth finally arrived, I thought my knees would buckle as I stood waiting for Professor Powers' secretary to buzz him.

"Miss Taeckens?" he said, as if asking whether my name might have changed since our last meeting.

"Yes, sir," I answered, trying not to let my nervousness show. This was our first encounter since I'd steamed out of his office almost two years ago.

"Come in."

I followed him, this time finding my seat without a hassle. He moved around his desk and sat down.

"I trust you had a good vacation?"

"Uh, yes, I did. And you?" He was sounding too nice, I decided. I tightened my stomach in hopes it would help absorb the blow I was certain he was about to send me.

"That's good, that's good." He cleared his throat, seeming nervous now.

What's he up to? I thought.

"I see here you've enrolled in my Braille transcription course."

"Yes."

"Well, I suppose you are rather proficient in Braille. Am I correct in that assumption?"

"Uh, well," I paused, wondering if this was a trick question. "Yes. I've been using Braille since I was eight."

"Good, good! Do you properly use all the contractions?"

Okay, what's he getting at? I asked myself, continuing to scrutinize his line of questioning. In my hesitation Professor Powers reassuringly said, "I have a proposal for you, Miss Taeckens, and I'm just trying to discern if you may have forgotten some of the more detailed rules of the language as I'm sure, like many other Braille readers, you've developed some of your own shortcuts to save time."

His assumption about my Braille use was accurate. Because punching out every dot, particularly on a slate and stylus, took great effort when writing extended text, most visually impaired folks developed their own shorthand system. It would be unlikely I could clearly read something Linda wrote and vice versa, unless we took special care to write properly.

So, do I remember all the specifics? I asked myself, thinking about how pcv stands for the word perceive, or how one should never use a double d sign in the middle of a word to represent the prefix dis-, which in Braille is the same dot formation as the symbol for dd, found in words like middle or cuddle.

"I'm pretty sure I remember them all," I told him, my curiosity growing.

"Well good!" he said sounding as if he might be smiling.

"Then what I want to suggest is, you forget about attending the actual class periods and simply take the proficiency test at the end of the semester. Grades for this course are solely based on this examination."

Did I hear him right? I asked myself, as I sat dumfounded at his offer.

"You must remember that the document you are required to copy will, of course, include the use of all the Braille symbols and contractions. I will accommodate you by giving you the material through an auditory modality. You can bring your own Braille writer or I can provide you with one, whichever you wish."

"Oh, I can bring my own," I said, totally astonished at his cooperative attitude.

With great joy, I almost skipped out of his office, hardly able to believe what had transpired. Dr. Powers had quite the reputation for his attendance policies and cutting no slack to anyone for any reason. Though a hint of suspicion crossed my mind, I figured I was relatively safe as I truly was proficient in the area of Braille.

So, the Monday after the Help Line encounter experience, only the fifth day into the term, I decided to enroll in one more class. Though I questioned my unusual craving for staying busy, I felt the thrill of being driven. Barreling through the landscape of activities, I began speeding like a freight train from one task to another, refusing to stop, even to think. Only the occasional moments like this caused me to pause and take notice of my questionable timetable.

I shook my head. As I worked to rid my mind of these thoughts, I hoped any doubts I harbored would vanish as well. Focusing on the reality in front of me did not make me feel any better. I groaned as I looked at the half-typed sheet in my typewriter. The two completed pages on the desk next to it told me I was only about halfway done. I stood up and walked over to my dresser.

It's been a week, I assured myself. I opened the jewelry box, but only counted four of my secret treasures. "I thought I had six," I said aloud. Calculating my last purchase, I remembered the exchange I had made with Dean the Sunday before last. I scored ten eleven days ago, I informed myself. Once more I did the math. "That means you dropped six in eleven days. That's one every other day," I announced. The worry I heard in my own voice brought memories of my high school years. *It cost you a friendship and your conscience,* I reminded myself. But the longing I had for the initial rush of the drug beckoned me, offering to give me the free-flowing energy I so loved to experience. As I stared at the little circle of energy which had somehow found its way into the palm of my hand, I made my decision.

"I can't give it up just now," I said, looking up at the haggard girl now gaping at me through smoky glass. She did not respond. She simply stared back at me, looking hopelessly forlorn.

You've got too much at stake right now. Just take one this time, and then don't buy any more, I said, a feeble promise mainly offered to appease the girl's anxiety.

But as I swallowed it with the bottle of Coke I'd been nursing all evening, I knew in my gut this freight train was already running out of control.

Chapter 28

The Power Within

April 1974

"Your name?"

"Geri Taeckens."

"Yes?"

"I have an appointment with the professor?" I said, wondering why this woman always asked the obvious question.

"The professor will be with you in a moment. Please take a seat."

"Thank you," I said, sitting down in one of the empty chairs. I dropped my trusty canvas bag down on the floor beside me and rummaged through it, looking for a hair band. Locating one in the inside pocket, I pulled it out and placed it around the end of my cupped fingers. Scooping up my hair, I fashioned myself a pony tail. I'd just as soon have my hair out of my face as I delved into this next activity.

This will be a breeze! I told myself, wallowing in the joy of having won my grievance.

As I sat there, waiting for Dr. Powers to arrive, I wondered who would be reading me the exam. I prayed it would not be him. Nervously I fiddled with the keys on my machine. I traced my finger around the identification numbers my father had etched into the metal casing before I left for college. He insisted on protecting this valuable tool he'd purchased for me when I was nine.

I'd accused him of being stupid for worrying about someone stealing this useless-looking contraption. Now I wished I hadn't given him such a hard time. *You should have just shut your mouth, Geri,* I told myself. Placing my elbows on the top of the machine and resting my chin on my upturned hands, memories of my last visit home crept into my consciousness. Sadness followed. The discussion I'd had with my folks still bothered me.

"I'm not getting any younger, Geri," my father told me, as we sat chatting in the living room of my childhood home.

"I know, Dad. But your life's not over. You should get out more. Do more."

"I'm almost sixty-five years old, for God's sake, and I don't feel good. I'm happy to stay home."

"But Dad, you used to play bridge and visit with your buddies from the shop."

"Well, I'm not up to that. I like to be close to my own bathroom. You need to stop worrying about me, Geri. If you want to make me happy, move out of that house and start going back to church."

"Dad!" I said, warning him not to get into this subject.

"Well, you asked what would make me happy. I surely can't figure it out. Your mother and I tried to raise you kids right, and not one of you practices the religion we taught you growing up."

"I know, Dad, but we all need to find our own way. Every one of your kids are good kids. That's what matters, isn't it?"

I hated watching my parents grow older. I wondered if the wisdom and invincibility they seemed to have possessed disappeared with age or if it never really existed. All I really knew was I felt scared for them and myself.

"Miss Taeckens. Bring your things and follow me, please."

Startled at the sound of his gruff voice, I lifted my elbows off my Braille writer, almost dropping it. Luckily, I caught it, but the clumsiness of my movements embarrassed me. Again, I felt my face flush just when I needed it not to. As we walked down the hallway, I prayed there'd be a reader for me. But alas, there was no one.

"Darn!" I said under my breath, dreading the time ahead with the professor. But a fate much worse awaited me. Instead of worrying about spending time with the head of the department, I should have been fretting about a much worse scenario. To my dismay, I quickly realized there would be no reader at all. Professor Powers's unspoken intentions sat on the table next to me. I recognized the familiar gray box right away.

"The tape is set up at the beginning for you. I'm assuming you know how to work the reel to reel?"

I wanted to slap myself. *How could I have been so naïve as to think I could beat this powerful man?* With little effort he'd figured out a way to trick me. There was no doubt I was going to fail this class, an absolute requirement for staying in the Special Education Visually Impaired curriculum.

While I processed my demise, I failed to respond to his question.

"Well, do you or don't you know how to use the player?"

Despite the satisfaction in his voice, I humbled myself in desperation.

"But, Professor Powers?"

"Yes? Is there a problem?"

"I am not going to be able to pass the exam if I have to listen to the material from a tape recorder."

He looked like King Kong puffing out his chest as he spoke. "Miss Taeckens, I told you at the beginning of the semester that I would provide you with the material in an auditory format. You didn't seem to have a problem then."

"I thought you meant you'd provide me with a reader."

"Well, I did. A reader read the material on the tape."

"But professor, I will not be able to hear the words letter by letter."

"Well, of course not," he chuckled. "It would take much too much time and tape to have a person read all of this material into a tape recorder letter by letter!"

"Exactly. Which is why I expected someone to be here with me to read the exam."

"Well, Miss Taeckens, as you well know by now, life is not always what we expect it to be. I'd suggest you get started. You've got a lot of transcribing ahead of you. Although I am willing to give you some extra time, you don't have all day."

With that, he walked out of the room.

I sat at the table staring after him. I couldn't believe he'd been so cruel. All semester, I figured I was home free on this subject. An automatic A. I'd be lucky if I squeezed out a D. Next to the tape player, Dr. Powers left a stack of Braille paper. I picked up the top sheet. Pushing the clips down to hold the paper in place, I rolled it into the contraption. As always, it disappeared, leaving only a thin strip for writing the first line. "I wish I could disappear with it!" I moaned.

I familiarized myself with the knobs on the tape recorder. I located play, flipped the switch, and waited for the first words of the narration. Professor Power's delighted voice announced, "This is examination for four dash seven four, winter term, for Professor Power's Braille Transcription course. Please place your paper in your Braille writer and prepare for the first sentence of the narration." He cleared his throat and I could hear the sound of paper being flipped over.

"It was early morning."

Crunch crunch crunch came the sound of the keys as I pushed them down to make the necessary combination letters and contractions.

"The sun peeked over the horizon."

Crunch crunch crunch. I paused.

Is horizon with a z or an s? I asked myself, trying to remember. *I think it's an…s, no, it's a z, I'm pretty sure.* Deciding I had to pick one, I began writing the word using a z.

Crunch crunch crunch…ding. Hearing the signal for the end of the line, I returned the space bar to the left. I pushed down on the lever that rolled the paper forward. The sound of my efforts caused me to miss the next word. Annoyed, I reached over, turned the lever to rewind, then restarted the tape.

"Peeked over the horizon, casting its rays over the meadow."

Completing the first sentence, I flipped the switch to off, and then ran my fingers over the dots on the page.

"I think it's perfect!" I said aloud. "So far so good."

Restarting the tape again, I listened for the next words of the dictation.

"Mrs. McGillacuddy looked out of her—"

Angrily, I shoved the knob back to stop and stood up. With definite purpose in my step, I walked out of the room and down to Dr. Powers' office. Without stopping to talk to the secretary, I walked through his opened door. As I did so, he looked up from his desk, and said, "Yes?"

I swear he had been expecting me. Firmly pronouncing his name, I said, "Professor Powers!"

"Yes Miss Taeckens," he answered, pretending he did not know what I was about to say.

"How do you spell McGillacuddy?" I demanded.

"I'm sorry, Miss Taeckens. I am not at liberty to offer any information during an examination."

"But Professor Powers, you know that without someone to help me spell some of these words, there is no way I can transcribe that material accurately."

"Oh!" he said innocently, "And why not?"

"Because, words like McGillacuddy are very uncommon words. I imagine there are others in the text that I will be unable to spell as well."

"Well, I'm sorry, Miss Taeckens, but part of transcribing is being able to spell."

"No, it's not. The other students can read that material letter by letter. They don't have to spell even the simplest of words if they don't want to. The way I am forced to take the exam is equal to taking a spelling test. This is not fair!"

"Now, Miss Taeckens," his voice was harsher. "I've already told you my view of the concept of fair. It's not my fault that you can't spell. Nor is it my fault that you can't see, for that matter. I have provided the material to you in an acceptable alternative format. I even checked with the University policy regarding reasonable accommodations to visually impaired students, and I'm afraid you are going to have to accept that I have met the appropriate standards."

Fuming at his audacity, I tightened my fists and pushed them hard against my hips. I did not want to lose control, but I could already feel my muscles begin to quiver. It took all my strength not to strike out at this pompous bastard. Taking a deep breath, I steadied myself and said, "But providing an exam on tape typically doesn't require a transcription of that test. If there is a policy that says taped tests are reasonable, I'm sure they're not referring to transcription exams."

"Well, the policy said nothing about such matters, so I'm afraid you're stuck."

Unable to contain my anger any longer, I stomped my foot and slapped my hand on the top of his desk. "But I'm not going to be able to pass this test!" I heard myself whine.

"Miss Taeckens, I told you once that I didn't think you were cut out for the education curriculum. Teachers need to be able to spell. They also need to be able to see. You are standing here, admitting to exactly what I tried to tell you two years ago. But you insisted. You said you could handle the challenges your visual limitations afforded you. Now, here you stand, whining to me about fair accommodations. I have waived the attendance requirements, extended your examination time, provided you with an examination in an auditory format, and that is still not enough," he said coldly. "The problem with those of you who are products of the special education system is that you've been mollycoddled, told you deserve special favors, while at the same time, brainwashed into believing ridiculous notions that you can somehow miraculously do what everyone else with vision can do. Well it's not so. You can stomp your foot and slap my desk all you want and it still won't make it so!"

Totally exasperated, I felt my body twist like a pretzel as my muscles knotted up with tension. There were so many things to respond to. Professor Powers was truly a master at mixing up his words so that falsehoods sounded like truths. Though I knew his logic was incorrect, my ability to verbalize what I knew while under the influence of rage was little to none. My face flushed hot as my cheeks filled with blood, my fists clenched so tightly I could feel the knuckles grow white.

"But, Professor Powers! You are purposely trying to make me fail this test."

Before the words left my lips, I knew it was the wrong thing to say. Accusations are not the way to go when defending one's point. Like any good loser of a fight, I grabbed my gut with my hand as I waited for his next punch. I knew it was going to hurt because, before he delivered it, he stood up, his large body towering over me.

"Miss Taeckens!" he boomed. "I will not tolerate such accusations. This conversation is now over. Either return to your examination or leave the building, but do not return to my office unless it is to drop off your transcriptions to my secretary."

I don't know how I did it, but despite my weakened condition, I stood there, visibly shaking, refusing to move. I turned my face directly at his, and hoped he knew I was staring him in the eye.

He said nothing as he looked back at me. I'm not sure how many years passed during those few moments, but finally, without changing my gaze, I broke the silence.

"I will make it through this program. I will become a teacher of the visually impaired if it takes me forever!"

More time passed without either of us moving. I had every intention of standing there until he showed some sign of giving in. Immune to the many stimuli which caused normally sighted people to flinch, I was able to avoid blinking for a very long time. Finally he tipped his chin. I imagined his eyelids dropping. With a nervous cough he said, "Return to your exam, Miss Taeckens."

Despite the knowledge I would fail the class, I knew I had won something indispensable. Deep within, I knew I possessed something Professor Powers could not cheat me out of. Resisting the urge to blurt it out, I proudly marched out of his office and completed the exam, right down to the last period. I knew I had failed, but also discovered I had learned the most important lesson. I placed the last page of my poorly transcribed document into the Braille writer and typed out one last paragraph for my instructor to evaluate:

Eyes can see. True vision requires integrity. It takes wisdom to know the difference and a heart to possess what is good.

Chapter 29

Incredible Journeys

Summer 1974

"Will passengers traveling Air Canada to London please make your boarding passes available and begin boarding at gate B-7."

A high pitched squeak escaped me as I bounced to my feet.

"Let's go, Geri girl," Cliff said, leading the way.

"Oh, Cliff, I can't believe we're really going."

"We're really going!"

Together we walked across the tarmac and boarded the plane. I was careful to keep my eye on Cliff's bright blue backpack. His reddish blond hair helped to set him apart from the others. I'd also taken note of his Rolling Stones t-shirt. Just in case we got separated, I could tell someone what to look for.

After settling into our seats, I reflected on all the events which had transpired prior to getting here. Somehow I'd made it through the most grueling semester ever, ending up with what could have been a 4.0. My expected E in the Braille transcriptions course pulled it down miserably. Only three days earlier I had traipsed across campus to meet with my advisor, asking her what I should do next. Joan suggested I take the transcription course at a university in Detroit. Though it would take some finagling for transportation, at least I would have a real opportunity for success.

With a plan in place and the excitement of the moment, I wallowed in my accomplishments. My newfound sense of hope had also been fueled by a decision I had made in March. After consuming twenty-nine capsules of Dean's magic energy boosters in seven consecutive days, I had found myself in a debilitating panic attack. I debated whether I should check into the hospital, as I was unable to stop myself from shaking. The fallout from my overindulgence required me to place the care of my two little charges in the hands of my roommates, using the excuse I had the flu. My addictive conduct almost blew my trip to Europe, however, with the near liquidation of my bank account. My many semester trips only cost me a measly $325 after Dean gave me a $25 discount.

This is when I firmly decided to use my own energy to speed through my demanding days. My ability to stick to my commitment liberated me to heights more far-reaching than any drug could have ever allowed, making this pending adventure even more exhilarating.

Sitting in the aisle seat of the DC-10, I reviewed the contents of my blue checkered bag. It was handcrafted of cloth by my thoughtful mom, with eight separate compartments, making it wide enough to hold the kitchen sink. I couldn't help smiling as I reflected on how she had illustrated the various features of her creation in her typical manner of quiet delight. Needless to say I was surprised when I discovered the $200 she and my father had slipped in the outside pocket. This brought my total budget up to $1200. After subtracting the $300 for the airline ticket and $165 for the Eurail pass, I had $735 left for food and lodging.

Though my folks were uneasy about me traveling with my male roommate, their attitudes had slowly changed. I'm not sure if the long trip without a resting spot was getting harder on my father, or if my folks were feeling sorry for my troubles with Professor Powers, but finally my dad agreed to come into my home. When he discovered a group of polite and well mannered guys, his fantasies about me being misused and abused disappeared.

Now rummaging through my handy sack, I felt the five hard metal tubes held together with the elastic band; the only catch to the generous donation from my parents. Though I had protested, I secretly felt relief knowing I could call on this symbol of blindness in case I got lost. There was also the fact I would be traveling home alone, as my diminished funds and Cliff's larger hoard would allow him to tour Europe two weeks longer.

"You don't have to use it," my dad insisted as he handed me the cardboard box containing the folded white cane. "I tried to find your other one, but it must have been misplaced," he explained. I felt so guilty as I pictured the same object still neatly tucked in my underwear drawer. *Why couldn't I have eased his mind all this time?* I secretly scolded myself.

"No one even needs to know you have it with you," he continued. "But if you do need it Geri, I hope you will use it."

The image of me walking down the street tapping this ridiculous looking white stick with a red tip made me cringe. Though I was somewhat aware that I didn't quite move with style and grace these days, carrying a cane would certainly extinguish any hope I had of ever being whistled at again.

The knot in my gut tightened as I thought about the combination of my new possession coupled with my visit with Linda two weeks earlier. A collage of recollections followed, bombarding me with emotions. My call to Linda was partly based on an unspoken agreement to take turns checking in with each other. I also needed her inherent understanding about my struggle with the mule-minded professor.

When she'd contacted me at the end of last semester, I'd been gloating about how I'd beaten him out. That's when she told me how her application to enter law school had been scrutinized. Before we hung up, we agreed our mutual plight deserved a date for lunch. I picked a Saturday in May, as I knew the kids would be away with their dad. I was looking forward to spending time with her, but I still wasn't real keen about being seen in public with a blind person. I also couldn't imagine how Linda and I would traverse a Chinese restaurant, her dining choice.

For three days I ruminated about this outing. We were to meet at her dorm and walk three blocks to the restaurant. I couldn't imagine how we were going to find the place, find a seat, read the menu, and pay for our meal. I knew the menus at Bob's Place, but Chinese food went beyond my scope of knowledge. When the specified Saturday rolled around, Cliff kindly drove me to her dorm.

When I entered the lobby, I realized I could not distinguish Linda from other students. I quietly called her name.

"Linda?"

"Geri, over here."

I turned to my left, searching the area where I heard her speak. A person in long hair and a blue top stood up. I moved closer.

"Linda?"

"Yeah, Ger, how ya doing?"

"Good. Hey, you look great!" I said, surveying her eyes carefully. I was impressed with how nice they looked with her complexion. Earlier in the year, Linda's biological eye had to be removed. The cosmetology consultant recommended switching from blue eyes to hazel, enhancing her appearance tenfold. In her present attire of blue jean bells and silky embroidered top, Linda looked perfectly normal; except for the cane she held in her hand.

We completed our greetings and headed out the lobby door. As we walked, I noticed Linda held her head up high, carrying herself with confidence and grace.

"You're looking spiffy, old friend," I remarked.

"Thanks. Got a friend in the dorm who goes shopping with me," she said, as she tapped her cane back and forth in front of her.

"That's cool!" I said, staying my traditional half step behind. The bright sunlight only allowed me to follow the upper part of her left side, but it was enough to keep us connected.

"Still not using a cane, Ger?"

"Nope! Don't intend to, either."

"Hmmm."

"Don't be startin' with me, Linda," I said affectionately.

"I won't, I won't," she laughed.

As we entered the dimly lit restaurant, I instinctively reached out to grab her arm. The adjustment to the new lighting temporarily blinded me. Realizing what I had done, I pulled my hand away.

"You can take my arm, Geri. It's okay." But I refused. Since we needed to wait for the hostess, I figured there'd be time for my eyes to adjust before moving again.

"May I hep you?" asked the hostess in her Oriental accent.

"Yes, we'd like a table for two," Linda said with poise.

"Vite dis vay," Linda followed the lady's voice, tapping her cane casually as she went. I followed the contrast of her hair against her shirt, glad I was now able to see.

A few steps later, Linda stopped.

"Ma'am?" Linda called to the hostess.

"Vite here," the woman replied, slapping the top of the table.

"Does she know you?" I asked, wondering how the waitress knew to alert Linda the way she did.

"Yeah, I come in here a lot," Linda said.

But our waiter was not so familiar. He brought us two print menus and quickly left before we could ask him to read them.

"So what's good here?" I asked.

"Depends on if you like hot or mild."

"I think I'm a mild person," I said with a smile.

"Don't know about that one," Linda said, sounding like she was smiling back. "My favorites are sweet and sour chicken and pepper steak," she explained.

"Ooh! They both sound good to me!" I said.

"Let's do it the traditional way. We'll each order one of them and then share."

"Okay with me."

The waiter returned. He looked at me and asked, "Vat does she vant?" Taken aback, I didn't quite know what to say at first.

"I don't know. You'll have to ask her."

Linda and I chuckled.

"I'll have the sweet and sour chicken," she said assertively.

"And I'll have the pepper steak."

"Lots of wait staff do that to me," Linda said once the waiter left.

"Really? That's awful. Don't you hate it?"

"Yes I hate it. They also like to talk to me as if I'm deaf. They raise their voices and overpronounce one…word…at…a…time," she said, demonstrating the pattern of speech.

As Linda and I ate our meal, conversing about our frustrations with being misperceived, I surprised myself at how easily I fell in with her. She expressed her desire to teach the world how blind people are like everyone else.

"All I ask is to be talked to, not ignored or infantilized," Linda exclaimed. "Unless I'm walking to classes with a friend, I really don't need to talk to anyone!"

"Do you get a lot of people trying to help you?"

"More than I want. Mainly I wish people would just ignore me like they do anyone else. There is hardly a day that goes by that somebody doesn't try to direct me to a place I don't even want to go. If I'm waiting to cross a street, I sometimes have to push folks away who practically pick me up and carry me across."

"Really?" I said, thankful I did not share in this dilemma.

"The best is the faith healers," Linda went on. "I bet I get five people a month coming up and putting their hands on me, telling me they are asking the Lord to heal me. What is it about people who think, just because I'm blind, they have a right to break past the social boundaries and touch my body?"

"So what do you do when that happens?"

"I tell them I don't wanna be healed, push their hands away, and tell them I wanna get to class, for God's sake."

We laughed.

"Why is it that everyone always thinks a blind person wants to see? I've never seen before and I don't need to now. But I do wish I could be treated like everyone else."

Linda's words triggered a flood of thoughts. I believed her. She was comfortable as a blind person, having no problem with missing vision. We'd argued the pros and cons of this point many times, sometimes leaving me secretly envious of her. Yet at the same time, I couldn't imagine life without a beautiful sunset, or the look of a meadow polka-dotted with dandelions. One thing I now realized I shared with her, however, was the desire to be treated equally. My fear of discrimination, of being viewed as a helpless person, was the motivation behind my effort to act as sighted as I could. Though I didn't have to deal with people trying to help me as often as Linda, it did happen. I noticed it most when I'd attend extended family gatherings or social events that included food. Whenever I'd get up to get something or prepare to pour liquid, someone would jump up and insist on doing it for me. I never failed to spill something when I was in the mode of proving myself. These situations were so embarrassing I'd often just give in and let people wait on me.

"Do you understand color?" I asked her, noticing her fingers had not lodged themselves in her new eyes.

"Nah, not really. I mean, I associate things with colors, like, pink is soft and fuzzy, and red is warm and velvety, brown is like corduroy, and black is hard like a black board. But to actually know what they look like, there's no real way to know."

"I don't know, Linda, I can't imagine being okay about such things."

"But, Geri, you have it hard that way, 'cause you know what you will likely be missing someday. Me, I don't care. Never had it, don't miss it."

Linda's words stung like a hot poker.

"There's no absolute I'm going to lose all my vision, you know."

"Maybe not, but either way, it's gotta be hard for you."

"Ah, I'm okay," I insisted, quickly putting my pretend self back to the forefront.

"You've lost more vision since I last saw you, haven't you?" she asked.

"A little, maybe."

"Hmmm."

Wanting to get off this subject, I expounded on my plight with Professor Powers. She shared details about her university's resistance to her admission to the School of Law.

"Well, it's a true case of blind justice, you beating them out like you did," I said, both of us roaring with laughter.

Together we got up and located the counter to pay our bill.

"Dat eaz four dolla and twenty-tree cents," the hostess said.

I watched Linda finger through her wallet. She handed the lady a bill and some coins.

"Here is a five dollar bill and the exact change," she announced, holding out her hand.

"How do you know that's a five?" I asked.

"I fold them. I put the tens long ways, the fives in half, the twenties in half twice, and the ones are straight."

"What about the hundreds?" I joked.

"Yeah, right. Maybe when I become a lawyer I can have a few of those, but right now, I rarely have to fold a twenty." We chuckled. "I can feel the different sizes of the coins," she continued, "which is good 'cause they're hard to fold."

More giggles escaped us as Linda completed her transaction.

My turn to pay came. I, too, fumbled through my wallet, but became embarrassed when I had to hold the bills up close to my eyes to read the numbers. In the poor lighting, I could not tell if I had a ten or a one. I finally had to ask.

"Um, ah, could you tell me what bill this is?"

"Vat you say?" came the response of the cashier.

"Is this a ten or a one?" I again asked, my faced reddening.

"Sorry." The cashier didn't understand.

"Here, let me get it for now," Linda said. "You can pay me back later when we can get someone to read it for you."

Her gesture told me the old tug of war game was back. Linda was going to show me how trying to see what I couldn't is not as good as being blind and using the proper accommodations. I was relieved to finally be done with the task of paying the bill, but I felt annoyed with both of us. Returning to the outside, I covered my eyes with my hand. The switch to the brightly lit day was physically painful. I wished I could wear sunglasses.

"Your hesitation tells me you're not seeing too well," Linda blurted out.

"Give me a second! I gotta get used to the sun."

"Geri, when are you gonna stop pretending you can see?" she scolded.

"But I can see," I insisted.

"Well, not very well. You couldn't find the right bill, that's for sure!"

"It was dark in there, Linda!" I protested.

"Other people can see their bills 'cause they're, s-i-g-h-t-e-d!" she taunted.

"Why you always wanna make me blinder than I am?" I asked.

"Because you always make yourself more sighted than you are."

After Linda retrieved her overnight bag from her dorm room, we headed back down the street to the main drag. We crossed at the light, and then turned right toward Banana House.

Feeling pumped up with a sense of adventure, we joked about being ladies of the evening. "Hope some cute guys see us and pick us up for a night on the town," Linda said. I didn't have the guts to tell her no one would even give us a look once they saw her cane.

As we walked, there were spots with no sidewalk. At one point I tripped over a metal cable that supported a billboard. In my high heeled wedgie sandals, it cut the base of my big toe, which promptly began to bleed. As I pulled my dad's trusty handkerchief from my purse, Linda began to fret.

"We should stop and call someone to pick us up, Geri."

"Nah, I'm okay."

"But you're bleeding!"

"Ah, it's nothing. Don't worry, I won't die."

"But there are going to be lots of things for you to trip on. It's not safe, Geri!"

"Come on Linda, it's not a big deal! You're such a worry wart."

"Maybe so, but I'm a healthy worry wart. At least let me lead with my cane."

"Oh Linda. It's not a big deal, for God's sake!"

"I don't care what you say, Geri. I'm not going any farther if you don't let me lead," she said.

"Come on, Linda, don't pull a parental control thing on me. After all, I'm twenty-two years old, for heaven's sake."

"Okay, then you lead the way but use my cane."

The idea made my heart sink. The very thought of it made me want to be sick.

"No way!" I said. "I don't need to use a cane. I'll follow you instead."

"Okay, but why don't you use it, just once?"

As we walked, Linda hounded me about how I shouldn't knock something until I tried it. She recited all kinds of statistics and rationales for why using a cane is a positive thing.

"How we ever gonna change the world if we can't be okay with ourselves? We need to revolutionize the image of blind men and women. Tell 'em all we're cool even if we tap a white stick in front of us. Don't be a hypocrite, Geri, come on and just use it for one block."

Finally, to shut her up, I agreed.

After crossing the next street, Linda stopped and handed me her extended eyeball as she called it. Although I'd held a cane many years earlier when attending That School, the rubber grip at the top felt foreign to me now. Recoiling at its touch, I almost dropped it. "You got it?" Linda asked, excitement in her voice.

"I got it."

"Good, now place your hand right in front of your belly button. Use just your wrist to swing the cane back and forth across the distance of your body."

"I know!" I whined, hiding the fact I'd forgotten the instructions taught to us kids so long ago.

We were presently walking in an undeveloped area. I felt the tip of the cane touch dirt. Lifting it up, I swung the probe to the right side. This time the sensation in my hand was different as it hit an uneven plot of grass. Surprised at the feedback it gave me, I remembered how the darn thing could be helpful. But when I heard a car pass by, the momentary feeling of appreciation disappeared.

I sure hope that wasn't somebody I know, I thought. Linda took my arm, and we began trudging through the uneven terrain. Earth to grass, earth to grass, earth to grass, the kinetic device explained. Suddenly, I felt myself dip forward as the cane slid downward.

"You're at the end of the block now. Did you feel that?"

Annoyed at her school teacher mentality, I sarcastically replied "Yes ma'am!"

"Great! See how much information you get from these ridiculous things!" Linda said, ignoring my irritation.

"Here you go. It's all yours now!" I said, turning to hand her the repulsive device.

"Keep going!" she insisted.

"Nope. We agreed, one block."

"Well, at least let it take you across. You can feel how it will hit the up curb when you reach the other side."

"I can see the other side," I insisted. "I don't need a cane to tell me anything."

"Oh, Geri, you are so exasperating. When are you going to stop fighting the inevitable?"

"Never! Now here's your cane back."

I honestly felt I should thank her, but I dared not give in and cross the line I'd been fighting against for so long.

Linda resumed her lead position. Without any more accidents, five and a half hours after leaving the restaurant, we stumbled our way onto the porch of Banana House.

"Your attention please!" the sound of the flight attendant's voice called, pulling me from my memories. I felt the plane move. Slightly startled at the unfamiliar motion, I touched Cliff's knee.

"Are we going up now?" I asked.

He laughed. "Not yet, kiddo. We have to drive out to the runway, and the stewardesses have to explain the safety precautions."

As she did so, I wondered if I would be able to protect myself in case of a crash. Unable to see the demonstration, and unwilling to ask Cliff to explain, I decided I would likely die.

Six weeks later, I boarded a similar DC-10, this time by myself. I'd managed to be able to follow the stewardess assigned to assisting handicapped passengers without taking her elbow or using the unfolded cane. As I fought off her overly helpful manner, asserting myself against her infantilizing instructions, I wondered how much longer I might be able to pull off such maneuvers.

"Here is your seat, honey," she said, taking my hand and touching it to the back of my assigned seat.

"This nice man will help you out if you need something before I can get back here to help you, won't you, sir?"

A nearly inaudible grumble came from the man.

Whispering as if I couldn't hear her, the stewardess bent over and said, "She's a blind girl. You won't mind helping her if she needs it, will you, sir?"

"I'm fine!" I said firmly. "If I need help, I will ask for it, thank you."

"Oh, you are such a brave one, aren't you?" she said, patting my arm with her hand. "Who's going to meet you in Windsor?" she asked, talking to me with that sing songy voice mothers use with a child.

"No one," I lied.

"No one? Well, how are you going to get home, honey?"

"I'm taking a cab," I lied again, hoping to give the impression of total independence.

"Really! Oh," she said, taking on a sorrowful tone now. "That's too bad! Who do you live with then?"

I was truly irritated at this woman's probing questions as I thought about Linda's comments regarding people crossing social boundaries.

"Myself," I snapped, pushing past her, hoping ignoring her would give her the hint to leave me alone.

Once we were in the air, I opened my checkered bag and pulled out the pen and spiral notebook I purchased the first day in London. I flipped past the many entries and found a blank page near the back. Taking out my wire rims, I slipped them on my face and began to print.

Date: July 20, 1974

Dear Diary,

I have just completed one of the most exciting adventures of my whole life. It was hard to say goodbye to Cliff and I wish I had more money to stay on with him. I hate dealing with obnoxious people who think because I have a vision problem, I'm stupid and need to be treated like a baby. Why can't they treat me like an adult? It's the hardest part about having vision problems. The right to be everyone's equal doesn't seem to exist.

When I completed my entry, I flipped back through the pages. Though I could only read the names of the countries I'd written about, the gesture helped me remember the highlights. The opportunity to wake up every morning with the only pressing concern of where to get breakfast turned out to be the best part of the adventure. In addition, my reflections on the incredible experiences of the thirteen countries and the many neat people we met rekindled the joy of each encounter. Touring the thrilling sites of London such as Buckingham Palace, witnessing the magnificence of the midnight sun in Sweden, overlooking Salzburg, Austria from atop an Alpine cliff, experiencing the awesome history imagined while standing in Rome's Coliseum, along with so many other beautiful sights, were all permanently imbedded in my mind's eye.

When I saw the entry for Amsterdam, I had to smile. While standing in a phone booth trying to call home, Cliff suddenly shouted out.

"Check out this little piece of graffiti, Geri! 'Blind People Are Out of Sight!'"

"Hey cool!" I said, deciding to make a mental note of the only positive reference to being blind I'd ever heard.

As I turned the page, I remembered how we'd often carried our backpacks many miles to find a youth hostel. It sure made for some hearty living. I felt strong and worldly and free, even though the underlying terror toward my growing vision loss tainted my joy. Fortunately, or unfortunately, a few experiences had forced me to face the truth about my struggles to see.

"Is everything okay?" asked the stewardess in her sickly sweet voice. I wanted to tell her I'd be better if she'd stop interrupting my thoughts, but instead I told her I was just fine. I started adding up in my head the number of miles we'd traveled by train, when suddenly one of the memories of our expedition pushed its way to my consciousness.

About the third week into our excursion, we were traveling all night from Oslo, Norway to Copenhagen, Denmark. The train was very full. This forced us to share one seat to avoid sitting on the floor. When we finally arrived, exhausted and weary-eyed, we threw on our backpacks and stood to detrain.

Though Cliff certainly knew I had trouble seeing, he'd never really spent much time with me in unfamiliar territory before the trip. In fact, most of our time together had been spent in Banana House, so he wasn't really aware of the extent of my growing difficulties. As a result, I worked hard to keep my struggle secret by using the tricks I developed with Cody so long ago. He had no clue how much I depended on following a half step behind him, or how little I saw when we toured museums. Our relationship had always consisted of hugging and joking and I felt more than ever the need to play the As Sighted As Possible game with him. Because of this lack of knowledge, he did not understand why I was so desperate when I asked him to go ahead of me in the aisle.

"Just go, Ger," he said, sounding a little grumpy with the lack of sleep. "Your pack is too big for me to pass in the narrow aisle."

Nervously I followed the person in front. When it came time to turn and descend the narrow stairs, then step onto the platform, I realized I was having trouble gauging the distance. There is always a gap between the train and tarmac, so I knew I had to be careful. But the gentleman's movements appeared slight as he continued on without a break in his stride. Likewise, I simply glided my foot out in a casual manner from the steps.

"Ah! Oh! Ouch! Oh, God! Oh ow! Oh, help!" The pain seared into my brain as the flesh of my naked shins became one with the track wall.

"Geri, Geri! Are you all right?" Cliff asked attempting to rescue me from under the train. The gap was so wide I had fallen several feet and dangled helplessly with my backpack caught on the stairs. Using my arms, I held on to the platform's edge, fearful I would slip down further. Like a turtle flipped on its back, I couldn't move in any direction. The weight of my body made it impossible for Cliff to lift me out. I thought my arms might be ripped from their sockets, as several hands frantically worked to yank me up before the train took off.

Finally, Cliff started counting, "One, two, and three." Everyone seemed to understand this American concept for working together, and with one big whoosh, I was liberated from my prison. Cliff no more than jumped off the train beside me, when its whistle blew announcing its motion. As it chugged out of the station, I wondered if my rescue had been delayed, if only the skin of my shins would be left.

With blood trickling down my legs, I reached into my bag and pulled out my dad's reliable white hankie, wiping them clean.

"Your meal is here honey."

It was my trusty babysitter standing beside me now, a tray of food in her hand. "Sir, can you put her tray down?"

"I can do it."

"Oh, that's okay, let the man do it for you."

Insistent on fending for myself, I beat him to the punch. Unfortunately, in my struggle to prove I could turn a plastic knob and release the hinged table, I knocked the woman's arm and the tray went flying.

"I told you the man should do that, dear," she said, trying hard not to sound upset.

Exasperated, I wished she'd go away. I'd be happy to skip dinner altogether to avoid her voice, I thought.

After she retrieved a towel and the liquid on my leg and floor were thoroughly sponged up, the stewardess returned with a fresh plate of food.

"Now you be careful, honey. I'm going to open your milk for you, so you don't spill it, but your soup is full. Maybe I should dump a little out for you?"

"No, that's fine," I quickly said. "Really, I can open my own milk. I'm sorry I bumped you, but if you hadn't tried to prevent me from—"

"It's okay, don't worry about the mess," she interrupted, not having heard a word I said.

My anger grew the more she spoke. *Can't I ever get through to these people?* I asked myself, once more thinking about Linda's words. Surrendering to an indomitable force, I simply sat back and let her arrange my meal. The man next to me, who had hardly spoken a word to anyone, made a surprising but enlightening remark. "She thinks you're a baby."

"I know!" I said, wishing I could hug him for noticing. Without another word, he went back to his dinner and I mine.

When the garbage was picked up, I tried to catch a nap. It was difficult however. I still felt the discomfort I acquired on our visit to Spain six days ago. It made sitting and relaxing difficult.

Cliff and I had been touring Barcelona. To beat the heat, I wore a pastel striped backless top and light blue hot pants with my hair piled high atop my head in a bun. Likewise, Cliff was barely dressed, wearing a white muscle shirt with cut off shorts. We sat down at a park three blocks from our hotel to rest. After eating a burrito purchased from a sidewalk vendor, Cliff was raring to go. The heat left me drained, and I desperately wanted to go back to our room to sleep.

"Sure you don't want to take a break, Cliffy boy?" I asked affectionately, hoping he'd change his mind.

"Ger, we only got a couple days here. I want to see the place."

"But Cliff, I just can't move anymore."

"Then why don't you go back to the hotel, and I'll sightsee on my own."

Even with the train incident, Cliff still did not understand the limitations of my vision. I'd managed never to leave his side through out the trip unless I stayed back at wherever we were staying. I'd always say I was tired if he wanted to do something I didn't. I considered asking him to walk me back to the hotel, but my obsession to sustain my image kept me from doing so.

"The hotel's down this block and two to the right, right?" I asked, wishing I hadn't.

"Yeah, it's the third door from the corner I think."

I had counted the awnings when we left that morning and noted three as well. I looked up at the sun. *They'll make a shadow on the sidewalk.* I thought, knowing I could no longer distinguish between sides of the building and doors, especially in the sunshine. *You could feel with your hands and count them you know?* I secretly suggested, but quickly dismissed the idea. They'll think I'm weird! I told myself. *Oh my God, why do you give a shit if some stranger sees you feeling a wall?* I asked, but I knew my rational self would never win out.

"So what's it gonna be, Geri, dear?"

"I think I'll go back and take a nap then," I said, checking my pocket for the key. I had left my mother's bag back at the hotel. In the hot weather of Spain, I wanted as little as possible touching my skin.

"You sure you're gonna be okay?"

"Yeah, it's only three blocks."

"Okay, I'll probably be back in a couple of hours then."

"Have fun!" I said, nervously watching a piece of his shirt walk away.

Gathering up the nerve to head off on my own, I hoped I'd made the right decision. With anxiety now triggering my adrenal glands, I didn't feel so tired any more.

"You should have just gone with him," I scolded out loud.

I gingerly stood up from the park bench and started walking down the angled sidewalk to the corner. I carefully crossed the semi-busy street and sauntered slowly to the next block. Again I negotiated the road, then turned right and traversed the next one. With every step anxiety was replaced with confidence. By the time I reached the end of the block, I was moving at normal speed.

"One more street to cross," I told myself, standing up straighter. "Then you need to start counting shadows."

I did as I directed, smiling with delight as I stepped on the first shaded area.

"That's one," I said, then proceeded to the next.

"Two." My excitement grew. "Three." Overjoyed at reaching my destination, I turned and quickly moved my hand to find the handle. Though there were very few people on the street, I prayed no one noticed I didn't grab it out right. Unfortunately, when I opened the door and stepped in, I realized I was not at my hotel, but a restaurant.

"Oh shit!" I said to myself, quickly stepping back out on the street. "Hmm," I pondered, struggling not to panic. It must be the fourth door? I considered how I might have made a mistake. That's right! I did count three. I guess I didn't include the door we came out of. With a new hope, I continued until I saw another shadow ahead.

"Yes, this is it, I'm sure," I said as I leaned forward to place my foot on the darkened spot. But it was not a shadow I stepped on. In fact, it wasn't anything at all. In one great swoop, I felt myself falling. I don't know whether I screamed or not, but I do remember hearing an odd sound when the air exploded from my lungs. With full force, I hit the bottom of a very deep ditch. As I lay on Mother Nature's dirty bed, I wondered if it might end up being my grave. It was the perfect size and I realized I couldn't move to escape, even if I wanted to.

With my lungs unable to inhale, I could not yet moan or cry out. Amazingly, an incredible sense of calm fell over me. There was nothing left in me to be upset with, so I just lay there in fascination, waiting to see what might happen next.

Soon, air filtered back into my lungs. Three Spanish-speaking men now stood above me at the top of the hole, which I figured to be about five foot deep. They bantered back and forth with words I didn't understand. Finally I discerned a familiar word.

"Ambulancia!"

Terrified I'd be carted off to a foreign hospital, I managed to get myself in a sitting position despite the pain shooting through my spine. Warm wet liquid flowed down my back. Having left some space in my cozy little crypt, one of the men jumped in beside me. Before I had a chance to figure out what the next move should be, he lifted me up by my hips, while the two guys on top pulled me out.

Plop! I was on the sidewalk again, as if I'd never fallen.

"Gracias!" I said, hoping I pronounced it correctly. "Do you know where the Hotel Grande is?"

"You Americano?"

"Yes," I said, praying he spoke English.

"You want Hotel Grande?"

"Yes, I don't see well," pointing to my eyes and shaking my head.

"You want to go to hospital?" Suddenly I realized he probably thought I meant I had hurt my eyes in the fall.

"No, no! To the hotel, please!" I begged.

"Over here." The man took my arm and pulled me along. We walked two shadows back and he opened the door.

"Gracias, Gracias!" I said with all the gratitude I could muster, breaking his grasp when I saw the door to the stairwell. The man was asking me something, but I didn't care, I just wanted to get to my room. I bolted up the steps to the third floor. Unfortunately, when I reached for the key, it was not there.

"Where's the key?" I frantically asked no one. I checked the other pockets, knowing the gesture was futile. *I must have lost it when I fell!* I told myself. Knowing I could not go back, I slumped down and began to cry. Wishing I had my dad's security hankie, I used the bottom of my shirt to wipe my tears. "You can't keep doing this," I told myself, feeling the exhaustion from all my efforts to see.

Reliving the moment complete with the pain, I was suddenly jolted to the present.

"We'll be landing in about twenty minutes, sweetheart!" came the irritating voice of the stewardess.

Rage replaced my momentary surprise.

"Oh, honey, I'm sorry. Did I scare you?"

"No!" I said, hoping to hide any expression of emotion which might have escaped me.

"Now I want you to listen very carefully."

Oh brother! I thought, making an angry face. Still recovering from her intrusive actions, I considered reaching out and slugging her.

"Are you listening?" she said, talking to me like a schoolteacher.

"Yes!" I snapped. "I'm listening."

"That's good. This is very important. When we land, I want you to stay right here in your seat. It's very important that you do this because I will come and help you off the plane. But first I must assist the other passengers. It might take a few minutes, but I promise I will come back for you. I'll take you to an airport agent in Toronto who will help you get through customs and get you aboard your connecting flight to Windsor, okay?"

I felt like telling her no, but I simply nodded my head.

"Are you sure you understand? There is no need to be afraid because I will come back for you, I promise. But it's very important, dear, that you stay…right…here!"

"I…under…stand," I said, mimicking her emphasis on each word.

During our descent, I thought again about Cliff. I pictured the face he wore when he saw me slumped on the floor half asleep three hours after we'd parted. "Ger! What's the matter!?" he asked, bending down to hug me.

"Oh, don't squeeze too hard," I said, pulling my arm away.

"Oh my God, Geri. What the hell happened?"

"Well, you might say I missed a step." I gave him a smile.

"You fell?"

"You might say that."

"What'd you do, trip over a curb or something?"

"I think the 'or something' might sum it up a little better."

"Well, what?"

"I was looking for our hotel and I went into the third door like we both thought, but it was a restaurant."

"Yeah, I checked it out on my way home. It's the second door."

"I guess I know that now," I gave him another half smile. "Anyway, when it wasn't the third door, I figured it must be the fourth."

"No it can't be the fourth, 'cause that's where they're diggin up...oh, Geri!" he gently reached over and kissed me on the forehead. "You fell into that ditch, didn't you?"

I shook my head affirmatively.

"Oh, you poor thing. How badly are you hurt?"

I leaned forward so Cliff could see my back.

"Oh my God, girl. You're covered in blood. So why are you out here?" he asked. It suddenly dawned on him that I should be in the hotel room.

"Must have lost the key when I fell."

"Oh, Geri," he said again, squeezing the lower part of my arms so as not to hurt me. "Let's go in and wash you up. They don't look deep, but we'd better be sure."

I followed his advice, and it turned out the cuts were fairly superficial. I was pretty sore for a bit, but it only really slowed our trip by one day. The discomfort was the worst when riding the train back to London. Sitting on the plane wasn't the best either.

As the jet tilted forward preparing to land, I considered the oddity of the two accidental events. Though he truly was concerned for my welfare, Cliff and I never talked about their cause.

I wonder if Cliff needs to see me as sighted as I want to be? I asked myself as I felt the harsh thud of the plane on the runway. A moment later, the pilot announced our arrival.

"Ladies and gentlemen, we are now in Toronto..."

As soon as the plane stopped and everyone's seat belts clicked open, I grabbed my bag and jumped up. I followed the crowd, praying the stewardess would not spot me disobeying her directive. As the hordes of passengers filed through the long aisle to the cockpit exit, I heard the nauseating voice of my enemy.

"Thank you for traveling with us. Have a great day!"

"Have a great day! Have a wonderful visit! Thank you for traveling... oh honey, wait!" she said as I slipped out of her reach. "Honey, come back. I'll be with you in a minute."

But this time I did not stumble or falter. As fast as I could, I brushed past passengers and followed the enclosed pathway into the airport. When I got inside I realized I did not know where to go. I knew at that moment, exactly what I had to do. Picturing Linda, I reached in my bag and pulled out my father's gift. Taking a deep breath I unleashed the binding. Instantaneously, the five metal rods sprung open. For the first time I stood alone, announcing to the world I was blind.

"Can I help you?" a lady asked.

"Yes, you may. I need some assistance to find my way."

Chapter 30

A Dead End

January 1975

7:55 a.m.
"Miss Taeckens?"
"Yes?"
"If you would be so kind to see me after class, I would appreciate it."
"Okay," I said, suspicious of what Professor Powers had in store for me. The first class of the semester hadn't even started yet, and he was already singling me out.

If he does anything to keep me from taking this methods class I'll— I thought as I found my seat. After passing out the course syllabus, Professor Powers cleared his throat and began his lecture.

"This class is to prepare all of you for your student teaching experience. Information learned here will be the most important of all. I will provide you with a variety of methods and strategies for teaching the visually impaired. If you are not able to demonstrate to me a competency in this area, your career in teaching the blind will never be realized."

As he droned on about how we will learn the importance of safety when setting up a classroom, my anticipation about what he wanted grew. It couldn't have anything to do with the Braille class, I assured myself, thinking about the clearance I'd received from the registration office. I reflected on the many trips the guys at Banana House had made for me. They'd taken turns the previous fall driving me to the university in Detroit. The professor there had been so reasonable. He even allowed George to read the transcription materials to me. Just as I had predicted, I passed the class with an A.

He's gonna mess up my student teaching plans, I warned myself, thinking about how close I was to being done with my course work. *Don't let him get to you!* I firmly advised, reminding myself of all I'd accomplished. *You're invincible remember?* I told myself, even though I hadn't been feeling quite so capable lately. *Don't forget what Jack says*, I reminded, forcing myself to think about how much I'd accomplished.

With no help from my old football team, I had continued to hold down eighteen credits during the previous semester. But despite Jack's encouragement, I found it difficult to give myself recognition for the 3.8 average I'd received. Although

Jack did not support the intensity of my schedule, he regularly praised me for the commitments I made. For four long months, I rode a total of seven hours each week to attend classes in Detroit. My nanny job had ended, but two additional families were on my babysitting list, and I added another shift at the Help Line. I also became part of a student movement which advocated for the rights of students with disabilities. Believing it was my job to do everything rarely gave me time to sleep. I attributed my loss of appetite to busyness, deciding giving was a better thing to spend time on than preparing meals. But since Christmas break, the energy which had allowed me to stay so busy had disappeared. I chalked it up to the holiday slowdown, and assured myself it would return once I got back into the swing of things.

When the hour ended, a surge of anxiety twisted the ever present knot in my gut.

I nervously waited while Professor Powers gathered up his things. When he did so, he indicated I was to follow him. I felt like a dutiful child, trailing behind him, my bag and coat over my arm, while holding my cane steady at an angle across my body. I was glad he couldn't evaluate whether I was using this alternative technique properly.

Despite the urge to resist its use, I had managed to stick to carrying the cane since returning home from Europe. I contacted the agency for the blind, requesting mobility instruction. Just as Linda had done, the instructor showed me how tapping the cane from side to side would give me tactile and auditory feedback. I pushed down feelings of embarrassment while learning under blindfold the techniques for orienting through veering sidewalks. They taught me other skills for using the cane except for the ones dealing with pity and shame. By the end of August, I had completed the three week course, scoring in the highest range of proficiency. With no skill development in the area of public and personal perception however, I promptly oriented my feelings out of bounds, telling myself I must just buck up and accept my fate.

"Miss Taeckens," Professor Powers said, sitting down behind his desk.

"Yes?" I replied, locating his unwelcoming chair. I leaned my cane up against the wall and hoped it wouldn't slide down.

"I hear you managed to sneak through the registration office to enroll in my methods class," he said.

"I didn't sneak," I replied, placing my hand on my knee to be sure my leg stayed put.

"Well, actually you did."

"How's that?" I asked, struggling not to react defensively.

"You are not allowed to enroll in a methods course until you have passed the Braille Transcription class."

"Oh, but I did, with an A, as a matter of fact," I said smiling now.

"Not as far as I am concerned."

"Huh?" I said, my anxiety rising.

"That's right!"

"But Professor Powers, I traveled a hundred miles twice a week last term to take the class at a qualified university accredited to teach special education for the visually impaired. I checked it all out beforehand, and I was assured it would be no problem."

"Well, obviously you did not clear it with me."

"No, I cleared it with the university," I said, hardly believing my worst fear might be realized.

"To your misfortune, you received inaccurate information. The only person who can authorize such a transfer is the head of the department, which of course, is me!"

"But Professor Powers!" My voice was panicky now.

"Yes," he said smugly.

I took a deep breath. I did not want to get upset. *You've gotta act mature!* I begged myself.

"Professor Powers," I said, steadying my voice, holding my knee more firmly. "The main objective of this course is to determine if someone can transcribe information into Braille. Having received an A suggests I can do just that. Why would you want to block me from continuing in this program?"

"Let me see…" he said, leaning back in his chair, folding his arms behind his head. "If I'm not mistaken, you walked into my office back in spring of 1972. I told you at that time that I did not believe the blind could teach the blind. I strongly suggested you take a different path for helping others. But you have persisted. I must admit I admire your moxie, Miss Taeckens, but at the same time I must tell you, you are not as clever as you think. One of the important realities about life is recognizing when it is not feasible to push through a brick wall. I am that brick wall. As long as I'm at this university, I will continue running this department in the philosophy I have held for many years. So, with that, it would behoove you to take a lesson from this experience and learn who is in authority and who is not. The registration department is not the authority. I, however, am!"

Silence followed. I sat stunned and numb at this impasse. This arrogant man was not going to give an inch. I could not come up with any recourse to overpower his unreasonable decision. Something within me changed. I now realized how fragile I truly was. I might as well have been made out of pick up sticks, as I felt the foundation of my being collapse. Without a word, I stood and walked out of his office.

"Good luck to you, Miss Taeckens. I'll trust you will drop my course soon so you don't get charged the tuition fee."

But I did not respond or look back. I left the building, my winter coat still hanging over my left arm. I felt no chill as I dragged beside me the cane I had worked so hard to use with confidence. Feeling totally numb, I moved automatically in the direction of Banana House. I barely noticed tripping over a raised sidewalk. The honking horn vaguely stimulated my eardrums as I blindly crossed the major street in front of the house.

   1 p.m.

   "Geraldine!"
A faint sound from far away threatened to arouse me from my slumber.
"Geraldine! Geraldine?"
I hate that name! Go away! I tried to say, but my mouth would not respond.
"Geraldine? Wake up Geraldine."
Why won't they go away? I want to sleep.
   "Talk to me, Geraldine, can you hear me? Come on, I can tell you're awake now. Open your eyes Miss Taeckens."
I tried to follow the command, but my lids had somehow turned into lead.
"Wake up, Miss Taeckens!"
Why can't I talk? I asked myself, trying to feel where my tongue might be.
There's something in my mouth! Just let me sleep! I said with out speaking, sliding back into the heavenly void of nothingness.

   2:30 p.m.

   "Miss Taeckens! Geraldine! Open your eyes!"
My eyes, where are they? I can't feel them. My head, they're in my head! I reassured myself now able to roll it back and fourth. *Am I floating?* I wondered, unable to detect anything around me.
   "Come on, you can open your eyes, Geraldine."
Someone's talking to me! I suddenly realized, struggling to figure out where I was. My hand, I can feel my hand…. But I could not lift it. Sleep called me again.

   4 p.m.

   "Geraldine. Can you hear me, Geraldine? It's time to wake up!"
The distant voice aroused me once more, but I could barely make out the words.
   "Wake up now. You are in the hospital!"

Hospital…what's a hospital? I struggled to surmise. Once more I made an effort to speak. What's in my mouth? I wondered again. Locating my eyelids with my mind, I opened them slightly.

"Good! That's good. Try to keep them open now," the voice of a lady said. But I could not do her bidding. Once more their heavy lids caused them to shut. I longed to find that quiet place inside my head.

"Wake up, Geraldine!"

Who keeps calling me by that name? I asked no one. Why don't they leave me alone?

"You are in the hospital, Geraldine."

The hospital? Suddenly the words registered. I tried to sit up, but I could not move. Someone had put a brick on my chest. My nose. There was something in my nose.

"My nose." I managed to say in a muffled voice.

"Yes, you have a tube in your nose, Geraldine. Do you remember coming to the hospital, Geraldine?"

"Geri. My name is Geri," I whispered.

"Geri, do you remember coming to the hospital?"

The hospital…I tried to remember. How did I get here? The desire to sleep threatened to override such questions. I didn't care where I was. I only wanted to go back to sleep.

"Keep your eyes opened, Geraldine," the annoying voice said.

"I want to sleep," I whispered.

"Do you know who brought you to the hospital?"

I attempted to think. How did I get here? Despite the pressure of gravity, I lifted my left hand to my face.

"Get it out!" I said, in a louder voice than before.

"Don't pull on that," the voice scolded. "You have a tube in your nose to help you. Do you remember your friends helping you?"

My friends? I considered, but my brain was so foggy. A vague recollection of Cliff's voice calling me came to mind, but quickly disappeared. I couldn't think. I felt so tired. I closed my eyes and began to drift away, but the annoying voice of the lady wouldn't let me.

"Geraldine! Stay awake now. It's important you stay awake!"

"My name is Geri!" I said angrily, my voice rising above a whisper this time.

"Good. I know I'm bothering you, but you must stay awake and tell me what you remember. Think about what you were doing before you came to the hospital."

Despite my irritation, I tried to do as the lady asked. Ted's image came in to my mind. The feeling of floating, no, being carried. *I had been carried!* I mused. Did Cliff and Ted carry me? The memory became clearer.

I pictured myself entering Banana House after the disastrous encounter with Professor Powers. But my conscious thoughts drifted back into nothingness. I could not yet remember the full story of how I came to the hospital. I could not recall how relieved I felt when I found the place empty.

Once I arrived at Banana House, I hurriedly calculated how much time I had before any of the guys would be back from class. It was almost ten. If I had their new schedules down correctly, they all either worked or had classes until five.

"I can do this and stay home," I recalled myself deciding, grabbing my glasses and magnifier from my desk drawer and then heading to the bathroom. Turning on the light, I opened the medicine cabinet door, knowing George stored his Valium in there. Jeff also mentioned some sleeping pills he took on occasion, so maybe they were in there as well. A slight tinge of guilt slipped into my otherwise empty being, but I quickly dismissed it with a plan to write an apology.

Placing my glasses on my face, I opened up the mirrored door. Five bottles of pills sat nice and neatly on the top shelf. One by one I picked them up and systematically searched the labels. I noted how calm I felt as I tilted the bottles and magnifying glass in various directions under the light. Manipulating the labels back and forth, this way and that, did not produce the typical frustration I normally experienced. Nothing could disturb my peaceful inner void as I methodically carried out my plan.

Eventually I was able to pick out the first letter of each prescription in order to complete my task. Confiscating a handful of the treasures I stuffed them into my jeans pocket. Closing the cabinet door, I caught sight of the ghostly figure in the mirror. With the florescent bulb no longer able to do the trick, I decided the image was an affirmative sign. This figure no longer can be humanized, I mused to myself as I flipped the light off. "You look like a ghost, so you'll be a ghost," I promised. "I won't make you go through this any more."

I took my finds and went to the kitchen, taking a glass from the cupboard. As I filled it with tap water, I noticed the pile of dishes on the counter. I'll do them while I'm waiting, I thought. A parting gift to my buds.

Like little pebbles collected by a child to give as an offering to a loved one, I gathered up my collection, opening my mouth and pouring the contents of my palm inside. Realizing it was too many for one swallow; I spit half of them back out, and took a drink. I repeated the process, and then slapped down the glass with satisfaction. As if having simply swallowed healthy vitamins, I filled the sink with soapy water and cleaned the dishes. When I was done, I headed to my room and typed a note.

Dear Banana buddies,

I'm sorry I had to do this, but honestly, I just can't fight it anymore. I can't keep the big secret I've been holding in my heart for so long. It's been very hard going blind, and I just can't make myself deal with it anymore. I wish I could blame Professor Powers for this, but actually he's the one who made me face the truth. I've learned my lesson. I just can't keep beating my head against a brick wall.

I'm sorry, Jeff and George, that I took your medicine. There's money in my purse and you can take whatever you need to replace them.

Thanks for all of you being such good friends. I'll be lots happier, wherever I end up.

Please tell my parents and family I love them, and I hope they understand.

Love,

Geri

With that, I put my favorite Simon and Garfunkel album on my turntable and lay back on my bed. As I drifted off to the unknown, I heard the voice of Paul Simon conveying the story of a most peculiar man.

Chapter 31

The Love Connection

January 1975

Day 21

"Geri, your ride's here."

I shot to my feet, perspiration generously moistening my palms as I fumbled to find the handles of my purse.

"Take your time. I'm sure he'll wait."

Despite this reassurance, I bolted down the hallway to fetch my things, nicking my hip on one of the rogue carts left astray in the hallway. I entered the doorway to my room.

"You leaving?" asked the voice coming from the chair in the corner.

"Uh, yeah!" I replied, frantically gathering up my suitcase and cane from the closet.

"Miss Muffett will be missed, just don't seize or desist." Realizing I needed to respond to the lady I had spent the last three weeks of my life with, I set my suitcase back down on the bed, dropped my purse beside it, and laid the cane over both.

"I'm gonna miss you too, Sophie. You're the best!" I said, walking toward her. She met me half way. Together we embraced, hugging each other tightly, knowing how deeply we had touched each other.

"Your shadow I'll be, as soon as you're free!" Sophie pronounced, sniffling back tears as she spoke. This was her way of saying she'd be leaving soon, maybe hoping to stay connected to me, I wasn't totally sure.

"It won't be long," I agreed. We held each other for several minutes, our cuddly winter sweaters adding warmth to our grip. Finally, she let go. Placing her hands on my shoulders, Sophie pushed me back, looking directly into my face. Despite her sallow skin permanently lined with worry, her dark eyes shone brightly, matching the warm smile she now gave me. Her brown hair streaked with gray looked disheveled. I had learned it was not a trait of her mental state, but simply the result of how it grew.

"You've stuck in your thumb and pulled out a plum, don't let anyone take it away. Keep making those pies, despite your poor eyes, and you'll keep having better days."

"I'll try to take your advice, Soph," I said, appreciating her kind wishes.

"Scared?"

"Yes." *Terrified!* I thought, wishing I could hurry up now.

"Well, you best be on your way, or you might miss out on the day." With one last squeeze, I gathered my things up once more and headed out the door. As I continued down the hallway to the nurse's station, other people emerged from the day room and corridors, wishing me well. The outpouring of affection rained down on me in a shower of sweet sadness. By the time I got to the desk, I was no longer able to hold back my tears.

"Now you take good care of yourself, missy," Dolly, the day nurse warned, pushing the box of tissues on the counter to me. "I need your signature on these papers, and then you can get the heck out of here!"

"Okay!" I said, once more unloading my belongings onto the floor. Dolly gave me a pen.

"Can you put your finger on the line?" I asked her.

"Sure!" It was easy to see her pink sculptured fingernail clearly identifying the spot, so I set the pen where it pointed and proceeded to squiggle out my name. Dolly explained what each document said as we repeated this process three more times. When I finished, Dolly came around the counter and gave me a big hug.

"Now, here is your prescription. Can your friend help you get it filled at the pharmacy?"

"Yeah, he will," I assured her, folding the lifesaving words and stuffing them into my jeans pocket.

"Good enough then. Your friend's waiting for you in the lobby. I'll get your coat."

"Thanks," I said, staring at the locked metal doors which had kept me safe for an eternity. There was no need for coats in this insane asylum, the name I had known it by prior to my visit. Contrary to outside impressions, the walls of this foreboding environment simply protected its residents from having to brave the cold harsh elements of the real world, while they battled the storms in their head. As Dolly helped me with my jacket, I worried whether I was truly ready to be released. Throwing my purse over my shoulder, I took my cane in my right hand, picking up my suitcase with the other. Before I could step forward, Dolly gave one last warning.

"And don't let me catch you coming back to the unit, missy."

I smiled at her as she dug her fingers deeply into my down jacket, gripping my shoulder affectionately through the protective layers as she had so many times before.

"I won't," I promised. Watching her step back into her office, I braced myself for the sound of freedom which frequently scared the hell out of me. Despite the fact I knew it was coming, I startled at the ear piercing buzz. The signal to leave was finally being discharged for me! Am I really ready? I asked myself, reflecting back on the previous three weeks. It seemed like I had been here forever. *You've come a long way*, I reminded myself, taking a step forward, while resisting the motion.

Days 1-4

After my body had been cleared of the multitude of pills I had taken, the tube was removed from my nose. Without my agreement, the emergency room staff, along with Jack's blessing, transferred me to the psychiatric ward of the same hospital I'd stayed at as a child. For the first few days, all I did was sit at a table in the corner of the day room with my head propped up by my elbows, my hands covering my face. I would have preferred staying in bed, but the rules of the ward wouldn't allow it.

"Everyone in the day room unless you have a specific purpose, and then it must be cleared with ward personnel," I was told in no uncertain terms. I soon learned the bearer of this information was Nurse Mitchell, alias Nurse Ratchet. This unaffectionate name had been assigned to her by the patients who likened her to the controlling character in the novel *One Flew over the Cuckoo's Nest*.

Dutifully, I dressed each morning and found my spot in the corner, hoping no one would notice me. Initially staff and patients left me alone. No one bothered me when I failed to brush my hair, eat, or engage in planned activities. I simply sat without moving, burying my head in my hands, maintaining a state of numbness as I gazed into the void. Only one tiny pinpoint of light occasionally broke through the darkness whenever another patient or staff person would try to connect with me. It would appear just above my eyebrows, inside my head yet far away.

The call of the psychiatrist inviting me into his office the first day forced me to briefly remove my finger veil. It did not break my silence, however. For five minutes he tried to get me to answer his questions. I simply shook my head "no" to all of them, including the one asking me if I was depressed.

"Well, we'll have you stay with us for a while and see what happens," he said, escorting me back to my corner.

Each evening my roommate tried to talk with me, but I simply pretended I was asleep. I wanted nothing from anyone and felt sorry Cliff had found me alive when he unexpectedly came home for a book he had forgotten.

As time went on, staff and patients kept asking me how I was. Though I maintained my vow of silence toward these unwanted intruders, I found myself internally responding to each of their interfering comments. I worked to focus harder on the void of nothingness behind my handmade curtain, but this very act seemed to make the tiny ember in my mind's eye glow brighter. Despite my irritation toward these trespassers, I became curious about the source of this illumination. Oddly enough, its origin was coming from the same region as the Fantasia movie I'd watched while smoking pot or doing acid. I preferred being left alone, yet I studied this phenomenon carefully each time someone introduced themselves or asked me why I was on the ward.

On the fourth day, a guy who had several times established himself as Gary came up to my table and sat down. Maintaining my pose, I continued to stare motionless into the darkness, which soon brightened to gray.

"How ya doing today? It's me, uh, Gary."

Just stay steady, I told myself. After several moments of quiet, he continued.

"Now listen," he said firmly. "You've been here, how many days?"

I didn't answer.

"Come on, girl, I know you want to talk. You've been here long enough now, that I know you want to say something."

Wanna bet? I said to him in my head.

"Hey, we all wanna connect to someone, even when we think we don't. I've watched you peek out from behind your secret hiding place. You're just scared to feel, that's all. We all get like that at the start."

I'm not! I mentally insisted.

"Hey, I'm making you mad, ain't I? That's good."

Go away! I silently screamed.

"See, you just grimaced behind your handy wall there. I saw it."

I wanted to open my hands and tell this guy to get the hell away from me, but I held them firmly in place. *No one's getting to me!* I proclaimed.

"There, you just did it again. Grimaced, I mean."

Several seconds passed. A pressure deep inside me began to build. Like a vat of hot lava rumbling and churning in the bowels of a volcano, the threat of a violent emotional explosion now terrorized me.

I have to get away from this person...but I can't! Frantically, I considered how to break free of this trap. Realizing it would require talking, I hung on tighter, digging my fingers into my forehead.

"Listen," Gary said. "It's hard! It's hard for all of us here. You got it rough. Everyone's got it bad sometimes, but it's not over!"

The affection in his voice calmed me a bit, even though I didn't want it to. As I mentally begged this guy to go away, he continued. His kindness threatened to make me cry.

"I'll bet it's your first time in a place like this. First times are scary. I remember my first time. Man, I was a fuckin' lunatic! Needed twenty-seven stitches across my wrist, check out the scar!"

I pictured him exposing his arm.

Does he know I probably can't see it? I wondered.

"Ah, come on, ain't ya gonna even look at my handiwork?" I didn't move. "Man, you're stubborn, that is for sure! Pretty, too. Need to brush your hair though. I'll bet you have pretty hair when it's combed. But you gotta get rid of that black shirt! Don't look good on blondes."

Please go away! I pleaded in my mind, hoping to telepathically get him to understand. He was softening my shell, and I couldn't have it. I desperately needed to stay anesthetized.

"I know I ain't no doc or nothin' but I'm an expert, you know," he laughed. "Got manic depression. Ever heard of it? I admit, I'm a bit on the up swing, but I'm leveling off with the lithium they're givin' me. Too bad in a way. Love them natural highs, but the crashes are hell! I look just like you when I'm down there. That's why I know how important it is to let folks pull you up. One thing I've learned is ya gotta say what's in the head. Keep it locked up, and it's like yer in a cellar, suffocatin' from the must and mold."

My effort to tune him out failed. Admittedly I knew what he was talking about. Secretly I wondered how I had been able to manage the incredible level of energy I expended during the previous semester. Though Professor Powers certainly pushed me over the edge, I found my vigor slipping over Christmas break. I had attributed my growing lack of enthusiasm to having fewer things to do. Spending time with my failing father had also taken its toll. I hoped I would feel better once my busy schedule resumed, but my confidence was shaky at best.

Get away from me! I internally commanded, now terrified I might have manic depression too.

"Ah, I'm just makin' you madder," he said. "I can see them fingers of yours tightenin' up. Okay, I'll leave you alone, but only for now. Look, you sweet thing, it's all about love, don't ya know. And to have love, you've gotta have connection! You've just temporarily lost contact with the world, that's all. You can get it back. But ya gotta let folks in. Trust me, I know this stuff. I forget it sometimes, gotta check in to this place for a bit, but I always get it back. You'll get it back too, just wait and see."

I heard him stand and felt his hand gently touch my arm. At the same moment, the pinpoint of light expanded. Pressing my fingertips even harder against my skin, I tried to look away from the swelling star, turning my eyes upward inside their sockets. For some reason, I felt desperate not to see the light, but I couldn't rotate my eyes far enough to avoid the intensifying glow.

With one swift movement, his large warm fingers cradled my upper arm, communicating all that was needed. A moment later the connection was gone, and the nebula disappeared. Contrary to my desire to get rid of him, I found myself sickened at the loss of the annoying stranger. Moisture began forming behind my lids. *Why couldn't I have said something to him?* I asked myself, the tears beginning to seep out between my fingers, my body remaining immobilized, powerless over the collapsing dam. I felt a mounting pressure force years of fermenting emotions into the tributaries of my being. With each compression of my heart, the painful substance gushed out into a current of tears, cleansing my soul. As I sat there, quietly spilling an eternity of sadness down my arms, a soft voice interrupted the sanitization process.

"Geraldine, I'm Dolly, one of the nurses here. How about coming with me for a bit?" Without hesitation, I followed her to a private room not far away. We sat at a small circular table, Dolly taking the chair next to mine. She handed me a supply of tissues. I continued to express my sorrow without words. Once in a while she squeezed my hand, telling me my feelings were normal. In time, the water works slowed.

"Better?" she asked.

I nodded my head.

"So tell me, why all the bad feelings?"

Still skeptical about breaking my silence, I remained quiet.

"You gotta start somewhere. It's not good holding it all inside. It's what got you here, you know."

I still couldn't think what to say. So many thoughts swam around in my head. Which one do I pick?

As if reading my thoughts, Dolly said, "Just say anything that comes to your mind. It doesn't even have to be a sentence. It doesn't have to make sense at all."

"I hate myself," I heard myself announce.

"Why do you hate yourself?"

"Cause I'm always trying to be what I'm not."

"And why do you think you do that?"

"Because I can't be what I want."

"What do you want to be?"

Pressing my lips tightly together, I held the answer at bay. Don't you say it! I firmly warned, knowing once I admitted it, I could never go back. A long time passed as Dolly waited patiently, yet making it clear she expected an answer. For some reason I found myself wanting to please her, but intuitively I knew I could never be the same if I shared the desire that could never be realized.

"If you can't tell me what you want to be, can you tell me what you don't want to be?"

Before I could stop myself, my lips flew opened and out came the words I had worked to keep hidden forever. "I don't want to go blind!" I yelled. In one great heave, the remainder of sediment contained in the reservoir of my soul catapulted forward. The sound of my own retching scared me, and I began to shake uncontrollably.

"I can't handle it," I wailed, grasping the edge of the table, hoping it would keep me from disintegrating. "I can't, I can't…" I wept, drawing up my knees and resting my heels on the cross bar of the chair. Bile erupted, threatening to gag me as it passed through my chattering teeth. Seizing a fist full of tissues, I placed them over my foaming mouth, wondering if I might pass out from the convulsing, part of me wishing I would.

Dolly got up and stepped out of the room, leaving me to believe I had scared her away. Momentarily she returned however, placing a warm blanket around my shivering shoulders. She gently patted my back. Her kind gesture made me cry harder, though the outpouring was less violent. Memories of being comforted by my father brought a terrible ache to my heart.

What would he think if he saw me now? I questioned, wishing I could tell him. He could never take it, I decided. It would break his heart if he knew I was here. Neither one of my parents could handle knowing I'd been feeling suicidal about the very thing they'd tried to help me accept. What if I had killed myself? I speculated, my anxiety rising. For the first time I felt glad I had failed.

"Geraldine?" Dolly finally said.

"Hmm?" I barely managed.

"Is this the first time you've admitted your fear of losing your vision?"

I nodded my head, still cradled in my folded arms.

"I thought so. You know, I certainly can't imagine what going blind could be like. I can't even say I wouldn't consider disappearing from this world. But I do know one thing."

I waited as this wise lady paused for contemplation.

"Life gives all of us challenges. But it also gives us each other. I have a hunch you can face your challenge, but you have forgotten the importance of the 'each other' part. Am I right about that?"

Once more I nodded my head in the affirmative. I considered her words carefully. My tears were down to a trickle now, and only a few occasional spasms made me gasp involuntarily for a breath.

"I never told anybody," I finally said.

"My gosh, missy, you been holding all that inside by yourself?" Dolly asked, tousling my hair with her hand.

"Uh huh."

"Well, I don't know whether to give you credit for being so brave, or to scold you for being so stupid."

Despite the intensity of the discussion, my elbows relaxed, lowering my head so it rested on the table. The cold surface against my cheek helped numb the severity of the moment.

"Stupid would be the right description," I said.

"I think you're right on that one, missy. Where did you get such a notion you had to deal with this all by yourself?"

"Maybe 'cause no one ever asks me!" I said, lifting myself up and propping my head on my hands. "I mean, they might ask me how much I can see or something, but never, never does anyone wanna talk about how I feel about it!" I almost yelled.

Dolly drew herself closer, staring directly into my face. For the first time I noticed her. Surrounded by snowy white hair, gentle blue eyes looked out from folds of soft skin indicating they had been smiling for years. Plump pink cheeks outlined with creases supported the notion she was a happy, wise lady.

"Geraldine, you have to listen to me very carefully," she said. Her use of my full name evoked my usual aversive reaction, telling me I had rejoined the world. "I'm not a psychologist, but I've been around a long time, so you're gonna have to take my word based on the credentials of long life," she said, giving me a momentary smile. "If you don't start talking, telling people who you are close to, what you are feeling, thinking, what makes you happy or sad, life will not be worth living. Folks can't read your mind," she insisted. "My dear! I don't mean to minimize the seriousness of your condition, but it is not the ability to see that makes things worth while, it's people and sharing that does that!"

"But nobody wants to hear about bad things, especially about going blind!" I told her.

"How would you know that, Missy?" she said leaning back, slapping her palm on the table. I bolted upright at the startling sound.

"Sorry," she said, reaching out and patting my shoulder. "I only wish I could pound some sense into you kids!" she said shaking her head. "You get these silly notions and think you're right. How can you know something you've never tried?"

I had no answer. Pulling the blanket tighter around my shoulders, I pondered why I had come to this belief when a powerful image from my youth came to mind.

"I couldn't have made the taboo of blindness all up in my head," I protested, wondering whether to tell her about the blind man I'd met so long ago.

"Well, if you've never mentioned it to anyone, where'd you get the idea then?"

"It's just understood. No one wants to go blind and no one wants to hear about it," I said, picturing my father, the tin can, and yellow pencils in my hand. The memory of how scared I felt when he swiftly pulled me into the store followed.

"Well, I'm not sure who the 'no ones' are, but I'll bet there's someone who loves you who would be willing to listen." More recollections of my father flooded my mind.

"Never cry over spilled milk," I could hear him say.

"I don't think my folks can," I explained to Nurse Dolly. "It would hurt them too much if they knew how much I hate the idea. Heck, they think I'm doing fine!" I laughed, a tone of irony apparent in my voice.

"So you think they'd like the idea of you being dead better?" she let out a hearty laugh. "I think it's you who can't deal with it, so you assume no one else can."

Instinctively I knew she was right, but decided not to say so. Exhaustion was now taking over and I wished I could lie down and sleep.

"Listen kiddo, something tells me you're a tough cookie, but no one can carry the burden of the world on their shoulders alone. Ever notice how hunched yours are?"

I nodded my head, picturing my stooped profile.

"With a little bit of support, my guess is you'll do all right. But like I said, I'm no psychologist. You need to do your best not to isolate yourself while you're here. There's lots of folks on this ward who got as much if not more wisdom than me, even if they need some time out for a bit. Get to know them. Join in the games or craft activities. I'm sure you can do many, even with poor eye sight. Give yourself a chance."

"I'll try," I said, standing to leave.

"That's all you can do, Geraldine."

Dropping the blanket over the back of the chair, I couldn't help wince at the sound of my full name. In my weakened condition, I dared not ask her a favor directly.

"Dolly?" I said sheepishly.

"What's that?" she asked, seeming to be excited at my initiation of a question.

"Do you think you could ask the other staff not to call me that?"

"Is some other nurse calling you missy too?"

"No, I mean my full name."

"Oh, Geraldine, you mean. Sure enough. What do you want to be called?"

"Just Geri."

"Well, okay Just Geri, I will be sure to arrange that. And if I slip up, you promise to pull on my ear to remind me." Giving me a knowing smile, she walked over and hugged me. Avoiding the start up of water works, I resisted fully surrendering to her round fleshy bosoms. Once again the memory of being cradled forever in my father's safe arms made me long to be a child. She closed the door to the quiet room. I walked unsteadily on fragile legs as Dolly escorted me back to my corner. This time I kept my hands down, exposing my face for all to see.

Chapter 32

An Even Greater Love Connection

January 1975

Days 5 through 13

The next day the doctor decided to prescribe antidepressant medication for me. Within a few days, I was eating and sleeping better. I was gradually able to tolerate conversations and discovered how similar we patients all were. Gary's earlier suggestion regarding this notion now made sense. I was able to realize each person's validity, regardless of how overwhelmed they might be by life's expectations.

Whether we were plagued by criticisms from internal or external voices, we all felt the same painful results. None of us wanted to be told we were unacceptable, whether we heard it from an imaginary devil or a real live person. I also discovered I was not alone in my struggle to accept my physical difference. I had been a part of the disability movement on campus, and our focus was to evoke a positive change in the public's perception. The resulting compulsion to present ourselves as happy and cool added to my pretense and promoted my denial. In contrast, the people on the ward with physical limitations were able to discuss the pain of their loss. I quickly learned I was not alone and enjoyed the freedom of sharing how I truly felt.

As time went on, I began to realize how devastating keeping secrets had truly been for me. A unanimous cheer rose from the crowd after overhearing me express this notion to Gary one evening at dinner. The comradery between the patients turned out to be more therapeutic than any analysis by staff. Nurse Ratchet didn't like us talking about emotional issues however.

"Tell that stuff to your psychiatrist!" she would warn, particularly when Nurse Dolly wasn't around. But we patients all knew her orders were ludicrous, as we rarely saw the docs. "They're out playing golf" or "Wait 'til your meds kick in!" were common retorts from the braver souls. Most kept quiet, however, as Nurse Ratchet would scratch a patient off the activity list if she thought someone was being disrespectful of her authority.

Although evening activities were nothing special, they became something for most of us to look forward to, breaking up the monotony of each day. Initially I had avoided them, but the others encouraged me, and before I knew it I was playing bingo, Concentration, and even charades. The thrill of laughing with others, being a part of such healthy activities, initially felt quite foreign to me. The fact that folks seemed to naturally step in to help, describing visual aspects of a game, warmed my heart. Unlike my old neighbor, Karen Worster, whose cruel treatment still haunted me, no one said I couldn't join in because I couldn't see.

With each passing day I grew stronger. The meds left me feeling a bit groggy, causing a funny taste in my mouth, but I felt calmer. My leg needed less external containment, and my desire to hide behind hands disappeared.

I discovered a more natural way to manage nervous energy when Dorothy, the art director, announced she would teach anyone interested how to cable knit a sweater. My mother had taught me some basic stitches as a child so I decided to take Dorothy up on her offer. I almost gave up however, as I quickly discovered I couldn't use my eyes to make the stitches anymore. With Dorothy's patience and encouragement, she was able to show me how to distinguish the pattern with my fingers. This included recognizing mistakes, as any true knitter must be able to fix their inevitable errors.

I also developed the courage to entertain a passion I had resisted for some time. When Sophie discovered I wrote music and played guitar, she brought one from home, insisting I perform for the patients. Though it was difficult to accept my audience's approval, their applause gave me a natural high I quickly learned to love.

Unfortunately, all the treatment and support could not take away the nagging ache in my gut. None of my friends from the Help Line or Banana House had contacted me. Except for Ted who initially brought clothing at the request of the hospital, I had spoken to no one besides patients and staff. I told myself I didn't really want to see anyone, but I secretly feared I'd been rejected for my terrible action.

The other nagging worry had to do with my parents. Despite Nurse Dolly's encouragement, I had not called them yet. Typically we spoke at least once a week; in two days it would be two. If I didn't call soon, they would try to reach me for sure as my twenty-third birthday was only eight days away.

As I readied myself for bed on the twelfth evening, I promised myself I would call them in the morning. I also decided I wouldn't tell them where I was. As Sophie and I lay in our beds waiting for sleep, we began our usual chat. I had already learned she suffered from headaches since childhood. By age thirty, she had developed a buzzing noise in her head, making her believe she had been wired by the FBI so they could control her thoughts. This was one of her many visits to the psych ward. Sophie explained she typically came in to take a break from life's demands, but this time it was because her husband of twenty years had left her. Though devastated, Sophie always took time to be concerned about others. As our friendship grew, she became convinced I too had been wired by the FBI. She was so fearful my privacy would be stolen, she promised to monitor my thoughts telepathically in order to block the FBI's intrusive messages. Between the lines of her insanity, however, I could tell intuitive wisdom prevailed.

"You stumped 'em well, with that flower that smells," Sophie said, referring to a word I used during the game of hangman.

"You liked my word chrysanthemum, did you?" I asked, chuckling.

"How smart you are, you must be from a star."

"You're not bad yourself," I said. "Don't you just love Charley?" I added, thinking about the word llama he'd picked in order to win the game.

"Sometimes bright, sometimes dull, if the devil don't get him, he hopes somebody will." We chuckled. Charley was always complaining about the voice of the devil getting after him. If someone could get him focused on a topic however, he usually knew everything about it.

"Tell a tale, folks will hear. Find him someone, he can call dear."

I had to think about this statement for a moment. Usually, it didn't take much to decipher Sophie's little riddle. Though initially I thought her strange comments were part of her mental illness, I soon came to realize this was her way of speaking the truth to someone without having to deal with their reaction if they didn't like what she said.

"So you think he's making it all up, the stories about the devil I mean?"

"Yup, he do, needs a girlfriend too."

We both giggled.

"Too bad he has to be discharged," I suggested. "He probably does better in a place where he's cared for and has instant friends," I said.

"Takes a brain, to know when to be insane!"

"You're probably right about that one, Soph," I said, chuckling at the thought of Charley giving some crazy line to the psychiatrist on duty in the ER, so he could get admitted and off the streets for a while.

Sophie made another sing-song comment.

"Geri's in the looking glass, what does Geri see? Instead of knowing it is her, it's Charley that she sees!"

I had to ponder her rhyme before I realized she was talking about me.

"I sure don't want to stay here, Soph," I replied, wondering if her suspicion might be true. Whenever I heard the buzzer unlocking the exit doors, I had this crazy fear I would somehow get sucked through the opening. This ridiculous notion was quickly followed by an uncanny urge to run as far away from the door as I could.

"Never worry, never fret, Sophie will block you from brats. FBI and Powers that be, I'll telepathically set you free.

"Thanks Sophie," I said, her kindness making me smile. Even though her offer to help me was in vain, I appreciated her desire to protect me from the perilous world outside. We fell silent, sleep beginning to slow my mind. I was almost in dreamland when, out of the blue, Sophie spoke.

"Geri's angry, Geri's sad, at your parents, who you pretend to make glad."

With my mind foggy from the medications, I almost passed over the opportunity to find out what she meant.

"Why would you suggest such a thing, Sophie?" I inquired blearily, turning so I was facing her.

"In your effort not to speak, you play the game of hide and seek."

"Sophie, what are you getting at?" I asked in an irritated tone. I was too tired to guess what she was attempting to say.

"You know, a tit for a tat, black black, I'll hurt you back?"

"No, I don't know," I said, my rising annoyance clearing the haze from my brain.

"They made you imperfect, it made you mad. Keep them in the dark, and like you, they'll be sad."

"Come on, Sophie!" I said, half laughing half whining as I propped myself up on my elbow. "That makes no sense. First of all, I surely don't blame my folks for my eye disease. Heck, they didn't know I'd get it. I tried to disappear 'cause I was overwhelmed. But now that I'm feeling better, I'm purposely not telling them so I don't upset them."

"The little blond girl who looks quite Dutch, I think thou doth protest too much!" There was cunning in her voice. I pictured her giving me her all-knowing smile.

"No, really, Sophie. Why would I be angry with my parents?"

"Oedipus killed his own father, you know, married his mother too. Don't 'spect he meant it though, as he said he had no clue."

"Oh, Sophie, you're crazy. Your words aren't making any sense!" I protested.

"Don't have to, just the way of the world. Emotions just are what they are, can't argue 'bout it, girl," she chuckled.

"Well, no matter, even if I were mad, which I'm not, I wouldn't tell them about what I did anyway."

"Ever hear about the princess who deceives the queen? She was found out and beheaded because she was so mean!"

"What, you think they're going to find out? You're wrong about that one," I told her firmly. "I will have to call them soon, but I ain't saying where I am."

"Santa knows all. Can't hide behind an insane asylum wall!" she said slyly.

"How could they find out?" I asked her. "If I don't tell them, and the guys at the house don't tell them, which I know they won't, there's no way—"

"So Geri will, afford the bill." Her words hit me like a brick. I hadn't thought about the insurance statements they'd be getting. As long as I was in college, I was covered under my dad's policy until age twenty-five.

"Damn!" I said, slapping my hand hard on the mattress. "I just can't tell them!"

"Through the looking glass or through the hole, which way will Alice in Wonderland go?"

"I wish I did live in Wonderland," I mused. "I'd split myself in two and go both ways if I did, and avoid reality all together."

"You're already it...like a banana split!" she giggled. "There's always two living inside. Phony and real, they both reside. Problem is which one is which?"

Is she talking about the FBI characters in her head? I wondered.

"Sophie, are you referring to the people that wire your brain?

"Nah! That's psychobabble, you know? Not the place where straight talk should go." I'd never heard Sophie allude to her delusions as being anything but fact. I smiled at the prospect that she knew better. I doubted whether she'd ever be able to say it outright, but her little rhymes were pretty obvious.

"So, if it's not that, what do you mean?"

"It's Dr. Jekyll and Mr. Hyde, where internal conflict does reside. Which one's right, which one's wrong, and where does Geri's plan belong?"

I was impressed with Sophie's insight. I had always wondered if other people had internal voices that battled back and forth like mine. Maybe she could answer my other question about this phenomenon.

"And how am I supposed to know which voice is which?" I asked.

"React from the head, you could end up dead. For it's devils' voices that give skullcap choices. But if you look for divine light, a pinpoint in the night, the answer to what where and why, are in the third eye. It's the wisdom of love, the essence of God up above, that's inside your mind. If you look, you will find."

Her words hit hard. I instantly knew what she meant. For one profound moment I was in the climax of my own movie, the orchestra playing 'tah dah' announcing my truth had been realized.

It is real! That light does exist! I thought. I had known it, but I had not been able to believe it. That star inside my forehead had been sending me the answers I needed. And now Sophie had confirmed it. The answer or truth about what I should think, feel, do came from within, and anything experienced in the state of love, was the same as experiencing God.

"God is love!" I said aloud.

"Geri's a whiz. She knows that it is," came Sophie's reply, as I heard her roll over, signaling she had completed her evening assignment.

But when lightning strikes, the flash lasts for only a split second. As fast and furiously as the inspiration had hit me, it disappeared as quickly. Smoldering doubt remained behind, once more leaving me with questions about the existence of God. The battle in my head continued, some voices telling me the divine radiance I saw was just my imagination. Interestingly enough, however, I had no difficulty maintaining my belief in the existence of the devil.

As I processed the likelihood of all these notions, I decided it was way too crazy for me to deal with. I still wanted to clarify my position with my parents though. Somehow if I could convince Sophie I didn't have to tell them where I was, I'd be right.

"Poppycock, Sophie," I said, knowing I was disturbing her. I heard the sheets rustle and figured she had turned back toward me.

"I don't think I'm being directed by the devil simply because I want to spare my parents from hearing painful news about their daughter. And I certainly don't believe for one minute that I am angry with either of them for anything!" I proclaimed, wishing I hadn't let so much irritation come out in my voice.

"Then Little Miss Muffet, should not sit on the telephone tuff it," Sophie pronounced, rolling back over, once more telling me our conversation was over. It continued in my mind however.

Could I be angry with them? I dared to ask.

A mental image of my parents, sitting in their respective arm chairs smoking and staring endlessly at the television back in Flint once again made my belly button twist itself in a knot. They'd both grown old and gray, losing their interests in friends and activities. Whenever I came home to visit, I found myself trying to convince them both to get out and have fun once in a while. Their sedentary existence grew more than worrisome, and I didn't know how to fix them.

How the hell am I gonna tell them I'm in a crazy house? I thought, realizing they were likely depressed themselves. A new image slid into view. The rocking chair my parents bought me at age ten was clearly visible. A heart filled memory threatened to make me cry as I recalled how they'd purchased it so I could sit close to the TV.

Before I had time to wallow in the sadness of this moment, the picture changed back to their lifeless images. Suddenly, rage took over and my arm shot forward, finding nothing to punch but air. I wanted to scream at them to move.

Why are you so weak? I yelled at them in my mind. More anger exploded from within, but they just sat there. The urge to slap the dumbfounded expressions off their faces overpowered me, so I took my hand and simulated the gesture. In an attempt to control myself, I gripped both knees with my hands.

You were always so weak! Too weak to help me! I silently screamed. Why couldn't you admit how awful going blind is? Instead, you made me pretend it was no big deal! Shaking uncontrollably now, I dug my fingernails into my legs, amazed at the depth of my rage. I'd never felt so much hatred before. Fearful I could not contain myself any longer, I rolled back and forth on the bed, trying to stay quiet for Sophie. Still seeing their stupefied looks, I persisted in my interrogation.

How could you be so stupid? How could you not see? I asked, desperate for them to answer. And then without warning, my mother's head dropped. She dabbed her eyes with the infamous hankie. Simultaneously my father's eyes lowered. They were filled with sadness. Bowing his head, he covered his face with both hands.

I'm sorry! I told them. Tears flooded my pillow. Wishing I had his hankie to hold, I gathered up the leftover pillowcase, squeezing it, hoping my love might reach them. You just didn't know how to talk of such things, I explained, believing this would help them feel better. With all my might I wished I could be with them, and vowed I would call and tell them the truth.

When the restless night finally ended, Dolly gave me the privilege of using the phone in the nurses' station. She had to ward off Nurse Mitchell in the process, telling her I needed privacy to deal with a family emergency. Gingerly I picked up the phone, my hands shaking so hard I could barely get the rotary dial to turn. When I heard the line on the other end start ringing, I thought I'd pass out from the anxiety.

"Hello," my mother's voice said.

"Hi, Mom."

"Oh, hi. Wondered when you'd call. How ya doing?"

"Uh, better," I said hesitantly.

"What do you mean, better?" she asked, her mother's antenna rising. I felt my adrenal glands release a dose of anxiety, as I prepared to confess my sin.

"Well, I've been having some trouble lately," I said, glad to be sitting.

"What kind of trouble?" her voice was now taking on that what-did-you-do-wrong tone.

"Uh, I've been kinda depressed lately, Mom."

"Oh honey, what have you been depressed about?"

"You know, I haven't been seeing too well lately. Do you know how hard that can be sometimes, Mom?" I asked, tears starting to roll down my cheeks.

"No, I can't imagine, but I worry about what it must be like," she said. "It's what I've always been afraid of for you, Geri."

Her comment took me aback. I had no idea she even thought of such things, let alone had feelings of fear. I reached for a handful of tissues, thoughtfully placed there by Dolly.

"What do you mean?"

"I mean, I pray for you every night."

Oh, please don't start the religious stuff, I silently begged, knowing this could threaten any hopes of getting what I needed from her, even though I wasn't sure what that was.

"I'd give anything to take your place, Geri," she continued. "I've been dreading the progress of your condition. So…how are you doing with it?" she asked tentatively.

"I guess that's why I called."

I waited, hoping she would say something, anything, to change my idea to share my secret, but she remained silent.

"I called to tell you, well, to tell you that I don't think I've done such a good job."

"What did you do?" she asked, panic in her voice.

"I'm all right now, Mom, but I did try to…hurt myself."

"Oh, Geri," she said, her devastation evident, the pain in her voice making me wish I had not called. In an attempt to rescue her from my awful admission, I quickly reminded her once again.

"Mom, I just need you to know I'm okay now. Really, I'm all right!" I said through trembling lips.

"Where are you?" she asked, still panicked.

"Uh, Mom, I'm in the hospital."

"Geri, what did you do to yourself? Oh God, I'm so sorry. I didn't mean to let this happen to you, Geri!" Seizing a chunk of hair, I pulled hard on it, holding back the anger now welling up inside me. Her expression of guilt was making it harder than I imagined. I feared I couldn't get through it. I thought about giving the phone to Nurse Dolly, but I instinctively knew I had to deal with her myself.

"Well, I took some pills, but I'm okay now, Mom. I just need to be in the hospital for a while."

"Oh, my God! You poor dear," she said, gasping for air, while I pictured her bending over with her hand on her stomach. The image was unbearable. The urge to hang up and disappear almost won out. I could hardly stand hearing her so distraught.

"I'm really sorry to upset you, Mom. But I had to tell you."

"Of course you have to tell us, Geri," she said, now sounding motherly and strong. "We are your parents, and we want to be there for you."

"Really, Mom?"

"Of course," she said, affection clearly expressed in her voice.

Convulsive sobs shook my entire body, as I squeaked out how sorry I was for having made my mother so sad. At the same moment, a warm blanket, compliments of Dolly, enveloped my shoulders, but it was my mother's voice that melted the ice between us. A long silence passed as we both worked to recover from this most profound discussion. Eventually I continued.

"Sometimes, you know, I didn't think you wanted to know how hard it's been for me."

"Oh God, Geri. If you only knew," she quietly wept. "I have felt so much guilt and worry about your vision loss."

"But I don't want you to feel guilty, Mom. It's not your fault!"

"Geri, I'm your mother. How could I not? Someday, if you have kids, you'll understand. But I have to tell you how I've racked my brain to understand. I've thought of all kinds of reasons for it. I was fairly old when I had you, of course, and I also drank a beer once in a while and smoked. Both your Dad and I talk of it frequently, but we figured you were getting along, so we didn't want to upset you by bringing it up."

Suddenly I began laughing through sobs. "You mean, all this time we've both been afraid to talk?"

"If I had known how depressed you'd become, I would have done anything for you, Geri."

"Oh, Mom, I would never want you to sacrifice for me. I need a little help dealing with the emotional part, that's all."

"So where are you? We'll be down to see you today."

"I'm at the same place I came for my eyes, only on the psychiatric unit," I said unable to keep the shame out of my voice.

"There's no need to feel bad about it, Geri. Your father is at the store, but we'll get in the car as soon as he gets back."

"You don't have to do that, Mom," I said, knowing how much she hated to drive on the expressway. "They're treating me really good here. I'm taking some medication for the depression, and I'm eating and sleeping lots better. Everyone here is really nice, too, especially Nurse Dolly," I said, turning in her direction. She was at her desk, pretending to ignore our conversation, but I knew she was listening.

"I want to come. And I know your dad will want to get there as soon as we can."

"You'll explain it to him then?"

"Of course."

"Be sure to tell him it's not anyone's fault. I just got into a bad state of mind and acted stupid. The good thing is I'm getting help and I'll be lots better now, especially since I've told you guys."

"I love you, honey," my mother said, crying once more.

"I love you too, Mom. I'm really, really sorry."

"Don't be getting yourself upset now. We'll be there as soon as we can. Can you give me directions where to go?"

"How about if you talk to Nurse Dolly. She can do that better than me."

We said our goodbyes, and I handed the phone to my Florence Nightingale, who had magically appeared at my side.

My folks arrived within two hours. My father was visibly shaken as we located a table in the visitors' lounge. He hugged me tightly, as more tears fell from my eyes. Pulling a hankie from his pants pocket, he handed it to me.

"You shouldn't be so silly, Geri. We love you very much!"

"I know, Dad," I said, doubtful he could understand.

"Do you think it would be better if I rented you a smaller apartment with a girlfriend? It might be less hectic for you, and you wouldn't have to try to find things with so many people living under one roof."

I squeezed his hand, realizing he was looking for simple answers to problems that could be easily fixed.

"No, Dad. That's not it. I just got depressed about my vision, that's all."

"But honey, you need to think good things about yourself. You're so bright and pretty. Maybe you could say some prayers, and God will help you realize how good life is."

A surge of anger made me grip his hand harder, followed by guilt for feeling annoyed. *Where is my strong capable father?* I asked in my head, as I hugged his frail bony frame. *He has become so pitiful*, I thought, remembering how he used to talk to me so knowingly. *He could do anything, and now he seems so weak!*

"You have to think of the good things, Geri."

"I know," I said, deciding I had to help him.

"I think I got upset because Professor Powers told me he wouldn't accept that A I got in the Braille class," I said, offering him a tangible explanation for my actions.

"What do you mean he wouldn't accept that A?" my father asked, anger clearly present in his voice. As I relayed the event leading up to my suicide attempt, I was glad I had been able to think of a problem that was more concrete. Going blind was definitely not it.

"Why do they have that man teaching at that school?" he shouted, pounding his fist on the table. Silently I rejoiced at my successful tactic to defocus my father from the real issue. Now he had someone to be mad at.

"I know!" I agreed. "I probably would have been okay if he hadn't kicked me out of his class that morning. I guess I just lost sight of things for a bit there, Dad. I promise, I'll never let that happen again. I promise!"

"Well, we still need to keep talking about other things, though," my mom said reassuringly, setting my mind at ease.

"We will, Mom." I winked at her, glad we were on the same wavelength.

By the end of their hour visit, I was exhausted. I had come to realize in those moments, my mother had now taken the role of the wise one. Together we had parented my father, who kept insisting on giving me money for phone calls and offering to run out and buy me snacks for later, just in case I got hungry in the middle of the night. I did agree to take one of his offerings however. Before they left, I reached out my hand to return his handkerchief.

"No, Geri," he said, patting my hand. "You keep it, just in case you need it." As I held the reassuring rag tightly in my fist, Dad slipped his hand over mine, squeezing it tightly. Despite his fragile condition, I felt the strength of his love and wished I could hold on to this moment forever. Instinctively I knew the memory of this precious exchange would have to suffice, however. At least I've got his hankie, I thought, consoling my aching heart. After all, this handy cloth had soothed many a sad moment. Without a doubt, it was the connecting symbol of our love.

Chapter 33

Unexpected connection

January 1975

Days 14 through 21

Although my visit with my parents rekindled our relationship, it magnified the fact that I was on my own. I knew there was no going back to childhood, to feeling safe and secure in the arms of invincible caregivers. I'd already figured out this fact of life, but the meeting with my folks seemed to make it truer. A renewed depression set in.

For the next few days, I isolated myself in the corner again, avoiding activities and people. Even Dolly's jovial affection could not shake me from my forlorn state. On the third day, however, she took charge of my despondent mood.

"Look there, missy," she said squeezing my shoulder. "You've had a very normal setback, and I've let you slide for a bit. But you gotta play at least one game of bingo tonight, or I'll never bring you a warm blanket again for as long as I live."

Following her prescription, I reinvolved myself with Sophie and the others, and within a couple more days, the depression lifted. One evening, as usual, the announcement for visitors came over the PA. The patients expecting their loved ones started filing to the lounge.

"Hey, missy!" Dolly said.

"Yeah?"

"You've got a man caller."

"Who is it?" I asked.

"Secret admirer, I guess. Asked me not to give his name. Nice lookin' fellow, though. I wouldn't pass him up if I were you," she said, giving me a warm smile and a wink.

"Come on, I know they've gotta tell you guys who they are."

"Mum's the word on this one. I promised," she insisted.

Curious now, I got up to find who it was. When I walked into the room, a man's voice said, "Hi, Geri." I went over to where I heard it. I immediately recognized the man sitting at the table. A large fast food drink sat in front of him.

"Dave!" I said, surprise evident in my tone. I hadn't seen him since he'd been ousted from the Help Line. Shortly after he started, the Crystals of the place told him there weren't enough shifts available. Knowing this was not true, I figured they couldn't accept a former frequent caller working beside them as their equal.

"Hope you don't mind me coming to see you," he said in his slow deliberate way.

"Uh, no," I said, struggling to hide my disappointment. It was Cliff or Ted I had hoped to see waiting in the lounge. Without getting up, Dave looked at me and continued.

"I heard about your suicide attempt," he said, nervously clearing his throat. "I've been worried about you. I wanted to come right away, but I know the rules."

I hesitated to speak. I too was still uncertain about this guy. He gave a nervous cough, clearing his throat once again. "Uh, yeah…I've been here a couple of times myself. It can be a good place for us when life gets overwhelming. They treating you okay?"

"Uh, oh ya, really well," I said, watching Dave play with his straw.

"Ain't Dolly great?"

"So that's why she could keep who you were a secret!"

"Yeah, Dolly and I are good friends," he said proudly, putting the straw's end up to his mouth. Dave continued to speak in his slow monotone style, the slight upturn in his tone telling me he was excited. Though I shamefully shared the mindset adopted by some Help Line staff, I found his visit rather intriguing.

"She's invited me to her house a few times to talk about books and philosophy. She's very well read, did you know that?"

"No!" I said, fascinated that a nurse on a psych unit would fraternize with patients after discharge. "It's okay for her to do that?" I asked.

"Sure. I mean, I suppose she could get in trouble if I complained, but Dolly never got into that rule stuff. Huh," he said, giving one of his trademark chuckles. "Dolly's pretty hip you know. She believes in her right to see patients once they're civilians. Huh! Imagine me a civilian. Funny, I guess I still think of myself as an eternal patient."

I stared at him, deciding I thought of him that way too. Once again his dichotomous nature confused me. I couldn't tell if I liked him or not. He was so odd, yet so honest.

"Wanna sit down?" he asked, tapping the table top with his makeshift wand.

"Oh, sure," I said, sliding out the chair near the window. I felt glad for Dave's company despite my uncertainty.

I glanced at the city beyond the window pane. The early winter night was speckled with golden squares and lines, the result of lit up office windows and street lamps. I felt myself relax with the warm glow of this scene. There was something about it which made me feel safe, allowing me to engage with Dave more freely.

Initially he asked me lots of questions about why I tried to kill myself. I was amazed at how little trouble I had answering him. I took my turn gathering my own information about him, learning more about his hospital stays and how Dolly had been the real therapist. Though I didn't mention anything about the light inside my head, I was well aware of it as he talked about his experiences with inner visions. He explained how he had to learn to tell the difference between visions caused by his disease and images which kept him going.

"Did you ever think about how you don't do anything without imagining it first?" he asked, placing the end of the straw in his mouth, blowing air through it while he waited for my answer.

"I'm not sure what you mean," I replied, weaving my hair in and out between my fingers. He mimicked the gesture of smoking, pulling the long tube away from his lips just far enough to be able to speak.

"I'm talking about how people think of what they're going to do prior to doing it, even before they get out of bed." Dave inserted his pacifier back into his mouth.

"I guess so," I said. "Do you mean like how I think about what I'm going to wear before I put it on?"

"That's right!" he mumbled, chewing on the end of his stick, a tiny hint of inflection in his voice. I had the distinct impression he was pleased with my ability to understand. Oddly enough, this gave me pleasure. My favorable reaction made me nervous however, evoking an urge to counter him.

"But we all do that! You can't say people think of everything they do ahead of time, you know."

Transforming his straw into a baton, he began directing his words as he spoke.

"Huh, of course we do. We're just not conscious of it," he said, sitting up straighter, marking each word by tapping his cheek with the straw as he spoke. "But we don't just think about it. We picture ourselves acting out whatever we do first. When you wake up tomorrow, be conscious of your thoughts and what you picture in your mind. Not only will you think about what you are going to wear, but you'll see yourself in it. You'll even be able to envisage how you look when you pull the covers off you, sit up, and step one foot on the floor."

"Really?" I said, feigning no knowledge of what he was saying, yet wondering if he saw moving slide shows in his head like I did. "So what's so big deal about that anyway?"

He cleared his throat. Leaning back, projecting an image of confidence, he said, "Well Ger, if you can't imagine yourself doing something, then you won't do it. People who get dementia, they have a heck of a time doing anything because they don't visualize much. If they do picture something, there's so much confusion, they're often stifled and end up just sitting there, like a vegetable." He gave another one of his half hearted chuckles. "But who knows, maybe vegetables have imaginations and we just don't know it!"

"Come on," I said, asserting my own sense of wisdom. "Vegetables don't have consciousness."

"How do you know?" he said, smiling. "Buddha says they do."

"Well, Buddha thinks we come back through reincarnation too," I countered. "Did you ever think that we might?"

"Heck, no. That would be impossible."

"Ever hear the term, ontogeny recapitulate phylogeny?"

"No, what does it mean?"

"Well, it refers to evolution. A zoologist named Ernst Haeckel, way back in 1866 proposed this theory about human development. He believed that human embryos go through all the same stages of every life form until they reach gestation.

"Really?"

"Yeah, if you compare the images of human development with the pictures of advancing species, they look similar. Ernst proposed that the progression moved from a fish, then a salamander, tortoise, a chick, a pig, a calf, and even a rabbit before life reached human form.

"Far out! I did notice how at one point a fetus looks an awful lot like a tadpole," I offered.

"I should tell you that Haeckel's theory was disproven for the most part, but it doesn't take a scientific proof to dispute that a sperm and an egg start out looking an awful lot like an amoeba, and then a lot of aquatic species as it goes through its changes."

"Wow! Never thought of it before, but that doesn't mean there's reincarnation."

"Well, you're probably right about that, Ger," Dave said, sucking air through his straw. "But you have to admit, life is pretty amazing when you think about it, you know. I mean it sounds just as crazy when you consider how two little microscopic cells come together and in nine months, you got a whole person."

I had to agree with him. I thought about the momentary discovery I'd made the other night with Sophie. If I applied the theory that God is love and that God's existence is expressed through light, which in essence, is energy, it made sense that the miracle of birth could take place as the energy of two people came together through love.

"Truth is stranger than fiction," he said, shifting forward in his seat. He methodically replaced the straw into the lid of his cup and took a drink, slurping the liquid like a child. "Ah," he said, momentarily engrossed in the experience of the taste.

When he completed his mission, he returned to the topic at hand.

"Think about electricity," he said, leaning forward, both arms curled up tightly against his chest, hands folded down into his wrist, looking similar to how babies hold their arms when they sleep. Despite the childish pose, Dave's face looked as if he was preparing to disclose some very adult information. "And the atom. I mean the smallest element, unable to be seen, can be split in two to make atomic bombs that can blow up the world."

"I know," I said, still twisting my hair, fear shuddering through me as I thought about such a dastardly invention.

"And then there's all the far out plants and animals produced on this planet," he said, looking down at his drink as if he might see them all in there. "Huh. Who knows what else is out there in the universe?" A closed lip smile crossed Dave's face as he sat back and stared up at the ceiling.

I couldn't help drink in the words which matched my own fascination with life as I gazed out the window and took in the view. This time it looked different as I thought about the vastness of space. *How did we ever come to be able to light up an entire city like this?* I asked myself.

"Humans are pretty amazing," I finally said. "To come up with figuring out electricity, running wires from wheels turned by rivers? Heck, I can't even understand how a light switch works," I said, marveling at the endless string of lights outlining the streets below. "And the buildings…I mean look at that tall one off in the distance. How'd we ever get all that brick twenty stories in the air?" My thoughts now racing with enthusiasm, I expounded on other great feats of accomplishment. "What about the Empire State Building?" I submitted. Dave laughed.

"If you think that's amazing, what about the pyramids?"

"I know!"

"Those people made those structures with out any modern tools."

"How'd they do it?" I asked, wanting to know more.

We leaned into each other, securing our connection, as if we were preparing to share the secrets of the universe. In keeping with his style, Dave cleared his throat, indicating he was about to make a profound revelation. As he began to tell me the details of the makings of the pyramids, I sat transfixed, ingesting every word of his history lesson. He was able to answer my many questions, never making me feel as stupid as I felt, thanks to the education I didn't receive at That School.

Mesmerized by each subject evolving through our conversation, I was suddenly stunned when, out of the blue, Dave skipped over the social appropriate etiquette he had disregarded on our first face-to-face meeting, and blurted out one of his intrusive questions.

"So you can see that building out there?"

Surprised by my lack of annoyance, I simply answered, "Yeah."

"That's pretty good, Ger. If you can see that, why can't you see something right in front of you?"

"I can only see it because it's lit up at night. In the daytime it would blend in with everything in the vicinity. Even if the building stood all by itself against the sky, the sun just makes a wash of things."

"But that's a good five miles away," Dave said, once more playing with his straw.

"I know. My vision don't make no sense," I assured him. "Not only can't I see any real detail on that building, but if I didn't know from past experience that it is a building, I wouldn't be able to tell. So much has to do with lighting, environment, situations of reference and other conditions, and I can't even know when I will see something and I won't."

"But you can see my face, right?"

"Yeah, at least here, sitting down, in this lighting with neither of us moving. There are times—"

But before I could expound any further on this subject, the bell ending visiting hours rang. An unexpected wave of disappointment hit me, reminding me of times I was homesick. I was glad David beat me to the question of whether he could come again, giving me something to look forward to.

"Go on missy," Dolly called, pulling me from my thoughts. "Get out of here before those doors come back and squeeze the stuffin' out of ya."

The affection in her voice helped move me forward. As I took my final step through the exit to freedom, I remembered this was the day of my birth.

I'm still alive! I told myself smiling, feeling grateful for the loving ties which now anchored me to the world.

Chapter 34

The Domino Effect

February 1975

Help Line trainings on the aspects of suicide explain that once one attempts to take their own life, they become branded. Everyone watches their every move, afraid to let the individual out of their sight, treating them with kid gloves.

This is what happened to me. I suddenly could no longer be trusted. I became viewed as fragile, my every move observed. Mostly people around me walked on eggshells, and conversations were careful for fear of tipping me over the edge again. Not that I blamed my friends and family for such behaviors. I had terrified them, and now I had to pay the consequences. In truth, I was still rather fragile.

Little was said between Ted and me the day he picked me up from the hospital. He shared a few tidbits about work and school, avoiding any questions about what my past few weeks had been like. I gripped the handle of the door as the discomfort between us grew. I wanted to have him turn around and take me back, but I asked him if he'd stop at the drugstore instead. He very willingly agreed, offering to run in for me while I waited in the car. Though I would have preferred him not to know what medication I was taking, I decided if this was easier for him, I would swallow my pride and accept his offer.

As we neared Banana House, Ted explained there'd be nobody home as the guys all had school or work. He had to leave very soon as well, as he was filling in at the Help Line for Dean. I hadn't expected a fanfare, but the fact that there'd be no one to welcome me back, particularly on my birthday, hurt my feelings deeply.

I did receive a phone call within an hour of my return. My folks wanted to be sure I got home okay and wish me a happy twenty-third. My dad must have asked me twenty times if he could come down and bring me home for a while, but I kept insisting I would be fine.

Two more calls from my folks came in before the night was over. The impetus behind the contacts included whether I had my medication or enough money for food, about coming home next weekend for a delayed celebration, and the fact that I mustn't forget to watch a good movie playing on the television which would take my mind off things. I had to smile at their loving efforts, but I couldn't help feeling guilty every time I hung up.

The fourth and final call came from a Help Line staffer. To my dismay, it was from none other than Crystal. I thought I'd die when I heard her sickening voice, oozing with mollycoddling comments. Between being referred to as honey, sweetie, and poor thing, I had to ward off Crystal's insistence to come sit with me. She managed to sting me with her insinuations, suggesting my being in the psychiatric unit could keep me from future jobs, particularly if I wanted to do anything in the helping professions.

The remainder of my evening consisted of knitting the sweater I'd started in the hospital, and watching the movie recommended by my folks. Between Sigmund wanting to play with my yarn and trying to concentrate on the story, I ended up being unsuccessful with both. I finally gave up and went to bed, though my restless leg and overall anxiety made sleep difficult. Instead I tossed and turned, thinking of the likely misperceptions others had developed about me. I fretted most about how I would ever get people to trust me again. Thankfully, Dolly had set up an appointment with Jack the next day.

I wasn't in his office more than a minute, when the water works started.

"I can't handle it Jack," I sobbed.

"What is it you can't handle, Geri?"

"They won't talk to me. It's like nothing happened, but there is this atmosphere. I know they're avoiding me. George could only muster a hi when he came home last night, and then he went directly to his room. I'm certain Cliff came through the back so he didn't have to see me at all. Jeff did ask me how I was feeling, but when I said fine, he went into the kitchen, got some food, and headed upstairs. It's awful, Jack. I need to go back!" Grabbing some tissues from the box on his desk, I wept while I listened.

"Geri, going back to the hospital is not the answer. You've just been released, and it's going to take some time for you to regroup with everyone. You have to understand, you scared the hell out of these guys. They're likely still afraid for you, and probably downright mad. I'm sure they don't know what to think or say, so they're avoiding you."

I shook my head in agreement.

"It's going to be up to you to help them understand."

"But I'm too weak to help them. I can barely help myself."

"Are you feeling suicidal?"

"No," I admitted, certain I wouldn't ever try doing something so stupid again.

"Then you're a lot stronger than you think."

I listened.

"It's going to take some effort though. It's like a muscle that hasn't been worked for a while. Your ability to deal with stress is at a low, though you are doing it."

"What can I do to make it get better?" I said, sitting up straighter now, wiping the tears from my face.

"Well, you can't hurry time, but you can start talking. You're going to have to be the one who initiates conversations. If you wait for others to reach out, you'll probably be waiting a long time. If you can't think of what to say, do things that tell them you're better.

"Like what?"

He thought for a minute. "You could cook them one of those great spaghetti dinners I've heard about!" he said with a chuckle. "Or talk about something you did in the day."

"Well, that'll be a whole lot of nothing," I said, throwing my chin on my hand.

Having missed the first three weeks of the semester, school was not an option for something to do. I doubted whether I could concentrate anyway. Jack had already sent word through Dolly that he recommended I wait a while before going back to my shift at the Help Line. He said there had been pressure by the board to give me a leave of absence as it might be too stressful listening to the problems of others. *Like I haven't been hearing about such things on the psych ward*, I thought.

"First of all, you could join the encounter group I'm running. It meets twice a week."

"Wow, two hours in two days," I said, exaggerating my words.

"You could try to locate more babysitting jobs," he suggested.

"Yeah right. The whole world probably knows about where I've been. Nobody's going to wanna hire a crazy college chick to watch their kids. Heck, I might chop them all up in little pieces or something!"

"What's this attitude thing you're copping, Geri? It's not like you at all."

"I'm different Jack. Don't you know once you try to kill yourself, you realize what a terrible person you've believed yourself to be? It's hard not to let the attempt confirm you must have been right. I'm so angry I did it. I don't know why I just didn't start talking about the thing that's behind it all."

"And that is…" Jack urged.

I knew Jack was aware of what I'd disclosed in the hospital. One of the documents I signed was a release of information going directly to him.

"I'm sure you read how I finally admitted how upset I am about going blind."

"I also read you've lost quite a lot of vision in the past while."

"Yup," I said, tossing my hair back wildly, transferring my chin to my hand.

"That's pretty heavy stuff. All the more reason you should come to my group. If you don't learn how to communicate with people, you are likely to continue bottling your feelings up inside. That's when you'll get system overload, maybe want to hurt yourself again."

"I've got the meds this time, Jack. They help keep me from feeling too much, don't ya know," I said sarcastically.

"You angry with me, Geri?" Jack asked matter-of-factly.

His question caught me off guard. I didn't want to answer. I felt my face twisting as I shook my head no.

"You are. You're mad at me," he said, as if discovering a curiosity of nature.

I couldn't answer.

"Can you think why?" he asked, giving no consideration to the possibility his assumption was anything but fact.

I couldn't speak, despite the growing awareness of why the word "YES!" was locked behind my lips.

"I didn't get it!" he finally said, his dark brown eyes staring upwards as if telling some invisible person about his revelation. "You've been trying to tell me how sad and scared you are about going blind, but I never got it, did I?"

Quiet tears dripped off my nose and cheeks. I couldn't move. There was still so much pain. *Will it ever end?* I thought to myself as Jack continued to process previous conversations we'd had.

"I guess it was so obvious, I never thought to ask."

I nodded slightly.

"This is it, isn't it? And I'm not the only one who missed what you're going through, am I?" His eyes once again turned upwards as he conferred with his consultant on the ceiling. I let him go on. Something about his discovery helped set free a deep sadness. He was breaking down one more barrier to my isolation.

"You know, Geri? You carry yourself so well. I mean you present yourself as so capable, and you are capable, but at the same time, you kind of send a message that you don't need anyone."

I nodded in agreement.

"When I think about your situation from a common sense standpoint, I can see why you'd be devastated. Yet, at the same time, you work so hard to project the image you can handle anything."

"I know," I admitted. "Yeah…"

"I gotta hand it to you," he said, face turned upward again. "You're sure good at it, Geri. I consider myself fairly sharp at catching such hidden agendas with folks, but you certainly fooled me."

"Maybe 'cause you can't handle it either," I said, hoping to sting him with the truth.

You're no better than anyone else! I secretly told him, angry he didn't live up to my expectations.

A long silence followed. Eventually, Jack leaned forward in his chair.

"You know, you could be right! I too could have been avoiding dealing with the pain of your vision loss. It really is so hard to even conceive of not seeing, maybe I didn't want to go there."

I sat rigid, refusing to let his warmth penetrate my heart.

"You were counting on me, and I failed you."

I simply glared at him.

"I am sorry for that. I guess I'm not Superman as you hoped," he said apologetically. Rubbing his chin with his hand, he continued. "I'm trying to think back here, Geri." Another pause. "But you know, it seems like every time you come in, and I ask you how you are, you bring up all kinds of issues. Of course many of them are about your vision loss, but they have more to do with feeling inferior, inadequate, or your problems with Professor Powers, rather than you telling me how you feel about the actual loss itself."

"I know," I said, dropping my eyes downward. "It's the hardest thing….but there is nowhere to get all these feelings out!" I half shouted, looking back up at him. "I mean, it's not like there is some specific moment in which I realize I can't see something any more."

"Yeah, I get what you mean," Jack said, his face looking thoughtful, his dark eyes staring off in the distance.

"Besides, most folks just can't handle the devastation of someone saying, 'Oh my God, I can't see!'" I said, exaggerating the example, desperate for him to understand the impossibility of my situation.

"I hear what you're saying, Geri." A long silence followed. "You're right! There really isn't a good place or time to say something so devastating."

"I know," I said, sadness replacing the anger now.

"Though it certainly wouldn't be a good idea going around telling everyone the details of your experience, you certainly could confide in close friends or me, don't you think?"

"It's too hard for you to hear, Jack! It's too hard for anyone to hear, even me!"

Jack rubbed his chin thoughtfully. After a long pause, he said, "Yes, I see what you mean."

"Besides, I'm so busy doing everything I can to be normal!" I said, stressing the last word. "And now I can't pull it off anymore." Once more tears began their journey down the pathway between the crevice of my nose and cheeks. "I'm so sick of crying about it though. I want it to be over! Sometimes I almost wish I were blind so I didn't have to worry about what it will be like any more."

"Yeah, I'll bet you do."

"My friend Linda, who's totally blind, always says she's the luckier of the two of us. She says she doesn't miss what she never had. I mean I'm glad I can see what a sunset looks like and flowers and all, but waiting for it to disappear is killing me." Once more the dam broke. I lowered my head in my lap. Covering my face with my hands, I wondered if the tears would ever end. But after a while, the water in the well turned to sludge, requiring a greater force to push the garbage from my soiled heart.

"I hate it Jack, I hate it!" I shouted, feeling my insides twist with the mixture of anger and sadness.

"I can hardly see folks' faces any more, unless it's in a specific lighting." More tears, then I blurted, "I get lost in places I've known for years. Oh God, I just can't handle it!" Choking sobs turned to weeping. I was grateful Jack let me cry for a while. Eventually his gentle voice spoke.

"You are a stronger person than you think, Geri."

I shook my head no.

"You are, but not for the reasons you think."

"What do you mean?" I asked through sniffles.

"Unfortunately, you've been under the impression that handling everything on your own means you're tough. As soon as it becomes too overwhelming, you become angry at yourself, think you're a failure, and that you don't deserve to live."

I considered his words. "I don't know how to be any different though. How can I hate going blind and not hate myself?"

"You have to believe that no matter what happens to you, you are okay."

"And how do I do that?" I said, working to regain some composure.

"By being nice to yourself. Believe that you need time to heal. Don't push yourself so hard. Say nicer things to yourself in your head."

"How can I do that, when everyone around me avoids me?"

"You need to learn to express your thoughts and feelings with the right people, and stop worrying about what others think. If you can do that, life will get easier. Though you certainly have some loss to grieve and will for a time to come, I believe it is your isolation that is your greatest enemy."

Considering Jack's notions, I blew my nose, sat up straight, and asked, "When is the group?"

"It meets Tuesday and Thursday from four to six. Since tomorrow is Thursday, you won't have to wait long. In the meantime, start talking to those boys, whether they want to talk to you or not. You know…" he said, pausing to organize his new idea. "It might not hurt to start with an apology. Somehow acknowledge the scariness of the situation those guys found themselves in. If you can speak about the elephant in the room, the rest will come more easily."

I thanked Jack and agreed to see him the next day at the group. When I got back to Banana House, I started pulling out the ingredients for chili. Realizing I needed more chili powder, I forced myself to walk to the grocery. Despite the anxiety I felt, I managed to get through the chaos of the snow and to the store. When I entered the establishment, I went right to the counter and asked if the clerk could find the powder for me. She happily obliged. On my way home, I concentrated on holding my head high, making proper wide sweeps with the cane, pretending like it didn't matter how I looked to the world.

I was home in no time. Feeling a bit stronger from my brave action, I made the chili and sat down in the living room to knit while I waited for someone to come home. I hoped having a dish that could be served any time would prevent me from feeling disappointed if my roommates had other plans.

Eventually Ted walked in.

"Got some chili for ya if you want it," I called to him as he headed up stairs to his bedroom.

"Great, be down in a minute. I'm starved and it sure smells good."

Immensely relieved at his interest, I headed to the kitchen to be sure everything was in order. Minutes later, Cliff came in as well. He too agreed to join us. Before I knew it, George was home and except for Jeff, we were all sitting at the dining room table eating. My stomach was so knotted up, however, I could hardly bring myself to eat. Outside of a few comments about their day, little was said. Remembering Jack's words, I finally mustered up the guts to speak.

"I don't quite know where to start," I said tentatively, waiting for a reaction. There was a long silence. Deciding there was no turning back, I forged on. "I mean, I guess I want to tell you how sorry I am for putting you guys through...well, for scaring you all like that."

After another long pause, Ted simply said, "It's okay."

More silence. Only the clatter of spoons hitting bowls could be heard. I had the distinct impression they all wanted to finish and get away from me.

"It's not okay," I said. "Really, I know you must all be really mad at me, and I don't blame you one bit. But I feel so awful that no one seems to want to be around me."

The clinking stopped.

"It's not that we don't want to be around you, Geri, but I don't think any of us quite knows how to handle you," Ted replied.

I began to cry.

"I'm sorry," I said, starting to get up from the table. "I shouldn't be messing up your dinner like this."

"You don't have to leave, Geri," Cliff said standing and gently touching my arm. "It's just... well, it was just so scary to see you like that," he said, reaching his arm around my shoulder. Hesitantly, I leaned my head into his chest, afraid to trust his affection.

"Geri Geri Geri," he said, hugging and rocking me back and forth in his arms.

Tears welled up in my eyes.

George coughed nervously, then said, "Yeah, Ger. We're all worried about you. We're not quite sure what to say, ya know?"

"I know," I said, moving my head up and down in the crook of Cliff's arm.

"You got to promise not to do stupid stuff like that, Ger," Cliff said, pushing me back away from him. "You're my bud. Can't have my traveling partner doing things like that."

"I'm sorry," I said, hugging him tightly, realizing we were all afraid to say the dirty word, suicide.

Despite my roommates' willingness to hear me out, I sensed they felt awkward. I didn't like infringing on their easy going lives at Banana House. I decided they probably had had enough for now. I know I had. Jack said it would take time, so I decided to put an end to this scene. Releasing my grasp, I stepped away from Cliff.

"Thanks guys for listening. I want to tell you I'm not going to do that again. I promise, so you don't have to worry or walk on eggshells with me or anything."

"Well, we sure hope not," Ted said. "We love you, Geri, but it's been pretty freaky."

"I know. I realize I got to stop pretending I'm fine and dandy all the time."

"Yeah, Ger, you don't have to be Super Chick, ya know," George said.

"Thanks, George. I know." As I made my next promise, I hoped I could keep it. "Honest guys, I'm gonna do better about rappin' to the right folks if I'm upset, instead of holding it all in." Though part of me wanted to share more about the cause of my desperate act, I decided I still could not talk about my impending blindness. I felt like I'd be forcing my Banana House buddies into a therapy session.

George stood and started toward the kitchen to put his dishes away. When he passed me, he reached out and gave me a squeeze. I returned the gesture, neither of us saying a word.

"Well, I'll be the bottle washer," Ted announced, picking up his dishes.

"I don't mind cleaning up guys. Really!" I insisted.

"Nope, you did the cooking, I'll do the cleaning." And he headed for the sink.

"Well, I gotta go study for an exam," Cliff said, giving me one last hug and heading to his room. I did likewise, turning on my stereo and placing a Moody Blues album on the turntable. Flopping on my bed, I listened as they sang the words to In Search of the Lost Chord.

Well, it was a start, I thought, closing my eyes and hoping it was the right one. Automatically, I looked upward inside my head. There it was, the little light I'd spoken to Sophie about. Its solid glow told me I'd done okay. Love was still within my reach.

Chapter 35

When It's Least Expected

April 1975

"Can you believe it? I can hardly believe it!" I announced, rushing through the back door of Banana House.

"What's up?" Ted asked, cutting me off at the path to the living room.

"Is Cliff here?"

"Yeah."

"Cliff's gotta hear this too!"

"Hey Ger, what's on your mind?" Cliff said, stepping out of his room.

"You guys will never guess!"

"Come on, spill the beans!" Ted said, tugging on one of my braids.

"You'll never guess who's retiring!"

"Jack?" Cliff asked, likely thinking about his job as adviser to the Help Line.

"I sure hope not," Ted countered.

"No, not Jack," I said, feigning annoyance.

"Then who? Stop keeping us in the dark," Ted urged, pulling my other braid now.

"None other than—Professor Powers!"

"All right!" Ted said, gripping me around my waist and lifting me in the air, barely getting my feet off the ground. Grasping his shoulders, I kissed him on the top of his curly head.

"Well, that's one way to skin a cat," Cliff laughed. "Boy oh boy, good old Professor Powers, kicking the department head bucket."

With my feet now back on the ground, it was Cliff's turn to hug me.

"God, I just can't believe it! I have waited for something like this for so long."

"Too bad you didn't get your grievance passed though," Ted remarked.

"I know, but honestly, I was beginning to think that would never happen. I ran right over to talk to Professor Dowmis. He's gonna be the new acting department head, and he said he's willing to sign the waiver, accepting my A from Detroit. I am so happy to be able to enroll in my methods classes and get the heck out of this university."

"Don't you have to student teach?" Cliff asked.

"Yeah, actually I gotta do two years of it. One in a Special Ed class for the blind and one in regular Ed, but I'm gonna love it! It's what I've been itching to do all this time."

"Far out!" Ted remarked.

"Yuppy! I can finally look forward to graduating in spring of '77."

"Right on, Geri girl!" Cliff said, pinching my cheeks as he always did.

"Well, I gotta head over to the center," Cliff said. "I'll catch you later."

A painful twinge pulled at my gut at the mention of the Help Line. I still had not returned. Except for Crystal, none of the phone staff or my para-pro colleagues had contacted me. I'd seen many of them around, but there was no mention of how I was doing or when I'd be back. The rejection was very painful. The place which once pulled me from depression and loneliness now evoked similar feelings. What would Mike think? I wondered, trying to imagine what he might be doing. Would he have reacted to me in the same manner? I asked myself, thinking about the rumors that had evolved out of my suicide attempt. As much as I wanted to go back to the phones, I figured for now I would avoid the place.

Although things between my roommates and I were better, I still felt a strain between us sometimes. I made myself scarce when the guys' girlfriends came to the house. Whether they intended to or not, I perceived condescension in their voices whenever they bothered to communicate with me. Friday night spaghetti dinners had stopped. I only cooked for the guys during the week now.

With time on my hands, I became more involved with the RDS, the Rights of Disabled Students group on campus. My grievance against Professor Powers had not been the only discriminatory action by university staff. Many physical barriers for wheelchair users and those with ambulatory impairments had made it impossible for some students to attend classes. Requests had been denied by university administrators to change instruction to buildings without steps or to move them from upper floors to ground level whenever elevators were not available. Deaf students were dealing with professors who failed to make written copies of their lectures or who refused to face the individuals so they could lip read. It was university policy to give extra time on tests for those requiring such an accommodation, but some instructors simply rejected the regulation, saying it was reverse discrimination not to allow equal time for everyone.

When I initially joined this group, I struggled with becoming too involved. I feared being perceived as one of those poor people who could only spend time with others who were visibly disabled. With the help of Jack and the group, my sense of being okay with myself improved, allowing me to discover the beauty of comradery with those who shared similar problems.

Between working with the RDS and babysitting for Joan and Tim and a few other professors who never heard a word about my emotional fiasco, I continued attending Jack's encounter group twice a week. Slowly but surely, I learned I did not have a corner on the market for having problems and gained a lot of support from members.

I transferred my increased tolerance to my parents, becoming more appreciative of my mother than I had ever been. Neither of us kept our promise about addressing my impending blindness, but the strain which used to hover

over our conversations evaporated. I went home to visit them more often, which made my dad very happy. He seemed to relax more, trusting I truly was doing better. His weakening condition scared the hell out of all of us, however. With all the bravery I could muster, I accepted my new role as parent toward him, providing comforting words and listening to his concerns whenever I could.

"Well, I'm heading out in about an hour," I called to the guys. "I'll make some soup and you boys can grab it whenever you want."

"Mmm! Sounds good!" Ted said, climbing the stairs.

"I'll get some when I get home tonight, Ger," Cliff said, the door slamming behind him.

After chopping vegetables, I threw them into a pot of water along with some spices and called my folks to give them the word about Professor Powers' timely decision. Needless to say they were pleased with the news. When I hung up I readied myself for my next undertaking. With a chill in the air, I pulled my jacket off its hook and threw it over my plaid shirt and jeans. I took my cane from the closet and headed out the door.

As I walked, I thought about the venture I'd been drawn to by a force I had no name for. I feared I might be gravitating toward it for the wrong reasons. Accepting it fully would be in opposition to what I fought against for my entire life. At the same time, I realized my goal to fit into the norm had not done me justice. In fact, it almost cost me my life.

In the two long lonely months following my release from the psychiatric ward, partaking in this endeavor satisfied a hunger I'd ached to fulfill since entering my grownup years. It contained many characteristics which my father displayed to me when he'd help me through a bout with Karen Worster or the loss of my very best friend. I felt soothed and satisfied as I gambled with this new undertaking, but I knew that if I plunged into this affair completely, I would have to leave many facets of my life as it existed.

As I neared my destination, I once more questioned whether I should be doing this. Why do I feel like a teenager sneaking behind my parent's back? I asked myself. You'd think I was stealing away to The House in Davidson, for heaven's sake!

Tapping my cane swiftly down the sidewalk, I drank in the smells of spring. The pungent odor of wet earth and soggy old leaves filled my nostrils. Several times I had to skirt around the pathway as the tip of my cane splashed water from puddles.

It won't be long before the flowers will be out, I thought. I looked up and gratefully caught sight of pale pink fingers reaching out from a cluster of gray clouds. A hint of warmth touched my cheek and I wondered how long I would be able to see such a view. *Well, you'll certainly always be able to feel it.* I reassured myself, smiling as I walked.

"Hi, Ger!" The voice near the river called.

"Hi, there!" I replied, cutting across the grass of Riverside Park to where I heard the voice. The smell of a cigarette wrinkled my nose as I neared.

"Like your braids," David said, a smile in his voice.

"Thanks."

"You always look so nice, Ger," he said, as he slowly brought what I assumed was his cigarette hand up to his mouth.

"You're too nice, David," I said, enjoying his pleasure at looking at me, but wishing he wouldn't smoke.

"Sit down," he said. I inched my way forward, sliding my cane thoughtfully in front of me, not wanting to fall over the edge of the bank. Recognizing my concern, David used a stone to tap the big rock he was perched on so I could find the spot. I laid my cane down on the ground and carefully felt with my hands, situating myself on the granite slab overlooking the water. With the river two stories below my dangling feet, I felt a thrill rush up my spine. I still like being high, I thought, glad to know this was a natural one, even though it certainly had potential for danger.

"Don't you just love the river?" David asked, starting another round of smoking.

"I know!" I said, the sound of babbling water easing me into repose. As I listened, the cascading stream outlined the rocks and boulders so amply positioned by nature's hand.

"This is how you find Nirvana," he said, letting out a half hearted chuckle.

"What is it about water that is so soothing?" I asked, not expecting an answer.

"It's the sound of life. Didn't you know that?"

"Never thought of it that way," I said, turning my face to the sun. David gave the butt of his cigarette a toss.

The joy I gained from this action didn't last long, however, as his hand moved to his shirt pocket.

"Things can live without sun or heat or just about anything, but water is the common denominator."

"I guess you're right!" I smiled. "All I know is I love being near it. But it'd be a lot more enjoyable if you didn't keep polluting the air with your cigarette!" I said, slapping his arm in a jovial manner.

"I won't light this one, okay?" he assured me, chuckling. "Just have to have something in my hands, Ger."

"Sounds good to me," I said, giving him an approving look. Leaning back against my palms, I caressed the soggy terrain with my fingers. I thought about how I'd need to wash the dirt from my fingernails and then Professor Powers came to mind.

I shared my news about his resignation. As I expected, David appreciated my relief. Somehow my excitement mixed with leftover resentments soon became insignificant. Instead, the calming atmosphere of the environment filled me with a sense of peace.

This was not the first time David and I had spent an afternoon mesmerized by this awesome scene. Even before the snow fully melted we'd been coming here, engaging in discussions about the beauty of nature.

I had reconnected with David after joining Jack's group. I was rather surprised to find he was a member. He'd enrolled in a math class he could have taught with his eyes closed, just so he could have access to the counseling center. Initially I resisted his requests to get together after group meetings. His continued insight mixed with kindness eventually pulled me to him like a gravitational force. His knowledge of life and his ability to speak freely about spiritual matters was refreshing, even if parts of him still repulsed me.

By the time the snow cleared, we'd moved our visits from Big Bob's to the park. Our twice a week connections were boosted to almost daily after David acquired his parents' used car. Although I insisted we meet at the river, we were able to explore other facets of the city if the temperature became too chilly.

"So Geri, you want to come to my parents' cottage this weekend with me?" David asked, his voice now breaking through my meditative state.

His question took a minute to register.

"Uh, really? You want me to come with you?"

"Sure!"

"What about your folks?" I asked, uncertain if he had obtained their permission.

"They said you're welcome to come if you want," he assured me, replacing the unlit tobacco in his pocket. "I know I'd like you to come. I could show you where my favorite places are in the woods where I took my acid trips and discovered my inner self," he said, looking downward, picking vegetation from the ground.

"Why are you so preoccupied with tripping?" I asked, slightly concerned with his apparent obsession with this topic.

"Can't help it, Ger. I still wanna know what those Timothy Leary types got that I don't. How could they take all those drugs and not end up in the psych ward like I did? They're the cool people!" he said, exaggerating the last two words.

"Oh, David. You put way too much importance on being able to trip. You said yourself you got a disease that's genetic."

"I know, I know. So, you think you'll come then?" he asked, looking up at me for a moment, then returning his gaze to the river. The sun on his hair accentuated its rich caramel color. His distinguished chin and long nose gave him an almost pretty boy look. Though he didn't have the appearance I was typically attracted to, there was something appealing about him, particularly when he took on an air of boyish uncertainty. His inability to mask his thoughts and emotions in order to come off sophisticated or cool, were both repelling and endearing.

At the moment, his childlike hopefulness for me to agree to come along captured my growing affection for him.

I admit this emerging closeness to David puzzled me a great deal. During times of self-reflection I tried to analyze whether I might be attaching myself to him out of loneliness or because I genuinely liked him. As I listed the pros and cons of his personality, I realized David possessed many of the essential qualities I held in high regard. I couldn't help admire how he had survived through many horrific, torturous episodes of the mind that most people would never have a clue about. The only cons I could identify included how he walked, spoke, and presented himself in a manner atypical to the norm. As normal was a major item on my life's agenda, it weighed heavily against my decision to spend time with him. But David's acceptance of himself was very appealing. He would never allow another's rejection to crush his spirit. I found this strength of character attractive and hoped it might rub off.

"Of course I'd love to go with you!" I said, touching his arm affectionately.

"Really?" he replied, a big crooked grin crossing his face. "My mom said we should ride with her and my dad."

"I'll be ready," I said, smiling back.

"So we'll pick you up at Banana House at eight on Saturday?"

A twinge of anxiety fluttered through my stomach. It made me hesitate.

"You don't want your buddies to know, do you?"

"It's not that," I said, trying to deny the embarrassment I still harbored about being seen with him. "I mean, pick me up at eight then."

"Really?" he said, sounding as excited as David could sound.

"Really," I agreed.

"Gee, Ger that's a big step for you, telling your friends you're hanging out with a schiz-o-phrenic," he said, drawing out the last word as he often did.

"Oh David!" I said annoyed, slapping him again on the arm. "Stop referring to yourself as that. You've got the most important characteristic of all."

"What's that?" he asked.

"Integrity!"

He smiled, chuckling at the notion. "You think so, Ger?" he asked innocently. My annoyance disappeared as I was once more drawn to him.

"I don't care what kind of disease I've got. Having you sitting next to me makes everything worthwhile."

I looked into his face. His warm smile touched my heart as I leaned toward him.

"Can I kiss you?" he asked, breaking the spell. I looked down at my knees in an attempt to hide my frustration. *Why does he always have to speak the obvious?* I thought.

"I guess not," he said.

"David, why do you have to say everything? Why can't you just let things happen?"

"Gee, I don't know, Ger. I've never been good at the social stuff. Even before my schizophrenia, I never got all that subtle amenity stuff my mom use to get after me about."

With no warning, I reached up and grabbed his shoulders. Pulling him close, I tipped up my chin and planted a kiss firmly on his lips. At first it felt awkward, but as David's surprise turned to affection, our natural bodily reactions did the rest. Though it was not a kiss of passion, I felt a warm glow emanate through my body. When our lips parted, David let out a boyish chuckle.

"That was nice, Ger," he said. I snuggled in close and we hugged each other for a very long time. Like magic, all the stiffness which made David seem robotic and unapproachable disappeared. Instead, I felt very comfortable as he cradled my head in his hands, stroking my cheek. As the two of us sat listening to the endless sound of the river, it felt as if we'd done this thousands of times before.

With my ear to David's chest, I couldn't help thinking of our encounter almost three years ago. I could now read his books of poetry, which were still stored in my closet. Remembering how disdainful he had appeared to me then was almost too weird to comprehend. I never would have expected to be sitting here in his arms listening to the beat of his heart. Like the river below, it pumped love freely into mine, and together we surrendered to the flow of life's journey.

Part III

Chapter 36

Revolving Doors

August 1975 to October 1976

    This year turned out to be a pinnacle year for me. My trip to David's family cottage was followed by many more. Exploring his childhood playground brought us even closer together as we expounded on the topic of metaphysics and other practical matters of life.

    When the summer came to a close, the residents of Banana House dispersed, ending another chapter of my life. With no one to share an apartment with, I invited Sigmund to join me and we moved into a little efficiency I found on Normal Street. Unfortunately, Sigmund must have missed his old stomping grounds as he took off one day shortly after we arrived. Luckily I found a replacement soon afterwards when a little black pup wandered into my life. I named her Jinxy on Sigmund's behalf, even though she was anything but a curse.

    September rolled around, and I began my student teaching under Mr. Sulvai, who just happened to be blind. He was not only insightful but lots of fun, teaching me that he could do anything but see. He was well aware of Professor Powers and his discrimination, which included refusing to allow university students to practice teach under him. I would be his first after a nine year ban during Professor Powers' tenure as department head.

    Throughout my busy days, David and his Old English sheep Dog, Fella, visited Jinxy and me regularly. Sometimes he'd read to me or help me with an art project I was making for the kids at school. Whatever we did, our four-legged companions always made sure we took a trip to the river. Daily visits turned to overnights and by November the four of us became a family.

    Our confidence grew as David and I shared the events of our day. I'd tell him about my concerns for continued segregation of blind kids in the schools, and he would try to explain to me some math proof he was working on. I gained more knowledge about how a totally blind teacher managed a classroom, and David gained friendships through contacts he made with math department professors. They'd hang out at Hungry Jack's, a restaurant next to Big Bob's, talking numbers and reviewing David's work of finding proofs for equations that no one had yet solved.

Though I never did experience the passionate longing for David I saw portrayed on the big screen, my fondness for him grew. He was truly committed to me. While my Banana House friends fell away and the Help Line happily went on without me, I became more convinced what I felt for David might be what love was all about.

My concern for normalcy still haunted me, however. Though I tried not to let it bother me, I found myself in deep conflict whenever the age old question about my new boyfriend was posed. "So what does he do?" was the first question out of everyone's mouth. At times I was tempted to say, "Oh, nothing!" but I ended up skirting the issue by jumping into comments about David's impressive achievements. I always made sure to emphasize his near completion of a PhD in algebraic topology at Berkeley, in hopes this might give him more validity. Except for my family to whom I was able to explain David's situation in more detail, weaving in the important attributes like kind, loving, helpful, thoughtful, and committed, most folks ended up thinking he was all a blind girl could get. At least this is what I imagined them to think, wondering it myself at times. But the qualities David possessed were exactly what I needed. Being able to hold down a job and bring home a paycheck would have been welcome, but David did not have the necessary stamina required for a forty hour per week job. If he worked part time, he'd not only lose his Social Security check, but also his government medical insurance, essential for his medical treatment.

I was amazed at how accepting my folks were toward David. They were not happy about us living together, however. In December, David and I decided to appease our tradition minded parents and headed down to the courthouse to purchase a marriage license. Much to our dismay, we learned the government believed two could live for the price of one. If we tied the knot, we'd be tying our money belts as well. Our two $300 Social Security checks would be promptly reduced to $50 more than half the amount of our total income. Saying "I do" would mean we don't get life's necessities.

Though slightly disappointed, David and I were practical. We believed in the bond of the spirit and not the approval of a justice of the peace. Unfortunately our parents did not view such commitments the same way we did. David's folks were bothered by our state of affairs, but mine were really upset. Although they understood about David's mental health limitations, they insisted I could not live in sin. Again, my father and I bantered about right from wrong, me begging him to understand our situation. I finally gave up hope for their blessing, agreeing not to sleep with him when we visited their home. Thankfully, time and experience have a way of helping ease things, and eventually they adjusted to our new lifestyle.

The remainder of the school year turned out to be relatively uneventful. I completed my student teaching under Mr. Sulvai, and in September of 1976, began my last year of practicum in a general education classroom.

This experience required a bit more ingenuity on my part, as I needed a lot more preparation to obtain and provide information in print format. It took many hours after school working with a reader to transcribe lessons into Braille or to create visual aids and displays. Unfortunately, David was becoming more preoccupied in his mind with math and mental phenomenon, so I had to scramble to find other human resources. By the end of the first month I was totally exhausted with all I ended up dealing with.

"Hey David?" I called to him after returning home from school one fall afternoon. As I worked to unjam the patio screen door of our new apartment, Fella and Jinxy anxiously pushed against it.

"Hang on, guys!" I affectionately scolded while I worked to get the door unstuck. Finally it gave.

"How ya doing, David?" I asked as Fella's big curly head pushed its way into my free hand. Jinxy followed his lead, jumping up on her hind legs to greet me.

"I got bad news."

"What's that?" I asked, bracing myself for his answer.

"The people upstairs…"

"Yeah?" Wishing I didn't have to hear this, I bent to hug both dogs.

"They're listening to me."

"What do you mean, they're listening to you?" I asked, looking at David huddled tightly in the red leather Lazy Boy his mother had given us for the new place.

"They're reading my thoughts, and they're laughing at me."

"No, they're not!" I insisted, walking to the dining room table and opening up the can of dog treats. Two wet muzzles poked at my hands. Simultaneously they gobbled up their tasty morsels and looked hopefully for more. Patting both of them on the head, I wondered how much attention, if any, they'd received all day.

"I told you yesterday I think you're only hearing their television," I reminded, walking into the kitchen to wipe my hands. I heard eight legs follow as I completed this effort and headed back into the living room. Both dogs bounded back to the door, indicating they needed to go out.

"Did you walk them today?" I asked.

"Sorry, Ger, I couldn't." Holding my tongue, I said nothing as I again fiddled with the screen. Once outside, both dogs promptly squatted, relieving their poor little bladders. I let them sniff as I worked to control the anger I felt for such neglect.

How much do I chalk up to his situation? I asked myself, dreading my return to the apartment.

When we did go back in, I sat on the turquoise couch across from David. Our decor wasn't exactly color coordinated, but it did have that thrown together look. Signaling the dogs with my hand to lay down at my feet, I stroked their backs as David's protests continued.

"No, Ger, you got to believe me," he said with desperation in his voice. "They're reading my mind!" I stared at the drawn looking figure across from me.

His large body looked so small tucked inside the confines of the overstuffed chair. I couldn't decide whether to be angry or feel pity for his idiocy. As I watched him drop his face into both palms, my heart softened, his gesture now reminding me of the time I needed to hide from reality.

The thought of the previous evening came to mind, explaining the exhaustion I now felt. For five nights David had not slept. Each evening he paced the long hallway between our back bedroom and the patio, wringing his hands and telling me how awful it was having the people upstairs monitoring his every thought.

"They think they're so cool," he said to me earlier this morning after waking me from a most needed sleep.

"Huh?" I asked, rubbing my bleary eyes with the knuckles of my hand.

"Those people! I can't let them win. Even though I have to go, Ger."

"You have to what?" I asked, trying to process what he was saying.

"I have to go, but I can't."

I reached over to the night stand and opened up the lid of my Braille watch.

"Where do you have to go? David, it's three in the morning!" I reminded him, feeling the two hands positioned at a forty-five degree angle.

"I have to go to the bathroom."

"Then go," I urged.

"I'm not gonna give those hip bastards the satisfaction of recording my bowel movements."

"But David, if you have to poop, then you should certainly do it!"

"I won't! I ain't gonna take a shit in front of those spies!"

As he spoke, I couldn't help notice the marked difference in how he delivered his words. David rarely used slang, and I no longer heard pauses or deliberations in his speech pattern. In fact, he spoke very rapidly, with a lot of emotion in his voice.

"What am I gonna do, Ger?" he demanded.

"I don't know David. You really need to use the bathroom if you have to go," I said, standing up now and rubbing his shoulder to calm him down.

"No!" he said, pulling away and marching down the hallway toward the living room. I started after him, the dogs now awake and attempting to rush past me. I quickly grabbed them both by the collar and returned them to the bedroom, closing them in. By the time I reached the screen door, David had already slid it open. I could hear him traipsing across the parking lot. The cracking sound of twigs breaking underfoot told me he was now entering the woods surrounding the complex. Silence followed. I resisted calling out to him for fear of waking our new neighbors. Holding my breath, I tried to think of what to do next.

Should I call the police? I wondered. What would I tell them? My mate ran away because he thinks the neighbors can hear him take a shit? Despite my distress, a forlorn smile formed across my lips. *Someday we'll laugh about this*, I assured myself, wishing that time would come soon.

After what seemed like an eternity, I could hear David's footsteps moving in my direction.

"David?" I called softly.

"Shush!" he said angrily. When he entered the doorway, I reached to give him a hug, but he roughly pushed me aside, bolting back to the bedroom. I shut the screen door and found him pacing, wringing his hands as he did so.

"You okay?" I asked.

"I fixed 'em," he said. "I took my shit in the woods."

"Good idea! Feel better?"

"I still think they might have heard me go out there."

"No, I don't think so," I said, humoring him. "You were pretty quiet."

I was quickly learning that in this state of mind, David could not be swayed. No matter how much I explained the impossibility of his beliefs, he could not shake himself from the nagging voices he now heard in his mind.

The recommendation to stop the meds came from David's psychiatrist when he began showing signs of tardive dyskinesia. This disorder was one of the potential side effects from psychotropic medication affecting two percent of the population who used the drugs. When David developed a dystonia, or muscle spasm, in his neck and tongue his psychiatrist immediately discontinued his chemotherapy. He said it would likely take two to three months for the symptoms of schizophrenia to show, a month for the blood levels to return to a drug free state, a month for the disease process to begin again, and a month before it reached its peak. David beat the clock. By eight weeks he was in a full blown psychosis. I had seen it in others, heard about it from David's mouth, but I believed David was intelligent enough to override what he knew were hallucinations. In my naiveté, I figured it wouldn't be too bad. I was wrong. Experiencing it first hand from a man who I considered to be brilliant was truly overwhelming.

Now, as I moved over to sit beside him on the arm of his chair, I wondered how much longer either of us could handle this nightmare.

"I need to go back to the hospital, Ger," he moaned into his hands. "I want to cry, but I can't. It's so awful, Ger. I just can't take it."

Wrapping my arms around his shoulders, hugging him hard, I tried once more to reason with him.

"David, you have to remember this is part of the disease. Don't you recall how you've told me it's all the schizophrenia playing with the synapses in your brain?"

"I know, I know, but that isn't what's happening now! Those people…they're hip, and they have that special kind of wisdom that allows them to see into my mind. I knew others like them at Berkeley. They smile at you, and make you think they're your friend, but then they laugh at you as they play with your head from a distance."

I wanted to cry. *What is happening to my mate, my friend?* I asked myself. My heart ached as I recalled how David had been the one to comfort me through bouts of depression. "This too will pass," he'd tell me as he gently rubbed my back and shoulders, sometimes for hours at a stretch. As I stroked David's hair, I desperately thought about ways to convince him his ideas were crazy.

As the days continued, so did the sleepless nights. Getting up in the morning at seven to make it to my teaching placement by eight became increasingly difficult. The further David slipped into his nightmare, the more depressed I became. It scared me how much I relied on him for my own sense of well-being. He seemed so strange and foreign to me, I hardly knew who he was.

Shamefully, I became aware of how much I still strove to be normal. Embarrassed and ashamed of my partner, I felt I couldn't tell anyone what was happening in my life, for fear they would not accept me. I didn't even let my folks know, certain they would suggest I leave him.

The longer I kept the secret of our situation, the more anxious I became. By the end of October, I couldn't manage the demands of school. I made up a story about being ill and asked my advisor to drop me from my student teaching assignment for the term, explaining I would return in January.

Shortly after I made this decision, I was ready to join David in his plan to check into the mental hospital. This is when I contacted Jack again. I had not seen him for well over a year, so I had to catch him up on my situation. Once again he reminded me how keeping secrets only created anxiety and depression. He encouraged me to talk more firmly with David's doctors to see if there might be another medication for him to try. His idea proved to be most helpful. When I described in detail how disturbed David had become, the psychiatrist immediately prescribed a new drug. In three months, David was almost back to his state of normal.

As this process took until spring of '77, I was unable to return to the university for the winter semester. My hope for graduating and getting on with my goal to teach and live on more than a pittance was once more postponed. It seemed the more I strived for normalcy, the more distant it became. Though it was hard at times, I did my best to focus on the love David, Fella, Jinxy, and I shared.

Chapter 37

Swinging doors

June 1977

In the midst of all the darkness a little gift of kindness happened my way. Like the saying goes, when you least expect it. In late March, I received a letter addressed to me from Canada, announcing I was the benefactor of $2,000 from my great aunt Grace. Although I never met her, she apparently had been moved by her niece's daughter's plight with going blind, so she made me a part of her will.

The only condition was that I use the money for traveling so I could see the world before the lights went out, so to speak. I had always wanted to explore new horizons, so I decided this was not the time to stand on principles. I strongly opposed the notion of disabled people soliciting alms or accepting financial discounts and sympathy gifts, but I figured there were exceptions to any rule. So instead of refusing to agree to "pity money" from someone who could no longer be educated on such discriminatory practices, I obliged her wishes. Accepting the fact I was an imperfect being who could not always live up to my own expectations, I happily made plans to travel by train across America without a hint of guilt. Though David was still not feeling his best, feeling a little leery about the whole idea, he did agree to accompany me.

After engaging each set of parents to doggy sit our pups, we hopped the Amtrak like vagabonds, carrying all we had on our backs in packs. Many details were out of sight for me, but I was quite able to absorb many of the more expansive views.

I was mesmerized by the muted hues of the Painted Desert, totally awed by a purple storm streaked with orange inside the Grand Canyon, found myself back in the land of psychedelica as the neon lights of Front Street in Las Vegas triggered the synapses of my brain, and mellowed as the sunset over the Pacific Ocean touched my soul. The last stop of our journey landed us at the ivied halls of David's alma mater. Thanks to his alumni status, we ended up in a dormitory at Berkeley paying nothing for our five day stay.

During the visit David took me down his memory lane, telling me about places he'd seen icons like Janice Joplin, Country Joe and the Fish, Ken Kesey, and others who were virtually unknown back then. He talked about his acid trips as we explored the botanical gardens and watched sunsets on San Francisco Bay. Despite the multitude of touring options, David's condition left him low on energy. He still experienced a bit of paranoia from passersby and constantly complained of visual distortions. I found myself feeling bored and lonely during his long afternoon naps. I came to realize on this journey how dependent I had become on David for getting around in unfamiliar areas. Even though I brought my cane, I kept it folded in my pack, still relying solely on his elbow for guidance.

As I sat in our dormitory room one afternoon while David slept, I found myself examining my continued need to pass as sighted. I wanted to go and enjoy the smell of the eucalyptus trees in the grove outside our door, but I worried about how I would find my way back. *You could always ask someone to help you*, I told myself, the mental image of me groping for a door and entering the wrong one quickly squelching my idea. *I hate having people think of me as incapable though*, I insisted. *Wouldn't it be neat to be on your own though?* I argued, trying to tantalize the independent side of my nature. *I can wait a while longer for David. It'll be easier*, I insisted, explaining this was a better choice in a foreign territory. But as I listened to the many youthful voices on the other side of our window, I couldn't stand being cooped up any longer. Before I could stop myself, I bolted upright, pulled my cane from the pack, double checked my pocket to make sure I had my key, and quietly slipped out the door.

I released the band from around the folded aluminum tubes and tapped my cane back and fourth, angry with myself for feeling ashamed. With little effort, I followed the cobblestone pathway for a short distance, located a bench and sat down. Breathing in the sweet smell of the eucalyptus leaves, I let out a sigh of relief. The aromatic scent mixed with the tinkling foliage made me feel like I was in the middle of a cough drop. As I absorbed the atmosphere, I overheard a person to my right talking on a phone. In a few minutes the receiver clicked and the sound of footsteps moved away. Suddenly, an idea came to me.

Getting up, I sauntered over to the area, trying to look nonchalant as I felt for the phone. I found it haphazardly nailed to a wooden pole and dropped a dime in the slot. I dialed in the universal 411, and waited for the information operator to answer. In a minute I had the number I requested. I hurriedly dropped another dime in and rotated the dial through the appropriate sequence of numbers, hoping in my excitement I hadn't mixed up the digits

"Hello?" the voice on the other end said.

"Mike, is that you?" I asked, my stomach fluttering, my knocking knees threatening to buckle out from under me.

"Yeah, who is this?"

"A voice from your past," I replied.

There was a short pause, and then, "Geri? Is that you?"

"Sure is! How ya doing?" I said, certain my knees would collapse beneath me any second now.

"Wow! Far out! How ya doing?" he asked.

"Really well," I answered, wondering if he would think so if he found out about my crazy mate sleeping his day away in the dormitory.

"And you? What are you up to?" I asked, sure he was probably some professor of philosophy or something by now.

"Hey man, I'm really really fantastic," he said. "So where you at?"

"Believe it or not, I'm here in Berkeley at the university."

"Wow, far out! Where are you staying?" I didn't want to tell him we were too poor to stay at a regular hotel so I said I had been strolling through the eucalyptus grove when I got the idea to call.

"I know right where you are. I'll be there in five. Don't move."

Without even a goodbye, I heard the dial tone in my ear. I found my way back to my bench as thoughts raced through my head. Twinges of anxiety rippled through my gut, as I scolded myself for being so hasty. *What am I doing?* I asked myself, hoping a half hour visit might make it possible for me to avoid mentioning my partner of two years. Though I knew David wouldn't care if I called Mike, I figured he might care about some of the old feelings now cropping up in my heart. *What if I had chosen to go with Mike?* I wondered, thinking about how warm and reliable he was. *He always said such wise things*, I recalled. *And he was so damn normal!* I twisted a lock of my hair as my apprehension grew.

What about my suicide attempt, the hospital stay, and being booted from the Help Line? Running my fingers over my jeans, I checked to be sure the cuffs weren't dragging on the ground. *At least I look okay*, I reassured, picturing myself in the v-necked navy t-shirt I wore. Tracing the outline of my buckled sandals barely covering my feet, I became doubtful. *They probably look cheap*, I decided, noticing a few cracks in the vinyl, wishing I could afford real leather. *He'll never notice*, I told myself. *Besides, Mike is very accepting, remember? But I'm so poor still. Haven't even graduated yet. Relax! There's no need to be ashamed of yourself. Seeing him again is what's important!* As I bantered back and forth, I absent mindedly pulled the dorm key from my pocket. Rotating its metal ring with my thumb and forefinger, my thoughts moved to the memory of our acid trip.

Suddenly, something occurred to me. *Where's the little light in my head?* I asked myself. *Why haven't I noticed it? Have I forgotten about the internal source of spiritual love?* I wondered, thinking about the conversation I'd had with Sophie so long ago. Striving to remember the last time I saw the twinkling star of my mind's eye, I closed my lids searching for its comforting glow. But the outside sun was too bright to allow for any distinction. Deciding this was not the time to ponder this question, I wondered how far away Mike might be. *You'd better look happy when he shows up!* I warned, quickly changing my thoughts to the excitement of seeing him again.

"Oh my God, you are so beautiful," came an old familiar voice. Instantly a smile spread across my face. Like a magnet and steel, we were drawn into an embrace. We rocked back and forth in each other's arms, moaning with "glad to see you" and "it's been such a long time." Finally, Mike pushed me back, holding me at arm's length.

"Let me look at you Ger! Man, you look so awesome. You know you haven't changed a bit!"

"Oh yes, I have!" I warned, reaching up and tugging on his beard which now hung to the middle of his protruding gut.

"Grown a little, haven't I?" he laughed.

"Hey, you look cuddlier than ever Mike," I said smiling. "I think it looks good on you." I half lied, still recovering at the unfamiliar feel of his body.

"Everyone says I look like a dark haired Santa Claus," he chuckled, pulling on his long scraggly beard. "Sit down," Mike commanded.

We found a spot on the bench. My cane rolled beneath my feet and I wondered if he had seen it.

"So how you been?"

"Good, and you?"

"I'm really well. And you?"

"I'm fine too!" I said, worried I looked anxious. We sat there smiling at each other, the awkward moment turning the knot in my gut.

"Wow, where do we start after all this time?" Mike said at last. He looked down at his lap, then chuckled. "I'll bet you're wondering about all this" he said, tapping his belly three times.

"No!" I lied.

"Ah, come on, just because we haven't seen each other, don't mean I forgot how you think, Ger."

Laughing now, my face reddened with embarrassment.

"Well, I guess I couldn't help notice," I said with a giggle, reaching over and rubbing his tummy affectionately with my hand, glad to experience his familiar nature. "More of you to love, that's all."

"That's right! That's exactly right. Geri, you have no idea how good my life has become since I came out here. I've really been able to let go and be myself."

"But Mike, you were always yourself! So much more than I was."

"I thought so, but now I know that was all part of the game."

"So, did you finish your graduate degree?" I asked, wanting to hear he had accomplished his desires.

"Hell no! Gave that stupid idea up three months after I got out here. Ger, don't you see, that degree stuff is all bullshit. Always knew it. Don't you remember me talking to you about the system and how it's only a money game by the powerful universities?"

I nodded, thinking back to our first meeting, wondering if this was deja vu.

"Well, I finally gave it up! The game, that is. Quit school and give my time where it really counts. It's all about love, Geri. You remember me telling you that?"

Again I nodded, trying to decide whether Mike had gone crazy too.

"Now I give my time to the soup lines, the homeless, the people that are real, who don't buy into the system that has no concern for people. I got tired of discussing the whys and hows of things, and now I'm just doing it! I love every minute of my life, Ger, every minute. I only spend time in activities of giving, sharing, loving, which makes life so much more meaningful."

He must have noticed the look of skepticism on my face as I pondered whether he was high on something.

"You think I'm crazy, don't you?"

"Not crazy," I said, realizing my hesitation was giving me away.

"Then what? What do you think of me?" his voice sounding slightly annoyed.

"Nothing!" I said defensively, twirling the key ring with both hands now.

"Geri, it's me, Mike. Come on, tell me the truth! I can handle it. It wouldn't be the first time I heard a bunch of negativity about my life choices."

Deciding I owed him my honesty, I said, "I'm not criticizing you, Mike. I'm just trying to digest the changes in you, that's all. Hey, if you're happy, that's what counts."

"But you expected me to have a degree by now, maybe even be teaching at the university, right?"

"Yeah, I guess so. But it's okay that you're not. Heck, I've been worrying what you'd think about me. I haven't graduated from undergrad school yet, so I got no room to judge." Speaking the truth with Mike came as easily as when we first met. The doubtful reaction I experienced from his physical expansion which had clouded my perception of him drifted away.

"Did you drop out too?" he asked, sounding like he hoped I had.

"No, I'm still in school, but with all that crap going on with Powers, and some other stuff, I had to drop out a few times. Hopefully I'll be done next spring."

"That's good, that's good!" he said, nodding his head vigorously while staring at me with a big smile on his face. "I always had faith you'd do something special with your life, Geri. Being a teacher is a wonderful path. If you can get through the phony requirements that are supposed to determine the capable from the incapable, then more power to you. I'm only sorry you had to go through all the crap with that idiot professor. I take it you got past him?"

I picked up the saga about Professor Powers from the point where Mike left off, eventually explaining how I'd won by default. I filled him in on other aspects of my life, including my coming to terms with the cane, depression and hospital stay. Despite the nagging thoughts of whether David was still asleep, Mike and I continued talking for the next two hours.

My initial impression of him steadily improved as he shared stories of his goodness. Though I couldn't fully agree with his method of financial survival, he assured me he needed welfare money in order to have time to give back to society in a way that really mattered. Instead of questioning him, I reminded him of my own use of government money to live.

This was a perfect lead into my relationship, so I refreshed his memory about Dave, the frequent caller, hoping I would pass the final test for Mike's acceptance. I soon discovered I had nothing to worry about. Except for his expression of disappointment at my having a mate, he listened closely as I explained all the sordid details about David's recent problem with medications.

I was surprised to find Mike was well aware of the plight of people with mental illness. He cursed the medical profession for not recognizing the need for better outreach toward those who struggled with psychosis. He told stories of how he supported many homeless people whose primary need was someone who cared enough to help keep track of their medical and mental treatments.

"It's through caring and love that folks want to stay well. If they just hand these folks a prescription and send them on their way, it don't work."

For the next five days, Mike, David and I hung together on the campus. The three of us swapped hippie stories and discussed personal discoveries about life. As Mike's acceptance of David unfolded, my admiration for him grew. His ability to ignore the typical social lines of distinction endeared him to me even further. I found myself looking forward to David's naps, so I could be alone with my old friend.

Each day, Mike guided me through the area, sometimes the two of us walking hand in hand. Guiltily, I grew more and more drawn to him, fantasizing about staying in California. Although he didn't say anything, I felt certain he was thinking similar thoughts. He appeared so happy and content, despite the fact I still harbored some doubts about his lifestyle. I couldn't help compare him to David and wondered what it would be like to be with someone who had so much enthusiasm and energy.

On the last afternoon of our stay while David was taking a rest, Mike came by the dorm and invited me to visit the Redwood Amphitheater, situated in the botanical gardens up in the mountains behind the university. We climbed the steep slope and sat on one of the bleachers made from redwood logs. Brightly colored blue jays flew close enough for me to see, snatching insects from the seats around us. I pivoted toward the bench above and behind me in hopes to get a better view.

"They're so tame!" I said to Mike, feeling great pleasure watching their curious movements, as they worked to find the delicacies hidden in the cracks and crevices of the wood.

"And so free," he added. Refusing to give up the miraculous view rarely seen these days by my weakening eyes, I resisted the urge to look at him while talking.

"You seem so free, Mike. I wish I could be like that too."

"Stay with me then, Geri."

Taken aback by his offer, I was unable to reply. Instead, I abandoned my watch, turning my body in his direction. I bowed my head as I became certain the desire I felt must be evident on my face. Neither of us spoke for a long time. He disturbed the poignant moment by gently touching my chin with his finger, guiding my face to his.

"You can if you want to, you know. You can be free too."

I looked at his scruffy beard and smiled. A blue jay running back and forth on the bench behind him searched frantically for food. Wondering how much longer I would be able to see such a sight, I took Mike's hand from my face and squeezed it tightly.

"I wish I could, but I have other commitments."

"But you don't have to keep them! Life is yours for the taking, Geri! Embrace it, follow your dream!"

With all my heart I wanted to surrender to this idea, to Mike, but as it had happened so many times before, something held me back. As I stared longingly into his face, imagining the details of his eyes, Mike leaned forward and kissed me. Like a parched desert traveler, thirsty from days of drought, I began to drink from his moist lush lips. I felt my being begin to flow into him, releasing my grasp from all that I knew, all that I cared about. Mike's warm tongue beckoned mine to join his fully, when a powerful force ripped through me, severing our connection.

"What's the matter, Ger?" he said, surprise and annoyance clearly evident in his voice.

"I can't, Mike, I can't!" I moaned, my aching heart threatening to tear through my chest to reach his.

"But Geri, I thought you finally…I mean, I was certain you'd finally realized you belonged to me," he said, taking both my hands and gripping them firmly in his.

Out of the blue, an image formed in my mind's eye. What I saw in the place I earlier feared had disappeared, was our two hearts meeting, my fragile heart being swallowed up by Mike's big strong one. He had found his niche in life, but I was still working toward mine.

"But that's just it, Mike. We're not meant to be. As much as I want you, as much as I've always wanted you, I could never surrender."

"But why?" he said, tightening his hold.

"Because, that's just it. I'd be surrendering!" Feeling the urge to break free of his grip, I continued my explanation. "It's the only way I can be with you, Mike. I've been holding myself back because I know, if I let myself, I'd give myself over to you. I could never be in love with you and maintain my sense of self. I would think of you as being better, wiser, more knowing than me, and I would end up handing you my whole self completely."

"You think I would abuse you if that happened?" he asked, relaxing his fingers slightly.

"No, I mean, maybe." Noticing a gap between his thumb and mine, I slid it out and curled it around his knuckle. "You wouldn't necessarily intend to Mike, but you would do it because you would grow tired of me if I became yours. Don't ask me how I know this, I just do."

I gave his hands a quick squeeze and hoped he wouldn't be offended as I pulled my right hand away. He was silent for a while, stroking his beard, digesting my words.

"I only hope when you go away from me, you'll realize you want to return."

"I know I won't," I said, taking a fist full of hair and pulling it hard, the resulting pain helping me stay with the harsh reality I knew I had to face.

"Always remember, Geri, my door will forever be open." As he said this, he released my other hand. A thought hit me.

"Mike?"

"Yeah?"

"Do you recall when I use to bug you about doing acid?

"Yeah," he laughed, throwing his head back a bit as he did so.

"Remember how you used to say there was no going back, how a door would open that could never be shut?"

"I do!"

"Well, there are lots of doors, Mike. Doors as big and as important as the door to an acid journey.

"Not sure I agree about that one, Ger," he said, leaning back on his hands now.

"Come on Mike, everything we do is a new venture that can never be erased from our lives. Acid certainly isn't anything to take lightly, but there are other events as significant. I have to admit seeing you has made me wish it might be different, but my relationship with David is a door I opened that I cannot shut."

"But Geri, you're not happy with him, I can tell," he said, leaning closer, running his thumb tenderly down my cheek. "What about love, freedom?" he continued. "Life should be lived to its fullest. If your heart is with me, why not follow it?" he begged, clutching both my arms in his hands. His sense of desperation quickly evaporated any urge I still had about drinking from his mirage.

"Because I have made a commitment to David, and for the most part, Mike, I'm okay with it, even though it ain't always easy," I said, inching away. "Freedom is not only the ability to follow one's urges, it includes commitment and responsibility to deal with the tough times as well as the good, which is what real love is all about."

"But you're not happy. I know you're not," he said, once more taking my hand, pulling it to his lips, passionately kissing my fingers. For a moment I feared he would devour me. My intuition was right. I now knew for certain Mike's sanctuary was filled with quicksand that would swallow me up if I dared to step in. My words came more easily now.

"Not all the time," I said, tearing my hand away, clearly communicating he was not to grab it again. "It's been a rough year, that's for sure, but I have been happy and will be again. Besides, there are other emotions like contentment, familiarity, that are worth living for as well. To simply shut a door without consequences is not possible."

Nodding his head, Mike admitted, "You're right."

At that moment, he resituated himself, bending his knees so his feet sat on the log between us, his arms wrapped around his legs. "I just wish I could have been behind one of the doors," he said sadly, dropping his chin on the top of the blockade he'd devised. Feeling safer now, I decided he deserved some acknowledgement.

"Mike, you have been behind one of those doors. You've affected my life in so many ways. Twice now, you've met me on a bench and filled up my loneliness, not to mention all the other rich times we've shared."

"Well, if I find you there again, I'm going to run the other way! What is it they say? Three strikes and you're out?" Mike chuckled, dropping his legs and returning to his original pose, slapping me hard on my arm.

Surprised at the level of aggression in his gesture, my summation of our relationship became firmly set in my mind. Maybe I wasn't Mike's inferior after all, I mused, giving him a knowing smile.

"I'm sorry if I brought unnecessary hurt to you Mike. It really wasn't my intention."

"Hey, come on now, Ger. I'm a big boy, I can take it. After all, what goes around comes around. I left you once, now you're leaving me," he said, reaching over and giving me a genuine hug. I returned his affection, squeezing him hard, whispering in his ear how much I truly loved him. We remained in this position for a long time, sadness now flowing between us. As I held him, waiting for the moment to end, the sound of fluttering wings distracted my attention. Looking in the direction of the sound, I caught sight of a blue blob ascending into the sky. In an instant, the colorful spectacle separated, little splashes of blue moving off in all directions. When they disappeared completely, I became aware my grip on Mike had loosened. The tension in Mike's arms slackened, and together we let go.

"Well, I guess it's time to move on, Ger."

"I guess so," I said, leaning back into him and kissing him on the cheek. Without a word, the two of us stood and began our journey down the mountain. Above me was the peep peep of one lone bird over head. I looked up and realized that I could only hear the flutter of his wings. *Don't have to see to know he's there*, I said to myself, the pain in my heart easing at this comforting thought.

I wonder if David's awake yet, I hoped, picking up the pace with the anticipation of seeing him again.

Part IV

Chapter 38

Mixed Blessings

July 7 1981

"Oww! Oh God, oh God, I can't take the pain! Please, please, please cut it out! I can't handle the pain. Please, just put me to sleep and cut it out!"

"Try to take deep breaths, Geraldine," a woman's voice said. "We're just about there."

"Don't call me Geraldine!" I screamed at her.

"That's right, Geri, I'm sorry about that. Can you take a deep breath now?"

"I can't, I can't. Just take it out. I can't stand it."

"Deep breath, deep breath," the woman's voice kept repeating.

"No no! You try to breathe with all this pain. I can't, I can't."

"Ger," I heard David's drawn out voice say. "They say you're going to be fine. They say it's not much longer."

"But I can't stand it. I don't care if they kill me, I just can't stand it."

Someone laughed.

"Don't laugh at me!" I scolded severely. "I can't take it anymore! I mean it! You've got to do something now!"

"I'm sorry," the woman said, brushing my soaking wet hair from my brow. "It's just that I remember saying the same thing myself not too many years ago."

I slapped her hand away. "Don't touch me!" I yelled. "Just stop this pain, right now! I mean it! Stop it! I'm not kidding!"

"I'm sorry, Geri. I do understand. I know it really hurts," she said. But her effort to soothe me only made me angrier.

"I said now! Stop it now!" I screamed.

"It won't be very much longer. I promise."

Somewhere beneath the horrendous pain tearing at my back and hips, I felt a twinge of guilt for being so horrid. I never would have dreamed something could be this torturous. My demanding voice softened into pleading whimpers.

"David, please get them to stop the pain. Please. Really, I can't stand it any longer."

"Gee, Ger, I'm not sure what I can do," he moaned, the anxiety in his voice only increasing my worry. Suddenly, everything changed. The back pain dissipated as the muscles in my groin contracted.

At this same moment, the woman who was manipulating my thighs announced,

"Okay, I think it's almost time. Now take a deep breath and follow my directions as best you can."

"I'll try," I grunted.

Before I knew it, the torture ended. The wretched tearing and ripping were magically replaced with a wonderful warm sensation now pressing against my arms and chest.

"Oh my God," I said, speaking my words softly. "I can't believe it. It's really here!"

"You have a beautiful baby boy there, Geri and David. Absolutely beautiful and healthy."

"Oh thank you," I said, caressing the bundle I held close to my heart. "David, can you believe it?"

"I wasn't sure you were gonna make it for a while, Ger," David said, worry still evident in his tone. "I was afraid you might go crazy or something, particularly when you told me to pack your things in a cardboard box. And then you said I had to take the lint from your hair and put it back in the blanket." As I listened to David's rendition of my recent babbling, I could see why he might have thought me insane.

I appreciated the understanding comments now coming from the female doctor on call. Though I had been upset when I learned my obstetrician had left for his vacation only yesterday, her firsthand knowledge of this ridiculously painful ordeal turned out to be very helpful. She simply poopooed my apologies for my bizarre behavior.

"Well, you did go a little crazy for a bit there, but I'm not sure you topped the weird notions I had when I had my first. Heck, I told my husband if he didn't get the popcorn out of my shoes I wouldn't be able to give birth," she said giving another hearty chuckle.

"Really?" David asked. "Gee, I never saw anyone get like that before, not even in the psych hospital," David added, still sounding stressed.

"I'm sorry I was so rude." Kissing my son on his fuzzy little head, I hoped to hide my face now flushed with embarrassment. I did not care to recall the things I'd done over the previous twenty-four hours. Not only had I grabbed at the doctor's collar and slapped her in the face, but I told her I would sell her soul to the devil if she didn't help me.

"Ah, forget it!" the doctor said. "You ain't the first and you ain't gonna be the last. You took Lamaze, right?"

"Yeah, but I forgot everything I learned."

"You and thousands of others," she chuckled heartily. "The way I figure it, if you can't refrain from letting out a yelp when you stick your hand under a hot tap, you probably ain't gonna handle childbirth by staying calm and collected."

This time I joined her, giggling at such foolishness, even though I still felt a little ashamed for blowing my plan to be a model for peaceful childbirth.

A couple of squeaks came from the living being now cradled in my arms.

"Hi there!" I said, lifting my baby closer to my face. "How ya doing?"

Two big round blueberry eyes opened wide and stared in my direction. The contrast between their rich color and the surrounding pale face made them easy for me to see.

"Oh, you are so cute!" I said, smiling broader than I ever smiled in my life. "He looks like Casper the Friendly Ghost, doesn't he?"

David did not respond.

"David," I called again, wishing he were more engaged in the joyous bundle now lying peacefully in my arms. "Don't you think he's so cute?"

Moving closer, David bent down over the two of us to take a look.

"Hi there!" he said, reaching with his hand and rubbing the little guy's head.

"He's a nice one," David said, giving me his half a chuckle which told me he was finally smiling. I realized this entire ordeal would be quite a strain for David, so I was glad to hear him relax a bit and begin to enjoy what we'd worked for.

"Can you really believe he's ours?" I asked, tears of joy beginning to roll down my face.

Our decision to have a baby did not come easily. I had always wanted a child, but there were many obstacles blocking us from parenthood. Mental illness, the stress of vision loss, educational and employment barriers, and resulting financial limitations, retarded the normal timeline for having a child. While the women's libbers and their husbands were raising two point five children by their mid-twenties, I was spending the entire decade trying to reach some level of emotional and financial stability.

"Ger?" David asked, the nervousness in his voice telling me he was about to request something he knew I might be upset with.

"What," I answered, hoping he didn't want to go have a cigarette.

"Now that the baby's here," he paused, clearing his throat.

"You want a cigarette right?" I said, hoping to beat him to the punch so I wouldn't feel so slighted.

"Uh, no. I mean, I'm wondering if it'd be okay if I went home now. I've been up for a long time, Ger, and I'm really exhausted."

Repressing the urge to burst out in sarcastic laughter, reminding him of what the true definition of exhaustion was, my higher level thinking took over, reminding me of the reality of David's fragile state. Without a doubt, I knew watching me go through labor for twenty-four hours was quite a feat for him. He'd actually done rather well for himself and for me.

"Sure. I'll just hang out here with my new boyfriend," I said, giving David an affectionate smile.

"Gee, thanks, Ger. I wish I could stay, but really, I never realized what an ordeal this would be for me…and for you," he said as an afterthought. Once more David's tendency to focus on himself during times of stress, reminded me of what I understood things might be like when making the decision to have a child. Although my capacity to react maturely was not always within my reach, today I would suppress my longing for attention for the sake of our baby. *After all, David is who he is*, I thought to myself. *And there's no use getting all upset about something I can't change.*

As I swallowed my disappointment, once again I couldn't help wondering if some of David's lack of energy was the result of can't or won't. *Remember all the good things he gives you, Geri*, I told myself, as I sanctioned his request.

"You have a good rest and come back as soon as you can, okay?"

"Sure, Ger. I will." He started to walk away.

"Hey, how about a kiss?" I asked, reminding myself his forgetfulness had nothing to do with not caring for me, but a part of his preoccupation with getting home.

"Oh, yeah!" he said, turning back toward me and quickly pecking my lips with his.

Before he could walk away again, I added, "Don't forget our new little Nolan."

"Yeah, sorry, Ger. I'm just really tired," he said as he bent down and gave our son a kiss on his forehead. "Well, I'm gonna go now, okay?"

"Yeah, get outta here, big daddy," I chuckled, glad I hadn't become upset.

Returning my focus to the tiny living being snuggled so comfortably in my arms, I marveled at the miracle of birth.

"So what's it like being out in the cold cruel world there, buddy?" I asked the staring eyes looking up at me. "Did you have fun growing in that nice warm belly of mine?" Though he did not answer, his wide eyes seemed to be trying to comprehend what I was saying. I kissed him again and then continued with our discussion of his arrival. Unfortunately we were interrupted.

"So what's this guy's name?" a woman asked, wriggling his little arm free from the fleece blanket which was tightly wrapped around him.

"Nolan David," I proudly announced.

"What a unique name! I'm measuring his wrist for his bracelet," she kindly informed me.

"I took it from my father's mother. It was her maiden name," I offered.

"Can you spell the first, middle, and last name for me?"

I did as she asked. I could hear her writing on what I assumed to be a clipboard, as I tucked my little boy's arm back inside the blanket.

"Thank you very much. I'll be right back."

"That nice lady's gonna get you a bracelet so you don't forget who you are!" I told my little bundle. "Nolan David. My little Nolan!" I announced, practicing the use of his name. He continued to stare at me, making me question the belief about babies being unable to see when they are born.

In a moment, she returned.

"Here we are!" she announced, taking his arm once again. In one swift movement I heard the snap of the clasp, and then she quickly wrapped him up again.

"Okay, I'll take him now," she said.

"Why?" I asked, holding him tighter, irritated at the suggestion.

"Gotta get him under the bilirubin light."

"The what?"

"We put all the infants under that light. It's a precaution, you know?" she said, shoving her hand between Nolan's back and my arm.

Resisting her effort, I asked, "What if we just skip that part?"

"Hospital rules!" she said nonchalantly, struggling against my hold.

Reluctantly I let her take my newborn, despite my intuition telling me to keep him close.

"How long will he be gone?" I asked, still uncertain about this whole idea.

"Oh, about a half an hour. They run a few tests, put the light on them, and then you'll get him back," she said, walking away. Before she managed to leave the room, I heard my little guy begin to cry.

"I'm not happy about this!" I called after her.

"Don't worry. He'll be fine."

Suddenly, I was left with a terrible feeling of emptiness. *How could I have lost him so quickly?* I wondered, thinking about how he'd been a part of me for nine very long months. *I wish David hadn't left*, I thought, wondering what to do with my childless arms. *What do the moms do whose babies are sick or…*the thought was too awful to consider. A few minutes passed, when an orderly came in and announced he'd be taking me to my room.

"How will they find me?" I asked, suddenly fearful I might somehow lose my baby. Chuckling, the man assured me I'd be found.

"I've got rooming-in, you know?" I half asked, half explained, glad I had chosen to follow the revolutionary belief which called for mothers and newborns to stay together during the first hours and days outside the womb.

"Your first, right?"

"Uh huh," I said proudly.

"Wait 'til the second and third come along. You'll want those nurses to do all the work."

"I'd never let a stranger take care of any of my kids no matter how many I have."

"That's what my wife said. She just had her fifth in five years. No rooming in for that woman," he laughed.

Once I was situated in my room, I lay in my bed anxiously waiting for my son's return. Unable to stand the quiet, I felt around for the TV remote. Finding nothing interesting to distract me, memories of how I came to this point in my life filtered into my thoughts.

After my visit with Mike in the summer of '77, it seemed David and I became even more secure as a couple. The medication he took for his schizophrenia brought him back to his solid self. Additionally, a newer drug helped reduce the symptoms of tardive dysconesia, freeing David from some of the jerky movements he experienced in his muscles.

I went back to school in September of '77 and began my last internship as a student teacher. David managed to find a proof for some mathematical theory which he submitted to a special math journal. Though he didn't receive any money for his discovery, he felt proud of his accomplishment, as did I.

The day I had worked for for seven years finally arrived. On April 28, 1978, I actually graduated from university with my degree in special education for the visually impaired. Mr. Sulvai phoned me shortly afterwards, informing me they needed a teacher in Youngstown, Ohio. With his help, I landed the job and David, Fella, Jinxy, and I left Michigan for a new adventure.

Sitting in my very own classroom after seven long and grueling years was a dream come true. I was thrilled to meet each of my eight preschool students, as they filed in on the first day. They all possessed a multitude of visual, cognitive, emotional, and physical abilities and differences, inspiring creativity in me and adding richness to my position. It took no time at all to fall in love with each and every one of the kids, as I watched them develop the ability to use their hands, noses, and ears, as they became less fearful to explore their world.

I was heartbroken when after only one year, in May of '79, I received a pink slip, informing me these children would all be moving to the grade one through three classroom. As there were no more preschool-aged blind students enrolling in the system, my services would no longer be needed. Though I certainly wished I could have continued, David and I were both glad to return to Michigan.

My search for a new teaching position was unfortunately met with a Catch 22. The requirement to have at least three years of teaching experience in the one hundred schools to which I applied was a real challenge. I was unable to figure out how to get three years of experience without being hired. This paradox made my efforts null and void.

Eventually, I did land a post at a center for mentally impaired adults, but the teaching conditions were despicable. With the movement toward deinstitutionalization, the facility had become almost barren of supplies. Nearly everything had been packed up and moved to state warehouses. The expectation to teach thirty or more blind adults with limited cognitive ability in a small room with nothing to do was more than frustrating. I badly wanted out of the job, so I applied for graduate school at the same university I spent my hospital days in as a child.

Though I resented the fact that Professor Powers' voice still taunted me inside my head, telling me I should pursue a social work degree, I did exactly that. The reason had nothing to do with him, however. After going through my own difficulties with self-acceptance, I became acutely aware of how many others struggled with the same thing. A person didn't have to be going blind to question their right to exist. Poor self-esteem, fear of fitting in, depression, the desire not to exist are not inherent to being physically different. I now understood that differences are identified as much by personal perception as they are classified by society. When I thought about the support I'd received from Jack, Dolly, and so many others, I knew I wanted to provide the same. I hoped my own experience would add to my effort in helping others through their personal journey as opposed to telling them what they should or should not be.

In September of 1980, I found myself entering grad school. As I stepped into another realm of my life, so did David. After being put on a new and improved psychotropic medication in May that year, David began to feel more energized and enthusiastic about life in general. While talking to one of his mathematician buddies, the professor asked him if he might be interested in teaching a couple of classes. Though apprehensive, he agreed and began a new career for himself. I had no doubt he would do well and reminded David of his excellent ability to explain things. He did not share in my confidence, but he soon learned his students really appreciated him. By the time his second semester of teaching came around in January of '81, students were clamoring to get into his class. By May of '82, I had graduated with my MSW. With two years of living as a successful couple, we figured we'd finally arrived at being normal.

"It really is a miracle!" I said out loud, as I sat smiling on my bed. I suddenly realized I still did not have my son. Fumbling for the call light, I found it and pushed what I hoped was the right button. In a minute, a nurse popped her head in my door.

"Can I help you?"

"Yes, can you tell me when I'm going to get my son back?"

"Oh, he's not back yet?"

"No!" I said, fearful something might have happened.

"Oh, I'm sure he'll be here in a minute."

"It's been a long time. I'd really like to hold him."

She chuckled. "Your first?"

"Yes, but even if he were my tenth, I'd want him with me."

"Oh sure," she agreed. "Well, it won't be long. Anything else I can do for you?"

"No thanks."

When she left, I found my way to the bathroom on legs which felt more like twigs rather than something to be used for walking. I reached down and felt for the missing bulge I'd known so well. I marveled at how flat my tummy now felt. When I was done, I was glad to return to my bed. I once more waited anxiously for them to bring my baby to me, but I couldn't stand doing nothing. I felt for the phone and dialed a number.

"Hello?" the female voice on the other end said.

"Well, he's here!"

"A boy?" she said.

"Yup! A beautiful baby boy. Nolan David is his official name."

"Oh, I'm so glad you stuck with that. I really like it."

"Thanks. Gotta keep my family heritage in there somewhere. So how are you feeling?" I asked.

"Five more weeks, and I'll be right where you are."

"I'll bet you can hardly wait."

My success as a new mother had been directly influenced by the woman on the other end of the line. Until she miraculously reappeared in my life only a year ago, I had pretty much given up hope of having a child. Although David's ability to work might have rekindled the idea, there were so many problems like finances, age, and my career, which was still on hold.

During summer break of 1981 the inspiration to have a baby began. I was sitting in my little basement apartment, two blocks from the university, when the phone rang. I could have fallen off my chair when I heard a soft familiar voice say, "Hi Ger."

"Oh my gosh, is that you?"

"I think so," she said.

"Cody Genteel?" I asked.

"Well, how the hell are ya doing girl?" she said. The image of her beautiful white teeth shining through her cherry lips reminded me of how much I missed her.

"I'm fine!" I replied, trying to recall the last time we'd talked. "And you?"

"Fine! Finally finished nursing school and got myself a nice new husband."

"No kidding! Oh Cody, I'm so glad for you," I said, thinking how abusive and kept she had been under her first husband's rule.

"Well, I thought I'd give you a call to see if you might want a visit from me."

"Absolutely! When?"

"Been thinking about coming down for the art fair and decided I'd look you up. My husband has to work, of course, so I hoped you might be up for it."

"Sure! Art fair's a great time around here. I love it 'cause we don't have to drive to it. I'm right down town, you know. The major events start two blocks from my place."

"Great!"

"Gonna spend the night, or drive back the same day?"

"Hmm, well, I guess I could stay," she considered.

"Oh Code, I'd love to have you. Of course I hope you don't mind the couch. It's pretty small, but if I remember correctly, so are you."

"Hell no! I can sleep anywhere. I'm just glad to see you. I think about you all the time Geri, but I never call. Finally I did."

"Gosh, I'm so glad you did. Cody, I don't know if you'll ever know how significant you were in my life back in those teen years."

"Well, you were pretty important to me yourself, Ger. There were days when I don't know what I'd have done without you!"

"I can't wait to see you, Cody," I said, sending my deepest affections for her through my voice.

"Me too. Can you give me the directions to your house?" I did as she asked.

After we hung up, my mind mulled over the past ten years. *There's so much to tell!* I thought, imagining how she might react to David and to my growing vision loss. I didn't feel worried about her ability to accept me, but I did wonder how I'd get past the initial greeting. She wouldn't notice much difference in my mannerisms in the apartment, but once we were in public territory, I would not be able to maneuver independently, at least not if we wanted to stay together through the crowds. I would have to take her arm, or have her follow me while I used the cane.

It turned out my intuition about her accepting nature was right. When she arrived a week later, we gave each other the hug of a lifetime. As we made our way through hordes of art junkies, Cody guided me as if we'd been traveling together for years.

The second evening of her visit, we were sitting in my living room after a hot day at the art fair. Cody stretched out on the couch while I perched myself on the beanbag cushion. David sat in his recliner now cracked and torn. Cody was catching me up on the latest news about girls we went to school with.

Chris Gabner had a nervous break down, and Deb became an engineer. I listened patiently, hoping she knew what had happened to Candice. I eventually asked.

"Oh, yeah, she's a lawyer now," Cody said, making me happy to hear she'd been successful.

We continued chatting about a variety of things when Cody announced some news.

"I'm trying to get pregnant, you know."

"No kidding! Oh, I wish I could have a baby. How long you been trying?" I asked a mixture of delight and jealousy exploding in my heart.

"Oh, just got started. About two months of being disappointed if you know what I mean?"

"Bummer! I'll bet you can hardly wait."

"It'll come when the time's right, I suppose. So why don't you get pregnant if you want a baby so bad, Ger?"

"Huh, yeah!" I said with a laugh. "There's no way we can afford a child right now, and I ain't getting any younger."

"Ah, heck! Who cares about money? You don't have to have money to have a kid. People who don't have money been having babies for years. Besides, you will some day when you're done with school."

"Well, you know," David said, "Ger and I wouldn't mind having a baby. It's the schizophrenia. I mean, I'm not sure I could handle the stress."

"Ah, come on!" Cody challenged. "Life is always stressful. Might as well get some good stuff with it. Babies are so nice. I work on a maternity ward in the hospital in Flint. Those little newborns are so cute and cuddly. Every woman that wants one should have one, don't you think?"

Her words sounded so convincing. A deeply buried desire stirred within me, followed by a practical thought countering such a ludicrous notion.

"But babies have to be taken care of," I reminded all of us. "If I end up being the breadwinner of the family, David would have to be responsible for child care. Eight hours is a long time for him every day."

"So, put the kid in daycare for part of the day or something. Work part time. Hire a babysitter when Dave needs a rest, for heaven's sake! Shoot, some folks put their kid in daycare eight hours a day and then hire a nanny in the evenings 'cause they're too tired to deal with anything when they get home from work."

"Oh, I wouldn't want to do that," I protested. "If I have a baby, I want to be the one who raises it as much as possible."

"Yeah, me too, but there's lots of ways to get around the things you guys are worrying about."

The more Cody shot down my arguments, the more excited I became.

"I don't know," David said. "It's an awful lot of work, those babies. My sister, she has a really nice one, but I remember her crying in the middle of the night. What if we got a sick one? That would be even worse."

"Well, of course, it's up to you guys, but there will always be 'what ifs.' And Ger, you've never let them stop you before. I just think you'd make a wonderful mom, that's all."

Once more, as she did in eighth grade, Cody believed in me, giving me hope about this idea I might not otherwise have considered. After she left, David and I continued talking about the possibility of a child. Eventually, we took action.

"Honestly, Ger, if this kid don't come out on time I don't think I will stand it," Cody was now saying.

Laughing, I replied, "Boy, do I understand that one. I thought Nolan would never come."

"But now you have him. You have to be so happy!"

"Yeah, and I have you to thank Cody. God, I will never forget you for helping me get here," I said, tears welling in my eyes. The letdown of emotions was met with a strange sensation in my bosom. It felt both pleasant and painful. Instinctively I knew I needed to feed my son. *Where is he?* I wondered, panic setting in. As soon as I could, I ended the conversation with my friend and once more hit the call light. After what seemed like an eternity, the same nurse entered my room.

"When will I get my son back?" I asked bluntly.

"He's not back yet?"

"No."

"Hmmm. Well, he'll be here soon."

"You said that a while ago. I need to feed him."

"Oh, well, don't worry. Someone will have given him a bottle by now."

"They'd better not!" I snapped. "I don't want him having a bottle. I want him to get his nourishment from me! What time is it anyway?"

"It's 5:45."

"Five forty-five! I had my baby at 4:20. They told me downstairs it would be thirty minutes at the most. Now I want him back! Is there something wrong with him?"

"Oh, no. He's fine, I'm sure. Sometimes they have several infants they have to check over. Don't worry, he'll be here."

"Would you please call and find out exactly where he is and tell them I want him in my arms now."

"I will," she assured me. "How come you haven't slept? You must be exhausted."

"I'm not tired. I'm excited. I finally have a baby to hold after nine long months, but someone has taken him from me."

"Okay, I'll check," she said.

I withheld a command for her to hurry up, hoping she understood my need.

More time passed with no word from the nurse. I hit the call light again. When she at last returned, I asked her the same question as before.

"Well, it shouldn't be too much longer."

"You keep saying that, but I still don't have him. I'm becoming convinced there's something wrong," I said, anxiety growing in my gut.

"Oh no! Nothing is wrong."

"How do you know?" I asked.

"They'd tell us. Now don't worry. Can I get you some juice or something to eat?"

"Get me my baby!" I demanded, slapping my leg with my hand.

I had planned to have my newborn in my arms when I called, but I decided to phone my parents anyway. Of course they were more than thrilled to hear the news, even though initially they were devastated I would have a child out of wedlock. At first my father attempted to bribe me to get married, offering me $1,000 to help cover the cost. But without the two Social Security incomes, David and I would never be able to manage.

I promised him, once we got on our feet financially, we'd tie the knot officially to make him happy. Throughout my conversation with my folks, my growing concerns nagged at me. When my son still had not arrived after my long conversation, I called for the nurse again. I waited for what seemed an endless amount of time. When no one came, I stood up and looked for something to put over my hospital gown. With great effort, I located my suitcase which had been packed for three weeks and pulled out a duster. Putting it on, I slipped on my flipflops and felt for my cane. It was nowhere to be found.

Too tired to keep searching, I decided to head down the hallway. Carefully I felt my way, avoiding carts and other objects scattered along the wall. At last I heard the sounds of the nursing station. Feeling for the counter, I located its edge and hung on tight so I wouldn't fall. The lady behind the desk was talking on the phone. When I thought my knees might give out on me, I coughed loudly. This caught her attention. Looking up she said, "Can I help you?"

"I want to know where my baby is," I said, my legs wobbling beneath me.

"Oh honey, you shouldn't be standing out here like this. Let me help you back to your room."

She informed the person on the other end of the line that she had to go and then quickly moved around the end of the counter. Gently, she took my arm. I didn't resist, uncertain of my strength. Together we walked back. As she helped me into bed, I explained to her how upset I was that my baby had not arrived yet.

"Well, I don't have much to do with all that, but I will tell your evening nurse. They're doing shift change right now, and it'll be about fifteen minutes before her charting is done. I promise, as soon as she's free, I'll tell her to come see you."

Hearing the reference to evening shift, my suspicions about the health of my son sky rocketed.

"What time is it anyway?"

"It's only 7:30."

"Seven thirty! I've been waiting for three hours! That's three precious hours I have missed with my little boy," I cried. "I absolutely know there's something wrong!" The nurse quickly grabbed a box of tissues from somewhere and handed them to me.

"Hang in there. Your nurse will be right here."

Soon a different nurse arrived. Tearfully I explained the situation and insisted she locate my son. To my surprise however, she proceeded to tell me what I did not want to hear.

"Well," the nurse began, "the doctor is thinking we might keep him in the nursery until morning. You haven't slept yet, and it would be best if you got a good night's sleep before taking over the care of an infant."

"What the hell is going on!" I yelled, anger overriding my weepiness. "I want my son. I have rooming-in privileges, and he was supposed to be here hours ago. If there is something wrong with him, I want to know!"

The nurse moved over to the side of my bed. She placed her hand on my arm, but I shoved it away.

"Geraldine, your baby is just fine."

"So why isn't he here with me?" I snarled. "My breasts are ready to burst and I know he has to be hungry!"

"We can alleviate your discomfort with a pump if you like. Don't worry about your baby. Infants really don't eat much their first twenty-four hours."

"Then why do breasts have milk ready for them?" I demanded.

"Well, it's not really milk just yet," Understanding the stages of lactating breasts, I told her I wasn't interested in arguing this point.

"Get. Me. My. Baby! Get him here right now!" I growled.

"Try to calm down there, Geraldine. We've paged the house doctor who's standing in for yours. He should be up momentarily to talk with you."

"Why do I need to talk to this doctor if my baby is fine?" I yelled.

"I'll go check to see if he's on his way yet."

"If you don't get my son to me in the next fifteen minutes, I'm coming down there to get him," I threatened.

"I'll be right back," the nurse said anxiously, as she swiftly flew out of the room. While I waited, I called David.

After many rings, he answered, his voice groggy.

"David, they won't bring Nolan to me. I don't know what's wrong!" I said half crying again.

"Gee, Ger, I was sleeping. What time is it?"

"It's almost eight. I've been waiting all this time for our son and they keep stalling about bringing him. He's probably crying or hungry or something, and I want to hold him."

"Uh, well, they'll probably bring him in a bit. I gotta go back and lay down, Ger. I'm really tired."

"David!" I yelled. "I'm worried about our baby! Can't you come up here, please?"

"Ger, I'm really sorry. I just don't think I can drive. You know how I get when I haven't slept. I get those visual distortions, you know. I'll have an accident if I drive."

Hopelessly, I knew David's state of mind could not be bargained with. I felt totally on my own as I hung up the phone. Soon after, a man entered my room. I heard the nurse come in behind him.

"Hello there," the man said, taking my hand. "I'm Dr. Shosel, sitting in for Dr. Towndel, your regular doctor. You must be the proud momma of that beautiful baby boy I just looked at." His smooth handshake and delivery of words reminded me of a used car salesman. Pulling my hand away, I adopted an instant mistrust of him as I firmly clarified my position.

"Yes, I am," I said sternly. "I want him here with me right now!"

"Yes, I can imagine that. I'm thinking we'll have one of the nurses bring him down for you to nurse and hold for a bit, then we'll take him back to the nursery for the night."

"I have rooming-in privileges!" I said forcefully. "I want him here with me until I leave the hospital."

The doctor hesitated. I pictured him scratching his head trying to think of what to say next.

"Ah, yes, I am aware of your request. But in light of the situation, I'm going to ask for your cooperation and allow the nurses to care for your child while you're here."

"Absolutely not!" I yelled, pounding my fist on the mattress. "I want my son, and I want him now!"

"Mrs. Taeckens," the doctor spoke calmly. "There's no need to upset yourself."

"I'm not upsetting myself. You're upsetting me. Now bring me my son now!"

"Well, Mrs. Taeckens. That's not exactly possible at the moment."

"Is there something wrong with my baby's health? 'Cause that's the only reason you could give me for me agreeing to your request."

"No, no! Your son is very fine. At eight pounds four ounces he's a very healthy lad indeed. It's just that, well, hospital policy states that rooming-in can only be provided to mothers who, shall we say, are—"

"Are what?" I demanded.

"Well, let's just say able to handle the care of the infant without assistance."

"Let's just say I can," I mocked.

A long pause ensued. I now pictured him with his hand to his chin, contemplating how to manipulate the situation.

"I'm sure, Mrs. Taeckens, you are a very capable woman. It's just that the hospital is a foreign place for you, particularly in the middle of the night. There are fewer staff on duty to assist you, and if your baby was to cry and you needed to get him, the lighting is not as bright at night. You might trip or hurt yourself or the baby. You wouldn't want that, would you? And neither would we."

I let out a bold laugh. "Ha! You're worried I might trip because the lights are off? What a joke. I don't need lights doctor or didn't you notice I don't see? That's what this is about, isn't it? You are discriminating against me because I am visually impaired, and you, as a sighted person, can't imagine how I could care for my son, so you are forbidding me to have him near me, even though that's what we both need the most after he's been inside me for nine months. Now bring him to me right now or I'm leaving this hospital immediately with him."

Having taken no breath throughout my tirade, fear of collapse now threatened the image of capability I was trying to project. The fury and anguish I felt at this man's audacity was almost more than I could bear. As this idiot began his reply, I couldn't help cursing the irony before me.

"Now, Mrs. Taeckens," Dr. Shosel said with a patronizing tone. "Let's not be hasty here. Like I said, we can have the nurses bring your son to you to hold whenever you want. Within reason," he added as an afterthought.

Why did my doctor have to go on vacation now? I asked no one as I mustered up the energy to respond.

"Don't you get it?" I asked, trying to call on any intelligence he might possess. "I don't want the nurses bringing him to me. I want him here with me being the sole person caring for him as I planned. Now get him here or I'm getting dressed."

I started to get out of bed. A list of names and phone numbers ran through my head as I realized I could not call David to come get me. *I can take a cab if I have to*, I told myself, not wanting to make an idle threat.

"Please, Mrs. Taeckens. Stay where you are. Please don't get up. Let's think for a minute." I could tell the doctor was finally catching on. I also figured he was trying to come up with something to appease me.

"Look!" I said firmly. "I am not settling for anything less than my son being here with me through the duration of my stay. He either is placed in my arms in the next three minutes or I'm out of here."

"Well, can you tell me this then," Dr. Shosel asked.

"What's that!" I snapped.

"Can you tell me what, if any, experience you've had with children?"

"Is this a standard question you ask all your mothers who get rooming in?" I inquired sarcastically.

"Uh, well…"

"Of course, it's not. This is discrimination. I'm filing a complaint on you for this. But right now I'm tired, and I want to see my son so I'll tell you that I have a ton of nieces and nephews who I've cared for from the time they were born. I am a teacher of preschool children and know how to use all my senses to care for myself and children. Now bring me my son or I leave!"

"So you've changed diapers, held an infant, fed a baby?"

"Now Dr. Shosel. Now!"

"Very well." He turned to the nurse and instructed her to get Nolan.

"Please be sure to call the nurses if you need any assistance," Dr. Shosel urged.

"Please get out of my room," I snarled. "You'll hear my grievance after I talk to Patients Rights in the morning."

"I'm sorry you feel that way, Mrs. Taeckens."

"How am I supposed to feel when you've robbed me and my son of his first precious hours of life with his mother?"

With that, the doctor turned and left the room.

I don't believe two minutes passed before the nurse brought Nolan and placed him in my arms. He was crying. I joined him.

"I'm so sorry little one," I said, holding him to my bosom. "You poor little thing. We've been together so long, and that nasty doctor took you from me," I said, keeping my voice soft so I didn't alarm him further. He continued to wail as I fiddled with my breast. Finally I managed to insert the nipple into his open mouth. Instantly, he stopped yowling and began to suckle. Wincing at the initial pinch, a warm sensation followed, flowing between the two of us as he drank from my lactating breast. Though I tried to fully engage myself in this miraculous moment, waves of regret continued to disrupt what should have been a most precious time.

"I have to let go of this," I explained to my young friend. "I don't want to let that mean old man take any more joy from us now, do I?" I said in the sing-songy style used by mothers everywhere. "It's a tough place to live little one," I cooed to my baby. "But you and I won't let it get to us, will we?"

As Nolan's little tongue vigorously swaggered back and fourth sucking all the nourishment he could swallow, a sense of peaceful satisfaction filled me. I wondered how long I would be able to protect this special life form. At least for the moment, his squeaks of pleasure helped ease my tension. As he conveyed his contentment with the world, only an occasional automatic gasp for breath signaled remnants of his first challenging ordeal.

"You're just a few hours old, and already you've been traumatized," I said sympathetically to my child. "You shouldn't have had to cry so hard for so long little buddy. Mommy will never make you cry like that again," I promised with all my heart.

Before long his suckling dissipated. With eyes closed, the tiny baby cradled in my arms slept peacefully. Slipping the covers up over both of us, I propped a pillow under my arm, making sure we were firmly supported. Before I lay back on my own pillow to rest, I bent down and kissed my little Nolan on his forehead.

From somewhere far away, I heard the words which had soothed me and others so long ago.

> I peeked in to say good night, and then I heard my child in prayer.
> And for me some scarlet ribbons, scarlet ribbons for my hair.

Singing the magical song to my very own child, tears of joy trickled down my cheeks. I am really a mom! I told myself. I'm really a full-fledged mother! Closing my own eyes, a warm glow enveloped me. Slowly but surely the little star of light I had not looked for in a long time, showed itself inside the empty space before my eyes. Smiling at the sight, I felt as if an old friend were now visiting me. Once more, the source behind this celebration was revealed to me. Without a doubt, I knew it was love.

Chapter 39

Bittersweet Goodbyes

November 1983

Day 1

"So if I call this number, they will come directly to my door?"

"Yes," said the woman on the phone. "It's best if you can schedule your ride a day or two ahead of time, but sometimes they have openings within the hour."

"So that's Thursday at one?"

"Yes, we'll see you then, Geri."

I hung up the phone and dialed the number the lady named Nina had just given me.

"One moment, please," a female voice said. Several minutes passed.

"May I help you?" I heard at last.

"I need to get a ride for Thursday."

"Which Thursday?" the curt voice asked.

"Oh, this Thursday, two days from now."

"What time?"

"Well, I need to be there at one o'clock."

"Need to be where, picked up at what address?"

"Oh, yeah," I said, feeling a little stupid for failing to supply such details. I gave her my address and destination.

"Need a return?"

"Huh?" I asked, not understanding the lingo.

"Do you want a ride back to your house?" she asked, deliberately emphasizing each word.

"Oh, yes, thanks. I would have forgotten that part," I half chuckled, hoping she would cut this newcomer some slack.

"So, what time?" she asked, sounding annoyed.

"Oh, uh, two, I guess."

"You guess or you want."

"I want."

"Okay, pick up Thursday at 12:45. Return 2 p.m. Do you have a card number?"

"Uh, no."

"You'll have to get a green card before you can ride the transit bus."

"How do I get that?"

"Go down to the main bus station. Take a picture ID and something that proves you have a disability, and they'll give you a form. Fill it out and they'll get you a card. Have to have it every time you ride."

Feeling overwhelmed, I asked, "How do I get to the bus station if I can't get a ride on the transit system?"

"I have no idea. Ask someone to drive you, I guess."

Irritated with the operator's curtness, I ventured another question. "My other problem is I can't fill out forms as I don't see too well."

"You can take it home and have someone help you."

Knowing I wouldn't have anyone to read for me until the day I needed the ride, I explained, "But I don't have a person to assist me until after Thursday."

"So what do you want me to do about it? I'm sure you can figure it out. I'll hold this reservation for twenty-four hours. You'll have to call back and give me your green card number; otherwise it'll be dropped from the system."

"But—"

Before I could finish my sentence, the irritating receptionist clicked off. The sound of the dial tone buzzed in my ear. I stared at the receiver in my hand. "Another Catch 22," I told it. *I wonder if I can really pull this off*, I wondered, replacing the receiver. Standing in my kitchen, I contemplated the many challenges before me.

Since David and I had separated only a month before, my initial inspiration about being independent was gradually fading. The few good friends I made in graduate school had moved away well over a year ago. Being a stay at home mom with an infant child did not lend itself to making new friends. The inexpensive apartment complex I was forced to live in during the past year made finding acquaintances difficult, at least the kind I was looking for. As far as I could tell only bikers and drug dealers lived around me. With my family fifty miles away, and nowhere in particular to go, I felt rather lonely in the town where I'd received my latest degree.

Moving to the sink, I prepared to wash the dishes. *I do hope I've done the right thing*, I pondered for the umpteenth time.

"It was the right thing to do!" I scolded aloud, bending down to attend to the little person now pulling on my leg. "You sure can be persistent, little buddy!" I said, picking him up in my arms, kissing him on the forehead.

"We had to ask Daddy to leave, didn't we, Noley Pie?" I said in a sing-songy way. "It's sad though, ain't it, guy?" I added in a voice suggesting something happy. I'd developed this technique for releasing my stress, hoping my son would respond only to my tone. Though I needed to talk about my recent decision, I certainly didn't want to upset my child.

"Daddy is a good daddy, isn't he, Nolan? He gets to come see you Thursday."

"Da-da," Nolan said, knowing exactly who I was talking about. Although unable to manage the day in, day out stress of having a baby in the house, David truly loved his son, taking good care of him during his visits. We still loved each other, too. It would have been so much easier to separate if we didn't. I knew by January our relationship was destined to change, but it took until October, right after Fella died, for me to insist that we stop living together. There is something about parenthood that can change one's tolerance for things. I had been able to accept some of David's oddities and self-absorption where I was concerned, but I couldn't accept it for my son.

After Nolan was born, David began slipping inside himself more and more. When September of '82 arrived, he announced he could not return to work. The hope for a decent income, marriage, and a better place to live were suddenly gone. I was devastated. The distress found its way into the muscles of my jaw and by December, I had developed chronic pain there. Until the dentist fitted me with a bite splint, I suffered for months, unable to sleep between Nolan's feedings and the discomfort I felt.

If this wasn't enough, Fella also became ill. He needed constant attention throughout the night. He required assistance to shift positions as his legs had become weak from a pinched nerve in his back. No matter how much I begged and pleaded for David's help, he refused. He said the reasons he couldn't were because of the voices or his own lack of sleep. The result was that I ended up having to hold things together by myself.

The days and nights filled with exhaustion continued. Slowly but surely my resentment grew, and I found myself becoming ugly with anger. David's kind and thoughtful gestures gradually ceased altogether.

One day in January, after losing my temper, I decided I would force him to be responsible. Certain Nolan was well fed, I moved his baby swing into the living room and slid him in. I knew he'd probably sleep for a while. Since David rarely left his recliner, I counted on these conditions as insurance Nolan would be okay. Repressing the anxiety that comes from leaving one's child for the first time, I called a taxi and quickly left the house. I returned two hours later with my hair cut and permed, not surprised to find David was still in the same spot.

"You look awful," he whined, as I stepped through the door.

"Well, it's a good thing I spent twenty bucks then. I wanna get the most for my money," I said sarcastically, checking to be sure Nolan was still sleeping.

"That's too much money for any haircut, especially one that makes you look like you put your finger in a light socket," he snarled. I sensed this might not be a quick argument, so I wound the swing's crank and put Nolan back in motion.

"Shall we add up how much money you spend on cigarettes?" I challenged, moving closer so I could keep my voice low.

"I need my cigarettes, Ger. They help me pace myself. If I didn't have them, I'd end up in the hospital."

"Why don't you go there then? It'd be a lot cheaper. That way I wouldn't have to look at you sitting there in that damn torn up chair of yours, staring into space all day while I take care of your dog and our child and every other damn thing that needs to be done around here."

"You said you'd take care of things if we had a baby. You're irresponsible for leaving me alone with him for so long."

"Irresponsible!" I yelled between clenched teeth, trying to muffle the intensity of my rage. "I can't believe your audacity, David. For over a year now, I haven't had five minutes to myself, while you hide out in the bedroom or smoke in your corner, poisoning the air for our child. When I said I'd take care of things if we had a baby, I didn't mean wiping your ass. My God, David, you can't even pick up your dirty underwear."

"I don't need my underwear picked up," he said. "That's your need. If you don't want it on the floor, then you should be the one picking it up."

"You are such an ass," I growled. "You are the most selfish bastard I've ever known." Glaring at him, I stamped my foot, shaking my fist in the air, blood pounding in my cheeks

"Thank heaven you still have enough sense to make sure he's safe," I snapped. From behind me came the sound of Nolan crying. My heart flooded with guilt as I went over to him.

"Hey there, little buddy! How ya doin'? Did you have a good sleepy pie?" I asked, picking him up from his moving chair. He continued whimpering. I patted his back, hoping to reassure him. I felt so torn between caring for my son and unleashing my rage at David. Pacing now, I carefully spoke, taking great effort to keep my voice low.

"You used to be so kind and thoughtful, but now you don't care about anyone."

"I'm not up for this, Ger. I can't handle the stress of all the demands," David moaned.

"Can't or won't?" I said sweetly. But David just went on defending himself, accusing me of being insensitive. When the urge to hit him almost won out, I knew it was time to leave the room. Nolan's diaper was wet, so I laid him on his changing table and unpinned the soggy cloth from his bottom. I hardly acknowledged his satisfied coos as I pulled a clean diaper from the stack below. I felt horrible for becoming so vicious, and started fantasizing about what to do.

What would it be like living alone? I thought, imagining myself asking David to leave. *What about your commitment, though?* Thoughts of my conversation with Mike so long ago came back to me. *You opened a door, and it can't be shut!* I heard my responsible self scold. *You said it yourself. No, that was Mike who said that*, I argued, trying to remember my exact words. *There is more than one door that can be opened, is what I said.*

"You're hanging on to technicalities," I said out loud to no one, closing the safety pin with my fingers. Ignoring the silent baby who now lay placidly beneath my hands, I continued to debate the rightness and wrongness of my fantasy. *But I can't take this!* I shamefully admitted, speculating the integrity of breaking my vow. *Am I foolish to think I could always stay loyal?* I pondered. *Is obligation the right foundation for raising a child if both parents are so unhappy with each other?*

What about David's commitment to me? Yes, but what about my need for a mate to share in the joy of our son? Suddenly, my heart filled with sorrow. Having no one to experience all the cute little things Nolan had done since his birth had certainly dampened the joy of motherhood.

I was filled with regret as I replaced Nolan's plastic pants and pajama bottoms. Suddenly I was aware of him. I noticed my little boy wasn't smiling. Another form of guilt threatened to make me cry, as I realized I'd been ignoring his coos and jabbers. It dawned on me how much my sadness transferred to him. It was time to do something to make my life better. To ensure my son's happiness, I would either have to find a way to tolerate David's state of being, or separate.

Needless to say, things did not improve. In order to keep Nolan from overhearing arguments, I simply avoided David as much as I could. Since David slept a lot, this was not difficult to achieve.

In May, a drop-in center for survivors of mental illness opened up in our town. With some prompting by his case manager and a few of his friends, David began hanging out there. In the meantime, Fella's condition became progressively worse. Finally, in late September, David agreed to let me put Fella to sleep. With little left to hold him to our home, arrangements were made for David to move in with his friend Duppy. He protested mildly when I talked about finalizing the arrangements, but we both knew it was the best thing to do.

"I think Da-Da can be a much better Daddy now that he and Mommy aren't unhappy with each other anymore," I said, smiling at my little boy. Nolan giggled back and the doubts I'd been considering once more slipped away.

"Laloo!" Nolan said, reaching for the phone.

"You wanna talk on the laloo?" I asked, sitting him on the nearby stool. As I handed him the phone, another member of our little family ran in and nudged my leg with his nose.

"Hey there, Herbert George!" I said, calling him by his formal name. He'd inherited this identification from one of my favorite authors, H. G. Wells. Herbert's timely arrival came two days after Jinxy died. I suspect she missed her buddy, as she passed away from a seizure three weeks after Fella's death. Feeling a void in our household, we welcomed Herby's timely arrival. It seemed fitting to give him the name of the author of The Time Machine. I assumed we'd be good for each other and invited him to move in. He accepted the offer graciously.

"Sorry, you're a bit too big for me to pick you up there, buddy!" The sixty pound shepherd husky mix simply licked my hand and wagged his tail. I thought again of the woman on the phone and had the urge to tell someone about her.

"Some people!" I told the both of them. "I hope neither one of you grow up with such rude manners!"

Nolan merely giggled at my smiling face and I gave him another big kiss on the cheek.

"Uh uh!" he said, and I knew he was pointing at something.

"What you want, Noley Pie?"

He continued grunting. I felt with my hand and saw he was jabbing the air with his finger. Following the direction of his arm, I surmised he wanted me to open the cupboard door.

"I know what you want, piggy!" I said, reaching in and lifting the lid off the cookie jar.

"Let's see who you've got," I said, tracing the outline of the treat. "Hmm, looks like a giraffe. See his long neck?" I asked, holding up the animal and running my thumb up and down the neck. "Ger-aff. Can you say that?"

But Nolan just wiggled and grunted, not caring a bit about what the object was called.

"Okay, here you go! Open wide," I said, pretending the animal cracker was an airplane. I zoomed it around, eventually placing it into his mouth. He laughed heartily. I blew a raspberry on his cheek, making him laugh even harder.

Just then, a paw slid down my leg, so I reached in and grabbed another cookie and held it above Herbert's nose.

"Sit." Obediently, Herby did so. I gave him the treat.

"Good boy! You surely learn fast, Herbert George."

Together the three of us sauntered into the living room. I sat down on the rocking chair and began to sing to my son. Herby lay at my feet while Nolan cooed along with Old McDonald and a variation of Bingo. Herbert appreciated our version best as we spelled out H, E, R, B, Y. Slowly Nolan settled in the crook of my shoulder. Knowing he needed a nap, I changed the tempo of the music and began our favorite lullaby.

I peeked in to say good night, and then I heard my child in prayer.
And for me some scarlet ribbons scarlet ribbons for my hair.

Thoughts of Edna and how she loved this song slid quietly into my memory. I said a silent prayer that my child would never have to endure the suffering she and her parents went through. A sense of melancholy came over me as I completed the last verse.

"It's a shame the safety of life is so short," I whispered to the sleeping baby snuggled in my arms.

"So many losses!" I told the air as I thought about the dogs, David's absence, and my father's death. Curiously enough, they all began fading from my life at the same time. Shortly following Nolan's birth, my father developed lymphatic leukemia. Despite many surgeries, radiation treatments, and chemotherapy, there was lots left of the cancer and little left of him. In June of '83, I received a disturbing phone call from my Mother.

"Your dad is on the living room floor and he can't get up."

"Call the ambulance!" I urged.

"He says he won't go back to the hospital. He's made it clear he wants no more treatments."

On hearing this news, Nolan, and I hopped a Greyhound bus to their home. When I saw my dad lying on the floor of their living room, too weak to get on the couch, I put my social work skills to use. For two hours, I debated with his doctor on the phone, trying to convince her that my father's wishes were valid. Despite her insistence she could save him, I was adamant he needed to die with dignity. Thankfully, she eventually accepted his right to spend his last days with the least amount of suffering and agreed to order a hospital bed, a visiting nurse and proper pain injections.

Although Dad wove in and out of consciousness, I was able to tell him many times how much I loved him. On July 5, 1983, two days before my son's first birthday, my father passed away. There are truly no words to describe the deep grief felt when part of the core of your being is no longer tangibly available. The man who had believed in me and given me so much had been reduced to 68 pounds at the end of his life.

"How did this happen?" I asked no one as I sat at the edge of his coffin in the early morning on the day of his funeral. With no one around, I grasped his cold lifeless hand in mine.

"How could you have been so strong and wise and now be gone?" I asked my dad. I closed my eyes to try to hold back the tears, and the warm glow of the light in my mind's eye appeared. "I'm not gone" was the wordless message I heard. "The love is still strong."

The same realizations I'd had in the hospital when talking to Sophie came back to me. God is love, and love can always be found if one takes the time to look. It comes from within and from those around me. This moment of truth was so real. But as before, it lasted only briefly, as this clairvoyant union evaporated into doubt.

Am I making this up? I asked myself. *This can't be my father talking to me, can it?* But when I opened my eyes, I noticed the deep sadness was gone. It's probably just my mind's way of helping me through this, I thought, recalling the loss and grief section of my psychology book.

"Whatever it is, Dad," I said, squeezing his hand one last time, "I think it must be true. You've sure given me a lot of love and hopefully I will give it to as many people as I can."

With the memory of this moment still fresh in my mind, I kissed my sleeping boy and the three of us all lay down for a nap. As always, I thanked the creator of sleep as I drifted into a peaceful slumber.

Chapter 40

Hello Dollies

November 1983

Day 3

When I awakened from my much needed nap, I got up and made several phone calls. On my third attempt, I located a former reader from grad school who was willing to help. Oliver kindly drove me to the transit station on Wednesday, where I received my ticket to freedom. From 6 a.m. to 11 p.m. I could now be driven door to door for only fifty cents per ride. Stuffing my green card in my wallet, I thanked Oliver for his gracious assistance.

Thursday finally rolled around. David arrived at noon, welcomed in by Herbert George.

"Hey there, boy!" David said affectionately. "Don't jump up now. Good boy!"

"You've got lunch duty, David. Nolan's in his high chair eating mashed potatoes." David threw his jacket on the chair while Herby ran back to his favorite spot underneath Nolan. I knew I could count on old H. G. when it came time for helping with cleanup duty. David walked into the kitchen protesting the scene.

"He's covered from head to toe in potatoes, Ger!"

"I know. He likes to feed himself."

"What do I do when he's done eating? He can't get down all messy like that!"

"So wash him up!" I explained, smiling to myself. "Potatoes clean up really easily off bare-chested babies."

"I don't know," David moaned. "I'm not sure it's such a good idea to let him get food all over the place like that."

"Do you mean it's not good for him or for you?" I chuckled as I headed to the bedroom to get ready.

"How long you gonna be, Ger?" he asked.

"About an hour and a half," I called from the other room. I heard him say something else, but couldn't make it out with my head stuck in the closet.

"Just a minute," I hollered. "I'll be out there in a sec."

I grabbed my rust colored skirt off its hanger and threw it over my head. Rummaging through my drawer, I located my beige cable-knit sweater. As I pulled the soft cotton fabric over my rather large hips, I patted my tummy, now slightly bulged.

"Hmmm!" I commented out loud, deciding that gaining fifteen pounds after having a child was okay. I pulled on my panty hose and slipped my feet into a pair of taupe pumps.

"I hope these go with this skirt," I mused, having no clue what taupe with brown highlights looked like. Though I could still see color, I could not pick up subtle hues. In my mind, brown was brown, beige was beige. I didn't understand the concepts of 'reddish tones' or 'on the gray side.'

I walked over to my dresser and picked up the newest fashion tool. A four-pronged pick now replaced the comb and ballerina brush I had used for most of my life. I fluffed out the soft tiny curls framing my face and cascading down the back of my neck. Leaning forward into the mirror, I worked to make out the outline of my image. The glare from the window on the opposite wall eliminated any chance of seeing. I walked over and shut the blinds then returned to my reflection. I now could see the outline of the bush I assumed must be my hair. I smiled and noticed the motion in the glass but could see no details other than the two dark spots I knew to be my eyes. Running my hand down the front of my sweater allowed me to focus my vision in on my upper body.

Much too plain, I told myself, so I pulled a string of brown wooden beads from my jewelry box and hung them around my neck.

"Ah, that looks better," I remarked, enjoying the contrast they made. *Not bad. Not too dressy, not too casual*, I thought, heading back into the kitchen.

"What was it you were saying, David?"

"I was asking you not to be long. I'm not feeling too well today. The voices are bad. Haven't slept in about four days."

"That's too bad, David. Are they looking at adjusting your medications?"

"Nah! It's just the stress, you know."

It was hard to hear about his struggle, but part of me believed his complaints were his way of paying me back for hurting him so. I tried not to show my guilt, but it haunted me every time I saw him.

"Okay, I think I hear the transit bus. Have fun, you two!" I said, bending down and kissing my son, avoiding being contaminated with mashed potatoes.

As I grabbed my coat and cane from the front closet, Nolan began to wail in protest. Herby, too, ran up hoping he could tag along.

He'll be okay, I told myself, pushing away my worry about David's capabilities. I reminded myself of their obvious bond, commending David for spending time with his son. *It's normal for him to cry when you leave*, I assured myself one more time, thinking about how I rarely left my little boy. Nolan's cries grew louder. I forced the guilt back and raced out of the house before I could change my mind.

As I climbed aboard the big lift equipped bus, I used my cane to tell me when the steps ended. I nervously felt for the money slot. Unable to find it right off, the driver directed my hand to the right place. I fumbled once more to find a seat, and this time managed on my own. *I sure hope I don't fumble too much when I get there*, I thought, as I rode to my destination.

"Hello!" I said, entering the Center for Disability Relations.

"Hi! You must be Geri. Welcome! I'm Sandy, the secretary. Nina will be with you in a minute. There's a seat to your right if you want to sit down."

"Thanks!" I said, grateful for the effective information.

In a minute, the sound of an electric motor grew closer. As it neared, I could see a figure sitting in a wheelchair.

"Hi there! I'm Nina. Glad to meet you." As she moved her chair a little closer, we touched each other's hands.

"I'm Geri," I replied, noticing the contracted position of Nina's fingers.

"Very glad to meet you," she said, inviting me to follow her. "We're going to meet in our conference room. Bob, the director, and the rest of the staff will be a part of the interview."

I was slightly less nervous after the success of the initial greeting as I followed the sound of her chair down a hallway. Entering a large room, I could see the outline of a man and two women arranged around a large rectangular table.

"You can have a seat here," Nina said, tapping a spot in front of me. I felt for the chair and sat down. She drove herself around to the other side, positioning her chair next to the man. After settling myself, I could see he wore a light blue shirt open at the collar.

"Why don't we introduce ourselves?" Nina began.

"Hey there, Geri, I'm Cheryl," a woman to my right said. "I know you can't see me, but I'm a wheelchair user like Nina. It'd probably be more effort than it's worth to try and shake hands, so I'll just tell you that I'm also very beautiful."

Everyone laughed.

"Ah, come on, guys," Cheryl said. "You gotta let me take a little advantage of her. It's not every day I get to convince someone of my gorgeous looks."

It was easy to notice Cheryl's long straight dark hair. She had big white teeth, which were quite visible through her wide smile. This was the extent of detail I could gather, though I sensed she was petite. As I considered whether it was vision or some other sense that might allow me to know this, the man across from me spoke.

"Don't believe her, Geri. She is gorgeous." He took my hand. "Hi, I'm Bob, the director of the agency. Glad you could come."

Returning a firm grasp, I said, "Nice to meet you. Who else do we have in the room?" I asked, hiding my nervousness as I demonstrated my ability to be assertive.

"Hi, I'm Mickie," the woman to my left announced. "I use a wheelchair too. If you could see me, you'd know I'm not gorgeous, as my arthritis has, shall we say, bent me up a bit?"

I turned to the left in an effort to make out Mickie's less than distinguishable features. I wasn't sure, but her head appeared to be tipped down as if she were talking to her belly. Mickie's hair looked medium brown against pale skin, giving her a washed out look. I resisted the urge to rescue her from feeling bad about her appearance.

She quickly added, "Don't go worrying about it though. I still know how to swing, and my boyfriend ain't got no problem with my weird positioning. It works better in bed, you know?"

Shocked at her words, I gasped, then joined the others as they laughed heartily.

"Well, I'm glad you found a good use for your situation," I added.

"Well, Geri," Nina began, "we're awfully glad you applied for the social work position. You certainly have an excellent résumé, so we'd like to start by asking what you can bring to a center that is set up to assist people with accepting their physical and mental disabilities."

How can I help people accept their disabilities? I thought as I scolded myself for having just used handicapped transportation for the first time in my life.

"Uh, well," I began. "I guess I can offer understanding and empathy. But the fact that I have been through a lifetime of trying to accept my growing blindness would be my greatest asset."

"That's good!" Mickie said.

"What is your visual characteristic?" Nina asked.

I smiled, deciding to adopt Nina's word in the future, as it placed a far more positive spin on my situation than the word disability.

"I have retinitis pigmentosa, a degenerative eye disease affecting the retina," I explained. "I have been losing my vision since at least age seven. I've struggled a lot with denial and tried to pretend I could see more than I really could."

Affirming comments came from those surrounding me.

"I have to admit it's only been in the past few years that I've been willing to acknowledge the likelihood I will go totally blind."

"Sounds familiar," Mickie said. "Of course, the loss of my mobility went a little faster than yours."

"Oh, really?" I asked with interest.

"Yeah, my rheumatoid arthritis hit when I was sixteen. I was on my high school gymnastics team, and I can remember forcing myself to get out on the gym floor even though I wouldn't be able to move for the rest of the day. By age seventeen, I got so I couldn't move at all."

"Bummer!" I said, being careful not to sound overly sympathetic.

"Not sure what would be better," Cheryl added. "Having some adjustment time or having it happen all at once. In my case, I didn't have a choice. I got hit by a drunk driver in an oncoming car."

"No kidding," I said, unable to contain my surprise. "Boy, that's too bad."

"I hold no grudges. Can't waste my time with that nonsense. It could have been me just as easily as the eighteen year old guy who hit me. Heck, I was a little bombed myself when I got hit. Probably kept me alive, 'cause my muscles were pretty mellow at the time. The docs said if I'd been totally sober, my body might have been more rigid, resisting the impact and causing my spinal cord to snap up higher. As it is, I only have paralysis from the nipples down instead of needing a breathing machine for the rest of my life. Or not needing nothin' at all." She chuckled at her afterthought.

I was amazed at her remarkable point of view, but I resisted the urge to ask her how she could consider paralysis from the chest down being such a great advantage.

"So you're recommending we all be a little drunk when riding in a car?" I said, keeping with the mood of the group.

"You got it, girl!" Cheryl chortled. "This one's a keeper, Bob. You're all right, Taeckens."

"Gee, thanks!" I said, holding back my excitement at being so readily accepted. "So with your accident happening fast like that, do you think it might have been easier to adjust better with no avenue for denial?"

"Don't get me wrong," Cheryl warned. "It ain't been easy and denial exists even when the facts are clear. For a long time I kept thinking the feeling in my body might come back or they'd come up with some kind of operation to re-connect my spinal cord. Actually, I did start to get some sensation in my arms and some patches on my stomach. When that happened, I really took off on this 'I'm going to be cured' kick, holding onto the sensations as proof I would get better. But when I finally realized that was about the extent of my recovery—physical recovery, that is—my real recovery began."

"What do you mean?" I asked.

"I mean, my mind had to recover from the truth about my situation. I had to get angry, cry, beg, bargain with God, and fall into a hopeless depression before I could get on with it. Took me two years to finally get to the point where I'd accept adaptive devices for writing, eating, drinking, and showing myself in public."

"So you feel pretty accepting of your situation now?"

"Fairly much," Cheryl said. "Don't get me wrong. I still wish I could walk or get myself dressed in the morning and shit like that, but I am no longer ashamed of who I am. I have my brain, my wonderful personality, and I'm a good lover."

Again her outrageousness caught me off guard.

Chuckling, she asked, "Whatsa matter? Don't tell me you're like the rest of the world who thinks crips don't got no sexual desires and abilities?"

"No," I smiled. "I just wasn't expecting to hear about everyone's sex lives at my interview, that's all."

Everyone laughed.

"We do have a unique group here," Nina agreed.

"Like I said, this one's a keeper, Bob," Cheryl said.

He chuckled, then redirected the conversation back to the interview.

"What experience do you have working with people who have been newly disabled?" Bob asked.

"I spent one of my social work internships at a rehab hospital in Detroit. I had to counsel and make discharge plans for people before they went home."

"What types of disabilities?" Mickie asked.

"Oh gosh, lots of different situations. One man had been shot in the head which resulted in a brain injury. Several folks had spinal cord injuries, and I worked with a few people with post-polio syndrome."

"Really?" Nina asked. "I have that, you know. I didn't think many of the medical people were acknowledging that syndrome too readily. Glad to hear it."

"Yeah, I heard about the controversy," I said, acknowledging Nina's situation. "Luckily, the docs at the institute understand it. The folks I spoke with really struggled with their general physicians, being told their pain was in their head or that nothing could be done for them."

"I can imagine!" Nina replied. "Since my doctor finally sent me to a rehab specialist, I'm getting the proper therapies and feeling much better."

"That's good."

"What about your experience with people with mental illnesses?" Bob asked.

I hesitated for a moment, considering how much I should share. But the open candid nature of this unusual group inspired me to divulge information about David. I briefly discussed my belief that mental illness is likely the least accepted, least understood, and most isolating disorder around. Emphasizing the need for adjustment counseling and peer support, I expressed a desire to help develop such programs. This segment of my interview turned out to be the most beneficial to me. I was surprised to learn the mission of the grant which would support the center's new position required programs to address psychiatric deinstitutionalization.

Before I knew it, an hour had passed. We were all laughing and talking as if we'd known each other for years when Sandy came in and announced my ride was waiting. As I left the room, Bob got up and shook my hand again and followed me to the entrance.

"We certainly are impressed with all you had to say here today, Geri."

"Thank you. I'm impressed with you and your staff as well. I've never been interviewed and had so much fun," I said with a chuckle.

"Well, we should know by next week some time if the grant funding this post comes through. If it does, I believe the staff and I are very interested in bringing you on board."

"Thank you very much!" I said, holding down my excitement at getting a job.

"We'd be starting you out at $16,000 a year plus benefits."

The sound of these figures was almost too much to take. Resisting the urge to hug him, I wondered if my dream to have my Social Security checks discontinued might really come true.

"Well, just let me know," I said, hoping my steady practical voice covered up my sense of desperation.

Despite the anxious anticipation growing in my heart, I felt a new sense of liberation as I rode home on the transit bus. I had spent time with others with physical differences through the RDS, but I had never met anyone quite like the folks at the Center for Disability Relations. Thinking about how okay they all seemed to be, I wondered if I could ever feel the same. For the first time ever I considered that disability could be a privilege. As I imagined myself becoming a part of such a community of healthy people, my heart swelled with an unfamiliar emotion. I finally realized it was pride!

Chapter 41

Wonders Never Cease

January 1984

    I stepped off the transit bus and hurriedly ran down the steps to my apartment and opened the door. After eight hours at work, I could hardly wait to get home and see my son. As I entered the apartment, the familiar sound of the jingling bells on his shoes told me Nolan was running toward me.
    "Hey there, Noley Pie!" I said, tossing my cane into the closet near the door. Together Herbert and Nolan demanded my attention, insisting they each get their due hugs before I did anything for myself.
    "Uppy, uppy, uppy!" Nolan repeated insistently as I patted Herbert on the head.
    "Good boy, Herby." I gently pushed him aside to pick up my adorable child.
    "Uppy-do! My buddy boy," I mimicked, lifting him off the ground. "Were you a good boy for Mary today?" He ran his fingers through the curly hair which now hung to my shoulders. His fingers moved around the frame of my face then across my cheeks and down to my mouth. He followed this ritual with running his nose along my cheeks and tasting my skin with his tongue. It was an odd greeting custom between a mother and son, but I knew it was likely due to being raised by a mother who interacts using all available senses.
    "He was, he was," said the wonderful lady who cared for Nolan each afternoon. She was David's relief from his morning duty. "Nolan ate real good today and went down for a nap at two. Slept about an hour and a half, which is surprising for him. Of course Herby stayed right with him the whole time, that wonderful soul. When he got up we played blocks and then he helped me make banana bread. I left it for you on top of the fridge. Made one for myself as well. Hope you don't mind?"
    "Heck no! Thanks, Mary. You are the best."
    She reached over and gave me a hug, then kissed the top of Nolan's head before leaving the apartment. I marveled at her incredibly giving nature and again wondered how I ever found her.

    In my effort to avoid day care, I had placed a small ad in the newspaper as soon as I got word from Bob that I'd be hired. Three people answered, but Mary shined above the others. Though my income had increased far above the government checks I'd received in the past, I still did not have much to give out for child care. As Mary could only earn a minimal amount due to limitations set by her own Social Security benefits, she was willing to take a less than competitive salary, accepting any food she could eat or bake as part of her wages. Though I insisted she not lift a finger in terms of dishes or housework, I never came home to a mess. The best part was her endless upbeat spirit and the fact she loved my son like a grandmother.

Whenever I told her how blessed I felt to have her in my life, she simply replied, "Oh honey, it's written in the stars, don't you know? We both need each other. Besides it's love that makes the world go round, and I can tell you and me got enough for everyone." Then she'd give me a big hug and I'd thank her again anyway.

"So you were a good boy today, were you?" I said to Nolan as I plopped him on my bed and changed into more comfy clothing. Herbert hopped up beside him. "Wanna go to the park with Mommy?"

"Pa-pa!" he answered with delight. Herbert's tail pounded the bed at the sound of this magic word.

Despite my exhaustion from a long day at work, I bundled both of us up and pulled the sled and my cane from the front closet. By the sound of his panting I could tell Herby had located his tennis ball and was more than ready to go. Picking up Nolan, I put him on my right hip, holding him firmly with the cane in a non-functional position in my hand. I opened the door and held it with my foot, so I could drag the sled behind me. With one great whoosh, I managed to get us all through the door without any fingers or tails getting pinched.

Once outside, I set Nolan on the sled and pulled it with my left hand while using my cane with the right. Walking in the snow was much more difficult than walking on clear terrain. I sometimes became confused as to where the snowy sidewalk ended and the boulevard began, but the sound of the moving traffic helped keep me oriented. Eventually I located the set of stairs three blocks from my house which led up a hill to the park.

Up and down the snowy mound we went while Herby quadrupled the distance chasing his ball. Only local residents knew about this little hideaway that had a hill with no trees. As it was tucked between three sides of houses bordering the unusually large block, Nolan, Herby, and I often found ourselves alone. When my legs would not withstand the effort anymore, I announced the news to my son.

"We gotta go home now, Pumpkin."

"Uppy, uppy!" Nolan insisted. So I agreed to one more time, three more times. Finally I convinced my two boys we had to go. With Herby's ball firmly clamped between his teeth, he followed as I pulled my son back home.

My eyes were half closed as I fixed some dinner, fed the three of us, cleaned the dishes, and readied us all for bed. Though he was unusually fussy, Nolan finally drifted off to sleep in my lap around ten. Herby and I soon joined him, as we both flopped into bed. It seemed like only seconds later when I heard my son crying in the next room. I got up and went to check on him.

"Whatsa matter, little one?" I asked, reaching down to touch him.

"Wow! You're really hot," I said, feeling his burning skin beneath my hand. Slightly panicked, I picked him up. His muscles and skin felt scorched and taut. I tried to soothe him, placing him over my shoulder, but he kept on crying.

The three of us entered the bathroom where I located the baby Tylenol in the medicine cabinet. I filled the syringe with one hand hoping not to spill it. Slipping the dropper into his mouth, I squirted the medicine in.

We moved into the living room. I switched on the lamp so he could see and began rocking him. Herby stood with his chin on my knee, staring at the crying baby in my arms.

"I'm not sure what's wrong with him," I told my caregiving partner, feeling Nolan's scalding forehead.

Nothing I could do would settle Nolan down. His cry, though persistent, sounded weak with noticeable congestion in his chest. His hot skin against my body told me his fever was rapidly getting worse.

"God, I wish I could read a thermometer," I told Herby who was now lying at my feet. After thirty minutes of rocking and pacing, singing every song I knew, it seemed like Nolan felt even hotter. His body started contracting as if he might be having convulsions. Terrified he could burn up, I began thinking of who I could call to help me read a thermometer. No one came to mind as my neighbors were not the trustworthy type. I finally decided to call my mom despite the early hour of the morning.

"Hello," she said groggily.

"Hi, Mom," I said, sure she could hear Nolan yelling loudly in the background.

"What's the matter?" she immediately asked.

"Well, Nolan's real hot, and I can't tell what his temperature is."

"Oh honey," she said sympathetically. "Can you wake up a neighbor or something?"

"I don't really think so. It's pretty late," I said, talking above Nolan's screams.

"What time is it anyway?" she asked.

"About three or so."

"Oh, dear. Well, you could try wrapping his body in a cool wet towel."

"Wouldn't that make him feel worse?"

"Probably, but it'll bring his fever down. Crying is good Geri. If he's crying, he's okay. I know it's hard to listen to, but I'd keep cool cloths on him until you feel his forehead cool down. Don't put the cold cloths on his head so you can gauge if the wet towel around his body is working."

"And if it doesn't work?"

"Well, then you need to call a cab and take him to the emergency room. Do you have any money for that?"

"Yes," I said, grateful I did. "Maybe I should do that anyway?" I asked, worrying I may have waited too long already.

"I think he's probably okay. Like I said, his cries are a good sign. It's when they get quiet that you have to worry. But if his head doesn't cool down, I'd take him just to be sure."

"Thanks, Mom."

"Call me back either way, won't ya?"

"I hate to wake you again. How about if I call you if he gets worse."

"Oh, Geri, don't be silly. I'm awake now anyway. Doubt I'll fall back asleep at this point. I'm just so sorry I can't be closer to come and help."

"Me too!" I said, aching for her to be with me. "I got Herbert here helping," I told her. "I think we'll be okay."

Mom gave a chuckle, and we said our goodbyes.

Following her directions, I put Nolan in his crib despite his protests. There was no way for me to hold him and wet down a towel. I thought Herbert would have a nervous breakdown as Nolan's screams intensified. He kept whining and trying to round me up, weaving his way in and out of my legs, unsuccessfully pushing me from my position near the bathtub.

"It's okay, boy." I attempted to reassure him as I leaned over the tub wringing out a thick wet towel. Returning to Nolan, I stripped him of his pajamas and wrapped the cold wet cloth around him. I was fearful he'd break a vocal cord from his piercing screams, but I continued pacing and singing in hopes I could soothe him.

With every passing minute, I wondered how long I should wait. I thought about parents who had colicky children and wished I could send them my sympathies. Again I longed for someone who could share in this most stressful situation, swapping breaks and discussing what to do next with him.

"I'm sorry my baby boy," I whimpered sympathetically. "It's gonna be okay."

But Nolan just screamed and screamed as I paced the floor of the apartment. Herbert followed every step, insistent on making sure I wasn't hurting his baby. Finally, after what seemed an eternity, Nolan began to lighten his cry to whimpers. Feeling his forehead, I could tell he was cooler now. Gingerly, I lowered myself into the rocking chair, exhausted from walking. Thankfully, Nolan allowed me to do this, as his body started to relax.

"I think he's doing better, Herbert," I said to my wonderful partner. "Thanks, boy, for helping out."

Herby settled down at my feet, pressing his muzzle over top of my bare toes.

I peeked in to say good night and then I heard my child in prayer.

And for me some scarlet ribbons, scarlet ribbons for my hair.

As I sang the words to the melancholy song, tears began to roll down my cheeks. With the fear from this terrible ordeal now subsiding, I scolded myself for not being able to see the thermometer. As I questioned my capability as a parent, I recalled another crisis we'd gotten through.

Remember the time you figured out he needed stitches? I asked myself, thinking of the incident in which Nolan tipped over on his miniature tricycle in the park. Instinctively I knew my tongue was the only part of my body that could tell me the depth of the cut. As fine tuned as my fingers could be, they were far too thick to determine such detail. It turned out he needed four stitches. The emergency room staff were also impressed not only for the skill of my tongue, but because I was willing to take a taste of my son's bloody knee.

You're not too bad, I said to myself, still marveling at how I knew what to do.

But you can't read a thermometer, I argued, continuing the battle with myself. How many other disasters could happen and you might not be able to protect him? I questioned. Remember how you knew he had a screw in his mouth? my other voice countered. Oh, yeah, my critical voice reluctantly acknowledged.

When Nolan was only nine months old, I had been cooking dinner in the kitchen when I dropped my spatula and ran into the living room. Locating my son on the floor, I again instinctively reached in his mouth and pulled out a tiny screw. At first I couldn't understand how I knew this. Then I realized it had to do with his breathing. As babies are mouth breathers, the sound of air going through his little nose alerted me his lips were closed. Above the noise of sizzling hamburgers and Sesame Street playing on the television, I miraculously became aware something sounded different.

"I still can't believe I heard that, Herbert," I told the sleeping dog. "I sure wish I'd known my body would take over like this all those years I stressed about not seeing. I should be more like you, Herby. You never fret. You just use your intuition and never worry about what's to come. Who said you guys are the inferior species anyway?" I asked him. But he did not answer. He simply continued resting peacefully on my feet.

I sure wish I had the answer to all this, I thought. The universe is truly an amazing place and yet I act like it's no big deal.

You have wisdom beyond what you know, my wise self said, as the familiar light came into view. Barely aware of my head's affirming nod, a warm glow descended over me.

"Maybe I do," I said aloud. "Maybe I do."

Chapter 42

Amity

August 1984

"Hey Geri, can you grab my pen off the floor for me?"
"Surely," I said, bending down to feel with my hands.
"Just a little to your left there," she directed. "Now up and to the right a bit."
I followed her directions.
"Now a bit left. You're getting warmer. Almost there!"
"Got it!" I said triumphantly, raising the object high in the air. "Where do I put it?"
"Feel the brace on my hand?"
"Yeah," I said, locating her arm, which was resting on her chair.
"Okay, look for the little slot that goes between my thumb and forefinger."
Running my own fingers over the plastic bands which crisscrossed Cheryl's unfeeling hand, I noticed a metal tube situated right where she said it would be.
"You got it," she said as I slid the pen in and returned to my desk.
"What ya working on?" I asked.
"Oh, that proposal for starting a new training for personal care attendants."
"Great! Have any concern we won't get it?"
"They'd better give it to us," Cheryl warned, lifting her arm from her shoulder to maneuver her pen on the paper. "Do you know how many people could live outside a nursing home if they only had someone to help get them dressed? It makes me sick that the government is more willing to spend money on residential placement than keeping people in their own private apartments."
I watched as she lifted her available forearm and rubbed it back and forth across her face.
"How 'bout lending me your fingers?" she asked, lowering her arm.
"Absolutely. What for?"
"I can't get this annoying hair out of my eye and it's driving me crazy."
"Sure." I found the straggling hair and wrapped it securely around her ear.
"Thanks my friend. That's better."
"No problem."
"Anyway, let's cross our fingers and hope we get this money."
I held up my hand and flashed the symbol requested.

"Knew I could count on you, Geri girl."

I gave her a smile as I shared what I knew about the subject at hand.

"Bob was quoting the stats to me the other day. It would be loads cheaper for Social Services to pay a person's rent, an attendant for eight hours a day, and public transportation than to pay for a nursing home."

"No kidding. Shit, I pay nine bucks an hour, which is half of what it costs the nursing home to hire an aide, and I only need assistance for eight to ten hours a day."

"Really! It's that much cheaper?" I asked, astonished.

"Yessum," she affirmed.

"I knew you had someone come help you get dressed in the morning and evening, but I didn't know you needed someone for that long..."

"Yeah, I do, but it's still not twenty-four hours, which is what nursing homes end up providing. I expect the government could get away with even cheaper wages, though I personally happen to pay better salaries than most."

"How come?"

"Mainly because the assistants deserve it. My lady not only helps me in the wee hour of five o'clock, but she has to spend the night and get up every two hours to keep me from getting bed sores."

I knew what Sherri meant by this. My experience working in the rehab hospital taught me about the hidden consequences of paralysis. Being unable to move or feel one's body could cause too much pressure on the skin. Infectious bed sores which could spread to the bone could end in serious illness, amputations, or death. It was, therefore, necessary for folks to be physically turned over.

Cheryl shoved her ceramic cup across her desk. The sound of rushing liquid followed.

"How can you drink that stuff?" I asked.

"Hey, it's my elixir of life. Don't drink, I stink."

I smiled.

"Well, I gotta admire you. Not sure I'd take such care of myself if I had to swallow something as boring as hot water."

Cheryl lowered her head and drank from her straw. I'd learned how she had developed many intricate ways for maintaining her independence, right down to her clever idea to use a hot water urn with a levered spout. All she had to do was push the valve with her wrist to fill her own cup. When she was done drinking, she went on.

"Then there's the bowel program. Of course nobody enjoys doing this shitty task. Anybody who's willing to stick a suppository up my ass and wait around for two hours while it all comes tumbling out—smell and all—deserves lots of money, my friend."

"I guess you've got a point there," I said, having forgotten about the bathroom detail. "How do you afford all this, if you don't mind me asking? The salary from the center sure ain't enough for such an extravagant lifestyle is it? I mean to pay for someone to oversee you take a shit?"

She laughed. "No kidding! I guess I'm lucky 'cause the insurance from the car crash pays for all that medically related stuff for me. Lots of folks who are disabled from an illness or birth or something don't have such luxuries. That's what makes me so mad. If the government could subsidize some of these folks, not only would some very capable people be able to work and get off Social Security, they'd save the government money by keeping out of expensive nursing facilities. Besides, just because someone uses a wheelchair don't mean they need skilled care. I mean we ain't sick, we just can't walk! If these lawmakers would get off their duffs and check out these places, do the math, and think about the fact they might be disabled themselves someday, they might make better decisions about how taxpayers' money is spent."

I nodded in agreement as Cheryl added, "Besides, if they thought about what they'd want if they were in my shoes, I'll bet they'd wanna hire some expensive chick to change their pants and do their bowel program. That'd get 'em off now wouldn't it?"

"Oh, Cheryl!" I laughed. "You do tell it like it is, don't you?"

"No other way than the straight skinny," she insisted.

Turning back to my desk, I continued my report on the peer resource training I had recently conducted. When I realized I didn't have the correct spelling for three of the attendants' names, I turned to Cheryl.

"Hey, can I bug you to read this and spell these names."

"No problem." I handed her the printed roster and typed as she spoke each letter.

"Now, could I get you to relieve me?" she asked.

"Sure!"

I waited until she maneuvered her chair out the wide three foot doorway and followed her to the bathroom. She rode up to the edge of the toilet and stopped. Shutting the door behind us, I came up beside her and lifted her right pant leg. As I had done three times daily since my arrival at the center, I bent down and picked up the filled leg bag strapped to her shin. I positioned the end of the attached hose over the toilet and opened the rubber valve. But instead of the urine pouring out in a nice even stream, the bag unexpectedly burst. In one great whoosh, urine sprayed all over both of us, saturating her pants and the skirt of my navy blue suit.

"Oh shit!" we said in unison.

"Ger, I'm so sorry!" she exclaimed.

"Heck," I laughed. "What are friends for if they can't piss on each other once in a while?"

"Oh, God. I am sorry."

"Forget it, Cheryl. I just hope I can find someone to bring me a clean suit before the meeting this afternoon."

"Oh God, we're presenting at the United Way today."

"Yuppers!"

"Oh, man. What a pisser."

"No kidding," I chuckled.

"Well, I'll drive us both home. You can change at your apartment and then we'll head to my place. If you don't mind, I'll have you snatch me a clean pair of pants and knee highs."

"That'll work. I can help you get changed when we get back here."

I retrieved a fistful of paper towels and mopped us both up and then wiped the floor. We notified Bob, who was entertained by our plea to take a half hour leave.

"By all means, please make yourselves presentable for the United Way presentation. We don't want our supporters to think we piss their money away."

We left the center in hysterics. With a flick of a button on her key ring, the back door of her van automatically opened and lowered into a ramp. I climbed into the passenger side as Cheryl rolled into the place where the driver's seat would normally be. She clicked another switch, locking herself into the wheel slots. I heard the back door electronically close. After slipping her arm into a sling-like apparatus, she started the ignition. I watched as she swung her arm in a circular motion, turning the van's wheels as she did so.

"And we're off!" she announced, "I can't wait 'til we get out of these clothes!"

At my apartment complex, I hopped out and hurried inside. In less than ten minutes, I had greeted David, my dog and son, jumped into a lighter blue suit, wiggled my way out of Nolan's goodbye grasp and cautiously rushed back to the van. Peeling out of the driveway, Cheryl raced to her place. I hastily unlocked her door, rummaged through her closet and found the items she'd requested.

When we returned to the center, I helped her change her clothes, not an easy task. I soon discovered there's an interesting phenomenon that occurs when stimulating the dormant muscles of paralyzed limbs. Instead of staying still, they react violently, as if angry for having their slumber disturbed.

"Whoa, down girl," I called, jumping back from a spasmodic kick.

"Sorry about that, Ger. They're extra wild, probably due to me being a little stressed."

"Maybe I should let them relax before I try putting on your clean pants. You don't mind going to lunch with a bare ass now, do you?"

"Well, I wouldn't mind, but Bob might get turned on, you know."

We both laughed. When the mission was finally accomplished, we tooled into the lunch room just in time to eat with the others.

The newest employee, Jody, was sitting across from me. She joined the center's team only two weeks earlier. Her hair and eyes were so dark I could easily see the outline of her face.

"So you got a little pissed off at Geri, did you, Cheryl?" Mickey asked.

"Just a bit."

"Heard it was quite a bit," Jody said.

"It was plenty," I agreed.

"So is everyone going to the social gathering tonight?" Bob asked.

"I've got to go to a baby shower," Cheryl said.

The rest of us confirmed we'd be there.

"Anyone able to give me a ride?" I asked, suddenly realizing I would need one without Cheryl.

"I'd be glad too, Geri," Jody said.

"Gee, thanks. You don't mind if my little boy comes with us, do you?"

"Heck no, I love little boys."

"Big ones too I'll bet," Mickey teased.

"Them too," Jody agreed.

As beautiful as she was, I was surprised to learn there was no love in her life. Despite an unsteady balance and some limitation with her coordination—the result of multiple sclerosis—Jody had a grace about her like no other woman I'd ever seen. Though she sometimes used an electric scooter, she often held onto walls with her hands when she only needed to go short distances. Despite her tremulous gait, her five foot nine stature made her look like a dancer as she glided along, or "wall walked," as she called it.

"I'll pick you up at six?"

"That's great."

We finished our day and left for home. As I opened the door to my apartment, Nolan came running up. An instant smile crossed my face.

"Mommy Mommy!" he squealed, as he leapt into my arms.

"Hey there, little buddy!" I said, matching his excitement. Herby jumped up too, wanting his share of attention. Reeling from the impact, I leaned my body against the door, hugging and patting them both.

"Hey there, Mary," I said, finally able to greet her.

"Hi there, Mommy dearest," Mary replied in her usual fashion, giving me the run down of the day. "Nolan and I made puppet socks today," she informed me.

"I show you, Mommy!" he said, diving out of my grasp and dashing off to the kitchen.

"See?" he said, bringing his creation to my hand.

"Oh, this is really cute," I marveled, feeling the two buttons sewn on for eyes.

"Don't forget to feel the ears," Mary urged.

"Oh, Nolan, did you help Mary sew the felt on?"

"Yuppie!" he squealed. After I thoroughly looked over the entire puppet with my fingers, Mary said her goodbyes and went on her way.

"So, you wanna go to a party tonight, Noodle Doodles?"

"Yuppie! Patty patty!"

"Yuppers!" I said, "That's right. We're going to a party. But first Momma's gotta get out of these clothes," I told him, directing my entourage into the bedroom so I could change.

After slipping into jeans and a scooped neck shirt that I knew was covered in tiny blue flowers, I packed up the diaper bag, took Herbert and Nolan outside so Herby could do his thing, and then returned my four-legged buddy to the apartment. Nolan and I waited on the front stoop, so I could hear when Jody drove up.

On the trip to the social gathering held at the Bear Club Lodge, I learned that Jody had in fact been a dancer in her youth. She'd been diagnosed with MS at age sixteen, but didn't really show symptoms until graduate school. Jody, the youngest of six, had five older brothers. She informed me her dark eyes and complexion were the result of her Jewish heritage. She had recently completed her master's degree in Social Work from the same university as me.

"So tell me about these social gatherings," she said.

Between Nolan's questions about her hand controls which looked nothing like Cheryl's, I gave her the scoop on the center's social program.

"We do them once a month. The center foots the bill for the food so folks can commiserate about whatever."

"So is there, like, a topic of the evening we all discuss? Or does someone give a presentation on the latest political issue or something?"

"Nah. That's more the stuff we do in presentations or individually with clients. Lots of the people who come to this shindig may not receive services from the center. They may have in the past, but it's not a requirement to eat. Heck, not everyone has a disability for that matter. It's really for anyone who wants to come. I find the atmosphere more conducive to folks chatting about issues though, as there ain't this expectation to pour out their guts, if you know what I mean."

"I do. Far out!" Jody said. "How many folks usually come?"

"Oh gee, it varies, but usually we have at least thirty, lots of family members too."

Jody turned her van into the parking lot and eased it into a spot. Nolan watched intently as she transferred from the driver's seat to her electric scooter.

"Was dat?" he asked, pointing.

"It's an Amigo. My friend," she said, giving Nolan a big smile. After activating her lift, she met us outside.

Nolan, still mesmerized by her unusual vehicle, asked, "Where's da moder?"

"It's right here," she said. "It doesn't have a motor, it has batteries."

"No moder?" Nolan asked, sounding disappointed.

"Nope, no motor, buddy. But it sure can go. Watch," she said, zooming forward. Nolan and I ran to catch her. When we caught up, he proceeded with his inquiry.

"Big wheel. Where big wheel?" For a minute I didn't understand what he was asking.

"What big wheel?" I asked.

"Cheryl big wheel?"

"Oh," I said, finally getting it. "Jody doesn't have big wheels like Cheryl. Her chair has little wheels."

"Yeah," Jody said enthusiastically. "I got little wheels. This is a scooter, not a wheelchair. Wanna ride?" she asked. To my surprise, my shy little Nolan hopped up on her lap and the three of us headed for the door.

By most people's standards, dinner might have appeared to be a catastrophe. Although the buffet table was abundant with food, it was not served in a neat timely manner. It didn't matter whether one walked or rolled, possessed spastic muscles, balance problems, was blind or deaf, everyone got in line and found a way to fill their plates. As we helped each other, trails of mashed potatoes, Jell-o, and other eatable remnants dripped into serving dishes or on the table. It might not have been pretty, but there was great beauty in the fact that not an ounce of condescension was heard. No one used the act of lending a hand to feel more capable or superior than another.

It amazed me how in this setting, I could be so independent when, in a room full of sighted people, I felt so inept. Jody marveled at the cooperative nature of everyone. She also commented on how good it felt to take her time getting her own food. Even Nolan, at the age of two, did his part. He fetched items for those who needed his help and cut his own carrot when he finally settled down to eat.

When the time arrived for us to leave, Nolan and I piled back in Jody's van.

"That was great!" Jody said, sharing in my sense of liberation.

"Ain't it though? I love being able to move in a crowd like that without folks being overly vigilant to my every need."

"No kidding! Shoot, when I'm with my brothers, I'm totally doted on. Not sure if it's my MS or the fact I'm the only baby girl in the family."

"Probably both," I said, chuckling.

"Hey, you wanna go to the movies with me next Saturday?" she asked.

"If you don't mind Nolan coming along, I'd really be into it."

"I hear a Muppet movie's playing," Jody said, her genuine interest tapping into my secret longing for a friend.

"Me gotta Kermie!" Nolan squealed.

"He does," I affirmed.

"Wow! You've gotta Kermit the Frog?"

"Uh huh," Nolan said, smiling.

"Well then, there is no getting out of it, Mom. Your son and I have a date for the movies. Of course you can tag along if you want, but Nolan and I will rendezvous on Saturday for sure," she said, reaching over and tapping Nolan's leg.

As he wiggled nervously, I wondered if he too desired a new companion to spend time with.

"You are the cutest!" she said, smacking her lips making a kissing sound. Nolan leaned back into my chest, a shy coyness coming over him. I bent my head and kissed him.

"Boy, I'd better watch out, Noley Pie. If I'm not careful, this lady is going to scoop you up and take over your affections."

He reached his hand up and felt my lips, gripping the bottom one and squeezing it hard.

"Ow! You little rascal."

"I think you're embarrassing him, Geri."

"I must be," I said, chuckling. After watching Jody express such affection toward my son, I thought I would explode with delight. The opportunity to share Nolan's beauty with someone was a rarity. I quickly cautioned myself not to get my hopes up. The novelty of spending time with a little one would surely wear off.

Despite my doubts, the anticipation of the upcoming venture helped ease the demands of the week. As promised, when Saturday came at last, Jody picked us up and we headed to the local mall to see *The Muppets Take Manhattan*. Each time Jody shared in Noodle's laughter, little bursts of joy squirted from my heart. Never in my wildest dreams would I believe I could find a childless adult to sit through and enjoy silly puppets running like crazy around a city. When the movie ended, Jody suggested we go window shopping. As usual, Nolan made his typical request.

"Uppy-do, uppy-do, Momma!"

"Oh kiddo, you are getting heavy, you know," I moaned as I reached down to pick him up.

"Wanna ride with me, little buddy?" Jody asked.

"Hey, yeah. You liked riding with Jody the other day, didn't you?"

Without a moment's hesitation, he leaped from my arms before I had a chance to let him down.

"Whoa, buddy, be careful there," I said, hoping he hadn't hurt her.

"Oh, he's okay," she said, hugging him affectionately as he squiggled himself on her lap.

"Where's moder?" he asked, placing his hands on the handle bars.

"Oh, you wanna drive, do you?" Jody asked.

"Me drive the moder."

"Okay, let's do it," Jody said. Before I could reposition my cane to follow, they were off.

"Now be careful not to hit those people ahead of us," I heard Jody say.

I gasped. "Nolan, you let Jody drive," I hollered from behind, wondering which one of us was crazy. Tapping my cane vigorously, I managed to get close enough to speak. "Nolan, it's too crowded in here for you to drive."

"Ah, he's okay, Mom, don't worry," I heard her voice trail away, as the distance between us expanded once more. Realizing my defeat against this fun loving couple, I slowed my pace and accepted my fate. I couldn't help smile at Jody's nonchalant attitude which had easily overrode my motherly instincts. As I struggled to keep track of my amigos on the Amigo, I listened for the sound of the motor. Thank heaven for their laughter as it was the only thing besides my cane I could hear. Rushing to catch up to this dynamic duo, I heard, "Wow! Look out!" followed by "All right, you did it!"

Opening my mouth to suggest an alternative traveling plan, I said, "Do you think this is a good—" but the sound of the scooter and their hysterical laughter again disappeared into the crowd. People moved in and out in front of me as I worked to keep track of my delinquent charges.

"Jody!" I finally called.

"We're over here!" I heard her say.

"Here, Mommy!" Nolan repeated, but another horde of people pushed their way in front of me.

For almost two hours I dodged and listened, as they rode and I walked up and down the length of the mall. We stopped once to have a drink and a cookie, but Nolan's passion to play chauffer urged us on.

"Pretty cool there, Noodles," I said, as Jody explained how fantastic my child was at maneuvering through thick crowds of people.

"He's only just two and he drives like Mario Andretti," she marveled.

"He loves motors," I agreed. "At home, we always have to have the vacuum out and he loves to turn it off and on."

"Do you do that?" Jody asked, bending her head to kiss him.

"Me wike the va-va!" he assured her.

As I observed the two of them, my hope for a friendship with Jody grew. Little bursts of anxiety threatened my feelings of optimism, but they were easily thwarted as we paraded around in public, sticking out among the crowd without an ounce of embarrassment.

Please let this last! I begged in my mind, praying this new friendship would never disappear.

Chapter 43

The Little Engine That Did

March 1985

"May I help you?" asked a dark haired woman in a red vest from behind the ticket counter.

"Yes, my friend needs to make arrangements for getting her electric wheelchair onboard," I explained to the clerk. The wraparound corral blocking Jody from the elevated booth was not wide enough for her to maneuver through. The barriers preventing her from taking care of her own business forced her to ask me to speak on her behalf.

"We will also need seat assignments," I added, holding out our previously purchased tickets.

I heard the clerk flip through the pages of our travel vouchers. When she looked up, she said, "I'm terribly sorry, but you'll have to have these tickets reissued for the 8:35 a.m. leaving tomorrow morning."

"What!" I said in astonishment.

"We only have one train a day taking handicapped people," she informed me.

"That's ridiculous," I insisted.

"Not really," she said. "In order to put you and your friend and her wheelchair on the train, the conductors need a lift. We have only one per day equipped with such an apparatus. That's the one that comes every morning. The 5:15 p.m. leaving from Toronto will be the one you need to take for your return."

"So, basically what you are saying is my friend and I get to have a whopping day and a half in Toronto, which means missing out on the play we're scheduled to see?"

"I'm terribly sorry, but the travel agent who booked this trip for you should have realized. The explanation of travel requirements for the handicapped is right there in the rules and regulations."

And who reads that fine print? I asked myself.

"Well, our travel agent didn't see that. Like me and my friend, she probably didn't even think to check out something so ludicrous."

Completely ignoring me, she asked, "Do you want me to reserve two seats for you and your friend for tomorrow?"

"No, I want you to give us a reservation for the one we are booked on today."

"Like I tried to explain, handicapped people are not allowed on this train."

"Not allowed?" I asked, astounded at her offhand reference to an entire group of people as if they were contaminated animals.

"Would somebody please clue me in on what's going on?" Jody asked, calling from the opposite side of the barrier. I turned in her direction. Several people were now lined up behind me.

"This lady is saying that people like us can't ride this train," I hollered for Jody and everyone to hear.

"What?" she yelled back. "What do you mean we're not allowed?"

"I know! I don't think they've heard of equal opportunity at this station yet."

In an anxious tone the clerk interjected, "It's not that you are not allowed, it's just that the one scheduled at this time doesn't have the proper equipment on it for you."

"What kind of equipment are you talking about?" Jody asked, maintaining a very audible volume as she spoke.

The clerk turned and called to someone behind her. "Maggie, can you take over for me here?"

At first I thought she might be asking her supervisor for help, which I hoped might improve our situation. But instead, the newcomer simply stepped up to the desk as the clerk moved out from behind the counter and walked over to Jody. I followed.

I wasn't absolutely sure, but I suspected the lady's motives were more about avoiding a public spectacle than any concern for respecting Jody's need to hear. Rounding us up like a team of football players to announce the next move, the clerk reiterated the same game plan to Jody.

"That is ludicrous!" Jody shouted.

"That's exactly what I said."

"Ladies, I don't make the rules. I only carry them out. There is nothing I can do. There's no way to get that thing on board."

"That thing happens to be my legs," Jody corrected.

"Uh, well, yes, but they're still not going to load it without a lift. The only train with such equipment runs in the morning as I have already explained.

"Look, they have to put people's luggage on. Let's just consider the scooter as part of the luggage," I suggested. "It comes apart into three pieces. I'm sure none of the components are heavier than many suitcases."

The clerk ignored my solution.

"As I said, I'm terribly sorry. You'll have to wait until the morning and take the specialized train for handicapped individuals."

Jody started to say something, but she was so dumbfounded only garbled sounds escaped her vocal cords.

"Listen," I said firmly. "We have spent a lot of money for a three-day weekend. We didn't get out of work until four, so we couldn't have made it this morning anyway. We have to be back Monday morning at eight. Like every other customer, we are entitled to the same benefits of multiple time options. The purchase of these tickets proves that. If I'm not mistaken, your rules also emphasize a no-refund policy, so you'll have to break one rule no matter what."

"The bottom line," I continued, "is that we are not going to have our much needed vacation be cut in half because you think luggage which comes in the form of a wheelchair can't be lifted into the baggage compartment. You either give us seat assignments and a baggage claim check, or we park ourselves on the train tracks so nobody goes anywhere."

A moment of silence followed as the clerk and likely several bystanders digested what I said. Unfortunately, instead of coming up with a workable idea, the lady was only searching for another defensive tactic.

"Even if we were able to convince the personnel to load the chair, none of them are authorized under our insurance policy to carry your friend on board."

"Her friend is sitting right in front of you, ma'am. You don't need to talk as if I'm not here," Jody said more politely than I might have. "Who says they have to carry me anyway?"

"You're able to climb the steps, ma'am?" the clerk asked, this time directing her question to Jody.

"No way!" Jody exclaimed. "But she can. Geri's lifted me many times in the past."

Speechless, the lady seemed perplexed. I was uncertain as to whether I actually saw her staring at my cane or whether I surmised this, but her next response told me my symbol of blindness was foremost in her mind.

"I would have thought you would need the same lift equipment as your friend here."

"Well, I'm not sure why you would think such a thing, but no, I don't."

Another moment of contemplation went by. Finally she shook her head. "There's no way you can carry your friend on board."

"Are you forbidding me to do so or do you not believe I'm capable?" I asked. "Because if it's the latter, all I can say is it's my eyes that are broken, not my legs. Jody and I have managed ourselves through many barriers. A few steps are not going to be a big deal."

"What about once she's on the train?"

"Excuse me," Jody interrupted. "Once again, I would appreciate you posing your questions about me to me."

The woman, notably nervous, sputtered as she struggled to formulate her next comment correctly.

"Well, you're likely going to have to use the bathroom. It's a lot different trying to keep one's balance with the swaying motion of the train."

"Listen," I said, mustering up a bit of kindness in my voice. "All I can say is, under the law, you cannot discriminate against any of your passengers. I realize you are only doing your job, but you don't question other people as to how they will get around, and you truly should not be asking us such personal questions as to how we are going to pee on the trip. If the employees simply treat my friend's chair as a piece of luggage, we can do the rest."

"Well, I can't promise anything," she said, relinquishing her adamant stance.

"Neither can we," I said, pausing for effect. "Now, if you will simply give us our seat assignments, we'll find our way to the platform when it's time."

The clerk turned and headed back to her counter. I heard the click-click of her stamper and in a moment she returned.

"Here are your seat assignments. I have no idea if the conductor will actually allow you on, but I've done all that I can do to prepare you."

"Thank you very much," I said sincerely.

"Yes, thanks," Jody added, as we headed toward the lobby.

"Can you imagine having only one train a day for gimps?" Jody said, choosing a word only those belonging to the disability culture were privileged to use without appearing offensive. "Shoot, what if people have to work like us?"

"It just ain't right," I said mournfully.

We realized we likely had another battle ahead, so we began discussing our tactics for every possible scenario. As the arrival time grew closer, we promised not to chicken out if it came to stationing ourselves on the tracks.

"We have to stand up for our rights," Jody exclaimed.

"You're absolutely correct. I just wish I didn't have to sometimes."

"It kinda takes the joy out of the trip, don't it?"

Eventually the rumbling locomotive thundered into the station. Jody and I, positioned next to the exit, zoomed out of the building and headed straight for the conductor.

We held out our tickets, pretending there was no issue. The conductor looked at them and then at us.

"Who gave you these?" he asked firmly.

"We purchased them through a travel agent," I said.

"Who stamped them with a seat number?"

"The clerk," Jody explained.

"Well, that shouldn't have happened. This train is not the disabled train."

"I think that's good," I said, hoping to lighten the mood. "We prefer ones that work."

"No, you don't understand. None of these passenger cars have a lift on them. We have no way of getting you on board."

"All you need to do is put the chair in the luggage compartment," Jody explained. "It comes apart in three sections and it's not very heavy. My friend and I can get aboard on our own."

"Nope. I'm sorry. The union doesn't cover crippled people on this route."

"Well, since we don't belong to the union, we will choose not to follow their rules," I replied, making an effort not to smile.

"Madam," the conductor said in a most exasperated tone. "None of my staff is allowed to lift something this heavy. Besides, it's not safe for her to be on the train without being strapped down."

"First of all sir," Jody said, attempting to engage his full attention. "You need to talk to me when you're discussing my particular business."

"Huh? Well, ah…" He was obviously taken aback, as I saw the brim of his cap turn abruptly toward Jody. I imagined his face reddening, as I suspected he only fully noticed her for the first time.

"Secondly," she went on, "how do you know what my safety needs are?"

"Look, we can't put you on," he insisted, becoming more flustered. "There are all kinds of rules and regulations. We just can't do it."

"Well, we just can't let you ruin our weekend vacation," I countered. "I'm sorry to put you in this predicament, but having only one handicapped train, as you call it, doesn't leave a lot of room for people with physical disabilities to get to Toronto. We've got two nights and three days there and an expensive ticket to a play. We're not going to allow you to leave us stranded here without a lot of opposition. You can either kindly put my friend's chair in the baggage compartment, and let us handle the rest, or we're parking ourselves on the tracks."

"Ladies," he said, half pleading. "I can't let you board. None of my staff will do what you're asking."

"Then you can put it on yourself. Like my friend told you, it comes apart, and it's not that heavy. I could even help you. But I would need to assist my friend on first."

The conductor made some barely audible sounds then reached in his pocket for something. For a minute I thought he might be contacting the police, but it soon became clear he was speaking to one of his staff.

"Charley, can you come down to six and give me a hand with something. It'll just take a minute." There was a pause, then, "Over."

As he replaced the walkie talkie in his pocket, he focused on Jody and me.

"I'll do it this time. But you better be sure you take the 5:45 back. I'm not sure you'll be able to bully your way on a non-disabled train down in Toronto. Those guys are strong union down there, and they ain't gonna budge for a couple of girls like yourselves.

"Thank you," we said in unison.

"You've helped save a much needed vacation," I added.

"Well, you've given me a reason to take one," he said, not trying to be funny.

Jody stood up. We slid our wallets from our coat pockets and stuck them in our jeans. Neither of us carried purses, as free hands were at a premium for both of us. Jody held on to me for balance as she took off her coat. I followed suit and tossed them both on our overnight bags perched in the back compartment of her scooter.

"It's too cumbersome with these on," I explained to the conductor politely. "Could you bring them to our seats once we're aboard?"

He reluctantly agreed.

Before embarking on the next phase of our journey, I handed the vouchers to Jody and asked her to find the seat numbers. She did so, sticking the tickets safely down her shirt.

I put my cane in my left hand. She turned so she was facing me. Crouching down, I bent my knees and placed my right shoulder in the crook of her diaphragm just below her breast bone. With one swift movement, I pushed up with my legs, lifting her off the ground. Like a very long sack of potatoes, she angled over my right shoulder, her rigid legs pointing straight out in front. Awkwardly I moved my cane with my left hand, careful to extend it past Jody's feet. I didn't want to ram them into the side of the entrance. Though Jody's ankle had endured a slamming door I'd failed to avoid once before, I didn't want to test her strength again. Besides, we'd already had to jump over a bunch of obstacles to go on this trip, and I wasn't about to add any more hurdles. Slowly but surely, I located the steps. The conductor must have caught sight of me at that moment because suddenly he was at my side insisting I let him help.

"Actually sir," I said pushing his outstretched hand away with my wrist. "If you would please let me handle this and refrain from touching me, it will make it much easier."

"But I'm afraid you're going to fall," he insisted.

"I've been on lots of trains and I know the layout," I told him, thinking about my disastrous experience in Denmark. There are advantages to making mistakes, I mused, fully aware I might never have understood the logistics of locomotives if I hadn't fallen under one. A slight smile crossed my face as I refocused on appeasing the conductor.

"I'm physically strong, so it's really no big deal. When you touch me, it throws my balance off."

"We've really got it under control," Jody added, her voice filled with grunts and groans. "It's best if you simply let Geri keep going."

In terms of discomfort, it was Jody who suffered most. With her weight primarily localized on one focal point of her rib cage, it tended to restrict her breathing, putting painful pressure on her torso. Ignoring the conductor's continued protests, I climbed the stairs methodically so as not to falter. With great effort, I weaved the two of us down the narrow aisle, Jody stretching her long neck back and forth to find our seat numbers. At last, she spotted them at the very end of the car.

"That lady did us all right after all," she said. Feeling the edge of the seat with my knee, I understood what she meant. Our row faced the way we'd come in, the opposite direction of the others. This arrangement made for a spacious area allowing more foot room. Best of all, it would make maneuvering Jody in and out much easier.

"Hey, this is great," I said, bending to situate her on the chair. In my excitement however, I failed to follow an important rule. In our experiences together, Jody and I had learned that moving too quickly could end up in a catastrophe. In my hurry, I failed to stay focused when lowering her butt on the cushion and almost dropped her on the floor. Knowing the limits of my strength, I panicked. It is one thing to lift someone from a standing position, another to pick them up off the ground. Not wanting her to spend her entire trip on the floor, I grabbed her by the armpit and painfully yanked her upwards, shoving her hard with my knee.

"Ow!" she squeaked.

"Sorry, Jode. Didn't want to lose you."

"No kidding," she sighed. "Heck, I surely don't wanna have to ask one of these union guys for help."

"Oh God, we'd certainly have to eat crow then, wouldn't we?" I chuckled. "There's nothing I hate more than being told, 'I told you so'."

"Well, I'm glad you caught me, anyway. And I hope no one else has the spots across from us."

The toot of the whistle announced our wish had come true. The time had arrived to leave the remnants of our fiasco behind. Straining against the force of inertia, the grinding wheels inched us forward.

"I think I can, I think I can, said the little engine that could," I recited.

"I remember that book, too," Jody announced.

"It was my favorite story as a child," I told her, remembering how I pestered my mother to read it again and again. "I think we've got a lot in common with that little choo choo," I remarked, drawing the parallel between the three of us struggling to deal with uphill challenges. As the locomotive whisked us from our humiliating incident, I felt my body relax to the swaying rhythm. Clickity clack, clickity clack, I heard the train wheels say as they moved us along faster and faster.

"Don't you just love that sound?" I asked.

"It's better than Calgon for taking us away."

We burst out laughing. A brief tinge of anxiety threatened to disrupt our growing bond. It had been a long time since I'd been on the same track with a girlfriend, especially someone as cool as Jody. I made a note to myself to enjoy her, instead of doing something that might push her away.

As the engine pulled us along, Jody and I took a tour through our lives. We hardly noticed the return of our coats with the warmth of our deepening friendship.

When we finally arrived in Toronto, we were on a natural high. Reversing the process, we got off the train, and the conductor presented us with Jody's chair. We thanked him again and tipped him generously. Since our hotel was only six blocks away, we decided to walk instead of hailing a cab. Slipping on our coats, we initiated the next leg of our journey.

The Harbor Castle was a towering hotel perched on the edge of Lake Ontario. I'd never seen such lavishness before as we entered the lobby complete with waterfalls and a concert pianist. As a bellhop dressed in fancy duds escorted us to our room, I felt like I was Cinderella again at the ball in the king's palace.

"Wow! Would you look at this place, Jode!" I marveled, running my fingers over the quilted spreads. "Never thought I'd be spending the night in such a luxurious hotel as this."

Like a schoolgirl doing an overnight, I kicked back on the bed, a rekindled youthfulness setting my spirit free.

"Ah, this is the life, ain't it?" I said, flopping back on a gigantic pillow.

Jody plopped herself in the overstuffed chair near the window, wholeheartedly agreeing with my appraisal of the place. We continued swapping secrets of our youth, discussing boys, drugs, and other deviant behaviors. I told my friend about my chairlift story, and she contributed a near-death experience with an avalanche while skiing stoned in Colorado. We'd both dabbled in getting high, but it sounded like Jody had not dealt with addictive urges. She didn't freak when I told her about my time in the "nut house" nor did I judge her as she unfolded inner struggles and self-destructive tendencies she'd had as a youth.

We continued our in-depth discussions as we toured the hotel and had a drink in one of the lounges. We returned by one in the morning and were still talking way past three. Only when the room fell silent did the homesickness set in. I thought of Nolan so far away and questioned my decision to leave him.

He's in Florida with his father and grandparents, for heaven sake! I told myself, trying to ease my guilt. *How could you keep a three-year-old from seeing Mickey Mouse?* I pictured my little one tagging along with his dad and grandparents at Disney World, and that eventually allowed me to sleep.

Jody and I explored the city on Saturday, using the combination of accessible buses and reluctant taxi drivers who weren't too keen on storing her unassembled chair. Though we enjoyed our visits to museums, Casa Loma, and Chinatown, it was the non-stop gabbing which was the richest part of each scene. By five it was time to return to our hotel to gussy up for the theater.

The sharp contrast of Jody's rich olive skin against her ebony attire made her easy to see. The high collar of her velvet dress accented her long neck, adorning her already exotic image. With some minor assistance, Jody put on her high leather boots, completing her very sexy outfit. Without a doubt, Jody's striking beauty was a pleasure to behold.

Oddly enough, the old feelings of jealousy I typically felt toward other females did not exist between me and my new best friend. Instead, I also felt pretty foxy as I decorated myself in a low cut red number with a satin bodice. Around my neck I placed a black onyx necklace which went with earrings given to me by my brother. To complete my look, I strapped to my feet a pair of black leather stilettos that were poor substitutes for shoes. With my artificial ringlets hanging in layers to my shoulders, Jody said if they were the same color, our hairdos would have looked like carbon copies. Unfortunately our waist-length wool coats tainted our Hollywood image, but cold weather overrode our desire to be cool.

We found our way down to the concierge's desk where we obtained directions to the theater where Cats would be performed. We also inquired about accessible restaurants. The gentleman behind the desk listed three dining establishments that he assured us served the finest cuisine. The Whaler was our only option however, after the attendant finally grasped the idea that accessible meant no stairs. Though his exceptional politeness felt rather foreign to me, I acted like it was an everyday thing. I graciously thanked him, putting on airs, as he secured reservations for us and then hailed us a cab.

The taxi driver held a similar view to those we'd met earlier in the day. He reluctantly obliged us anyway, placing Jody's chair in his trunk while she steadied herself with my arm. She gingerly lowered herself into the back seat and I climbed in the other side.

"To the theater," I announced, feeling wealthy and free.

In my wildest dreams I could never have imagined the extravaganza displayed in a bona fide theater. The performances at my niece and nephew's high school were the only live plays I'd ever seen performed. I couldn't see the props or the details of the actors' faces, but the brilliant spotlight allowed me to catch the gist of their movements. Only once did a tinge of sadness for my disappearing vision interrupt this thrilling event, as I watched kitty cats dance and roller skate to the jazzy tunes of this musical bonanza.

"That was awesome," I said to Jody as we left the theater.

"No kidding," she agreed. "Wow, what incredible performers."

"Were you ever able to move like that?" I asked.

"I wasn't too bad, but not quite that good," she chuckled.

"It's gotta be hard to watch people move about the way you used to, huh?"

"Sometimes it's unbearable, but not tonight. These guys were terrific. How about you? I expect it must be frustrating for you, too, not to be able to see all the details."

"Yeah, sometimes it is," I said, recalling the earlier acknowledgement I'd had about eventually being unable to see. "For the most part I don't think about it much, though." It was enough to know I'd be able to talk with her about it someday, but at the moment I was loving the mood and didn't want to spoil it.

As we entered the crowded lobby, I reached out and took the back of Jody's chair.

"I'm hanging on so we don't get separated," I announced.

"Good idea."

When we got outside, Jody's attempts at hailing a taxi were futile. As we had discovered earlier in the day, very few cabbies wanted to stop for a wheelchair, particularly when they didn't know it came apart. We thought about hiding Jody in the wings of the marquee while I flagged one down, but decided it'd be easier to walk the eight long blocks in the end.

Except for a growing pinch in my little toe, traversing the busy city at night was pretty awesome. We agreed the occasional gawking stares and sympathy comments were much more tolerable when we were together.

"There's power in numbers," I said, as we proudly walked and rolled down the street. An invisible force seemed to connect our spirits as confidence flowed between the two of us.

"To the Dynamic Duo!" Jody cheered

"We're invincible!" I shouted approvingly.

Our frame of mind came in handy as we approached our destination. The barrier-free establishment so highly recommended by the concierge must have grown taller since the last time he ate there. Twelve steps stood between us and the entrance. Checking the surrounding area, we could find no back door or other way in. Sizing up the wide deep steps carefully with my cane, Jody and I decided to give them a try.

We removed our coats to lighten the load and Jody put our wallets in the top of each boot. Once again I hoisted her over my shoulder.

"Are you ready?' I asked with a charge in my voice.

"Ready!"

Teetering on disaster in my red dress and three inch heels, I stuck out my cane and somehow managed to get us to the top.

"Can you see the door handle?" I asked, turning slightly, unable to feel for it with my occupied hands.

"Yeah, it's just out from your right elbow," Jody directed, so I moved to the right and reached out with my left hand to grab it. But as I did so, the door flew open. It knocked into Jody's legs, throwing us both backwards. I must have looked like a clown in a circus, as I took rapid tiny steps sideways, then back, bending slightly forward before falling off the step. Luckily Jody's long legs hit the pavement at just the right angle, pushing us upright like one of those plastic Weeble toys that pop up after you try to knock them down. Pivoting around, I turned and moved back against the building, knocking Jody's head into the glass window.

"Ouch!" she yelled, followed by a quick, "I'm okay." With no clue what he'd done, the perpetrator continued on down the stairs.

Once more I ventured toward the door, this time successfully maneuvering us both inside. Sliding my cane awkwardly forward in my left hand, I struggled to hold Jody securely with my right. As my ankles grew weaker, I gingerly walked forward in search of the restaurant's host when an unexpected barrier stopped my cane.

"What the hell?" I said aloud, again shifting so Jody could see.

"Oh my God!" she said in her shrill voice. "You are not going to believe this."

"Don't tell me. More steps?"

"More steps," she reiterated. Tracing the outline of the barrier with the tip of my cane I counted each stair as it ascended.

"One, two… holy shit! How many are there?"

"Thank heaven, there's only three," Jody informed me, "but still…"

"We're gonna have to bring that concierge to dinner with us next time so he gets what we mean by barrier free."

"No kidding," Jody grunted, her lungs sounding close to collapse.

"I think I can, I think I can," I jokingly said aloud. With great effort, I pulled hard with the muscles of my right leg while pushing with my left, finally reaching the top.

At last we were on flat ground. I could see a white blob moving toward us. As it neared, I surmised it was a man dressed in a white tuxedo.

"May I help you?" he asked, a bit of uncertainty in his voice.

"Yes. We have reservations for Walker and Seemore," I announced, holding Jody firmly over my shoulder.

Responding to my unexpected wit, Jody burst out laughing. I, on the other hand, managed to keep a straight face.

"I'm sorry, the name is…?"

"Taeckens," I said with a smile.

"One moment, please," he said. My mind placed a puzzled look on his face.

"I don't think he got my joke," I moaned.

"Geri, you are too crazy," Jody chortled

"I'm crazy?" I challenged. "This place is crazy. Who'd ever think a restaurant with no steps would have so many?"

"Stop it!" Jody said with a snort. "It's killing my gut to laugh like this."

"Well, you'd better stop, or we're both going to end up on the floor," I giggled.

Just then the maître d' returned. "Yes, I have your reservation."

Before he led us to our table, Jody explained about her chair. Again he took off, returning momentarily with news it would soon be retrieved.

"The attendant will place it behind the reservation desk for you, if this is permissible," he said.

"I'd like to ride it to the table, if you don't mind," Jody countered.

"I believe that would be a difficult arrangement, madam. If you follow me, I'm certain you will agree," he said with his foreign accent. I wondered what he really must think.

Following behind, I quickly lost track as his quiet footsteps disappeared in the cushy carpet.

"Would you mind if I take your arm, sir?" I called. "I don't see too well, and it's a little difficult for me to maneuver with my friend on my shoulder."

More snickers escaped Jody's lips as the gentleman allowed me to take his arm. Like a parade announcing the beginning of a circus, we began our procession through the restaurant. We had not advanced far when our escort stopped to announce, "Madam, there are five stairs down to the tables. How would you like me to proceed?"

So that's why he didn't want to give her the chair, I thought to myself, as I answered with no sign of surprise.

"You can just go ahead, it's really no problem," I replied, acting like nothing was odd. Jody's giggles increased, threatening my ability to counterbalance her oscillating weight. Holding fast to the quivering elbow of my escort, I resisted the urge to inquire if this was the Twilight Zone. I decided against it, figuring he wouldn't get it, and fearing it would only shake him up more.

As the theater of the absurd continued to play out, I became curious about the minds of our audience. To be a wealthy, upper class someone dining in luxury and expecting things to be 'just so', must have affected the clientele in some shape or form. What did they think of this circus team of women, dressed in fashionable attire, traipsing through this exclusive place like two members of the Flying Wallendas?

Over dinner Jody and I conferred about our deviant behavior. Admittedly we agreed we felt great satisfaction at disturbing the status quo.

"If you can't join 'em, shake 'em up!" I said, glad not to be riddled with the embarrassment which had once ruled my existence.

"They'll get over it," Jody suggested, after describing the looks of disgust on some of their faces.

"We still have to go back through," I reminded her.

"I'll be sure to give them an extra wide smile."

I wish I could say the last part of our evening went smoother than the first. However, the twelve steps down to the bathroom and three more down to the stalls made us both wonder if the building engineers had been paid by the number of stairs they designed. We also questioned how important emptying one's bladder truly could be. Thankfully my ankles and Jody's rib cage held their own as the maître d' arranged for Jody's chair to be returned to the sidewalk. We thanked him politely, glad to escape the house of stairs and headed back to the hotel.

Our decision to walk the nine blocks to our weekend haven rather than hail a cab turned out to be another fascinating venture. In our obsession to be independent, we failed to consider those parts of reality which might cramp our style. The result proved to be rather stimulating indeed. Halfway there, Jody's battery went dead.

I must admit pushing an electric vehicle with wheels that rely on the power of electricity adds great muscle mass to one's calves. It surely ain't the greatest for feet squished in leather bound stilts however, unless one is fostering the development of the largest blister in the world.

Back at the hotel, I lay in a tub of hot water while Jody curled herself on the chair.

"What a night!" she called. "Hope you can walk tomorrow."

"No kidding!" I laughed. "I hope your chair charges up."

"It should be fine by eight," she assured me.

"Wish I could just plug my body into the wall like that. I have a hunch I might be functioning with half the juice tomorrow."

Jody let out a snicker. "You have as much fun as I did?" she asked.

"It was the best!"

As I opened the tap and let more hot water pour in, I smiled at all we'd been through. Never would I have believed I could feel so much gratification for dealing with so many disasters.

"I guess we can face anything if we've got each other, Jody B," I said, suddenly feeling I might cry.

"It's true, it's true!" she happily agreed. "We did it, you know! We faced it all!"

"No kidding," I added, my heart warmed by the smile I couldn't see. "This is…truly a night to be remembered, Jody Beeswax!" I said, affectionately playing with her name.

"That it is, that it is, Geri-deen," she said, her twist on my formal name giving me a smile I made sure she could hear.

"What a team!"

"From here on out, it's Walker and Seemore, all the way!"

Chapter 44

The Moment of Truth

May 1986

"Howdy!"

"Hey there, Beeswax," I said, reaching for the door handle of her van. Before I could release the latch, Herbert George ran up and stuck his muzzle into my leg. As usual, it was stuffed with his tennis ball.

"Oh, Herbert, how did you get out?" I lovingly scolded. "You can't go with us today. I'll be right back, Jody. I gotta take him in the house."

"Poor Herby. Sorry boy!" she called through the opened window. I patted his head as I pulled him toward the door.

Since I had moved into a duplex apartment in May of the previous year, Herbert George had become her personal greeter. I always knew when she was about to arrive because five minutes before she'd drive up, he'd snatch up his ball and wait at the door and whine. The moment it opened, he'd run down the ramp so kindly built by Fred, my sister Grace's husband. Herby's timing was perfect. He'd leap onto her lift the instant it leveled out. Circling twice, he'd move to the side in order to make room for her to roll onboard. Jody said he looked so proud as he escorted her down, his ball still clutched in his jaws.

On this particular day, there was no time for such ceremony. As this ritual typically took ten minutes, it would put us in a time crunch. Today Jody and I were meeting Cheryl and two others to present on a panel at a university seminar. I didn't suppose being covered in dog hair would be the best thing for her professional appearance. As Herbert was primarily white, the black pants Jody typically wore would look more like tweed.

"Sorry, Herby. You know how I hate keeping you from your best friend," I told him, but my consoling words did nothing for the forlorn look I felt on his face. As I returned him to the empty house, a tinge of resentment came over me. I truly enjoyed public speaking, but I wasn't happy about doing it on a Saturday. David had kindly offered to take Nolan to his parents' summer cottage. Though I knew Nolan would have a great time, I hated being away from him on my only two days off. With a hug and a kiss, I assured Herbert I'd be back in three hours.

Clunking back down the wooden ramp in my two inch beige pumps, I pictured how they looked with my sage green dress. *What the heck does sage green look like anyway?* I wondered. Throwing open Jody's van door, I climbed in.

"So what color is sage green?" I asked, hoping Jody could explain it. So far she'd been the best at descriptions of odd colors.

"Hmm. Well, it's on the beige side of green."

"Beige! How can green be beige?" I asked, more confused than ever.

"Well, I mean it's more toward the brownish greens, rather than yellow or blue."

"Can you compare it to an object?" I asked, unable to picture anything other than kelly, olive or lime.

"Well, do you remember the color of an aloe plant?"

"Uh, kinda."

"Well that's sage green."

"So I'm right about it being a light color then?"

"Yeah, very."

"I thought I saw a hint of green, but wasn't sure. The lighting in my house is so dim, you know?" I explained, wondering why I felt the need to excuse my question. I tipped my head downward and stared hard at the material now spread across my lap. I waited for my eyes to adjust, sure the bright sun would reveal its hue. Concentrating hard on the image of the aloe plant I once possessed, the color seemed to come into view. My tummy relaxed. I ran my finger around the v-neckline, then fondled the row of shiny brass buttons. I winced as my hand rolled over the bulge in my stomach. I still held on tight to my additional fifteen pounds, but I hoped I didn't look too bad. After all, the sales clerk who'd described the style to me assured me the full gathered skirt and belt with brass buckle accented all the right places.

"So, you up to doin' some dirty talking?" I asked, referring to our task at hand.

"Isa ready!" she said enthusiastically, moving the van away from the curb. "I gotta tell ya, Ger, I've been sitting out here looking over all your flowers and admiring your wonderful spirea bushes. I don't know how you keep them so full. They look so inviting!"

"I don't do anything with them," I said disconcertedly, trying to conjure up the image of these cascading white flowers. My increasing ability to picture objects in my mind soon helped me remember how beautiful they looked. These lacey works of nature with their long flowing branches were a definite asset to my home. Interestingly enough, they bordered the north side of my yard, the same side my mother planted hers on, back when I was a kid. Memories of us picking them together sparked a melancholy feeling in my heart. Despite her complaints about their petals falling like confetti and making a mess, you could find them decorating our living room every spring.

"Ger? You with me?" Jody asked.

"Huh? Oh, yeah," I replied.

"Don't tell me you're nervous about our gig today?"

"Oh, no."

"You okay?"

"Yeah, I was thinking about Nolan having to be away for the weekend," I lied, wondering why I did so. Feeling strangely desperate to change the subject, I asked, "So how was your date last night?"

"Not bad! We went to dinner, came home, and listened to music and…"

"And what?"

"Well, let's just say he's not a bad kisser."

"Anything else he's not bad at?" I taunted.

"Actually, we're not that far along in the relationship yet, but I tell ya, he's a cutie! So, did you and Stan have a nice evening?"

"Oh, it was okay. I do have to get out of that relationship, though. As crazy as I am about him, it's really not going anywhere," I admitted, wondering how many months I'd been saying this. Although the man I'd been spending time with had many fascinating qualities, one of them being his Russian birth, he was totally intolerant of children. I juggled this little inconvenience by seeing him only when Nolan was asleep or with his dad. I adored his knowledge of classical music and drank in every word of the obscure literature he read to me, but I wanted and needed more.

"I don't know why I find inattentive men so attractive," I said, thinking of two similar relationships I'd had since my separation from David.

"Know what you mean. After the third date, I'm wondering when Denny's gonna turn out like that last schmuck I got myself hooked up with."

"No kidding," I gave a half-hearted laugh. "That guy was pretty far out for sure."

"Was it his obsession with guns or his mother's apron strings that make you think that?" Jody asked with a chuckle.

"Actually, I think it was his philosophy about women that topped it off for me. When he tried to talk me into a ménage a trois that night while we were waiting for you, he kinda turned me off."

"Oh yeah!" Jody chortled. "I forgot about that one."

"Why do we women always want to save these screwed up men?" I asked.

"I don't know," she sighed. "Sometimes I get scared I won't get a man. Every time I lose more functioning I figure I'm one step closer to spending the rest of my life alone. Now that I can't even wall walk any more, well…" she broke off.

"I know," I said empathetically. "But Beeswax, you are so beautiful and charming and funny. I can't imagine a truly good man passing you up."

"You're sweet," she said, smacking her lips, making a kissing sound. "What would I do without you, Geri-Deen? I know you could be right, but it's so hard to get a man to look past the wheelchair. You know the stats. I'm preaching to the choir here, but we all know looks are what brings 'em in. Heck, even if a guy didn't get turned off by the chair, once they saw the jungle gym I use to get out of bed, they'd run faster than a jaguar.

"You're probably right," I said, thinking about Jody's growing inability to transfer independently. Her diminished body strength had not only required the installation of an in-house lift, she also had to switch from a scooter to a regular electric wheelchair. Like me, it had taken a few near-death experiences for Jody to recognize her losses and make the necessary adaptations. After becoming overheated while transferring from her driver's seat to her chair, Jody collapsed in a closed van one 90 degree day. If someone hadn't walked by and heard her, she would have likely melted away. This is when she decided to purchase a van similar to the one Cheryl used. Though initially Jody admitted these changes were hard to accept, in time, she appreciated the new freedoms they afforded her.

"It's the same with the cane," I said, responding to her truthful statement about first attractions. "Remember Joel?"

"Oh yeah. Too bad about him."

"I know. He was so cool, and he loved Nolan, but he just couldn't get past the fact I couldn't see. Shit, it still upsets me. I thought for sure he was really the one."

"Me too! I pretty much figured you two would be getting married some day."

"God, I was so disappointed. I was so angry I went home and wrote *Blind Man's Bluff*."

"I remember. Great song!"

"Thanks, but I surely wish my great plan of singing it to him would have worked. He never did see the light," I chortled.

"Ah, can't teach anything to those mutations they call men," Jody laughed.

"I suppose. To be honest, I wish I could live up to what I really believe in."

"What's that?"

"Well, I know I don't practice what I preach, but I sure as hell wish I'd stop giving myself over to guys who don't treat me right. I mean, there really is a life with or without a man, ain't there?" I asked, half joking.

"I'm right there with you, Geri-deen. Not that I wanna give up the idea of having a man to cuddle up with at night, ah say, maybe for the rest of my life?" she laughed. "But I gotta admit, most of the good times have been with you guys!"

"So what ya complaining about? Heck, you've got two steady beaus already, you know?"

We laughed.

"You'sa right about that one, Geri-deen. That Nolan and Herby boy, they are my men!"

Jody turned the van into the parking lot. After she completed the electronic steps to get out of her vehicle, we walked and rolled into the university medical building, still chuckling. We found the rest of the panel members sitting on the stage. This would be the fourth time we'd be doing a seminar for Dr. Betty

Mooney. As the director of the sexuality department of the medical school, her passion was addressing the intimacy needs and rights of persons with disabilities. Dr. Mooney was a phenomenal woman, not afraid to speak out against the conservative beliefs held by the establishment. She had a real knack for discussing taboo topics without ruffling too many traditional feathers. The issues Jody and I had discussed in the van were not foreign to others who had a notable difference. Many of us looked to Dr. Mooney as a guru. She was easy to talk to about the subject of sex.

When I worked at the rehabilitation hospital, I learned how doctors would address all aspects of a newly disabled person's life, except for the most important one. They'd order all kinds of physical and psychological therapies and provide accommodating devices for mobility and daily living. However, adaptive tools for intimacy needs were never mentioned, let alone prescribed.

In contrast, Dr. Mooney had an incredible ability for integrating words like sexual aids or penile enhancers into conversations without missing a beat. A client hardly had enough time to become embarrassed as she fired questions about what positions and erotic stimuli they might enjoy.

As Dr. Mooney modeled the okayness of talking about sensual needs and desires, she helped clients, with or without partners, to see themselves as sexual beings.

"Everyone's entitled to feel sensuous," she'd say to her clients. "Embrace yourselves. You're full fledged human beings! Looks don't make a person sexy. It's how you feel about yourself that does."

Sexual histories and physical assessments were only part of Dr. Mooney's services. Clients had opportunities to experiment with different devices, sometimes right at the clinic. Couples were also taught how to hire and utilize human assistance. If both partners were disabled, being able to obtain such hands-on support was crucial.

Though we typically spoke to second year medical students, today we'd be addressing university administrators. As the topic of sexuality was still rather controversial, Dr. Mooney wanted to expose these influential individuals to the real thing. We'd be discussing facts and myths about sexuality and disability, sharing personal frustrations and successes. Though a bit nervous, we all hoped to convince the allocators of funds to continue supporting this program.

The day proved rather successful. The participants were initially uptight with the explicitness of our conversation, but our humor and Cheryl's audacious nature eventually helped them relax and enjoy themselves. Before we left, Dr. Mooney shared her hopefulness and thanked us for our help.

Exhausted from talking about sex all day, Jody and I rode home in relative silence. As I slipped out of her van, I felt the warm sun on my face. I did not experience the usual rush of pleasure, however. Instead, a sullen mood came over me as I made my way up the ramp. As I unlocked the door, Herby greeted me, wagging and jumping, hoping I'd throw his ball.

"Hi, boy," I said, patting his head. "I'll take you out in a minute, okay? Gotta get out of this dress first."

He reluctantly climbed on my bed. I sensed him pensively watching every move I made as I pictured him in his readied position. I put on my jeans and red t-shirt, hoping they would give me some comfort, and moved toward the door. But the bothersome feeling held me back, as Herbert catapulted forward.

"What is wrong with me?" I questioned aloud. "I'm not usually skittish about being alone."

Instead of responding to Herbert's desperate pleas, I checked my answering machine, which was empty.

"Just a minute, boy," I said, shuffling through a stack of papers on my desk. I edged my way to the kitchen, Herby right on my heels. When my hand touched the sink filled with dishes, I felt the compulsion to clean. Despite Herbert's protests, I went from one task to the next, wiping the counter, table, and fridge. Finally Herby's frantic whines told me I couldn't put him off any longer.

"I'm sorry, boy. I know you've probably got to go real bad. I don't know why I'm making you wait." *Why am I feeling so uptight?* I wondered.

Setting down my wash rag, I dried my hands on a towel. Three more times I distracted myself from making it to the front door. Practically jumping out of his skin now, Herbert urged me on.

At last, I opened the door to let us both out. Positioning myself on the north side of the ramp, I accepted the ball Herby stuffed in my hand. He dashed to the south, anticipating the pitch. I gave it a whirl. I heard him catch it. He scurried back and forth with delight. I did not smile at his joy. Despite my abnormal disinterest, I repeatedly obliged him. Between throws, I kept looking up to the sky. The air felt normal, but my instincts told me it might rain. Again and again, Herby shoved his prized possession into my palm. Over and over, I plunged it into the air.

An impending sense of doom nagged at me. Like a magnet being pulled by an invisible force, I kept inching my way north. I'd throw the ball, take two steps, throw the ball, take two more steps, even though I wanted to stay put. Suddenly, there I was, grazing the thing I'd been secretly avoiding. I closed my eyes, attempting to hold back the rush of fear now surging through me.

Why am I feeling so scared? But before I could answer, Herby was back. My fingers obeyed his command. As he once more disappeared, I reached out and touched the forbidden scene.

You have to, you know, I gently warned, wishing what I knew was not true.

Searching for courage, I asked myself for the strength to face my fate. An eternity passed. Still I waited. I could not dare to look.

You've just got to do it! You know you do!

More moments ticked by. Finally, from deep in my soul, I force my lids to let go.

I opened my eyes. There it was…

Nothing!

Just one more time…? Please? But the void in front of me did not disappear. Only my fingers touched the colorless bundles which no longer revealed themselves to me. Silent tears pushed up from my gut, but I stopped them before I could cry. Instinctively I knew it'd be far too painful, so I just stood there, fondling the delicate blooms. From far away, Herbert's muzzle nudged my leg. Absently I slid the ball from between his teeth and gave it a toss. Without warning, I snatched up a handful of the unseen blossoms, the branches shaking from their loss. Flinging the damaged morsels to the ground, I walked in shame toward the house. An unaware Herbert continued to prod me, insisting there was still time to play.

Once inside, I opened the front closet door. Knowing the thing I needed was close, my quest became suddenly urgent. Locating my hanging jacket, I frantically slipped my hand first in one pocket then the other. There it was.

"Thank God!" I cried out, grateful to have found it. Unraveling the wadded pacifier of old, I gripped my dad's hanky with all my might. But before I gave it a reason to be used, I made one last ditch effort to disprove what I knew.

Slowly, I moved around the room, trying to focus my eyes on whatever object I came to. But the answer stayed the same. How long haven't I seen anything? I asked myself, searching my brain to know how it could have happened. In my mind I still saw the variegated afghan lying against the back of my brown couch, the crazy paisley pattern of my chair, the outline of the red brick fireplace against the cream colored walls. I've been here for almost a year. How could it have all slipped away without my knowing it? But further testing gave me the same result. I realized that even the light of the lamp and the sun had disappeared without my notice, leaving me to see nothing at all.

I flopped on the couch and stared into a blank room. Only hours ago, it was richly decorated with outlines and color. Drained of emotion, I sat perfectly still, my dad's treasure tucked firmly in my palm. Though the clock kept on ticking, I had no awareness of time.

Out of the blue, something warm touched my wrist. Herbert's affectionate kisses aroused more than my consciousness, however. His loving gesture had triggered expressions of grief.

I began to cry. A current of sorrow steadily streamed from my being, stirring up feelings which were so bittersweet. Though deeply painful, I found it satisfying. As I wondered if it would ever end, part of me wished it wouldn't. In time however, the reservoir emptied, yet I knew something else remained.

I've gotta get rid of the rest of this crap. I told myself. Just then the image of Jack in his contemplative pose came to my mind's eye. When I saw his eyes move from the ceiling to mine, I knew he'd tell me what to do. "You've got to talk about these things," I heard him say. Knowing he was right, I turned to the closest friend at hand.

"It finally happened, Herby," I told my dog, shaking uncontrollably now. "I really can't see anymore. Can you believe it, boy?" I leaned over and hugged his neck. As I felt the warmth of his soothing body, leftover tears broke free. The shower of sadness did not last long. It's really over, I mused. I don't have to worry about going blind anymore. The muscles in my body collapsed, as the last bit of hope slipped away.

I suspect Herby sensed my relinquished state, as he asked to climb aboard.

"Okay boy, you've done your duty," I said, scrunching myself against the couch. He snuggled in tightly. I wrapped my arms around him and gave him a loving squeeze.

"Oh, Herby," I said. "I just can't stand to feel sad about this any more."

A swish of his tongue told me he agreed.

As we readied ourselves for sleep, my comforting rag still in hand, a peaceful calm washed over me. Moments later I drifted off into sleep.

Chapter 45

Love is the Answer

October 1993

A sunlit meadow
A blue horizon
Swaying Trees
And dandelions
A lovely vision
For all to see
Nature's portrait
Of reality.

The greenest greens
The bluest blues
Intangibly
They speak the truth
But sunset comes
With graying dusk
And fades the colors
To emptiness

A darkened void

Where beauty dwelt

Tears at my heart where love was felt

With hopeless tears

I realize

No more for me

The dawn's sunrise.

A lovely vision

For all to see

But not for me

Only in my dreams.

As my thumb slid down the bottom three strings of the guitar, I heard the resonating sound of the minor to major chord resolving the anguish of my composition. The stillness of the room brought hopeful anticipation. I had faith the insights of my poetic creation would be understood.

More silence followed. As if debating whether to applaud such an expression of grief, one by one, members of the faceless audience dared to clap their hands. The gesture quickly spread among the eighty-six conference attendees, building into a crescendo, seeming to last forever. Maintaining my composure, I held my smile at bay, even though my insides were bursting with happiness. This song had been a long time coming. Finally, I was now able to share it with others.

"Thank you," I said, as the generous response subsided. "I want you to know, though this song expresses some painful emotions about my experience with losing vision, it's also one of the most healing songs I've ever written." The sounds of murmurs and shifting bodies suggested the crowd did not yet grasp my meaning.

As I stood before them, waiting to complete my story about self-acceptance, I reflected back on all the things that had transported me to this stage of my life. After awakening from the deepest of sleeps the morning after my unseen discovery, an amazing sense of lightheartedness lifted me out from under my trusty dog still sleeping soundly next to me. The internal voice which had guided me from pain to luminescent beauty so many times before, was now telling me I was on my way. I didn't fully know what this meant, but I intuitively trusted this mystifying message. With the dreaded moment having come and gone, I figured I might as well make my way to the kitchen to make breakfast.

The lyrics of this cathartic ballad came later on in the day. Herby and I were walking through the park near our house. As we climbed the hill used for sledding in the winter, a portrait began forming in my mind's eye. There before me was the familiar mound of dandelions. Peeking through the Crayola-green grass, they looked like a gala of yellow polka-dots. With each step, the internal shaft of light continued to sketch a picture of nostalgia. As the expanse of nature opened up before me, a winding pathway wound itself through the cherry grove, snaking up and around the side of the hill. Suddenly my mystical illustrator became inspired to set this magical scene in motion. Overhead, I heard the sound of birds singing. The noise made by their fluttering wings allowed me to follow them in flight as they darted in and out of branches. Similarly, the soothing whoosh of swaying foliage was now visible. I could clearly see the variegated greens sweep silhouettes of cotton clouds across an ocean of blue sky. A smile crossed my face as I tapped my cane and climbed to the top. After locating a swing, I sat down, soaking up the rays of the warm solstice sun.

I turned my head to the direction from which I had come and imagined the peaceful view of the rolling hill. "A sunlit meadow," sang my internal sage. "A blue horizon," the ethereal voice went on. With each simple description of what I could no longer see, tears of sadness flowed from my eyes. This time it was pure relief I felt as the rest of the musical tribute unveiled the eventual promise of dreams. I knew without a doubt I would always be able to look for what I needed in the sacred gallery of my mind.

The auditorium was again silent. I returned my guitar to its case on the table to my right and continued with my presentation.

"It may seem like a contradiction," I said, addressing my listeners' confusion. "But it wasn't until I could finally and directly grieve the loss I had dreaded for so long, that I was able to begin to feel okay about myself.

"The stories of my crazy risk-taking behavior I have shared with you are all examples of how I tried to hide the truth about my situation. The energy it took for me to pretend to be what I was not drained me of life's pleasures, as well as kept me from liking myself for who I was.

"Any facade covering up the fear of loss without an active and honest expression of sadness will impinge on anyone's enjoyment of life."

This time I heard a murmur of understanding from the crowd. I was grateful to move the group to this level as I reached down and stroked my friend. Feeling replenished by the touch of her thick velvety coat, I couldn't help reflect on what an asset this sixty-pound chocolate lab named Heath Bar had become.

After Linda obtained a dog guide in the mid-70s, she continually bugged me to check out this method for getting about. As usual, I resisted her suggestion, explaining the white cane worked perfectly fine. In the back of my mind, however, I occasionally thought about this option. By the time Nolan was seven, I began to seriously consider it. I visited a few guide dog schools, deciding the K-9 method of travel was more my style after all. Of course in our endless game of tug-of-war, Linda took credit for my decision. I gladly gave it to her. So, on my thirty-eighth birthday, after being away from home for twenty-six days, Heath and I arrived at the airport, happily greeted by my son and Jody.

Focusing my attention back on the audience, I continued to elucidate on the beauty of facing up to life's challenges.

"I have shared with you many aspects of my life which interfered with my happiness and confidence. For me, impending blindness was the major obstacle I had to figure out. Of course there are many challenges in all our lives, but because this was such an obvious and traumatic experience in mine, it's the one I use to exemplify how a supposed misfortune can be turned into prosperity.

"My personal journey has provided me with many paths of opportunity to better my life. The barriers have forced me to stop and consider the best way for moving forward. I have had to become stronger, more thoughtful, and clever in order to find the directions to where I want to go. Admitting who I am, my strengths and limitations, has turned out to be the key for ensuring my survival in this complicated roadmap of existence.

"Of course, recognizing the power of love from without and within is the spiritual element I was finally able to find after all those years of searching. Little did I realize I'd possessed this wisdom as a child. Whenever I took those many trips downtown with my father, feeling the love between us, my mind was always satisfied. Everyone has such times in their lives. Everyone can have a satisfied mind!

"We all have personal journeys. Each and every one of us has challenges to face. You have all experienced loss and other difficult hurdles. If you look back and examine what things best helped you make it through tough times, what do you think helped you the most?"

Silence filled the room as I stopped to give time for contemplation.

"Out of the muck grow lilies," I submitted to my fellow travelers. "Without the dirty grind of life's mucky quagmires, we would never have budding flowers or relationships. Without the exchange of love with all of the special people in my life, my journey would have been so much harder, if not impossible. Even the Karen Worsters, Joc Kewls, Crystals, and Professor Powers of the world helped to bring me to this point of acceptance. And acceptance is the key. It is honesty, love, persistence, and finding and following your own inner spiritual wisdom that gives us meaning. It is overwhelming catastrophes like blindness, which become the amazing vehicles to happiness."

Again, I allowed time for the audience to digest this. An astounding atmosphere was forming in the room. An unseen connection held us together as each individual processed the notions at hand. A warm feeling of satisfaction ran through me, as I offered up yet another thought.

"If I could get an operation and see tomorrow, would I jump at the chance?"

My companions shifted uncomfortably in their seats. I smiled broadly.

"Well, I probably would go for it, but I have to tell you it wouldn't be easy.

More murmurs and rustling followed my audacious claim.

"No, seriously! I know it's hard to fathom, but my blindness is now my friend. Not being able to see is part of my identity. It's who I am, and it's helped me to become honest. Besides, I get a lot of credit for things that most might not. Heck, you all cook a meal or do the dishes and it's no big deal. Me, I do the same things and everybody thinks I'm amazing!"

Chuckles and laughter erupted. Their response spurred me on.

"I realize I sound as if my journey is over, like all I have to do is sit back and glide through life with no more woes."

I heard a brave soul in the back let out a hearty chuckle. I smiled.

"Well, at least one person understands what a joke that would be!" This time we all laughed. "Don't we all wish it were so simple? But just think how many exciting challenges we'd miss out on if it were all so easy."

"Yeah, right," said a voice in the front.

"Ah, come on, you mean to tell me you'd give up the hardships in life?" Again the crowd chuckled.

"Well, you never know what the pathmaker above will bestow upon us," I said smiling, looking upward in an exaggerated motion.

"All I'm saying is the things that can seem to be the worst, can end up being the best thing that ever happened."

More mumbles and whispers.

"Don't get me wrong, my life is far from perfect. Heck, I continually make all kinds of mistakes despite my knowledge about how to live in good grace. Sometimes in the depths of a painful situation, I forget about honesty and having faith, and I fail to follow the spiritual wisdom within. I'm sure you all know what I'm talking about. Everyone knows when they've gone against what is right. I suspect you all know the resulting feeling of an unsatisfied mind as well."

The sound of "yes" and "uh huh" floated from below the stage. The binding energy which had been evolving was now flowing between all of us, inspiring me to share another significant part of my life.

"Listening to my spiritual voice is what led me to being comfortable with who I am. This acceptance in turn allows me to truly love or be loved." I winked to my right at the spot I knew to be occupied by someone very special to me.

Continuing on, I said, "Only after I came to terms with myself, did I stop looking for that thing, or man, out there who was going to save me from myself, who would make me feel okay. But you know what they say—when you least expect it!" I pointed my finger and gave a nod.

Rustling noises helped me picture the audience turning their heads.

Before venturing into my summation, I smiled once more, glad to be able to embarrass the special someone who two years earlier, miraculously came into my life.

My mind couldn't help slipping back to the time when Nolan, Jody, Heath, and I were vacationing in Northern Canada. It was there that a voice from a nearby picnic table commented on my dog. Before the three of us knew it, we were sitting with him and his friends. The force of the attraction pulled us close. Within seconds I knew it was love at first sound. A bushman by nature, Billy Park showed me his view of the world, while adapting to my way of seeing. As time went on, he embraced my son fully, accepting Nolan as his own while respecting David's place in his life. My wonderful husband never resisted my desire to cross country ski or climb steep cliffs. He simply grasped how I could use every sense I possessed to triumph over physical obstacles we dared to rise above. As I discovered the awesome sights Mother Nature had to offer, I once again learned beauty is in the eye of the beholder.

As I pushed these fond memories away for now, I steadied my excitement for what I was about to say.

"In closing, there is one more individual I want to take particular notice to thank for his never ending guidance. He is a man of great integrity, strength, and wisdom. Though he has never been recognized for any of these qualities, he continues to prevail in his own right. He gave me an extraordinary gift of insight I don't believe I could have obtained from any other person."

A poignant moment filled the air.

"Who is this man I'm referring to?" I asked my companions. Their loud silence assured me they were mulling over my question. "Oddly enough, he is the blind man on the street corner I met so very long ago."

A united gasp left the amalgamated crowd. I waited.

"You are surprised at this?"

Rustles and whispers confirmed my suspicion.

"I expected you to be. You see, like me, the image of the poverty stricken individual I described to you at the beginning of this seminar is the last person anyone would think of as being so significant. None of us would think to consider this person as being anything but pathetic, let alone have the value I now attribute to him.

More sounds of confusion were heard. I went on.

"I would now challenge you all to give up your previous notions about this person and think about the viewpoint I am about to offer."

I let another moment pass as I formulated my final words. At last I spoke.

"Despite the endless parade of sympathy, disdain, ridicule, and misinterpretation of his character, the blind man managed to triumph. Day after day, he sat on his bench collecting a pittance from anyone who dared to notice him. But like the Fool on the Hill described in the song by the Beatles, he did what he had to do to survive. I commend him for this. And I thank him for helping me see that no matter what we appear to be, we are what we see ourselves to be.

"In closing I propose to you that, in all honesty, this paradox of life is truly The Blind Man's Bluff!"

Epilogue

Blind Man's Bluff

When I was just a young girl,
My daddy said to me,
"We must take care of this blind man
Because he can not see.
Sellin' pencils is his livin',
And it's up to you and me,
To provide him with these pennies,
And give him sympathy."

Now little did I realize,
That later in my life,
I would be just like this blind man,
With no vision in my eyes.
Well the horror that ran through me,
When I pictured in my mind,
Sellin' pencils on a corner,
It made me wanna die.

So I contemplated thoroughly,
Just what I had to do,
To make it in this world,
Without being reduced,
To a helpless individual,
Whose talents are unused?
Well against all odds,
I took a chance,
And now my dream's come true.

I beat the odds.
I beat the odds.
Counter to childhood predictions,
I don't solicit alms.

I beat the odds.
I beat the odds.
I'm a whole and valid person.
My freedom I have won.

Now you ask me how I did it.
Well the road was long and tough.
There were many misconceptions,
In this game of blind man's bluff.
There were obstacles of concrete,
And terrain at times was rough.
Information on all kinds of things,
Was often out of touch.

So I became an educator,
On disability,
And I used my other senses,
To take care of my needs.
And I gracefully made blunders,
While still remaining me.
Though I still had my emotions,
That needed some release.

So I learned how to laugh,
And I learned how to cry,
And I learned how to get angry,
With dignity and pride.
And for those who can not look past,
My disability,
I can only say,
There are none so blind,
As those who will not see.

I beat the odds.
You can beat the odds.
Counter to childhood predictions,
You can be just what you want.

We can beat the odds.
We can beat the odds.
We are whole and valid people,
And freedom can be ours.
Yes, we're whole and valid people,
And freedom can be ours.